earthscape

earthscape

A Manual of Environmental Planning and Design

JOHN O. SIMONDS

VAN NOSTRAND REINHOLD COMPANY
————————————— NEW YORK

Acknowledgments

Those to whom I am indebted are legion. To list any is to risk omitting many. They are

students and teachers,
writers and scientists,
architects, planners, and engineers,
colleagues and clients,
family and friends.

Many will recognize in these writings some personal contribution. For this, and to them, I am grateful.

The creative guidance and work of book designer Jan V. White has been so telling, however, that he is singled out for special thanks.

The Author

Van Nostrand Reinhold Company Inc.
115 Fifth Avenue
New York, New York 10003

Van Nostrand Reinhold Company Limited
Molly Millars Lane
Wokingham, Berkshire RG11 2PY, England

Van Nostrand Reinhold
480 La Trobe Street
Melbourne, Victoria 3000, Australia

Macmillan of Canada
Division of Canada Publishing Corporation
164 Commander Boulevard
Agincourt, Ontario M1S 3C7, Canada

16 15 14 13 12 11 10 9 8 7 6 5 4 3 2

Library of Congress Cataloging-in-Publication Data

Simonds, John Ormsbee.
  Earthscape: a manual of environmental planning.

  Includes bibliographies and indexes.
  1. Environmental protection. 2. City planning.
3. Regional planning. 4. Landscape architecture. I. Title.
TD170.S55   363.6   77-9485
ISBN 0-442-28016-5

Photo Credits

Cover

Natural area preserved within the planned community of Pelican Bay, Florida
Photograph by *Ed Chappell*, courtesy of Westinghouse Communities of Naples, Inc.

Frontispiece

View of Toledo, Ohio
  Courtesy of Sasaki Associates, Inc.

Author

Photograph by *Lynn Johnson*

Page

    1 *Grant Heilman*, Lititz, PA
  11 *Grant Heilman*, Lititz, PA
19–24 The Botanic Garden of the Chicago Horticultural Society, Chicago, IL
  25 *Jim Gauss*, The Botanic Garden of the Chicago Horticultural Society, Chicago, IL
29–30 *Anthony M. Bauer*
  35 *Alvis Upitis*, Minneapolis, MN
  47 *Grant Heilman*, Lititz, PA
  49 *Grant Heilman*, Lititz, PA

Case Study Planning and Design Team Participants

John O. Simonds	*Environmental Planning*
Philip D. Simonds	*Landscape Architecture*
Paul D. Wolfe	*Urban Design*
C. Richard Hays	*Recreation Planning*
Geoffrey L. Rausch	*Landscape Design*
Jack R. Scholl	*Community Planning*
George J. Sloss	*Research and Analysis*
Richard O. Hagan	*Site Systems*
John C. Laatsch	*Transportation Planning*
Robert J. Vukich	*Site Planning*
James E. Voss	*Impact Assessment*
Richard A. Graig	*Regional Influences*
Kirk Elliott	*Topographic Mapping*
R. Jackson Seay, Jr.	*Planning*
Edward E. Werley	*Site Construction*
C. Steven Victor	*Ecological Factors*
Donald Vogan	*Component Design*
Clifford Johnston	*Plan Development*
Joseph Lukitsh	*Graphic Presentation*
Edward Dumont	*Illustration*
Sharon Dupont	*Transcription*

52–61 *Grant Heilman*, Lititz, PA

65–81 Leisure Properties, Ltd., St. George Island, FL

95 *Grant Heilman*, Lititz, PA

100 *Grant Heilman*, Lititz, PA

105–113 *George Hull* and *W. C. King*, The Chattanooga Times, Chattanooga, TN, Color photos by courtesy of the Chattanooga-Hamilton County Regional Planning Commission, Chattanooga, TN

123 *Grant Heilman*, Lititz, PA

139 *R. M. Keddal and Associates, Inc.*, Bethel Park, PA

145–148 Clarke & Rapuano, Inc., New York, NY

155 *Weyer-Toledo*, Toledo, OH

157 *George Hull*, Chattanooga, TN

164 Courtesy Sasaki Associates, Inc.

175 *C. J. Deland*, U.S. Department of Agriculture Soil Conservation Service, Washington, D.C.

182 Chatham Village Homes, Inc., Pittsburgh, PA

213 *Grant Heilman*, Lititz, PA

221 *Brian Brake*. From Peking, A Tale of Three Cities, by Nigel Cameron & Brian Brake. Published by Weatherhill, New York & Tokyo, 1965

225 Department of Housing and Urban Development, Washington, D.C.

227 *Gene Kinney*, State Highway Department, Portland, OR

232 Department of Housing and Urban Development, Washington, D.C.

247 Department of Housing and Urban Development, Washington, D.C.

249 Federal Highway Administration, Department of Transportation, Washington, D.C.

255 *Gerald Ratto*. Model by Architects: Wurster, Bernardi and Emmons, Inc., DeMars and Reay, San Francisco, CA

257 *Grant Heilman*, Lititz, PA

270 *Grant Heilman*, Lititz, PA

289 *Grant Heilman*, Lititz, PA

295 Wisconsin Natural Resources Department, Madison, WI

297 *Grant Heilman*, Lititz, PA

301 Virginia Department of Highways, Richmond, VA

302 *Philip Flournoy*, Virginia Chamber of Commerce, Richmond, VA

304 Virginia Department of Conservation and Economic Development, Richmond, VA

309 Virginia State Travel Service, Richmond, VA

319 *Grant Heilman*, Lititz, PA

333 National Aeronautics and Space Administration, Washington, D.C.

335 *Theodore Osmundson*, San Francisco, CA

Foreword

These are times of great promise.

Even as the condition of the habitat of the human race ebbs swiftly to its tragic nadir, there are many hopeful signs.

There is, for example, the gathering force of indignation at all forms of pollution and against those who pollute. There is growing alarm at the depletion of our natural resources and the rapid deterioration of our countryside. There is an urgent clamor for inspirational cities and for communities where life is satisfying and where unspoiled nature may be found close at hand. There is emerging a new and insistent demand for beauty in our surroundings and for quality in our lives.

Much has been written about the threats to our living environment:

The new critical levels of contamination,

The ecological blunders,

The despoliation,

The waste,

The sprawl,

The litter, the blight,—the whole range of visual obscenities.

The facts are gloomy and sickening, but they must be told and vividly retold until the idea of such widespread and recurring calamities becomes utterly repugnant. We cannot afford, however, to let ourselves become discouraged to the point of resignation.

There is a brighter side. It is the seldom-mentioned saga of national parklands preserved, of lakes reclaimed, of river systems under study, of the comprehensive planning of states and counties and towns, of successful conservation and community improvement programs being conducted on both a massive governmental scale and through the efforts of dedicated individuals. We can take further encouragement from the fact that within our schools and universities there is being generated a keen new interest in the relationship of people to their environment and a whole developing science of ecological planning.

Happily, this new determination is coupled with a technological capability that makes it possible *now* to reverse the downward trend of degradation. Clearly, within this century we will have both the knowledge and the means to create here in America a veritable paradise on earth. This book has been written to help point the way. It is dedicated to the Young . . . who hold in their hands the shape of tomorrow.

Preface

Some years ago the author set out to write a comprehensive treatise on the whole broad field of environmental planning. Many months later, with reams of notes and several hundred pages of draft text filed away, less than one-tenth of the subject outline had been covered.

Meanwhile, in winter the skis and poles lay gathering dust in the rafters. In summer the sailboat tugged idly at its moorings, and trout rose unheeded in the nearby streams and pools.

Finally, with good sense it was decided to convert the original work into a primer. The tome was reduced to a simple book of practical principles. These deal with the means by which our living spaces can be made more useful and pleasant. They are organized in a logical sequence of sections, each introduced with a page or two of observations, and laced with a generous array of photographs, and "thinking" diagrams. Case studies adapted from actual project commissions have been included to demonstrate the practical application of the principles described. In sum the material constitutes a working manual of environmental planning and design. Although "boiled down," the manual is quite complete.

It is believed that this book will be useful to students, laymen, and experts alike. The author, at least, has learned a great deal in putting it all together.

And now he is going fishing.

John O. Simonds

SCOPE

ENVIRONMENTAL CONCERNS

	FOREWORD	OVERVIEW	1 THE EARTH	2 AIR	3 WATER	4 THE VISIBLE LANDSCAPE	5 NOISE	6 PATHS OF MOVEMENT	7 THE PLANNED COMMUNITY	8 URBANIZATION	9 REGIONAL PLANNING	10 DYNAMIC CONSERVATION	LOOKING AHEAD
1. Contamination	●	●	●	●	●	●	●		●	●		●	●
2. Visual Blight	●	●	●		●	●		●					●
3. Waste Disposal		●	●		●	●		●					
4. Noise						●	●	●					
5. Erosion		●	●		●	●							
6. Scarification		●	●		●		●				●	●	
7. Ecology	●	●	●	●	●	●	●	●	●	●	●	●	●
8. Natural Resources	●	●	●	●	●		●	●		●	●	●	
9. Historic Landmarks					●		●		●	●		●	
10. Open Space		●		●	●			●	●	●	●		
11. Sprawl and Scatteration	●			●	●			●	●	●	●		
12. Trafficways			●	●	●	●	●	●	●	●	●	●	
13. Strip Development							●			●			
14. Urban Decay		●			●		●		●			●	
15. Urban Renewal		●			●		●		●			●	
16. Land Reclamation		●			●		●		●				
17. Vanishing Wilderness					●			●		●	●		
18. Wildlife		●	●		●		●			●			
19. Population		●		●				●	●	●	●		●
20. Planning	●	●	●		●	●	●	●	●	●	●	●	●
21. Design	●	●	●	●	●	●	●	●	●	●		●	
22. Civic Action	●	●	●	●	●	●	●	●	●	●	●		
23. The Government Role	●	●	●	●	●	●	●	●	●	●	●	●	
24. Conservation	●	●		●	●			●	●		●	●	●
25. Energy		●		●	●	●		●				●	●

Contents

Overview

Pollution—the American problem is enormous, but it is absolutely tailored to the American genius. To solve it needs energy, resource, invention and a certain ruthlessness. And also, perhaps, the American feeling for wild nature. There has always been a touch of Thoreau lurking behind the face of the consumer economy. I shall have been a very bad observer, and a worse prophet, if America is not out of comparison less polluted in ten years' time.

C. P. SNOW
"Hope for America"
Look magazine
December 1, 1970

As best we can now determine, man as a recognizable human creature first slunk through the Pleistocene grasslands of the earth some one million years ago. His needs then were the same as those of the other animals—food, water, and shelter in a cave or tree bough to protect him from the elements and the terror of the night.

Until the past few thousand years of his existence, man's harmful effects upon the earthscape were probably negligible. There is evidence, in fact, that he took great care to preserve the natural condition. Contemporary study of such primitive people as the African bushmen and those living Stone Age relics, the aborigines of Australia, gives testimony that their sometimes elaborate tribal laws and taboos were in large part developed to protect their water holes, hunting grounds, and supply of useful plants.

The earliest writings record also, however, man's proclivity for tampering with nature. Many experiments were ingenious and show a keen understanding of natural cycles and processes. Irrigation projects, terracing of diked paddies, reclamation of fertile delta lands and in time the sophisticated development of the Nile and Yellow River basins are examples of man working hand in hand with nature, sometimes on an astonishing scale.

In most cultures, down through the ages, there have been farms and vineyards, orchards, villas, and pleasure gardens demonstrating the rewards of attuning one's life to nature. The man-nature idea was inculcated in the first legends and in time has become a central tenet of whole systems of thought. Such is the case in the teachings of Taoism and Zen. Perhaps the fullest flowering of the concept of man in harmony with nature was exemplified by the life patterns and culture of Japan at the end of the nineteenth century, when nature appreciation was a vital compulsion and a guiding principle in the planning and design of every home and garden. Visitors to the Islands of the Rising Sun were amazed to find the whole of Japan laid out as a great all-embracing park with farms, temples, and villages beautifully interspersed. Conservation was an established way of life. (It is disheartening to note that with Japan's twentieth-century leap into industrialization, the traditional tenets of enlightened land planning have been tragically abrogated.)

From ancient times one can trace also the sordid record of man's abuse of nature and the waste of her bounty. His first significant transgression against his natural habitat came, no doubt, through the use of fire. Flames must have then, as now, escaped from fire pits by accident to leave devastation in their wake. By simplest deduction he would soon learn to turn fire against attackers and to drive and slaughter game. Much later he would learn to clear land for his first crude plantations by burning off the bush.

A second offense against nature came about through man's leveling of the forests to provide timbers and planking for dwellings and ships. The groves of Syria, Palestine, and Lebanon were almost totally destroyed. The Phoenician fleet was launched at the expense

Legislation

In the battle against pollution the most powerful single weapon is *legislation.*

It is somehow in the nature of things that the brat and the bully seldom change their ways until they have been forcibly persuaded. And so it has been with most polluters. Mill owners, truckers, and even the untidy neighbor in the block have been ready with the glib retort and quick to flex their muscles. It has been only recently, when an aroused public has called for and received decisive political action, that the tide has begun to turn against the horde of despoilers.

The necessary legislative controls may be enacted on many levels, from federal and state statutes to local codes and ordinances. Company standards, club regulations, and even family rules of conduct can all make their contribution.

Enforcement

Within each level of government it is essential that the authority for pollution control be centralized in one office. As a normal condition, the responsibility for environmental protection is presently so fragmented that most problems "fall through the cracks." Most public administrators would agree that every state, county, and city government should assign to one agency or official the responsibility for all forms of pollution control. This central authority would be charged with the protection of the environment against pollution of the air, water, surface, and subsurface of the earth by sound, heat, light, radiation, chemicals, biologicals, and other organic or inorganic matter adversely affecting or potentially harmful to humans.

Just as the basis of effective legal controls is that they are reasonable and adequate, so it is that the enforcement of these laws must be fair, firm, and uniformly applied. There can be no exceptions. Fines imposed for violations or nonconformance should be scaled to serve as stringent deterrents.

As a working rule, penalties should be considerably *in excess* of the total benefits gained by noncompliance. They should also be sufficient to cover the costs of the remedy, *plus* the cost of enforcement.

The ecologic imperative

The basis of all life upon our planet is the process by which solar energy is converted into organic compounds by means of photosynthesis in green plants. This function is in turn dependent upon an infinitely complex and delicately balanced life-support system involving the whole of our universe. Each of us, as a living organism, draws vitality from this system—an eternal circle of life, death, and reuse.

The photosynthetic, life-sustaining process is dependent upon

Government . . . is that power by which individuals in society are kept from doing injury to each other, and are brought to cooperate to a common end.

ALEXANDER HAMILTON (1794)
Quoted in *Public Officials and Their Heritage*
Public Administration Service
Chicago, Illinois, 1958

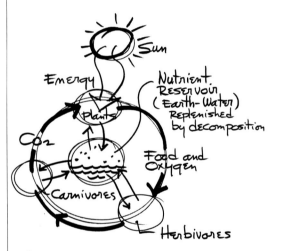

THE LIFE SUPPORT SYSTEM

Photosynthesis takes place in the chlorophyll cells of green plants — consuming carbon dioxide, producing carbohydrates, and freeing oxygen.

Braun and Cavagnaro have pointed out that each plant and animal takes from its environment the water and food it needs to live and returns to the land, sooner or later, its entire substance. The economy of living here is a balanced plan for survival, an eternal circle of life, death, and reuse, beautifully frugal and exacting.

The phytoplankton, those vegetable algae that teem in the sea and are the beginning of the marine food chain, through photosynthesis absorb the light of the sun and are sustained by it; a similar phenomenon occurs with vegetation on land.

In the seas, as on the land, all life, all movement, stems ultimately from solar energy, transformed sometimes over millions of years, sometimes in a few days or even a few hours.

All natural fuels—wood, coal, oil—in burning give back the solar energy acquired at the time of their formation.

Hydraulic energy, produced by natural waterfalls and man-made dams, is made possible because water was evaporated by the heat of the sun, to fall later as rain, snow, or sleet and accumulated to supply the power plants that produce electricity.

The various forces of nature—winds, waves, storms, ocean currents—derive from the sun and would disappear if the sun were extinguished.

JACQUES PICCARD
The Sun Beneath the Sea
Charles Scribner's Sons
New York, 1971

With Earth's first Clay They did the Last Man knead,
And there of the Last Harvest sow'd the Seed:
And the first Morning of Creation wrote
What the Last Dawn of Reckoning shall read.

EDWARD FITZGERALD
"The Rubáiyát of Omar Khayyám"
A Pocket Book of Verse
Washington Square Press, Inc.
New York, 1962

Science is the discovery and the formulation of the laws of nature.

PAUL B. SEARS
The Steady State; Physical Law and Moral Choice
The Subversive Science
Houghton Mifflin Company
Boston, 1969

Francis Bacon called scientists to the great task of creating Utopia. Their success has been so complete that it threatens disaster.
[Reason] . . . now bids them consider the responsibility of Science to Man.

RENÉ DUBOS
"The Dream of Reason"
Horizon magazine
July 1961

the presence of air, sunlight, and water. It takes place within the limits of our biosphere, which comprises that part of the Earth's crust, waters, and atmosphere where living organisms can subsist.

In a crucial sense, then, pollution may be considered as any act which defiles the earth matrix, the air, the soils, or the water supply and thus disrupts the fragile balance of life. The examples and the lessons are to be found everywhere around us. We can observe the direct result of pollution in the Lake Erie fish kills off the foul mouth of the Cuyahoga River. We can trace the less obvious cause-effects in the unhatched clutch of eggs in a stork's nest deep in the Okefenokee Swamp, or in the decimated migrations of the western yellow warblers. We cannot easily ignore the poignant warning of Rachel Carson's *Silent Spring*. Nor can we forget Hiroshima.

The ultimate consequence of pollution is the diminution of life.

It has become all too clear. Unless we act decisively to correct the tragic error of our ways, and outlaw forever the crime of defilement, the damage will soon pass the point of no return. For as significant as the *extent* of pollution is the alarming *rate of increase* within the past decade. We are joined in a race with time.

The incontrovertible facts

Among those scientists of many disciplines most profoundly aware of our culminating rush toward global catastrophe, the warnings are clear and emphatic. Should the accelerating rates of pollution and resource consumption continue without abatement, the world would become unfit for human habitation within the next few centuries, if not the next few decades.

It is clear that the costs of environmental protection—even healthful survival—will be more than many will wish to bear. The idea of limitations and personal sacrifice for such abstract goals is bound to have its detractors. Yet we have recently faced and accepted the fact of automobile emission controls, water rationing, and severely restrictive energy cutbacks. These are but the beginning. There will be fewer comforts and even fewer luxuries in the years ahead as we come to understand the necessity, and compensating benefits, of preserving our natural heritage.

We must attack, as an act of ultimate survival, every threat to the life-support system.

In the final analysis, our well-being in all aspects of life—physical, inspirational, social, and economic—depends upon the balance of nature. A central purpose of our lives, therefore, and one affecting all individual and group action, must be the safeguarding of our terrestrial habitat, the biosphere, the earth, the water, and the air.

The voices signal the approaching possibility of disaster. But, more important, they point out too that the antidote for Doomsday is quite within our reach if we will only stretch for it.
LOUDEN WAINWRIGHT

Henceforth, the laws to govern us must be the laws of ecology, not the laws of a self-destructive laissez-faire economics. And what the laws of ecology say is that we, we fancy apes, are forever related to, forever responsible for this clean air, for this green, flower-decked, and fragile earth.
HUGH H. ILTIS
"The Paradox of Human Ecology"
Bio Science, Vol. 20, No. 14
July 1970

Ecology as a science is relatively recent. It has emerged as a field of study only in the last thirty years, growing with the deepening of the environmental crisis, and perhaps profiting in some degree from the development of the systems theory.

There is no specifically human ecology. There is only one ecology, and man is part of it—properly as member, too often as destroyer, ultimately as victim.

Since there is no instance in history of an advanced technology reversing itself, one has to assume that the new primitivism is not the answer, that the answer is control and direction of our awesome power over nature and the control of our own numbers. We are a weed species. That in itself is a revolutionary perception, and the beginning of wisdom.
WALLACE STEGNER
Life magazine

You can't be serious about the environment without being a revolutionary. You have to be willing to restructure society.
GARY SNYDER, quoted in
Life magazine

Ecology is more revolutionary in its implications than either civil rights or peace. Made a guiding principle in our affairs, it would turn our society upside down, questioning its aims, assumptions, and methods, alter its mentality, overthrow its gods. And possibly save it from itself.
WALLACE STEGNER
Life magazine

Life is an experimental form of surface chemistry; it happens only where earth and water meet air and sunlight. It is a borderline creation, like the frost of dawn, and may last no longer than frost does, by space time.
ERNEST BRAUN AND DAVID CAVAGNARO
Living Water
Copyright © 1971 by The American West Publishing Company, Inc.
Used by permission of Crown Publishers, Inc.

Further Reading:

Anderson, J.M.
Ecology for Environmental Sciences: Biosphere, Ecosystems and Man
John Wiley & Sons, Inc. (Halsted)
New York, 1981

Baker, Edna
An Island Called California: An Ecological Introduction to Its Natural Communities
University of California Press
Berkeley, Calif., 1985

Curry-Lindahl, Kai
Conservation for Survival, An Ecological Strategy
William Morrow & Company, Inc.
New York, 1972

Dubos, René
So Human An Animal
Charles Scribner's Sons
New York, 1968

Ehrlich, Paul R., et al.
Human Ecology: Problems and Solutions
W. H. Freeman and Company
San Francisco, 1973

Forman, Richard T. T., and Michel Godron,
Landscape Ecology
John Wiley & Sons, Inc.
New York, 1986

Lee, James A.
The Environment, Public Health, and Human Ecology
Johns Hopkins University Press
Baltimore, Md., 1986

Lyle, John Tillman
Design for Human Ecosystems
Van Nostrand Reinhold Company Inc.
New York, 1985

Reid, Keith, et al.
Man, Nature and Ecology
Doubleday & Company, Inc.
Garden City, N.Y., 1974

Ward, Barbara, and René Dubos
Only One Earth: The Care and Maintenance of a Small Planet
The United Nations Conference on the Human Environment
W. W. Norton & Company, Inc.
New York, 1972

Ecology, the science that interprets the biosphere, is the study of the relationship of living things to each other and their environment.

1

The earth

Land, then, is not merely soil; it is a fountain of energy flowing through a circuit of soils, plants, and animals. Food chains are the living channels which conduct energy upward; death and decay return it to the soil. The circuit is not closed; some energy is dissipated in decay, some is added by absorption from the air, some is stored in soils, peats, and long-lived forests; like a slowly augmented revolving fund of life.

ALDO LEOPOLD
A Sand County Almanac
Oxford University Press
Fair Lawn, N.J., 1969

Photosynthetic cells contain chlorophyll, the only substance that can fix the energy of the sun in a form suitable to life.

Two billion years ago, or so, plants began producing and liberating more oxygen than they consumed. This eventually gave way to a division of labor in the world of life. New organisms evolved which gave up the chemistry of production and lived instead by consuming the plants.

About 200 million years ago, land plants changed dramatically. The conifers developed, the first plants independent of the need for free water to support their reproduction. At about the same time, great uplifts took place on the continents, and the conifers became dominant on the uplands.

Still, plants needed water to live, and had to hold back some of the water rushing past them. Soil formation solved this problem, and provided a means of recycling the basic nutrients needed for plant growth.

At present, as far as we have yet been able to ascertain, no form of life exists, in a natural state, except on planet Earth.

Our sphere, sweeping at incredible speed through the emptiness of space, is locked into orbit by the immense gravitational forces of the solar system. Infinitesimal in comparison with other of the heavenly bodies and the vast interspatial framework, our globe is nonetheless mightily contrived. Consolidated over eons of time from the primordial vapors, its heavier core is a mass of white-hot iron, overlaid with viscous basalt. The molten mineral fluxes of lighter specific gravity have been gradually swirled to the surface by centrifugal force, and solidified into a shell of rock some twenty-five miles in thickness.

As the Earth's outer crust has slowly formed, it has been folded and contorted by enormous internal pressures. Violent contractions and surging volcanic upheavals have formed the mountain ranges and the lesser ridges, peaks, and valleys of our planet. The ocean basins, as they have filled with torrential rainfall from the cooling clouds of steam, have received as well the salt-laden runoff from the eroding land masses. Their rocky floors have been fractured and further depressed by the overwhelming weight of water. Whole continents have been torn apart in the dynamic process, wedged asunder, or crushed together under tremendous stress.

Over some areas of the globe the original igneous rock lies exposed as a naked sheath. Elsewhere it is covered with deep layers of sandstone and limestone laid down on the bed of warm Paleozoic seas by sedimentation and the skeletal remains of the earliest marine plants and creatures. Where the land mass has been exposed to the elements, it has been worn away, and the weathered particles have been washed or blown into the crevices and hollows to form a thin layer of topsoil. In this precious substance the earliest terrestrial grasses and plants were able to fix their roots and take their nourishment.

The first life on earth appeared about three billion years ago. The first living cells would hardly be distinguishable from simple chemical-mineral blobs. In time, through the long process of evolution, there appeared the single-celled algae, which are believed to be the first organisms capable of photosynthesis.

Today, as from the time of their beginning, people prosper in those areas where the topsoil deposits are deep and rich, where they can graze their animals and grow their grain and other crops. It is only within very recent years that agricultural peoples, with their age-old understanding and awe of nature's processes, have discovered and become absorbed in the use of power machinery. They have come to put their trust in machines and industrialization, and have turned their backs on nature. In their mechanized zeal they have scooped and hauled their way across the face of the earth and tunneled deep into its subterranean strata. They have plowed or burned off the protective sods and covers of the lowland fields and felled the timber from the upland watersheds. They have allowed billions of tons of the vital topsoil substance to be blown away or washed into the sea. They have altered river courses and leveled mountains to satisfy their immediate needs, without concern for the devastation they have wrought, or for the inevitable consequences.

And yet the tough earth, in its broad forms at least, has managed to survive the onslaught. But our newest devices and techniques are so fearsome in their power that some, like laser mining, sonic drilling, and atomic blasting, can wreak terrible and irreparable destruction. Those of us who yet cherish the earth and would protect and develop it as humanity's ultimate habitation must demand, and achieve, a moratorium. It is time for the people of our nation to reappraise our values; to reassess our goals. It is time to devise broad new legislative programs to strengthen the authority and powers of the guardian agencies. It is time to establish great centers for research and teaching in the natural sciences so that we may help new generations find again a way of life attuned to nature's way—before we have lost the choice. Otherwise, it will soon be too late. The warning signs are everywhere about us, eroded deep into the valleys and blasted out of the hills.

We have a responsibility to the earth . . . to ensure for all people clean air to breath, good water to drink, and fertile topsoil to till.

Soil erosion by water alone carries away some three billion tons of topsoil from the fields and pastures of America each year.

This soil contains over 40 million tons of essential nutrients—phosphorus, potassium, and nitrogen.

One fourth of all our croplands have already been destroyed by wasteful farming and grazing techniques.

In many countries fields have been tilled and animals pastured for centuries without depleting the soils or detracting from the beauty of the landscape.

Since the achievement of Independence, he is the greatest patriot who stops the most gullies.
  PATRICK HENRY

Every time you see a dust-cloud or a muddy stream, a field scarred by erosion or a channel choked with silt you are witnessing the passing of American democracy.
  STERLING NORTH

The wealth of a nation is in its soil, its water, its forests, and the things they produce and reproduce.
  RICHARD L. POLLET

Be provident if you wish to remain worthy of the land . . .
  VIRGIL

It is a questionable economy to spend millions of dollars on dams as part of a flood control scheme, unless at the same time we are doing all we can in the way of forest and soil conservation and rehabilitation, so that floods will be minimized rather than aggravated. Similarly, it is not sensible to spend millions of dollars to reclaim land, in order to create new farms, if at the same time we fail to take the appropriate steps to save existing farm lands from being washed into rivers.
  HARRY S. TRUMAN

If it is un-American to conserve our forests and grass-lands, in a very few generations it may be un-American to eat.
  LESTER VELIE

We Americans need again to have and be conscious of land hunger, river hunger, sea and sky hunger. . . . This isn't sentimentality. It's a matter of getting back to national health.
  SHERWOOD ANDERSON

Quotations selected from *Conservation Quotes*
U.S. Department of the Interior,
National Park Service
January 1953

Topsoil

A lengthy scientific treatise has been written describing the vital processes that occur within the first few millimeters above and below the surface of the ground. It is within this zone that earth, air, and water intermix in the presence of sunlight. Here miracles of chemistry, osmosis, transpiration, decay, transmutation, and regeneration take place. It can be said that the health and comfort, as

Topsoil is composed of disintegrated rock and the remains of plants and animals.

It is that upper surface of the earth's crust which can support the growth of indigenous vegetation or cultivated crops.

In nature, soil is formed when rock is weathered by ice or frost action, by rain, by the heat of the sun, or by oxidation. A two-inch layer is approximately a thousand years in the making.

Soil may be deposited, or removed, by the action of glaciers, wind, or running water.

With its protective vegetative covers intact, the topsoil accumulates. With the foliage and fibrous root system removed and the friable earth exposed, the entire topsoil section of an extensive acreage may be blown or washed away in a single storm.

When the soil mantle is depleted or allowed to wash away, the agricultural wealth and strength of a nation are diminished.

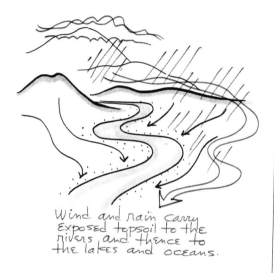

Wind and rain carry exposed topsoil to the rivers, and thence to the lakes and oceans.

We haven't got too much time left to insure, . . . that government of the earth, by the earth, for the earth, shall not perish from the people.

PHILIP SNOW
''Hope for America''
Look Magazine
December 1, 1970

Disease, warfare, and civil strife have certainly played important roles in the collapse of ancient civilizations; but the primary cause was probably the damage caused to the quality of the soil and to water supplies by poor ecological practices.

RENÉ DUBOS
B. Y. Morrison Memorial Lecture
Annual Meeting, American Association for the Advancement of Science, Washington, D.C., 1972.
(Lectureship established by the Agricultural Research Service of the U.S. Department of Agriculture)

well as the food and water supply, of the human race are utterly dependent upon the workings within this fragile matrix. These in turn are largely dependent upon the presence of topsoil and humus.

It might be assumed, therefore, that one of our greatest concerns would be the preservation of the subsoil deposits and topsoil film created over the centuries by the infinitely slow decomposition of bedrock. Yet few of our builders or lawmakers have the slightest sense of its value, and we watch every day as other acres of land are denuded and the precious supply of topsoil is buried or washed away.

Conserve the nation's topsoil bank

Wherever topsoil may remain—be it in woodland, wetland, parkland, cultivated field, or kitchen garden—it is to be considered national treasure. Whenever this loamy resource is depleted by one cubic yard, our productivity and well-being is to that extent decreased. Yet within the past decade, and without apparent concern, we have stood by as an estimated 4 percent of our total supply has been irretrievably wasted.

When our topsoil is gone—if it is to be gone—our verdant land will be barren. Many once abundant regions, like the "Fertile Crescent" of the Middle East, have thus been transformed within a few centuries of exploitation into arid wastelands. When the fact of our folly is sensed at last, the dissipation of this vital substance through erosion, filling, grading, covering, or any other wasteful practice, will no longer be condoned.

Make topsoil conservation a condition of all development and construction

The filing of a plan for the stripping and disposition of topsoil from all land to be disturbed, and the posting of a performance bond before permits are issued, are reasonable requirements.

Rebuild the topsoil section

While nature's patient process of weathering rock into fertile soil has not yet been duplicated on any significant scale, the final stage of converting low-grade soils into topsoil has been practiced for many centuries and is at present the only means by which topsoil may be feasibly replaced. It consists of blending the required admixtures of humus and nutrients into the mineral base of clays, shales, or sand, to produce varying types of loam. With the required materials at hand this can be successfully accomplished by tested formulas.

A relatively new and promising technique is the scientific blending of processed sewage, garbage, and other wastes to restructure and enrich low-grade soils.

Erosion

Where the absorptive surface cover of the watersheds has been destroyed, as by the clear-cutting and burning of our forests, or the "sod-busting" and improper cultivation of our prairie lands by poor land management, or by uncontrolled development, new land-use regulations must be framed by which surface erosion and runoff may be checked. Many regulatory and corrective programs have already been initiated on an effective scale.

Reforestation, coupled with the practice of selective logging, can be the salvation of our still extensive timberlands. The construction of hundreds of thousands of agricultural surface-water holding ponds under the guidance of the Federal Soil and Water Conservation Program has clearly proved its value. The contour plowing of farm fields, adopted as standard procedure only within the past half-century, has not only retained precious water and improved the crop yields; it has conserved hundreds of millions of cubic yards of topsoil that would otherwise have been carried down the streams and rivers and lost to the sea.

The planning and regulation of all new developments, with full consideration of their effects upon the protection of the natural watersheds, is long overdue.

Stop erosion and sedimentation

The total cost of erosion and sedimentation in the United States runs into billions of dollars annually. This includes the expense of water purification, the dredging of rivers, canals, and harbors for navigation, the reshaping of highway ditches, and the cleanout of drainage systems for cities and towns. These costs are in addition to the loss of topsoil, the depreciation of land values along the water bodies, or the expense to private owners of coping with water-borne silt.

All in all, sediment, in terms of sheer volume, outranks domestic sewage, industrial wastes, and chemicals as a major cause of water pollution. And yet few localities have laws to prevent erosion or the generation of sediments.

Preserve the ground covers

Most soils in their natural state are protected by vegetation from the blowing winds or from being washed away by the runoff of falling rain. Such vegetative cover may range in type from the loose-knit dune grasses and sedges along the coast to dense wetland alder thickets or to the towering stands of spruce and fir that compose the upland forests. As a soil protector their function is much the same in all cases, for their roots, shoots, and tendrils, together with decaying leaves, twigs, and branches, form a tightly interlaced mat that absorbs and holds the water, allowing its percolation into the earth.

Where the protective ground covers have been removed or destroyed, the unchecked surface runoff is concentrated into rivulets and streams which soon cut ruts into the soil and eventually further erode them into deep and ever-deepening gullies. The downstream covers are in turn torn loose, and great areas of land may thus be rendered useless. A further serious consequence is that the eroded soil deposits often do great damage to farmlands and to the rivers and lakes which they discolor and fill with silt.

When so much harm can result so quickly from a single break in the ground-cover fabric, all concerned with soil conservation must be on the constant lookout to keep the protective matting in repair.

Plan land development in harmony with the natural runoff patterns

Farmers have learned that when their plowed furrows run downhill, the melting snow water and falling rain soon wash them deeper and deposit much of the topsoil at the lower edge of the field, or into a passing stream. By plowing *across* the face of a slope and "with the contour," the runoff is retained to conserve both the valuable water and the soil. From a plane one can see the graceful and highly func-

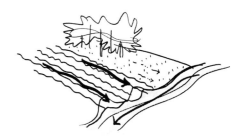

Natural vegetation and cover crops are land and soil stabilizers.

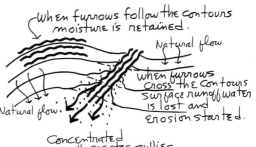

When furrows follow the contours moisture is retained.

Natural flow

When furrows cross the contours surface runoff water is lost and erosion started.

Natural flow.

Concentrated runoff creates gullies and sedimentation.

CONTOUR PLOWING PRESERVES THE LAND AND CONSERVES THE TOPSOIL COVER

At the commencement of the seventeenth century the soil [of the New England colonies], with insignificant exceptions, was covered with forests, and whenever the Indian abandoned the narrow fields he had planted and the woods he had burned over, they speedily returned . . . to their original state. Even a single generation sufficed to restore them almost to their primitive luxuriance of forest vegetation.

GEORGE PERKINS MARSH
Man and Nature
Scribners, New York, 1864
Reprinted, Harvard University Press
Cambridge, Mass., 1965
A John Harvard Library Book

A citizen of western Henrico County paid $5,000 more for his property than a neighbor across the street because his lot bordered on a lake and included a pond. A small stream fed the pond and lake. Now about four years later, the pond has become a silt basin, filled with sand and grit washed into it from upstream development. The lake has also begun to fill.

Residents of Lake Barcroft, a major housing community, also paid a premium for their property. They have since spent more than $300,000 dredging sediment out of the lake. The sediment has washed down from upstream development. Dredging is still needed about every two years.

In Chesterfield County, the three-acre, man-made lake in Brighton Green all but disappeared last year when it filled with silt, which washed off nearby land that had been stripped of vegetation for housing development.

The Virginia Outdoors
Published by the Virginia
Commission of Outdoor Recreation
Richmond, Va.
June 1972

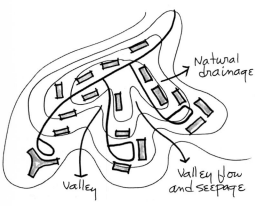

plan roads and structures in harmony with the contours and natural land forms.

PLAN WITH THE CONTOURS

tional patterns of the contour plowing of agricultural lands, and can also in some cases observe the disastrous consequences that occur when the principle has not been adopted.

The principle applies not only to farmland but to the design of residential and other properties as well. Where the flow of surface water has been considered in the placement of the buildings, the alignment of drives, and the arrangement of the parking, recreation, and garden areas, all things work better together. Less grading is required, ground-cover disruption and replacement may be minimized, and the problems of erosion are reduced or eliminated.

The lessons of contour plowing should be applied to the layout not only of single properties but to the planning of extensive systems of land use. Since gutters, swales, and huge storm drainage ditches run beside and parallel to most transportation and transitways, the consideration of "running with the contour" insofar as feasible should be an important factor in the comparative analysis of their alternate routes.

Subdivision platting, park and open space planning, and even zoning, also set the broad framework of land use and thus determine the relationship of streets and sewers to the conformation of the watersheds. This critical fact is too often overlooked.

Accommodate the surface runoff from all disturbed land areas

When the land is disturbed by grading or construction operations, the surface-water runoff patterns are changed and usually concentrated. Erosion is bound to occur unless the storm water is intercepted and redirected or put to some good use, as in a holding pond or irrigation system. Often the most severe erosion occurs during the construction period. This should therefore be precluded by preplanning and by building-inspection requirements.

Conduct concentrated storm drainage to an acceptable outfall

Where water is collected, as in a gutter, swale, or drainage pipe, it is incumbent upon the owner to see that it is conducted to a storm sewer, to a stream or pond, or to some off-site point of discharge. If water is to be directed across neighboring properties, an easement or other legal agreement is usually required. There is time-honored precedent in the codes of land law to ordain that an owner who alters, increases, or concentrates the flow of water from land is responsible for any damage it does to the properties below.

Sustain the sheet flow of ground water to downslope lands

Too little storm runoff may be worse than too much. New highways or canals, for example, often disrupt the natural flow of surface and subsurface groundwater and destroy the ecological balance of the entire affected watershed. On a smaller scale, a homeowner's prized magnolia may wither and die because of a minor change in the drainage pattern of the neighbor's lot beyond the boundary hedge.

Where regrading or construction is contemplated, care should be exercised in maintaining the established and desirable movement of both surface and ground water.

Intercept and divert destructive storm-water runoff, fill the gullies, reestablish ground covers, and rebuild eroded lands

Erosion in any form is such a destroyer of land and of property values, such an "uglifier," and such a serious environmental menace that wherever noticed it should be stopped immediately, before it gets further out of hand.

If the local authorities when notified are lethargic in responding, an appeal to the county agricultural agent or to the district Federal Soil and Water Conservation officer should get effective remedial action.

Protect farmlands from wind erosion

Wind is a destroyer, too.

Those who remember the pathetic "exodus of the Okies," or who have themselves experienced the overwhelming dust storms of the windswept flatlands, will realize the value of sustained crop cover and shelterbelt plantings.

The driving force of unchecked winds can quickly lay bare exposed farm fields, removing the topsoil and reducing whole counties to desolation and ruin. The dust clouds, or muddy runoff streams extend the area of damage. Eventually they dump their load into the lakes or other water bodies, causing unsightly turbidity and destructive siltation.

Check the wind erosion of beaches and dunes

Along the coasts and lakeshores, where the natural covers have been destroyed by overuse or development, the winds soon open up and enlarge the earth wounds. Small drifts of sand develop into great shifting dunes which encroach upon and inundate vegetation, farmlands, and homesteads.

The first wind-opened lesions of the soil can be treated with a few hours of effort by a single property owner. By acting promptly, the owner can protect and supplement the existing natural growth or may install mulches, erosion netting, or inexpensive windscreen fencing. Once the wind erosion has reached epidemic proportions, however, only governmental action can effect a cure.

Excavating, filling, grading

Each time the surface of the earth is laid open by grading equipment or construction, a chain of disruptive reactions is set in motion.

With vegetation and absorptive ground covers removed, the accelerating process of erosion is initiated. New storm-water runoff courses are formed. Soil structure is altered and its stability reduced. Bird, animal, and insect habitats are destroyed. Even the quality of light and levels of sound are changed. The character of the whole visible landscape is affected, usually for the worse. One morning's roaring work by an earthmoving machine may permanently scar a roadside or community. The consequences, in sum, are so critical that we can no longer allow an insensitive contractor or a hell-for-leather bulldozer operator the freedom to gouge and shove the earth around at will.

Require an earthwork permit

In the future, and the sooner the better, all excavating, filling, and grading operations involving heavy equipment will proceed only by permit from the local office of environmental control, and then only under the watchful eye of a trained observer who understands the full significance of the surveillance.

Enact legislation to control excavation, filling, and grading

Most sizable construction projects will require some grading by heavy equipment. The negative effects on the environment both during and

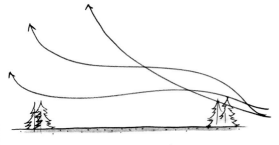

Shelterbelt plantings protect vulnerable fields.

INSTALL TREE ROWS AS WINDBREAKS

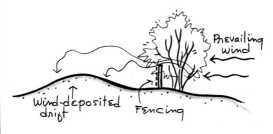

The drifting of sand can be arrested by the use of fencing or screen plantings.

The seeding or planting of native ground covers or windbreaks is also feasible.

CHECK DUNE MIGRATION WHERE DESIRABLE

Man is rich in proportion to the number of things that he can leave alone.
Henry David Thoreau
Walden, Chapter 2

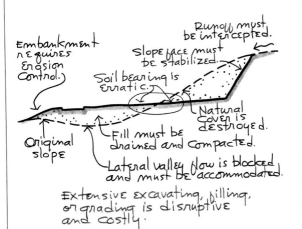

Extensive excavating, filling, or grading is disruptive and costly.

AVOID HEAVY EARTHWORK WHENEVER POSSIBLE

after the earthmoving operations can be minimized by the enforcement of an earthwork ordinance. The list of requirements might well include the following procedures:

1. Review the plans to ascertain that the site development has been designed to fit the topography and that the extent of the earthwork is justified.

2. Investigate surface and subsurface conditions including landscape features to be preserved, soils, utilities, and possible mine workings.

3. Reduce erosion by limiting the area and time of exposure and by the provision of drainage diversion channels.

4. Use culverts or temporary bridges at points of stream crossings by equipment.

5. Construct catchment basins to trap silt and debris before they enter the mains or streams, or cause property damage.

6. Abate dust generation and clean up the mud.

7. Preserve existing vegetation, where possible, to serve as buffer and erosion control.

8. Use erosion nets, mulch, or temporary seeding over unstable areas.

9. Locate storm drainage outfalls at or near stream elevation.

10. Repair damaged areas and install ground-cover surfacing and planting as soon as feasible.

Borrow pits

The extraction of sand, gravel, and other construction materials has pocked and disfigured many square miles of the landscape adjacent to our cities and highways. Since the materials are bulky and low in cost, they are usually excavated near the sites where they will be used. Unless the locations and workings are subjected to controls, the depleted properties will be left with steep, unstable banks or pits. Often they remain water-filled, as a health and safety hazard, or awash with scum and trash as a visual blight to the neighborhood for many years to come.

Only within recent years have public agencies and sand and gravel companies, under the pressure of growing public resentment, developed procedures by which the final land and water forms are designed in advance of digging. The expended parcels are graded out, seeded, and sold as highly desirable building or recreation sites. What is now done in exceptional cases should be made mandatory.

Preplan the finished landscape

By using available survey and core-boring data it is a simple matter to prepare plans by which, in the process of excavation, borrow sites and gravel pits may be transformed into real estate assets rather than liabilities. The topsoil may be stripped, stockpiled, and reused. The overburden and deleterious soils may be shaped into sculptured landforms surrounding streams, lakes, or lagoons. Often the newly created landscapes may be far more attractive, and salable, than the existing properties which surround them.

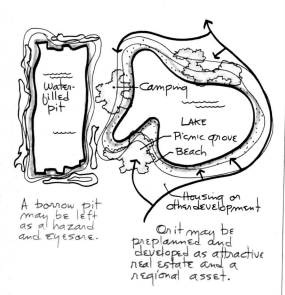

A borrow pit may be left as a hazard and eyesore.

Or it may be preplanned and developed as attractive real estate and a regional asset.

BORROW PITS AND STRIP MINES NEED NOT BLIGHT THE LANDSCAPE

The sand and gravel industry is in a unique situation insofar as rehabilitation is concerned. It utilizes heavy earth-moving equipment, and often has large volumes of material, unsuitable for processing, available for creating functional land forms. Since it is necessary to move all this material in order to extract the desired natural resources, it becomes a matter of manipulating the equipment in a manner that will achieve the most desirable land areas.
ANTHONY M. BAUER
Simultaneous Excavation and Rehabilitation of Sand and Gravel Sites
A Research Project of the University of Illinois
Sponsored by the National Sand and Gravel Association, Silver Spring, Md., 1965

Los Angeles has mineral deposit planning. The City surveyed sand and gravel deposits in the San Fernando Valley, evaluated them by drilling, and zoned a number of them as gravel pit sites. After the deposits are quarried, they will be used for waste disposal, and then restored for other urban uses.
PETER FLAWN
Environmental Geology
Harper & Row, Publishers, Inc.
New York, 1970

Text continued on page 26.

Land reclamation

The creation of a new land-water setting
for Chicago's Botanic Garden

When the Chicago Horticultural Society set about to construct a new botanic garden, a suitable site was not to be found—so one was *created* to meet the demanding specifications. A whole new landscape of hills, streams, lakes, and islands was shaped from depleted fields and grossly polluted drainageways. Wasteland unfit for human use and providing but marginal habitat for birds and wildlife was converted into a garden framework of unique topographical interest and great beauty.

This is the story of the transformation. It exemplifies the possibilities of preplanning extraction pits, sanitary fills, and the restoration of millions of acres of stripped, eroded, or otherwise degraded lands that lie in the wake of man's abuses, like festering sores upon our American landscape.

The material presented has been abstracted from continuing planning proposals being developed for the Botanic Garden of the Chicago Horticultural Society.

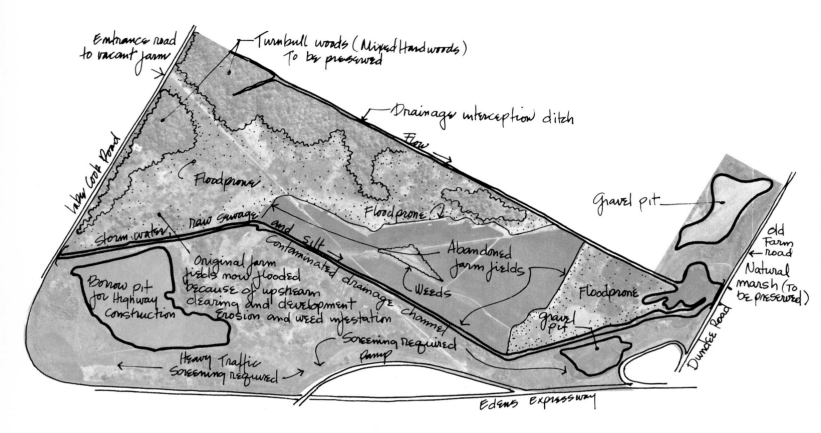

Labels on the illustration:
- Entrance road to vacant farm
- Turnbull woods (Mixed Hardwoods) To be preserved
- Drainage interception ditch
- Flow
- Floodprone
- Floodprone
- Gravel pit
- old Farm road
- Natural marsh (To be preserved)
- Lake Cook Road
- Storm water
- raw sewage and silt contaminated drainage channel
- Original farm fields now flooded because of upstream clearing and development Erosion and weed infestation
- Abandoned farm fields
- Weeds
- Floodprone
- Borrow pit for Highway Construction
- gravel pit
- Screening required Ramp
- Heavy Traffic Screening required
- Dundee Road
- Edens Expressway

The existing conditions

In its program for a new botanic garden the Chicago Horticultural Society required a site of approximately 300 acres. Of this total, some *40 acres* would in time be developed intensively as display and teaching gardens, *5 to 10* acres would be devoted to a research and experimental center and maintenance compound, and the balance to parking, nature preserve, bird and wildlife sanctuary, and peripheral screening. Ease of access from the entire Chicago metropolitan region would be essential, as would suitable soils, site drainage, air, water, acoustical, and visual qualities and microclimatic conditions. A thorough reconnaissance showed that, even with a generous acquisition budget, no suitable property was obtainable.

Borrowing from the experience of the Cook County Forest Preserve District, which in the days of the Civilian Conservation Corps had created prime parklands from a silted and contaminated section of the Skokie marshes, it was decided to build a new garden site out of the weeds, ooze, and scrabble.

An abandoned farm and borrow pit was selected near an interchange on the north-south Edens Expressway. Preliminary testing showed that with extensive regrading, water quality control, and screen planting, all essential criteria could be met.

On the face of it, the existing situation would seem to be far from promising. (See illustration.) Much of the original farmland had been flooded out as a consequence of clearing and uncontrolled development in the upstream watershed. A deep drainage ditch transecting the farm was charged with silt, refuse, and raw sewage. In times of heavy rainfall the ditch would overflow to flood and erode all but the highest farm fields. As these became impoverished, they too had been deserted and left to the overgrowth of noxious weeds. Several large gravel extraction pits had been left in the wake of the construction of the adjacent roadways. The sight and sound of passing traffic on the expressway would require earth mounding and heavy tree planting to furnish an adequate noise and visual barrier.

On the positive side, the higher land to the north and east had been left in a stand of mixed hardwoods. Across the balance of the eastern boundary lay the rolling fairways and greens of a country club and golf course, affording long-range protection. On the lower floodplain a deep section of topsoil had been deposited above a rubbery strata of glacial till. The water retained in the borrow pits gave promise of a potential series of lagoons and waterways. The soil excavated in their construction could be shaped into well-drained plateaus above the flood level—and into a composition of mounded peninsulas and islands. The sculptured landforms would provide a measure of wind protection and afford a variety of exposures. The expansive water surface would ameliorate the summer heat, increase the humidity to the benefit of the plantings, and temper the damaging effects of late spring and early fall frosts. Scenically, the landforms and waterways would be reminiscent of the lovely garden islands of Soochow and the Yuan Ming Yuan to the west of Peking. When reshaped and provided with freshwater pumped from Lake Michigan, the land-water setting would have few rivals as the site of a fine botanic garden.

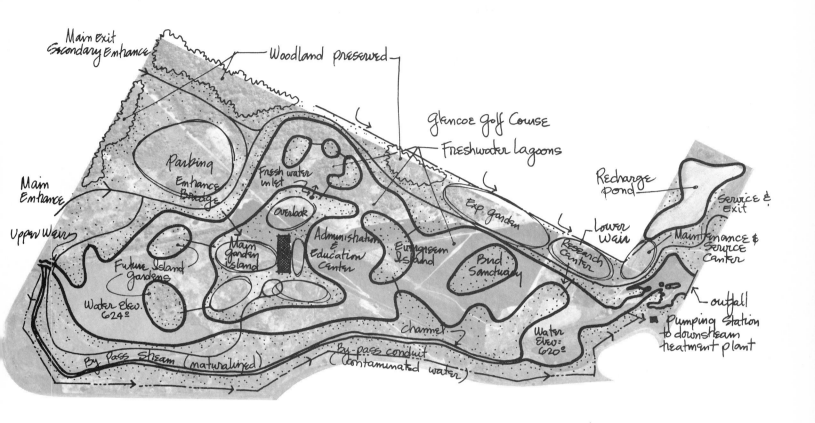

Labels on map: Main exit / Secondary Entrance — Woodland preserved — Glencoe golf Course — Freshwater Lagoons — Recharge pond — Main Entrance — Parking Entrance Bridge — Fresh water inlet — Overlook — Exp. garden — Service & Exit — Upper Weir — Main garden Island — Administration & Education Center — Evergreen Island — Lower Weir — Research Center — Maintenance & Service Center — Future Island gardens — Water Elev. 624° — Bird Sanctuary — outfall — Pumping Station to downstream treatment plant — By Pass Stream (naturalized) — By-pass conduit (contaminated water) — Channel — Water Elev: 620°

The plan for conversion

To preplan a site for a given purpose—such as a horticultural garden—it is important to first have in mind at least a general plan of the completed installation. A new landscape can then be custom-designed to accommodate the proposed layout.

The land-use components

The major land-use areas of the garden were first conceived in diagram as to best possible size, shape, and interrelationship. These included the main garden island on which would be built the educational and administrative center. The structure would be built on a knoll commanding the most dramatic views to the north and south and relating directly to the display and demonstration gardens. These would be linked by water-edge pathways from which one could cross by bridge to the smaller islands.

The interconnecting island concept would provide a delightful garden setting of ever-changing views. Circulation would be direct, security maximized, and shorter hauls by the earthmoving equipment would make

the lake excavation and earth sculpturing more economical. On the "mainland," areas were likewise designated for parking, the experimental gardens and research center, and for the maintenance building and service courts. Interfolding hillocks would be rolled up along the Edens Expressway to help screen the traffic and contain the bypass overflow channel. The established woodland would be left intact and the more remote areas of the site would be blended into the last remaining vestiges of the original Skokie "Marsh." This historic preserve would be left in its natural state as a bird and wildlife sanctuary.

Trafficways

Anticipating future garden attendance in the range of a million persons each year and peak day visitation of over 35,000, great care was taken in the planning of all types and routes of movement. The roadway capacities and points of ingress and egress were determined in a series of meetings with state and county highway officials. Paved parking compounds for 1,200 cars were provided, with

overflow parking on stabilized turf for an additional 600 automobiles. The garden elements were intentionally spaced out to provide maneuvering distance and avoid traffic congestion. All internal drives were planned as "parkways," and their alignment and profiles designed to reveal an unfolding panorama of woodland, gardens, and lakes, while yet shielding traffic movement from the main garden views.

Walkways of varying width were planned to provide routes for all types of pedestrian movement, and in some cases to "govern" the rates of desired flow—for "ways" and related "places" must be designed together in terms of capacities.

Hydrology

The expansive areas of water had their genesis in the need for earth fill to lift the gardens out of the muck and above flood levels. Landscape architectural plans and sections were prepared in conjunction with those of the engineers to balance the "cut" and "fill," and to best utilize the various types of soils in the land and island construction. First the

MAIN ENTRANCE

PARKING

LAKE COOK ROAD

ACCESS DRIVE
TO MAIN ISLAND

OVERFLOW PARKING

TURNBULL WOODS

JAPANESE GARDEN ISLAND

EVERGREEN ISLAND

ILLINOIS TOLLWAY

ADMINISTRATION AND EDUCATION CENTER

work areas would be cleared of weeds and brush, all topsoil stripped and stockpiled, and a temporary bypass channel cut. Then as the water bodies were excavated, the selected subsoils could be placed and compacted in layers to build up the new landforms.

To intercept the contaminated stream, a weir was planned at the upper end of the property. From this point the low-level flows

of polluted water would be conducted around the gardens by a subsurface conduit to a new pumping station at the south, and thence to a downstream treatment plant. The upper levels of cleaner water would be allowed to overflow the weir and form an open bypass stream which would accommodate all but the heaviest rainfall and stream surges which would only then enter the lake. At off-peak demand

hours fresh water would be introduced into the lake system in order to maintain the desired levels.

The earthwork and garden construction were started in the fall of 1966. Three years later the land sculpturing was completed, the lake basins filled, and the new landscape seeded and green in its temporary cover of grasses.

SCALE:
0   100' 200' 300' 400' 500' 600'

NORTH

RESEARCH AND PRODUCTION AREA

DUNDEE ROAD

MARSH ISLAND

MAINTENANCE
BUILDING

SKOKIE LAGOONS

TO CHICAGO LOOP ➤

EDENS EXPRESSWAY

The island gardens

The objective of the Chicago Botanic Garden is to provide education in all aspects of horticulture within the framework of a beautiful landscape setting. While each area of the site—be it woodlot, bird sanctuary, or experimental plot—is important to the work of the scientific institution, it is on the main island grouping that the more intensive teaching program will be conducted. Here, on a broad saddle between two knolls, and commanding striking views in all directions, the educational and administrative center has been constructed. Housing offices, meeting rooms, auditorium, library, and display houses, its function will be to concentrate and extend the learning and teaching activities of the embracing horticultural gardens.

In crossing the bridge from the tree-shaded parking "rooms" to the central island, one will enter a pedestrian domain. Only by a gated access drive and circuitous approach can visitors, staff, and service personnel gain admittance by car to an enclosed parking court and entrance. Elsewhere on the islands the garden walks and spaces are to be kept traffic-free and serene in order that they may be enjoyed and the plantings studied without distraction.

On the larger island will be installed, stage by stage, a full complement of demonstration gardens, seasonal walks, floral displays and tree, shrub, and herbaceous collections. The smaller, outlying islands, to be reached only by pathway and footbridges, are being planned for the display of collections of evergreens, hawthorns, flowering crab apples, and other selected plants.

It will take many decades for Chicago's Botanic Garden to attain its full splendor. But Nature is patient as she watches the slow transformation of this reach of land and water from pristine marsh, to polluted sump to, in time perhaps, one of the great horticultural gardens of the world.

In the Western Hills beyond Peking are still to be found the island groves and waterways of the fabled Yuan Ming Yuan, or "Garden of Perfect Brightness." This garden paradise of the ancient Chinese emperors was, perhaps more than any other, the prototype for the new Chicago Horticultural Society Botanic Garden now taking form north of the Skokie Lagoons. In both, the expansive garden setting of lakes, hills, and channels was created in its entirety from a marshy floodplain. In both, plants from the farthest reaches of the world would be introduced into the extensive horticultural collections. And in both—for their time and place and purpose—the stated objective was to create a garden second to none.

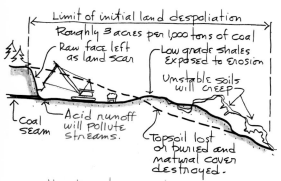

Limit of initial land despoliation
Roughly 3 acres per 1,000 tons of coal
Raw face left as land scar
Low grade shales exposed to erosion
Unstable soils will creep
Coal seam
Acid runoff will pollute streams.
Topsoil lost or buried and natural cover destroyed.

With adequate regulation and bonding the fertile soils can be stripped and stockpiled, the overburden replaced to existing or improved contour, and ground covers, crops, or forest restored.

COAL STRIPPING — THE CURSE AND THE CURE

The Interior Department estimates that $250,000 million would be needed to repair damage caused by strip mining in Appalachia. In addition, about 10,500 miles of Appalachian streams are contaminated by acids, sediments and metals from exposed coal beds.

"Environment: The Price of Strip Mining"
Time magazine
March 22, 1971

Strip mines

The surface mining of coal, ores, clays, or phosphates also utilizes heavy earthmoving and processing equipment and large stockpiling areas. These drastically disrupt and deface the rural and suburban terrain in which they occur. The land is scalped, topsoil is buried, debris is scattered, erosion started, and streams and lakes polluted with silt and other wastes. Noise, mud, dust, truck traffic, and unsightly workings are typical features. These, combined with the scarred and derelict lands left in their wake, all make surface mining operations, as generally conducted, incompatible with good land use. The initial flush of tax contributions to the local coffers is lost many times over by the long-term depreciation of land values which they cause.

There is no reason to stand by while the landscape is ravaged just because an operator holds, or has leased from a marginal farmer, the "right" to strip the land. Surface mining must be treated as any other land use, and controlled by zoning, bonding, and effective legislation.

In the United States strip mines have already despoiled more than 2 million acres of our land; yet only 5 percent of the strippable coal has so far been removed. Extensive new deposits are being unearthed in Arizona, Montana, North Dakota, and Wyoming.

Enact effective legal controls and enforce them

Since local ordinances, in rural areas particularly, may not be adequate to provide workable controls, it is up to the next higher jurisdiction—the county or the state—to assume responsibility. State guidelines as to policy, model ordinances, bonding requirements, and inspection procedures are helpful to local communities wishing to better regulate surface mining operations. Where the state agencies themselves are lax, the federal government must exercise firm control until satisfied that local regulations are adequate and are being strictly enforced.

Require a performance bond

As a condition of surface mining or material extraction it is established practice in most progressive localities to require that prior to the start of work a bond be posted to cover the full cost of restoration. If a plan and specification for the work are made part of the permit granting, if the bond is adequate, and if all requirements are enforced, the results will be gratifying.

Restore the stripped and mined-out properties

Communities saddled with depleted surface mines or extraction pits, which are usually tax delinquent, have little recourse but to rehabilitate the blighted or blighting acreage at public expense. Often a locality may partially recoup the cost by converting the land to recreation uses or to forest preserve.

As a glowing example of what can be achieved, the public-spirited owner of the Harmon Creek Coal Company in western Pennsylvania pioneered techniques of regrading, seeding, and replanting of the huge mined-out holdings. This work was carried out concurrently and coordinated with the stripping operations. In time, the potential wasteland was transformed into an idyllic landscape of clear streams, lakes, and wooded slopes to be donated as the site of a new state park.

Deep mine extraction

Most of the environmental problems resulting from the subsurface mining of coal and other minerals could be eliminated by the simple and logical requirement that owners be made responsible for any contamination or subsidence resulting from their operations.

Contamination usually occurs in the form of sulfuric acid or iron sulfides which are leached from rock strata when they are exposed to precipitation or dripping mine water. The telltale rusty discoloration of the outfall streams is common in mining territory and gives evidence that they have become unfit for use and noxious to fish and wildlife. The unsightly seepage from a single mine opening can pollute the water and stain the countryside for many miles downstream. The damage will continue until the pit is sealed or the leakage plugged.

Subsidence of the land above the mined-out seams is also a common hazard. If the owners were to install a permanent type of shoring, backfill the mine, or leave a system of unmined columns to support the overburden, settlement could be virtually precluded. But they make do, instead, with temporary planking and supports, or "pull the stumps" of coal or ore as they leave, to retrieve the maximum profit and let the structures or the land above suffer the consequences.

Redefine mining and mineral rights

This needs to be done at both the state and federal levels.

The prerogatives enjoyed by possessors of mineral or subsurface rights are dubious held-over privileges derived from the early days when mining occurred mostly in the outback country where the negative effects were seldom noticed or considered. Presently, large-scale mining operations are often conducted within and beneath densely populated cities and suburbs. It would be supposed that the limitations and liabilities would by now have been redefined, but this is not so. Inexplicably, homeowners and members of the business community alike have accepted displaced foundations, cracked building walls, and dangerous cave-ins without challenging the power of the mining interests or their state and federal lobbies. In the face of the changing public temperament it is time that they did.

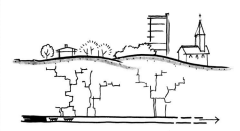

Many property owners are blithely unaware that the ground beneath their homes, or other structures, has been mined out or is still subject to unrestricted mineral rights.

SUBSURFACE RIGHTS SHOULD BE REEXAMINED AND CONTROLLED

Drilling, ditching, dredging

It is probable that these three activities, together with other related forms of extraction and earthmoving, have wrought more havoc upon the face of the earth within the past twenty years than the destructive human animal has managed in all the years before.

When digging and earthwork were accomplished only by the straining power of men, horses, and oxen, the need for a project would have to be clearly evident before the task was undertaken.

Not all the winds, and storms and earthquakes, and seas, and seasons of the world, have done so much to revolutionize the earth as MAN . . . *since the day he came forth upon it, and received dominion over it.*

H. BUSHNELL
Sermon on "The Power of an Endless Life"
From the title page, *Man and Nature*
George P. Marsh
Scribners, New York, 1864
Reprinted, Harvard University Press
Cambridge, Mass., 1965
A John Harvard Library Book

Damage was usually confined. Present-day projects of massive ecological impact, such as the trans-Everglades canal, seem to have been proposed simply because the wetlands were there and the means of destruction at hand. With the advent of colossal power machinery and atomic blasting, we have the capacity, and seem determined, to lay waste one of the most bountiful and beautiful of all the lands that mankind has found for a home.

Perhaps the seriousness of the threat, and the shocking disasters which surround us, will stir us at last to demand the controls so clearly required.

The offshore oil spill at Santa Barbara in 1969 covered 800 square miles and washed 2,000,000 gallons on shore.

California subsidence due to oil extraction has caused damages estimated at over $100 million within recent years.

Regulate the construction and operation of drilling sites, processing areas, pumping stations, and pipelines

The pumping, storage, transmission, and processing of oils, gas, and chemicals have etched their unfortunate record across our countryside. Who is not familiar with the stench and smear of the pumping stations and seepage ponds? Where can we find a landscape not marred by the ditching for cross-country pipelines? What oceanfront county has not lost saltwater marshes and beaches to the onslaught of the dredge?

Consider the menace of cross-country ditching

As if the poor earth hadn't troubles enough, a new threat has appeared on the scene, the super-rotary ditcher. Some can gouge out a trench 6 feet across and 10 feet deep at the rate of 2 miles per day. The damage that can be caused in one day's work is unbelievable. Huge quantities of topsoil can be chewed into and mixed with the subsoils; sheet and ground water are intercepted and diverted; root systems are destroyed or weakened; and both wind and water erosion are brought into play.

Such equipment must join the parade of other monster power machines that need to be tamed and brought under firm control.

Confine the use of dredging equipment to precisely defined lines and fields of operation

The natural processes which occur along the edges and on the beds of the larger water bodies are vital to the life cycle of many types of fish and wildlife. Dredges, used to cut channels, extract building materials, or create buildable land, disturb not only the site of the cuts but also the site of the fills. Often the result is a double tragedy.

The state of Florida, as one example, has inadvertently become a demonstration ground for all the ills attending indiscriminate dredging. Rivers, coasts, and keys alike have until recently been ravished without restraint. At last the state and the more progressive counties are taking exemplary action to protect their land and water resources.

Human activity has already scarred the face of the earth and upset many ecological systems, but men have not yet learned to predict or forestall the unwanted side effects of landscape alterations. With characteristic heedlessness, however, we continue to plan even larger alterations ignoring the fact that construction of monumental projects entails the risk of monumental blunders.

R. L. NACE
Quoted, *Water, Earth and Man: A Synthesis of Hydrology Geomorphology and Socio-Economic Geography*
Edited by R. J. Chorley
Methune, Barnes and Noble, Inc.
New York, 1969

Base permission upon performance

In any operation which causes, or threatens to cause, the *significant* disruption of the earth's surface, structure, drainageways, or aquifers; or which may result in pollution; or which may in any way effect a harmful imbalance in the natural processes, those in charge must be made responsible to the public. It is proposed that the public interest be represented by the federal, state, and, in turn, the local environmental protection agencies.

Licenses and bonds are to be required of the owners of all firms engaged in the activities of excavating, mining, or drilling. An application will be required for each specific project. Work will be initiated only after full investigation, the issuance of a permit, and the assignment of a responsible inspector who will be present during the entire procedure. Licenses will be renewed and permits issued only to those with a record of satisfactory performance.

Waste piles, dumps, sanitary fills

Wherever the good earth has been abused by the diggings, leavings, and heapings of man; wherever the drainageways or underground water tables have been befouled, there is need for remedial work. For such lesions and infections tend to spread and disfigure the complexion of the regional landscape and to poison the ecosystem.

Often an editorial, or the protest of a citizen group, is enough to spur the offending landowner or the local government to action.

Stop the violations

In most well-governed communities the ordinances required to prohibit unsightly or unsanitary conditions are already on the books. If they are not adequate, or if they are not being fairly enforced, it is time to get out the petitions.

Clean up the mess

Messes, like most other problems, don't just blow away. Unless corrected they tend to spread and proliferate.

A noted park administrator achieved for his recreation areas the reputation of being the cleanest and most attractive in the nation. His rule was simple. Before opening the parks to the public in the morning, his staff would remove all traces of litter and graffiti, repair any ruts in the turf, and wash down the walls, pavements, and tables. Confronted with such sparkling surroundings, the people responded by helping to keep things clean. Such is human nature.

Convert liabilities into assets

Waste areas, bypassed and avoided by developers, often provide a community with its last opportunity to acquire open space lands. By removal and processing of the refuse and by regrading and planting the sites, they can be transformed into highly desirable recreation areas and valuable building frontage.

Mystic Bay, Indianapolis: Aggregate mining operations being conducted to yield a lake and earth contouring for a preplanned community.

Mystic Bay, after reclamation.

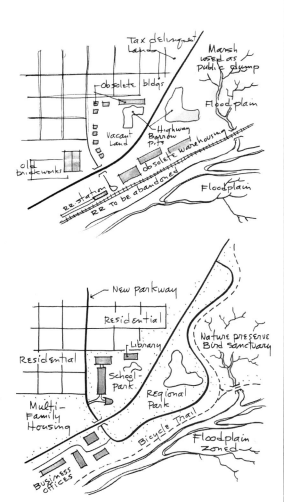

REASSEMBLE UNUSED AND VACATED PARCELS
AND CONVERT THEM TO COMMUNITY ASSETS

Reclamation, regeneration

Mention has been made of the opportunities for converting landscape eyesores into pleasant and useful community spaces. This promising aspect of land conservation deserves more thorough consideration.

In every built-up region one finds those neglected properties which detract from the appearance of the neighborhood and depreciate real estate values. Such parcels may be blighted by vacant or deteriorating structures or by undesirable uses. They may be narrow strips or fragments bypassed and left because of their unsuitability as building sites. They may comprise extensive wastelands created by strip mining, gravel pits, or heavy fills. They may include swamps or wetlands misused as public dumps, or eroded gullies choked with debris. Often they are backed up against railroads and transmission rights-of-way, or follow along and include steep slopes or watercourses. Many such properties have become tax delinquent. Others are owned by any one of a number of governmental agencies.

While in their neglected state these remnants are detrimental, they may well be, in many instances, the last and best hope for neighborhood rehabilitation and for bringing nature back into the built-up urban districts. The open space land is there, unrecognized as such because of its unsightly condition, but waiting to be reassembled into usable patterns and rehabilitated. With cleanup, reshaping, and replanting, these properties may be used to protect and enhance the waterways, reforest the slopes, and screen the traffic and transit routes. A whole city or region may be revitalized, given form, breathing space, and recreation places by the reclamation of such derelict lands.

Remove blight and obsolescence

A first step in the upgrading of a community landscape is the removal of offending trash, debris, weeds, and all other forms of pollution. This can be accomplished only if the local government assumes its proper role, provides a budget, and assigns responsibility to an agency official whose duty will be to organize and publicize the effort, to enlist the aid of citizens, and to provide the necessary guidance, staff, and equipment.

A second function, best performed by the same agency, will be the definition and enforcement of a satisfactory level of maintenance of all properties. Where necessary, vacant and obsolete structures will be removed. This program may be carried forward under the authority of existing or amended ordinances governing the public health, safety, and welfare.

If cleanup and maintenance is not performed by the owner after sufficient notification, the local government will perform the required work and back-charge the offender. If necessary, the right of property lien and police powers may be exercised.

Reshape the disfigured earth

Where the land has been subjected to erosion, uncontrolled landfills, strip mining, or pit extraction, there will be a need for regrading and recontouring. If this is accomplished with a new use and development plan in mind, a prepared site may usually be provided for less than the cost of comparable land. Drainageways, water features, ground covers, and planting may create a new and attractive landscape asset.

Restore the topsoil section

Depleted farm fields, contaminated watersheds, slag dumps, or mined areas often require major soil-restoration measures as part of their rehabilitation. Concurrently with the enforcement of effective controls against further degradation, restorative procedures will be put into operation. These may include erosion prevention and the sealing off or treatment of mine wastes and other contaminants. The stabilized land surfaces will then be cleaned and scarified in preparation for topsoiling. The new topsoil section may be applied directly if a supply is available, as from well-managed sanitary fills. Otherwise a satisfactory section can be constructed, by the addition and intermixing of such materials as sand, humus, agricultural limestone, or other soil conditioners.

Reestablish the natural covers

The seeding of reshaped land and revitalized soil to crops or to native grasses will preserve their condition and tilth. The healing process can be accelerated by hydro-seeding and mulching or by the application of reforestation techniques.

Often in the more extensive areas of regrading, as along highways or watercourses, the most effective and most economical means of reestablishing native growth is to stake out an undulating mowing line beyond which nature is allowed to take its course. Volunteer windblown, water-borne, and other seeds will soon initiate an ecological progression of grasses, weeds, and brush which will in time produce a climax wetland, meadow, or forest.

Reclaim extraction pits, fills, and spoil piles

Since there will be a continuing and no doubt increasing need for fossil fuels, chemicals, minerals, and construction aggregates, their further extraction is to be anticipated. With creative planning and proper regulation this necessary disruption may be used to generate new recreation and open space lands. The chief requirements are that the issuance of all permits be made subject to the filing of a restoration

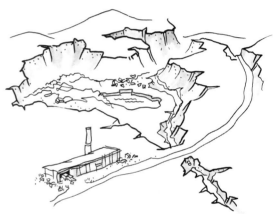

CONVERT LANDSCAPE LIABILITIES - - -

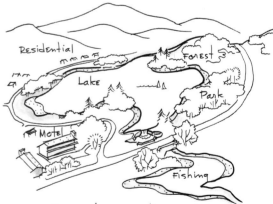

With new heavy earth-moving equipment it is now feasible to reshape and reclaim lands which have been stripped or otherwise abused. A whole new landscape may be so created.

- - - INTO COMMUNITY ATTRIBUTES

plan; its approval by a responsible agency; the posting of a bond; and the assurance that the restoration plan be fully realized.

By this simple device strip mines and gravel pits may be transformed into a new landscape of reshaped landforms, water features, and plantings; sanitary fills may be developed as new agricultural lands; and quarries may be converted into attractive sites for housing, public gardens, playgrounds, or parks.

The prerequisite of restoring or improving the ravished land should be considered no more than a fair and reasonable condition of depleting a natural resource.

Reassemble the unused parcels

Leftover slivers and odd-shaped pieces of land can be fitted together into lineal parks between which, along which, or around which, sound development will be attracted. Tax-delinquent properties, unbuildable parcels, and excess governmental holdings may also be incorporated into the open space network. As other properties become vacant or nonconforming, they may in turn be acquired to round out and complete the system.

Rezone the slopes and floodplains

These marginal or unbuildable lands are the hope of congested urban areas. Their use for housing or other building construction is expensive because of foundation problems and site-improvement costs. There is the ever-present danger of slippage or flooding. Furthermore, the provision of public services, streets, utilities, lighting, and fire and police protection often costs more than the tax revenues received.

By the rezoning of steep slopes and flood-prone lowlands to an open space category, a sprawling metropolis can be separated into logical neighborhoods or districts, each surrounded by greenbelts. These will ventilate and beautify the region while providing routes of movement and transmission. This is land conservation at its very best.

Landscape protection

In the United States a large proportion of all construction and landscape development is awarded by competitive bidding and carried forward in accordance with plans and specifications prepared by architects, landscape architects, and engineers. This being so, it is incumbent upon the planners to ensure that the contract documents provide for a reasonable level of environmental protection and pollution control.

In this context, pollution is defined as the presence of physical, chemical, or biological elements which adversely affect human welfare, unfavorably alter ecological balances, or degrade the quality of air, water, or land.

Where construction is undertaken without professional guidance, the local government must assume the full responsibility for environmental protection.

Maintain the quality of the land

All areas within the project boundaries, except those clearly intended to be modified by development, are to be preserved in their existing condition, or so improved that they will be compatible with both the new construction and the surrounding landscape.

For one kind of land, the case for zoning is abundantly clear: the flood plains that border our rivers and streams. . . . Building on flood plains hurts people. It is not only a question of what happens to the unfortunates who live in the houses that will be inundated but to the people downstream.

By allowing developers to waterproof the flood plains, communities have been increasing the flood damage potential faster than the engineers can build dams to compensate.
WILLIAM H. WHYTE
The Last Landscape
Doubleday & Company, Inc.
Garden City, N.Y., 1968

Prevent landscape defacement

Except in those areas designated for clearing, storage, or improvement, the contractor shall preserve the ground cover, existing ground forms, landscape features, and vegetation. Prior to the start of work barricades shall be erected to protect freestanding trees and temporary fencing or well-marked post and line barriers installed along the limits of construction.

Maintain an orderly project site

From start to completion of construction the property shall be maintained at all times in a clean, safe, and sanitary condition. Natural drainageways are to be kept open and unpolluted and additional temporary drainage structures installed as required. Sanitary facilities shall be located away from streams, wells, or springs. No on-site burning shall be permitted. All waste materials shall be stored within approved enclosures or hauled away in covered vehicles. No litter or trash are to be in evidence. Noxious weeds are to be mowed or removed to prevent seed dissemination.

In addition, and within reasonable limits of tolerance, the operation shall be so conducted that neither noise, temporary lighting, fumes, dust, nor other forms of pollution will become a problem.

Take steps to preclude erosion

Reduce, insofar as possible, the extent of cut and fill operations and the length of time that readily erodible soil will lie exposed. Immediately upon completion of grading of any sizable area, the soils shall be protected by the use of temporary vegetation, seeding, or mulch, or by the establishment of permanent covers.

Protect the water resources

It shall be the responsibility of the contractor to investigate and comply with all federal, state, county, and municipal laws concerning the pollution of watercourses and water bodies. Streams, lakes, or reservoirs are not to be polluted with fuels, lubricants, chemicals, sewage, bitumens, acids, or other harmful materials.

The rate of runoff from the construction site is to be retarded and controlled. Sediments resulting from dewatering, grading, and construction shall be trapped in silt-retention basins. Other erosion and sediment control devices such as berms, dikes, and drains shall be provided as necessary. The fording of streams by equipment shall be limited in order to reduce turbidity; where frequent stream crossings are to be necessary, temporary culverts or bridges are to be installed.

Preserve fish and wildlife habitat

To prevent the disturbance of fish or wildlife cover beyond the actual construction area, a contractor must have the express permission of a game warden or conservation officer to cut brush, alter watercourses, or spray with insecticides or chemicals.

Restore disturbed areas

Upon completion of construction the contractor shall be obliged to obliterate all signs of haul roads, storage areas, and temporary structures. Extraneous materials and objects shall be removed from the site. Trees, plants, ground covers, or other landscape features which may have been damaged shall be restored or replaced.

The finished project, if well conceived and well constructed, will leave no blemish upon the landscape and will in all ways enhance the community of which it is a part.

Further Reading:

Bradshaw, A. D., and M. J. Chadwick,
The Restoration of the Land: The Ecology and Reclamation of Derelict and Degraded Land
University of California Press
Berkeley, Calif., 1981

Dale, T., and Carter, V. G.
Topsoil and Civilization
University of Oklahoma Press
Norman, Okla., 1955

Griggs, Gary B., and John A. Gilchrist
Geologic Hazards, Resources and Environmental Planning
Wadsworth
Belmont, Calif., 1983

Hudson, Norman
Soil Conservation
Cornell University Press
Ithaca, N.Y., 1971

Law, Dennis L.
Mined Land Rehabilitation
Van Nostrand Reinhold Company Inc.
New York, 1984

Leopold, Aldo
A Sand County Almanac
Oxford University Press
Fairlawn, N.J., 1969

Leveson, David
Geology and the Urban Environment
Oxford University Press
New York, 1980

Marsh, George Perkins
Man and Nature
Scribners, New York, 1864
Reprinted, Harvard University Press
Edited by David Lowenthal
Cambridge, Mass., 1965

Sendlein, L. V., and H. Yazicigil, eds.
Surface Mining, Environmental Monitoring and Reclamation
Elsevier
New York, 1983

Smith, M. A.
Contaminated Land: Reclamation and Treatment
Plenum Publishing
New York, 1985

Attitudes toward the land must ultimately be based on attitudes toward life.

CLARENCE GLACKEN
Quoted by Pierre Dansereau
Challenge for Survival
Columbia University Press
Irvington-on-Hudson, N.Y., 1970

2

Air

Whereas the Columns and Clowds of Smoake, which are belched forth from the sooty Throates of those Works [London factories] are so thick and plentiful, that rushing out with great impetuosity, they are capable even to resist the fiercest winds, and being extremely surcharg'd with a fuliginous Body, fall down upon the City.

I propose therefore, that by an Act of this present Parliament, this infernal Nuisance be reformed; enjoyning, that all those Works be removed five or six Miles distance from London before the River of Thames . . .

JOHN EVELYN
Fumifugium, Or the Inconvenience of the Aer and Smoak of London Dissipated
The *Diary of John Evelyn*
London, England, 1661

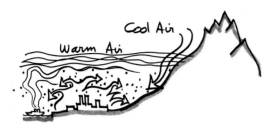

The serious consequences of air pollution are increased manyfold in those areas subject to the phenomenon of atmospheric inversion.

Normally warm air rises from the heated land mass into cooler atmosphere and carries with it the fumes and particles resulting from combustion. Winds and breeze help in the dispersion.

On foggy windless days, when air is trapped beneath a warm air blanket, the buildup of air pollution can often reach lethal proportions.

INVERSION

From the admitted uncertainty about the precise effects of air pollution, pesticides, and similar threats to public health has sprung the fantastic doctrine, parroted by many industrialists and even by some public officials, that so long as there is the slightest reasonable doubt about the effects of a suspected health hazard, we should do nothing to control it.

C. W. GRIFFIN, JR.
Controlling Pollution
Prentice-Hall, Inc.
Englewood Cliffs, N. J., 1967

Air is the breath of life.

We have always believed the supply of this essential element to be inexhaustible. We are now learning, however, that almost within our lifetime clean, uncontaminated air has become scarce. Even in remote reaches of the Arctic Circle and the South Sea Islands the amounts of airborne poisons have reached concentrations lethal to birds and fish and, indirectly, to humans.

On a worldwide basis the rain of death by pesticides and herbicides continues almost unabated. Despite the popular assumption that their aerial distribution has been for the most part outlawed, thousands of tons of such lethal substances as DDT, Dieldrin, and Chlorodane are still sprayed from planes each year to poison millions of acres of cropland, marsh, and waterway. Even populous towns and cities are not spared as, inexplicably, this mass contamination is permitted to occur.

In London, back in 1952, the human toll from air pollution was direct, immediate, and easy to establish. Then, over 4,000 persons were killed in a five-day period when fog capped down over the hapless populace the deadly fumes from the city's stacks and chimney pots.

Lesser catastrophes have struck in other cities around the world, as in Tokyo and Los Angeles where as many as a hundred people have died each day for several days running from smog inhalation; or Donora, Pennsylvania, with twenty deaths and half the total population of 14,000 sickened in a four-day "inversion."

And so it goes. But the greater tragedy lies in the unpublished (because unverifiable without much further research) statistics on the average dwellers in the urban and industrial centers who, with blackened lungs, die the slow and gasping death of lung cancer, emphysema, and other respiratory disorders induced by the very air they breathe. Or of those whose health and stamina are gradually undermined by particulate and chemical air contamination until they succumb to heart failure or other diseases.

Meanwhile, even in some of the most exemplary residential communities, or on the highways which interconnect them, levels of air pollution have become so extreme that "stay at home" alerts are frequent. It is abundantly evident that our atmosphere must at last be protected against such abuse.

Our atmospheric habitat

When one considers the vastness of the universe, the relatively microscopic earth speck with its unique atmospheric conditions is such a rarity that one can only wonder how it came to be. Yet it exists, and because it exists, so do we. For only planet Earth, of all the heavenly bodies known to us, is enveloped with just the right combination of vapors to support human life.

At sea level, the air is composed of approximately 78 percent nitrogen by volume and 21 percent oxygen. The remaining 1 percent consists of carbon dioxide and traces of other gases. These swirl incessantly about the globe, driven by winds which result from the uneven heating of the Earth by solar energy. Floating about with the air currents are minute particles which from the time of Earth's beginning have been spewed forth by volcanoes or blown free in the form of dust. Cosmic detritus, attracted from the far reaches of space, has also accumulated over the eons. Gradually, human activity has added to the atmospheric pollution until presently approximately 200 million tons of chemical and particulate impurities are released into the air each year over the United States alone. This is almost a ton for each of us. This stupendous mass of foreign material is lofted from strata to strata until today no level of the atmosphere is free of contamination.

It is at the lower levels, where the air is naturally more dense, that the pollution is concentrated and where from a plane it can be seen as a murky stain spreading for miles downwind of industrial centers and cities.

Since each particle of matter acts to seed condensation in the form of clouds, fog, rain, ice, or snow, even the weather and climate are affected.

The stratified layers of particles, and especially the veil of carbon dioxide between the sun and our planet, form a filter which allows solar rays to penetrate but which tends to preclude the Earth's built-up heat from escaping. Apparently this "greenhouse effect" has not yet been detrimental—perhaps because of the overall periodic cooling cycle which we are experiencing. There is serious speculation among the geophysicists, however, that when in time the atmospheric accumulation is compounded with the warming phase, the polar ice caps will be melted to a degree heretofore unknown and that extensive areas of the Earth's coastal plains may be inundated by the overbrimming oceans.

There is, of course, the more immediate problem that whatever kind of pollution is released into the air by anyone must come down sometime, somehow, somewhere, on someone.

Contamination

Who are the offenders? The chart on the next page shows the sources of the five major types of air pollutants.

Carbon monoxide. This colorless, odorless exhaust-pipe gas can be deadly in such confined spaces as garages or poorly ventilated tunnels. In heavy traffic or enclosed parking areas it can slow the driver responses and cause dizziness, headaches, and fatigue. People with heart disease, asthma, or anemia are particularly susceptible to the harmful effects of this dangerous pollutant.

Hydrocarbons. Another emission of the automobile exhaust pipe and the smokestack, hydrocarbons are the unburned products of the combustion of organic fuels. They are the primary source of smog, the most troublesome irritants to the eyes, nose, and throat, and a serious threat to sufferers of respiratory disorders.

Air is the swirling mixture of gases and vapor that surrounds planet Earth.

Without air there could be no form of life. Humans, like most plants and animals, could live for some time without food or water, but without air they would die within a few minutes.

It is the oxygen of the air that makes life possible. It combines with other substances in the process called *oxidation*. This releases heat and energy, the basis of growth and movement.

Air is a substance having weight. Every square inch of the earth at sea level sustains a pressure of about 14.7 pounds. The pages of this open book have over a ton and a half of pressure bearing down upon them.

Air, like the sea, is constantly in motion and links all habitations, no matter how remote, into a world community.

The flowing air mass around us is extremely susceptible to contamination which is rapidly dissipated into the surrounding atmosphere for an area extending many square miles and to a height of many thousands of feet.

A large percentage of the polluting chemical and particulate matter is returned to the earth by precipitation. Much, however, is absorbed or retained, and carried by air currents as high as the stratosphere to form an ever-thickening shroud of deleterious matter.

Aside from its blighting effects upon plants, humans, and other animals, air pollution is the chief eroder and corroder, causing billions of dollars of damage annually. According to recent studies, it will in time have a telling effect upon even the climate and weather.

About one million years ago the Ice Age began to send its rapacious fingers down from the north polar ice cap. Because of intricate changes in climate, triggered perhaps by variations in the carbon dioxide content of the earth's atmosphere or by accumulations of volcanic dust which intercepted the sun's heat that otherwise would have reached the earth, large sheets of ice began to accumulate where none had been before.
JAMES A. MICHENER
Centennial
Copyright © 1974 by Marjay Productions, Inc.
Random House, Inc.
New York, 1974

. . . in populous city pent, Where houses thick and sewers annoy the air.
MILTON
Paradise Lost

Much of "The facts of air pollution" has been quoted directly, with permission, from the booklet, *Air Pollution Control*, published by the National Association of Counties Research Foundation, 1001 Connecticut Avenue, N.W., Washington, D.C., 1971.

Particulates. The solid particles that come from smoke, especially from wood and coal form the sooty dust that soils clothing, discolors buildings, and damages paint. Particulates also have harmful effects when inhaled and tend to accumulate in the lungs.

Sulfur oxides. Fossil fuels of high sulfur content give off in the process of combustion the foul-smelling gases which are all too familiar to dwellers in industrial and densely populated urban areas where coal is burned as the source of heat. Sulfur dioxide is the notorious ruster of metals, the destroyer of crops, the reducer of visibility, and the most harmful irritant to eyes and the mucous membranes.

Nitrogen oxides. Emitted mainly from exhaust pipes, residential chimneys, and industrial stacks, nitrogen oxides have an unpleasant odor and are injurious to animals and vegetation. They are the chief offenders in producing the photochemical smog that blankets so many cities.

Other pollutants. Equally destructive and injurious, these include radioactive particles, metals in suspension, and photochemical smog.

In sum, air pollution in its many forms is a killer and devastator. To untold thousands of humans it brings suffering and premature death. It is debilitating to livestock. It damages timber, crops, and all forms of vegetation. In addition, it causes extensive economic loss through damage to materials—eroding stone, corroding metals, making rubber crack and nylons run. It shortens the useful life of everything that it touches.

Emissions of major pollutants

	Carbon monoxide %	Hydro-carbons %	Particulates %	Sulfur oxides %	Nitrogen oxides %
Motor vehicles	64.8	45.7	1.0	0.9	36.5
Aircraft	1.9	1.1	0.3	0.3	1.7
Railroads	0.1	0.3	0.3	0.6	0.4
Vessels	1.1	0.8	0.3	0.9	0.8
Other motor fuels	5.8	5.1	0.3	0.6	7.6
Stationary sources*	1.2	2.4	20.4	73.0	42.1
Industrial processes	7.9	14.7	41.0	22.5	0.8
Waste disposal	5.2	5.3	4.0	0.6	1.7
Forest fires	6.2	7.7	25.0	0.0	6.7
Agricultural burning	5.5	4.6	6.8	0.0	1.3
Other	0.3	12.3	0.6	0.6	0.4
	100.0	100.0	100.0	100.0	100.0

* Fuel combustion in such fixed locations as homes, municipal incinerators, oil refineries, and power plants.
After an *Air Pollution Chart* prepared by Roy G. Scarfo.

The facts of air pollution

It is believed by many that air pollution is the price we must pay for progress. This is far from the truth. First of all, what *is* progress unless it includes the assurance of a wholesome place in which to live? Moreover, there are case histories to prove that many communities and industrial cities have learned to achieve increasing prosperity while providing an attractive environment, in which people can breathe clean air.

The supply of air is limited. The oxygen-bearing stratum, upon which all life depends, extends upward little higher than our tallest mountain peaks.

The air we breathe is becoming increasingly polluted. Each year, far greater loadings of pollutants are discharged into the atmosphere. Global air currents intermix these contaminants throughout the entire atmospheric sheath.

Most pollution is caused by people. It comes mainly from the burning of fossil fuels in the home, factories, and motor vehicles. It comes from chemicals released by or used in factories or mines. It comes from the disposal of waste materials and from manufacturing processes. Nature adds its dust and fumes, but people are by far the worst offenders.

Contaminated air is a hazard to human health. Aside from the "people kills" directly attributable to smog inversions in many United States cities, there has been an increasing incidence of diseases traced to airborne pollutants.

Many urban areas are frequently subjected to concentrations of carbon monoxide exceeding 30 parts per million. At such levels body functions can be affected and chronic disorders induced.

Polluted air is harmful to plants and animals. Forests subjected to certain types of pollution are often killed outright. In other cases, the devastation is more gradual. Orchards are blighted, vineyards wither, and the yields of hundreds of thousands of acres of farmland and garden are reduced or destroyed. The quantity and quality of the livestock "crop" are also significantly reduced.

The hazards of travel are increased. The incidence of accidents on the ground and in the air is greater when visibility is reduced.

Air pollution and smog are depressing. They degrade the human spirit. New Yorkers living amid the yellowish haze spewed forth from thousands of apartment-house incinerators literally inhale a portion of their own trash. In St. Louis, according to a recent survey, over a third of the citizens are plagued and dismayed by the city odors. The pride of Denver—the prospect of the Rocky Mountains viewed from the streets—is often obscured by clouds of man-made pollution. And who has recently looked out across Los Angeles, the "City of the Angels"?

The climate is affected by airborne gases and particles. Statistics show that in winter North American cities have over 100 percent more fog than rural areas and less than half the ultraviolet radiation, which is an essential ingredient in the growth of plants.

Air pollution grows worse. As the population increases, there is more demand for energy and combustible fuel and there are more heaps of trash for incineration. The steady rise in per capita income

A miasmic cloud rises from every . . . city and blackens the clear blue sky above. This is the awesome reflection of the population explosion of men and machines wracking the city below. A city-bound traveler cresting the hill nearby is suddenly confronted with the cloud hanging over the city. He shudders as his car rolls down the hill and into that man-made muck.

From *An Environmental Policy for Connecticut*
Report of the Governor's Committee on
Environmental Policy
New Haven, Conn.
June 1970

Each year we add 270 million tons of highly toxic carbon monoxide to the atmosphere. Most of this comes from the automobile.

All major tree species within 5 miles of a smelter in Montana were found to be dead or dying as a result of the fumes.

A healthy economy requires a healthy ecology.

Hundreds of new chemical compounds are released into our atmosphere each year without any knowledge of their ultimate effects.

A governmental appraisal of the total costs (purchase price, fuel consumption, maintenance, etc.) of emission controls as compared with other automotive "extras" is as follows:

Emission (pollution) abatement devices	7–12%
Air conditioner	9–20%
Automatic transmission	5–8%
Conventional vehicle, over compact models (approx)	150%

It seems to me that air pollution should be viewed in the larger context to which it belongs. It is part of one of the most vital problems that confronts man today: how to control the spreading contamination from many sources that is rapidly causing the deterioration of our environment. In biological history no organism has survived for long if its environment became in some way unfit . . .

RACHEL CARSON
Silent Spring
Houghton Mifflin Company
Boston, 1962

has enabled the average citizen to own more goods, to replace them more often, to travel more, and in other ways to improve his way of living. But these gains have been made at the cost of an ever-increasing discharge of pollutants into the atmosphere.

Property values are reduced. In many industrial cities, the value of real estate varies in almost inverse proportion to the intensity of the ambient smoke and fumes. By whom are the property owners to be compensated?

Atmospheric degradation can be stopped. Even though thousands of varied sources are still befouling the public skies, most of the devices needed for controlling emissions were invented long ago. The required technology is at hand. To date, however, Americans have lacked the collective concern, and the resolve, to face up to the problem and solve it.

The costs are not prohibitive. In terms of money, an expenditure of less than one-half of one percent of the gross national product would reduce air pollution by at least two-thirds. The savings to the taxpayer each year would far exceed the investment.

The controls cannot be self-imposed. It is not reasonable to expect that homeowners will restrict their pollution output on a uniform basis. And in a competitive society, industry will not willingly forgo a competitive advantage. Its record to date has been dismal. It is generally conceded that effective air pollution abatement can best be achieved only by state and local governmental action with national emission standards, matching funds, and with federal authority to step in and take over where performance lags.

An achievable goal

The Sierra Club has demanded the end to "any significant deterioration of air quality." It has also joined ranks with many other environmental protection groups to plug for the *reduction* of present levels of all types of air contamination to new and acceptable criteria yet to be defined.

Reduce emissions and concentrations

Air quality is achieved mainly by the *reduction* of emissions or by the *dispersion* of the pollutants into a larger volume of air, with the consequent reduction of concentrations.

Reduction of emissions is accomplished by limiting the number of vehicles or dispersion units at any one point, by their mechanical improvement, and by the application of enforceable standards and controls on their manufacture and use.

Avoid the trapping of polluted air

Since most pollutants are heavier than air, they tend to "pond" and build up concentrations in low areas or basins. Air movement by gravity flow can be increased by aligning trafficways along ridges or through broad valleys with consistently falling or rising gradients.

Isolate sources of air contamination

Dispersion into larger volumes of air usually involves larger land areas also, to be subjected to increased air contamination. It is therefore desirable to locate transportation routes, factories, processing plants, and other sources of noise or air pollution as far away from sensitive areas as possible and with the provision of buffer strips.

Relate sources to topographical drainageways

Dispersion of polluted air into suitable receptor areas can be aided by relating to natural drainageways and by creating free-flowing unobstructed channels for air movement. The orientation of source areas and routes to take advantage of prevailing winds and breezes is a logical advantage that seems to be seldom considered.

Protect vulnerable activity areas

Areas most sensitive to air (and noise) pollution are hospitals, schools, playgrounds, residential neighborhoods, and places where people congregate.

Improve transportation ways and vehicles

Transportation routes and highways particularly are presently the major source of air and noise pollution. Improvement will come in several ways. Their roadways may be reduced in scale as by the reduction in the number of lanes. Their routes in many cases may be aligned to avoid planned residential or institutional areas.

Transportation vehicles must be drastically improved. A whole new concept of automation, cargo hauling, fuel transmission, and people-movers is long overdue. Since the self-propelled vehicle in some form is almost certain to be with us for many decades, it is incumbent upon manufacturers to create "clean" engines and automobiles.

Plan more efficient systems of movement

The efficient movement of people and goods is a public benefit of a high order. Highways and transit systems must therefore be recognized as essential components of every agreeable community and region. It is not a matter of *whether or not* they shall be permitted, it is rather a case of *where and how* they are to be located and designed to provide the most public benefit at the least social cost.

Both air and noise pollution are intensified by intermittent vehicular movement. Within urbanizing regions the provision of free-flowing parkways and truck routes as well as rapid transitways is an essential means of relieving the hellish stop-and-go traffic that so commonly jams and pollutes our local streets.

The outlook

Encouraging as recent events may be, we are still losing ground in the battle against air pollution. On a worldwide basis, we will discharge more waste into the air today than yesterday, more tomorrow than today. And the end is not in sight, for despite our most optimistic predictions, we cannot presently foresee a reversal of the trend.

Why? There are several reasons:

1. *Growth.* While our national *birthrates* have declined, the number of babies born in this country continues to rise each year, and their life-span increases. By the year 2000 we may expect an additional 75 million people to swell our population to the 300

When civilization was getting underway some 5,000 years ago the total world population was probably no more than 20 million persons. That's about the amount of the increase in the past 6 months.

Increasing longevity is one important reason for our surging population growth. Another is that our anticipated life-span has increased by more than 10 years since 1930.

Life expectancy in the United States is presently more than 70 years. This is roughly double what it was in the time of Caesar or Pericles.

U.S. Population

Source: *Statistical Abstract of the United States, 1974. U.S. Department of Commerce, Government Printing Office, 1974*

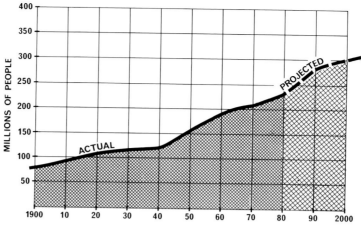

World population

Source: *The Limits of Growth—A Report for the Club of Rome's Project on the Predicament of Mankind, a Potomac Associates Book, Universe Books, 1972*

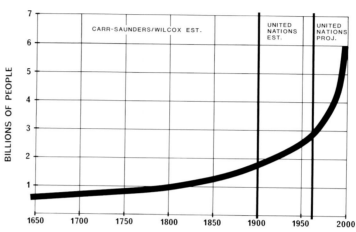

U.S. Demand for energy (in barrels per day)

Total Energy Values converted to barrels per day of oil equivalent (B/DOE)

This chart shows the meaning to the United States of the difference between the era of relatively cheap and available fossil fuels now ending and the emerging era of a requirement for an ever increasing supply of nonfossil energy sources and for imported energy fuels. Note that even a significant decrease in energy demand and a major increase in domestic fossil supplies will only provide a few years respite in the nation's energy dilemma.

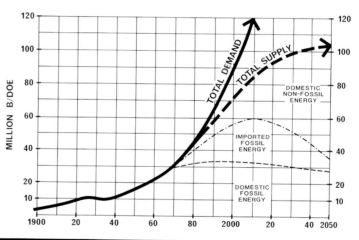

Food furnishes only 1.4 percent of the energy we use. Most of the remaining energy is obtained from fuels.

Instead of just the basic 2–5,000 calories needed to sustain life and carry on a day's work, there is now available to each American an average of 180,000 calories of energy.

GEORGE HARRISON
The Conquest of Energy
Morrow Publishing Co.
New York, 1968

million mark, or four times that at the start of this century.

2. *Migration.* Of the horde of new polluters, over 45 million will be added to our thirty largest metropolitan areas where the present levels of contamination, already extreme, will be intensified by the need for augmented power, heat, and means of transportation.

3. *Demand.* The demand by each individual for goods and energy has increased year by year on a sharply ascending curve in response to more income and leisure time and our new technology. It is this factor more than any other that has precipitated our impending fuel shortages.

It would seem evident that such luxury tastes must be curbed until new sources of pollution-free energy production can be developed and brought on-line. Some potential sources such as nuclear *fusion* (as differentiated from nuclear *fission*) will be nearly 100 percent efficient, producing no waste products or waste heat to pollute the air or water. This promising form of energy production makes use of relatively inexpensive isotopes which are in almost unlimited supply. It may require many years of further experimentation, however, before the practical peace·ful utilization of the fusion process can be attained.

Another contender put forth as the fuel of the future is hydrogen, one of the most abundant elements on earth. It burns cleanly over a wide range of conditions, and the only major by-products of its combustion are heat and water.

Hydrogen can be used as fuel for vehicles, homes, industrial plants, and electrical energy production. Experimental hydrogen-powered automobiles are already running—with more efficiency than those using gasoline. The problems at this stage are the cost of producing hydrogen from water, and the size of the tanks required to store it in its liquid or gaseous form. Research is expected to remove both these drawbacks before the century ends.

Other future possibilities for pollution-free energy production include the use of the tides, wind, geysers, space platforms, and solar energy.

4. *Apathy.* In the losing fight against air pollution the attitude of the public is also a crucial factor, for what the people demand, they will have. Perhaps in the public mind we finally have the air pollution problem under control. Far from it. But in the last few years, at least, we have made a good beginning.

A strategy for protection

The atmosphere functions as an enveloping earth shield and the vital source of the moisture and oxygen essential to all life. For the first time since creation our air supply is under massive stress. What can be done to protect it?

Within the past three decades the United States has taken first tentative steps and then giant strides in the field of air pollution control. As early (or as late) as 1955 the federal government expressed its concern by the passage of the Air Pollution Act. This was followed in 1965 by a bill providing for the investigation and regulation of pollution from motor vehicles. It was the Air Quality Act of 1967 and the Clean Air Act of 1970, however, which together with amendments provide the U.S. Environmental Protection Agency (EPA) with sweeping powers and the mandate to clean up the air.

Essentially the EPA has embarked upon a program to improve air quality in all ways possible. Its role is to provide leadership, guidance, technical and financial assistance, and ultimate control. Its primary goal is to reduce pollution to levels conducive to human health. Its secondary goal is to otherwise promote the public welfare

Natural gas is the cleanest, but scarcest, of the fossil fuels.

Atomic power looks clean, but is the dirtiest. High-level radioactive waste must be isolated from the environment for up to 25,000 years, a problem for which there is probably no technical solution.

Fusion: By fusing together the nuclei of easily obtained isotopes of hydrogen, helium is formed and a large amount of energy is released. This is the principle of the hydrogen bomb. A controlled fusion reaction has never been obtained, but experimental results in the United States and Russia are encouraging. Fuel supplies would be virtually unlimited. The reactor would produce no radioactive wastes.

The affluent society has shown an enormous appetite for energy and an indifference to the consequences of that indulgence.
ROGERS C. B. MORTON
"Resources: Are We Running Short?"
Consulting Engineer
March 1973

Every 15 minutes the sun sends to earth as much energy . . . as could be released by burning all the world's forests, and all its remaining coal, gas and petroleum.
GEORGE HARRISON
The Conquest of Energy
Morrow Publishing Co.
New York, 1968

If we are to make truly substantial progress in cleaning up the air of the United States, we will have to focus our attention on much more than merely installing control equipment on air pollution sources. We will have to make common cause with those who are concerned with controlling population increase, with development of new towns, with new mixes of public policy addressed to improving transportation systems, and with new programs to deal with the very formidable problems of urban design.
ARTHUR A. ATKISSON
Bulletin of the National Tuberculosis and Respiratory Disease Association
American Lung Association
1740 Broadway, New York
February 1971

and to prevent damage to animals, plant life, and property. It has moved decisively, and with growing public support, in the face of strong opposition from some segments of industry and officialdom.

Air quality control is an emerging science. Those intrigued with its possibilities and involved with its application to environmental planning and improvement are convinced of the following needs:

Standardize terms, equipment, and methodology

The wide variations in all three at present lead to confusion and the discrediting of otherwise sound and useful data.

Conduct research

In addition to its own intensified efforts, the federal government would do well to grant funds to those universities, agencies, and private scientific groups which are conducting research in the atmospheric sciences. It should also continue to support and encourage investigation into air-related health problems, new techniques of heat and energy production, and effective methods of air pollution abatement. Voter support of these efforts is needed to assure an adequate flow of funds.

Survey the existing conditions

There is presently no uniform method or system for measuring the various types and degrees of air pollution. Nor is there a coordinated network of monitoring stations to record and evaluate existing levels and trends, against which performance can be checked. These two essential programs must be a next order of business for the EPA.

In addition to continuing checks at the national level, there is need for international surveillance of the chemical and physical processes in the atmosphere, perhaps under the auspices of the World Meteorological Organization.

Establish federal emission criteria

There is urgent need also for the formulation and publication by the Environmental Protection Agency of a comprehensive table of permissible emission standards. This should show for each pollutant not only the maximum amount of emission permitted, but also the level of contamination triggering an "alert," "warning," and "emergency" stage. To be meaningful, the limits of permitted emissions must be related to land-use zones, for it is evident that higher levels of air contamination might logically be permitted in some areas—as in heavy industrial districts.

Publish mandatory criteria well in advance

It is important that the attainable performance standards be established and scheduled well ahead of enforcement deadlines to provide sufficient lead time for the necessary research, development, and remodeling required to achieve compliance.

Accelerated conversion, without adequate testing, may create more problems than are solved.

Develop, and enforce, uniform emission controls

It can be readily observed—as in the cloud of filth pouring from the exhaust pipes of many diesel trucks on many highways, or from the stacks of factories or power plants at their sides—that clean air can be achieved only when emissions can be legally limited and accurately measured and controls fairly and strictly enforced.

Control contamination at the source

The pollution of air can be eliminated only at the chimney, the smokestack, the tail pipe, the smoldering refuse dump, the spray nozzle, and the blast site.

Abolish the gasoline engine

There is compelling evidence to the effect that the conventional gasoline combustion engine has outlived its usefulness. This ingenious machine, which gave rise to industrialization, has long since been the chief culprit in polluting the atmosphere. Few engineers believe that this type of power source, which depends upon a series of wasteful rapid-fire explosions, can ever achieve the efficiency required to eliminate air contamination.

If present air pollution levels are to be held, let alone decreased, long-range emission-control standards must look far beyond the best performance ratings to be expected of the gasoline and diesel engines. The design of machines to meet criteria, rather than criteria to match machines, will do much to stimulate the development of innovative energy units.

Eliminate the incomplete burning of unrefined fossil fuels

The combustion of low-grade coals and oils releases heavy concentrations of hydrocarbons, sulfur oxide, nitrogen oxide, and particulates, as well as less visible gases which are equally destructive. The use of such fuels should be made contingent upon their further refinement or upon the adaptation of equipment and processes, presently developed, which reduce the emission of pollutants to a fraction of present levels.

Assign the costs where they belong

While it is true that standards of environmental quality affect our economic competitive ability, the cost of industrial cleanup is a logical industrial, not governmental, responsibility. It is reasonable, and standard procedure, that manufacturing costs be passed on to the consumer.

Encourage state action

While the EPA and other federal agencies have provided the impetus, it remains for each state to adopt and implement its own air pollution abatement program. Many states are dragging their feet. Because air pollution does not follow political boundaries, the EPA has been given the power to step in where states or localities fail to act. But pollution control is best and properly kept in the hands of the people most directly affected.

Initiate local programs

The National Association of Counties Research Foundation, as an aid to county and local governments, has outlined the following specification for a sound program of air pollution control:

1. Develop a public policy on air conservation.

2. Provide an organizational framework, capable staff, and adequate funding.

3. Formulate one-, three-, and five-year objectives.

4. Assess existing air quality and estimation of projected pollution levels.

5. Assess, on a continuing basis, the emissions from all existing

Many technological and economic factors inevitably affect the selection of means of avoiding or controlling the emission of a pollutant, but the choice lies fundamentally among five alternatives:

1. *Select process inputs, such as fuels, that do not contain the pollutant or its precursors.*
2. *Remove the pollutant or its precursors from the process inputs.*
3. *Operate the process so as to minimize generation of the pollutant.*
4. *Remove the pollutant from the process effluent.*
5. *Replace the process with one that does not generate the pollutant.*

The American Chemical Society
Cleaning Our Environment—
The Chemical Basis for Action
American Chemical Society
Washington, D.C., 1969

Simply letting pollution continue will be far more expensive than spending what it takes to curb it.

WILLIAM D. RUCKELSHAUS
Administrator, U.S. Environmental Protection Agency
Washington, D.C., 1971

Voluntary private and industrial action is a beneficial first step, but it penalizes the good guy. The fair way—firm and uniform policy, law and standards.

RUSSELL E. TRAIN
Chairman, Council on Environmental Quality
In an address before the Allegheny Conference on Community Development
Pittsburgh, Pa., 1970

Each city, state and nation must assume the responsibility to ensure that activities within its jurisdiction do not degrade the environment either within or beyond its borders.

GEORGE SLOSS
Unpublished memo

Further Reading:

Austin, Richard L.,
The Yearbook of Landscape Architecture: The Issues of Energy
Van Nostrand Reinhold Company Inc.
New York, 1983

Calvert, Seymour, and Harold M. England
Handbook of Air Pollution Technology
John Wiley & Sons, Inc. (Wiley-Interscience)
New York, 1984

Carr, Donald E.
The Sky Is Still Falling
W. W. Norton & Company, Inc.
New York, 1982

Carson, Rachel
Silent Spring
Houghton Mifflin Company
Boston, 1962

Esposito, John C., and Larry J. Silverman
Vanishing Air: The Ralph Nader Study Group Report on Air Pollution
Grossman, New York, 1970

Freeman, A. Myrick
Air and Water Pollution Control
John Wiley & Sons, Inc. (Wiley-Interscience)
New York, 1982

Hagevik, George
Air Quality Management and Land Use Planning
Frederick A. Praeger, Inc.
New York, 1974

Landsberg, Helmut E.
The Urban Climate
Academic Press
New York, 1981

Merrill, Richard, et al., eds.
Energy Primer: Solar, Water, Wind and Biofuels
Portola Institute
Menlo Park, Calif., 1974

Robinette, Gary O.
Energy and Environment
Kendall-Hunt
Dubuque, Iowa, 1973

Russell, Clifford S., Winston Harrington and William J. Vaughan
Enforcing Pollution Control Laws
Johns Hopkins University Press
Baltimore, Md., 1986

Should things go wrong at any time, the people will set them to rights by the peaceable exercise of their elective rights.

THOMAS JEFFERSON (1806)
Quoted, *Public Officials and Their Heritage*
Public Administration Service
Chicago, Ill.

pollution sources and those expected to exist in the future.

6. Develop the necessary information about factors that influence the transport of air pollutants.

7. Assess the effects of the ambient air quality of a community or region on people and their environment.

8. Establish air quality goals, or standards, and the legislation needed to achieve them.

9. Design remedial measures calculated to bring about the air quality desired.

10. Develop a long-range air-use program, fully integrated with all other future community plans.

11. Develop an understanding of the broad impact of changing science and technology on air resources.

12. Initiate an effective information and educational program.

Promote citizen participation

Individuals and groups have many means of exerting their influence. In a guideline for citizen action, the National Air Conservation Commission has proposed a set of procedures which make such good sense that they have been paraphrased in their entirety as follows:

1. *Set priorities.* It is likely that there will be so many aspects of pollution needing improvement that you won't know where to begin to correct them. Concentrate on those areas where you think you can have the most effect.

2. *Promote good relations.* Keep on speaking terms with the agency people, even if you have to lock horns on some issues. Give them credit when they deserve it. Publicize the good things they're doing. Have luncheons for them. Give them awards. Tell the media the good news as well as the bad.

3. *Note inadequate performance.* Discover the reason for the inadequacy. It may be budget, lack of experienced workers, uncommitted personnel, or political high jinks. If it is budget, offer help in getting increased appropriations. If it's a lack of experienced people, help in the search. Suggest training both volunteers and professionals; you can assist in the arrangements. If it's a matter of uncommitted personnel or politicking, try supportiveness, friendliness, and gentle persuasion. Your awareness of the facts, even though unstated, will not be lost on those involved.

4. *Search out weaknesses in the law.* Confer with official agency staff and rule-making bodies to discover the gaps. Prepare drafts of legislation to correct matters. Seek the help of legislators, the agencies, and interested groups to get the laws introduced and passed.

5. *If necessary, wage an open fight.* Gather all possible forces to work with you. Demand public hearings. Arouse and educate the public by meetings, mailings, and distribution of literature. Write letters to the editor. Round up your reserves among the specialists; and send out news releases describing the situation and your position.

Keep the pressure on city hall

Tough legislation backed by the force of public opinion holds the key to the purification of our atmosphere. Political pressure, which is what it takes, can be applied at all levels of government, from the floor of the council chamber to the desk of our chief executive.

3 Water

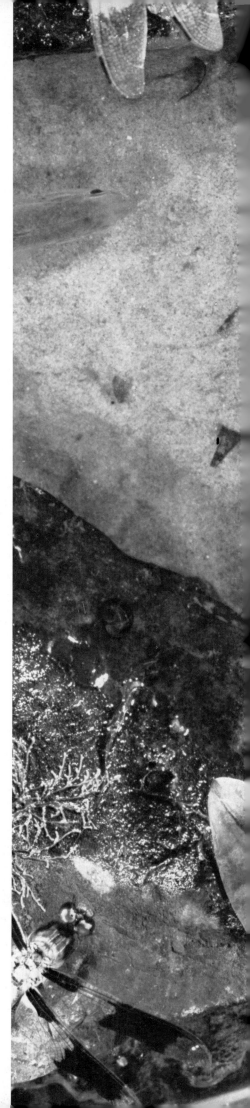

Man, wherever he lives, whatever his culture, waits for the rain. Often he waits in hope, sometimes in fear, sometimes in vain, for the waters of the world do not always suit man's needs or desires as they move through their predestined circle to and from the sea. Yet if he is wise, man has within his power the ability to exercise a measure of control over the movement of waters, and in so doing, he may, to a significant degree, control his own destiny.

While the laws that control our water cycle cannot be changed, they can be understood and made to work in man's behalf. The blending of natural law and human endeavor is the essence of resource management.

LEROY L. PREUDHOMME
Editor, *River of Life*
U.S. Department of the Interior
1970

It takes about 1,000 pounds of water on the average to produce 1 pound of food.

One bushel of corn requires from 10 to 20 tons of water in its growth.

The amount of energy of falling water harnessed by power plants in the United States and converted to electrical power is roughly equivalent to the energy that could be produced manually by five times all the people who live here.

Nearly all industries require vast quantities of water.

Civilizations rise and flourish where fresh water is abundant, and vanish when the supply is depleted or fails.

The water reserves in the United States are being drawn down farther each year by wasteful practices and inept water resource management.

Water, like air, is essential to all living things.

History could be told in its simplest terms by tracing the story of man's search for fresh water and his struggles to maintain a supply. From the dawn of civilization he has followed the watercourses and camped beside the marshes and lakes. He and his people have fought for and defended their water holes and springs. They have dug and lined myriad wells in the earth and sand. They have terraced hillsides and mountains to utilize the precious fluid to the utmost in the irrigation of crops. They have learned to drill to incredible depths to tap the underground streams and water-bearing strata.

In contemporary times, with our huge pumping stations and extensive aqueduct networks, we have come to assume the supply of water to be self-replenishing and adequate for all our needs. This is no longer so. More water is being drawn from many of the earth's surface and underground reservoirs than is flowing into them. Burgeoning cities have had to reach farther and farther into the hinterlands to tap ever-additional and ever-diminishing reserves. Still, in times of drought, many municipalities have had to ration their drinking water. On both coasts the subsurface freshwater tables have been drawn down so far by overuse in some areas that saltwater intrusion has become a serious problem. At present rates of consumption the time is soon approaching when our demands for water will exceed available supplies.

We are running out of potable water. This is a fact of life that won't go away, and it is one that has to be faced. There's another fact, too, and it is that the *quality* of the water we drink and wash with and swim in today is far from what it used to be, and we have to face up to this, also.

To address the dilemma and move to constructive solutions, it is helpful to have a rudimentary understanding of the apparently simple, but actually extremely complex, *hydrologic cycle*. This is basically a closed system in which precipitation in such forms as dew, rain, or snow is absorbed by the earth or stored in water bodies to be returned by evaporation or transpiration to the atmosphere.

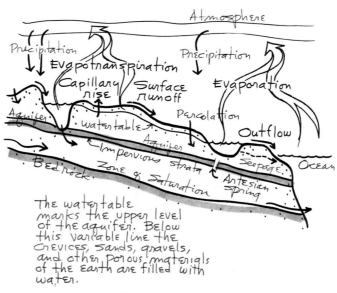

The water table marks the upper level of the aquifer. Below this variable line the crevices, sands, gravels, and other porous materials of the earth are filled with water.

THE NATURAL HYDROLOGIC CYCLE

From the time when the first clouds formed with the cooling of the earth's water vapor, and the first rains fell, the process of recycling has been continuous.

A more complete diagram shows the oceans to be the ultimate storage basins, while the aquifers within the earth are slow-moving streams of fresh water that must be continually replenished unless they are to run dry.

The oceans, which cover almost three-quarters of the globe's surface, hold 97 percent of *all* the earth's water. Of the 3 percent balance, being the world's total freshwater supply, approximately 75 percent is locked up in the polar ice caps and over 24 percent exists in the form of groundwater. Less than 1 percent is present in the atmosphere and all the terrestrial streams, rivers, lakes, and wetlands combined.

Water is one of the most abundant yet precious substances on earth. In those places where it is not to be had, no life can be sustained.

The average rate of water consumption in the United States for all urban purposes is about 155 gallons per capita per day. Flushing a toilet requires about 6 gallons; taking a shower 10 or 20 gallons; a bath as much as 30 gallons.

The average lifetime per capita requirement of a person living to be seventy is in excess of $1\frac{1}{2}$ million gallons.

Fresh water occurrence

	Approximate percentage
Ice sheets and glaciers	75.00
Groundwater (2,500′ to 12,500′ depth)	14.00
Groundwater (to 2,500′ depth)	10.60
Lakes and water bodies	.29
Soil moisture	.05
Rivers and streams	.03
Atmosphere	.03
	100.00%

With well over 99 percent of the world's fresh water either frozen into the polar ice and glaciers, or moving deep within the sands and gravels of the earth, one wonders at the abundance of free water that pours seaward down our streams and river valleys, or that is contained in the shimmering expanses of our marshlands and lakes. This free water is the glory of our landscape. It is the source of many of our favorite forms of recreation—our fishing, swimming, and boating. It is also the key to our well-being, sustaining much of our vegetation and food supply and providing most of the water which we use. Yet everywhere our waterways and expanses are subjected to the full sorry range of mistreatment.

As a timely lesson in resource management, it would be well to consider a typical river system as an example of what can and must be done to sustain and protect our water supply. Let us start at the beginning . . .

The seas around the world are presently rising 2 to 3 inches per 100 years because of the glacial melt.

The Soviets, in a plan to warm the Arctic Ocean and help melt sea ice, have conceived of a way to place a barrier across the Bering Strait allowing the flood tide to bring warm water in, but not allowing it to ebb out. The climatic effects are at present unforeseeable.

Upland water sources

Most rivers or their tributary streams rise in remote wilderness headlands where they are fed with the melting ice and snows. When the slopes were in their pristine condition, the spring thaws and flows were retarded by the moss and duff of the forest which released the water slowly. But over the years unscientific lumbering, overgrazing, and hydraulic mining have denuded much of the land and exposed it to the unraveling of erosion. Where the protective growth has been destroyed, flash floods now rush unchecked down

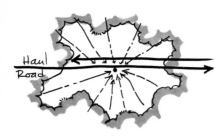

Often immature trees are destroyed and erosion started as logs are dragged back to a central spar beside the tractor haulways.

UNCONTROLLED LOGGING CAUSES MASSIVE FOREST DESTRUCTION

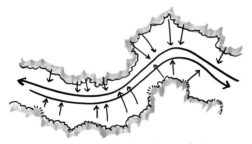

Mature timber harvested along pre-described bands by permit.

SELECTIVE LOGGING OF CONTOUR BANDS

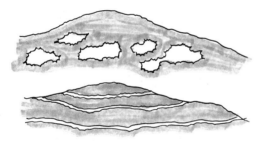

Contour logging preserves the slopes and yields visual improvement over uncontrolled scalping.

FOREST WATERSHED PROTECTION

The river

To trace the course of a stream from its source to the sea is to observe a miracle of nature's forces at work.

the precipitous slopes, carrying pebbles and rocks which grind their way along the streambeds to deposit huge quantities of debris and sediments on the valley floors below. Then, after the floods, the beds run dry.

Fortunately, most of the upland watersheds are in the public domain. Under the care of such agencies as the U.S. Forest Service, the National Park Service, and the Bureau of Land Management, they may be administered in the best interest of the public. This has not always been the case, for too often in the past—in spite of the remonstrances of the agency chiefs and their staffs—the public welfare has been betrayed as leases, franchises, and special privileges have been arranged by some elected officials in exchange for political support. With new environmental fervor evident both within and outside the government, we may expect, yea, must demand, a new high level of surveillance and performance.

Restore the cover

Watershed protection must be designated as the primary purpose of lands contiguous to upland tributary streams. Where growth is intact, preserve it. Where it has been destroyed, restore it to the native or naturalized plant covers best suited to the situation and the use.

Initiate new methods of timber cropping

Ban as obsolete and wasteful the uncontrolled cutting of forest lands. Hundreds of thousands of acres of prime woodland are presently mutilated each year as unscientific logging destroys the understory along with the removal of mature trees. Fire-prone slashings are left strewn about on the forest floor, and churning tractors open up a maze of ruts to start massive slope erosion.

The aerial "lift-out" of selected logs by overhead cableways, helicopter, or balloon-winch rig is often feasible and leaves the forest land unscarred. In other situations where the clear-cutting of uniform stands of timber or pulpwood is prescribed, the practice of contour logging and reforestation is to be ensured in so far as is reasonable. The emergence of a new science of forest management in our country bodes well for the watersheds.

Prevent overgrazing

The leasing of grazing lands will in the future be conditioned upon a scientific study of the regenerative tolerances of the existing cover. Preleasing reconnaissance will determine the use and intensity, and periodic seasonal checks will ensure compliance and the healthy condition of the pastureland. Slopes presently eroded will be rehabilitated and new crops developed for their nutritional value and for their ability to retain and build up the light soils.

Prohibit hydraulic mining

The mining of slopes by subjecting them to jets of water under high pressure opens gaping rifts in the upland valleys and plateaus. Once such massive erosion has started, the land deteriorates rapidly, and restoration, if possible, is extremely difficult.

Reduce the flash floods with impoundments

The regulation of seasonal runoff by the construction of dams on the tributaries runs contrary to the wilderness code. Yet, where the natural conditions have been altered, there are obvious advantages to containing the spring freshets and "paying out" the water when it will be most needed. In addition to flood control and irrigation, other benefits may include recreational uses and hydroelectric power generation.

Each proposed reservoir is unique. Each has its positive and negative values. Each is to be considered on its own individual merits and on the basis of thorough study of all the related factors.

Streams

Few features in nature offer more interest and year-round delight than our streams.

Along their edges are to be discovered the first buddings and leafings of springtime. In the heat of summer they trace a cool and refreshing course across the sun-parched land. In the autumn the lush vegetation along their banks seems to have the richest glow and color. And in the winter, when the open fields are white and windswept, the stream banks with their cover provide welcome sanctuary for small game and the birds.

These things being so, how can we have allowed such widespread desecration of these beautiful waterways? How can we have permitted so many thousands of miles of their meandering beds to be channelized and armored, or enclosed in concrete pipe?

Leave the stream channels undisturbed whenever possible

Their beds of dense clays and gravels and their edges protected by stones, roots, and grasses are erosion-resistant in their natural state. They serve also to sustain the water table and provide ground water by percolation into surrounding soils.

Maintain the streams as landscape features

Each watercourse is a natural garden, self-sustaining and refreshing. Landowners and municipalities would do well to protect their watercourses as prized community assets.

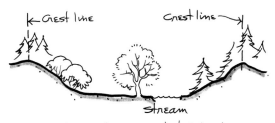

Where stream-related lands are to be acquired for drives, parks, or other public uses, the taking should be from crest line to crest line — or better, to the visual limits beyond — to maintain the integrity of the valley or ravine. This principle was successfully applied in the design of Cleveland's "Emerald Necklace," an early and exemplary circumferential parkway belt that followed the watercourses.

ACQUIRE THE FULL WIDTH OF THE VALLEY OR FLOODPLAIN

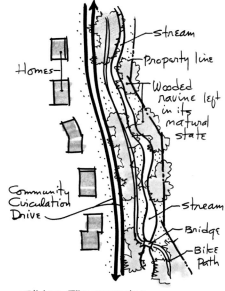

SHARE THE STREAM WITH THE PASSERSBY

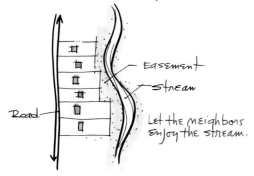

Where buildings are planned to abut a river or channel, leave room for a pedestrian easement and walkway beside the edge. The entire neighborhood will benefit.

LET THE PEOPLE WALK ALONG THE BANKS OF THE WATER

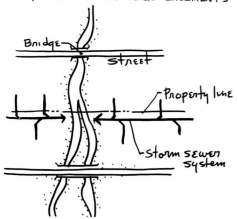

Road — Easement — Stream

Let the neighbors enjoy the stream.

PROVIDE WATER EDGE EASEMENTS

Bridge — Street — Property line — Storm sewer system

Where streets cut across a streambed expensive bridges or culverts will be required and a closed storm system must usually be installed to conduct runoff to the waterway. Moreover, the temptation to "squeeze out" additional street frontage will often result in the ditching and walling of the stream, or placing it in a culvert which is buried under fill. This is to be avoided.

LIMIT VEHICULAR CROSSINGS

Preserve existing streams in their natural condition

Sound land planning recognizes the wisdom of shaping communities around the watercourses which will then irrigate and drain welcome open space. These waterways will in turn form the framework of the interconnected regional "greenway" and "blueway" systems which are ideal locations for walking and bicycle paths, bridle trails, and related recreation places.

Align the trafficways beside the streams

Where the topography so permits, the stream may be shared with those who move through the environs by vehicles or on foot. Some of our most pleasant communities have been laid out with this plan arrangement.

Provide for water-edge circulation paths where lots abut streams

Sometimes streets and drives near watercourses are best aligned in such a way as to produce a band of usable parcels which back upon and overlook the stream. The stream and its edges may then be preserved by deed or easement for community use as greenway linkage to schools, parks, or other focal points. In such an arrangement the waterway contributes its full measure to the property owners and to community life.

Plan streets and drives parallel with the watercourses

This will eliminate many vehicular crossings and permit the stormwater runoff from the adjacent properties to enter the stream by sheet flow.

Use the streams to conduct storm water

Streams are the natural drainageways and the best possible conductors of storm-water runoff. Ideally, rainfall is directed to the watercourses in the form of sheet flow, which irrigates fields and gardens along the way and helps to recharge the groundwater.

An artificial storm-drainage installation with its miles of buried pipe and manholes is an expensive and inefficient substitute for nature's original system. It is probable that with sound landscape planning less than 5 percent of our extensive storm-sewer networks would ever have been built.

Keep the streams clean

Sanitary sewage is never to be discharged into a watercourse except after tertiary treatment has restored it to drinkable quality. Silt-bearing or fast-moving runoff is best conducted via interception swales and ponds. Detergents, or oily drainage from service areas, must first be trapped and filtered. Waste and trash no more belong in an open stream than on the kitchen floor.

Ponds, freshwater marshes

In the "taming" of our American wilderness the pioneers and their contemporary successors have acted upon an overpowering compulsion to drain the freshwater swamps and marshes. In many instances this was a means of gaining additional farmland. In other cases, it was a senseless and sometimes wanton destruction of a vital link in the fragile ecological chain.

Eighty percent of the freshwater wetlands which existed in the United States in Colonial times have since been drained. The elimination of these natural holding and recharge basins has resulted in an enormous subsequent loss to the downstream property owners. Erosion, flash flooding, and seasonal drought have since continued to plague them—often without their knowing why. When the "total" costs are computed, it can be readily seen that the conversion of wetlands to agricultural use or "development" is seldom economically sound or ecologically wise.

Many such wetlands still exist simply because of the cost or bother of filling them in. Some are in their natural state; others polluted and trash-filled to the point of disgrace. All are to be retrieved and preserved to enrich our urban and rural landscapes.

They are our natural museums—the domain of the frogs, spring peepers, pollywogs, dragonflies, cattails, and water lilies, of herons and redwing blackbirds, of "crawdads" and ring-tailed coons.

Our world would not be nearly so good a place were it not for the existence and lessons of Thoreau's beloved Walden Pond, and for the remaining ponds, rapidly dwindling in number, still left to us for safekeeping.

Preserve the ponds and marshes

They and the vegetation which they support perform a necessary function. Aside from serving as freshwater holding reservoirs and percolation beds, they also provide a breeding ground for fish and wildlife, and a nesting place for the birds which regulate the teeming insect population.

Include the wetlands in the regional open space system

Planning agencies have a key role in the conservation of our remaining ponds and marshes. They can save them en masse. Acting in the best public interest they may designate them, and our streams, as part of the regional open space preserve. They may promote their acquisition

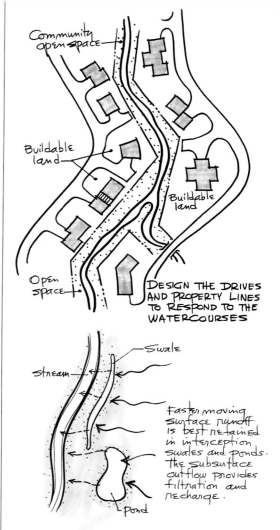

DESIGN THE DRIVES AND PROPERTY LINES TO RESPOND TO THE WATERCOURSES

Faster moving surface runoff is best retained in interception swales and ponds. The subsurface outflow provides filtration and recharge.

RETAIN THE STORM DRAINAGE

Primary wastewater treatment is a simple gravity process that separates and settles the solids within a tank, removing 25 to 30 percent of the BOD (a unit of biochemical oxygen demand).

Secondary treatment is a biological process that speeds up what nature does in waterbodies. Good installations remove approximately 90 percent of BOD as measured by chemical tests.

Tertiary, or *advanced wastewater treatment* involves a variety of processes designed to meet specific requirements. Upward of 99 percent of measured BOD can be removed in some instances.

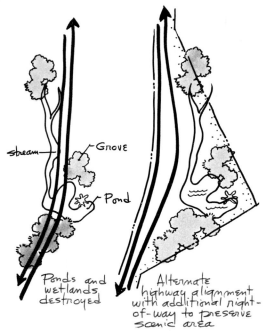

INCLUDE AND PRESERVE
THE NATURAL ROADSIDE FEATURES

stream — Grove — Pond

Ponds and wetlands destroyed

Alternate highway alignment with additional right-of-way to preserve scenic area

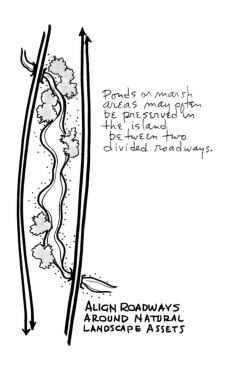

Ponds or marsh areas may often be preserved in the island between two divided roadways.

ALIGN ROADWAYS AROUND NATURAL LANDSCAPE ASSETS

as fish and game lands. They may recommend their inclusion under floodplain zoning. They may propose protective restrictions upon their use in land development projects. Interested citizens would do well to encourage and support the planners and public agencies in these important endeavors.

Include ponds and wetlands within highway rights-of-way

State and county highway departments, with new budget allocations for environmental improvements, may design the wetlands into their highway corridors as scenic features and as buffers against roadside development. There is much to commend this approach, for troublesome highway noise and glare would be abated at the minimal acquisition cost of low-value marginal lands. There would be no need for the construction of expensive shielding devices or screening plantations. Storm water from the road shoulders could flow directly into the waterways rather than into massive storm-sewer systems. Roadside maintenance would be reduced, for natural ponds take care of themselves. This "conservation" approach supports the farsighted contention of the Federal Highway Administration that the best way to "landscape" a highway is not to decorate it with "horticultural parsley," but rather to so locate and design it as to preserve, and provide views to, the natural features of the landscape through which the roadway moves.

In many urbanized districts, highway corridors afford the last opportunity for the protection of native growth and the provision of wildlife sanctuaries.

Encourage wetland preservation by providing the developer with incentives

Since the number of dwelling units and the permissible square footage of floor area are often geared to the total acreage of the development tract, the developer can plan around the ponds and marshes, preserving them for public use while clustering the buildings on the higher and more usable land.

Less fill and grading will be required. Streets and utility systems will be more efficient, and the visual quality of the neighborhood enhanced. Planned community development (PCD) ordinances and zoning provisions for clustering are new tools which make even more feasible such enlightened considerations.

Recognize the key role of private owners in preserving ponds and marshes

It is probable that most owners bought their properties or built their homes because of their appreciation of the pond life or their enjoyment of the views. As development closes in, and as land prices and taxes rise, the wetlands are often threatened. An owner may do many things to help preserve wetlands for continued enjoyment, for example:

1. Donate them to a conservancy, with limitations as to their use. Such restrictions can usually be written to the donor's own specifications;

2. Sell them to the public agencies as natural areas, fish and game lands, wildlife sanctuaries, or park preserves. Again, the terms can often be written to best suit the owner's wishes and to help with estate and tax planning;

3. Preplan the acreage to conserve the natural areas and features while selling off, or leasing, building sites with adequate setbacks and restrictions;

4. Develop them for income production, as in fishing or camping sites or picnic facilities; or

5. Help form a local conservancy association to which several or more owners can deed their joint holdings of streams, ponds, and marshland. This can provide welcome tax relief, the benefits of common management, and a superlative gift to the adults and children of the neighborhood, for their long-range instruction and pleasure.

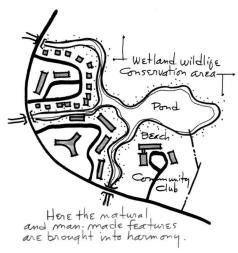

Here the natural and man-made features are brought into harmony.

PRESERVE WETLANDS AND WATER EDGES FOR COMMUNITY USE

Lakes, reservoirs

In regions blessed with natural lakes or sizable manmade reservoirs, those in authority have the responsibility for making them available for the enjoyment and use of the entire community. There are sometimes exceptional cases of single ownership or special function that dictate exclusive rights. Usually, however, the water and its surface should be in public ownership. And the people should be able to get to it.

With sensible planning and regulation such bodies of water can enhance the living and property values of the whole surrounding region, rather than of a single band of waterfront parcels alone. Too often such narrow strips of private land seal off altogether the view and the use of the water.

This is not to imply that the neighbors should have the right of access to the water through private lands or to trespass on private property along the shoreline. Where properties are deeded to the water's edge, these lines are to be respected. It is not reasonable to expect that existing rights in land should be abrogated or that property be confiscated by zoning or imposed governmental controls without due compensation.

It is suggested, however, that the land between the water's edge and the abutting property lines as legally described should "go with the water" and be considered part of the public domain. Additional public access areas and circulation ways as needed should be acquired by easement, lease, or purchase. It is further proposed that in all transactions relating to public water-edge lands, as well as in all rezoning or platting of lakeshore property for development, the reservation of public access to and along the shoreline should be an important consideration.

In every case the use of the water and its edges should be limited by strict regulation to ensure that the quality of both the resource and the environment will be maintained.

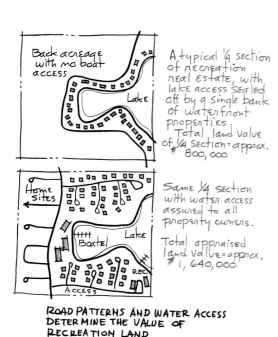

A typical ¼ section of recreation real estate, with lake access sealed off by a single bank of waterfront properties. Total land value of ¼ Section = approx. $800,000

Same ¼ section with water access assured to all property owners.

Total appraised land value = approx. $1,640,000.

ROAD PATTERNS AND WATER ACCESS DETERMINE THE VALUE OF RECREATION LAND

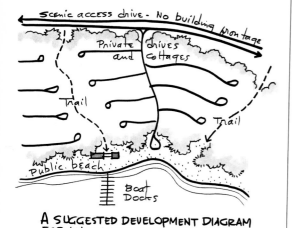

A SUGGESTED DEVELOPMENT DIAGRAM FOR WATERFRONT RECREATION LANDS

Retain the natural character

With the great need for water-based recreation, our lakes and reservoirs can no longer be treated as private preserves to be rimmed to the water's edge with cottages and commercial honky-tonks. Nor can they be allowed to deteriorate. Experience has shown that without regulation most resort areas soon become a hodgepodge of jerry-built construction. All interests within the lake environs can be better served by the application of reasonable planning principles and controls. These include:

1. The preservation of the beach and shoreline vegetation by the requirement of building setbacks and permits to cut, clear, or "improve" the lake frontage.

2. The strict enforcement of adequate water supply and sanitary sewage regulations.

3. Appropriate subdivision ordinances.

4. Zoning and regulation of commercial enterprises.

5. Provision of frequent access drives with parking space, launching ramps, and community docking facilities.

6. Public ownership of conservation areas embracing the feeder streams, marshes, and outstanding scenic features.

Cluster the dwellings and other structures

In place of the traditional band of shoreline or roadside *strip* development, new lakefront or woodland neighborhoods composed of building clusters have many advantages. Shared installation and operation of wells, disposal systems, docks, and beach improvements substantially reduce costs, and large areas of the natural landscape can be saved.

In this example the waterfront acreage is narrow and mostly unusable. For lake access, most cottage owners must cross the public road.

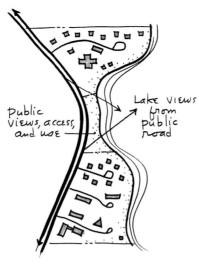

Lake or reservoir

Water frontage and building sites are constricted

PLAN WATEREDGE LANDS AND RELATED ROADWAYS TO REALIZE THE FULL LAND USE POTENTIAL

Public views, access, and use

Lake views from public road

USABLE WATERFRONT ACREAGE AND PROPERTY VALUES ARE INCREASED BY IMPROVED ALIGNMENT OF THE PUBLIC ACCESS ROAD

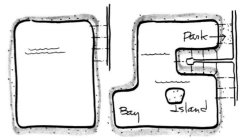

Park

Bay   Island

16 Acres of water surface. 3,400 lin. feet of water frontage. Uninteresting views.

16 Acres of water surface. 4,350 lin. ft. of frontage (exclusive of island). Lake is rich in visual quality.

Note: Water edge parcels are often valued at from 2 to 5 times comparable "dry" lots.

IN SHAPING EXCAVATED LAKES OR IMPOUNDMENTS, CONSIDER THE VIEWS AND THE LENGTH OF USABLE FRONTAGE

Make full use of the shorelands

Their value is often only partially realized. Proper land use and roadway planning can increase the enjoyment of the resource, property values, and the tax yield to the local government.

Preplan man-made water bodies for optimum conformation

Many reservoirs, extraction pits, or water-management holding basins can serve a double purpose. Not only their primary function but also their visual qualities and development potential are important factors in their planning and design.

Provide views and water access for the highway users

The attractiveness of an area, as well as its economic growth, is largely a matter of what one sees from the highways. Since few natural features have as much appeal as water, it would seem reasonable for a community to share with all citizens, as well as its visitors, views across the water bodies, as well as public access to points along their shores. The alignment of such scenic roads and the location and design of the access areas is work requiring professional skill.

Control the use of the water surface and shoreline

Lakes and reservoirs when considered, as they should be, in terms of their highest and best use can be zoned and regulated as effectively as any land area or trafficway. Planning and zoning would normally cover subdivision regulations, sanitation control, limitations on water drawdown, the use of the water surface, and other matters relating to the public welfare.

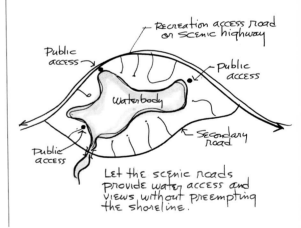

Recreation access road on scenic highway

Public access

Public access

Waterbody

Public access

Secondary road

Let the scenic roads provide water access and views without preempting the shoreline.

Over half of all water pollution comes from storm water runoff, erosion, and siltation.

Cleveland's harbor has to be dredged every year, with over 880,000 cubic yards of sediment removed.

Many miles of beach along the Great Lakes have for years been closed to swimming because of the high coliform bacteria count. Enlarged and improved sewage treatment plants in many lakeside cities must be installed before the condition can be corrected.

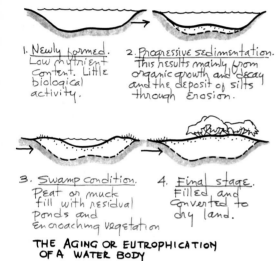

1. Newly formed. Low nutrient content. Little biological activity.

2. Progressive sedimentation. This results mainly from organic growth and decay and the deposit of silts through Erosion.

3. Swamp condition. Peat or muck fill with residual ponds and Encroaching vegetation

4. Final stage. Filled, and Converted to dry land.

THE AGING OR EUTROPHICATION OF A WATER BODY

One of the most serious water pollution problems is eutrophication. . . . In the first stage—lakes are deep and have little biological life. Lake Superior is a good example. Over time, nutrients and sediments are added; the lake becomes more biologically productive and shallower. This stage has been reached by Lake Ontario. As nutrients continue to be added, large algae blooms grow, fish populations change, and the lake begins to take on undesirable characteristics. Lake Erie is now in this eutrophic stage.

Council on Environmental Quality
From the First Annual Report of the Council on Environmental Quality, 1970
U.S. Government Printing Office

In matters of planning, zoning, or enforcement, where local powers are not adequate, it falls to the next higher authority, the county, state, or federal government, to act until the lower jurisdictional body has developed its own controls.

Prevent siltation and turbidity

Thousands of lakes and reservoirs have been discolored and ruined for most types of recreation by waterborne sediments. These are caused by the unchecked erosion of farmlands and fields or areas of new development within the watershed. Expert advice on the prevention of erosion and siltation is provided without charge by the regional offices of the U.S. Soil and Water Conservation Service. The improved water quality of streams and lakes is but one of the many benefits of its effective program.

Ban all forms of pollution

Many bodies of water, including ponds, reservoirs, and even extensive areas of the Great Lakes have become virtual cesspools. Swimming is prohibited because of the health hazard, and the water has become discolored and foul. It may be said that such lakes are "suffocating" from lack of oxygen, the great purifier. Normally the oxygen content of a lake is constantly replenished by surface aeration and by the photosynthesis taking place within waterborne plants and algae. Pollution corrupts the process.

Protect the health of the water body

When the demands for oxygen in the water exceed the supply, the decomposition of plant and animal life becomes anaerobic (without oxygen) and gives off the nauseous odors of decay. The undecomposed detritus builds up, destroying the bottom feeding and spawning beds, and the pond or lake becomes shallow and warmer. Eventually it is converted to swamp and then dry land. This phenomenon, called *eutrophication*, occurs in nature over eons of time by the slow addition of nutrients washed down by the feeder streams or leached out of the surrounding soils.

The eutrophication of a pond or lake is a natural process of aging by ecological succession. Since it is based on the amount of nutrients and biological productivity, it can be drastically affected by man. "Dying" Lake Erie, for example, has aged more since the turn of the century because of man-caused pollutants than it would normally have aged in many thousands of years.

With exposure to man-made pollution the process of eutrophication is greatly accelerated. The input of nutrients and other contaminants is increased by the runoff of wastes, fertilizers, and pesticides from farms, and by such by-products of urbanization as sewage, solid wastes, and industrial oils and chemicals. The oxygen content of the water is exhausted in the process of conversion. First the bottom and

soon the entire water body will become septic.

Some lakes, heavily polluted, have passed from a healthy to putrefying condition in less than a decade. Only rigid pollution control can stop, and reverse, the trend.

One of the most successful campaigns ever waged against water pollution has been centered in the Great Lakes. The stakes are high, for one out of every seven Americans and one out of every three Canadians live close to their shores.

Until 1970 there seemed to be little hope of stemming the massive degradation that was turning them into open sewers. Commercial catches of trout and whitefish were being declared unsafe for consumption. The water surrounding most cities was unfit to drink. Mile after mile of contaminated shoreline was roped off and posted to protect the health of would-be bathers and swimmers. And each year the condition worsened.

Then in 1970 a study by the International Joint Commission projected such a calamitous future for the huge freshwater bodies that the United States and Canada were finally spurred to action. Within two years these countries had signed a pact to clean up the lakes, and the EPA had been given the authority and funds to tackle our share of the job. Since then more than a billion dollars has been expended by the governments of Canada and the United States on the world's biggest cleanup project. Although there is still a long way to go, the results so far have been spectacular.

Resuscitate the "dying" lakes

Once water pollution is brought under control, the quality and vitality of water bodies can be restored in many ways, including:

1. The use, recycling, and purification of the water before its return to the source.

2. Flushing, by the controlled seasonal tapping of upland water reserves and watershed holding basins.

3. The pumping of fresh makeup water from the underlying aquifers.

4. Scientifically supervised dredging.

5. The mechanical removal of noxious weeds.

6. Chemical treatment and control.

7. Aeration of limited areas by forced-air jets and bubblers.

8. Reshaping the water edges to permit increased solar penetration.

9. Reduction of air contamination to promote increased photosynthesis.

10. Selective cutting of wooded edges to admit channelized crosswinds and breezes for increased surface aeration.

A water body in a state of natural harmony maintains a balance where nutrients and organic materials combine with dissolved oxygen in a cleaning cycle. If the oxygen demands of this chemical process exceed regenerating capacity the chain is broken and the cleansing aerobic decomposition becomes septic. Organic decay slows, adding to the available nutrients and stimulating algae growth, all of which increases the need for oxygen and quickens the cycle. Eventually, through bottom siltation and active algae production, shallow water thickens and a swamp is born.

PAUL DORR WOLFE
Unpublished memo

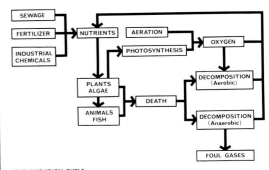

THE OXIDATION CYCLE
IN A NATURAL WATER BODY

The Detroit River, the once sewage-filled and malodorous link between Lake Erie and Lake Huron, has been cleaned up to the point where steelhead trout fingerlings are now thriving within the city limits.

Not long ago more oil was routinely flushed into the industrial Detroit River each month than was involved in the entire Santa Barbara spill of 1969, an event that shocked the nation.

Duck kills from oil in the marshes off Point Mouillee, Michigan, once were as high as 40,000 a year; now they are less than 100.

DDT concentration in Lake Michigan and mercury concentration in Lake St. Clair have dropped by more than 60 percent since 1970.

The amount of chemicals needed to make Chicago's water fit to drink has declined by over 40 percent within the past eight years.

The gratifying improvement in water quality in the Great Lakes has sent ripples of hope throughout the country, for if these waterbodies which together comprise the world's largest area of freshwater can be cleaned up, it can happen anywhere.

We recommend that outstanding water areas and water courses in the United States . . . be designated national scenic and recreational landmarks. . . .

Water and waterfronts need special treatment in all city plans. Historic waterfronts, especially, should be preserved, restored and protected. . . .

New techniques for extending the use of waterfront lands to metropolitan residents should be developed. There is far too little actual water's edge available to the typical city resident.

GRADY CLAY
Chairman, Panel on Water and Waterfronts
Beauty for America
Proceedings of the White House Conference on Natural Beauty, Washington, D.C., May 1965
U.S. Government Printing Office

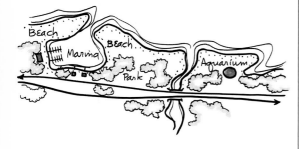

URBAN WATERFRONT IS BEST RESERVED FOR PUBLIC VIEWING AND ENJOYMENT

Preplan and zone the use of all major new impoundments and adjacent lands

Their immense potential value to the region can best be realized by planning in advance of construction.

Local jurisdictions, concerned with their long-range growth and development, will help to coordinate the master planning. It is their role to designate patterns of land use and traffic movement and to provide for the best possible use of the water and its shorelines. Where local planning expertise is lacking, as in some remote areas, the state can provide aid and guidelines.

Acquire the necessary land

The most suitable sites and right of way should be reserved from the start for the planned recreation uses. The time for their acquisition is while they are still available and before the cost has become prohibitive. Often the contribution of all lands required for public use is made a condition of the reservoir construction.

Develop the recreation opportunities created by impoundments

Throughout the countryside numerous lakes formed for the purpose of flood control, power generation, or conserving soil and water now also provide fishing, boating, and swimming. Where these water bodies are large enough for public use, sufficient and suitable land should be designated and acquired to provide the full range of water-related recreation uses. This might include forest preserves, wildlife sanctuaries, campsites, marinas, beaches, and picnic areas. Scenic access roads, parking compounds, and boat-launching ramps are also important components.

Reserve the urban waterfronts for the use of the people

City dwellers, and their guests on the trafficways, will be grateful for the opportunity to enjoy the views and water edges. Such cities as Palm Beach, Chicago, and Seattle, as examples, have demonstrated the advantages of reserving these lands and waters as recreation grounds for the whole metropolitan area.

Rivers, channels, canals

From the days of the early explorers America's rivers have provided an important means of transportation and a source of profit and pleasure. So bountiful have they been that we have assumed them capable of taking all manner of neglect and abuse while still meeting all demands upon them. With population and economic growth these demands have become counteracting.

City dwellers consume prodigious quantities of fresh water daily, much of this drawn from the rivers.

Industry requires huge additional reserves for its washing and cooling processes.

Sewage and industrial wastes, after treatment, are usually returned to the waterways as the most convenient means of disposal. (It is hard to believe, but it is true, that many communities, and some large cities, still dump raw sewage directly into the source of the regional water supply.)

The same waters are used for swimming, fishing, and boating

and often provide essential shipping and transit lanes. Impounded, they are used to generate much of our power.

As these conflicting uses have created problems, a variety of state and federal agencies have been directed to deal with each as if it were separate and independent. Experience has shown this proliferation of agencies treating isolated segments of a complex situation to be sadly inefficient. A river basin, from mountain spring to delta, is a highly sensitive *system*. Under the stress of large and opposing needs, it can be effectively planned, developed, and managed only as an interrelated *system* and only as a whole.

Look to the wild rivers

These beautiful stretches of water which pour down through the headlands of our major river basins are the unifying elements of much of our prime wilderness preserve. They are the delight of the white-water canoeists, the naturalist, the trout and salmon fishermen, and all true lovers of the great outdoors. Being isolated and frequently the target of the power and lumber interests, their condition, and often their very existence, is at stake. They need the protection of a concerned and vocal body of influential friends.

Preserve the natural channel

Stream beds and riverbanks in their natural state represent the resolution of many forces. The convolutions of the channel and the irregular edge formation and growth fulfill important functions. These include the holding of soils, checking the ground surface runoff and erosion, and flood control. They also serve the less apparent functions of water absorption, percolation, and transpiration, and provision of food and cover for aquatic and other forms of life. When disturbed at any point, the balance is thrown out of adjustment, usually to the detriment of the downstream channel or bordering lands.

While improvements may be necessary and desirable, they should be made only with an understanding of the effects upon currents, erosion, and the ecosystem. This underscores the need in each region of a comprehensive hydrological and ecological survey.

Save the islands and sandbars

Islands and riverbed sand and gravel deposits are being rapidly dredged out of existence.

Here again the improvements of navigation or the extraction of construction materials may well be valid endeavors. To judge their validity, the consequences must be weighed against all other possibilities. Islands, once removed, are lost to the communities forever as open space nature preserves, picnicking and camping areas, and scenic landmarks.

Dredging companies, barge lines, and even many governmental agencies have assumed "rights" to the rivers which are not always theirs, nor are they in the best public interest. It is time that these be reappraised and redefined.

Rivers belong to no one.

Rivers belong to everyone.

If you have within your view or experience a favorite river island, set about with your friends or local councilmen to protect it. Otherwise, in time, it will almost certainly disappear.

Include within the public domain as much waterway land as possible

In urban centers, as well as in suburban or rural regions, public ownership of the watercourse edges provides the ultimate use.

Everything is connected to everything else.
BARRY COMMONER
The Closing Circle
Knopf, New York, 1971

For most Europeans, nature means beautiful meadows, disciplined forests, daintily tilled farmlands, streams and polished banks, manicured parks and gardens. Such humanized types of landscape also contribute to the nature scene in this country. But the more common and deeper nostalgia in the American mind is for another type of scenery wilder and on a much grander scale than that associated with the word nature in the European mind. Words like the Rockies, the Far West, and even the Appalachians still give to the concept of nature a peculiarly American quality.
RENÉ DUBOS
Environmental Improvement
(Air, Water, and Soil)
The Graduate School
U.S. Department of Agriculture
Washington, D.C., 1966

Any form-manifestation in nature is a true expression of the meaning behind this form-manifestation; and this is a rule from which there is no exception in all the universe.
ELIEL SAARINEN
The City, Its Growth, Its Decay, Its Future
Reinhold Publishing Company
New York, 1943

The increased tax yield of the first band of properties surrounding the Cook County Forest Preserves (Illinois) is more than enough to cover all costs of acquisition, improvement and future operation. Beyond this, the value of all real estate within the vicinity has risen substantially.
CHARLES G. SAUERS
In conversation

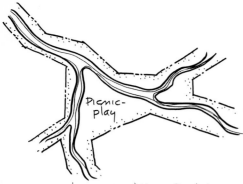

Rivers, streams, and their floodplains, if acquired and developed under public ownership, can provide a community with an interconnecting system of greenways and blueways. Within such water edge lands may be constructed drives, walks, and recreation areas. Around their sides will be drawn the better types of housing, institutions, and business uses that seek an attractive environment.

ACQUIRE THE RIVERS AND FLOODPLAINS

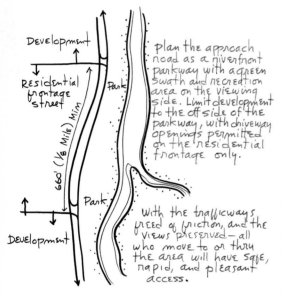

Plan the approach road as a riverfront parkway with a green swath and recreation area on the viewing side. Limit development to the off side of the parkway, with driveway openings permitted on the residential frontage only.

With the trafficways freed of friction, and the views preserved — all who move to or thru the area will have safe, rapid, and pleasant access.

MAKE THE STREAM OR RIVER A COMMUNITY FEATURE

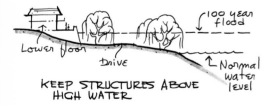

KEEP STRUCTURES ABOVE HIGH WATER

There can be no better long-term community investment than to acquire and hold all such available lands. Once assembled they will assure a superb open space holding around which will be attracted in time the cream of future development.

Relate towns and cities to the rivers and channels

Strive in long-range planning for a more direct and dramatic relationship. Consider water-edge parks and parkways. Provide scenic overlooks. Open up all possible views of the watercourses from public ways and places.

Provide a complete system of park and recreation uses along the waterways

The scenic, interconnected blueways that lace through most metropolitan areas provide an ideal location for recreation features. These might well include marinas, a zoo, public gardens, concert shells, an arboretum, stadium, forest preserves, nature trails, and riding paths. Private recreation facilities such as boating and tennis clubs should also be encouraged. New walks, bicycle paths, drives, parking turnoffs, and picnic spots would further enhance the environs as would the addition of small ponds along the feeder streams, and naturalized plantings.

Control the use of adjacent lands

To help ensure harmonious relationships, new zoning provisions should be framed for residential, cultural, commercial, and industrial campus uses along the canals and rivers.

Developers would welcome opportunities to terrace down to the waterways, to open up attractive views to and across them, and to connect into pedestrian walks and parkway drives that move along their sides. The Canadian parkway treatment of the banks of the Niagara River above and below the falls is a splendid example of what can be achieved.

Plan in harmony with the waterways

Rivers, canals, and channels are lineal elements in the landscape. Development along their edges is best planned in compatible lines and sweeps. Drives or paths along the watercourses are best designed as flowing, sequential lines of movement.

Consider the floods

Where waterways are subject to periodic flooding, buildings should be permitted only above projected one hundred-year levels. Hardship, municipal damage suits, and extensive repairs may thus be precluded, and ecological impacts reduced.

Parklands, farm fields, truck gardens, and even scenic roadways not damaged by intermittent high water may be planned within the floodplain.

Regulate the treatment of river edges and channels

The edge conformation and structures have a direct effect on the hydrodynamics of the watercourses, affecting currents, sedimentation, wave action, navigation, and water quality.

Explore the possibilities of stream and riverfront improvements

Few towns or cities take advantage of their streams and rivers, which are usually hidden away between the backs of buildings, polluted to the point of shame, or lined with brush and trash. Such was the case of the river in San Antonio before a group of citizens discovered its possibilities and converted it into a park and garden showplace. It has

Text continued on page 82.

Water resources and land development

Author's note

St. George is a barrier island. Almost without exception such national topographic superlatives should be preserved in their natural state, and in their entirety, for wildlife management or boat-access recreation.

Unfortunately, in the case of St. George Island, such uses had been precluded at the time of this study by the prior construction of a wide access bridge from the mainland. Much of the adjacent island land had been platted and sold for summer homes, which were without adequate water supply or waste disposal facilities. Pollution was rampant. Dunes and scrub were being demolished by off-road vehicles. The balance of the unplatted land seemed destined for comparable uses and destruction—as a hazard to the contiguous marshlands and the bay. Because of these existing conditions, no public agency or conservancy group approached by the residual land owners had interest in acquisition.

In consultation with the agencies concerned, it was concluded that under these very special circumstances a limited, well-planned resort village would present the best alternative, on the condition that it:

1. Provide fresh- and waste-water systems that could be tapped by the platted parcels.

2. Preserve and protect by bufferage the entire remaining perimeter of the island and all related sensitive land and water areas.

3. Be confined to a first phase area planned on the uplands in accordance with PUD procedures and subject to detailed review and monitoring.

4. Land-bank the balance of the unplatted tract, subject to an ecological survey and comprehensive county-wide planning.

The following case study is included to exemplify water management considerations and an advanced approach to the planning and protection of (non—barrier island) lands in coastal regions.

A water management program for a new resort community on St. George Island, Florida*

A report based on the premise that sound development can and must be made compatible with the protection of the ecological communities susceptible to change in water quality and flows. It demonstrates how, through sensitive planning, people and their constructions can be brought into harmonious relationship with the physiographic features and forces of a given site.

The study describes the mapping of salient ecological determinants and gives examples. It then outlines the process by which the land-water tract was divided into five broad categories which were to govern its use and planning.

Because of the critical need to conserve fresh water and to preclude the flow of contaminants into the marshes and adjacent oyster beds, special emphasis has been given to water management.

*A preliminary study.

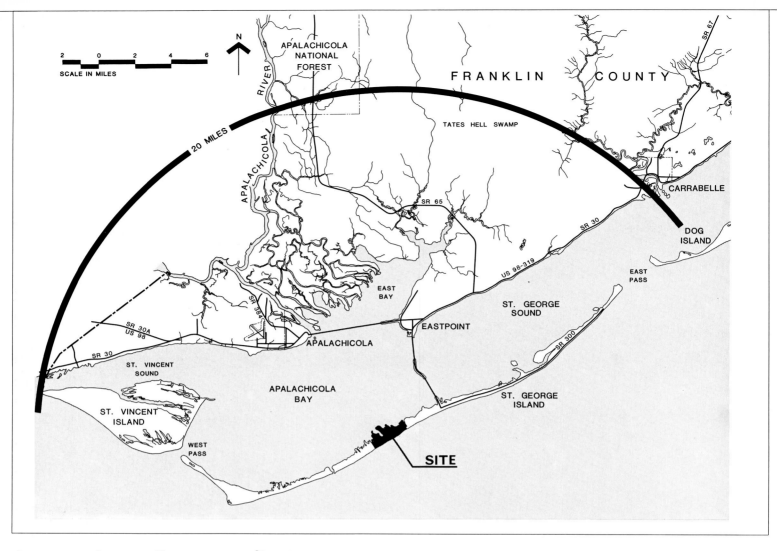

A proposed recreation community

Overview

St. George Island is one of the last major barrier islands in the state of Florida as yet uncommitted for development or acquired as part of the public domain in the interest of conservation. Big and Little St. George Islands together form a 28-mile-long strip of dunes, pine-palmetto cover, and marshland between the Gulf of Mexico and Apalachicola Bay. The bay and adjacent St. George Sound are renowned as one of the world's most productive oyster-gathering grounds. With the harvesting of shellfish and finfish their chief means of livelihood, the people of Franklin County are justifiably concerned about the rapid deterioration of the regional waters due to increasing pollution. Citizens view the further uncontrolled development of their area, and St. George Island in particular, as a serious threat to their industry and economy.

Development of the island

Ecologically, the crucial fact of the St. George Island complex is the existence, at the head of the causeway, of a rapidly building subdivision of some 1,067 acres which includes a large commercial site.

No water or sewage facilities exist or are considered feasible under present development conditions. Controls on building construction have been nonexistent. Dunes are presently being leveled. Shallow wells are being drilled on the same lots where discharge from septic tanks leaches through the porous sand into the water table. Garbage and trash are dumped into open pits. Trail bikes and dune buggies roar freely over the island, destroying vegetative cover. Campers and picnickers strew their refuse along the beaches and dunes. Pollution is rampant and destruction goes on apace. It is evident that should the present type of development be permitted to continue, or the present uses to spread unchecked, there would be little hope of preventing massive degradation of the island and its surrounding waters.

Of the total island, some 1,750 acres at the eastern tip have been purchased for a state park. At the opposite tip, the area from the St. George Island channel to the west has been designated by the state of Florida as "endangered land" and is, it is hoped, to be acquired as a nature preserve.

Aside from the existing subdivision, the state park, and a portion of Little St. George Island, the remainder of the island is owned by a consortium which plans a residential and resort community on an 800-acre tract. Plans include the installation of a water supply and advanced wastewater treatment system to initially serve the 800-acre community, but which can be expanded to serve the entire island. Also included are self-imposed environmental protection controls far exceeding in stringency any yet in force in the state. Although the island proposals have been developed in close coordination with the responsible agencies and have been generally commended, there is still, in the minds of some officials, "reasonable doubt" as to the consequences of further island development.

The alternatives

In most cases where the use of a large tract of critical land is under consideration, there are three possibilities.

If the land is in its natural state, it may well be eligible for purchase by a public agency or a foundation as a nature preserve, wildlife sanctuary, or recreation area. In the case of St. George, the owners have encouraged such acquisition and will continue to do so, but available funds are limited and the island is far removed from the population centers where open space or recreation lands are most urgently needed.

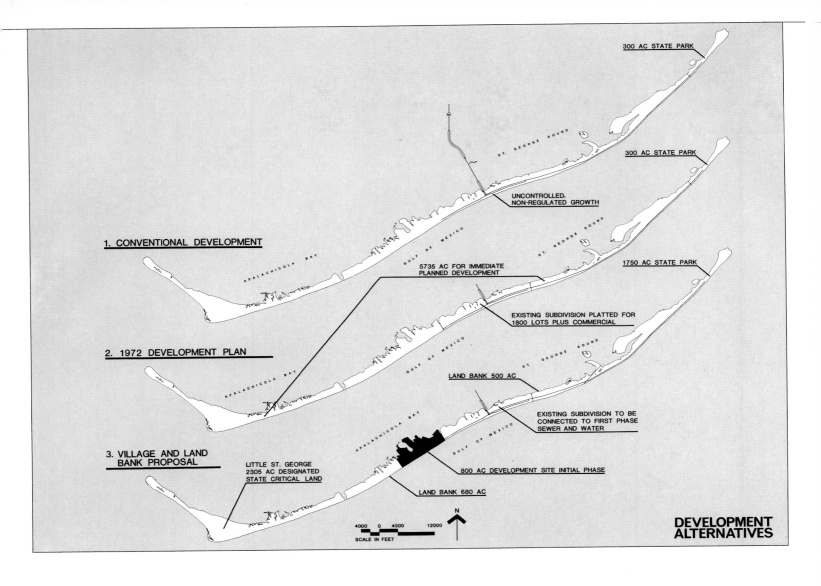

1. CONVENTIONAL DEVELOPMENT

2. 1972 DEVELOPMENT PLAN

3. VILLAGE AND LAND BANK PROPOSAL

A second, and far less desirable alternative, is the sale of the property as raw land divided into parcels without the benefit of an overall plan or the provision of community amenities or public facilities. Such fragmentation is the reason for the chaotic conditions which presently exist on the island. It thrusts upon the local government the responsibility and burden of installing the necessary public facilities. This approach, as experience has shown, can lead only to more problems and increased public expense.

The third possibility entails the comprehensive planning of the tract, or a unified portion thereof, with all trafficways, land uses, and engineering systems designed and approved as a total package. It is this latter approach to which the owners and their planning team have addressed themselves.

As the best alternative, the owners have selected 800 acres of their most suitable property for development of a prototypical resort community to demonstrate the best that can be achieved environmentally and ecologically in coastal development. This site was selected because of its high elevation, its broad width, and the lack of any producing oyster beds in the area, all factors which will minimize the risk of environmental damage.

Preservation

To assure the ecological protection of the bay and sound, all marshes are to be designated as permanent preservation lands. They are not to be disturbed by construction or the presence of the villages. The dunes which border the Gulf along the entire length of the island are also to be preserved in, or restored to, their natural condition. Except for local access paths, and perhaps a future clubhouse and fishing pier, no development is to occur within a band extending from the water's edge to the approved setback line landward of the dune crest. The full stretch of sandy beach will be available for use by the residents and public.

Between the dunes and the lower-lying wetlands, which are owned by the state, is a broad strip of sandflat and pine-palmetto cover. This swath extends on either side of the causeway and present subdivision. It is a beautiful natural environment within which the scenic parkway and collector loop roads will be aligned.

All development will occur in compounds adjacent to the parkway. The dwellings will range in type from single-family homes, villas, and garden apartments to low-rise condominiums and a resort hotel. By applying the

"cluster" principle of building groupings, extensive areas of the scrub and pine forest are to be left in their natural state.

The Village

(A working test model)

To allay lingering and understandable concerns, the owners currently plan to "land bank" all property outside of the platted subdivision except for the site of the above-referenced 800-acre recreation village which will be created over an extended "build-out" period. It will demonstrate the best techniques of environmental protection and serve to prove that responsible development can take place successfully in any area with similar finite balances between the land and the sea.

The village site will embrace some 800 acres of undeveloped land lying directly west of and adjacent to the existing subdivision. Of this total tract, over 274 acres of salt marsh, beach, and dune are to be preserved intact. An additional 183 acres will be devoted to an 18-hole golf course, racquet and swim club, and supporting recreation areas. The scenic parkway and drives will contribute additional open space, as will extensive conservation easements within the residential parcels. The eventual residential units within the vil-

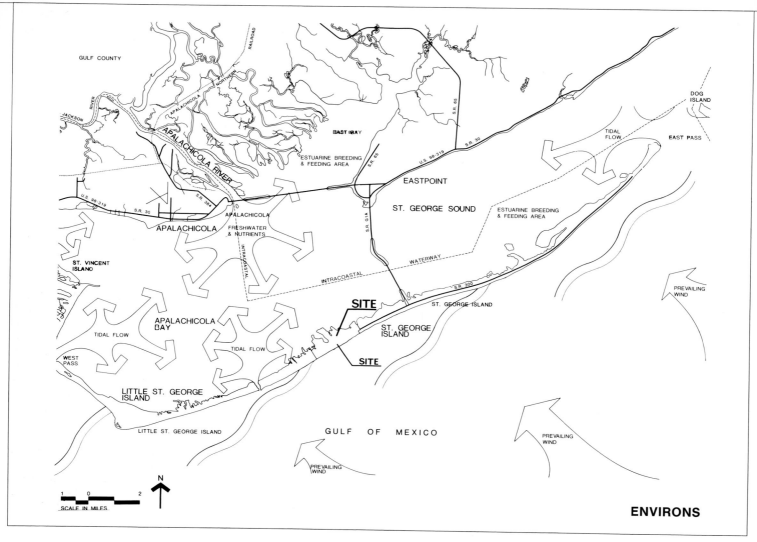

ENVIRONS

SCALE IN MILES

1 0 2

N

lage are to be constructed over the next twenty years at a mean average annual building rate of 160 dwelling units. When completed, the village will be an informal recreation community of exceptional quality and a welcome county asset.

As a condition of development, the owners have contributed funds with which the appropriate agencies will install along the water edge of the bay and gulf a series of monitoring stations. These will be manned by governmental scientists and used to detect the slightest trace of pollution. Should contamination become evident, all contributing conditions are to be "cured" before further construction proceeds.

Such an approach is unprecedented, for it commits the owners to very substantial initial costs on the basis of their confidence that the working model will test out. In short, the risk is on them. While the eventual goal of the development group is to build a successful resort community, the immediate concern—let there be no mistake—is *environmental protection.*

It is generally conceded that the planned improvements, and especially the installation of water supply and sewers, will help to correct the unsanitary conditions which pres-

ently exist. The new village will set a high standard, encourage sound construction regulations, and provide shops and more recreation for all who come to the island. Further, it will serve as a substantial tax base and will provide many employment opportunities for a county whose economy is presently sagging.

Many questions remain. The local residents and leaders must yet be convinced that their fishery won't be harmed. The resorters now on the island would prefer, quite understandably, to have the beaches all to themselves. They wonder what changes the new village will bring. The agencies, too, have their special concerns which relate to such matters as public health, navigation, and vehicular traffic. But all seem to favor the new approach which is more limited and which provides for long-range and staged development under close scrutiny and control.

Few opportunities remain in the Apalachicola Bay area for the creation of desirable, high-quality, resort communities. With the plans now being considered, St. George can be one of them.

The island, the bay, and the estuary

In flying over St. George Island, one sees spread out in panorama a classic estuarine system.

The Apalachicola River, flowing down from headwaters and tributaries in Georgia and Alabama, debouches the waters of the nation's sixth largest river basin into Apalachicola Bay and St. George Sound. These great shallow mixing bowls of fresh- and saltwater, nutrients, and river-borne sediments provide almost ideal conditions for shellfish culture. It has been estimated that with scientific aqua-farming, these two oyster fisheries alone could produce each year a crop sufficient to supply the world's present consumption. The waters teem also with shrimp, clams, crabs, and various sport and commercial fish. But perhaps the greatest value of the estuary and its tidal marshes lies in their vital function as a nursery for most of the varieties of shell and game fish taken the length of the Florida coast.

Three large offshore islands enframe the bay. St. Vincent to the west is a federal preserve, and Dog Island to the east is under private ownership. Stretching eastward from St. Vincent, St. George Island lies like a curving protective arm against the winds and waves of the Gulf of Mexico. The narrow strand is blessed with wide beaches and low dunes along the Gulf, a central pine-palmetto forest, and wide tidal marshes.

The river and its estuaries, the bays, sound, offshore islands, and the tidal surgings of the Gulf together form a complete ecological unit.

The estuarine system

As may be imagined, the biologic workings of a bay system are infinitely interrelated and extremely complex.

The bays and sounds comprise one of Florida's richest marine breeding and feeding grounds. They are shallow, with brackish water ranging in depth to 9 feet above a sand base and layers of sediment. Here, and along the bayside marshes, freshwater, nutrients, and decaying vegetation brought down by the river from upland forests and swamps are commingled by the winds and tides into a saline solution containing CO_2 and inorganic ions. These are converted by photosynthesis into the simple starches of the basic aquatic food chain. This conversion is dependent upon the presence of sunlight and the chlorophyll contained within the cells of phytoplankton, algae, or other marine plants. The often microscopic phytoplankton (plants) become the chief source of food for grazing zooplankton (animals) and other lower forms of aquatic life. Or they may be ingested directly by oysters and by smaller fish which in turn become the food of the larger species.

It can be said that within the catalyst bay and sound, the energies of the fetching river, the blending winds, and the warming sun are transformed into food and life.

The offshore islands, and especially St. George, provide a barrier against the scouring effects of the winds and waves which would otherwise flush away the rich bottom sediments of the protected waters. They help to sustain the freshwater hydraulic head against the invasion of the salt tides. And finally, they support the marshy bay fringe so important to the system.

Although vast in extent, the estuarine ecosystem is intricately balanced. It is dependent upon finely adjusted tolerances in seasonal salinity, nutritional values, and temperature. These in turn are affected by rates of river flow, currents, and wind action. While natural imbalances may be temporarily harmful, the presence of man-made pollution in increasing amounts presages biologic disaster, eutrophication, and the eventual death of the bay.

Monitoring

In an effort to better understand and protect the fishery, the county government has, for the past several years, been at work on biologic studies and a permanent baywide network of monitors. Four stations have recently been installed adjacent to the island to collect and record base data in the vicinity of the proposed village site.

The monitoring operations will consist of periodic physiochemical probes to test those properties associated with the aquatic community structures and population distributions. The biotic parameters checked will include counts and condition of phytoplankton, invertebrates, fishes, and plants and food-chain analysis. The abiotic factors will include those of temperature, salinity, turbidity, and the presence of nutrients, dissolved oxygen, pesticides, trace metals, and other pollutants. Both diurnal and seasonal changes are to be recorded.

The purpose of the stations is to detect any significant changes in water quality in order that possible problems may be fore-stalled and unhealthy conditions corrected. The ultimate aim of the system is to assure zero discharge of pollutants into the marshes, bay, and sound.

Problem and opportunity

The people of Franklin County are well aware that new building construction has traditionally meant the dredging and filling of wetlands, bulkheading, channelization, and the discharge of sewage into the fishing grounds. Citizens are concerned that unplanned development will destroy their fishing and change their unique and pleasant way of life. The concern is justified. The threat is real and serious, for historically when development has moved into the lands adjacent to an oyster fishery, the beds are soon placed "off limits" by public health officials. The cry is now out to "Save the bay!"

The potential sources of trouble are threefold. The river itself which pours down its supply of freshwater, detritus, and nutrients is now becoming polluted. Unregulated growth along the bay shores is adding its share of contamination. And now, with the completion of the causeway, the further development of the island is a virtual certainty. If history is to repeat itself, there would seem to be little hope for the threatened fishery. One by one, others like it have been closed.

But perhaps there may yet be marshaled the necessary combination of scientific research and control, governmental cooperation, and sound planning to reverse the trend and "put it all together." It is fervently hoped by many that the Apalachicola region may become a laboratory and working model of the best that can be achieved in coastal land and water management.

It is within this context that the planning of the recreation village on St. George Island has been initiated.

APALACHICOLA BAY

GULF OF MEXICO

400 0 800   1600
SCALE IN FEET

AERIAL

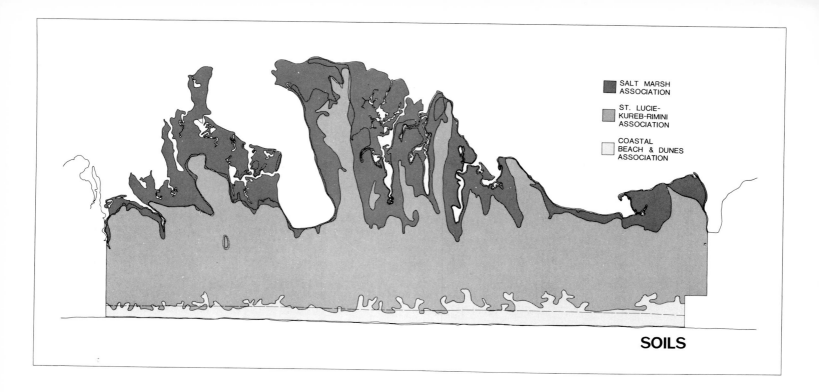

SALT MARSH ASSOCIATION

ST. LUCIE-KUREB-RIMINI ASSOCIATION

COASTAL BEACH & DUNES ASSOCIATION

SOILS

Ecological survey

A first step in the planning process is the collection of all necessary background and survey data. These are often recorded in the form of a series of reference "eco-determinant" maps and supporting documents which record all physiographic, social, and economic and other pertinent information.

The examples shown are from a series which includes that information most useful in the conceptual land planning of the island and first village. Each planning team member, consultant, and scientist-adviser has contributed special knowledge to the preparation and analysis of these maps.

Physical constraints

The physiographic characteristics of the island impose severe restrictions on its use.

Climate: The climatic conditions of the Apalachicola region in general, and of St. George Island in particular, will be a primary factor in the alignment of roads, the designation of land-use areas, the siting of structures and the design of the buildings themselves. While many climatic influences may be dealt with intuitively in the master planning studies, actual site and building designs in the advanced planning stage must reflect thorough analysis.

High winds and tidal fluctuation: Although no hurricane* has been officially recorded on the island, the effects of Hurricane Agnes, which passed nearby in May of 1972, were drastic. Aerial photographs taken immediately prior to and following the storm indicate that storm waters swept entirely across the island over a length of approximately 7 miles where the protective dunes were low. These were practically leveled by the storm, and the profile of the remaining sand barrier was substantially altered. Unless the lower protective dunes can be restored and stabilized, the permanence of dwellings, or even roadways,

*Defined as a violent tropical cyclonic storm with winds exceeding 74 miles per hour.

0 - 5% SLOPE

5% - 15% SLOPE

PLUS 15% SLOPE

SLOPES

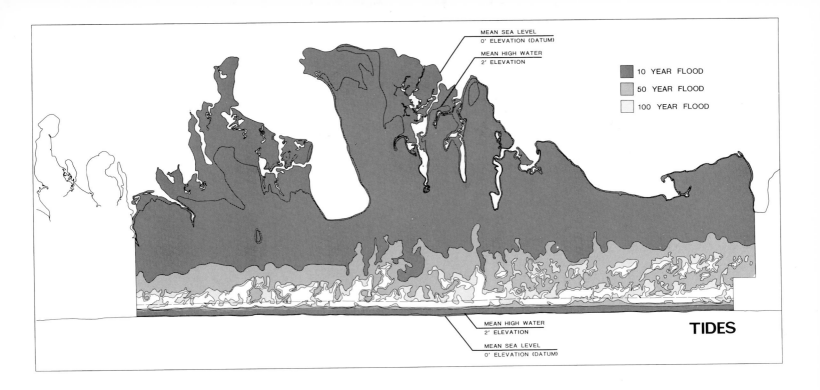

MEAN SEA LEVEL
0' ELEVATION (DATUM)

MEAN HIGH WATER
2' ELEVATION

■ 10 YEAR FLOOD
▨ 50 YEAR FLOOD
□ 100 YEAR FLOOD

MEAN HIGH WATER
2' ELEVATION

MEAN SEA LEVEL
0' ELEVATION (DATUM)

TIDES

is in jeopardy. Regeneration of the dunes would be favorably considered by the State Bureau of Beaches and Shores, and state participation in such a program has been suggested as a possibility.

A second factor in tidal consideration is the HUD insurance requirement that the floor level of structures in this area be a minimum of 9 to 10 feet above mean sea level, or from 7 to 8 feet above mean high tide. This drastically limits the extent of normal slab-on-grade construction, and suggests a post-and-beam island architecture.

Living quarters would thereby be lifted well above grade, giving protection from insects, welcome exposure to the prevailing breezes, improved views, and shade for cars which could be parked under the buildings.

In addition, Florida State law also provides that all buildings must be located behind a "coastal construction setback line." The precise location of this line has been established in cooperation with the State Bureau of Beaches and Shores. Construction must be located sufficiently landward of the dune crest line to prevent damage to its structural integrity.

The dunes: In addition to the possible rebuilding and reshaping of the dunes, their protection from overuse and from the ravages of "off-the-road vehicles" must be ensured.

The owners will cooperate with state and local officials in enforcing the legal prohibitions against any vehicles on the dunes seaward of the setback line. Residents of the village will have full and free access to the beaches through membership in a homeowners' association. The general public will be encouraged to use the public beaches in the state park.

The wetlands: The tidal marshes fringing Apalachicola Bay are the most productive and valuable land-water areas in the county. They are also the most vulnerable to pollution. Since the health of the bay and the abundance of its yield of fish, oysters, and

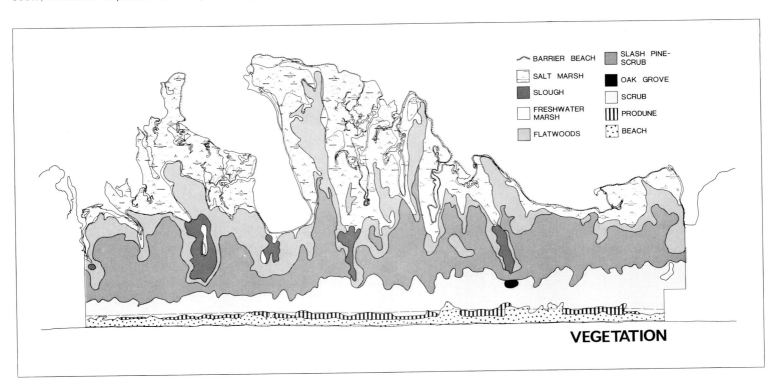

BARRIER BEACH
SALT MARSH
SLOUGH
FRESHWATER MARSH
FLATWOODS
SLASH PINE-SCRUB
OAK GROVE
SCRUB
PRODUNE
BEACH

VEGETATION

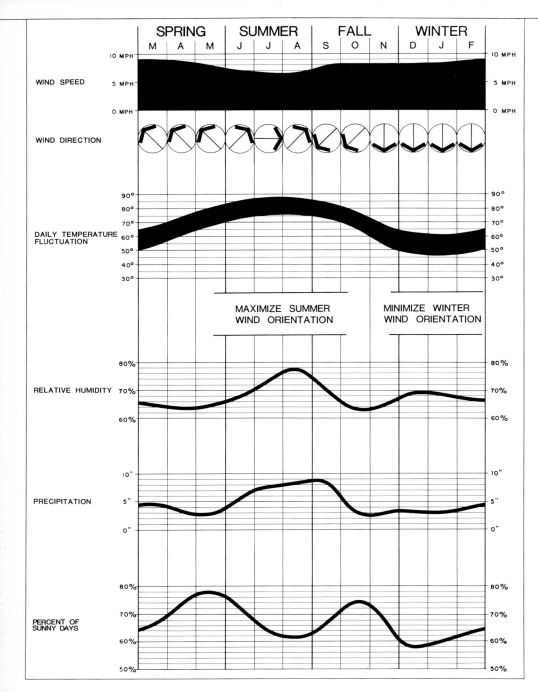

SPRING | SUMMER | FALL | WINTER
M A M | J J A | S O N | D J F

WIND SPEED — 10 MPH, 5 MPH, 0 MPH

WIND DIRECTION

DAILY TEMPERATURE FLUCTUATION — 90° 80° 70° 60° 50° 40° 30°

MAXIMIZE SUMMER
WIND ORIENTATION

MINIMIZE WINTER
WIND ORIENTATION

RELATIVE HUMIDITY — 80% 70% 60%

PRECIPITATION — 10" 5" 0"

PERCENT OF SUNNY DAYS — 80% 70% 60% 50%

shrimp are directly dependent upon the preservation of these wetlands, their protection has become a first consideration in the planning of the village.

Water: Fresh water presently exists on the island in limited quantities. A test well drilled at East Point on the mainland has a capacity to provide enough potable water for the entire village. A pump and a treatment plant will be installed at a collection point in the well vicinity. Water will then be transmitted to the island where a concrete ground water storage tank will be installed for storage and distribution. Potable water and advanced waste treatment will be made available to the existing subdivision as soon as economically practicable. Shallow wells on the island may be utilized to provide some of the water for irrigation and other auxiliary uses.

Vegetation: The existing vegetation, while sparse in many areas, is typical of Gulf barrier islands. If preserved, reestablished where disturbed, and supplemented with indigenous plant materials, it will provide a memorable island setting. It is proposed that native vegetation be maintained and that the introduction of exotic plants be prohibited except for limited areas of intensive development.

It has also been proposed by the Bureau of Sports Fisheries and Wildlife that the seeding of dove grass be considered in the dune stabilization program, since St. George Island lies astride a principal dove flyway. Other native plants which provide food and cover have also been recommended.

Soils: The soils of the island are composed largely of sands and other porous materials. Clays and humus are generally lacking. Topsoil is practically nonexistent. Both the load-bearing and absorptive capacities of the soil must be tested on a systematic basis so that in the process of excavation, the best use will be made of selected materials.

BAY

SALT MARSH | SLOUGH | FRESHWATER MARSH | FLATWOODS | SLASH PINE-SCRUB

Landscape analysis: To understand the nature of the land upon which the first village is to be built, it is well to take an overview to discover the chief landscape features and their interrelationships. A visual sweep of the island from gulf to bay reveals a topography of dramatic changes and rich vegetative variety. From the south, the floor of the Gulf of Mexico slopes up to a relatively stable beach which extends for over a hundred feet from the mean high-water line to the toe of the frontal or primary dune. The sugar sand is deep and, when dry, is subject to the drift that has built here a dune barrier some 20 to 30 feet in height, and upon which the vegetative covers remain for the most part intact. It is to be noted that in other parts of the island, where the cover has been destroyed, the dunes have been subjected to severe wind erosion. The secondary dunes are crowned with interlocking patches of wind-sheared scrub. The close-knit, picturesque growth helps to stabilize the lateral sand drift and should be left undisturbed insofar as possible. A transitional belt of slash pine scrub lies between the dune tailings and flatwoods. Toward the north, the undulating ground levels out to form a relatively high pine-palmetto plateau. Here, where most of the dwellings will be grouped, the scattered clumps of slash pine provide a sparse but spectacular overstory with their storm-contorted upper limbs and tops. Between the scrub and the tidal marsh are found occasional freshwater bogs which, in times of downpour, serve as natural holding basins and a filter between the high land and the bay. Beyond to the north, along the whole length of the village site, lie the broad saltwater marshes. By consensus, these wetlands and the adjacent bottoms must be protected in their entirety as the aquatic nursery for the oysters, crabs, and other fish which inhabit the bay beyond.

Each of the realms described, while interacting with the others, is a natural system in itself and worthy of detailed study.

GULF

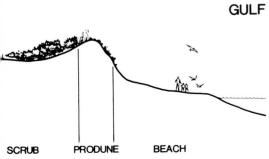

SCRUB   PRODUNE   BEACH

73

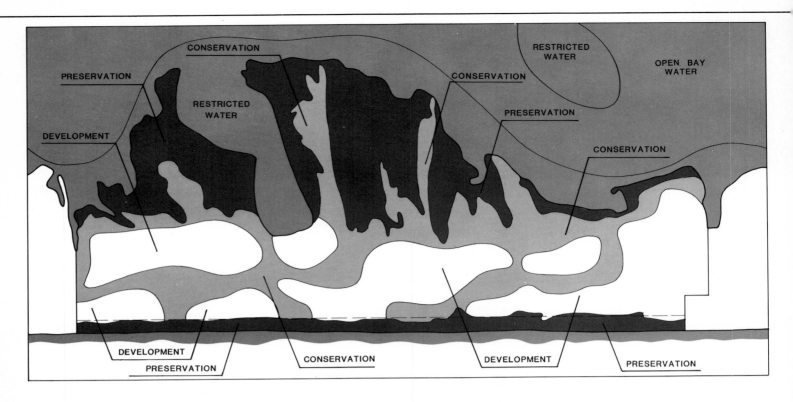

Zones of suitability

A study of the landscape environs begins to reveal areas or zones of varying fragility and ecological significance. Each suggests those uses for which it is suited, and others for which it is not. Some areas are of a landscape character deserving complete *preservation* as a nature preserve or open space enframement. Such are the frontal dunes, the tidal marshes, and portions of the freshwater swamp. With the possible exception of occasional raised observation walks or platforms and confined access trails, the existing condition is not to be changed in any significant way by human presence or constructions.

Other less sensitive or less productive areas are suited to limited use. In such *conservation* areas, the best of the springs, groves, and other natural features will be conserved and protected. In and around these, recreation areas and paths of movement will be arranged with care to bring people and nature into compatible relationship. Here people may enjoy the natural scenery and live amidst thriving oaks, pines, and palmetto clumps and the associated flora and fauna. Such *conservation* areas will be governed by use restrictions and will serve as the buffers between the *preservation* areas and zones of more intensive development.

Designated *development* areas are those in which the natural landforms and vegetation are of minimal significance. These may be modified by grading and used freely as construction sites, provided precautions are taken to eliminate any possible degradation of the bordering zones. Here again, the better landscape elements will be saved insofar as feasible and the building clusters, parkway, and other construction fitted in amongst them. New plantings and ground covers of native materials will be established to blend all installations into the natural surroundings.

As with land areas, certain stretches of water are also of ecological importance. Oyster shoals and marine grass beds, for example, should be left undisturbed. Although

there are legal difficulties in restricting the use of navigable waters, the owners will co-operate with local and state officials in trying to secure legal approval for the restrictive zones described below.

To assure the integrity of the several zones, they have been meticulously defined over various reference maps with all factors considered. Starting from the open water and moving inward, the zones are proposed as follows:

Open waters

These will include all waters of the bay and Gulf excepting those which may be designated as "restricted."

They will be open to all those forms of water-related activities which cause no significant pollution or unacceptable levels of stress upon the natural estuarine system.

Suitable uses
All water sports.
Commercial and sport fishing.
Construction of offshore recreation facilities on the gulf side only, provided environmental criteria are met.

Not permitted
Dredging or filling.
Seawall construction.
Docks, piers, or other construction within bay waters.
Destruction of the reefs or plant life.

Restricted waters

These include the oyster reefs, marine grass beds, and water areas especially productive in shellfish, commercial, or sportfish propagation.

Suitable uses
Boating by sailing craft.
Commercial fishing by licensees.

Scientific monitoring and marine experimentation.
Aquatic preserves.
Aquaculture leases.

Not permitted
Any other uses.

Preservation

These lands of particular ecological sensitivity are to be preserved, essentially, in their natural condition. Aside from their vital role of

protecting the bay systems and shorelines, they will afford aesthetic values to the community and will serve as a bulwark against the storms.

Suitable uses
Raised access walks and nature trails with confining guardrails.
Observation decks and platforms of post-and-beam construction.
Dune stabilization devices.
Protective fencing.
Dune renourishment and establishment of supplementary ground covers.

Not permitted
Use of recreational or other vehicles except for maintenance carts on confined cartway.
Trespassing on the primary dune.
Public use or trespass on the bayside shore.
Building construction.
Excavation, filling, or grading.
Pollution in any form.
Disturbance of archaeological or historic sites.
Dredging, filling, or seawall construction.

Conservation

While *conservation* areas, as herein designated, are not considered to be critical to ecological balance, they contain many features of landscape significance which are to be preserved insofar as feasible. They may be unsuited to intensive use because of the physical limitations of the soil or the probability of wind erosion or flooding. They may be utilized for local drives, walks, bicycle trails, golf fairways and greens, and other recrea-

tion uses. Buildings of post-and-platform construction may be permitted with adequate restrictions and controls. Broadly, however, conservation lands serve best for limited use, open space recreation, and greenbelt buffers to preservation zones.

Suitable uses
Local access drives and parking compounds.
Pedestrian walks and bicycle trails.
Golf-course installation.
Tennis courts, swim clubs, and other recreation areas.
Limited building and other construction.
Recharge swales and holding basins.
Public use of the beach for swimming and shelling.
   (Gulf exposure only)
Lifeguard station and cabanas.

Not permitted
Use of off-cartway recreational vehicles.
Major roadways or construction.
Excavation, filling, or grading.*
Felling of trees or destruction of ground covers.*

Development

This zone includes those lands which are intrinsically suitable for more intensive development. Although there may be physical limitations such as drainage problems, or unstable bearing conditions, it is anticipated that these can be overcome without disruption to the surrounding environs. It is to be noted that all uses and construction are to be in accordance with plans approved by the appropriate agencies and governed by applicable laws, codes, and ordinances. In addition, it is intended that all development is to be subject to deed restrictions and the issuance of permits based upon review and approval by the management of detailed layouts, types and methods of construction, and stringent antipollution controls both during and after construction. All first-floor elevations will be above 100-year flood levels. Within the broad *development* zone, several subzones have been designated on the basis of suitability for varying degrees of land-use intensity.

Suitable uses
Vehicular parkway and circulation roads.
Residential construction of all proposed categories.
Golf clubhouse, spa, and recreation courts.
Community center.
Convenience shopping.
Possible future airstrip.
Service station.
Utility and wastewater treatment plant.
Forest and agricultural uses.

Not permitted
Major commercial facilities.
Industrial or manufacturing uses.
Trailer parks.
Sanitary landfills.
Livestock, barns, pens, stables, or pasturage.
*Without written approval of the Environmental Control Officer.

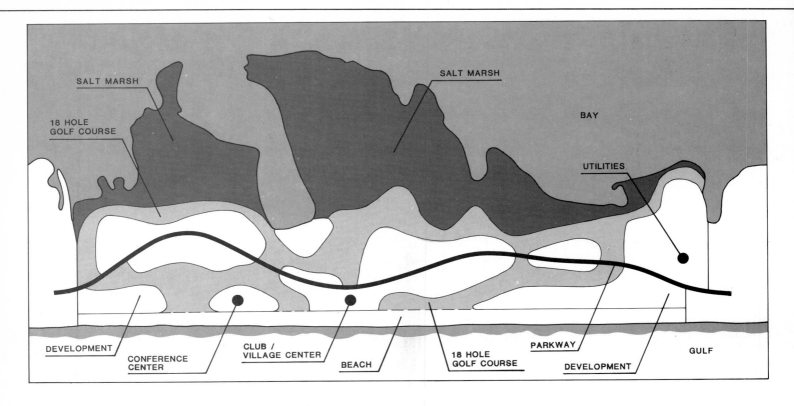

SALT MARSH

18 HOLE
GOLF COURSE

SALT MARSH

BAY

UTILITIES

DEVELOPMENT

CONFERENCE
CENTER

CLUB /
VILLAGE CENTER

BEACH

18 HOLE
GOLF COURSE

PARKWAY

DEVELOPMENT

GULF

A conceptual plan

Just as the land has been analyzed to find those uses for which each area is best suited, so has the planning team considered each plan component also, to determine its best location and design characteristics. The various plan elements and land-use areas of approximate size and shape have been tested out in most reasonable relationship one to the other and to the lay of the land.

Scenic parkway and drives

The several types of trafficways are arranged to provide access and interconnection. The parkway spine, being dominant, is so aligned as to establish a theme of varying views and dramatic scenic exposures. It serves also, together with its drainage swales and median, as a protective surface drainage barrier between the multifamily development areas and the fragile marshes which lie along the edge of the bay. The circulation loop roads and culs-de-sac, too, seek out and reveal the best of the landscape features as they weave between and around them.

Golf course

The golf course, as a design element, must be considered from many points of view. Since the first concern of the golf architects will be the quality of the play, they will want the most favorable orientation, topography, and enframement. They will be interested, too, in the relationships to the clubhouse and access roads, and will check and recheck the soil types and existing drainage patterns. The architects will be seeking to enhance their buildings with the best exposures from and across the fairways and greens. Marketing consultants will be well aware that an important aspect of the course will be the appreciation of land values along its sides and they will seek to extend the benefits. The botanists will be intent upon the interactions of the course and the plant communities, while the marine biologists will promote its use as a buffer and filter between development and the

bay. The engineers will envision the irrigation system as an advanced phase of the waste-water treatment and disposal. And the landscape architects will want to be assured that all installations respond to, preserve, and accentuate the best of the landscape features and contribute in full measure to the environmental enhancement of the new community.

Community center
The community center with its club, spa, recreation areas, and general store will be planned as the village focal point. Here the approaches, spaces, and the structures with their terraces, courts, and flying decks will take full advantage of the views and breeze. They will achieve in all ways possible a harmonious integration of architecture and nature.

Dwellings
Villas and apartment clusters will be grouped compactly around tree-shaded courtyards. Parking bays and entrances will face inward upon the "motor gardens." Living areas, patios, and screened decks will be oriented outward to the breeze and to the views. The free arrangement of dwellings in clusters has many advantages. It is less disruptive of the groundforms and vegetation. It requires shorter runs of access drives and utilities. It confines the parking and service functions and thus minimizes pollution. It assures a higher degree of privacy and preserves more usable outdoor open space.

Utility Plant
The utility plant is also a service facility with demanding placement requirements. A location central to its service area will reduce the lengths of reach and the size of mains and equipment. Its relation to the marshes and bays must provide a failsafe means of protection in case of a breakdown or temporary surcharge due to storms or other emergencies. Although it is to be well designed and fully maintained, such an installation tends to reduce adjacent land values and is best kept isolated within its own domain.

Open Space
All open spaces are to be combined into an interrelated system which will surround and interlace the entire community. They will embrace the length and breadth of the beach and foredunes, include the tidal marsh preserves, and incorporate the golf course, parkway, recreation areas, and all conservation easements. Open space lands and waters not dedicated for public use will be maintained by the village association.

The Village
Buildings, facilities, trafficways, and the open space framework have been brought together in the conceptual plan to establish the broad outlines of a complete recreation resort village. The plan sets the general pattern for all those myriad relationships and experiences which make for community life. If the planning as it proceeds confirms the fact that the relationships developed are sound, then the village will be attractive and harmoniously adjusted to respond to the natural forms, forces, and features of the island site.

The goal of the conceptual planning and design process has been to provide a pollution-free environment where life, and the most healthful forms of recreation, may be enjoyed within the exhilarating setting of a coastal nature preserve.

Environmental protection

As has been noted, the *conceptual plan is a diagram of relationships.* It is to be refined and developed, and perhaps revised, as each element, and the plan itself, is subjected to further study. In the continuing design process, as from the start, all aspects of the community are to be considered in the light of four guiding objectives.

These are:

1. To create a resort community of the highest order, as an integral part of an attractive and prosperous region.

2. To preserve the bay, the Gulf, and all shoreline and beaches in their natural condition as a magnificent land-water setting.

3. To protect the estuarine ecosystem against pollution in any form.

4. To plan the St. George Island property as a laboratory and working model of the best that can be achieved in coastal land development.

In working to achieve these goals, the concerns for environmental quality have resolved themselves for the most part into the elimination of all possible forms of pollution. To this end, all potential sources have been listed, together with the safeguards proposed.

Misuse of the beaches
The beaches below the mean high-water line belong to the state and will be available for the use of the residents and the public. The beaches above the mean high-water mark will be owned and regulated by a village home-owners' association. The beaches will be open for use by the residents and their guests, subject to such reasonable restrictions as may be imposed by the association.

Dune erosion
The primary dunes are the island's protective barriers against wind-driven tides and storms from the Gulf. The loose sands of which they are composed are extremely susceptible to erosion. Once the fragile vegetative covers of sea oats, vines, and scrub growth are disturbed, the rapid disintegration of the dune is imminent. The frontal dune system is, therefore, to be made "off limits" to all vehicles and uses except for raised beach-access walkways and scenic overlooks.

Destruction of vegetation
Also to be protected are the thin soil mantle and vegetative covers of the balance of the island. The trees, shrubs, and other indigenous plants comprise a natural system in dynamic equilibrium. They ameliorate the microclimate by providing shade, wind-screen, evapotranspiration, conserving air and ground moisture, and by recharging the groundwater table. They serve as wildlife habitat and form a landscape of great beauty. Sound planning will seek to bring development patterns into harmonious relationship with the natural order in such a way as to enhance the workings of both.

Trafficways and parking areas
In terms of environmental impact, the alignment and section of roadways and parking compounds are as important as the materials of which they are constructed. They are to be located to "run with" and blend into the landforms and to be placed, wherever possible, *between* the trees and groves and other landscape features.

The scenic parkway has been located and is to be designed as a storm-water barrier and filter between the development areas of higher intensity and the waters of the bay. Berms, local roads, and parking courts are to be constructed of porous materials. Paved surfaces are to be minimized.

Marinas and boat use
No marinas, landings, or private docks are to be permitted within the village. Boat access and moorings now existing at the causeway marina will be used, and possibly improved upon eventually for the use of the village residents.

It is urged that all boat use of the waters surrounding the island be made subject to regulations as to type, condition, and operation which will preclude all forms of pollution.

Service facilities
The village store, filling station, launderette, and all similar public and private service areas and facilities are to receive special study. Such potential "point sources" of contamination are to be located and planned with care to eliminate the possibility of degrading the environs.

Dredging and filling
Permits for offshore dredging are currently being granted by the state only when it can be demonstrated that there will be no harmful effects. Because no marinas or landings are being planned for the village, and because of the wish to preserve the adjacent bay bottoms and edges, and the beaches, in their entirety, no dredging of canals or building of seawalls is to be considered within the village confines.

Building construction
The hazards of erosion, siltation, and contamination are perhaps the most acute during

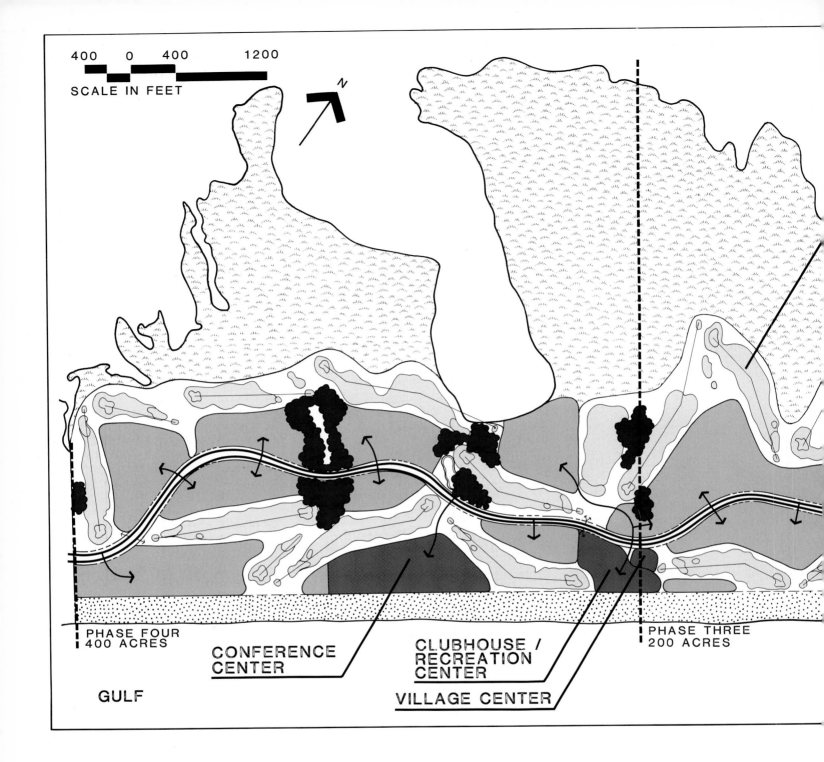

SCALE IN FEET
400 0 400   1200

N

PHASE FOUR
400 ACRES

CONFERENCE
CENTER

CLUBHOUSE /
RECREATION
CENTER

VILLAGE CENTER

PHASE THREE
200 ACRES

GULF

the construction period. It is, therefore, to be mandated that the plans and specifications for all earthwork, road building, or other construction include a detailed section on pollution control. It shall cover such aspects as the provision of protective barricades, signing, interception ditches and settling basins, material storage, and the disposal of surplus materials and refuse. It shall also provide for the prevention of erosion by the installation of temporary or permanent storm drainage, mulching, netting, and ground cover seeding. All clearing, burning, excavation, filling, and grading is to be performed under bond and made subject to the prefiling of a plan to assure erosion and pollution control.

Storm drainage and surface runoff

While the sheet flow of the natural rainfall on undisturbed areas is beneficial to the bay, contaminated storm runoff from rooftops, parking, and service areas and from the parkway pavement must be intercepted. Should the level of pollution from oil or other sources be considered hazardous, the runoff will be collected and so processed that the potential problem will be resolved.

Siltation

On a narrow barrier island particularly the accelerated movement and settling out of windborne or waterborne soils or other particulate matter can have deleterious effects.

The blowout of a frontal dune can bury whatever lies behind it. Concentrated storm-water runoff can cut deep gullies into the duff and sands. The resulting siltation can soon overwhelm an existing plant or animal community. Siltation is best controlled at the source. Dune protection and the use of all effective erosion controls are considered to be essential.

Water supply and saltwater intrusion

The primary supply of potable water is to be pumped from wellfields on the mainland in quantities sufficient to provide for the needs of all village uses and users on a ten-year projection. Supplementary wells may be

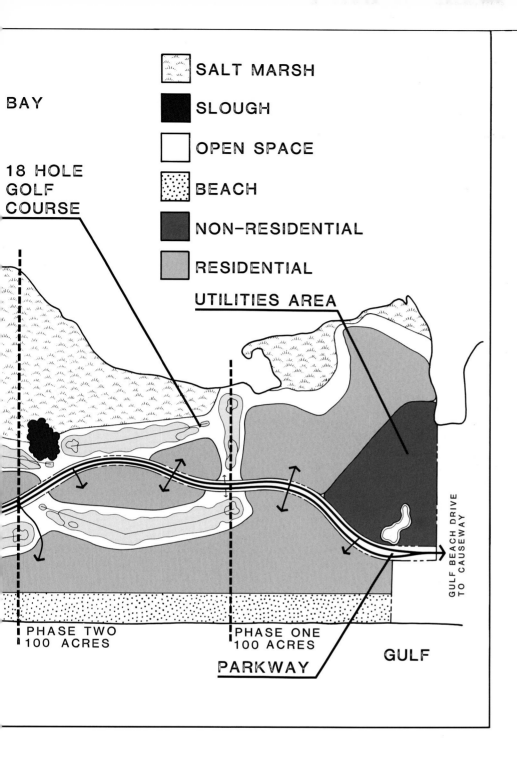

Legend

- SALT MARSH
- SLOUGH
- OPEN SPACE
- BEACH
- NON-RESIDENTIAL
- RESIDENTIAL

BAY

18 HOLE GOLF COURSE

UTILITIES AREA

GULF BEACH DRIVE TO CAUSEWAY

PHASE TWO 100 ACRES

PHASE ONE 100 ACRES

PARKWAY

GULF

---

discharged by offshore outfall into the Gulf.

The golf-course irrigation system is to be designed as a form of advanced wastewater treatment for "burning off" residual nutrients.

All water used for irrigation is to be kept from flowing into the bay or marshes. It is to be retained by berms or recharge lagoons and pumped back to irrigate the golf course, parkway, and other nonsensitive areas.

Fertilizers

The type, amount, and placement of all fertilizer used shall be made the responsibility of the management, which shall keep accurate records of its ordering, storage, and application. The use of fertilizer by private homeowners or their tenants will not be permitted.

Garbage disposal

Each dwelling is to be equipped with a garbage disposal unit on-line with the treatment plant. Garbage from public or other major dining facilities is to be stored in refrigerated containers for removal by truck from the site.

Solid waste

Trash and other solid wastes will be stored in approved watertight containers in enclosed service areas at each dwelling or other building. Collection will be by privately owned companies franchised by the county or community management, with off-island disposal as approved.

Trace metals and PCB

Contamination by polychlorinated biphenyl (PCB) or such trace metals as copper, zinc, lead, cadmium, or mercury is not considered to be a problem, since strict controls on their use and disposal will be enforced in the form of building restrictions, construction regulations, and solid-waste disposal specifications.

Pets and livestock

No pets, livestock, or domestic fowl of any kind are to be kept within the island community.

Insect control

No pesticides or herbicides are to be used on-site except under the direction of the superintendent of maintenance and by trained crews. Selected materials, methods and rates of application, and controls, are to be as approved by the consulting biologist, botanist, and entomologist, and are to be consistent with all county, state, and federal health ordinances, regulations, and practices.

Operation and maintenance

The maintenance of all roads, rights-of-way, exterior grounds of public and private buildings, golf-course areas, and all beach, dune, marsh, conservation, or preservation areas is to be conducted by trained crews operating under the supervision of the management. Administrative responsibility shall be centered in a management company. It shall be governed by a charter which shall be made part

---

drilled on-island for secondary uses as long as it can be demonstrated that saltwater intrusion will not be induced by the freshwater drawdown.

Sewage disposal

A wastewater treatment plant to be located at the eastern limit of the village will have the capacity to serve all existing and proposed development for the area of St. George Island lying westward of the bridge. This plant will provide advanced waste treatment of sewage with the reuse of all treated water for local irrigation and recharge of the freshwater aquifer.

The design engineer is to provide a com-

prehensive program for nutrient loadings and quantitative models for controlling the disposition of all water and possible contaminants introduced to the island in any form. Hydraulic and nutrient loadings are to be based on 25-year storms.

The treatment plant will be designed with a standby auxiliary system and without a bypass. It is to be operated by a Class "A" Wastewater Treatment Operator.

Irrigation

Insofar as feasible, all treated effluent from the plant is to be used either for irrigation or as makeup water in the recharging ponds. As a possibility, excess treated effluent may be of all sales and lease agreements. It is considered to be essential that the management shall have the authority and adequate staff to impose and enforce whatever sanctions may be required to assure environmental quality and to protect the bay.

Aside from those measures required to preclude the contamination of the bay and sound, there are others which can also have a telling effect on environmental quality. These deal with air, noise, and visual pollution. They include also those guidelines and controls which help to ensure fine architecture and landscape development. It is intended that all concerns are to be addressed and receive full attention.

Conditions for development

As a condition of undertaking the St. George project, a firm commitment by the project development organization has been made to the county and state that the proposed community will not harm the fishing industry or the estuary. This has underscored the urgent necessity for emphasis on the ecological considerations throughout the planning process. The self-imposed conditions for development may be summarized as follows:

1. Comprehensive schematic planning for the total island and its environs.

2. Phased development and commitment to a construction schedule and periodic reviews. Procedure from stage to stage to be based on performance.

3. A limited first-phase community of no more than 800 acres and a density not exceeding 3.75 dwelling units per gross acre.

4. Controlled (and monitored) protection of the bay and sound against any significant project-caused pollution in any form.

5. Preservation of the dunes, wetlands, and water edges in their natural condition.

6. Preparation, and county acceptance of, a comprehensive environmental impact report.

7. Creation of a centralized administrative unit with strict construction and operation controls and means of enforcement.

8. Provision of leadership in reversing the trend of deterioration of the island. (An important first step will be the installation of the potable water supply and advanced wastewater treatment systems.)

The village

An essential feature of all fine communities is that they take their form stage by stage from an overall plan which determines from the start the patterns of traffic movement and land use.

Features

In this village plan, a distinguishing feature is the broad scenic parkway which sweeps through the slash pine forest to interconnect the residential compounds and the community center. Local loop roads and winding trails of shell or gravel will complete the trafficway system. Within each neighborhood compound villas and apartments will be grouped around the motor courts with cars stored in parking bays or beneath the structure where floors will be raised above the 100-year flood elevation and take full advantage of the scenery and breeze. Cars will thus be kept confined, while views from the dwellings will be oriented outward to the forest, dunes, and marshes, or toward the golf course which weaves between the neighborhoods to overlook Gulf and bay.

Also dominant is the spacious enframement of nature preserves and conservation lands. These, together with the parkway and golf course, will provide an open space system embracing the entire village. Within this beautiful natural environment, building clusters will be interspersed and paths and bicycle trails will be threaded.

A third distinguishing feature of the plan is its response to the need to protect the bay waters. Since contaminants are concentrated where people congregate, the higher-density residential uses and more intensive activity centers such as swimming pools, recreation terraces, and the village store are located in areas of minimum sensitivity and with maximum care in pollution control. Even the cluster arrangement of all building types is devised to minimize the disruption of the landscape and provide open space lands between the groupings and the marsh.

The scenic parkway has been designed in plan and section as an effective drainage barrier between the more populous compounds and the bay. The golf course has also been placed as a buffer and filter for surface runoff. Sheet flow from the greens and fairways will be directed away from the marsh to retention swales, and in turn, to ponds where fresh makeup water will be added. Stormwater runoff from roads and developed areas may be intercepted and collected in shallow recharge swales or in deeper ponds where it should be circulated, supplemented with treated wastewater, and reused for irrigation.

A complete resort community

With a broad base of single-family housing designed for a wide range of modest to higher family incomes, the master plan provides also for villas, patio homes, garden apartments, and several low-rise condominium clusters grouped near the village convenience mall. Plans for the future include a conference center and eventually a beach resort complex and inn. One hundred twenty-five conference center–related dwellings are scheduled. It is estimated on the basis of comparable resort community experience, that approximately 90 percent of the dwelling units will be acquired for seasonal use.

Residents will be served by a general store complex where one can find a well-stocked grocery, hardware, and druggist shop and other conveniences. There will be a restaurant, cafe, and a tennis and swim club. The community center will include a pro shop and spa and will face upon a wide sandy beach accessible to all residents by a short walk or bicycle ride. There will be play areas, game courts, overlooks, and nature trails. Recreation, in a beautiful natural setting, will be a way of life.

A commitment*

The master plan of the village must be considered both a guideline and a pledge. It must give the residents assurance that growth will be orderly and in accordance with established limitations of land use, density, and other predetermined controls. Yet it is best kept sufficiently flexible in detail to accommodate necessary change and to permit expected improvements.

* All plans and proposals outlined in this preliminary study (1975) are tentative and subject to final governmental reviews, revisions, and approvals.

Village site. Land-use allocation (800 acres)

	Preservation	Conservation	Development
Residential	8.4 acres	3.2 acres	243.7 acres
Conference center			12.0
Convenience/commercial			1.0
Golf course	13.9	164.0	
Clubhouse			5.1
Airport			20.8
Utilities			20.0
Parkway			27.1
Open space		6.0	
Salt marsh	94.8		
Beach	57.8		
Land below 2-foot contour	122.2		
	297.1 acres	173.2 acres	329.7 acres

A broader view

Within the past few years, Floridians throughout the length of the state have come to share a growing concern for the rapid spread of unplanned development. They have in increasing numbers expressed a desire for governmental controls to ensure the protection of the state's outstanding natural attributes. The concern is clearly evident in the fact that a number of the most stringent state environmental bills to be enacted in the United States have been passed in recent sessions of the Florida legislature.

To understand the reasons for this concern, one must know that while many developers have produced exemplary communities, the overall Florida record of large-scale land development has been dismal. Speculation, misrepresentation, and poor planning have ravished some of the most beautiful coasts and richest agricultural lands of the state. The unfortunate citizens left in the wake of such exploitation have been saddled with fragmented subdivisions, inoperable utility systems, erosion, pollution, high taxes, and many other vexing problems. It can thus be appreciated that even entrepreneurs with the best of intentions and the most enviable of records must demonstrate step by step, and detail by detail, that their product will be in all ways a long-range community asset.

To this end, it is proposed that on St. George Island great care be given in each area and stage of development to cooperative planning and consultation with each of the state departments and divisions having jurisdiction. It is further proposed that, in addition to the normal legal safeguards, a set of environmental quality controls be formulated to run with the land as binding covenants. These, together with the system of monitors described, should guarantee that the village can be completed with many positive values and no significant negative impacts.

In looking to the bay and its protection, one must look far beyond St. George Island. There is a larger area of concern which embraces the whole of the Apalachicola River basin and includes all of Franklin County. For only with an unprecedented and massive approach can the river, bay, and sound and their natural environs be preserved for long as a healthy ecosystem. From the springs of the rising river tributaries to the estuarine delta, the whole is linked together in a pattern of cause and effect.

There is need for a comprehensive study of the entire region—a study which will appraise the problems and possibilities and lead to a many-faceted program of conservation and sound development. Such a study—to be launched and coordinated, it is hoped, by the state—would be directed to such projects as:

- *A comprehensive regional plan* showing the disposition of all trafficways and land uses and including a supporting zoning ordinance.

- *A river-basin study* directed toward an analysis of the alternative types of agricultural, industrial, housing, or recreational development and their consequences.

- *Continuation of the current Sea-Grant Program* of scientific investigation of the physical, chemical, and biological features of the estuary.

- *A soil and water conservation program* to stabilize the soils and flows of the watershed in such a way as to assure high levels of productivity.

- *A study of aquaculture* as a means of increasing the extent and yield of the bay-sound fishery.

- *An historical and archaeological program* to define and catalog those structures and sites of highest value and to propose legislation and methods of funding designed to preserve them.

- *A regional recreation plan* to outline the means of conserving and developing the land and its natural resources in the best interest of the locality and the state.

The Apalachicola region is now at a critical period in its history. It can proceed without planning and expect little short of economic and environmental disaster. Or with coordinated effort—and in view of the new public interest in environmental matters—the state and county can demonstrate the best techniques and methods of coastal land and water management. In considering an overall program of regional conservation and improvement, it is proposed that this village on St. George Island should be a welcome example and help to lead the way.

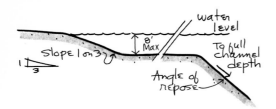

WHERE PLANT GROWTH IS TO BE
ENCOURAGED DESIGN THE CHANNEL
SECTION TO PERMIT FULL SUN
PENETRATION AT THE EDGES

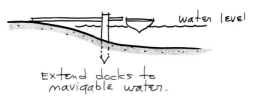

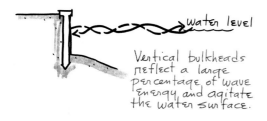

SLOPE THE BANKS OF WATERWAYS
WHEREVER FEASIBLE

No clean stream can be anything but beautiful . . .

Even in its natural state no stream can be called "pure." Admixtures are always present in the form of dissolved minerals, soil particles in suspension, or the leachings of leaves and animal wastes.

Water pollution has occurred when the composition or state of the water has been modified to an extent that makes it less suitable for the purposes to be served.

The United States takes water out of the lower Colorado River for irrigation and returns it to the river with such high salinity that it has serious adverse effects on agriculture in northern Mexico.

Our major rivers, filled with toxic effluent and industrial wastes, discharge their poisonous loads into the sea.

Thirty percent of all DDT compounds ever produced have found their way down the watercourses to the oceans.

Text continued from page 64.

reoriented the entire city and increased manyfold the value of the property at its sides.

The Trinity River of Dallas, the Riverside Drive of New York City, and the Intracoastal Waterway of Palm Beach and Fort Lauderdale are further examples of what can be achieved when the banks of the watercourses are developed and featured as lineal urban parks.

Conserve the watercourses

No community should waste one lineal foot of stream or river bank by permitting fills or unplanned alteration. No matter how littered or foul the stream, preserve the edges for public use or private development. The end of pollution and the restoration of water quality is just a matter of time.

Rehabilitate abandoned canals and channels

Private developers and redevelopment authorities would do well to seek out and rehabilitate the old canal systems.

Some of the most delightful water-edge living in America, as in Europe and the Orient, is to be found where homes and shops are clustered along the edges of such man-made waterways. Many cities and regions have rediscovered and refurbished old canals, locks, and channels as prime real estate and frontage.

Plan the river as a water parkway

Rivers and canals, as navigable waterways, can serve to give agreeable form and structure to the regions through which they pass. A trip down the Rhine is filled with examples. Perhaps the most telling lesson is that as a busy shipping and industrial channel, it was allowed to become so foul that in spite of the stringent antipollution regulations now in force it will take many years before an acceptable level of air and water quality can be restored. Such commendable progress has already been made, however, that salmon are now again being taken in its headwaters.

Its pollution control measures for vessels and for river-edge lands have become a model. Water flow is controlled at the tributaries. Riverbanks are stabilized and marked at each kilometer station. The valleys are zoned and the rivers are flanked with farmlands, vineyards, and forests. Each village and city has its attractive water portal. Sand beaches are formed at the riverside parks by the currents and well-placed groins. The entire river basin is administered by a joint authority, with uniform signals and regulations.

By comparison, most navigational rivers and channels in America are ugly and chaotic. Their study and transformation is long overdue.

Protect and upgrade the quality of the water

Since rivers and their tributary streams are the chief repositories and carriers of pollution, they must be guarded from contamination at all points and from all sources. The major pollutants are present to some degree in almost every river system. They include:

1. *Sediments.* Particles of soil and minerals introduced by erosion, unscientific farming, and unregulated construction cause damage throughout the length of the watersheds. Such sediments discolor the water, fill the channels, lakes, reservoirs, and harbors, smother the feeding and breeding grounds of fish, and reduce the aeration of the water by the penetration of sunlight.

2. *Plant nutrients.* When large concentrations of nitrogen and phosphates are discharged into the stream by sewage, industrial waste, or the leaching of fertilizers from farmfields, the waters bloom with

algae. Fish and natural water plants are displaced, and eutrophication is hastened.

3. *Oxygen-reducing wastes.* Fish, aquatic plant life, and water quality all require the presence of free oxygen in the water. This vital element is depleted or eliminated by the introduction of organic wastes from sewage, animal manures, food processing plants, and many industries. The lower reaches of most riverways are oxygen deficient.

4. *Infectious organisms.* Disease-causing agents such as coliform bacteria and viruses are introduced into the streams by sewage and by food processing and packing plants. Humans become infected by contact.

5. *Organic chemicals.* Many of the new synthetic pesticides, detergents, and industrial chemicals are toxic to the fish, plants, birds, and animals that inhabit our waterways. Some are poisonous, even in low concentrations. Others produce stench and discoloration. Most resist conventional water treatment.

6. *Minerals and inorganic chemicals.* These are by-products of mining, the petroleum industry, farming, and manufacturing plants. They are composed mainly of trace metals, salts, acids, oils, and other chemical compounds which are detrimental to all users of the contaminated water.

7. *Heat.* Thermal pollution reduces the capacity of water to absorb oxygen, break down wastes, or support aquatic life. Most such heated water is discharged by industrial and power-generation plants which require enormous volumes of water for washing and cooling.

8. *Radioactive materials.* The most significant sources have been the fallout from nuclear weapons and devices, and the use of radioactive substances in industry and research. Radioactive pollutants are relatively new and their long-term effects are not yet understood. It is recognized, however, that they comprise a serious potential threat to the world environment.

Create a water resource or river basin commission

As major flood control, water supply, or other developments are planned within a watershed, it is important that each state have the governmental machinery to bring together all the arguments for and against the proposals, and to consider alternatives in the light of future problems and benefits.

Few states presently have a central office or agency through which all water-related studies, plans, programs, and proposals can and must be cleared.

Help to promote a study of the entire river basin

There are noteworthy examples.

The Potomac River Study outlined goals and objectives and developed workable techniques by which they could be achieved. Although far from complete, the study report demonstrated beyond question the need for such an examination of the river basin as a whole and interdependent system. It also set in motion a commendable series of projects designed to maintain and improve the Potomac's value and usefulness.

A survey and report on the Hudson River built upon and extended the Potomac effort. Many other ecological, engineering, economic, social, and recreation considerations must in time be included

Out of the hills of Habersham,
   Down the valleys of Hall,
I hurry amain to reach the plain,
Run the rapid and leap the fall,
Split at the rock and together again,
Accept my bed, or narrow or wide,
And flee from folly on every side
With a lover's pain to attain the plain
   Far from the hills of Habersham
   Far from the valleys of Hall.

All down the hills of Habersham,
   All through the valleys of Hall,
The rushes cried Abide, abide,
The willful waterweeds held me thrall,
The laving laurel turned my tide,
The ferns and the fondling grass said Stay,
The dewberry dipped for to work delay,
And the litte reeds sighed Abide, abide,
   Here in the hills of Habersham,
   Here in the valleys of Hall.

High o'er the hills of Habersham,
   Veiling the valleys of Hall,
The hickory told me manifold
Fair tales of shade, the poplar tall
Wrought me her shadowy self to hold,
The chestnut, the oak, the walnut, the pine,
Overleaning, with flickering meaning and
   sign,
Said, Pass not, *so cold, these manifold*
   Deep shades of the hills of Habersham
   These glades in the valleys of Hall.

And oft in the hills of Habersham,
   And oft in the valleys of Hall,
The white quartz shone and the smooth
   brook-stone
Did bar me of passage with friendly brawl,
And many a luminous jewel lone
   Crystals clear or a-cloud with mist,
Ruby, garnet and amethyst
Made lures with the lights of streaming stone
   In the clefts of the hills of Habersham,
   In the beds of the valleys of Hall.

But oh, not the hills of Habersham,
   And oh, not the valleys of Hall
Avail: I am fain for to water the plain.
Downward the voices of Duty call
Downward, to toil and be mixed with the
   main,
The dry fields burn, and the mills are to turn,
And a myriad flowers mortally yearn,
And the lordly main from beyond the plain
   Calls o'er the hills of Habersham,
   Calls through the valleys of Hall.

SIDNEY LANIER
"Song of the Chattahoochee"
Selected Poems of Sidney Lanier
Charles Scribner's Sons
New York, 1947

in such river-basin studies to make them comprehensive and fully effective.

Continuing studies, exploring all characteristics and use potentials of stream and river networks, will soon become a prerequisite to further development within each watershed.

Tidal estuaries

The tidewater wetlands produce a rich crop of phytoplankton, microscopic organisms which form a vital link in the aquatic food chain. These saltwater marshes are the bountiful marine pastures for many forms of life. Their food energy production is prodigious, exceeding that of the most fertile upland farm fields.

Here in the tidal estuaries, the sensitive spawning and feeding grounds of clams, oysters, and other shell and fin fish, the feeder streams and rivers debouch. If the watercourses are polluted, as most have now become, the havoc wrought can soon destroy both sport and commercial fishing for many miles around. Nesting and migratory wild fowl will be killed or driven off and the tidelands left to putrefy.

There are other forces which also point to the early extinction of the estuaries. Long bypassed by developers, they are now under heavy pressure by those who would dredge and fill them as ocean-front real estate.

In the fight to conserve the remaining coastal islands, bays, and wetlands, all possible friends and defenders must join in concerted action before it is too late. As an example of what can and must be done, the state of Florida has undertaken a study of all its coastal lands, introduced guidelines for development within the defined coastal zones, and enacted stringent legislation to regulate "dredge and fill." Public opinion has been strongly supportive.

Petition for a moratorium

Conservation and civic action groups would do well to list the local areas of critical concern including all endangered coastal wetlands. Mark them on a U.S. Geodetic Survey quadrant or other easily available map obtained from your planning agency. Request your state and local governments to halt all further construction within their jurisdictions until each proposed project can be reviewed by the appropriate agency in terms of environmental impact assessment. Follow through with requests on the same petition that the state enact an uncompromising coastal or waterfront zoning bill.

Urge a comprehensive study of the coastal wetlands

This could be conducted either within the state university or responsible state agency or both in cooperation. Or perhaps, as in Florida, a new joint council could be created for the specific task. The purpose of the study would be fourfold. It would:

1. Define the geographic limits of concern, which may in certain cases extend for many miles inland from the coast.

2. Initiate an on-going scientific investigation of the complex workings and interrelationships of the coastal ecosystem.

Wetland: An inland or coastal area that is periodically flooded or immersed in fresh or saline water.

Plankton: The microscopic floating plant and animal organisms of lakes, rivers, and oceans which are basic to food chains producing the higher forms of fish and aquatic mammals.

Food chain: The pathway by which living things obtain, use, and transfer the energy derived from the sun.

Instead of reclaiming salt marshes for use as lettuce fields, man should learn how to preserve, enhance, and share in its natural productivity.
    WESLEY MARX, editor
    The Frail Ocean
    Ballantine Books
    New York, 1967

An oyster can build up a bodily concentration of DDT 80,000 times that existing in the waters that wash its bed.
    ROBERT F. KUNZ
    "An Environmental Glossary"
    Saturday Review magazine
    January 2, 1971

Until recently, unless useful as deep-water ports, estuaries have been ignored by man as unsightly blemishes on nature's beauty. This indifference has allowed them to flourish in a natural state, whereas forests have been axed and hills leveled. Today, because of their treasured seaside location, estuaries are on the frontline of development. They have qualified for burial by earth fill, better known as "land reclamation."
    WESLEY MARX, editor
    The Frail Ocean
    Ballantine Books
    New York, 1967

3. Formulate a workable policy to govern land use and protection.

4. Propose the legislation required to effectuate the policy recommendations.

Organize a watchdog group

This group of citizens in action should have as its urgent charge the immediate and continuing protection of a specific stretch of bay or estuary. If well-conceived and -directed, and if reasonable in its arguments, it will gather support from many sources—the press, sportsmen, commercial fishermen, resorters, bird watchers, conservationists, students, scientists, politicians, and all those who enjoy and wish to preserve such natural landscape features.

It is surprising to seasoned political observers how effective such action groups have become. Armed with articles, photographs, slides, handbills, posters, and petitions, they have representatives present at all possible community meetings of church and service groups, school assemblies, public hearings, park and planning authorities and commissions. Their direct and vocal involvement, their depth of support, and their numbers are persuasive factors wherever votes are counted and decisions made.

Form a conservancy

If the estuaries, bays, islands, or other environmental features are to be preserved, they must not only be "saved," they must also be acquired and administered on a sound and permanent basis. The "conservancy" is a tested and proven vehicle for this purpose. A nonprofit organization, it has charter and legal powers granted to it by the state or municipal government. It is tax exempt. It may solicit members, funds, and gifts of property. Its objective is usually to assemble and administer, or turn over to an appropriate society or governmental agency with compatible goals, all such scenic, historic, or environmental resource properties as may seem to its membership and board to be in need of protection.

Broaden the area of concern

Groups formed to protect a particular land or water area may find that there are many ramifications. A wetland "saved" may then be endangered by happenings on the adjacent properties or by the disruption of the larger natural system of which it is a part. Pollution from cities far upstream can have a deleterious effect. It can be seen that while each local contingent works on its project of primary concern, it would do well to add its support to the larger cause of total environmental improvement.

Beaches, dunes

Along much of the continental perimeter, where land and ocean meet, the waves roll in to break upon sandy beaches. Where the supply of sand is sufficient and the wind currents strong, a rise of dunes may be formed to the landward. In rare cases these may tower to a height of 500 feet above mean sea level. Usually, however, the dunes are low and undulating, and constantly on the move. Fine grains of sand are driven up the windward face to tumble down the lee side, where they come to rest at the angle of repose. As new material is added, the dune creeps gradually inland

The tidal wetland fringe along New Jersey's 130-mile coast from Sandy Hook to Delaware Bay is now protected by state law which regulates its use.

As I watch the great marsh, I speculate about the energizing forces at work out there—at the fantastic systems of structures in nature, the surging energy of growth and instinct. The development process is an incessant journey, and since nature formed man's beginning, should it not now serve as man's guide?
  BENJAMIN THOMPSON
  Quoted in *From Sea to Shining Sea*
  A Report on the American Environment—
  Our Natural Heritage
  By the President's Council on Recreation and Natural Beauty
  U.S. Government Printing Office
  1968

What we the living require is most of all each other. Essentially, what we require is that when we look at a salt marsh we no longer say, "fill it, build on it, turn it to a profit," but say instead, "We need the air you replenish and the fish you spawn; we need the sound of birds calling upon your shore, and the expanse of your water to sooth our eyes and our spirits. Fellow creatures of the marsh, you are a part of us and we desire your company, you have a right to this place."
  ERNEST BRAUN AND DAVID CAVAGNARO
  Living Water
  Copyright © 1971 by The American West Publishing Company, Inc.
  Used by permission of Crown Publishers, Inc.

The ocean may appear to end at the shore, but its vital processes extend into our bays, up our rivers, and even into our mountain streams, where not only salmon but also sandy beaches are born.
  WESLEY MARX, editor
  The Frail Ocean
  Ballantine Books
  New York, 1967

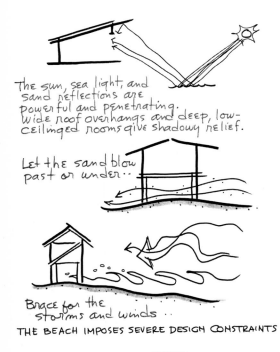

The sun, sea light, and sand reflections are powerful and penetrating. Wide roof overhangs and deep, low-ceilinged rooms give shadowy relief.

Let the sand blow past or under..

Brace for the storms and winds..

THE BEACH IMPOSES SEVERE DESIGN CONSTRAINTS

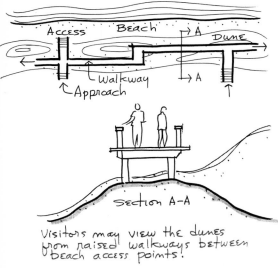

Visitors may view the dunes from raised walkways between beach access points.

PROTECT THE DUNE GROWTH FROM DESTRUCTION

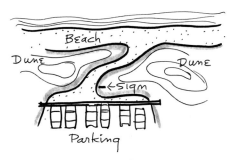

Parking areas should be remote and pathways confined.

PROVIDE LIMITED ACCESS POINTS TO BEACHES AND FRAGILE DUNE AREAS

to cover and smother whatever may lie in its path.

Usually the inward drift of dunes is more or less checked by the loose net of vines that enmesh them, or by the fibrous roots of such grasses and shrubs as sea oats, bearberry, or spreading juniper. When the fragile cover is destroyed and the dry sand laid bare to the winds, the drift is accelerated. Roads may be clogged, croplands covered, or homesteads inundated.

In their conformation the beaches, dunes, and the associated tidal wetlands have been perfectly formed by nature to serve as a resilient buffer against the onslaught of the wind and sea. The heaving tides and crashing rollers break upon the sloping beach plane to dissipate their force and thus inhibit the erosion and regression of the shores. A section from shoal to water edge to dune to upland meadow and forest, at any point along the coast, reveals a miraculous system of forces in motion and in equilibrium. Where this balance of nature is tampered with, destruction in some form is bound to occur. Those who have studied the coastal frontiers are certain that insofar as possible they should be left undisturbed, and that no uses should be permitted that will cause significant changes.

Preserve the barrier islands by leaving them alone

In their natural state they are superbly shaped to absorb the force of the ocean storms and protect the inner coastline. They are as dynamic as the winds and currents that form them. To build upon their slowly shifting sands is unfeasible. To attempt their stabilization by bulkheading or other engineering structures is enormously expensive—and ultimately futile.

Protect the dune cover

Dune buggies and trail bikes or motorcycles must be categorically outlawed, except on isolated courses reserved for their sole use. Not only are they a serious hazard to picnickers and sunbathers on the beach, but they rip and tear the grasses and vines that knit the dunes together. A single vehicle can in one day do irreparable damage to many miles of beachfront.

Even the barefoot public must be kept away from the vulnerable plants which stabilize the drifts.

Provide crossovers

As an added safeguard to the dunes and estuaries, public access should be provided at frequent intervals. Access from limited parking areas, located well to the landward, is best provided by confined pathways or bridges. A nature-interpretation display explaining the natural system and the need for its protection would make a fitting marker for the start of the crossover trail.

Establish adequate setback lines

The seaward limits of cultivation or land development can be determined in each particular instance only after a study by experts of the long-range effect. It is the responsibility of each builder or developer to prove the merit of his plans.

Where adequate protective measures are included in the design, paths, buildings, or other structures may be brought into fairly close

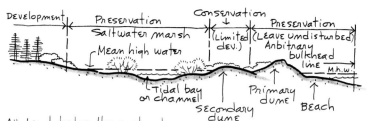

Development | Preservation | Conservation | Preservation
Saltwater marsh | (Limited dev.) | (Leave undisturbed) Arbitrary bulkhead line
Mean high water | | M.h.w.
Tidal bay or channel | Secondary dume | Primary dume | Beach

All land below the natural mean high water line should be in public ownership. A building setback line from the beach should extend to the landward toe of the primary dune, where one exists, or to the limits of highly productive or essential stabilizing growth. Within conservation areas limited development may occur as long as the more important landscape features are protected.

A DEVELOPMENT GUIDELINE FOR
COASTAL BEACHES AND WETLANDS

proximity to dunes, tidal inlets, or bays. In no cases along a public beach, however, should a private development of any type be permitted below the seaward mean high-water line or between the beachline and the fronting dunes.

Design ocean-related construction in response to the natural constraints

There are many conditions peculiar to beachfront, dune, and tidal wetland sites that require special consideration. These include resistance to wind and wave action, flooding, protection of the natural covers, visual intrusion, and the effects on the marine and bay ecology.

Establish beach-use capacities

Recreation agencies have found that there are definable limits to the amount of use to which a beach can be subjected. Overuse of any type, be it boating, fishing, swimming, sunbathing, or even shelling, can in time reduce or destroy the quality of the resource.

Use capacities can be established only after a detailed ecological survey of each area has been made. The number of visitors will then depend upon the natural character, the width of the beach, and the type and distribution of the users. Usually the number of visitors can be regulated by the number of parking spaces and access points provided. In other instances gating or the regulation of visiting hours may be required.

Acquire the beaches as public lands

Of the 5,000 miles of oceanfront in the United States approximately 4,500 miles is in private ownership. Of the remaining 500 miles some 150 are held by public agencies. The balance is still up for grabs. In land acquisition for public use the highest priority should be given to the purchase of additional shoreline.

In their natural state the beaches provide one of the most attractive recreation places to be found. But the great sweeps of beachland are no longer available. Those open stretches that remain must soon be acquired and held as a national trust.

Check beach erosion

Much valuable water frontage is lost each year by wave and wind action. Not long ago, for example, a group of men sat in conference negotiating for a strip of beautiful beach property on the Gulf of Mexico. Millions of dollars worth of real estate were involved in the

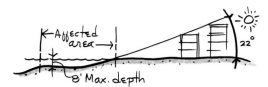

Affected area | 8' Max. depth | 22°

As a rule of thumb, a building and planting height limitation of 22° rising from the water edge has been suggested by marine biologists. This would allow approximately 90% of the daily sunlight to penetrate to the plants in shallow water. It would also permit afternoon sunlight on the beach where this is desirable.

This consideration is to be treated as but one of many factors and waived altogether except where extensive blockage might occur, or on shores adjacent to critical productive waters.

CONSIDER THE SHADOW EFFECTS OF
WATERFRONT BUILDINGS AND PLANTINGS

Post-and-platform construction is well suited to the dunes

On the tidal bays . . .

ADAPT BEACH CONSTRUCTION
TO THE CONDITION

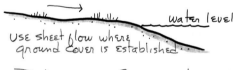

Water level

Use sheet flow where ground cover is established

Water level
Sump

Direct the storm runoff to sumps or percolation beds where erosion or contamination pose a problem. The unchecked discharge from storm sewer outfalls can be especially destructive.

INTRODUCE STORM RUNOFF
TO BAYS, WATERCOURSES, OR
WETLANDS BY SHEET FLOW
OR PERCOLATION

All French beaches are in the public domain.

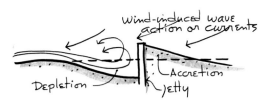

Wind-induced wave action on currents

Depletion

Accretion

Jetty

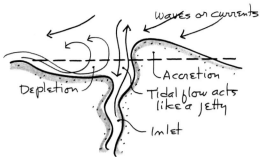

Waves or currents

Depletion

Accretion

Tidal flow acts like a jetty

Inlet

A stream or tidal channel acts as a jetty or groin.

BEACH EROSION AND BUILDUP

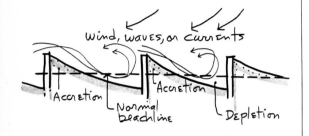

Wind, waves, or currents

Accretion

Accretion

Normal beachline

Depletion

All too often beach "improvement" takes place at a neighbor's expense.

BEACHLINE MODIFICATION IS BEST BASED ON SCIENTIFIC ADVICE

Together, the ocean, the living earth, and the atmosphere form one great system which makes all life possible on this planet.

Our oceans are being killed by pollution, over-fishing, and careless coastal development.

The beautiful coral reefs, teeming with exotic fish, may not survive another generation. And the sea otter, so long abundant off the California coast, is today rare and threatened.

Human abuse of the seas, if not corrected, is leading to the gradual extinction of the marine life we have known and treasured.

There is very little time left.

JACQUES-YVES COUSTEAU
From a brochure of The Cousteau Society, Inc.
777 Third Avenue, New York, NY 10017

transaction. In an adjoining office engineers and hydrologists, poring over surveys and a series of aerial photographs, were discovering that during a twelve-year period since the first surveys were made, the tidal currents had been altered by the dredging of a new off-site channel, and the land under discussion had all but disappeared.

While the simple principles of beach erosion are well understood, further study is needed in the development of corrective techniques so that reliable advice may be provided. Consideration should be given to the creation, by federal and state legislation, of beach erosion districts through which a group of concerned owners can work together on corrective measures. Uncoordinated efforts to stabilize the frontage of one property at a time can do more harm than good.

Regulate the installation of seawalls and jetties

Groins, seawalls, and jetties should be permitted and constructed only as part of an areawide beach improvement program. Such devices can be effective in stabilizing or building up the beach, or they can cause a disaster. A jetty that may protect or build up a sandy strand for one property owner may wipe out the beach next door.

Here again, in the planning of all beach improvements the advice and consent of experts is required procedure.

Renourish eroded beaches

Where beaches have been washed away by storms or by man's tampering with the inlets or water edges, it is possible that they can be restored. With hydrological study, a stable waterline and beach contour can often be reestablished with hauled material for a base and with sand cover pumped from the ocean floor.

Much costly experimentation with beach and shore "improvement," however, has demonstrated the wisdom of keeping development well back, leaving the shorelines undisturbed, and letting nature take its course.

The oceans

In studying the charts of this watery sphere one is struck by the immensity of the saltwater oceans which cover most of the surface of planet Earth, sometimes to depths exceeding 6 miles. Surely man could do little to affect the vast and intricate workings of these briny deeps.

And yet, from the ecological point of view, the problems presented by the oceans, in their present state of advanced deterioration, are formidable. Still, the rectification of all man-caused imbalances are within the realm of present scientific capability. We know what we have done in the past to disrupt the natural workings of the oceanic system. We know what we are presently doing and a good deal about the effects. We know what we *must* do to end the corruption and restore the oceans to their health, and we will do it or they will perish.

It may take a century; it may take ten; but with the swelling volumes of garbage, sewage, trash, and poisons being sloughed off into the ocean basins, as the ultimate receptors they will in time become septic and devoid of significant life. All evidence supports this damning fact.

What is to be done?

While the problems are difficult and complex, and while the commitment of funds and effort required for the task will be monumental, the approach to the solution is disarmingly simple. And there can be no other approach to the protection and intelligent use of the oceans. Clearly, what is required is a massive and concerted campaign *on an international basis,* launched concurrently on three fronts, to gain three essential objectives. These are:

1. The halting of all further ocean contamination.
2. The intensification and coordination of research in oceanography and marine biology.
3. The formulation of an international commission to administer the use of the oceans and their resources on an equitable basis.

Many of the institutions and much of the legal framework needed are already established.

The situation has become appalling.

The need for decisive action is clear.

It is up to our government, among others, to propose and support those measures which will unite all nations in this common cause.

At sea, flying flocks of ducks and auks often swoop down on patches of oil, where the deep-sea roll is less heavy. These oil patches serve as veritable death traps. The oil-soaked birds can neither fly nor dive, and their plumage no longer protects them against cold and wet. Thus the oil-smeared birds either starve or freeze to death, or become so wet and heavy that they drown.

The grounding of a German ship off the estuary of the Elbe in 1955 caused a release of ,000 tons of oil that killed about 100,000 sea birds. . . . It has been calculated that until recent times, tanker fleets have discharged annually while cleaning their tanks, between one and two million tons of oil into the sea.

In other marine regions, formerly rich fisheries have disappeared entirely due to overexploitation. A tragic example is that of the waters around the Juan Fernandez Islands off Chile, where an abundance of economically important fish and crustaceans, particularly lobsters, was once the basis for the island economy. These resources were exploited too heavily, with no regulation. The lobsters have long since vanished and so have many fish species. The populations of the remaining fish are so thinned out that the fisheries are no longer profitable.

A drastic example of how the lethal methyl mercury can poison fish living in the open sea is the tuna. In December, 1970, it was *found in the United States that millions of cans of tuna contained dangerous levels of mercury. The poisoned tuna came from all eight major commercial fishing areas off the United States, where even higher levels of mercury were being found in some swordfish.*

On September 3, 1970, a fish kill in Escambia Bay, Pensacola, Florida, which involved the death of 10–15 million menhaden was one of forty-two kills that occurred in the same bay that year. The extent of these kills varies from hundreds to thousands, to millions. All are due to nutrification. Most of the kills occur in the small bays off the big one. The algae and plankton populations grow rapidly due to over-nutrification resulting from industrial discharge into the bay. When the menhaden come in to feed on the plankton, there is not enough oxygen for the large amount of fish.

Radioactive waste dumped into the sea is another potential danger. It, too, may have serious consequences, not only for marine life but also for man, who is the last link of many food chains. Radioactivity from nuclear fallout can be found in any fifty-gallon sample of water taken anywhere in the sea.

Man's destruction of marine vertebrates other than fish and birds has reached criminal proportions in the past, and the slaughter continues. Sirenians, sea otters, seals, *whales, and sea turtles have for centuries been among the most mistreated groups of animals in the world. The fact that these animals . . . are natural resources of high economic value has not prevented man from reducing the populations of many species to the verge of extinction.*

Disastrous effects on marine life zones are continuously caused by oil discharges from ships in the open sea. Like the extermination of whales, this form of piracy results from the unfortunate situation that international waters are considered to be a "no man's sea," where neither nations nor individuals have responsibility.

Dumping of solid wastes into the open sea has in recent years taken place indiscriminately and in large quantities. All fish in the North Sea and eastern North Atlantic contain a particular type of chlorinated hydrocarbon, which apparently originates from industrial dumping and has resulted in mass death of plankton and lowered condition of fish.

Despite the fact that the oceans cover almost three quarters of the earth, there is at present an almost total absence of international law. Except for a few fish conservation and fishery treaties and certain national laws, there is no efficient legislation or treaty governing the utilization of the oceans and the sea bed.

KAI CURRY-LINDAHL
Conservation for Survival
William Morrow & Company, Inc.
New York, 1972

In 1933, 28,907 whales were caught (in all the oceans), and they produced 2,606,201 barrels of whale oil. In 1966, 57,891 whales were killed, or almost exactly twice as many as in 1933. But twice as many whales yielded only 1,546,904 barrels of oil, or just about 60 percent of the 1933 yield. The reason is that as the larger kinds of whales were driven toward extinction, the industry shifted to harvesting not only the young individuals of large species, but with time, smaller and smaller species.

PAUL R. EHRLICH AND ANNE H. EHRLICH
"The Food-from-the-Sea Myth"
Saturday Review magazine
April 4, 1970

We have looked to the oceans as the ultimate source of additional food, but this is a false hope. Already many of the more desirable shell- and fin-fish are being harvested to the point of near depletion; and the yield of the basic plankton mass has its own exhaustible limits.

Minerals are almost everywhere for the taking if we can develop the energy and technology to extract them. In a mere cubic mile of seawater, for example, is more magnesium than has yet been mined in the history of metallurgy.

JOHN MCPHEE
Encounters with the Archdruid
Copyright © 1971 by John McPhee
Farrar, Straus and Giroux, Inc.
New York, 1971

The technological penetration of the ocean is daring, inspiring, and quite possibly, potentially disastrous. If the ocean is to be a jumbo resource, its exploitation must be carefully husbanded. The ocean can no longer take care of itself. It requires as much respect for its weakness as its strength. The concept of an all-powerful ocean is today obsolete.

WESLEY MARX, editor
The Frail Ocean
Ballantine Books
New York, 1967

France and Italy pollute the Mediterranean outrageously, affecting all the bordering countries, but have refused to meet with them to even talk about the problem.

Water resource management: The procedures by which water can be maintained in an adequate and qualitatively useful supply.

Halt the further contamination of the ocean basins

This will require a joint statement of purpose, a bold and forthright manifesto, endorsed by the leading maritime nations as a binding pledge. It must include a time-frame within which new processes for the disposal of all types of wastes can be brought into being, and all forms of pollution phased out completely. In addition to a planning and development function there will be need also for effective surveillance and policing.

The main problem of the oceans is that they have been used as the world's dumping grounds. They can no longer take it. In recent recognition of this fact the United States is leading a drive for the environmental protection of the oceans by outlawing the dumping of all toxic materials and by imposing controls on all other forms of ocean disposal.

Intensify research in oceanography and marine biology

Far too little is known about our marine resources. They are being drastically affected each year by the accumulative effects of contamination and refuse disposal, by the bilge and spillage from shipping and off-shore drilling, and by coastal land development. The oceans are being overfished and otherwise overexploited.

They hold great promise as sources of food, minerals, and fossil fuels. They serve increasingly as air, surface, and subsurface transportation and transmission routes. They are the new frontier in the search for scientific data and knowledge about the world in which we live. Increasingly, many vital decisions are being made regarding the protection and utilization of the oceans and their stores. In weighing proposals and effects, and in devising controls, precise scientific data, accurate oceanographic surveys, and comprehensive ecological studies are essential.

Create an international commission to govern the use of the oceans

By tradition each nation has jealously guarded its sovereign rights and privileges and has been understandably reluctant to delegate powers to a higher authority. But such delegation has been granted in those few cases where no workable alternative existed and where calamity was otherwise at stake. It can be seen that these conditions now operate in regard to the care and regulation of the world oceans.

Only at the international level can a unified approach be taken to the formulation of policy, the enactment of laws and regulations, and the administration of controls in regard to such matters as ocean navigation, transportation and transmission, military rights, fisheries, mineral and fuel extraction, and environmental protection.

Such a commission could be the outgrowth of existing institutions including the United Nations. It must have the technological resources, the prestige, and the power to command respect and achieve compliance.

Water management

The science of water management is as old as civilization, but in recent years it has taken on new dimensions and importance. In broad terms it deals with three aspects of water and its use. Its objectives are to assure the supply, protect the quality, and promote its efficient consumption.

In many developing areas of our land the fresh water flowing from hydrants and faucets has been reduced to a trickle. To compound the problem, we are faced with the unprecedented demands of our booming technology and the needs of a rapidly expanding population. In searching for new means by which the fresh water reserves may be sustained, we can find a number of possibilities. These include watershed protection and reforestation, new techniques of precipitation catchment, and the tapping of new sources.

Most problems of water supply and pollution are the result of exploitation. Traditionally, fresh water in most of the United States has been so plentiful that people have helped themselves freely to as much as or more than was needed. And generally they have let the used or wasted water flow back untreated into the source, without concern for the effects upon their neighbors. As the users have become grouped more closely together, the problems of water quality and supply have become intensified.

Today, with soaring water demands and critical shortages in some regions, we are looking to the science of water management with new respect and interest.

Protect and reforest the watersheds

All bodies of water are formed and replenished by the natural drainage from an upper reach of land. This seeps and flows along the watercourses and eventually makes its way to the ocean. Its flow determines to a large extent the amount of fluctuation of the water in the soils and water bodies at any point along the course.

If the watershed is denuded of absorptive covers—trees, grasses, mosses, or forest duff—the system is susceptible to erosion, siltation, and a maximum rise and fall in water levels. Springs run dry, water tables are lowered, and water reserves stored in the great subsurface aquifers are gradually depleted. Even the climate and the quality of the atmosphere are changed, for vegetation cools, cleanses, and moistens the air through the process of transpiration, in which the carbon atom of carbon dioxide is combined with the hydrogen atom of groundwater to produce the free oxygen which we breathe.

Develop more efficient means of precipitation catchment

Surface contouring and treatment to entrap natural precipitation and divert it to use or to reservoirs is a technique not yet perfected, although the Indonesian paddy fields and the furrowed slopes above the harbor of St. Thomas give a clue as to how it can be accomplished.

The natural precipitation in most areas (a world average of 33.8 inches annually) could, if conserved and recycled, fulfill the needs for all fresh water.

Tap new sources of water supply

The desalination of seawater holds promise. Although many installations are now in operation, the cost of conversion is presently too expensive for wide application. As needs increase, however, and as techniques are improved, we may turn to the sea as a major source of potable water.

Other possible sources include the melting of glacial or polar ice and rainfall induced by cloud seeding.

Prohibit the discharge of untreated sewage into watercourses or water bodies

Good sense dictates that permits for new construction be granted only upon prior commitment by the developer or responsible agencies that sewage disposal facilities will be available and that these will meet all

. . . it is imperative that we push full speed ahead using present knowledge while developing new control technology to clean up and make useful as much water as we can, for as many people as we can.
JAMES M. QUIGLEY
*Envirnomental Improvement
(Air, Water and Soil)*
The Graduate School
U.S. Department of Agriculture
Washington, D.C., 1966

It is common practice to design sewage disposal plants to divert untreated raw sewage directly into watercourses when the plant machinery breaks down.

The right to produce is not the right to pollute.

Industries using good quality water for their processing must return an equal amount of good quality water to rivers and lakes.
WALTER J. HICKEL
River of Life
U.S. Department of Agriculture, 1970

In sum, under the Water Pollution Control Act and the Clean Air Act, environmentalists can use the public hearing to make known their views on proposed discharge permits and compliance schedules. They have access to information needed to measure the effectiveness of the permits and compliance schedules. They can determine if laws are being enforced. And, if necessary, they can take court action against violators.
MARVIN ZELDIN
Audubon magazine
September 1973

From 10 to 40 percent of the fuel in the tanks of outboard motors is discharged into the water unburned.

Many rivers and lakes serve two conflicting purposes: they are used both as sewers and as sources of drinking water for 100 million Americans.

Many water-treatment plants are hopelessly outmoded. They were designed for a simpler, less crowded world. About three-fourths of them do not go beyond disinfecting water with chlorine.

As in the air, contamination of any kind spreads quickly throughout a water body or the earth upon which precipitation falls or through which groundwater moves.

The increasing pollution of our streams, rivers, lakes, and oceans—and the fields and forests which they sustain—has increased so drastically within recent years that scarcely a cubic foot of water now exists in nature without measurable contamination in some form.

It is only within the past few years that the results of water pollution have become so evident and devastating that effective controls are beginning to be enforced. In some large areas, as in the Great Lakes system, for example, the flow of pollution is being stemmed and degradation reversed. Lake Erie is now cleaner than it was five years ago.

An *aquifer* is a porous underground water-bearing strata.

That's your Aquifer. Underground and invisible. Four million years ago when the Platte was being carved into the silt thrown down from the Rockies, there was this impermeable basement of shale and limestone. On it rested deposits of highly permeable gravel and sand, in some places two hundred feet thick, and as you can see, up to ten miles wide. For millions of years this catchment lay hidden, covered over by whatever topsoil came along. It now forms a lens whose interstices can be filled with water. It's really a massive subterranean reservoir, and it acts as the balance for our entire Platte system.

JAMES A. MICHENER
Centennial
Copyright © 1974 by Marjay Productions, Inc.
Random House, Inc.
New York, 1974

existing standards for environmental protection.

A further, and closely related, condition of development should be the assurance of an adequate supply of fresh water without diminishing present levels of service or depleting the available reserves.

Assess to each offender the full corrective costs

Where the hazard of pollution exists, the minimum charge for operating permits should cover the expenses of adequate policing and controls. Mandatory performance bonds and liability insurance should be adequate to pay for all damages *plus* any corrective measures which might possibly be needed. In cases of violations or incidents of contamination, additional fines of sufficient magnitude to minimize future risks should be levied. The idea is to set the charge high enough to force the polluter to stop.

Stop the pollution of streams by acid mine wastes

Seal off the discharge of existing mines which are no longer working. Control by regulation the flow of acid and other wastes from active mining operations. Uniform laws and enforcement are needed to reduce the economic disadvantage of certain localities, but under no circumstances can the commonplace corruption of our watersheds be allowed to continue. Since the costs of corrective programs are usually too heavy to be borne wholly by districts plagued with abandoned strip- and deep-mine workings, state and federal funds will be required.

Prohibit the dumping of dunnage, garbage, sewage, or other wastes

This essential mandate is long overdue on both fresh- and saltwater bodies. It can be enforced as effectively, by annual licensing renewal and inspections, as have been traditional requirements regarding running lights, safety equipment, and navigational procedures.

Ensure against the intrusion of saltwater into our freshwater reserves

Along our coastlines an increasing threat is being posed by the infiltration of seawater into the aquifers. As the hydrostatic pressure of the landward water table is reduced by drawdown, the normal flow to the oceans is reversed. Preventive techniques include the construction of extensive systems of dams and barricades, coupled with the regulation of freshwater consumption within the limits of adequate supply.

Outlaw the manufacture of compounds which damage water quality

Prohibition on use alone, being much more difficult to control, is not sufficient.

A further prohibition against manufacture for domestic consumption or for export is evidently needed since huge quantities of DDT, for example, have been produced for distribution abroad after restrictions were placed upon its use in the United States.

Preclude all other forms of pollution

As a governing rule, no new development, manufacturing, processing, or operation of any description should be permitted—save in an emergency—if it will result in the significant degradation of any water resource.

Use the water efficiently

Water rationing has never been popular. But in many localities it has now become necessary to place limitations upon homeowners, as well as agriculture and industry, as to the types, times, and amounts of permitted use of water. It will be necessary to tighten such regulations as needs increase in relation to supply.

Commendably in many areas the right to develop land is based upon the submission of a comprehensive plan showing not only the extent of the available water and the effects of the projected draw, but also a schedule of proposed water-use regulations and a full description of all recycling procedures which are to be applied.

Regulate freshwater consumption

The time has come when the unlimited use of this essential commodity can no longer be permitted. In many areas its use for irrigation or as an industrial coolant, as examples, may have to be reduced or even banned. In some cases these functions may be served as well by treated or even untreated fluid wastes. Otherwise, if new sources of fresh water cannot be tapped, the bulk consumers may have to relocate to other areas where suitable water is in adequate supply.

In any event, it is incumbent upon planning authorities to run a check upon the quantity needs and uses of all existing or potential consumers, with an eye to the future regulation of freshwater resources as related to land use.

Create subsurface holding reservoirs

Natural underground limestone caves, or depleted mines, may well be used for bulk water storage.

An ingenious plan has been proposed for the city of Chicago whereby the outfall from the combined storm and sanitary sewage system will be dropped through shafts into deep underground storage tunnels drilled for this purpose through the underground rock strata. In these subterranean chambers the first stages of sedimentation and water treatment will take place.

The energy of the falling fluid in the drop shafts will generate electrical power to meet peak-load power requirements. In off-peak hours the surplus power will be used to pump the water to the surface for further treatment and purification. The problems of sewage disposal will thus be relieved and freshwater reserves replenished.

Recharge the aquifers

The rapid runoff of precipitation and groundwater is wasteful, for it prevents natural percolation into the earth and water tables where it might otherwise have been stored. In addition to checking the surface drainage, other means must be found by which the underground water reserves may be replenished. Such water-management procedures will include the collection and pumping of surface runoff into natural wetlands or into man-made holding ponds or percolation basins. Treated sanitary waste may be used and disposed of in this manner and for irrigation, for even raw sanitary sewage can be converted to a quality fit for human consumption for a few cents per thousand gallons.

Apply the advanced techniques of water management to community planning

The traditional and wasteful practices of "drill, pump, and spill" have long been outmoded. We have learned how to do it better. But much that is known about more efficient methods of water conservation, use, and recycling has not yet been generally applied. Nor have many innovative approaches used with local success been adopted as standard procedure.

Unfortunately, sound water resource management—like other forms of environmental protection—is seldom voluntary. It seems to occur only when "built in" to the goals and comprehensive planning of each municipality, and when enforced as a mandatory condition of all land use and development.

There are some welcome exceptions.

Soil acts as an enormous reservoir for water. The underlying layers of clay, shale, and fissured rock store groundwater in great quantities.

Most groundwater will eventually return to the ocean, but it is believed that some has been locked in the earth for thousands of years and may even have fallen as mist or rain before human history began.

Further Reading:

Braun, Ernest, and David E. Cavagnaro
Living Water
The American West Publishing Company, Inc.
Palo Alto, Calif., 1971

Carson, Rachel
The Sea Around Us
Oxford University Press
New York, 1951

Ducsik, Dennis W.
Shoreline for the Public: A Handbook of Social, Economic and Legal Considerations . . .
MIT Press
Cambridge, Mass., 1974

Laws, Edward A.
Aquatic Pollution: An Introductory Text
John Wiley & Sons, Inc. (Wiley-Interscience)
New York, 1981

Leonard, Jonathan Norton
Atlantic Beaches
The American Wilderness/Time-Life Books
New York, 1972

Mann, Roy
Rivers In The City
Frederick A. Praeger, Inc.
New York, 1973

Marx, Wesley, ed.
The Frail Ocean
Ballantine Books
New York, 1967

Matthews, William H., Frederick E. Smith, and Edward D. Goldberg, eds.
Man's Impact on Terrestrial and Oceanic Ecosystems
MIT Press
Cambridge, Mass., 1971

Robinette, Gary O.
Water Conservation in Landscape Design and Management
Van Nostrand Reinhold Company Inc.
New York, 1984

Rothenberg, J., and Ian G. Heggie, eds.
The Management of Water Quality and The Environment
John Wiley & Sons, Inc.
New York, 1974

Tourbier, Tody, and Westmacott
A Handbook of Measures to Protect Water Resources in Land Development
Urban Land Institute
Washington, D.C., 1981

4

The visible landscape

Propriety stems from the mutual respect which a true society should maintain amongst its members, which is not quite the same thing as manners. . . . Propriety never seeks to stifle, rather it is self-expression within a civilized framework.

GORDON CULLEN
Townscape
Reinhold Publishing Corporation
New York, 1961

Visual pollution, or clutter, is an offense against the landscape, and thus against society—for the landscape is society's home.

To pollute the visible environment is an act of obscenity, of corruption. While each small act, often committed thoughtlessly, may seem minor, the sum of these can soon despoil the streetscape of a city, mile upon mile of highway, or the whole of a rural countryside. On the way to work in the morning one may drive through a blizzard of signs and billboards, pass an abandoned gravel pit left in weeds and stagnant pools, or view vacant and derelict buildings left standing to blaspheme a neighborhood. In walking from parking garage to office one may see blowing trash and papers, or an ugly web of utility wires in silhouette against the sky. All may be in themselves visual *misdemeanors*, yet they add up to a *crime*.

The limits of what and how much may be added to, subtracted from, left standing in, or dumped upon the landscape is a matter of fitness and propriety.

If an object or structure serves a good and useful purpose, does not adversely affect the health, safety, or welfare of the public, and does not detract from the quality of the landscape, it may probably be said that an act of visual pollution has not been committed.

It all boils down to what an individual or group may or may not be permitted to do, and what they may be required to do. Educational campaigns have done much to improve the visible environment, but ultimately it becomes a matter of providing and enforcing reasonable controls. As a start, the following guidelines are suggested.

Billboards and signs

The most effective single way in which the appearance of the average street or highway could be improved would be to take down the billboards. Their unsightliness is so evident that they would have been outlawed years ago were it not for the strategy of the powerful billboard interests. They have moved quietly in the various states to engage as legal counsel, at handsome retainers, the law firms in which a large percentage of our congressmen and legislators served or have a continuing interest. Any statute to curb the billboard kingdom "rights" or limit their activities naturally meets with short shrift, as even a recent president discovered.

Yet come down the billboards must, and shall, when the representatives of the people are made emphatically aware of the public will.

Regulate the use of roadside signs and billboards

Often they are so closely spaced that they not only obliterate the scenery but even block each other. Tough zoning controls are needed to protect view and vistas, and to preserve the quality of the roadway and the adjacent neighborhoods.

Provide travel-information centers

Where tourist information is needed, as at approaches to cities or other destinations, an attended roadside station can replace and better

And I brought you into a plentiful country, to eat the fruit thereof and the goodness thereof; but when ye entered ye defiled my land, and made mine heritage an abomination.
JEREMIAH 2:7

Roadway signs are designed and intended to convey information to the motorist speeding by: gas here, food there, lodging up the road, etc. But the increasing competition for the driver's attention has turned the signs into swirls of conflicting graphics and verbiage. The lights cause glare, the billboards obscure the landscape and sometimes the roadway, and the wordy messages confuse and distract the driver. In the end, the signs also fail in their purpose, to convey basic information.
RICHARD REIN
Unpublished memo

*I think that I shall never see
A billboard lovely as a tree.
Indeed, unless the billboards fall
I'll never see a tree at all.*
OGDEN NASH, as quoted by Victor Gruen
The Heart of Our Cities
Simon and Schuster
New York, 1964

serve the purpose than thousands of square feet of roadside advertising scattered along the way. Such centers can disseminate current directional maps and provide factual information on lodging and local attractions. Where the demand may be less heavy, the information could be mechanically dispensed at scenic pulloffs or rest areas.

A town or city wishing to promote its attractions could do far worse than to staff such hospitality centers with youthful volunteers.

Install scenic and historic trail markers

As a guide-on to interested travelers, a uniform and well-designed series of trail markers for scenic or historic roads and walks should provide easy identification. These need not be conspicuous or mar the beauty of the scenic route they trace. As welcome substitutes for the blatant tourist-baiting road signs, they can politely conduct the traveler to the various points of interest.

Develop a system of well-marked beltways

Even when circumferential arterials have not been planned around a city, a combination of existing roads, drives, and parkways may be linked by distinctive signing into such a loop or series of loops. Well-placed colored discs, for example, may mark a blue route, or red or yellow route, that may help drivers thread their way through or around a region. This device may give the traveler helpful guidance without the need for the placement of large directional signs at every intersection. It may also relieve the communities of through traffic and congestion.

Group informational signs into clusters

Designate areas for the controlled placement of tourist-attraction advertising and directional signs. These may be grouped at key points, roadside parks, or rest areas. Elsewhere they will be prohibited and the highway freed of the distracting billboard clamor.

Enforce building-identification sign controls

Most businessmen would welcome an arrangement by which all storefront signs along the streets and highways could be reduced in size and ornamentation while yet identifying their shops or offices on a fair and equal basis. Installation and maintenance costs would be less, energy consumption would be reduced, and the street made more attractive. Many cities have enacted exemplary codes which define the size, type, number, and placement of commercial advertisements.

Overhead wires and utility poles

With the visual blight caused by utility poles and overhead lines so obvious and so universal, there is understandably a swelling outcry that all wires be put underground. In the case of local power distribution and telephone lines this can be easily accomplished. There is no longer an excuse for the installation of unsightly poles or overhead wiring. For a small fraction of building construction costs, all power and telephone distribution lines can be buried in underground conduits where they are out of sight, easily accessible for pulling and repair, and protected from winds, falling limbs, and the weather. The community appearance is greatly improved thereby.

In clearing away the clutter we reveal the city. The sight of it from afar can be compelling—Dallas across the cotton fields, Chicago from the Lake Shore Drive, and never more so than when first discovered at the crest of a hill or a sweeping turn of the road. And it is at just these spots that the clutter is often the densest . . .

WILLIAM H. WHYTE
The Last Landscape
Doubleday & Company, Inc.
Garden City, N.Y., 1968

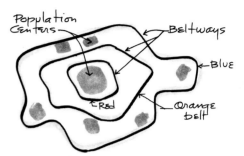

Well-marked beltways (as by colored discs or distinctive symbols) can help guide strangers —and residents— through the metropolitan maze.

DESIGNATE A SYSTEM OF CIRCUMFERENTIAL BELTWAYS

Roadside billboards hide the views.

Where needed, informational and directional signs may be clustered at pull-offs.

CONTROL THE PLACEMENT OF ROADSIDE SIGNS

REMOVE THE UTILITY
POLES AND WIRES

Increased property values more than offset the cost of underground installation.

In the past, local governments have rarely asserted control over transmission lines and other utility projects. Recently, however, some municipalities in New York State have taken steps to regulate the character and appearance of transmission lines. Their right to do so has been sustained by the courts, notably in Long Island Lighting Co. v.s. Horn *(1966), in which the Town of Orangetown, in Rockland County, has adopted a zoning law requiring a permit for the construction of a new transmission line. Nevertheless, such steps toward municipal regulation of power transmission lines are relatively rare.*

Curves or turns in an overhead transmission line route usually require some additional towers, or larger towers, to take up lateral stress. Nevertheless, in certain landscapes, a curving route often represents an acceptable compromise between the conventional straight line or overhead route and the far more expensive alternative of putting the line underground.

BRUCE HOWLETT AND FREDERICK J. ELMIGER
Power Lines and Scenic Values
A Report by the Hudson River
Valley Commission, 1969

So is the service and the factor of public safety.

While underground *distribution* is recommended as standard procedure, the subsurface *transmission* of bulk power for long distances is not yet technically feasible. Raw power is transmitted at extremely high voltages to compensate for the voltage drop or loss from friction in the cables. In underground installations, aside from the exorbitant costs of cooling and insulation, the high voltage produces a flow of "charging current" in the insulated cable which within a limited distance demands its full carrying capacity. Various means of overcoming this difficulty are under study, but to date no solution has been found by which the cost of underground power transmission systems can be brought within reasonable limits. In urban areas, for short carries, however, the underground method must be considered in spite of its heavy cost.

Bury the light and telephone wires

Local overhead distribution lines and the forest of light and telephone poles which support them are as obsolete as the dodo. Many municipalities now require by ordinance that all such new installations be placed underground. Other progressive communities are also requiring the staged conversion of existing overhead systems by the utility companies.

Control the routing and installation of power transmission systems

Municipalities cannot very well prohibit the construction of facilities required to serve their needs for electrical energy. They can, however, regulate the placement and design of such installations by requiring a permit for their construction and the right to review and approve all plans. Utility companies may thus be persuaded or compelled, as the case may be, to comply with reasonable standards of safety, rational planning, aesthetics, and other factors affecting the well-being of a community.

Combine them with other uses

The increasing demand for interconnected networks of high-voltage power transmission lines, coupled with the public antipathy for conventional installations, has recently focused attention upon improved design and location techniques.

It is no longer reasonable, at least within urbanizing regions, for a utility company to usurp mile after mile of valuable real estate for rights-of-way devoted to the single purpose of carrying their massive transmission towers and their sky-filling proliferation of cables. The newer towers are lighter in mass and often graceful in profile. Cables have been clustered into streamlined conduits. The right-of-way swaths have been reduced in width and are often shared with other uses such as fuel transmission pipelines, parking lots, and industrial buildings. Transformer stations have been concealed by screen walls, mounding, and tree planting. Such innovations are to be encouraged, expected, and demanded.

Align transmission towers and lines through the most compatible areas

When routed through industrial districts or transportation corridors, they usually inflict the least damage on the landscape and most directly serve the consumers of high-voltage power.

Remove them from the public view

The less obvious they are, the better. As a rule, they should be kept away from areas where people congregate and from routes where people travel. In the latter regard, because the viewing field of transit passengers is to the side, the best possible location for power transmission lines may be directly overhead where they are out of sight. Such lines looping along an interstate freeway or parkway, however, would all but destroy the desirable scenic values.

Blend them into the landscape

The Hudson River Valley Commission in a report, *Power Lines and Scenic Values*, has outlined several simple but effective principles to be applied in cross-country transmission-line routing:

1. Avoid sites of great scenic value, including prominent ridge lines, lakes, and barren sides of mountains or hills.

2. Keep alignments along the bottoms of lower slopes and valleys and between hills.

3. Avoid crossing hill contours at right angles; avoid steep grades which expose the right-of-way to view.

4. When crossing principal roads, jog alignments to avoid extended tangents along the right-of-way on either side of the road.

5. In rough or very hilly country, change the alignment continuously in keeping with the scale of the topographic changes.

6. Where feasible and in keeping with the prior criteria, run lines along the edges of differing types of land use, with special emphasis on preservation of forest growth.

7. For lower-voltage subtransmission lines, undergrounding is desired when alignments parallel major highways or scenic areas. In these instances, provision for the subsurface installation should be considered when construction is undertaken.

8. If a proposed route can be realistically shifted from a scenic area to one already industrially developed, the route should be placed through the latter.

From the environmental point of view the chief objective in the location of power and telephone lines is to reduce their visibility. Having consolidated all possible transmission and transportation corridors, and having reduced right-of-way clearing, lines, and structures to the technological minimum, then conceal the lines and cleared swath within the folds and cover of the countryside.

Junk, trash, and garbage

Junk cars, scrap metal or lumber, paper, fibers, glass, raw garbage, and even industrial sludges are generally all grouped together in the category of *solid waste*. This comprises all types of refuse excepting sewage or materials ground up, as by garbage disposal units, to be flushed into sewage systems.

In the United States, on an average, each of us throws away in one day more than 5 pounds of trash and garbage. The resulting mountain of waste must be hauled away and put somewhere—all at an astronomical cost, and all contributing to pollution in one form or another.

By tradition we have carted our refuse off to dump it somewhere "out beyond" in rotting, rusting heaps. As our population has

Avoid the visual scars and erosion caused by straight steep climbs across the hill contour.

Ensure minimum interference with natural landmarks, and the least possible disruption of natural lines and profiles.

Where feasible, use existing transportation corridors to avoid wasteful duplication of rights-of-way, isolated parcels, and visual turmoil.

PRECONSIDER ALL ASPECTS OF CROSS-COUNTRY POWER TRANSMISSION

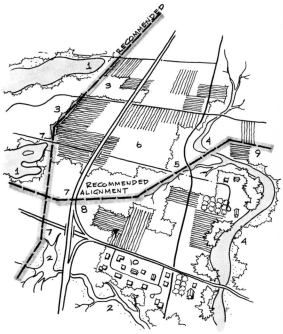

1. Avoid water bodies
2. Bypass open-sky wetlands
3. Follow the natural edges
4. Stay clear of major river valleys
5. Follow the secondary valley floors
6. Do not traverse open farm lands
7. Cross trafficways at a right or obtuse angle
8. Provide short right-of-way sight lines at highway crossings
9. Move with the grid of fields and subsection lines
10. Give wide berth to nonindustrial development

TRANSMISSION NETWORK ALIGNMENT

In one year over 450 million cubic yards of sewage sludge and liquid wastes were dumped off the eastern shore of Long Island alone.

Our total annual discharge of debris into the oceans has been equal to nearly half a ton for every man, woman, and child in the United States.

Instead of "wasting" sludge as an ocean pollutant, it could be much better converted to fertilizer and compost to rebuild depleted land.

Americans consume nearly half the earth's industrial raw materials. Not surprisingly, the way of life that requires such large amounts of natural resources also produces enormous amounts of wastes.

The solid wastes produced in the United States now total over 4.4 billion tons a year. Of this 360 million tons are household, municipal, and industrial wastes. In addition there are 2.4 billion tons of agricultural wastes and 1.8 billion tons of mineral wastes.

The vast quantities of nonrenewable resources, such as ferrous metals, which are permanently lost in the solid-waste stream present a growing and unnecessary economic and resource drain.

Today a new concept of solid-waste management is evolving; it assumes that man can devise a social-technological system that will wisely control the quantity and characteristics of wastes, efficiently collect those that must be removed, creatively recycle those that can be reused, and properly dispose of those that have no further use.

Many American cities and countries are presently planning solid-waste disposal plants which, with various combinations of shredders, filters, centrifuges, and magnets can recover such reusable materials as metal, paper, and glass. The organic materials are converted at high temperatures to energy in the form of gas or steam. With their feasibility established, such plants can reduce both the hazards and cost of solid-waste disposal.

expanded, the deluge of urban garbage and trash first began to fill ravines and then whole valleys—to the consternation, discomfort, and very real health hazard of the neighboring communities. As an alternate solution, some coastal cities blithely barged their mess out through their harbors and dumped it into the sea. But the sea, biologically offended by leaching oils and residual poisons such as methyl mercury and DDT, has responded with decimated harvests of shellfish and contaminated yields of seafoods of all types. Trash and other waste materials rejected by the ocean have washed back upon us to litter our beaches and often to coat them with malodorous films and scum. In the United States the sea is now officially "off limits" as a dumping ground.

In desperation, some cities have turned to burying their refuse. In this process the material is first compressed or ground to reduce its bulk and then bulldozed between alternating layers of earth into extensive "sanitary" landfills. Refuse out of sight, however, is not necessarily refuse out of mind, for standard landfilling procedures have their drawbacks, too. Aside from the problems of trailing and blowing litter and the odors inherent in the hauling and filling process, there is the ominous possibility that subsurface water sources may become contaminated. Moreover, as the waste materials decompose, the fill will continue to subside for decades and perhaps even centuries, thus making the land unsuitable for many purposes.

By a process recently introduced in Germany, both trash and garbage are ground to fragments and incinerated under intensive heat to a liquid state. The superheated liquid is then exploded by contact with water to produce a slaglike granular substance which is clinically sterile and a stable fill material. But here again, as in most means of refuse disposal, there remains the matter of air or thermal pollution or of other vexing side effects.

If we can't hide it, burn it, sink it, or bury it—what then can we do with our waste? The most promising areas of breakthrough lie in a variety of procedures which may be generally classified as "recycling," or reuse. Much of the problem of waste disposal will be resolved when it is recognized that this seemingly limitless mass of unwanted material is in fact an untapped resource of great potential value.

Man can no longer throw away his refuse, for there is no more "away, . . ." As the earth becomes more crowded . . . one person's trash basket is another's living space.
THEODORE C. BYERLY
Environmental Improvement (Air, Water, and Soil)
The Graduate School
U.S. Department of Agriculture
Washington, D.C., 1966

Every American city shows these alternating bands of glory and garbage, and often the garbage has been what it is for a long, long time.
ROBERT FUTTERMAN
The Future of Our Cities
Doubleday & Company, Inc.
Garden City, N.Y., 1961

Goop, the goulash of environment, is not a simple thing due purely to the automobile or to exurbia or commercial pressures. The American mess is worse than any other mess in the world for a combination of reasons, not all of which came over with Columbus, some are America's own contribution. They are like the components of an explosive that had been smoldering together for years and that finally went off after the Second World War.
IAN NAIRN
The American Landscape: A Critical View
Random House, Inc.
New York, 1965

As man has come to appreciate that the earth is a closed ecological system, casual methods that once appeared satisfactory for the disposal of wastes no longer seem acceptable. He has the daily evidence of his eyes and nose to tell him that his planet cannot assimilate without limit the untreated wastes of his civilization.
EDMUND S. MUSKIE
Environmental Improvement (Air. Water, and Soil)
The Graduate School
U.S. Department of Agriculture
Washington, D.C., 1966

Institute "recycling" procedures

While the reclamation of most discarded material at present requires subsidy, many new techniques for such recycling are being studied and applied. The processing of solid waste is usually a matter of selective sorting or stripping, incineration and/or shredding to reduce the bulk, and then the application of one or more separation and conversion procedures. In some instances the end products may be reused as raw materials—scrap, basic metal, glass, or industrial chemicals. In other cases they may be used in a converted form such as construction materials or soil conditioners.

Perhaps refuse has been a problem simply because it has been traditionally treated as a problem. The cost of its collection and processing or disposal has been considered a burden to be borne by the

Recycling: The reutilization of expended man-made products and natural resources.

Because there is a pervasive throwaway psychology in the U.S. we do not come close to realizing—or even envisioning—the potentialities of recycling. In many instances where recycling is dismissed as economically or technically unfeasible, the possibility has not been carefully examined.
The Editors, *Fortune* magazine
The Environment
Harper & Row, Publishers, Incorporated
New York, 1970

Sewage in its processing may be converted through incineration or chemical treatment into useful end products. Solids may be transformed into feed or fodder or supplements for livestock, into fertilizers, or a variety of related agricultural products. The liquid content, when separated and treated, may be used for irrigation or, with further purification, may be made suitable for human consumption. Even contaminated hospital effluent may be converted to drinking water as sweet and pure as that drawn from a mountain spring.

We have a massive problem of disposing of solid waste. And yet our solid wastes by and large contain better grade ore than much of that which we mine.

S. DAVID FREEMAN
"Outlook for the Future"
Consulting Engineer
March 1973

Not all urban wastes go to sanitary landfills. Modern cities slowly rise on a mound of debris, just as ancient ones did. It has been estimated that London is building upward at a rate of 1 foot per century.

Mount Trashmore in Virginia is a man-made sanitary landfill that has transformed a badly scarred marshy pit known as the Badlands into a ski slope and toboggan run. Reaching an elevation of 125 feet, the "mountain" consists of 3-foot layers of compacted garbage capped by 1-foot layers of clay.

Strip mining mars more than 150,000 acres each year. This would be enough to accommodate the country's entire annual output of solid wastes if placed as a sanitary landfill of processed residues.

taxpayer in one form or another. It is doubtful that a satisfactory solution can ever be found in such a negative approach. It is proposed, rather, that the breakthrough will come when garbage and other refuse is recognized for what it is, one of the world's richest and fastest replenishing resources; when it is "mined," processed, and recycled as a self-sustaining, profit-making enterprise.

Convert the waste into a public asset

As an example, one propitious endeavor is the conversion of biodegradable organic material into a clean-burning fuel, methane gas, which is in diminishing supply and high demand. In this procedure, bulk unsorted garbage from the collection trucks is reduced by "shredding" to coarse particles. This decreases the volume and facilitates the separating out of the heavier inorganic substances which may then be otherwise reclaimed. After the separation stage the pulverized organic matter is subjected to a biological treatment by which as much as 50 percent of the bulk may be converted into high-quality methane. The by-product is an inert humus which may be placed in structural fills. This residue which has been completely stabilized has great advantages over the untreated refuse normally used in landfill operations.

This extraction and sterilization of the organic content of garbage opens up also the possibility of large-scale composting, or the production of artificial topsoil. Treated organic sludges mixed with leaves, straw, grass, clippings, pulp, or pulverized wood chips, all machine-blended with low-grade soils or sand, could conceivably be at last a source of that vital substance, topsoil, which has been so disastrously wasted and depleted. Composting by municipal sanitation departments can produce an abundant supply of odor-free rich loam or mulch for park and roadside plantings or for sale on the open market.

Reprocess wastepaper

Newsprint, magazines, and most other paper products are among those most easily processed for reuse. A paper collection program initiated by every town or city would serve a useful function. Well-designed collection bins could be located throughout the community and serviced by a section of the sanitation department or by a charitable organization, either with or without a subsidy. Besides reducing the amount of refuse to be incinerated or plowed into landfills, the recycling of paper will help to conserve our forests. A ton of paper thus reused may save as many as twenty full-grown trees.

Remelt and reuse the glass

Many thousands of miles of our beaches and highways are strewn with empty bottles and shattered glass. Responding to growing public indignation, the glass-container industries have undertaken two remedial programs. One is to stimulate the return of glass bottles (which may be reused some twenty times); the other is to remelt the throwaways. The premise of successful reclamation programs is simple: bottles and jars that have enough value will not be scattered about the landscape.

Recycle the metals

Aluminum soft-drink and beer cans have also become notorious for their part in the roadside litter disgrace. Left to the weather they are almost indestructible, but collected and remelted they are an economical source of new metal. There is promise in the fact that it takes fewer kilowatt hours of power to process aluminum from scrap than to produce new ingots from ores. If an additional incentive is needed to ensure the remelting of metal and glass containers, a licensing fee or tax can be imposed upon the manufacturers—to be rebated upon evidence of their having collected and repossessed one expended unit for every new unit produced.

Metals when separated from other solid wastes may be almost completely recycled. As public attitudes stiffen, as ore reserves dwindle, and as economic sanctions and incentives are applied, scrap metals, abandoned jalopies, and junk will be sought out for their residual value—to disappear forever from the American scene.

Rate consumer goods according to their effects upon the environment

Much may be expected from awakened public concern about waste disposal and from changing consumer habits. Many consumers have become determined to buy less and to waste less. They are refusing to purchase those goods which come in bulky crates or cartons that must be discarded. They are demanding a ban on nonreturnable containers. They favor those products whose producers are "ecologically minded" and who provide the means for recycling, or promote antilitter campaigns. It can be expected that a system of rating consumer goods in terms of environmental merit factors will soon be initiated.

Organize volunteer cleanup squads

Grade school, high school, and university students with a newly aroused compulsion to *do something* about litter and pollution might well be organized as a volunteer labor force. Service could be occasional as on a specially designated day, or it could be provided under the leadership of an "elite corps" as part of a systematic training in environmental science. The number of work hours contributed, and the focalized concern and action, could be of far-reaching significance. Such training would do much to instill constructive attitudes. It could also lead to specialized study or to a position as a city or county environmental agent.

Close the economic gap

Spurred by federal grants and by private industrial research programs, experimentation in waste processing and reclamation is gathering momentum. Until the technology has been advanced to the point where the recycling of all types of solid waste is profitable, the gap must be closed by governmental subsidy. Some of the funding may be borne by direct appropriation from state and federal operating budgets. Some may be provided through licensing of the manufacturing of the products which will later be disposed of. Some of the financing should be provided by industrial taxes which will in turn be passed on to the product consumer. Mandatory performance on the part of the manufacturer and distributor must be set at feasible levels.

Such possibilities give promise that our industrial technology, which has produced history's greatest heap of solid wastes and greatest volume of pollutants, may in time eradicate pollution and waste altogether.

Litter

In the war on filth the launching of an intensive cleanup campaign serves as a booming opening salvo. The impetus of a citizens' action committee is usually needed, together with the help of public officials and the organized support of the news media. In drawing up a plan of attack the three essentials seem to be active neighborhood

Recycling is hindered by heterogenous materials:
1. The aluminum ring left from the twist-off cap on the bottle makes it uneconomical to grind the bottles into cullet for glassmaking.
2. The aluminum can contains a small amount of magnesium.
3. Lead solder and tin coating on the otherwise steel (tin) can lowers its salvage value.

Over 2 million tons of copper are used in the United States each year.

More minerals have been extracted and used in this century than in all the others combined.

The United States has six percent of the world's population and uses sixty percent of the world's resources.
JOHN MCPHEE
Encounters with the Archdruid
Copyright © 1971 by John McPhee
Farrar, Straus and Giroux, Inc.
New York, 1971

Community rehabilitation seems to call first for drastic steps to stimulate the community interest of every citizen by letting him participate actively.
WALTER GROPIUS
Rebuilding Our Communities
Paul Theobald & Company
Chicago, Ill., 1945

Nothing in nature is wasted.

Can our wealth, our technology and our political ability produce a livable urban environment, or are we damned to live in the waste of our mistakes? This question may well be one of the crucial tests of our civilization.
LAURANCE S. ROCKEFELLER
From "The Quality of Our Environment—
The Challenge To Landscape Architects"
An address before the American Society of Landscape Architects
Niagara Falls, Ontario, 1968

leadership groups, the strategic placement of local field headquarters, and the full and enthusiastic cooperation of the local sanitation department.

The districts most in need of cleanup are readily apparent. The conversion of a vacant store "in loco" puts the project leader close to where the action is.

Litter can best be defined as any kind of waste that is located outside the solid-waste cycle. If a tissue is thrown into a litter can, it becomes solid waste. If it misses the can and hits the ground, then it is litter.

Litterbugs in Detroit can be sentenced to four hours of "litter school."

Kentucky drive-in restaurants are required by law to place signs warning against littering and to provide a minimum number of litter baskets.

The Coast Guard has recently reported that in one year more than 200 vessels were involved in major accidents caused by floating objects.

An alternative to banning disposables outright is to tax them in an amount equal to the deposit on returnable containers. This would make returnables a better buy and penalize only those who buy polluting containers. The tax collected could be used for litter collection.

According to *Time* magazine, in one recent year, Americans junked 7 million cars, 100 million tires, 20 million tons of paper, 28 billion bottles, and 48 billion cans.

In one state during a three-year period, 621 accidents were reported caused by vehicles striking or swerving to avoid a foreign object.

Less than 50 percent of the nation's cars have litter bags, and only 6 percent of the boats.

Organize the streets

The most effective cleanup drives are tackled on a street-by-street or block-by-block basis. The neighborhood leader—ward boss, matriarch, teenage hero, minister, rabbi, or priest—is enlisted. He or she is persuaded to "talk things over" with the local residents. If convinced that something can be done, they may select a day or weekend when everybody is to get together for the big "dig-out." Maybe they will and maybe they won't, but the odds are favorable. In the spirit of the old barn raising, trash and refuse are hauled to the curb where they are picked up in trucks provided by the city. Cellars, vacant lots, backyards, alleys, and empty buildings cleared of debris bring a new sense of accomplishment and pride.

A key factor is that the people on the block, or within any given district, commit *themselves* to the project and share a sense of decision, participation, and success in the result. Perhaps the biggest single factor in the general air of frustration within the cities has been that the people have felt that nothing they do or say seems to make any difference. To have a say as to whether or not even a cleanup effort should be attempted and how or when it should be done, and then to have a part in it, can have a bracing and tonic effect.

Give recognition and publicity

Before-and-after photographs, with action shots of the process and a "post facto" review of results by participants and leaders, all serve to stimulate interest in the adjacent streets. Awards and news coverage also help give momentum to the continuing drive. Don't forget kudos to "City Hall." Politicians need all the credit they can get. Their jobs depend upon it.

Keep up the momentum

In the wake of successful cleanup campaigns there is often enthusiasm for other improvement projects. The most important is the initiation of a regular trash and garbage removal system with periodic and well-publicized "cleanup" days. More frequent pickups, of smaller disposable bags or containers furnished by the sanitation agency, would do much to alleviate the collection problem and to preclude malodorous accumulations of ripe garbage and the scatteration of trash. Even if they cost more—which is doubtful—daily or semiweekly collections would remove (along with the refuse) the most common problems of the city dweller. Perhaps no other single urban improvement program would have such a good effect.

Vacant buildings may be converted into neighborhood centers. Empty lots may be leveled or terraced as garden courts or play lots. Window boxes and planters may appear under garden-club sponsorship. Shade and flowering trees may be planted along the streets, with new lighting, signs, and benches to follow. With a minimum of outside organizational guidance and aid, quiet miracles may be performed.

As an example, the Pittsburgh Renaissance was spearheaded by *Pa Pitt's Partners*, a foundation-sponsored cleanup program that transformed the appearance of whole city wards within a few short months.

Text continued on page 114.

Visible landscape

This summary report deals primarily with recommendations for enhancing the visual quality of a city and its supporting region.

The study was sponsored by the Area Beautification Committee of the Greater Chattanooga Chamber of Commerce and the Chattanooga–Hamilton County Regional Planning Commission. It addresses itself to the preservation and orderly development of the area's magnificent resources—its mountains, valleys, open space, and waterways. It is concerned with the streets and highways along which the people drive and from which, in the main, they come to know and appreciate their countryside and city. It considers those public places and ways through which one can or would like to walk. It suggests an enlightened treatment of the rich heritage of historic areas and landmarks. It deals with the individual community cores and features, which together compose the structure of the city.

In short, this report discusses each of these elements, their interrelationships, and the means by which they can contribute to a comprehensive program of urban landscape improvement.

This beautiful landscape is threatened. It is being disrupted and despoiled at an alarming rate. Forested areas are being slashed. Hillsides are being gouged back by heavy construction equipment, exposing ugly barren soil which is left open to erosion. Valley floors are being leveled, marshes filled with litter and trash, and streams and rivers polluted.

The people of Chattanooga and Hamilton County, as they move from home to work or to shop or play, are often faced with jarring contradictions of scenic splendor and visual blight. From wooded residential areas one drives past automobile junkyards, through uncontrolled sign clutter and down bleak unshaded streets laced with overhead utility wires.

Even within the central city one finds empty lots choked with weeds and strewn with refuse. And here, surprisingly, those public squares, plazas, playgrounds and riverside parks which normally provide centers of urban life and activity are almost totally lacking.

Fortunately, there is today an increasing awareness of the need for more effective controls, more enlightened development, and more amenities. There is in many quarters a growing concern for the stewardship of the land.

It is not too late. The strength and quality of the landscape setting is so dominant that it has so far withstood the growing desecrations. But the margin of time is growing short. That which has been harmful must be corrected. That which is threatened must be protected. And that which is needed and has not been provided should be provided—now!

Purpose:

1. Explore the project region and develop a checklist of the problems and possibilities of environmental improvement.

2. Outline a broad program to serve as an overall guide to local governmental officials, civic action groups, and private interests.

3. Develop, for general application, a body of workable techniques and procedures.

4. Describe specific projects, noting their scope, priority, cost, and means of implementation.

Process:

As in all sound planning studies the first stage has entailed a survey of existing conditions. The second involved the formulation of rec-

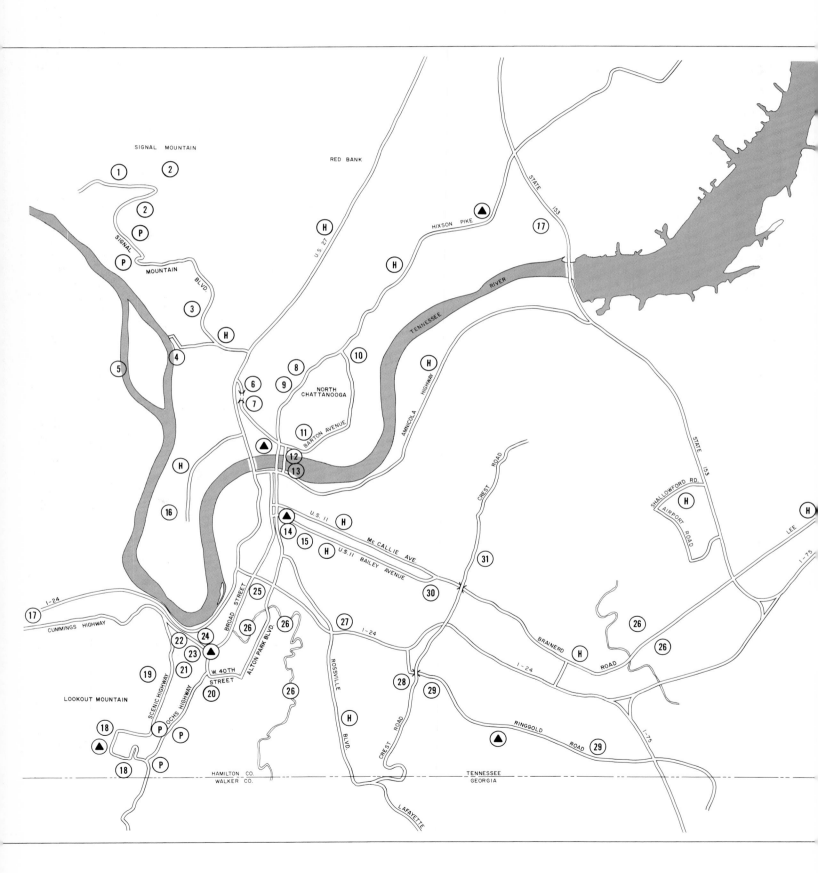

ommended procedures suggested by the survey. In this, the third stage, a listing is made of projects for early accomplishment. While varying in type and magnitude they would, in sum, eliminate many unfortunate conditions which prevail, and make a significant contribution to the beauty and distinction of the Chattanooga environs.

Landscape impact projects

1. Theme Planting, Signal Mountain Community Core to Signal Point
2. Identification Signs, Signal Mountain
3. Visual Screening of Unsightly Yards
4. Burris Bar Boat Slip and Picnic Area
5. Williams Island Acquisition for Future Water-Related Recreational Park
6. Stringers Ridge Tunnel Improvements
7. Cherokee Boulevard Improvement
8. Dallas Road Planting
9. Passive Park Area, Dallas Road and Market Street
10. Paved Street Island, Hixson Pike and Barton Avenue
11. Identification Sign, Little Theater
12. Little Theater Boat and Fishing Park
13. New Park and Playground, Spring Street
14. Active Vest-Pocket Park, Ninth Street
15. Passive Vest-Pocket Park, Ninth Street
16. Moccasin Bend Park Development
17. Tourist Information Centers
18. Identification Signs, Lookout Mountain
19. Pedestrian Way Development, Incline Station to Point Park
20. New Signing, Landscape Development at Entrance to Ochs Highway
21. Cravens House Entrance Improvement
22. Cummings Highway Overlook
23. Paved Street Island, Broad Street and St. Elmo Avenue
24. Railroad Viaduct Improvement, Cummings Highway and Broad Street
25. Travelers Square Development
26. Chickamauga and Chattanooga Creeks Recreation Development
27. Montague Park Development
28. Bachman Tubes Improvements
29. Identification Signs, East Ridge
30. Paved Street Island Improvement—Bailey and McCallie Avenues
31. Crest Road Development, including Sherman Reservation
P. Overlooks and Pulloffs. See Total Highway Program (page 112).
▲, H. Highway improvement. See Total Highway Program (page 112).

Provide access to the river. Boat slips proposed adjacent to the Little Theater would accommodate patrons coming by rivercraft and give a welcome land-water access point. Access would also be provided to the Audubon Society Wildlife Refuge on Maclellan Island.

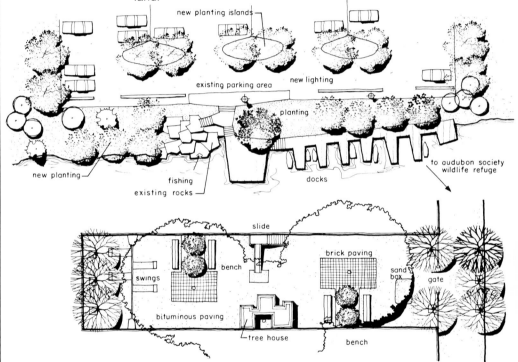

Install a series of small play lots. Such active play spaces utilizing narrow vacant lots throughout the city would give children a safe and pleasant place for play and improve the neighborhood.

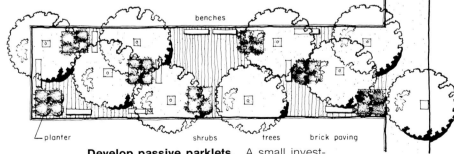

Develop passive parklets. A small investment in land cost and improvements can provide a delightful oasis for crowded city dwellers. Neighborhoods are stabilized; real estate values enhanced.

107

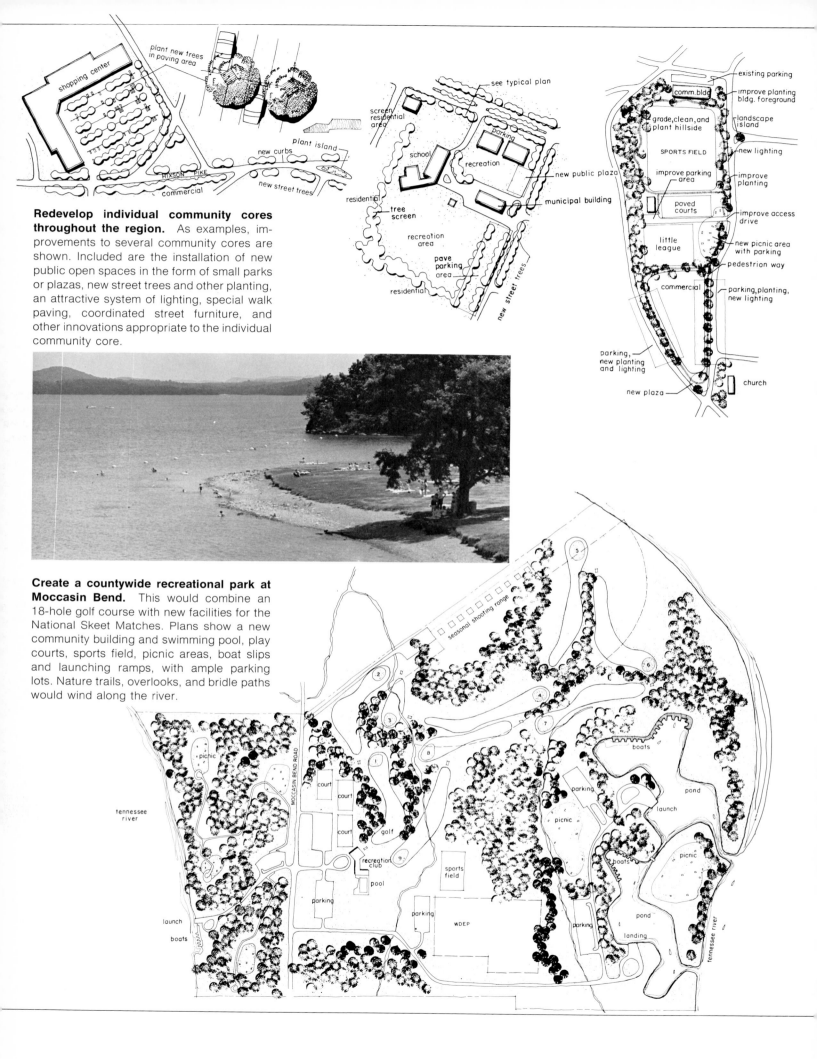

Redevelop individual community cores throughout the region. As examples, improvements to several community cores are shown. Included are the installation of new public open spaces in the form of small parks or plazas, new street trees and other planting, an attractive system of lighting, special walk paving, coordinated street furniture, and other innovations appropriate to the individual community core.

Create a countywide recreational park at Moccasin Bend. This would combine an 18-hole golf course with new facilities for the National Skeet Matches. Plans show a new community building and swimming pool, play courts, sports field, picnic areas, boat slips and launching ramps, with ample parking lots. Nature trails, overlooks, and bridle paths would wind along the river.

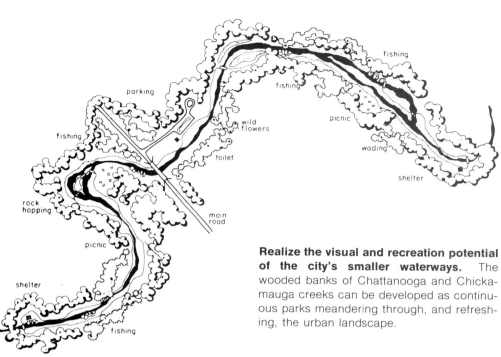

Realize the visual and recreation potential of the city's smaller waterways. The wooded banks of Chattanooga and Chickamauga creeks can be developed as continuous parks meandering through, and refreshing, the urban landscape.

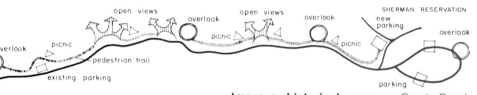

Improve historical areas. Crest Road, which traverses historical Missionary Ridge, can be substantially improved with the provision of new parking facilities, pedestrian walkways, lighting, and a series of pulloffs and overlooks to enable visitors to stop, read the many historical markers, and enjoy the splendid views.

Develop opportunities for water-based recreation. A new park at Burris Bar could provide launching ramps, fishing sites, and picnic areas at the water's edge.

Rediscover the water courses. The Tennessee River, Chickamauga Lake, and the Chattanooga and Chickamauga creeks compose the major waterways of the region. Few urban areas of the country have so inviting a potential for water-related living and recreation. Yet the city to date has almost ignored its streams and their possibilities.

There is little access to or enjoyment of the river. There is not one riverside park, developed and useful to the public. Views of the river are rare and occur only when one is well elevated. Even potential river views from the bridges are obscured by the guardrails.

Chattanooga and Chickamauga creeks, long neglected, require major cleanup and pollution control.

Chickamauga Lake is beautifully situated, easily accessible and well suited for all forms of water-related recreation, yet little of the shoreline or supporting land area has been set aside and developed for public use.

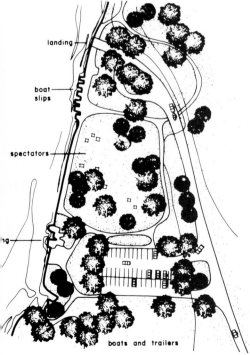

Install a coordinated system of signs and markers. It is proposed that the marker system be composed of three sign types—the route marker, the pathfinder (which tells how to get to specific attractions), and identification signs to be placed at major intersections and at entrances. Signs would be so designed that they could be grouped in sign centers.

The blizzard of existing and competing signs which blight the landscape would in time be replaced or removed.

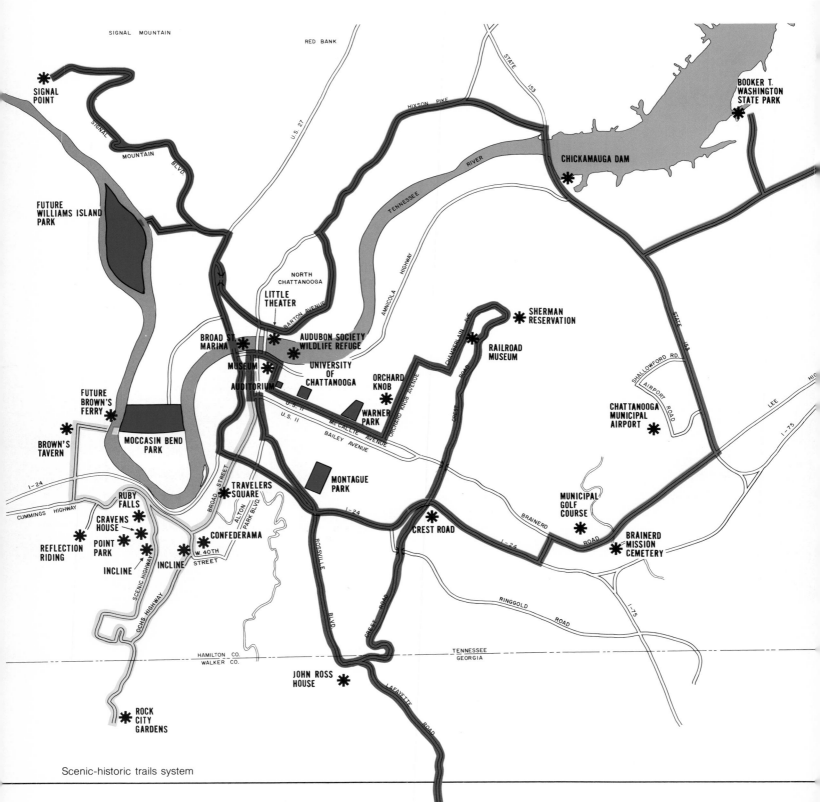

Scenic-historic trails system

Enhance the highway corridors

Remove visual pollution. Well-enforced sign ordinances, new street hardware, and a street planting program can transform such chaotic trafficways into pleasant vehicular and pedestrian routes of movement.

Construct a series of overlooks. Here an existing overlook has been improved by the provision of a raised viewing platform spacious enough to accommodate several picnic tables.

Provide scenic pulloffs. The widening of a road or street, together with selective tree thinning and the installation of walls and plantings to enframe the views can add to the pleasure of driving.

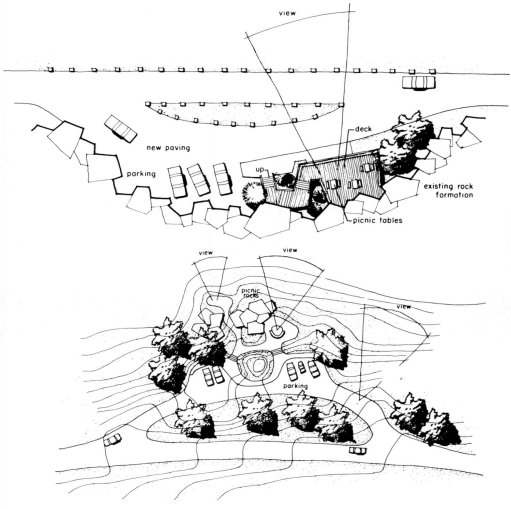

Open views to the river and mountains. The scenic assets are all but hidden from the public view by signs, ungraded banks, and rank roadside vegetation.

Design the new arterials as limited-access parkways. Movement throughout the metropolitan area should be safe and pleasant, displaying the best features of the region. Roadways will often have variable-width medians and rights-of-way.

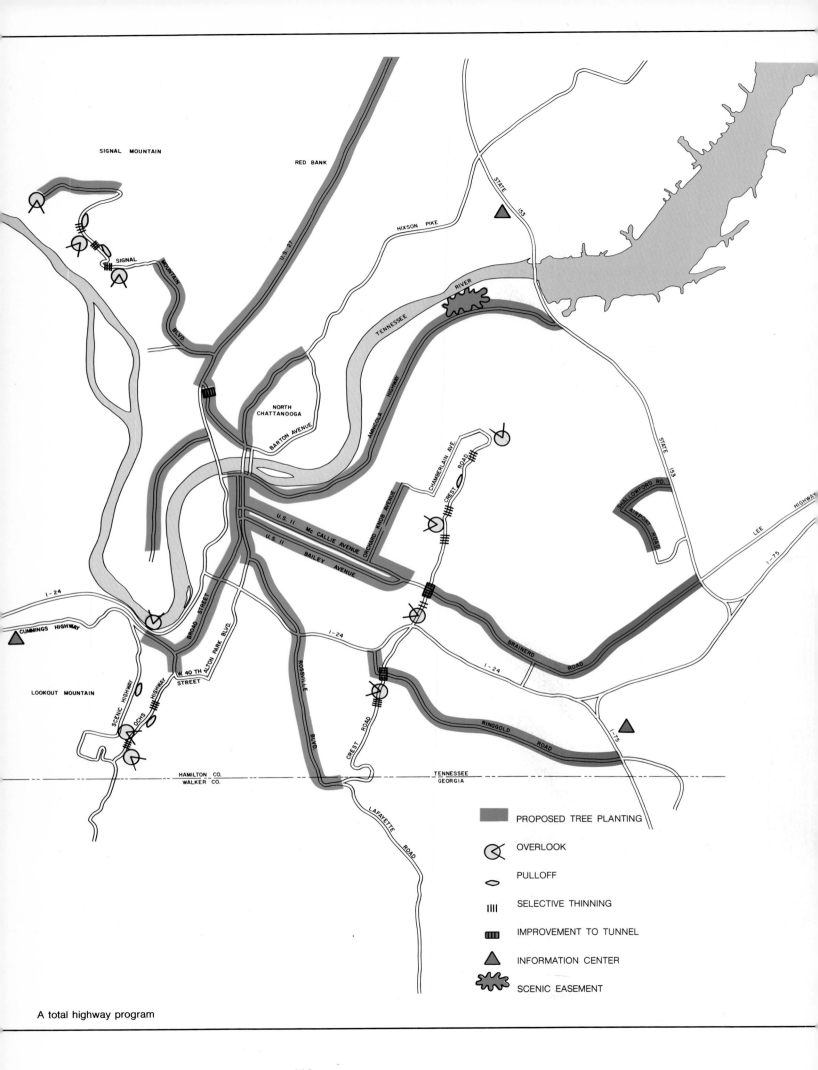

SIGNAL MOUNTAIN

RED BANK

STATE 153

HIXSON PIKE

TENNESSEE RIVER

SIGNAL

MOUNTAIN BLVD.

U.S. 27

NORTH CHATTANOOGA

BARTON AVENUE

AMNICOLA HIGHWAY

CHAMBERLAIN AVE

CREST ROAD

STATE 153

SHALLOWFORD RD.

AIRPORT ROAD

LEE HIGHWAY

I-75

ORCHARD KNOB AVENUE

U.S. 11 McCALLIE AVENUE

U.S. 11 BAILEY AVENUE

I-24

BROAD STREET

ALTON PARK BLVD.

W. 40 TH STREET

BRAINERD ROAD

I-24

I-24

CUMMINGS HIGHWAY

ROSSVILLE BLVD.

CREST ROAD

RINGGOLD ROAD

I-75

SCENIC HIGHWAY

OCHS HIGHWAY

LOOKOUT MOUNTAIN

HAMILTON CO.
WALKER CO.

TENNESSEE
GEORGIA

LAFAYETTE ROAD

PROPOSED TREE PLANTING

OVERLOOK

PULLOFF

SELECTIVE THINNING

IMPROVEMENT TO TUNNEL

INFORMATION CENTER

SCENIC EASEMENT

A total highway program

Looking ahead

While much of the nature of the Chattanooga–Hamilton County region is seeded in the past—fully as much of its future character and quality must lie in the fact of what the people *will* their city and county to be. If the improvement is to come the people must want for their children and grandchildren a better way of life and a better place in which to live it. Hopes and desires must be translated into plans; plans must be put into action.

The compulsion of citizens for excellence can be measured in terms of their institutions, goals and programs. The present governments are implementing the programs which the public has demanded. They are working in the long range public good. They are guiding public policy toward the creation of many future improvements. But present efforts are not enough. Environmental planning to be effective must be approached on a massive, total, and continuing basis. Beyond normal—even accelerated—governmental efforts, there should be a whole range of supplementary programs directed toward the protection and care of the landscape and toward the best possible development of the region for the use and enjoyment of man. There is urgent need, for example, for such citizens', quasi-public, or official organizations as:

A nature conservancy
As a citizens' group, operating with funds raised by bequest and by private subscriptions, the conservancy could work to designate, protect, and perhaps acquire the natural superlatives of the region. The Western Pennsylvania Conservancy is a successful prototype.

A river-basin study commission
The Tennessee Valley Authority might well be encouraged to implement a comprehensive study of the Tennessee River Basin, such as one recently completed for the Potomac. Included would be recommendations for measures to ensure that a full range of recreation uses be integrated with all riverside communities. Clean water, flood control, and the sound long-range economic development of the entire watershed would also receive detailed attention.

A riverfront development authority
An official city-county body with powers granted to it by the state could work for the coordinated and orderly development of the river and its tributary streams within the study region.

No other single effort could contribute more to the future well-being of the area's citizens. Attention is directed to the work of the Niagara Parks Commission in Canada.

A citizens' planning association
A well-conceived citizens' action group could bring together the best minds and most dedicated leaders of the region to work for the common good. It could unite all groups such as the Area Beautification Committee and the Downtown Development Committee which would give broader influence in the shaping of the total environment. Such an association usually works with and through the local governments. The Chicago Central Area Committee and the Allegheny Conference on Community Development are inspiring examples.

A horticultural society
Such a society could stimulate interest in horticulture, landscape design, and the creation of public gardens.

A historic landmarks commission
Such a commission with powers granted to it by the state could work to establish, designate, and preserve historic landmarks and to acquire by gift, lease, or by condemnation such historic assets as might from time to time be threatened. The Historic Landmarks Commission of Virginia is a good example.

A regional park authority
The authority could help to supplement local park and recreation facilities and develop a system of regional park and forest preserves.

Until such broader efforts can be put into motion, and indeed as a generator of such efforts, the initial environmental improvement program herein described has been presented for immediate implementation. It is the product of many meetings and much thought. Officials, staff members, and many concerned citizens have given able assistance and offered invaluable suggestions which have been incorporated. The resulting program deserves the support of every citizen and the backing and full thrust of the city and county governments which have been its sponsor.

It is a good beginning.

Text continued from page 104.

A series of further physical and social improvements have followed over the years by popular demand backed up with enthusiastic local participation. Philadelphia, Los Angeles, and a host of other cities and towns have launched highly successful cleanup-fixup drives which prove how much can be done.

Wage a three-pronged campaign against litter

The three most effective ways to alleviate the problem of litter are to:

1. *Educate the public.* Keep America Beautiful, a nonprofit organization, has sponsored national educational programs with remarkable success.

2. *Provide adequate disposal facilities and collection.* Much of the litter is caused by persons who would prefer to be good citizens but who don't have access to litter receptacles.

3. *Enact and enforce antilitter laws.* These exist in most states but most could be simplified and updated. Statutes and regulations clearly displayed and fairly enforced can work wonders. Fines and sentences also help things along.

Vacant properties

Urban decay is usually concentrated in and around vacant properties, with their weeds, heaps of trash, and scurrying rats. Like an open sore they soon infect the healthy tissue around them. Pride in the neighborhood fades; people and enterprises move away; property values drop; and dilapidation spreads in an ever-widening circle.

Serve notice of violation

When a property, used or vacant, has become an eyesore through misuse or lack of maintenance, a violation of local codes has usually occurred. If not, new codes are in order.

An inspection in prompt response to routine police reporting or neighborhood complaints is a sign of good local government. If justified, notice to the property owner should describe the specific violations and improvements required, the period of grace, and the penalties for nonperformance. In cases where the owner does not respond, the municipal department can act for him, adding the costs to his tax bill or placing a lien against the property.

Catch and punish vandals

The willful destruction of property is a costly form of pollution. Where community attitudes are lax or permissive, small acts of property damage can soon engender a destructive tide of vandalism and even violence. While "informational" and "educational" crusades may be beneficial, the direct approach is the best approach. Offenders must be apprehended and made to pay for their misdeeds.

Require protection and upkeep

Before the first windows of a vacated building can be shattered, or the doors battered in, the owner should be advised officially to protect and maintain the structure. A notification statement giving full particulars is helpful. Before occupancy or reuse is permitted, the structure and its grounds must be restored to compliance with local health and building regulations.

In beauty I walk
With beauty before me I walk
With beauty behind me I walk
With beauty below me I walk
With beauty above me I walk
It [the day] is finished in beauty
It is finished [again] in beauty.

Night chant
Navajo, c.1890
From *Sacred Circles*. Two thousand years of North American Indian art. An exhibition of the Hayward Gallery
London, 1977

With inexpensive housing in such short supply, local governments would be well-advised to relax the strict building regulations imposed on new construction in cases of permitting rehabilitation. With "a few boards, a bucket of paint, and a will" enterprising tenants can often work small wonders with an obsolescent building and breathe new life into a sagging neighborhood. *Incentives* are in order.

Remove the derelicts

Abandoned buildings and those not kept in good repair should be demolished promptly at the conclusion of an adequate period of time, after notification, for bringing them up to a safe and healthful standard. After the structures have been demolished and all rubbish removed, the cellars should be filled and the lots graded and otherwise improved in keeping with surrounding properties. Again, should the owner fail to act, the appropriate department must act for him and at his expense.

Put the vacant properties to use

With self-help guidance, local volunteers, and a minimum outlay of funds for tools, spray paint, and equipment, vacant homes, stores, or other buildings may be converted into welcome neighborhood activity centers, and empty lots into play spaces or parklets. The planting of a tree under the supervision of the city forester, for example, or the placement of a bench or basketball hoop provided by the department of recreation, can do much to lift the spirits and improve the block.

Most property owners would welcome an offer by neighbors or a local citizens' group to use and maintain the vacant property until such a time as a new buyer or renter could be found. Tax relief in the interim period can be a further incentive. Often, the vacating of such parcels provides an opportunity for the municipality to purchase or lease the land for one of its new programs to put recreation or other community services in the places where the people are. The problem is so critical and the possibilities so great that municipalities would do well to establish a center for the sole purpose of listing vacant or obsolescent properties, ensuring their proper treatment and converting them into community assets.

With renovation by willing hands the spirit and life of a block or street can be regenerated. The Georgetown district of Washington and the Annapolis central city have shown what can be done.

Obsolescence is not so much a matter of age or outward appearance as the waning of inner energy.
GERHARD SIXTA
In conversation

Views and viewing

Within any landscape there are agreeable and disagreeable features, but what one knows of the area is mainly what one observes. If what can be seen is dull or dreary, then the city or county is dreary and depressing. Conversely, if from automobile, transit car, or ferry one is exposed to dramatic vistas of the ocean, rivers, mountains, or plains, or to sweeping views of the city, then the region is attractive. If people walk to their offices, schools, or shopping places through refreshing spaces or exciting places, then their days and their lives are more pleasant and rewarding.

Anyone familiar with the rudiments of photography knows that what one sees of the world is mostly a matter of selectivity. And so it is with the visual aspects of landscape planning, in which the attractive features are "selected out" of the natural and man-made landscape and the observer is brought into the best possible sequences of relationship. The more desirable facets of the countryside or metropolis are revealed and enframed by the planning of paths of movement, and by the location and design of public ways and gathering places. The monotonous or ugly features are removed, if possible; otherwise they are screened or circumvented. Simply by taking full advantage of the scenic opportunities that exist within almost any metropolitan area, it may be visually transformed into a place of wonder and delight.

Develop the scenic possibilities of existing roadways

Nationwide surveys have revealed repeatedly that *driving for pleasure* is listed by most families as a favorite form of recreation. This being so, it would behoove highway departments at all levels of government to explore and develop the scenic potential of existing roads. A study of each roadway would show that views ranging from *pleasant* to *spectacular* could be opened up for the enjoyment of the highway users at a nominal cost. Little more may be required, for example, than the elimination of a wall of billboards at a curve, the removal of a sagging fence, the grading out of a roadside ridge that blocks the view, or the judicious thinning of vegetation to reveal the scenery beyond.

As part of the same study the provision of viewing pulloffs and overlooks may be considered, as well as the addition of natural plantings to screen out objectionable roadside areas or features. Once initiated, such scenic improvements usually become so popular that they are made part of a continuing program, staged out as budgets allow.

Consider the visual aspects of new street and highway alignments

An important factor in roadway location and design, often completely overlooked, is the viewing experience of the traveler. In the consideration of alternative alignments and profiles it is only reasonable that weight should be given to the visual qualities of the districts traversed and the scenic features to be revealed. Other factors being equal, the best alignment is that which by location and grade provides the most desirable views both to and from the highway.

Attractive highways cannot be achieved simply by the addition of nursery stock to a canyon or ridge of uniform cut and fill slopes. They are instead the result of planning the road in harmonious relationship to the natural topography and existing neighborhoods. They are produced by the preservation of streams, rock outcrops, groves of trees, and clumps of native vegetation. They entail the pleasant contouring of the earth forms and the skillful manipulation of screening and enframement. In short, the same landscape architectural approach that is applied to park and parkway design is needed in the team planning of all our streets and highways.

Reveal and enframe the major vistas

Most views seen from our public roads have been produced unintentionally. Yet as a highway is routed through almost any area, the opportunity exists for the designer to provide a pleasantly evolving sequence of visual impressions. It is sometimes a matter of adjusting the road profile to top a rise at a point where the view is most dramatic, or of swinging a curve a bit wider to unfold an exhilarating panorama of city or countryside.

Where the outward scenery is unattractive, existing earth forms or vegetation may be left or reinforced to provide screening. New contoured earth shapes may be rolled up as a visual barrier where required, or the roadways may be depressed or separated so that the viewer's attention may be focused inward upon well-modulated slopes.

The visual enjoyment of a highway is sometimes an experience beyond analysis. To sweep along a freeway and into a city at dusk, as the sunset fades against the buildings and shadows deepen while myriad lights flick on among the darkening cubes is to see the urban landscape in a new and magical way. Similarly, an early morning haze on the harbor can produce a deep and lasting emotional impression of a city.

The Freeway in the City
A Report of the Urban Advisors to the
Federal Highway Administration
U.S. Government Printing Office
Washington, D.C., 1968

Where the external scenery is attractive, expose it to the highway viewer.

Where the outward views are unpleasant — as across spoil areas — either reclaim the landscape or create earth forms to provide visual containment.

SHAPE THE ROADWAY SECTION TO MODULATE THE VIEWS

Abrupt vistas or visual impressions of short duration are to be avoided. They are annoying and sometimes even dangerous in causing driver distraction. Views from high-speed highways are best when gradually unfolded and enframed.

Develop an urban parkway system

Without exception, arterial circulation through areas of intensive development should be by controlled-access parkways. The roadway capacities would thus be greatly increased over normal friction-laced trafficways, and travel would be safer and more pleasant. Such highways should be lineal parks designed especially for motorists, who could enjoy the scenery as they sped along beside the rivers, through wooded ravines, past the beaches, or atop the ridges overlooking the city. Rights-of-way should be widened to include and preserve the natural features and to provide room for scenic walks, bicycle trails, and overlooks.

Often new parkways may be aligned intentionally through public dumps, borrow pits, sanitary fills, or floodplains. With the opportunities for large-scale earth shaping and reforestation, whole new landscapes may be created along the roadway flanks.

Create gateways to the cities

With forethought and imagination the major highway approaches to cities can be designed as portals of startling beauty. The same is true in the planning of rapid transit systems, air terminals, and port facilities. New York City's East River Drive, Pittsburgh's Fort Pitt Tunnel and Bridge at the Golden Triangle, and Milwaukee's proposed waterfront park are examples of what may be achieved in making the views of a city memorable.

It is significant to note that the scenic possibilities of freeway design have been in the past so generally overlooked that the breathtaking panorama from the Bay Bridge in San Francisco is blocked from the sight of the motorists by the metal panels of the bridge rail that extend above eye height.

Provide parks and open spaces

Aside from their many other attributes the visual qualities of urban parks are alone enough to make them essential. In size and type they may vary greatly, as from the gemlike focal points at Washington's radial street intersections, to the fountain plaza of Portland, Oregon, the charming riverside parks of San Antonio, Central Park of New York City, or Fort Lauderdale's magnificent oceanfront beach. Such oases within the desertlike expanses of pavement and masonry provide refreshment to the city dweller and enrich the urban landscape with attractive vistas and views.

Public open spaces need not be lavish or large to be significant.

CREATE OUTDOOR PLACES

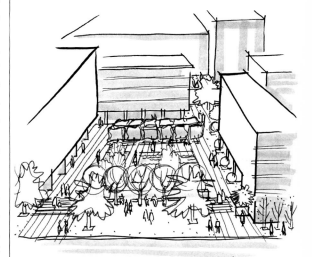

Midblock plazas and throughways open the city wide to pedestrian use and add visual delight.

A single tree can create an oasis

PLANT A TREE DOWNTOWN

The streetscape

Our living landscape is composed of *ways* and *places*. Ways are the paths of movement of people and vehicles. Places are activity centers where people work, trade, learn, worship, and relax. The streets of a city are lines of concentrated activity where ways and places are combined and where life and movement are intensified.

In the planning of such business or residential streets it is important that all functions be considered and interrelated, that the movement of vehicles be accommodated to provide safe and convenient access, and that the walkways and open spaces upon which the buildings face are suitably planted and furnished with all the amenities that can contribute so much of pleasure to city life.

The worst condition is a straight and unterminated ribbon of paving streaming with high-speed through traffic, and flanked by unrelieved concrete sidewalks which are bounded in turn by an unbroken line of building facades, all converging at the horizon.

The best condition is a meandering local street carrying local traffic, with infrequent cross streets, and interrupted occasionally by a building, a plaza, or a park, to give human scale and interest. The pedestrian areas are variable in width, sometimes widened to receive an island of planting, a bus shelter, a sales stall, or an illuminated display case, or sometimes expanded into a court around which the buildings are spaced. Midblock pedestrian ways or arcades provide welcome through-connection from street to street and give prime locations for the wine, cheese, leather, dress, jewelry, and other specialty shops which make a city urbane.

Such shopping and residential streets as Ocean Avenue in Carmel, Chicago's Michigan Avenue north of the river, Worth Avenue and its side streets in Palm Beach, Stroget of Copenhagen, Lijn Baan of Rotterdam, or the narrow Via Condotti of Rome near the Spanish Steps, are economic proof of the plan arrangement and mix. Their soaring ratios of sales volume per square foot of floor area reflect the fact that they draw customers from around the world to shop in their delightful courts and alleys. Such business-office-apartment avenues as the Champs Elysées of Paris, Kurfürstendamm of West Berlin, or the Ginza in Tokyo also have their lessons in urban streetscape planning. A comparison of office and apartment rents in varying situations will give solid affirmation of the value of attractive ways and places.

Create new public squares and plazas

Each new space opened up within the crowded city lets in the air and sunlight and adds interest to the street and surrounding buildings. It increases sales and real estate values, too.

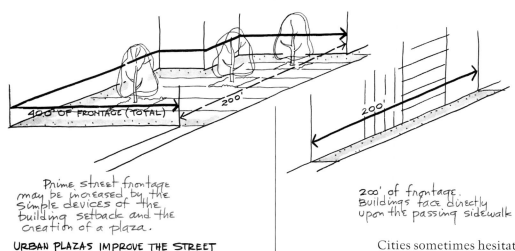

Prime street frontage may be increased by the simple devices of the building setback and the creation of a plaza.

URBAN PLAZAS IMPROVE THE STREET

200' of frontage. Buildings face directly upon the passing sidewalk

Cities sometimes hesitate to take the required properties from the tax rolls, or to assume the burden of upkeep. Yet the increased tax revenues generated by New York City's Central Park or Paley Park, as examples, far outweigh all municipal costs. The presence of the Cascade Gardens and Plaza in Rockefeller Center, as another case in point, has made the Center a national landmark and sustained rental values at peak for over thirty years.

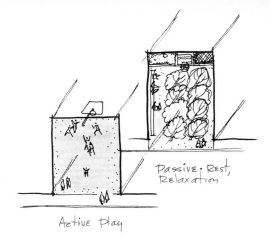

Active Play

Passive, Rest, Relaxation

USE THE VACANT CITY LOTS

Construct waterfront parks

Open park spaces and walkways which give access and views of the canals, streams, rivers, lakes, or beaches provide welcome relief to the buildings and pavement. They afford the best possible frontage for hotels, apartments, and business offices.

Plan a series of small parklets on narrow, vacant, city lots

These often transform problem properties into refreshing breathing spaces in the densely built-up blocks.

Line the streets with shade and flowering trees

Few investments can do as much to enhance a building or avenue. A systematic tree-planting program by the municipality, or a campaign by a civic action group, can transform a sterile trafficway into a verdant *allée*.

A theme tree such as oak, sweet gum, magnolia, or flowering cherry, or in warmer climes, the black olive, mahogany, or palm, might be considered for each street or district of the city.

Install attractive street and area lighting

Select a family of coordinated and well-designed standards and globes.

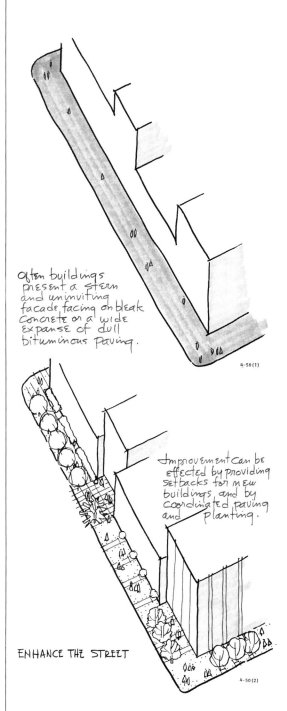

Often buildings present a stern and uninviting facade facing on bleak concrete or a wide expanse of dull bituminous paving.

4-50(1)

Improvement can be effected by providing setbacks for new buildings, and by coordinated paving and planting.

ENHANCE THE STREET

4-50(2)

Furnish the streets for the city dwellers' convenience, comfort, and enjoyment

Embellish the pedestrian ways and places with benches, planters, drinking fountains, waste receptacles, and good-looking graphics. Attractive canopies or shelters at transit stops are welcome additions. Well-designed and well-placed magazine and flower stalls and telephone booths also help to enliven a streetscape, as do sculpture, murals, fountains, and night illumination.

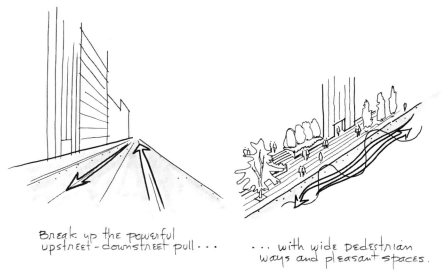

Break up the powerful upstreet-downstreet pull...

... with wide pedestrian ways and pleasant spaces.

Consider the use of handsome walk pavements

At walk intersections, building fronts, shopping malls, or other public gathering places, squares or patterns of colorful tile, brick, or exterior terrazzo will give relief from the normal stretches of dull concrete.

Screen the parking areas

On-grade parking areas are necessary service facilities which may add to, rather than detract from, the urban scene by the application of a few simple design controls. These should regulate points of entry and exit, signing, appearance of the attendant's booth, type and levels of

Parking lots and cars
seen from the city walks
and streets are less than
attractive.

By depressing the parking level
and providing boundary walls
and plantings they may be
converted into visual assets.

SCREEN THE PARKING COMPOUNDS

Further Reading:

Appleyard, Donald, et al.
The View From the Road
Joint Center for Urban Studies
MIT Press
Cambridge, Mass., 1964

Ashihara, Yoshinobu
The Aesthetic Townscape
MIT Press
Cambridge, Mass., 1983

Beauty For America: Proceedings of the White House Conference on Natural Beauty
U.S. Government Printing Office
Washington, D.C., 1965

Blake, Peter
God's Own Junkyard: The Planned Deterioration of America's Landscape
Holt, Rinehart and Winston, Inc.
New York, 1964

Bush-Brown, Louise
Garden Blocks for Urban America
Charles Scribner's Sons
New York, 1969

Clay, Grady
Close-up. How to Read the American City
Frederick A. Praeger, Inc.
New York, 1973

Goodland, Robert, ed.,
Power Lines and the Environment
Cary Arboretum, Millbrook, New York, 1973

Jacobs, Allan B.
Looking at Cities
Harvard University Press
Cambridge, Mass., 1985

Kovacs, M., ed.
Pollution Control and Conservation
John Wiley & Sons, Inc. (Halsted)
New York, 1985

President's Council on Recreation and Natural Beauty
A Proposed Program for Scenic Roads and Parkways
U.S. Department of Commerce
U.S. Government Printing Office
Washington, D.C., 1966

lighting, and the provision of a hedge or decorative treelined screen-wall along the facing streets. The depression of the parking area from one to several feet where feasible also helps to screen the cars and pavement.

Regulate the commercial signs

Take forceful measures to eliminate the chaotic clutter of signs and announcements which now profane most city streets.

Identification is necessary, and must of course be permitted, but on an equitable basis which spells out clearly by ordinance the permitted types, locations, and sizes of signs and advertising.

Initiate design controls

Many municipalities have prepared and issued a manual of landscape development standards which govern all new site construction and serve as guidelines in rehabilitation.

Such a manual governs not only pedestrian paving, street furniture, and lighting, but all other aspects of site and landscape planning as well.

Encourage area improvement

Inaugurate a program of public and private building rehabilitation. Here the city and county governments, perhaps spurred by citizens or the press, may lead the way. They can demonstrate their interest, and give example, by the improvement of public buildings and lands.

An effective crusade could be started, for instance, by the simple requirement that not less than 1 percent of the cost of all new public buildings be devoted to the installation of fountains, lighting, planting, or other site amenities beyond the normal landscape grading, drainage, seeding, and walk paving.

The countryside

When the word *scenery* comes to mind, one's thoughts turn to the open countryside. But the countryside is fast disappearing, at least from the view of the public roads. Exposure to highway traffic has brought with it the construction of industrial plants, motels, restaurants, truck stops, gas stations, and the whole range of enterprises which depend upon highway access and users. Countless frictions are thereby imposed upon the roadways. New connections and service roads must be built. Sewers, water mains, and power lines must be extended. As the improved land values increase, taxes rise with them, and the area farmers who have tilled the same fields that their grandfathers tilled are no longer able to make ends meet or continue with their farming.

New growth at the sides of Interstate 5 to the north of Seattle is claiming the fields of the prosperous bean farmers. The vineyards are also thus being squeezed out of California's Napa Valley. Farther to the south the artichoke farms are giving way to strip development along U.S. 101. Across the country, dairy farms, tobacco lands, pastures, orchards, gardens, and groves are all threatened by the same fate. What then is the solution to this dilemma?

It is not that development should be, or could be, stopped. It is rather that hop-skip patterns of growth are uneconomic, both for the entrepreneur and the agriculturalist, as well as for the communities which must provide the services. The answer lies in zoning and land-use controls for all highway corridors and interchanges and for the lands which surround them. Growth should be concentrated into residential or industrial parks, business-office campuses, and commercial centers where utilities already exist or where they are readily available. Prime agricultural land should be so designated and its use for the other types of development absolutely prohibited. While the main concern is for the more efficient use of our land resources, a secondary benefit is the protection of the rural landscape as viewed from the public roads. This, too, is important.

Aid rural communities in resource planning

Each state should assume responsibility for the provision of guidelines, incentives, and interim legislation to help localities in responding to new pressures imposed by highway and transit access, or rapid population growth.

Acquire additional right-of-way to conserve roadside features

Traditionally, highway departments have been authorized to purchase only that width of right-of-way which is required for actual road construction. In many cases it has been necessary to acquire a strip through a woodland or farm and to pay separation rights in excess of the cost of the total property. It is proposed that in such cases the entire property be acquired and held to protect the scenic quality of the roadway, or that excess land be leased back or sold, with restrictions, for purposes in keeping with the highway use. It is conceivable that the revenues thus received could be used for highway construction and operation, and would go a long way toward allaying the huge budgets presently required. After all, there is no reason for the random landowners or speculators to profit from the sale of roadside lands whose value has greatly appreciated solely because of the roadside presence.

It is further proposed that highway enabling legislation be revised to permit purchase of flanking lands of natural scenic value. By this means long swaths of unused woodland or floodplain could be preserved as a roadway enframement for the enjoyment of the public.

Create scenic-historic parkways

Within each state there are opportunities for the delineation of primary road systems which would link and traverse areas of unusual scenic and historic value. Such roads would weave between and around the cities, with convenient turnoff points. Farms, towns, and other appropriate uses at the sides would be zoned and protected, with access provided by local service roads. The entire highway corridor would be constructed as a parklike roadway and widened wherever necessary to encompass streams, ponds, or extensive conservation areas. The use of scenic and conservation easements would be employed, and travelers would be shown the region at its best.

Provide roadside parks and recreation areas

Several states, such as Michigan, Ohio, and Virginia, have for years provided tourists with welcome roadside picnic spots in the shade of a tree or beside a stream, overlooking a woodland or farmstead. Also, spaced out along the highways are rest areas and larger recreation parks for the comfort and enjoyment of their people and traveling guests. Few highway expenditures have yielded such rich returns.

Further Reading (cont.):

Simonds, John O.
Landscape Architecture: A Manual of Site Planning and Design
(Second Edition)
McGraw-Hill Book Company
New York, 1983

Stegner, Wallace, and Page Stegner with Eliot Porter
American Places
E. P. Dutton
New York, 1981

Tunnard, Christopher and Boris Pushkarev
Man-made America: Chaos or Control?
Yale University Press
New Haven, Conn., 1963

U.S. Department of Agriculture, Forest Service
National Forest Landscape Management, Vol. 1.
U.S. Government Printing Office
Washington, D.C., 1973

U.S. Dept. of Agriculture, Forest Service
*National Forest Landscape Management, Vol. 2
The Visual Management System*
U.S. Government Printing Office
Washington, D.C., 1974

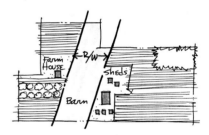

When highway right-of-way acquisition must disrupt the efficient operation of a farmstead or other enterprise, the entire property should be purchased.

Often the cost of the entire tract is less than the sum of the right-of-way land appraisal, relocation, provision of alternate access, and separation expenses

ACQUIRE THE ENTIRE PROPERTY

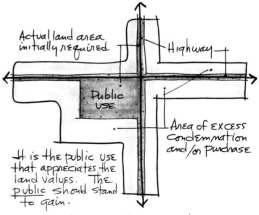

Actual land area initially required

Highway

Public use

Area of excess condemnation and/or purchase

It is the public use that appreciates the land values. The public should stand to gain.

In the acquisition of land for any public use or installation—such as a highway, airport, marina, national park, or military base—it is wise to purchase sufficient contiguous land for protection and future expansion. In the interim the land can be leased for compatible uses and supporting services—under restrictions.

ACQUIRE EXCESS LAND
FOR GROWTH AND PROTECTION

5 Noise

. . . noise is receiving widespread recognition as one of the major environmental problems of our age, with the forces of government and industry directed toward an accelerated search for solutions.

WILLIAM R. TALBOTT
''Noise''
Highway User Magazine
March 1972

It is absolutely impossible to sleep anywhere in the City. The perpetual traffic of wagons in the narrow winding streets . . . is sufficient to wake the dead . . .

The Satires of Juvenal
Rolf Humphries
Indiana University Press
Bloomington, Ind. 1958

America is the noisiest country that ever existed.

OSCAR WILDE, quoted by Richard Saltonstall, Jr.
Your Environment and What You Can Do about It
Walker and Company
New York, 1970

Noise has become a new form of trespass, a new invasion of privacy.

CHARLES ABRAMS, quoted
The Fight for Quiet
Theodore Berland
Prentice-Hall, Inc.
Englewood Cliffs, N.J., 1970

Decibel: A unit of measurement of the intensity of sound. Zero on the decibel scale approximates the lowest level of sound audible to the human ear. A sound level of 140 decibels (a sonic boom) can rupture eardrums.

High decibel noises, like the roar of the jets, are not the only levels that cause harm and should be regulated. Noises you do not notice can slowly deteriorate the microscopic cells that send sounds from your ears to your brain. In response to noise, small arteries constrict and thus pressure is put on the heart through an increase in the pulse rate.

You may think you have gotten used to a noise but your bodily system has not, and over a period of time your muscles, nervous system, and heart are taking a strain while your listening acuity is being dulled.

Certain low-frequency sounds of the city, although not within normal hearing range, can nevertheless cause blurred vision, nausea, headache, and a general feeling of malaise. They may result from traffic, the operation of heavy machinery, or even air conditioners.

Medical and acoustical experts have warned that noise levels frequently experienced by city dwellers are injurious to human hearing and can be the cause of permanent deafness.

Prolonged exposure to loud noise results in a permanent impairment or loss of hearing.

Noise is unwanted sound. It is usually rated according to peak noise as measured in decibels on the A scale of a sound-level meter and referred to, simply as so many dBA. The fewer the better. Noise abatement consists of reducing to an acceptable level, or preferably lower, the amount of sound received at critical locations.

While existing or projected *levels* of "sound pressure" can be measured with precision, the *effects* of noise upon the recipient are dependent upon other factors as well. Roaring, rumbling, or clanging sounds, for example, may have quite different audiopsychological impacts than a sharp report or screeching. Whether or not sounds are steady or intermittent has a bearing upon a subject's tolerance also, as does his mood or activity. Noise and vibration levels acceptable in a factory or a busy office, for instance, might be unacceptable in a home or classroom. Another important factor is the presence or absence of ambient background sounds ("accoustical perfume") which tend to cover up an interjected noise. Generally, however, it is the *amount* of noise that counts.

To give a sense of the relative magnitude of commonly experienced sounds, typical sources and noise levels are listed below.

Typical sound levels for common noise sources in dBA

Overall quality	dBA	Outdoor	Indoor
Uncomfortably loud	130	50-horsepower siren at 100 feet	
	120	Jet takeoff at 200 feet	
	110		Rock 'n' roll band
Very loud	100	Jet flyover at 1,000 feet	Newspaper press
	90	Motorcycle at 25 feet	Food blender
Moderately loud	80	High urban ambient sound; passenger car, 65 miles per hour at 25 feet	Garbage disposal, clothes washer
	70		TV audio, vacuum cleaner
	60	Air conditioner at 20 feet	Electric typewriter, conversation
Quiet	50	Light traffic at 100 feet	Average residence
	40	Birdcalls, lower-limit urban ambient sound	
Very quiet	30		Soft whisper
Just audible	20		Television studio, leaves rustling
	10		
Threshold of hearing	0		

Source: U.S. Department of Health, Education and Welfare.

A decibel rating of 70 outside dwellings or public buildings is about the maximum acceptable under most conditions. To the human ear, a 70-dBA level seems about one-third as loud as an 85-dBA reading. As a rule of thumb, every reduction of 10 decibels corresponds in turn to halving the apparent loudness of the sound.

The Noise Control Act of 1972 has categorized major noise sources as construction equipment, transportation equipment, motors, and electrical equipment.

These together, have produced a sound level that has been increasing in crescendo at an alarming rate, until doctors and scientists now recognize noise as a major cause of hearing impairment and often a contributing factor in nervousness, high blood pressure, and stress.

Noise abatement

Tests have indicated that people can become accustomed and adjust to relatively high levels of background sound, which nevertheless have a telling effect on their comfort and well-being. They are particularly distressed by those occasional noises, such as a sonic boom, or the roar of a passing motorcycle, that stand out above the norm. This would suggest two areas of concentration in noise control—both the reduction of the level of background sounds and the elimination of "peaks."

Eliminate noise wherever possible

1. At the source

2. At the path

3. At the point of reception

Since it is by definition undesirable, the removal of unwanted sound is bound to effect an improvement.

Muffle the source

This may be achieved by the redesign of the vehicle, engine, structure, or hull, or some component thereof, to eliminate friction, impact, or vibration. It may be accomplished by enclosing or shielding areas of sound emission. It may be a matter of modifying the characteristics of the sound, or the provision of absorptive devices. Usually, redesign for noise abatement yields side benefits of improved performance and efficiency.

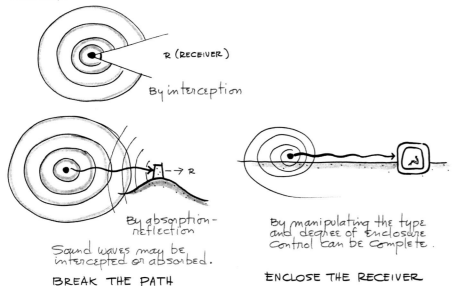

R (RECEIVER)

By interception

By absorption-reflection

Sound waves may be intercepted or absorbed.

BREAK THE PATH

By manipulating the type and degree of enclosure control can be complete.

ENCLOSE THE RECEIVER

Increase the distance between the source and the receiver

The level of sound decreases in inverse proportion to the distance between the receiver and the source of emission.

Break the path

To be effective, sound barriers must block the direct path of the noise.

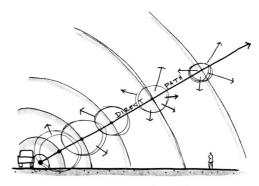

From any point on the direct path of sound projection, secondary sound waves of lesser magnitude travel outward in all directions.

THE TRANSMISSION OF SOUND

Recent studies have shown that noise at intervals or long duration besides bringing on gradual deafness, damages the heart and vision, produces indigestion and stomach ulcers, builds up hypertension, and causes mental disorder that sometimes leads to suicide.

Tests in which animals are assailed with noise at levels not far above those many people are routinely subjected to produce horrifying results within a short time—cannibalism, homosexuality, loss of fertility, and outright heart failure.

RICHARD SALTONSTALL, JR.
Your Environment and What You Can Do about It
Copyright © 1970 by Richard Saltonstall, Jr.
By permission of the publisher, Walker and Company
New York, 1970

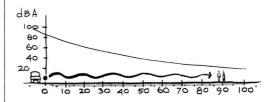

The isolation by distance of the emitter, or the receiver, is one positive means of sound abatement. The farther the source, the better.

INCREASE THE INTERVENING DISTANCE

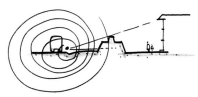

Sound shielding can be achieved by earth mounding, walls, or tunnel enclosure.

DEPRESS, OR ENCLOSE, THE SOURCE

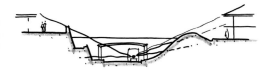

To be effective, sound barriers must block the direct path of noise. Next to complete enclosure earth mounds, masonry-clad dikes, or massive walls free of vibrating elements and impervious to sound waves, give maximum protection.

INTRODUCE A DENSE BARRIER

Architectural planning can effectively limit intruding noise. A building can be so designed that functions compatible with more noise are placed in the noisier locations, and so that more sensitive areas can be shielded by less sensitive areas. The use of air-conditioning that permits occupants to close windows and doors, and careful attention to the acoustic details of framing, wall construction and surfaces can also greatly reduce noise levels.

PETER A. FRANKEN
Vice-President, Bolt Beranek and Newman Inc.
From a paper presented at the American Medical Association's Sixth Congress On Environmental Health
Chicago, Ill., April 1969

Earth mounds, masonry-clad dikes, or massive walls free of vibrating elements and impervious to sound waves give maximum protection.

Reflect the sound waves

Sound waves, like light waves, may be directed; they may be diffused; or they may be broken up by coarse, grooved, studded, or baffled receptors.

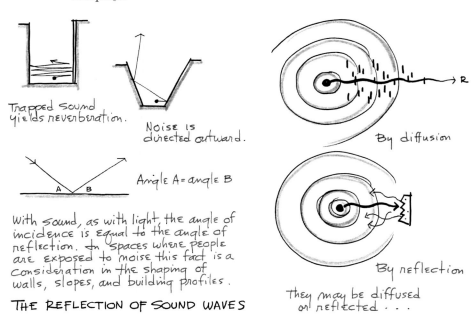

Trapped sound yields reverberation.

Noise is directed outward.

Angle A = angle B

With sound, as with light, the angle of incidence is equal to the angle of reflection. In spaces where people are exposed to noise this fact is a consideration in the shaping of walls, slopes, and building profiles.

THE REFLECTION OF SOUND WAVES

By diffusion

By reflection

They may be diffused or reflected . . .

Shield the receiver

Much can be achieved also by site planning and landscape design. With careful plan layout approach courts, activity areas, and service compounds can be devised as highly efficient sound traps and barricades. Areas susceptible to noise impact may be lowered and dug into the sheltering earth, or shielded by embankments and mounding. Earth contouring can virtually roll the noise aside. Spaces can turn their backs to the sources of annoyance and focus away, or inward. They may be enclosed with massive rough-textured walls supplemented with dense screen plantings.

Absorb the rest

This may be achieved at any point of sound generation, transmission, or reception—either by the use of sound-absorbent walls, screens, or applied ground-surface treatment such as turf, exposed-aggregate paving, loose fiber mulches, or raked gravel.

Contrary to common assumption, the absorptive value of trees, shrubs, and vines is quite limited. They lack the mass and density required of an effective barrier; their twigs and foliage vibrate and are permeable to airborne sound. A fringe of pine or oak trees at the edge of a highway, for instance, will reduce by no more than a few decibels the sound of a passing truck. Bank plantings of honeysuckle, ivy, or low evergreens will help with another decibel or two as a supplementary aid.

As a visual barrier, however, plant material has a positive psychological value. Existing growth preserved, or new plantings installed to provide such a screen, can be highly effective, for what is out of sight is often out of mind.

Valuable existing and vegetative cover may be preserved as a community asset by leaving the natural slopes undisturbed. This can often be accomplished by judicious horizontal and vertical highway alignment and by the use of retaining walls, rip-rap, and terracing.

Enforceable standards

In the United States the establishment of mandatory and uniform levels of maximum noise emission, from sources of all types, is long overdue. For some reason, perhaps because of lack of precedent, few agencies or governmental bodies have faced up to the problem.

Noise impact criteria must be based both upon environmental protection and reasonable efficiency in the design and operation of production centers, structures, vehicles, and trafficways. Communities tend to be ultraconservative in wishing to preclude any additional noise intrusion. On the other hand, manufacturing, transportation, and operating interests forcefully oppose limitations on levels of noise emission. In resolving the conflict, both wisdom and determination are required.

Establish maximum permissible levels of sound

As a guide, to be modified in the light of further experience, the following table of recommended standards is proposed.

Maximum permissible noise level in dBA °
(Three years from date of code enforcement)

Noise source	Place of measurement	Zones				
		A	B	C	D	E
Airports—all types	Airport property line	80	NP	NP	NP	NP
Aircraft—overflight	Ground level through-					
	out city	80	75	70	60	55
Passenger cars	25-Foot distance	80	75	70	70	55
Trucks and busses	25-Foot distance	80	75	70	70	55
Motorcycles, snowmobiles	25-Foot distance	80	75	70	NP	NP
Construction equipment	25-Foot distance	80	75	**	**	**
Other equipment, tools, etc.	25-Foot distance	80	75	**	**	**

* These proposed dBA readings are approximate and in practice might be modified by such technical factors as sound classification, frequency, length and time of occurrence, and exceptions.

** By permit, new construction or repair only.

NP Not permitted.

Zones:

A   Heavy industry, railway yards, airports.

B   Light industry, freight terminals, trucking routes.

C   Commercial, expressway, and transit corridors, waterways permitting power craft, active recreation areas.

D   Residential, schools, churches, hospitals, campuses, office parks, parkways.

E   Passive recreation, conservation areas, nature preserves.

Adopt and apply the standards

It is recommended that such a set of standards be adopted and enforced by local governments. As a first requirement it is important that one department or officer be designated and empowered to coordinate all noise-control activities. Then, with clear authority, the coordinator can outline necessary procedures and set about to ensure their implementation. Again, in the absence of effective local legislation or enforcement, the next higher jurisdiction, the county or the state, may step in to assume interim responsibility.

Municipalities must do what they can to help themselves, and what they can do to get others to act in common cause of controlling destructive noise.

Acceptance or designation of responsibility for urban environmental noise pollution is a first requirement.

MELVILLE C. BRANCH
Outdoor Noise and the Metropolitan Environment
American Society of Planning Officials
Special Report
Chicago, 1970

Decibel zoning

Noise will never be completely eliminated from our living and working places. The problems, however, can be greatly alleviated by the grouping of land uses in relation to their relative noise production and their limits of tolerance. This requires a systematic planning approach. As a first step, sound-level surveys will indicate existing locations and magnitudes of noise generation. They will indicate, clearly, the need for controls. They will also provide the basis for the establishment of zones within which regulated levels of sound emission will be permitted.

Good land management will not only guide the development of vacant lands by establishing zones of compatible sound levels and land use; it will also provide for the orderly conversion of existing and nonconforming uses.

This suggests the preparation of an "isodecibel" map for each planning district under consideration, showing by contour the varying bands (zones) of maximum sound intensity permitted.

Conduct noise-intensity surveys

With a suitable city map as a base it is informative to plot field readings of existing noise levels. Any good sound meter may be used to record for each location tested a series of readings taken at various times of the day or week to check the highest and lowest incidence of

A regional isodecibel zoning site.

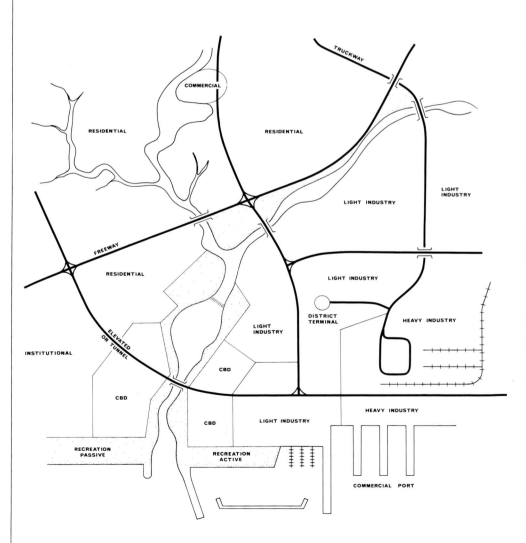

sound. From the readings logged from each location tested, the mean dBA level can then be computed and recorded.

Readings are usually taken at all street and highway intersections, at the top and bottom of all steep grades, and at points where street traffic must stop and start. They are also taken at points 25 feet from all major sources of outdoor sound, excluding sites of temporary repairs or construction. The sound from passing vehicles, motorboats, and overflying planes is usually noted, together with a comment as to source.

For future reference in sound-abatement testing it is helpful to take additional readings at points 25 feet from the entrances and facing walls of apartments, schools, hospitals, churches, and at such other areas as zoos, parks, or public gardens where noise levels are critical.

Correlate land uses and noise levels

On the basis of sound-level surveys the existing and projected types of land use should be examined in relation to their degree of noise generation and tolerance. Where an existing use is located in an area of excessive noise, either the use must be phased out or the noise controlled.

While high noise-emission transit-transportation lines, for example, are often compatible with industry and shopping centers, they should be separated in the location and design stage from offices and schools and further removed from hospitals or residential parks. Uses most sensitive to noise should be protected by bands of intermediate sound generation. Areas producing higher levels of sound might be so

The most promising approach for avoiding future transportation noise problems involves providing sufficient distance and shielding between the vehicular source and the residential neighbor. Thus we must develop a rational program of land resources allocation, including not only the highways (or flight paths or rapid transit corridors) that are associated with the sources, but also adjacent noise buffer zones that could contain industry, outdoor recreation, shopping centers, and other less-noise-sensitive activities.

CHARLES ABRAMS
The Commerce Technical Advisory Board Panel on Noise Abatement, 1968

Legislatively as well as technologically, the U.S. lags far behind other countries in setting standards and instituting controls to curb noise.

RICHARD SALTONSTALL, JR.
Your Environment and What You Can Do about It
Copyright © 1970 by Richard Saltonstall, Jr.
By permission of the publisher, Walker and Company
New York, 1970

A regional isodecibel plan (theoretical). Maximum permissible dBA ratings for the zones are indicated.

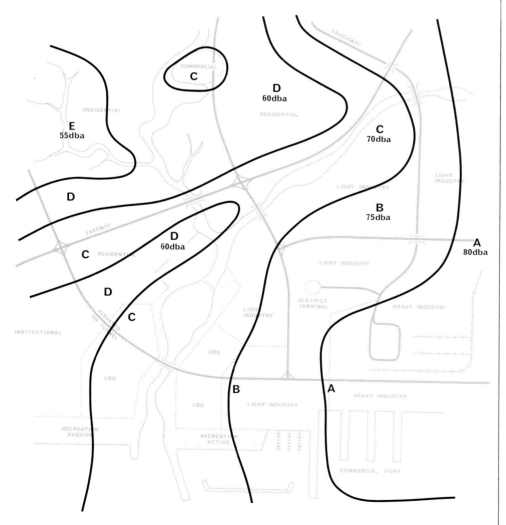

Noise is getting worse all the time—by approximately one decibel a year.

It causes loss of hearing and sleep, interferes with relaxation and thought, creates stress, and destroys the serenity of the out-of-doors.

There are no meaningful noise controls over the sources which bother people most—trucks, motorcycles, planes, automobiles, and construction equipment.

Further Reading:

Baldwin, Malcolm F.
The Off-Road Vehicle and Environmental Quality
The Conservation Foundation
Washington, D.C., 1974

Berland, Theodore
The Fight for Quiet
Prentice-Hall Inc.
Englewood Cliffs, N.J., 1970

Bragdon, Clifford R.
Noise Pollution: The Unquiet Crisis
University of Pennsylvania Press
Philadelphia, 1972

Committee on Environmental Quality
Noise: Sound Without Value
Federal Council for Science and Technology
Washington, D.C., 1968

Crocker, Malcolm J.
Noise Control
Van Nostrand Reinhold Company Inc.
New York, 1984

Jones, Dylan M., and Anthony J. Chapman, eds.
Noise and Society
John Wiley & Sons, Inc. (Wiley-Interscience)
New York, 1984

Lara-Saenz, A., R. W. Stephens, eds.
Noise Control Scope Twenty-Four
(Scientific Committee On Problems of the Environment)
John Wiley & Sons, Inc.
New York, 1985

Miller, Richard K., and Albert Thumann
Fundamentals of Noise Control
Fairmont Press
Atlanta, 1985

Saltonstall, Richard, Jr.
Your Environment and What You Can Do about It
Walker and Company
New York, 1970

Transportation Noise and Its Control
U.S. Department of Transportation
U.S. Government Printing Office
Washington, D.C., 1972

arranged that the noise would be concentrated at the center while tapering off toward the more quiet surroundings.

Zone the landscape according to acceptable levels of sound

Only by the adoption of mandatory noise-level standards related to a zoning map, or land-use categories, can noise control be administered as a manageable aspect of planning.

Translate concern into action

Noise control is expensive. While much can be achieved through intelligent land-use planning, almost all aspects of noise reduction include factors of cost for additional space, shielding, muffling, or redesign. But when noise becomes first an irritant, then an intolerable environmental condition, and finally a menace to hearing and health, the expense is one that must be allocated and borne.

With noise levels and peaks mounting steadily to critical proportions, the need has become so obvious that people are demanding relief whatever the cost. Airline and highway officials are drastically revising their plans and budgets in response to growing indignation at noise pollution. Industry is being forced to comply with new standards. Legislators are being put on the alert.

The public is learning that noise need not be tolerated. If the tranquility of a waterfront resort is shattered by the roar of speedboats, a reasonable time must be allotted by ordinance for the redesign of the engines, or the boats ordered off the water. If the peace of a park preserve or residential countryside is disrupted by snowmobiles, they must be confined to restricted areas or prohibited from operation until modified and soundproofed. Powerboats, trail bikes, and many sports cars are noisy because they have been designed to be noisy. If the din is objectionable enough to enough people, they have effective recourse in demanding new legislation and strict law enforcement. As in so many other aspects of life, an informed public, moved to action, has surprising political clout.

No one has power except from the people. . . .
This is the condition of a free people . . . to
be able to give or to take away by their votes
whatever they see fit.
  CICERO (49 B.C.)
  As quoted in *Public Officials and Their Heritage*
  Public Administration Service
  Chicago, 1958

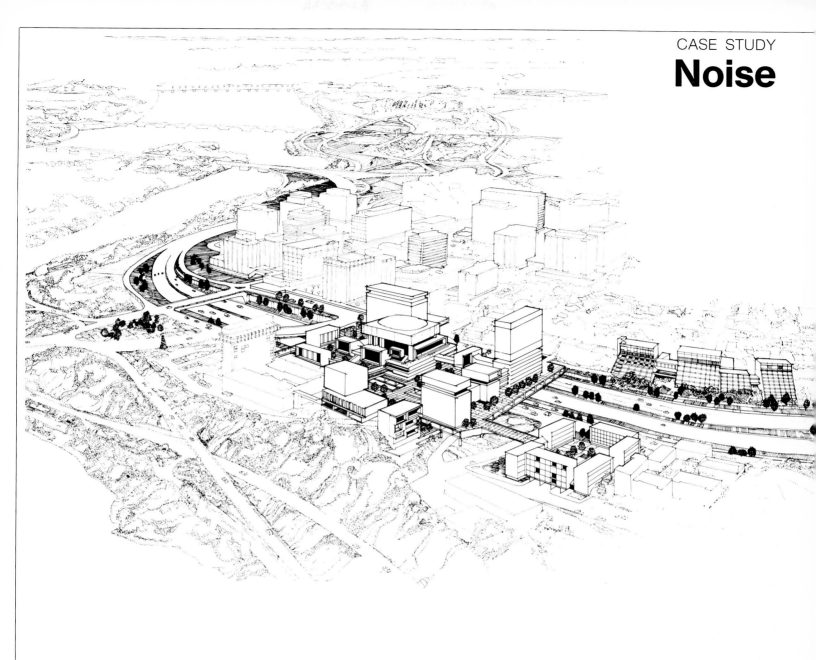

This case study presents a proposed solution to the problems of noise, separation, land-taking, and disruption attending the construction of an urgently needed segment of the I-66 freeway approach to our nation's capital. The highway, together with many of the suggested ameliorating features, has since been installed.

This example demonstrates the acoustical (and other) problems and solutions relating to the proposed construction of an interstate highway segment through the urbanizing region which lies across the Potomac from the nation's capital.

The material has been condensed from a comprehensive study conducted in cooperation with the Virginia Department of Highways and the Federal Highway Administration and completed in 1973. Its purpose was to devise

those feasible means by which negative highway impacts can be ameliorated and the benefits increased.

In the initial briefing the planning team was instructed to:

1. Ensure the harmonious integration of the highway into the adjacent communities.

2. Assume the highest standards of, and innovative approaches to, highway design, construction, and operation.

3. Conduct the study in such a manner that, when completed, this section of Virginia Interstate Route 66 and its environmental quality would become exemplary.

In the progress of the work, roadway-generated sound was to become a central concern. It is dealt with particularly in this case study

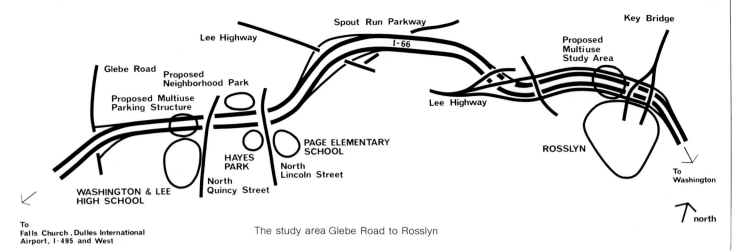

The study area Glebe Road to Rosslyn

summary. While the material presented is not purported to be a full or scientific treatise on the subject, it should give an instructive insight into the problem of highway noise and what can be done to reduce it.

Virginia is proud of her roadways, which rank among the most beautiful in the nation. Her rural, primary, parkway, and freeway systems have been precedent setting.

But, as Commissioner Douglas B. Fugate has noted, there are new and far-reaching considerations emerging in highway design, especially in urban areas. Highway departments, with great demands upon their resources, are finding that it is no longer enough to provide safe and efficient traffic movements to and within metropolitan areas. It is being recognized that urban highways must not only preserve the natural and man-made assets of the communities through which they pass; they must be closely coordinated with existing and future land-use patterns. They can and must provide an imaginative framework for the entire evolving metropolitan region. Planned in cooperation and coordination with local governmental agencies and civic action groups, they may set the pattern for, and give impetus to, city improvement, revitalization, and orderly growth.

The route along the Washington and Old Dominion Railroad right-of-way has been well selected to preclude disruption of major natural and man-made features and to minimize the need for acquisition of private properties. The roadway will of course bring with it a certain amount of noise, fumes, and glare; these must be eliminated or abated to reasonable levels of acceptability. There will be severed streets and connections; new vehicular and pedestrian connections must be provided. The right-of-way taking has reduced the inventory of parcels available for development; such areas are to be restored where feasible through the possibilities of multiple use. An important aspect must also be the consideration of all means by which the highway may contribute to the well-being, workability, and quality of the surrounding community.

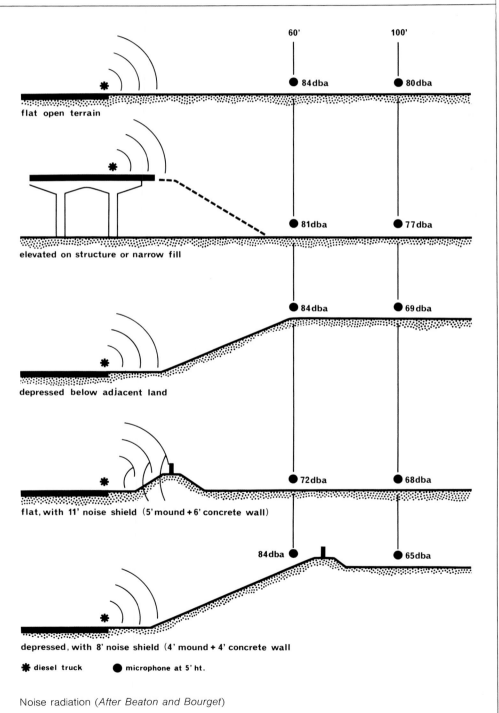

flat open terrain

elevated on structure or narrow fill

depressed below adjacent land

flat, with 11' noise shield (5' mound + 6' concrete wall)

depressed, with 8' noise shield (4' mound + 4' concrete wall

✳ diesel truck   ● microphone at 5' ht.

Noise radiation (*After Beaton and Bourget*)

Noise abatement

The prospect of noise emission from motor vehicles on *Interstate Route 66* is one of the foremost problems in terms of community reaction. This is one of special concern in the section between Glebe Road and Rosslyn where homes, apartments, schools, and other structures lie in proximity to the roadway.

In the design of noise-abatement devices for highway-generated sound a first task must be to establish criteria for acceptable levels. This is difficult since in the United States neither legal standards nor generally agreed-upon ratings of permissible noise existed at the time when this work was initiated. It was therefore decided to consider the levels of sound which would be experienced by those who live and work adjacent to the proposed freeway and at the points at which the sound would be received.

As a working premise it was determined that a desirable goal would be the achievement of mean sound-pressure readings of less than 68 decibels at a point 5 feet above grade at the nearest building walls. Generally, all highway-related sound levels within the community were to be reduced as far as feasible. Special emphasis was to be given to areas of particular sensitivity—such as schools, business offices, parks, and recreation areas.

It is found in highway planning that the owners of adjacent properties are particularly disturbed at the prospect of traffic-generated sound. When irate citizens storm the public highway hearings, they are speaking mainly of noise.

Their concern is made graphically clear in a series of sections (page 132) showing the sound levels to be expected along the roadside from the passing of a single diesel truck. This source is used as the reference standard since the diesel truck is normally the major source of peak decibel reading for highway noise.

Sound levels typically experienced

Experience has shown that public reaction to noise peaks can be quite accurately charted as follows:

Peak noise near residence In Decibels	Reaction
Over 85	Legal committee activity with influential or legal action
80–85	Petition of protest
77–80	Letters of protest
73–77	Complaints likely
70–73	Complaints possible
62–70	Complaints rare
Under 60	Acceptance

An indoor noise level of 35 to 45 decibels is suggested as a maximum for apartments and houses. An exterior noise level of 70 decibels can usually be reduced to 45 decibels by closing windows facing the source. If windows facing the noise source are partly open, an exterior noise level less than 60 decibels is desirable.

The physical measurement of sound or noise is difficult because there is no instrument which will directly measure human responses to sound. The most simple instrument for measuring sound, and perhaps the most underrated, is the sound-level meter. When positioned for measurement, the sound-level meter yields a direct reading in decibels.

The reading obtained from the meter is the overall sound-pressure level, which is an expression of sound pressure as it is related to a reference. The general reference of sound pressure is 0.0002 microbar. Typical overall sound-pressure levels obtained with a sound-level meter are shown in the following chart.

The following table illustrates the types of noise levels, in decibels, that are common to various land uses and street intersections.

In the VA I-66 study, as a means of comparison, readings of existing sound levels were taken along the major adjacent trafficways under the direction of the Highway Research Council. By means of a well-tested computer model, projected readings were then computed at a number of key control points along the freeway route on the basis of the preliminary roadway design.

A series of revised readings were finally projected at the same control points on the basis of proposed sound-abatement designs. The designs involve various combinations of road lowering, bifurcation, sound shielding by textured earth dikes or mounds, and the introduction of multiple-use structures and/or masonry sound-barrier walls. The designs were adjusted until the desired degree of noise abatement was achieved.

In exploring the various means by which highway-generated sound could be reduced to acceptable levels, each, in turn or in combination, was applied to the preliminary highway designs which were revised accordingly for testing. Models and designs were then modified to give optimum performance. It was only after the entire corridor had been studied that an itemized total estimate of the proposed improvement cost was assembled. At that time the full improvement program was reviewed and approved with minor exceptions as being within the range of feasibility.

The more practicable of the sound-abatement methods, devices, or structures applied include the following:

Change in roadway elevation

As a means of reducing the direct sound impact upon adjacent receptors, the raising of the roadway by embankment or elevated structures was explored. Although there were obvious acoustical benefits, the difficulties of cross-street grade separation and ramp connections, and the more desirable gradients of the original design, supported the original highway proposals.

The lowering of the roadway in several critical areas, however, proved to be beneficial not only in acoustical and visual improvement, but also in yielding additional fill material required for new earth contouring and sound dikes.

Bifurcation

A major improvement was effected by separating the eastbound and westbound roadways through a critical 2-mile sweep. By this means a mounded and planted divider island

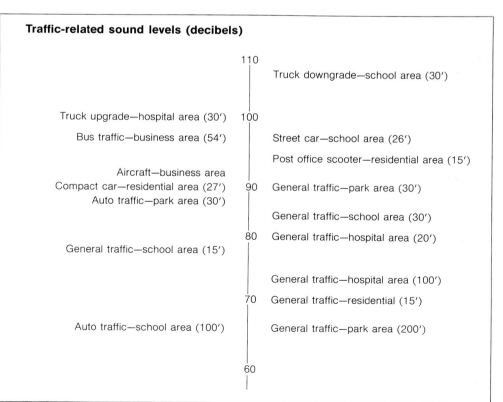

Traffic-related sound levels (decibels)

	110
	Truck downgrade—school area (30')
Truck upgrade—hospital area (30') 100	
Bus traffic—business area (54')	Street car—school area (26')
	Post office scooter—residential area (15')
Aircraft—business area	
Compact car—residential area (27') 90	General traffic—park area (30')
Auto traffic—park area (30')	
	General traffic—school area (30')
	80 General traffic—hospital area (20')
General traffic—school area (15')	
	General traffic—hospital area (100')
	70 General traffic—residential (15')
Auto traffic—school area (100')	General traffic—park area (200')
	60

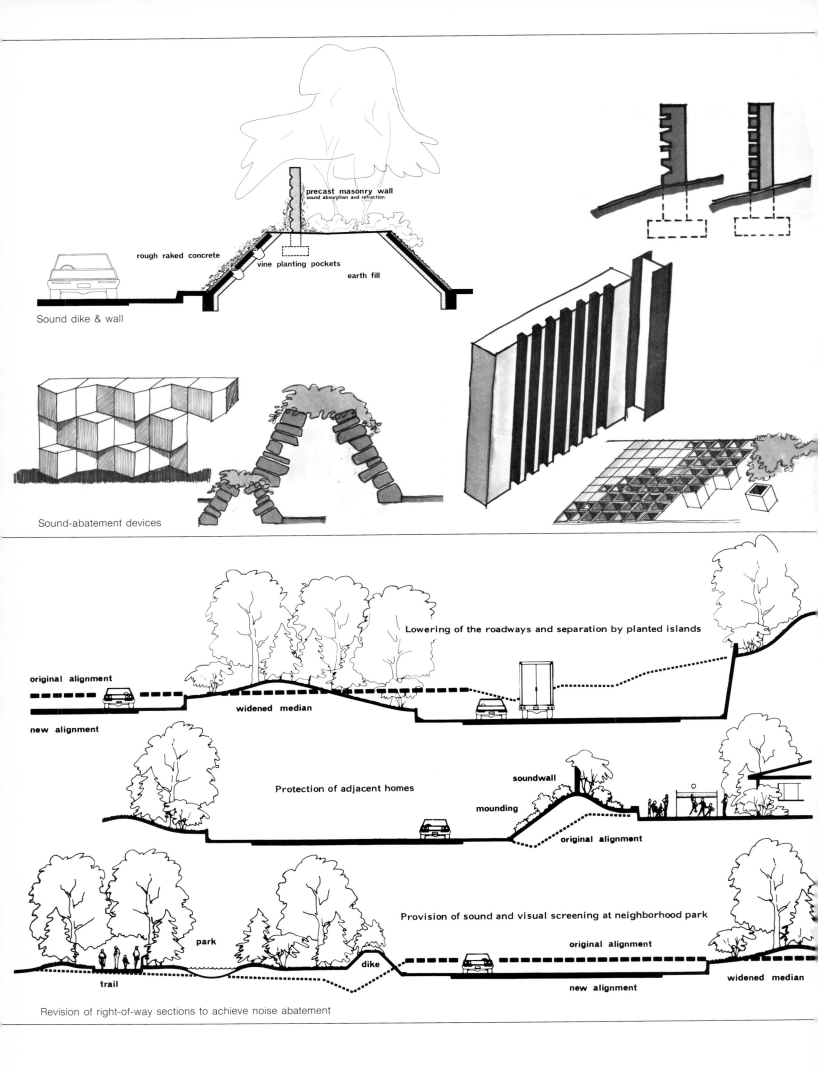

precast masonry wall
sound absorption and refraction

rough raked concrete

vine planting pockets

earth fill

Sound dike & wall

Sound-abatement devices

Lowering of the roadways and separation by planted islands

original alignment

widened median

new alignment

Protection of adjacent homes

soundwall

mounding

original alignment

Provision of sound and visual screening at neighborhood park

park

original alignment

trail

dike

new alignment

widened median

Revision of right-of-way sections to achieve noise abatement was introduced, the expanse of paving to be seen from any one vantage point was reduced by half, the glare of oncoming lights was eliminated, and noise sources were depressed and largely contained within retaining walls or embankments.

Earth mounding

The sound-absorbent qualities of earth make its use in contouring, mounding, and embankment a primary means of noise control. With and without a facing of masonry or rip-rap, it was used throughout the length of highway under study—with uniformly effective results.

Sound dikes

Where width for sound shielding was a limiting factor, sloping masonry-clad dikes with earth fill and planting were found to be highly functional. In some cases, they were topped with masonry walls to provide maximum shielding.

Sound barriers and diffusers

Masonry walls of various conformations, materials, and textures were analyzed for their sound absorbent-reflective characteristics. Generally, those with the most mass and density and with the roughest texture were found to be best.

Devices in combination

Using the many proven means of abatement in numerous combinations, the preliminary highway designs were modified through the process of comparative analysis until the agreed-upon objectives were achieved. The sections and treatment varied from station to station in response to conditions within and adjacent to the corridor, and to satisfy all requirements.

As an example of projected sound-abatement performance, a generalized iso-decibel map shows the approximate levels of mean sound pressure in decibels which will

prevail within the critical Glebe Road to Lee Highway environs when I-66 is put into operation.

It was made evident by the study that the existing sound levels on local streets will continue to have more adverse effect on the community than the sound which the proposed freeway will introduce. It is to be noted that the map does not reflect the reduction of noise to be achieved by new or existing vegetation (which was not included as a factor in the computer simulation). Nor does it indicate the lowering of noise levels on the existing streets which may be expected when the volume of stop-and-go through traffic is reduced by the presence of I-66.

Other design considerations

Beyond the problems of noise abatement the study team addressed itself to the provision of all possible additional environmental improvements. These included such features as the provision of new recreation ways and

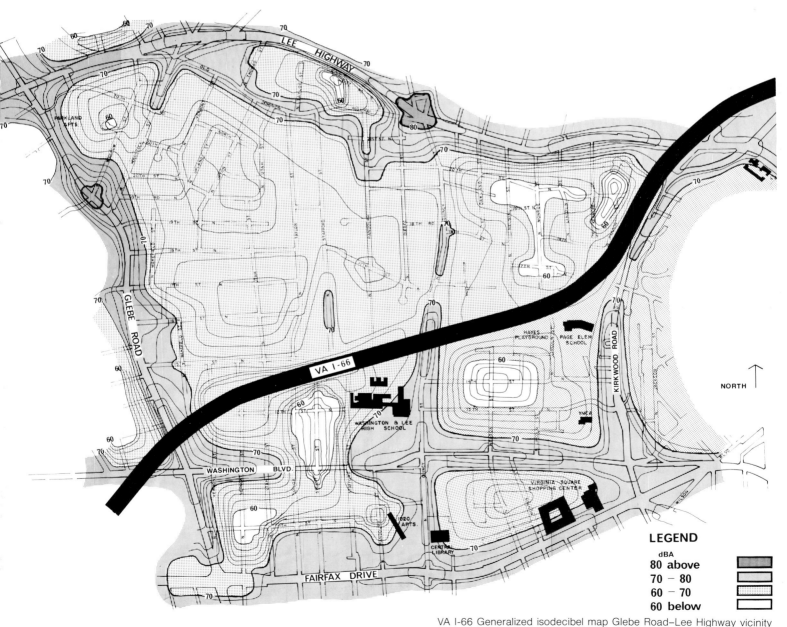

LEGEND

dBA	
80 above	
70 – 80	
60 – 70	
60 below	

VA I-66 Generalized isodecibel map Glebe Road–Lee Highway vicinity

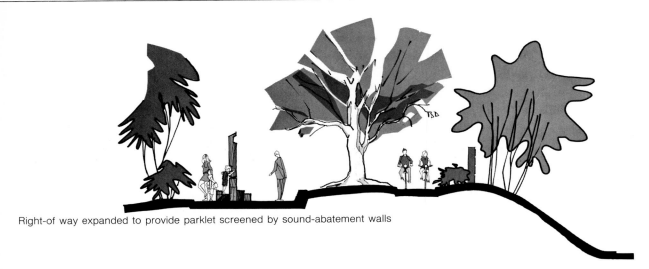

Right-of way expanded to provide parklet screened by sound-abatement walls

places, roadway enhancement, and multiple-use opportunities.

Parks and open space

Portions of the railroad right-of-way and other properties acquired for highway development will be available for improvement as a parklike enframement and can be set aside for public use. The roadway boundary fence will be placed well within the right-of-way. This will permit use by Arlington County of approximately 22 acres of parkland within the Glebe Road to Rosslyn corridor.

Included in the 22 acres of additional parkland are a 4½-acre neighborhood park and a 1½-acre parklet. In addition, community access will be preserved and extended by several miles of planted and illuminated walkways and bicycle paths. To ensure continuity of pedestrian movement throughout the neighborhood grade-separated crossings, pedestrian overpasses, and widened walkways are planned.

The development of I-66 through the study area will substantially increase, rather than reduce, the public open space inventory.

Other public and private uses

While large areas will be reserved by the Department of Highways for screening and landscape planting, much of the right-of-way required for construction of the freeway will be returned to the public after grading and improvement, as open space land. Where feasible, improved property will also be provided to schools for their use. In other instances, where suitable, land adjacent to institutions or private dwellings may be made available to the owners by easements or lease agreement.

Bridges and overpasses

The design of the bridges and overpasses is being modified by the Department of Highways to reflect the revised roadway alignment, width, and grade. Essentially, however, it is proposed that as simple and expressive engineering structures their form remain unchanged. It is strongly recommended that no decoration be applied, as by formed textured

patterns, or by brick or stone veneer. Such a treatment, installed at considerable public expense, only makes the bridges look dated and ponderous.

It is proposed that the bridges and overpasses be kept as light and graceful in profile as possible, with a concrete finish in a warm off-white. An added feature would be the use of color in the metal girders which could match that of the highway lighting standards and other hardware in a coordinated system of subdued and attractive colors.

Roadway paving

An investigation has been made as to the comparative desirability of various paving types in relation to their environmental impact.

It is concluded that, of the three major alternate types of pavement under consideration, the order of desirability is as follows:

Preferred. Bituminous concrete, medium texture.

Less Desirable. Continuous ribbon concrete.

Least Desirable. Conventional concrete slab.

The factors considered included relative safety, noise abatement, striping and lane demarcation, daytime and nighttime glare, staining and discoloration, and general landscape character. Relative costs, wear resistance, maintenance, and other such engineering factors were not made a part of the study.

Safety. Available evidence indicates that under comparable conditions bituminous pavement of medium surface texture is as safe or safer than normal concrete.

Acoustical Rating. Sound-level tests by the Highway Research Council, including recent comparative tests in Virginia, favor the bituminous concrete over either of the other types of concrete installations.

Lane Demarcation. On the basis of contrast in color values, surface aggregate and configuration, and relative permanence of the

striping, the bituminous concrete is preferable for clear traffic lane demarcation.

Air quality

Emissions of internal-combustion engines can be controlled realistically only at the source. Federal standards call for a 90 percent reduction in automobile exhausts within the next decade. The design of the highway can deter air pollution, however, by assuring smooth and efficient traffic flow and by encouraging quick dispersal of exhaust emissions.

Air pollution is generally heaviest on city streets edged with tall buildings and clogged with slow-moving, stop-and-go traffic. High pollution levels in the vicinity of other local streets can be reduced to the extent that I-66 reduces congestion and promotes free-flowing traffic on those streets. I-66, a limited-access highway, will carry traffic through a wide corridor descending to the Potomac River. High concentration of air pollutants is not foreseen on the basis of preliminary calculations.

Lighting and hardware

A fresh approach to direct and indirect highway illumination was made possible by a supplementary engineering study. The emphasis was the coordination of the lighting proposals with the overall environmental protection and improvement. New types of signing, lane demarcation, hardware, and signalization are also proposed.

Planting

The landscape planting of I-66 within the study area has been conceived to enhance the corridor and integrate the highway with the existing natural and scenic features while relating to and complementing the architectural character of the established neighborhoods. Schematic plans have been prepared to meet the following objectives:

• Provide the motorist with a safe and relaxed travel experience.

• Utilize the functional characteristics of the various plant materials to best provide pollu-

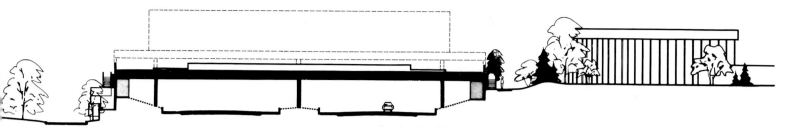

Section. Parking structure and future recreation deck to be built over the roadway.

tion abatement, glare control, privacy, and enframement.

• Identify and complement community features; create portals to the various neighborhoods and harmonize features of multiple use into a unified landscape. Sheath the highway with plantings of native shade and flowering trees to create the visual interest and scenic richness that typifies the Virginia landscape.

It is urged that ample budget be devoted to the installation and maintenance of the landscape development. The textured dikes and earth contouring will provide a strong and pleasant framework which, with well-studied planting, can transform the whole corridor into a handsome lineal park.

Multiple use

A primary purpose of the study has been to identify the kinds of multiple uses most suitable for inclusion within the highway right-of-way and upon adjacent properties. Such uses should complement, serve, and strengthen existing developments to remain. They should provide essential parking and additional building sites. They should, where feasible, augment the county's tax base. They should enhance the experiences of driving upon the highway and of living and working within the freeway environs.

Within Arlington and Fairfax counties there is opportunity to benefit from the full range of multiple uses. These include *air rights*. The space directly above the corridor comprises a vast new supply of available open space that can accommodate growth in directions not before considered possible.

Within the Glebe-Rosslyn sector two major air-rights structures are proposed as possibilities. The first deck of a multilevel parking terrace at Washington and Lee High School will initially provide much-needed storage for 384 cars to serve the school, the administration building, and the community. To provide recreational multiple use of the structure, six tennis courts will eventually be provided on two of the four decks while an open play space and parking will occupy the other decks. At off-peak hours a major por-

tion of the parking area could thus be converted to recreation purposes.

The parking terrace has been designed for expansion to accommodate an eventual 950 cars and a recreational pavilion providing either all-weather tennis courts or a wide range of alternative recreation facilities for the school system and citizens of Arlington County.

In Rosslyn there exists a unique opportunity for the planning of a civic and recreation center atop a multilevel parking structure. Such a terraced plaza, built on air-rights space above the freeway, would provide a parklike focal point for the urban core and unify the intensive commercial, business office, and apartment development which has recently occurred on either side of the I-66 right-of-way. (See illustration on page 131.)

Community benefits

The major environmental improvements and community benefits for I-66 between Glebe Road and Rosslyn are summarized:

• Construction by the Virginia Department of Highways, within the right-of-way, of a 2.7 mile segment of the regional bicycle trail and pedestrian parkway system.

• Provision of air-rights space for a 950-car parking facility and sports pavilion adjacent to the Washington and Lee High School.

• Construction by the Department of Highways of the first deck of the parking structure to accommodate 384 cars. This deck and its foundations will provide support for the future construction by the county of two additional decks and a multiuse sports center.

• A new neighborhood park of 4.6 acres. Included will be the improvement of an existing stream, the creation of a freshwater pond, and the establishment of an arboretum for nature study.

• Potential air-rights at Rosslyn provide the opportunity for the development of a unified civic-park center. Supporting parking decks and terraced plazas can unite the entire urban core into a magnificent regional focal

point. Approximately 22 acres of greenbelt land will be added to Arlington County's park and open space inventory. For the total 9-mile study section (extending to the I-95 Beltway) there are additional community benefits.

• The highway is to be enframed and screened with plantings of native shade and flowering trees. Considerable expenditure for landscape development has been budgeted to provide an immediate effect.

• Sound levels will be significantly reduced by earth moundings, sound-barrier walls, and by the lowering of critical roadway sections.

• The natural fall and open section of the highway, free of entrapped air ponding, provides a near-optimum condition for air pollution abatement. By reducing through stop-and-go traffic on local streets, the overall air pollution index of the area should be significantly reduced.

• New pedestrian crosswalks will be installed and others widened, to provide community linkage and to increase the safety of children en route to the schools.

• Roadway engineering improvements will include lowered vertical alignment, a planted median, extended safety-barrier height as glare shield, bituminous surfacing, and internal storm drainage.

• The integration of METRO mass transit into the transportation system for the I-66 corridor, with joint use of the right-of-way between I-495 and North Frederick Street.

• The entire highway corridor including the roadway, slopes, and highway-related environs has been studied as a work of landscape architecture to improve the travel experience of the motorist and the living experience of the citizens in the adjacent neighborhoods.

Note:
Although the construction of this highly controversial sector of I-66 is not to be implemented in the form described by this case study—many of the noise abatement and other environmental improvement features proposed have been adopted elsewhere.

6

Paths of movement

We must reject the kind of "ei-
ther-or" approach which maintains that the nation's transportation goals are inconsistent or
in contention with other personal and community aspirations. The question is not, for
example, whether to preserve an
historic site or to build a highway. Rather, the question is,
"How do we provide needed mobility and, in the same process,
contribute to other important
social goals—such as the preservation of historic sites?"

LOWELL K. BRIDWELL
The Freeway in the City
A Report of the Urban Advisors to the
Federal Highway Administration
U.S. Government Printing Office
Washington, D.C., 1968

In the United States, as in most developing countries, it would appear that the problems of transportation have become too complicated and too overwhelming for anyone—even the experts—to deal with. The various routes of movement for vessels, trains, trucks, buses, and the private automobile have become so intertwined, crisscrossed, and snarled that everything seems to interfere with everything else, and especially with the people who are trying to live and work within our metropolitan areas.

There seems little opportunity to sort out even the present conflicts—for the additional millions of miles of travel continue to soar each year.

The cause of the snafu is simple. The problem is that cities, like the transportation networks that serve them, to a large extent "just grew." Warehouses and mills crowded next to the wharves. Hotels and businesses lined up along the streets near the depots, with housing packed in behind. Streets were extended. The railroads tied harbors and mills and depots together. And over the years, new highways and airports have elbowed in as best they could to provide the additional access demanded by the public. Once the initial patterns were set, everything has just gone on from there—growing denser and squeaking or roaring more loudly as the pressures have increased.

The essential fact is that at no time in most municipalities have trafficways and land uses been studied together in terms of the most efficient and supportive relationships. Nor have the various modes or routes of movement been planned together as interrelated systems. Is it any wonder, then, that they are not?

It could be well argued that until quite recently the idealized planning of a more workable city would have been a waste of time. For in the formative days city governments lacked the powers or the legal machinery by which master plans could have been implemented. Neither the uses to which the lands were put nor the major routes by which traffic would move could have been preestablished. The rights of land use went with the land and to the people, groups, or agencies who owned the real estate. Such rights in property were considered to be inviolate.

Many things have changed in the past few decades. Entirely new concepts of "land rights," "public good," and "governmental authority" have evolved. The zoning process has withstood the court cases to test its legality, and it is now widely applied. Urban renewal, after a number of awkward starts, is coming into its own as an effective tool in the reshaping and revitalizing of our urban areas. It is only quite recently, too, that the disciplines of urban and regional planning have been developed on a scientific basis, and that planning departments have been formed within the various levels of government. These can now avail themselves of computer techniques, systems analysis, and improved methods of technological assessment. Even more recently, the U.S. Department of Transportation and Congress have ordained that all federally aided highways be planned together with local governments and on a comprehensive, continuing, and cooperative basis.

Perhaps the time has come at last when we can begin to put it all together. It will take a fresh new look.

Streets and highways

No one can make a convincing case that the use of the private automobile as a means of commuting is efficient, for the average cost per passenger mile traveled far exceeds the real and total cost to the individual and public of the same distance traveled by transit. Yet each year the number and *ratio* of passenger cars increases, and the miles of new streets and highways stretch on and on and on. To own and drive an automobile is, clearly, for the average American, an ingrained compulsion. It is not to be curbed by costs, highway taxes, or even by legislation, for few legislators would think to take from the voter his most prized possession, his car.

The way people move

Method of passenger trips between cities

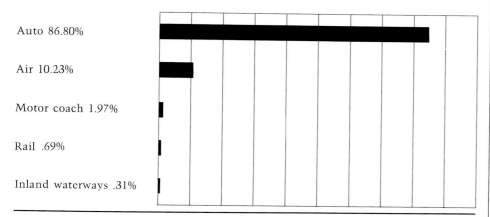

Auto 86.80%

Air 10.23%

Motor coach 1.97%

Rail .69%

Inland waterways .31%

Source: Interstate Commerce Commission and Transportation Association of America.

Since the habits of ownership seem to be a given factor, improvement must come in the form of improved vehicles, in new types and patterns of roadways and in new relationships of streets and highways to home, communities, cities, and the regional landscape.

First, as to the car itself. The clear necessity to conserve our fuel may at last signal the demise of that symbolic whooper-dooper, chrome-plated, super-American automobile. All who travel abroad should long since have been convinced of the economy and many

Energy data for passenger transport

Mode			
Intercity	Btu expended per passenger mile	Urban	Btu expended per passenger mile
Bus	1,600	Bicycle	200
Railroad	2,900	Walking	300
Automobile	3,400	Mass transit	2,800
Airplane	8,400	Automobile	8,100

Source: E. Hirst and J. C. Moyers, "Energy Efficiency in the United States" *Science*, Mar. 30, 1973. © American Association for the Advancement of Science.

Although 4-cylinder automobiles consume about half as much gasoline per mile as their 8-cylinder "big brothers"—approximately 80 percent of all American-made cars still sport 8 gas-guzzling cylinders.

A mandatory ceiling on automotive horsepower for private passenger cars—irrespective of the weight of the vehicle or number of cylinders—could at one stroke reduce by half our present gasoline consumption.

Without drastic use-curbs, the 6 million or more barrels of oil presently converted to gasoline each day in the United States will exceed 10 million barrels daily within the next ten years.

Larger cars require for their driving and storage roughly double the amount of space needed by a "compact."

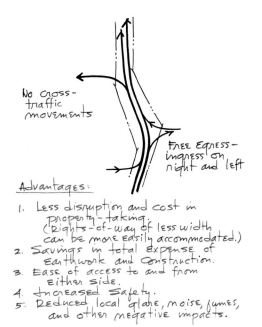

No cross-traffic movements

Free Egress-ingress on right and left

Advantages:

1. Less disruption and cost in property-taking. (Rights-of-way of less width can be more easily accommodated.)
2. Savings in total expense of earthwork and construction.
3. Ease of access to and from either side.
4. Increased safety.
5. Reduced local glare, noise, fumes, and other negative impacts.

THE WIDE SEPARATION OF ONE-WAY HIGHWAY PAIRS

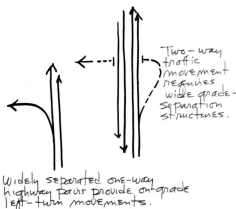

Two-way traffic movement requires wide grade-separation structures.

Widely separated one-way highway pairs provide on-grade left-turn movements.

ONE-WAY PAIRS REDUCE CONSTRUCTION COSTS

other advantages of the more compact, more maneuverable vehicles.

As long ago as the early 1930s planners were experimenting with residential neighborhoods in which automobiles and delivery trucks approached from, and were parked or garaged at, the periphery of the living areas. Homes, schools, and neighborhood life were focused inward to pedestrian parks, walkways, or plazas. This sensible concept is now being applied, with modifications, to many of the finer communities being developed in the United States and abroad.

By all reason the same principles will be extended to the planning of compact metropolitan centers around which, and between which, all vehicular trafficways will be routed.

It is proposed that in the not-too-distant future, arterial thoroughfares will no longer slice through our communities and cities to mutilate and divide them. Roadways, garaging, and transitways will be kept to the outside of the cores, or so integrated with the urban structure as to serve the centers and subcenters directly while eliminating all conflicts between vehicles and pedestrians. Highways and transitways will share the space at their sides, the ground rights beneath them, and the air space above with buildings, parking decks, and recreation facilities. Often the two-way arterials will be split into two widely separated one-way pairs of lesser width and of parkway characteristics; these will impose less environmental stress on the communities served, and have other benefits of savings in land acquisition and construction costs. They will be safer and they will look better, too.

Transportation-transit "ducts" will be planned into the urban structure and reserved (with interim uses) for modes of travel yet to be conceived. The need for freight vehicles on city streets will be eliminated by the construction of in-city and intercity freight tunnels, tubes, or beltways providing direct connection between all major airports, seaports, and other freight terminals. In such new cities people, vehicles, and goods will move freely, activity centers will function more efficiently, and life will be more humane.

Between the urban centers, future roadways will weave through the open countryside within multiple-use corridors of varying width which will embrace and preserve the farmlands, forests, and natural features of the terrain. They will sweep between parklike interchange nodes designed and expanded as open space community focal points, around which the highway-related motels, restaurants, service areas, and business offices will be grouped on their separate frontage roads and motor courts.

Movement through the outer cities will be by spacious parkways, with transport vehicles diverted to separate routes. As arterials and circulation roads approach the city centers, they will divide by level or alignment into one-way lanes. They will become architectural in character and will move around, through and underneath the structures in vehicular chases or terraces, or along the rooftops. They will never disrupt the activity levels of the major urban cores. On-grade traffic within the central city will soon be outmoded.

The future is sure to bring radical changes also in transportation modes. It is predicted that the most creative evolution will come in the improvement of the wheeled vehicle, and in roadways and expressways with entirely new characteristics. We may soon become accustomed to using three-wheeled "roundabouts" resembling enclosed and air-conditioned golf carts for our local travel. For greater distances we may consign ourselves to lightweight wheeled capsules which may be locked into electronically controlled "trajectories" along new types of high-speed roadways, or linked together for automated travel on air-cushioned guideways, to "cut out" again, for driver takeover, after having passed programmed interchanges. Individual units may be fitted together for express transportation to distant points within a carrier shell. We may expect long-distance movement of automated vehicles and passengers at super speeds by jet tube or jet rail.

Vehicles of the future will be equipped with force-field units to preclude collision. They will be cleaner, quieter, lighter, more efficient, and more compact. Certain it is that the privately owned 2-ton, 300-horsepower prestige symbols we now parade about the highways will be as obsolete as the circus wagons and steam calliope.

Plan circulation into the cities

As mobility is increased, horizons expand.

The whole idea of planning is to guide the evolution of the most favorable relationships between the kinds of things that will go on the land and the trafficways that will serve them.

Coordinate highway and all other transportation considerations in the comprehensive planning of each region

The entire process can only be tackled as a joint venture between the various agencies involved. Here is an ideal opportunity for the application of the *systems analysis* team approach that has been so successfully used in the study and solution of other complex problems. Examples include logistics in warfare, the design of advanced mechanical systems, and the launching of interplanetary spacecraft.

Keep the citizens informed

No matter how painful the public hearings—and they can sometimes be rough—it is important to let the people of the affected communities know what is being planned for them. Exposure gives feedback and highlights the problems, needs, and concerns. If the proposals are sound, this will become evident and they will gain public support. This, too, in a democratic society is a matter of importance.

Apply an interdisciplinary team approach to all street and highway planning

The planning process depends for its success upon close cooperation between the professionals involved, the engineer, the planner, the landscape architect, and the architect, each of whom has essential knowledge and skills to contribute. Other members, called upon as needed, will include specialists in more general fields such as sociology, economics, political science, and ecology.

Plan a hierarchy of streets and highways

They will vary widely in function and capacity, from local residential streets to commercial avenues, institutional boulevards, bus transit-

Four out of five United States families own at least one car. They add up to over half the cars in the entire world.

Between 35 and 55 percent of the land area of most American cities is devoted to highways, streets, or parking lots and garages.

In a very real and tragic sense, the automobile has taken over our cities.

Each year urbanizing regions assign increasing proportions of their land to trafficways, without reducing apparent congestion.

The increasing numbers of automobiles within our cities not only disrupt cohesive activity centers and destroy the essential networks of close pedestrian interconnection; they also contribute substantially to the din, and to the worsening air pollution.

Fifty years ago the automobile, destined to revolutionize the American way of life and travel, was a novel plaything of the wealthy. The travel modes of 50 years from now are seeded for the most part in inventions yet to come.
MARVIN R. SPRINGER
The Freeway in the City
A Report of the Urban Advisors to the
Federal Highway Administration
U.S. Government Printing Office
Washington, D.C., 1968

The circulation routes of the city, whatever the city's size, become its fundamental urban structure. If that structure breaks down, the city as a functioning whole ceases to exist.
DAVID LEWIS
Address at Pennsylvania Chapter American
Society of Landscape Architects
Hershey, Pa.
October 1966

Highway engineers can make, and have made, a persuasive case against the efficiency of conventional rail transit systems. Rail transit proponents in turn can cite damning statistics against the conventional use of the automobile as a means of moving warm bodies or freight.
The problem has been that both groups have traditionally considered the two methods as opposing and exclusive. Yet as engineers these professionals are our hope in solving together complementary and mutually supportive modes of transportation for the movement of people and goods. Only with such a total approach can a total solution be found.
PHILIP D. SIMONDS
Unpublished memo

It has been well said that every highway is a political statement.
The Freeway in the City
A Report of the Urban Advisors to the
Federal Highway Administration
U.S. Government Printing Office
Washington, D.C., 1968

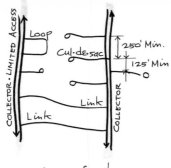

Keep frontage
off the collectors.

THE USE OF THE CUL-DE-SAC,
LOOP, AND LINK FRONTAGE ROADS

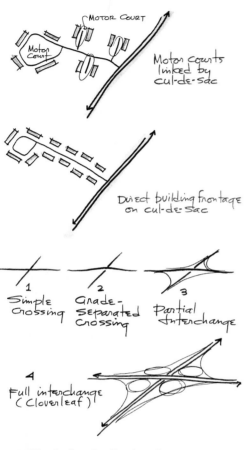

Motor courts
linked by
cul-de-sac

Direct building frontage
on cul-de-sac

1
Simple
Crossing

2
Grade-
separated
Crossing

3
Partial
Interchange

4
Full interchange
(Cloverleaf)

EVOLUTION OF THE HIGHWAY INTERCHANGE

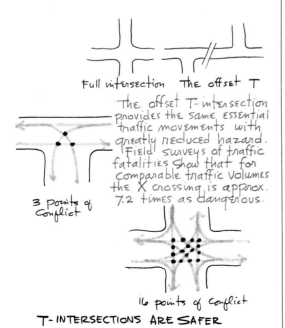

Full intersection   The offset T

The offset T-intersection
provides the same essential
traffic movements with
greatly reduced hazard.
Field surveys of traffic
fatalities show that for
comparable traffic volumes
the X crossing is approx.
7.2 times as dangerous.

3 points of
Conflict

16 points of conflict

T-INTERSECTIONS ARE SAFER

ways, trucking routes, and interarea freeways. Each, serving its specific purpose, will have its own distinctive form and character. All, working together, will function as a system.

Design local streets for low-speed circulation

Often narrow and curvilinear, they are best planned as loops, links, or short culs-de-sac. While by custom providing direct frontage for homes and apartments, they serve preferably as attractive circulation ways between planted residential motor courts and pedestrian plazas, around which the housing may be arranged.

Make use of the superblock

The short-block grid layout of traditional American streets makes no sense at all.

If streets are supposedly planned to facilitate traffic movement, how could one conceive of a less efficient traffic pattern than one which inflicts a crossing every two to three hundred yards? If streets are designed for pedestrian movement and safety, why should a child have to cross a succession of dangerous roadways on the way to playfield or school? If not then planned as safe and pleasant pathways for cars or people, what *is* the reason for stop-and-go through street grids? Could they have been considered desirable building frontage? Hardly, for why would one wish to face home, school, or office on a noisy, polluted traffic stream when instead it could face inward upon a pleasant tree-shaded park or courtyard?

A more rational solution for the design of traffic movement and living spaces lies in the superblock planning. By this well-tested device, the blocks are lengthened, and cross streets reduced in number or eliminated. Both vehicular and vehicular-pedestrian crossings are grade-separated wherever possible, and building frontage is not permitted on the major circulation ways.

Eliminate all at-grade highway crossings

Lanes of vehicular movement are dynamic lines of force. Whenever they cross, or even merge, there is potential hazard. Each time the flow of traffic is interrupted at a crossing, the efficiency of both the roadway and the vehicle is drastically reduced. Fumes and air pollution result; noise is increased by the acceleration and deceleration of the vehicles, and lives are endangered.

Grade separation of all new highway intersections, while more expensive initially, would result in freer traffic movement and increased capacities. Such crossings are safer; they look better; and they make better long-term economic sense.

Require the use of the T-intersection in new communities

Where streets or roadways must cross at grade, the use of two spaced-out T intersections in lieu of a full X crossing will prevent many accidents and probably save many lives. The number of vehicular pathway intersections is reduced as are the number of decisions and points at which they must be made. Where pedestrian crossings must be included at or near the street intersections, the advantages of the T are further increased.

Reserve the public trafficways for the movement of traffic

The dubious advantage of exposing homes and enterprises to view from the public streets may satisfy the homeowner's penchant for exhibitionism, or the apartment dweller's pride of address, but it also exposes the occupants, in turn, to the noise and hazard of passing vehicles. It may be a form of advertising for commercial ventures, in that their shops or offices may be seen by all who pass, but the rush of traffic may preclude ease of access or parking for their customers. Studies have shown, in fact, that except in the case of highway-related uses such as service stations and garages, frontage on arterial streets is usually more detrimental than beneficial to business. A further consideration is the drastic reduction of the traffic-carrying capacity of the roadways due to the conflicts of local movements.

Preclude building frontage on residential collector streets

These are best kept as free-flowing channels for the distribution of traffic at moderate speeds within a parklike setting. They add much to the quality of a neighborhood, especially when the right-of-way is widened to embrace such landscape features as streams, ponds, and native trees, or expanded by contiguous park and recreation lands.

Local streets branching off at intervals of 250 feet minimum provide the building frontage and driveway access to homesites.

Permit no parking on any public street

Roadways are best designed for the free movement of vehicles.

In advanced street and highway planning, all parallel parking strips or bays adjacent to traffic lanes will be eliminated. They add paving width, reduce visibility and capacities, and increase both friction and hazard. In areas of new development all parking space will be off-street, and provided within, or at the rear of, the abutting parcels.

Blend urban streets into the neighborhoods

New roadways are best "fitted in" to the topographical setting and to the existing patterns of land uses and streets. Every effort should be made to preserve the best of those community areas and features that give it its own unique quality and character. It is to be remembered that the purpose of highways is to provide access to, not through, established community centers.

Fit the highways between cohesive districts

While providing rapid and pleasant access, such roadways do not disrupt. They may even serve as welcome boundaries—as between industrial and recreational areas, or between commercial centers and residential parks.

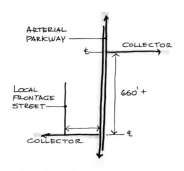

Arterial and collector roadways are best reserved for traffic movement, without building frontage.

THE ARTERIAL, COLLECTOR, AND LOCAL FRONTAGE STREET

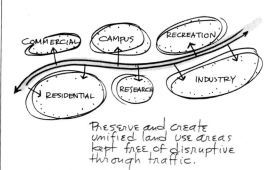

Preserve and create unified land use areas kept free of disruptive through traffic.

BYPASS THE ACTIVITY CENTERS

The design of the street is design for movement.

LOUIS I. KAHN
Perspecta 2

The design and location of the highway is usually dictated by such socioeconomic factors as minimum route mileage, least land acquisition cost, safety, public benefit, and toll charges or other cost-defrayment or cost-allocation schemes.

While these are valid considerations, other important economic factors should be considered; namely, the value depreciation of property along noisy expressways and the high cost of sound-proofing apartments, schools, churches and houses located nearby.

The Federal Council for Science and Technology
A Report of the Council's Committee on Environmental Quality
U.S. Government Printing Office
Washington, D.C., September 1968

Direct building frontage with ingress-egress on arterial highways is inefficient and dangerous.

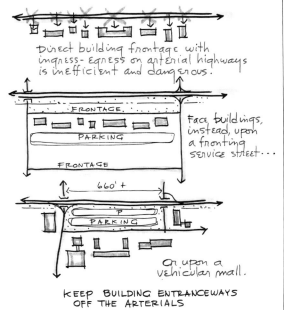

FRONTAGE
PARKING
FRONTAGE

Face buildings, instead, upon a fronting service street...

660' ±

PARKING

Or upon a vehicular mall.

KEEP BUILDING ENTRANCEWAYS OFF THE ARTERIALS

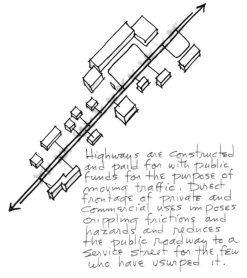

Highways are constructed and paid for with public funds for the purpose of moving traffic. Direct frontage of private and commercial uses imposes crippling frictions and hazards and reduces the public roadway to a service street for the few who have usurped it.

ELIMINATE ALL STRIP DEVELOPMENT ALONG HIGHWAYS

Design all urban arterials as controlled-access parkways

There is no valid reason any longer to permit the "strip commercial" or "apartment wall" development with frontage on these primary distributors. The resulting friction of stop-and-go let-offs, deliveries, and servicing all but precludes the free movement of vehicles for which the roadways were built.

If buildings must be seen from the urban arterials, let them face upon a parallel access street while the now freely moving traffic moves through a parklike corridor. Travelers, shoppers, apartment dwellers—all would benefit.

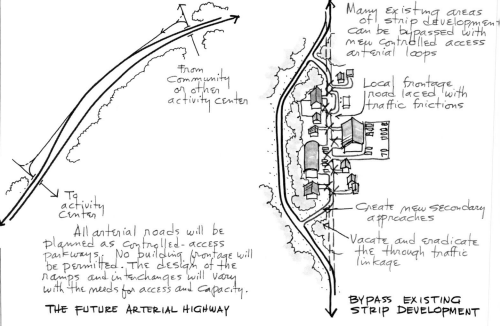

From Community or other activity center

To activity center

All arterial roads will be planned as controlled-access parkways. No building frontage will be permitted. The design of the ramps and interchanges will vary with the needs for access and capacity.

THE FUTURE ARTERIAL HIGHWAY

Many existing areas of strip development can be bypassed with new controlled access arterial loops

Local frontage road laced with traffic frictions

Create new secondary approaches

Vacate and eradicate the through traffic linkage

BYPASS EXISTING STRIP DEVELOPMENT

Promote the multiple use of the roadways

Within urban areas most roadways and other routes of transportation have traditionally traced a path of environmental degradation. Aside from the noise, fumes, and visual blight which they generate, their rights-of-way slice a wide swath between the uses on either side.

Most of these problems can be ameliorated by the application of the innovative but proven concept of "multiple use." This involves the use of the space above, below, and alongside the road for other than highway purposes. As examples, roadways, parks, plazas, office buildings, freight terminals, or parking garages can share the same land area but at different levels. All such construction must be planned ahead with ample "lead time," and designed in close coordination with the highway engineers.

By this one device, the roadway can be contained and concealed, building and storage space increased, valuable real estate returned to the tax rolls, and neighborhoods reunited. On federally aided highways, there is presently nothing to preclude this. The Department of Transportation has the legal authority and has repeatedly demonstrated its willingness to cooperate in such ventures.

Provide for subsurface deliveries and storage of vehicles

In the cities of the not too distant future, it is predicted that all deliveries and waste removal will be provided by underground distribution-collection terminals. The movement of freight and service vehicles, and the parking of private automobiles, will not be permitted on the city streets.

Provide transport trucks with their own system of roadways

Within the urban regions at first, and eventually cross-country, the slower-moving vehicles should be provided their own separate routes. Along these truck routes, or freightways, could then be planned the industrial, warehousing, and light-manufacturing parks dependent upon trucking. Freeways, freed of the cumbersome transport vehicles, would be much safer, more efficient, and less costly because of the reduced paving section and maintenance required. Fuel savings for both trucks and passenger vehicles would also be dramatic.

Bypass the city centers with freeway construction

Except under special circumstances, freeways should bypass the city centers, providing several choices of ingress and egress via controlled-access parkways to the inner distributor ring. Outside, and to a limited extent just inside this ring road, will be located the parking structures or compounds providing rapid transit access to the central business district.

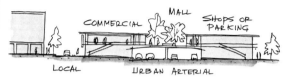

PLAN VEHICULAR ACCESSWAYS INTO THE URBAN ARCHITECTURE

Urban arterials may be depressed, elevated, or structurally integrated to provide joint uses of the right-of-way.

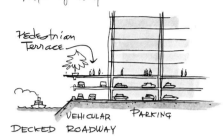

Pedestrian Terrace
VEHICULAR PARKING
DECKED ROADWAY

COMMERCIAL MALL SHOPS OR PARKING
LOCAL URBAN ARTERIAL
ROADWAY AT GRADE

SHOPPING PLAZA RECREATION ETC
LOCAL ACCESS
URBAN ARTERIAL
ROADWAY DEPRESSED

A street wants to be a building.
  LOUIS I. KAHN
In conversation

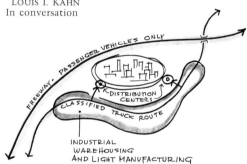

FREEWAY: PASSENGER VEHICLES ONLY
DISTRIBUTION CENTERS
CLASSIFIED TRUCK ROUTE
INDUSTRIAL WAREHOUSING AND LIGHT MANUFACTURING

Trucks and tractor trailers do not belong on the urban freeway system.

PLAN TRUCKWAYS, WAREHOUSING, AND INDUSTRIAL USES TOGETHER

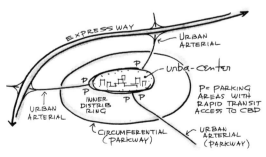

EXPRESSWAY
URBAN ARTERIAL
urban center
INNER DISTRIB RING
P = PARKING AREAS WITH RAPID TRANSIT ACCESS TO CBD
URBAN ARTERIAL
CIRCUMFERENTIAL (PARKWAY)
URBAN ARTERIAL (PARKWAY)

KEEP FREEWAYS OUT OF THE CITY

Surveys of several in-city freeways have shown that fewer than 4 percent of those traveling within the urban centers have any wish to be there.

147

Until quite recently most highways were built on the basis of the *cost-benefit ratio*—because that's what the taxpayers wanted. By this criterion the best alignment was that which provided the most miles of travel between given points at the lowest total cost for land acquisition, highway construction, and operation. Little consideration was given to visual qualities, to the disruption of farms, parks, or neighborhoods, or to the structuring of sound regional growth. We deserved what we got. Today, because of changing public attitudes, most contemporary highways are planned from the start to respond to such environmental factors.

Each city, county, region, and state would do well to avail itself of the various federal programs now in force to improve the quality of our highways. Many have not. Funds may be obtained for such purposes as control of outdoor advertising and junkyards, landscape development, acquisition of scenic overlooks, and the construction of rest and picnic areas.

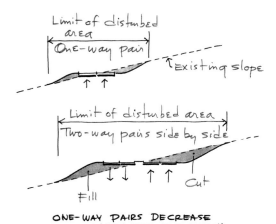

ONE-WAY PAIRS DECREASE LOCAL LANDSCAPE DISRUPTION

Steel or concrete highway structures should not be faced with decorative metal panels or masonry veneers. Beauty in freeway design rises from a combination of careful planning, the direct and sensitive use of materials, and able detailing. Steel and concrete if expressively used, are beautiful in themselves.

The Freeway in the City
The Report of the Urban Advisors to the
Federal Highway Administration
U.S. Government Printing Office
Washington, D.C., 1968

EXPRESSIVE CONCRETE STRUCTURES REQUIRE NO ORNAMENTATION

Align the roadways to eliminate ugliness and blight

Often a highway can be so routed as to replace borrow pits, strip mines, and refuse dumps. Sometimes the best arrangement is a joint venture between the highway department and the local park and recreation agency. With regrading and landscape development, the eyesores may be transformed into prized community assets.

Move lightly across the landscape

Both in location and design the highway should sweep easily through the landscape avoiding not only the man-made landmarks, but also those natural features of most scenic and ecological value. Sensitive highway planning can all but preclude the unsightly scars left in the wake of blasting and heavy grading.

Preserve the best features along the way

Until recently, the standard width of a right-of-way for each classification of federally aided highway could only be increased as needed to permit construction. Now, the amended enabling legislation gives highway departments the right to acquire excess land. This creates the opportunity to "build in" to the roadway such scenic features as groves, streams, and wetlands, which might otherwise in time be

destroyed by adjacent development. It can be seen that the best way to shield and "landscape" a highway is to acquire and preserve the best of the natural features and growth that already exist.

Screen the highways from the host communities

What the neighbors see, hear, and smell of a highway is as important as what the travelers see of the surrounding neighborhood. There are many things that can be done in the planning and design stages to reduce the negative highway impacts upon a community. Among these:

1. Locate the right-of-way so as to provide maximum insulation between the highway and abutting development.

2. Divide the two-way road into two one-way roads separated by a mile or more wherever it is practical.

3. Design the alignments to "roll with" the topography, thus requiring less disruption.

4. Depress the road to increase the shielding effect of the side slopes or walls in areas of unusual sensitivity where it is often feasible.

5. Preserve or plant tree screens.

Create beautiful highways

Beauty is seldom achieved by the application of ornament. It is, rather, a quality perceived when all the components are compatible and expressive. The most beautiful highways are usually those distinguished by restraint and utmost simplicity in the design of the roadway, structures, and appurtenances.

Designate as "scenic byways" all local roadways of exceptional landscape or historic value

All across the nation are to be found local roads of great charm and historic significance. These are to be identified and their character protected for the enjoyment of the public and as an attraction to visitors.

Scenic byways are best planned to permit only low-speed travel, with the narrow and circuitous cartways and local uses preserved. "Improvements" consist mainly of restoration, often by a historic society, and the provision of wayside recreation and rest stops and picnic areas. The existing uses, or compatible new uses, are protected by ordinances, and the route is marked by uniform trail signs. The benefits of local pride and tourist appeal are quickly evident.

Plan a system of recreation parkways

The remarkable popularity of the scenic highways and parkways built and operated by the National Park Service attests to the desire of most Americans for esthetically pleasing roads built primarily for recreation driving. These might provide for each state a vehicular greenbelt linking most of its recreational facilities, historic and scenic places, and natural wonders.

Scenic access roads will be provided to major recreation areas including particularly the state's larger water impounds. Special criteria and standards will be drafted to ensure the most desirable alignments and to protect the natural and scenic values—for traveling to recreation areas is an inseparable part of the recreation experience.

Some states are well along in the creation of a larger-scale scenic-historic roadway planned to connect and display the natural and historic superlatives, and to give citizens and visitors a memorable viewing of the countryside at its best. California and Texas have led

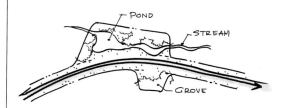

As a scenic roadside feature..

ACQUIRE SUPPLEMENTARY HIGHWAY RIGHT-OF-WAY

The ravage of scenic country roads has become a very serious matter in recent years; for as the city spills over into rural areas, the scenic roads are invaded not only by home owners but also by commercial and industrial establishments.

CHARLES A. GLOVER
Quoted, *The Highway and the Landscape*
Brewster Snow
Rutgers University Press
New Brunswick, N.J., 1959

The highway as a cultural asset is long overdue for consideration in the United States. With few exceptions, all the really inspiring rights-of-way, from the Via Appia to the Blue Ridge Parkway, contain strong esthetic elements which produce extraordinary scenic beauty. Every day we are missing opportunities to bring this beauty into our lives.

CHRISTOPHER TUNNARD AND BORIS PUSHKAREV
Man-Made America, Chaos Or Control?
Yale University Press
New Haven, Conn., 1967

The scenic parkway, such as the Taconic or the Garden State, is a typically American contribution to environmental planning.

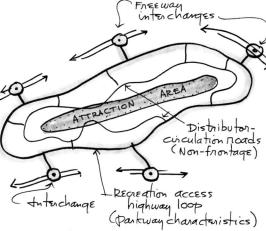

Provided the roadways are so planned the approach to the recreation areas can be recreation too.

PROVIDE SCENIC ACCESS ROADS TO RECREATION AREAS

After years of deliberation, Congress has now directed the Secretary of Transportation *"to determine the feasibility of establishing a national system of scenic highways to link together and make more accessible . . . recreational, historical, scientific, and other . . . areas of scenic interest and importance."*

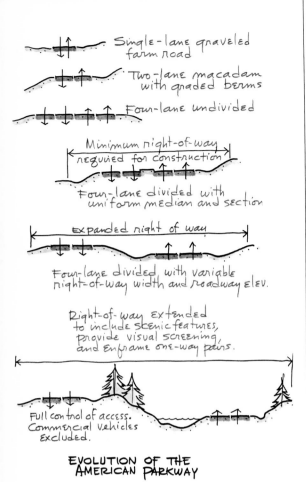

Single-lane graveled farm road

Two-lane macadam with graded berms

Four-lane undivided

Minimum right-of-way required for construction

Four-lane divided with uniform median and section

Expanded right of way

Four-lane divided, with variable right-of-way width and roadway elev.

Right-of-way extended to include scenic features, provide visual screening, and enframe one-way pairs.

Full control of access. Commercial vehicles excluded.

EVOLUTION OF THE AMERICAN PARKWAY

Circulation patterns should be regarded as major instruments for achieving better urban forms.

PAUL D. SPREIREGEN
The Architecture of Towns and Cities
McGraw-Hill Book Company
New York, 1965

Highways should lead, not follow, development.

JACK SCHOLL
Unpublished memo

Planned cities and urban redevelopment around the world demonstrate approaches to living and moving that can be applied to existing cities to arrest decay, restore vitality and guide further growth. They involve not only ways of improving mobility and accessibility, but also methods of making transportation contribute in a positive way to a quality urban environment.

WILFRED OWEN
The Accessible City
The Brookings Institution
Washington, D.C., 1972

Present highways are to a large extent the three-dimensional representation of existing laws. If more creative highway planning and design concepts are to be realized, they must be preceded by legislation to permit and encourage them.

MICHAEL RAPUANO
Unpublished memo

the way. And in Virginia the George Washington Memorial Parkway, the Blue Ridge, and the Colonial Memorial Parkway between Yorktown and Jamestown are someday to become segments of a grand statewide circuit.

Consider new highways as restructuring elements

With future highway alignments coordinated with all other means of transport in a region's comprehensive plan, they may establish a more functional development framework and stimulate healthy growth.

With a sound and flexible transportation and land-use plan as a guideline, a city can be gradually shaped, and reshaped, in accordance with the plan as it evolves. When we realize that most of the construction we see today in our cities will have been demolished within the next fifty years—we can sense the possibilities.

Plan well ahead

All forms of transportation are best studied together, at an early stage, with proposals for land development. Once the trafficways and development patterns have been brought into best relationship, the rights-of-way should then be acquired. The time to purchase land is when it is still vacant. Once building has started to occur, the right-of-way acquisition becomes extremely expensive and disruptive.

Amend the state and federal highway acts
to provide for environmental protection

Since highways can be no better than the laws which authorize and govern their construction, it will be well to review and revise these basic enabling acts and keep them updated. Few, if any, are presently adequate to provide the full range of environmental improvement measures now so urgently required. The basic Federal Highway Act itself, while not superseding state legislation, does have great force because of the 90 percent (federal) to 10 percent (state) funding provisions. It, too, is in need of revision to provide for such essential highway considerations as:

1. *Advanced planning.* This will ensure coordination with the long-range goals and planning of other state and federal agencies and with local planning departments.

2. *Advanced acquisition.* With a revolving fund to provide for the acquisition of right-of-way well ahead of construction, great savings could be effected. Other benefits accrue when highway acquisition precedes and stimulates, rather than disturbs land development. The long-range designation of such corridors and interchanges will help to give more desirable form to the regions—especially where planning and acquisition is conducted jointly with park, housing, and redevelopment authorities.

3. *Expansion of permitted uses within the right-of-way.* The definition of *highway construction* will be broadened to include multiple-use foundations and structures, surface parking areas, sound abatement installations, rest and recreation areas, bicycle and hiking trails, and scenic overlooks. There will be provision, also, for the widening of rights-of-way, where feasible, to include wooded areas, ponds, streams, and rock formations as part of the highway landscape.

4. *Off-site construction.* Make clear and specific the right of the highway departments to consummate scenic and conservation easements and to engage in construction beyond the normal right-of-way limits. This will provide the area needed for selective

clearing, pulloffs, recreation areas, and other landscape improvements.

5. *Disposition of excess property.* Provide for the sale or lease of residual lands, under protective controls, to public agencies, adjacent owners, or developers. Funds received could be used to help defray the cost of highway construction, roadside development, and upkeep.

6. *Sale or lease of ground rights and air rights.* At present the wording of most highway acts is so vague on this point that the multiple-use potential of the corridors has been slow in its realization. New language is needed to spell out clearly the permitted uses, restrictions relating to safety, appearance, access, and maintenance, and to continuing rights and controls. The matter of taxation of multiple-use facilities and the disposition of revenues also needs clarification.

Provide alternative means of moving about

Let the American families have their beloved automobile(s), as long as they can afford them. But let us provide as well increasing opportunities for those who seek to walk or ride their bicycles to work along safe and pleasant pathways. Explore, where appropriate, the possibilities of daily transit by waterborne launch or hovercraft. Consider the aerial tramway. But develop for sure the reserved bus lanes required to speed commuters to and from employment centers without the interference of heavy transport trucks or endless lines of private automobiles. Plan rapid, automated connections between the urban centers and the peripheral parking compounds. And learn at last the lessons of Sweden in planning new communities and transportation as one integrated system.

Watching a major metropolitan freeway at 5:15 P.M. on a business day, several things are immediately apparent. One, that traffic is moving at a pace far below freeway speed design. Second, most of the cars carry only one person, the driver. Also apparent is a pall of poisonous fumes.
There has to be a better way, something better than the automobile and better than most existing public transportation.
BURT RAYNES
Mainliner magazine
United Airlines
September 1973

Transit

On the face of it, rapid transit—the group movement of people between residential areas and regional activity centers—is so essential and rational an operation that it can only succeed. Then why is it that in our country rapid transit installations to date have been at best a moderate success and at worst a dismal failure? Why must they be so heavily subsidized and yet attract such a small percentage of the urban commuters? There are several reasons:

1. *Rapid transit has been a back-alley operation.* On-grade routes have traditionally followed the railroad freight lines which have carried passengers each day past dreary miles of warehouse sidings, slaughterhouses, tenement fire escapes, and trash-strewn railway embankments. Underground trips have been roaring, rattling forays through soot-encrusted tunnels. Rolling stock and trackage have been obsolete; stations and equipment shoddy, and service perfunctory. Buses are often crowded and grimy and must inch their way at peak hours along jammed thoroughfares,

Cars, with an average load of 1.5 persons, can carry about 2,400 people per hour on one expressway lane.

Rapid transit lines have extremely high capacities. For a route with eight cars, 50 seats per car, and no standees, operating on a 3½ minute headway between trains, capacity is 9,600 passengers per hour in one direction.

Along with such proven carriers as the swish monorail trains of Florida's Disney World, urban transit planners are considering also new forms of moving walkways, chairways, "horizontal elevators," and tubeways through which passenger compartments will be propelled by electromagnetic force at high velocities.

At present the two leading contenders for basic rapid transit are the "midi-bus," looping on and off reserved bus lanes, and the streamlined, fixed-rail express trains between concentrated residential and business centers.

. . . if public transportation fails in Chicago and its riders are added to the auto population on the now crowded highways, the impact could be devastating. We would need 148 additional expressway lanes costing in excess of $25 billion and it would require that every fifth building in the Chicago Loop be converted to a mammoth parking lot.

MILTON PIKARSKI
Mainliner magazine
United Airlines
August 1973

Of the 2 million people who enter Manhattan to work on week-days only about 140,000 come by car. Even this number fills the highways, bridges and tunnels into the island to capacity in rush hours . . .

"Attacking the Mass Transit Mess"
Business Week
June 3, 1972

bumper to bumper with passenger cars and diesel transport trucks. All in all, it would be difficult to plan a more uninspired and uninspiring form of travel than has been offered the American public in the name of transit. There are, of course, promising exceptions.

2. *Transit routes and stations have not been planned as unified elements of the districts which they serve.* They have had to beg their way into the new communities and—largely because of their unfortunate image—have been relegated to the industrial districts and the dumps. The pickup and discharge points have thus been removed both physically and psychologically from the public to be served.

3. *Commuter trains fail to serve the urban centers.* Most regional activity nodes—the business-office districts, the commercial focal points, the governmental cores, and the cultural centers—have moved away from the railroad lines and stations. Since rail transit systems have remained with the railroads, they deliver commuters "down by the tracks." Long walks from station to destination are an inconvenience. Transfer by bus is an annoyance and added expense. If rapid transit is to succeed, it must be both *rapid* and *direct*, and take people, agreeably, where they want to go.

4. *Americans have a stubborn affinity for their automobiles.* The car—an American fetish—has become the suburbanites' security blanket. Uncomfortable if caught more than a few strides from a "set of wheels," they have insisted upon, and been granted, the right to take their automobiles to work with them—even though each car usurps some 300 precious square feet of storage area within the urban confines, and vast sweeps of highway corridor and public street to give ingress and egress. The shopper must take the family automobile to the bakery, unless the teenagers have already commandeered it for a run to the pool.

As long as the automobile is invited within the metropolitan centers—or allowed into precincts where transit alone belongs—the success of transit, and the centers, is in question.

The progressive transit systems of the future will be planned with a bold new approach. They will be conceived as an essential and attractive component of a whole new way of living in a whole new type of urban metropolis.

Let us assume an arrangement by which transit is planned as *the* means by which people are moved between their living quarters and the urban centers. Communities will then be spaced out along the linear transit routes. The stations will be designed as attractive portals. They will front upon the community shopping mall with its convenience and fashion shops, its markets, restaurants, theaters, and civic center. There will be fountains and sculpture, and in warm weather there will be flowers and café tables under awnings and benches under the trees. About the mall will be grouped the high-rise apartments tapering sharply downward in profile to garden apartments, townhouses, single-family dwellings, and to greenbelt and agricultural lands beyond, which will form the boundaries and surroundings. As transit-oriented towns they will be compact. Families with cars will be encouraged (by patterns of streets and garaging) to live toward the outskirts for easy accessibility to the freeways and open countryside.

Vehicular access to the shopping mall will be from the outer edge inward, sometimes at a lower level. The outer band of each community will thus be designed for the automobile. The central mall and adjacent apartment areas will be reserved for the pedestrian. Movement by transit from community to community and on into the city will be an experience of convenience and delight.

So much for the new transit villages and towns. As to the urban centers, *the primary reason for their existence is to provide a maximum concentration of related activities.* The more compact the center (whatever its nature) and the more closely related the components (whether they be offices, theaters, restaurants, or shops)—the more desirable it becomes as real estate and as a business address. If this be so—then no business, cultural, or recreation center can afford to be split or fragmented by vehicular trafficways—or to be burst apart by huge parking lots or garages. Automobiles must be excluded and left "stabled" at the outer edge of the central city where they can be stored adjacent to the circumferential beltway. Service vehicles will also be excluded from the pedestrian levels of the center—with goods delivered via service tunnels, or by moving beltways or tubes from outlying terminals served by regional transportation routes.

People will arrive at the urba-centers either by buses looping in from the outside—or by rail at strategically located stations from which they may move on foot through parklike, surface pedestrian malls or be transported under cover by lifts and moving walks or chairs to adjacent office towers.

When driving individual automobiles into the city has become prohibitive in cost (because of increased parking charges), even less efficient (because parking garages have been moved to the outer edge of each center, where they belong), and less desirable (because transit has become *more* desirable)—then cities will again become "hived" hubs of business and cultural activity, new communities will be formed around their transit stations, and transit will come into its own. This is not to say that the automobile is soon to disappear from the American scene. In areas of lower population density particularly, the driver-operated vehicle—whatever its form—will long be with us as an essential means of transportation.

For many the new look of mass transit will be surprising. Sleek buses will stream along their own busways through lineal parks, with no stops except at attractive all-weather stations. Aerial cars, high overhead, will skim cross-country on cables suspended from widely spaced towers. Between lake and coastal cities new quiet types of hovercraft will provide rapid interconnection. Elsewhere, capsule cars will be jetted through pneumatic tubes.

The advanced forms of rail transit will be highly sophisticated,

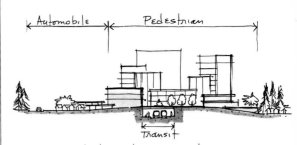

Rapid transit communities will be formed compactly around the pedestrian cores from which the automobiles will be excluded. Transit lines and stations will be grade-separated.

THE NEW TRANSIT-RELATED COMMUNITY

KEEP DELIVERIES, SERVICE, AND PARKING FUNCTIONS OFF THE PEDESTRIAN LEVELS

Urba-center: A nodal concentration of urban activities, together with all essential support facilities and services.

because to be successful, they will have to be. The cars will glide noiselessly, at super speeds along subsurface or elevated guideways. Passenger units will be smaller, computer-operated, and electronically controlled. Being compact and lightweight they can be more rapidly filled, more frequently scheduled, and easily manipulated. They can also be more quickly accelerated or decelerated and rifled from target to target with a minimum of energy. At peak hours from one to thirty units as needed may be whisked into the boarding station, labeled automatically for varying destinations in response to passenger demand (registered by scanning of tickets and passes.) Units may be dispatched independently, or as linked multiples, for varying destinations.

When redeveloped urba-centers, new transit and transportation systems, and new communities are planned together, as interrelated elements of a unified region, the cities, routes, and satellite towns will operate with a new efficiency and purpose. City dwellers and "exurbanites" will be afforded the opportunity to enjoy both urban life and communion with nature. And the cities will thrive, with a new vitality, because they will function again as true hubs of culture and commerce. Their position of dominance will be assured by the provision of rapid and pleasant access from the radiating residential sectors.

Build separate busways

Bus transit between outlying centers and the "downtown" has been well received in forward-looking communities where reserved bus lanes have been provided. These can be constructed either within highway, transit, or utility rights-of-way or on their own separate alignments and can accommodate through and local buses and car-pool vehicles on a high-speed nonstop sweep through the countryside between local pickup and discharge points.

Connect the centers

Well-conceived transit systems will be so devised as to provide direct and rapid connection between nodes of residential concentration and regional activity centers. Terminals will not be located within those districts in which the planned densities are to be low. To function successfully both rail and bus transit require a high count of potential commuters within easy walking distances of terminals and pickup points.

Reshape communities around the outlying transit stations

As in many of the pleasant new towns of Europe the station can serve as a gateway to the public square with its offices, shops, restaurants, trees, and fountains. Or it may open out into the central plaza of a business district, an industrial park, or an educational campus. An essential feature will be the concentration of people and activities about the transit access points.

On a typical morning community dwellers may walk along pleasant pathways leading from the clustered apartments or homes to the coffee shops, flower stalls, and newsstands beside the transit station. The "kiss and ride" commuters arriving by automobile may be discharged at the station under cover. Others, arriving by minibus or "roundabouts" (perhaps leased at low cost by the transit authorities), may store their vehicles in shaded lots or convenient garages.

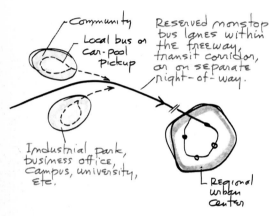

EFFICIENT BUS TRANSIT

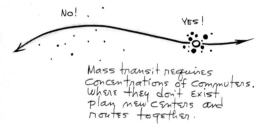

LINK THE NODES

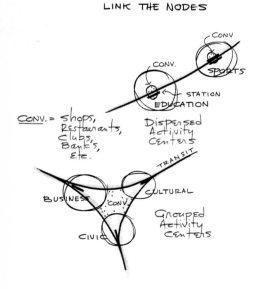

TRANSIT-RELATED ACTIVITY CENTERS

Text continued on page 166.

Paths of movement

Urban blueways and greenways

The stated purpose of this early proposal for the City of Toledo, Ohio, was the design of a major riverfront park. As the studies progressed, it became clear that the success of the new urban complex would depend largely upon its extensions into, and linkage with, the surrounding business and residential community. A primary consideration, therefore, was the provision of a wide range of agreeable access alternatives including pedestrian, vehicular, and waterway approaches.

Plans for the city's street and arterial highway network were modified to bypass the park site while providing improved ingress and egress to peripheral car-storage compounds. New parkways were described along the river edges. The municpal transit system was extended by a loop to the parkside entrance portal. Marina and landings were designed to accommodate passenger boats and pleasure craft approaching from the river, the bay, and the Great Lakes beyond. Terraced malls and enclosed skyways were conceived to furnish all-weather ties to the neighboring office towers and proposed shopping plaza. Also planned concurrently was a regional system of pedestrian pathways and bicycle trails that will trace their way along the streams and natural drainageways. They will be aligned through an extensive system of open space park and recreation lands and forest preserves which are presently being assembled. These lands will envelop much of the riverside and bayfront, and penetrate deeply inland along the tributary streams. They will embrace the best of the area's woodlands, marshes, beaches, and scenic features, interlace the communities, and link the activity centers.

Thus, in time, the waterfront park and its extensional accessways and conservation lands will open up and give new form and orientation to the entire Toledo environs.

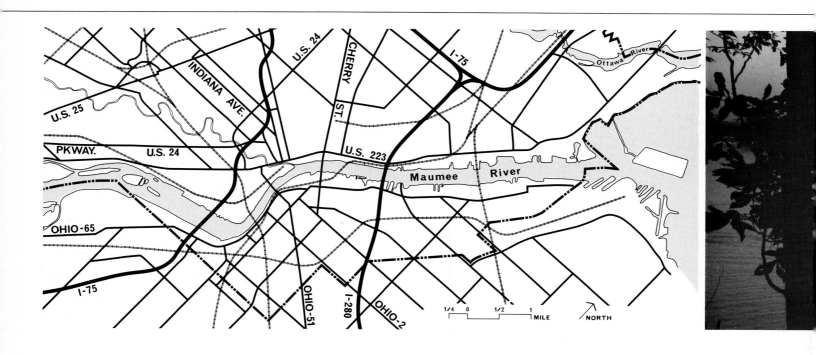

Toledo looks to the river . . .

Today in Toledo it is possible, for the first time in a century, for people on both sides of the Maumee to look to the river—and see broad stretches of it! Few American cities can boast as much. All Toledoans can and should take special pride in the fact that through the combined efforts of many individuals and leadership groups, the city now owns major parcels of land on both sides of the river adjacent to the busy urban centers. This open land provides opportunities for present and future generations to make decisions con-

cerning the reuse of this valuable asset, choices to be carefully studied and balanced to assure that all will benefit to the greatest possible degree.

In looking to Toledo's waterfront and central city, the plan and program resulting from this study have consolidated the best of the recent reports and thinking into a single document. The conceptual plans are not to be construed as definitive, but rather as early-action proposals in many instances and as long-term opportunities in others. The schematic plans for Promenade Park show in detail the location and interrelationships of

those projects currently under consideration. As architectural plans are finalized, the detailed layout of the park must be concurrently adjusted in collaborative effort to achieve a unified development.

Numerous individuals and citizen groups have participated enthusiastically in the formulation of these plans. Proposals include a restructured city center terraced down to the water's edge and facing across to an International Festival Park. Concerted support of this bold concept will help to assure the emergence of a dramatically beautiful and dynamic river metropolis.

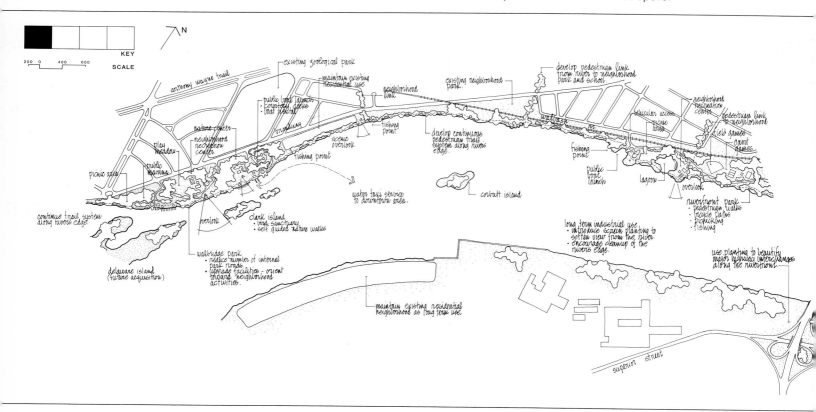

. . . and can envision

A city stepping down to the river's edge, and fronting upon a magnificent waterscape.

A city joined together, rather than separated, by the Maumee.

A city proud of its industry, which in turn expresses pride in the city by enhancing the urban environment.

A city providing an ideal setting for new apartments, office buildings, civic structures, shops, and restaurants attracted to the riverside and bay.

A city protected by a sound flood-control program for the entire Maumee River basin.

A city with clean, usable water—its entire watershed secured by scientific methods of erosion control and reforestation against the waste and blight of siltation.

A city with a balanced river-bay eco-system providing desirable habitat for all living creatures.

A city refreshed by open spaces which reclaim and envelop its waterways and shores.

A city of river, lake, and park-related neighborhoods and communities.

A city looking not only to the future, but also to the past, and committed to retain those elements of its cultural heritage that will enrich the lives of all.

A city capitalizing upon its bay and water frontage.

A city provided with safe and pleasant routes of interconnection—where freeways, parkways, waterways, transitways, bicycle trails, and walkways are all planned together as an interrelated system.

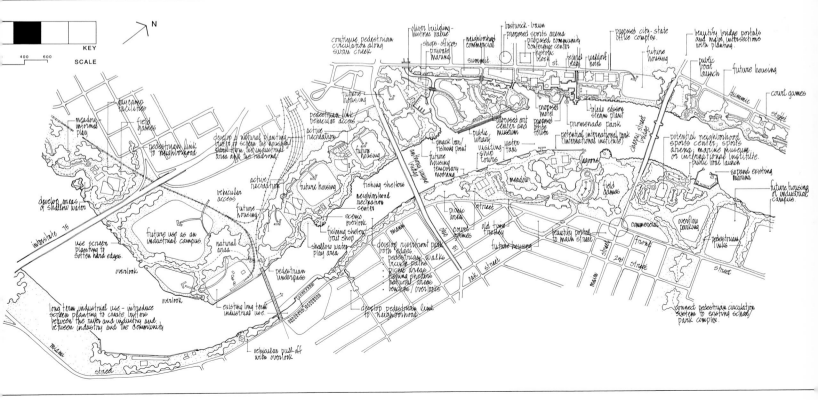

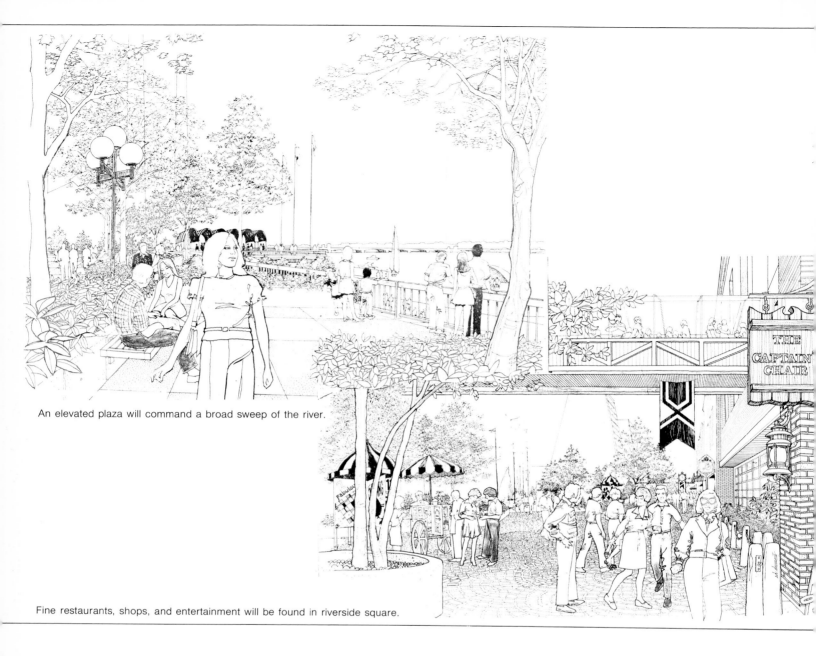

An elevated plaza will command a broad sweep of the river.

Fine restaurants, shops, and entertainment will be found in riverside square.

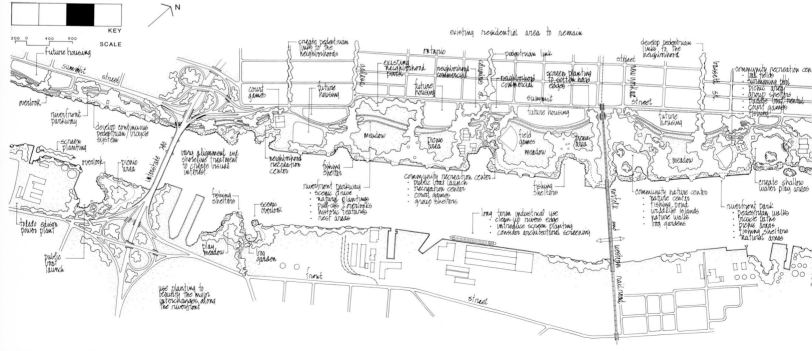

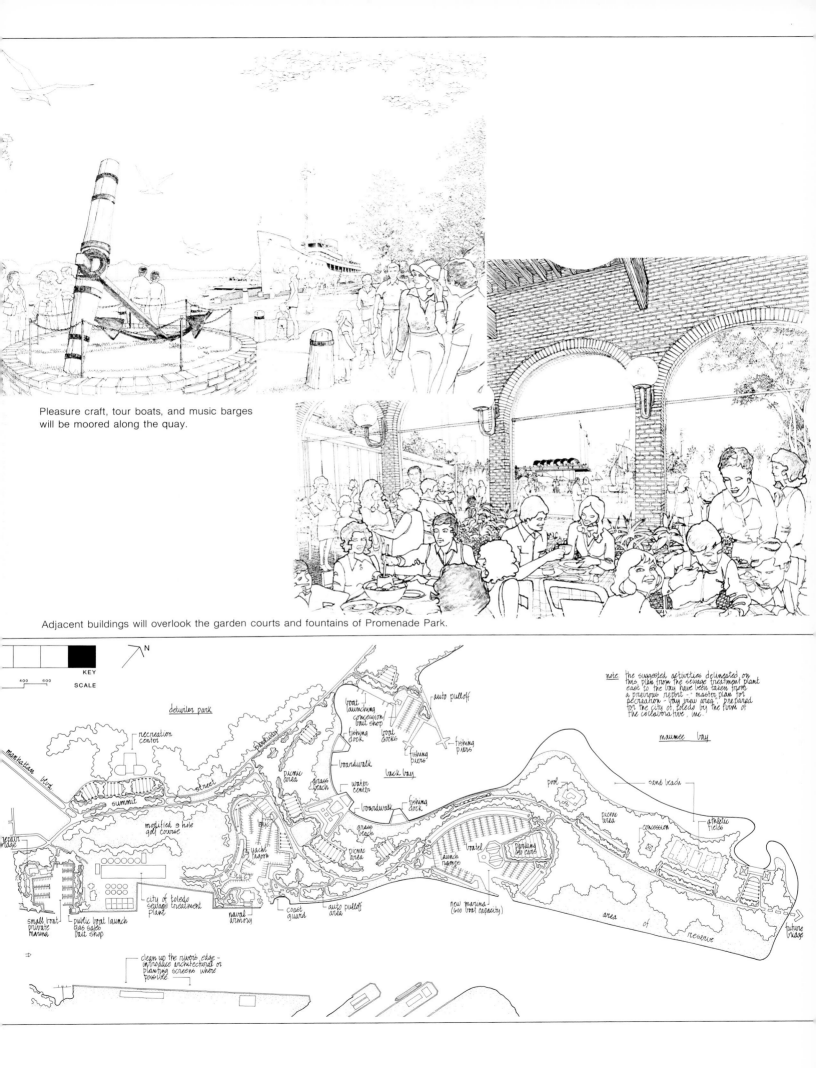

Pleasure craft, tour boats, and music barges
will be moored along the quay.

Adjacent buildings will overlook the garden courts and fountains of Promenade Park.

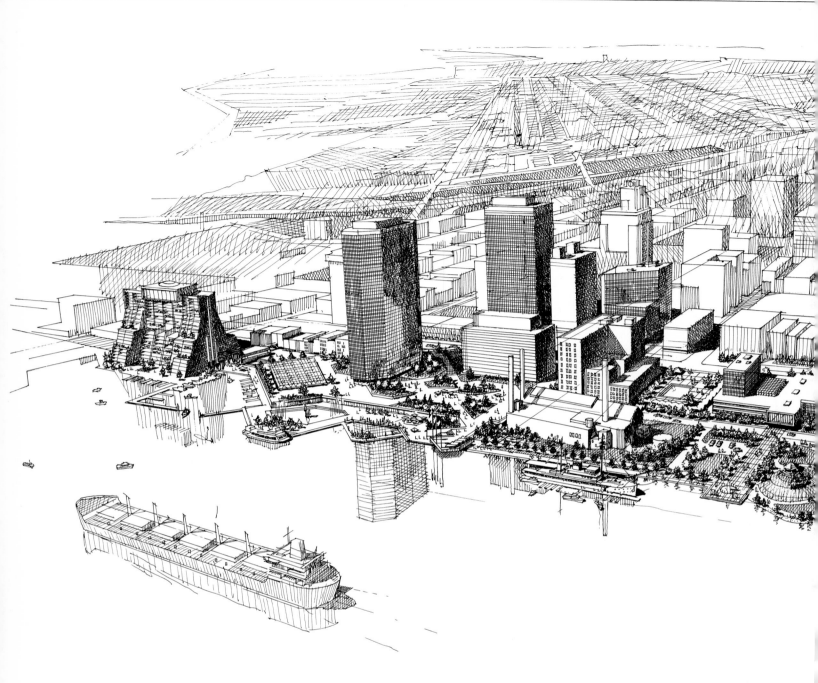

Toledo looks to the river as an integral part of the city

The central purpose of this study has been to establish the concept and broad outlines of a new urban riverfront park. From the outset, however, it has been recognized that no park or other city component can be planned independently. Structures, routes of vehicular and pedestrian movement, and landscape enframement must all be conceived together, and work together, as a unified living and business environment.

Creative urban planning is at best a search for the most fitting relationships . . .

of land uses to each other and to the topography,

of building to building and space to space,

of buildings and spaces to traffic and transit ways,

and all to the surrounding environs.

It was for these reasons that the consultants were wisely charged by the city administration to plan Promenade Park as an integral part of the supporting business district and the entire interconnecting system of waterfront holdings.

Plan all components together

Let the riverfront park open upward and into the city. A network of attractive pedestrian walkways, plazas, and malls will refresh and revitalize the downtown, enhance real estate values, and provide inviting ways and places leading down to the water's edge.

Let the park approaches extend both ways along the river, far up the tributaries, and lakeward to the bay. Such a blueway-greenway system will provide not only safe and pleasant access to the downtown, it will also describe the best possible structuring for the future development of the region.

Let Promenade Park and the embracing central city face across the Maumee to a new River East International Park.

These grand and strong relationships will form the framework for the new City of Toledo.

Provide direct transit and vehicular circulation and peripheral parking

As Toledo reorients and builds toward the river, it will be highly desirable to divert

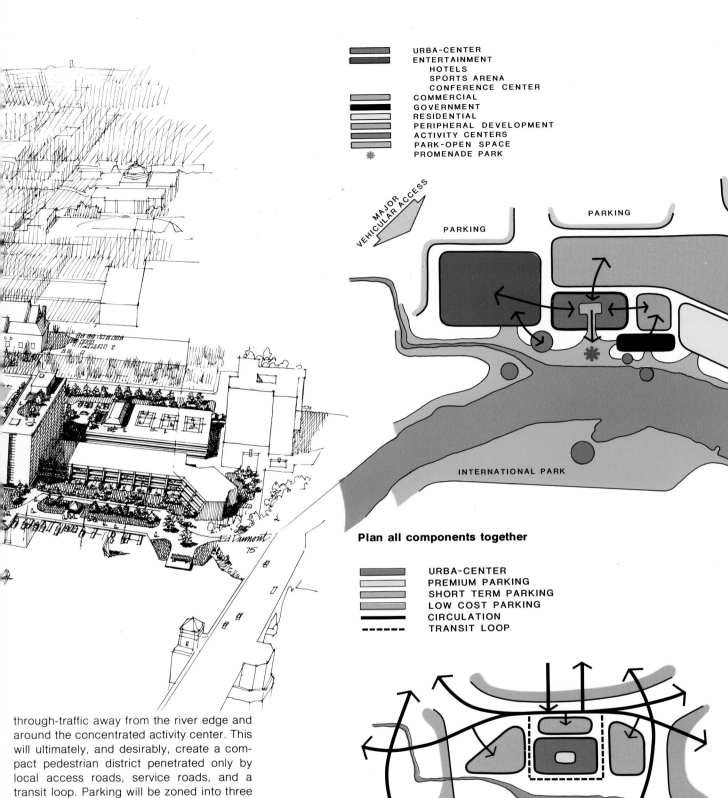

MAJOR VEHICULAR ACCESS

PARKING

PARKING

PARKING

INTERNATIONAL PARK

Plan all components together

CIRCULATION AND PARKING

Provide direct transit and vehicular circulation and convenient peripheral parking

through-traffic away from the river edge and around the concentrated activity center. This will ultimately, and desirably, create a compact pedestrian district penetrated only by local access roads, service roads, and a transit loop. Parking will be zoned into three categories as follows:

1. Premium parking which will occur internally within the highly concentrated urba-center.

2. Short-term convenience parking.

3. Low cost peripheral parking which will serve daytime workers in Toledo's downtown.

Premium and short-term space will serve as the primary source of parking during the evening hours.

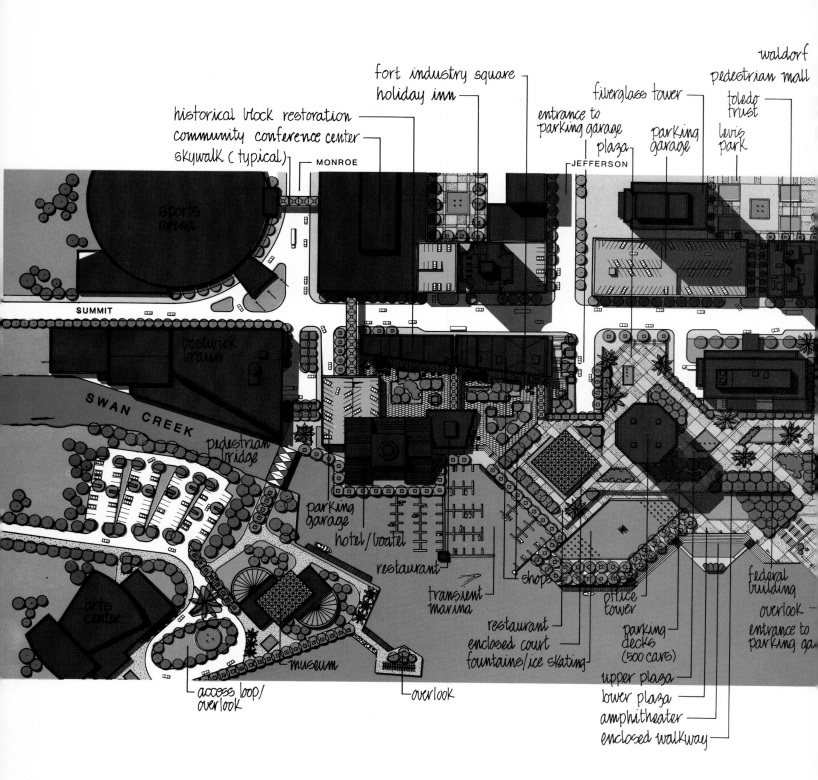

historical block restoration
community conference center
skywalk (typical)
MONROE

fort industry square
holiday inn

entrance to
parking garage
plaza
JEFFERSON

fiberglass tower

waldorf
pedestrian mall
toledo
trust
levis
park

parking
garage

sports
arena

SUMMIT

bostwick
braun

SWAN CREEK

pedestrian
bridge

parking
garage

hotel/boatel

restaurant

transient
marina

shops

office
tower

parking
decks
(500 cars)

federal
building

overlook
entrance to
parking ga

arts
center

museum

access loop/
overlook

restaurant
enclosed court
fountains/ice skating

overlook

upper plaza
lower plaza
amphitheater
enclosed walkway

Toledo looks to the river and plans a major waterfront park

The park and its extensions into the center city must complement and supplement the adjacent business community.

The park and its environs are to be urban and urbane in character. While the approaches from up and down the river will be more natural, in keeping with the adjacent residential communities, Promenade Park has been conceived as a series of rich and beau-

tifully furnished courts, gardens, lawns, and plazas stepping down to the river's edge.

It is to be constructed of fine building materials and paving that will reflect and engender quality in all related structures.

Promenade Park is to be beautifully appointed with handsome shelters, walls, planters, benches, and other furniture. It will have splashing fountains and attractive nighttime illumination to highlight its features and pro

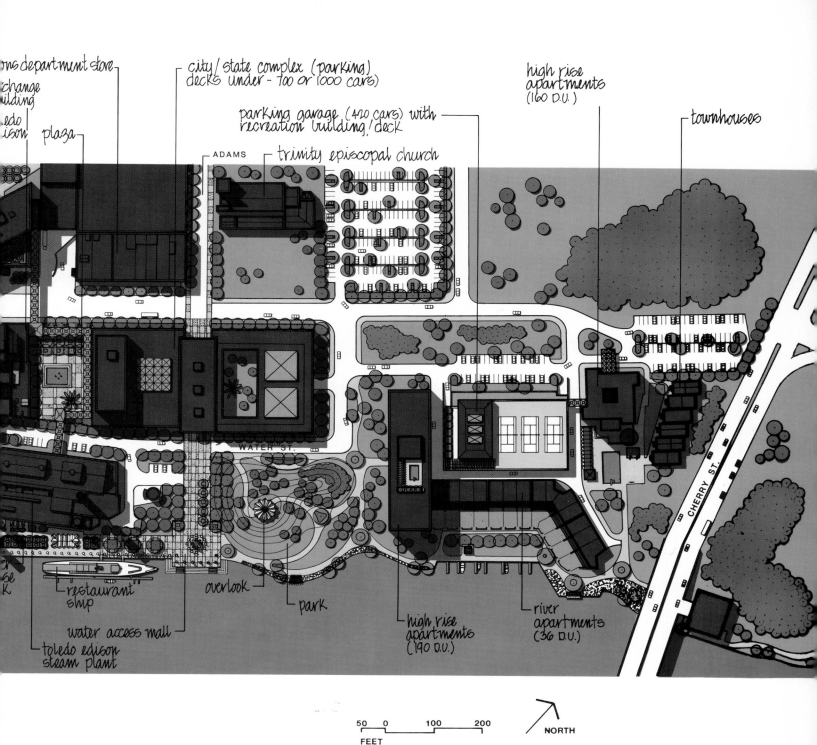

department store

change building

ledo ison

plaza

city/state complex (parking decks under - 700 or 1000 cars)

parking garage (420 cars) with recreation building/deck

high rise apartments (160 D.U.)

townhouses

ADAMS

trinity episcopal church

WATER ST.

CHERRY ST.

restaurant ship

overlook

park

water access mall

toledo edison steam plant

high rise apartments (190 D.U.)

river apartments (36 D.U.)

50   0   100   200

FEET

NORTH

vide a high level of safety for the patrons.

It must be designed for the use and enjoyment of people, provided with all the amenities, and enlivened with art shows, music, and a host of daily and weekly activities. It will be used in the daytime and evening in all seasons of the year.

The park will accommodate great numbers of people for major events. It is so planned that small groups and individuals will

also be comfortable whether they are strolling or otherwise occupied.

It will retain and feature buildings and other historic elements and have a welcome measure of nostalgic appeal.

It will be easily accessible to pedestrians, transit riders, and those arriving by car. Adequate parking is to be provided.

Within the river-edge park approaches there should be allocated and built, with high

priority, the finest array of active and passive recreation facilities in the whole Midwest.

The expanded Promenade Park complex will combine new and existing structures into a dynamic business, civic, and cultural center at the river's edge. It will be a dominant regional focal point and the site of many of the city's most important activities and future events. It will become the crown jewel of Toledo's park and open space system.

163

Toledo looks to the river—and acts

Summary of the action recommendations

1. *Approve this report in principle,* as the consensus statement of many contributing agencies, study groups, and citizens. Its proposals for early action and its guidelines for the long-term reshaping of the city and the supporting region are paramount to Toledo's continuing renaissance.

2. *Proceed immediately to develop the program and final plans for the River East International Park.* The inclusion of elements such as the International Institute and Festival, the trolley, ethnic sports, and a marine museum are to be encouraged. The development of the program and master plan should be initiated soon to assure that this major facility, which potentially will enjoy a national reputation, develops in a logical sequence. Care must be exercised to include only those elements which will nurture the international flavor.

3. *Appoint a full-time downtown waterfront development coordinator.* Supporting staff and sufficient funding should also be provided to coordinate the plans, develop the implementation potentials, initiate the programs, and promote the activities which are beginning to emerge.

4. *Explore all avenues for project financing.* Incentives should be provided to stimulate the development of the proposed hotel, parking, apartments, office buildings, retail areas, and historic renovation proposed in the plan.

5. *Create a nonprofit civic organization dedicated to the improvement, beautification, and development of the lake and waterway edges.* This organization would work actively to support existing agencies such as Clear Water, Inc., and policies such as the ones set forth in the Water Resources Planning Act of 1965. It would also help to initiate beneficial legislation and promote water-oriented activities such as ski shows, boat parades, a water-edge band shell, and symphony barge.

6. *Establish a public relations program.* Utilizing the theme "Toledo Looks to the River," posters, signs, slide presentations, traveling displays, models, and brochures could be used to inform and gain the support of the entire community.

7. *Enlist the efforts of existing public service organizations in planning the activities for the downtown riverfront.* Groups such as the Junior League and the Arts Commission of Greater Toledo can be highly effective in re-establishing the downtown as the "Action Center" of Toledo.

8. *Use the lands now owned along the river and bay for interim recreation.* Much of the land could be converted to open meadows with borders planted to seedling trees.

9. *Formulate and accelerate a continuing waterfront acquisition program while lands are still available, or as they become available.* The Middlegrounds and other abandoned rail-line areas and facilities should receive a high priority.

10. *Promote a rational dredge-fill policy.* Since dredging must occur to ensure navigable channels, the resulting landfill should be used to create a planned river-edge landscape of beauty and distinction.

11. *Eliminate blighting influences near the downtown area.* Such elements as the salt and aggregate piles, the sugar storage tanks, and the Harbors and Bridges storage shed should be removed or relocated. All vacant buildings should be torn down and all obsolescent structures removed or rehabilitated.

12. *Promote industrial participation in an annual cleanup along the water edge and a campaign to provide permanent screening and planting of unsightly areas.*

13. *Endorse floodplain zoning as recommended by the Ohio Bureau of Natural Resources and the Corps of Engineers.*

14. *Promote comprehensive river-basin studies for the Swan Creek, Ottawa River, and Maumee River watersheds.*

15. *Construct, within the "blueway and greenway" open space matrix, a series of complete and well-staffed neighborhood, community, and regional recreation areas.* Initiate a ten-year program and budget to create a blend of facilities which will provide a well-balanced system of parks for the active and passive user. Highly organized improvements such as ball diamonds, hard-surface athletic courts, swimming pools, play-equipment areas, pathways, park shelters and centers combined with an assortment of sitting areas, scenic overlooks, and open meadows will make the entire water-edge system an invaluable community asset.

Toledo has had enough studies, enough reports, and enough proposals and discussion. It has undergone an unprecedented year of intensive self-examination and cooperative planning. It has formulated a joint and creative guideline for the long-range development of a notable city. This is a time for decision, and commitment.

Two views of downtown Toledo today showing the magnetic attraction of a riverfront and riverfront development.

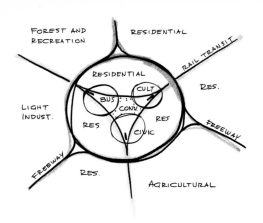

INTEGRATED SYSTEMS OF
HIGHWAYS AND RAIL TRANSIT

*The very key to satisfactory city organization
is concentration without congestion.*

EDWARD HIGBEE
The Squeeze—Cities without Space
Apollo Editions
New York, 1962

*The fantastic growth in the number of office
buildings on Manhattan has swept away
countless viable neighborhoods and pleasant
communities and converted the center of the
island into a crowded, noisy jungle by day and
a deserted dangerous one by night.*

"Attacking the Mass Transit Mess"
Business Week
June 3, 1972

*The real problem is political. Different transit
related agencies—city, county, state—must
find a way to work together productively and
harmoniously and still arrive at the same objective—moving people easily, efficiently and
economically.*

DAN HEARN
Mainliner magazine
United Airlines
August 1973

Text continued from page 154.

Redevelop metropolitan centers around rapid transit nodes

For transit to best serve its purpose, urban activities will be concentrated near the transit stations. Each business, cultural, and civic
complex of high intensity will be grouped within agreeable walking
distance. All will be linked by swift transit vehicles to each other and
to the region which supports them.

The concentration of transit-related intown cores or urba-centers
of varying functions and forms will improve the efficiency of both the
land use and the transportation systems.

Set the best working capacity for each node and gear the transit system to it

Communities and cities, like schools and office buildings, have optimum working limits beyond which they become crowded and inefficient. Sound planning dictates that as the urban cores and supporting
transit systems are planned together, the ultimate capacity for each is
predetermined and fixed. Additional satellite centers and routes can
be created as they are needed.

Join forces to achieve a total system

The consolidation of the federal highway, mass transit, and transportation programs under a joint Department of Transportation was a
necessary and propitious move. A next step is to effect a truce and
cooperative working relationship between the warring mass transit and
highway lobbies. Both have everything to gain. Only when all aspects
of transportation have been made part of a coordinated and balanced
system will people, cars, and goods move freely and will all interests be
well served.

Explore all possibilities

While some of the transit proposals under experimentation seem like
dreams for fantasy land, they bear watching. Among the great variety
of maxi- and minibuses, trains, aerial trams, horizontal elevators, and
personalized people-movers are the prototypes of our future vehicles.
With modification and refinement they will someday, in combination, serve new cities which, if we could now foresee them, would
seem as fanciful.

Apply advanced technology

When the same high level of ingenuity that has carried the astronauts
to outer space has been applied to the design and operation of our
rapid transit systems, we may yet coax reluctant commuters out of
their automobiles and get them to the desk on time.

Upgrade the existing facilities

Cities with severe problems of traffic and pollution cannot wait for the
development of the super transit system, or for a massive infusion of
federal funds. They must piece together from available bus routes,
trackage, and other resources the best they can achieve, and work hard
at improving it. The best transit mix and modes for any municipality
will evolve out of the experience of a dedicated team that keeps
seeking better solutions.

Use transit to spark new communities

Advanced transit concepts provide the opportunity for urbanizing
regions to "do it all over again and do it right." Stockholm in Sweden
has shown the way of "saving" and revitalizing the center city by
extending new radial lines out into the open countryside where rapid
rail transit stations would be planned as the nuclei of such compact
high-density "new towns" as attractive Farsta and Vallingby.

Air as a trafficway

The wild blue yonder of yesteryear has become overdomesticated. The salient fact of air travel today is that the lanes are hopelessly jammed. There is simply not enough room over our larger cities to accommodate the number and types of aircraft presently in use. Air passenger miles of travel are expected to more than double again within the next ten years.

The tedious waits at the airports, the slowly descending spiral of stacked-up planes and dismal balance sheet statistics all point the way to new forms of flight and new systems of regulation. There are a number of possibilities.

Improve the aircraft

As a passenger vehicle the contemporary plane leaves much to be desired.

It requires huge runways and glide paths.

It produces a deafening racket.

It is one of the chief air polluters.

It is designed for both people and commercial cargo, to the detriment of both.

Most aircraft are grossly oversized.

It is time to change the emphasis, by controls if necessary, from the most powerful and biggest to the most efficient and best.

Classify and segregate aircraft by type

It doesn't make sense that military aircraft should be based at metropolitan airports, or that private or cargo planes should clutter the runways of major passenger terminals. Future airports for each type of service will be located to meet their own specific requirements. All will be spaced out to relieve traffic frictions and provide more direct connections to transit and transport routes.

Improve the airports

Most have been permitted—through lack of foresight and planning control—to draw to their vicinity a multitude of conflicting activities such as housing, hotels, strip commercial, freight warehouses, business offices, and even regional entertainment centers. The air terminals of the future will be planned solely as isolated ports.

Impose uniform and adequate regulations

No aircraft should be licensed to fly in the United States unless it is properly equipped to meet Federal Aviation Administration requirements for operations under instrument flight rules. The filing of a plan should be required for *all* cross-country flights. Rigid enforcement of these regulations would do much to reduce delays, crashes, and the number of fatalities.

Centralize surveillance

Those who have flown in private planes, to be guided from vector to vector along their course by the crackling and often indecipherable voice directions from local towers, will know such methods to be as dated as helmets and goggles. In these times of swarming air activity

Almost 300 million passengers will be flying over domestic routes this year.

The superports being planned to accommodate the crush are enormous. The new Dallas–Fort Worth port is larger than the island of Manhattan.

The environmental impacts of air transportation are threefold. They occur as the planes are in the air; they occur in other forms at the ports; and they occur in all forms of port-to-metropolitan-area transportation.

Some of the means available to protect airports and the public include purchase of development rights over abutting properties, purchase of excess land and resale or lease for compatible use with restricting covenants, buffer zone planning, and public land use controls. They are most effective when used at the time of development or expansion of an airport.

From Sea to Shining Sea
A Report on the American Environment—
Our Natural Heritage
By the President's Council on Recreation and
Natural Beauty
U.S. Government Printing Office
Washington, D.C., 1968

We are beyond the old "barnstorming" days, but some private plane owners don't know it. They pose a serious threat to all who share the air.

Col. Willard W. Wilson
In conversation

Most of the increasing rash of commercial aircraft accidents involve collisions with private planes.

To support the case for the separation of general aviation and larger air carrier ports one need only consider the wide variance in plane maneuvering speeds and space requirements, and in levels of pilot proficiency.

the coordination of flight plans, scanning, plotting, and directional control can only be handled by fully automated regional operations centers.

Reduce air traffic

Since the space available over urban centers cannot be expanded and since it is currently overused and dangerously overcrowded, the use must be reduced. This suggests the dispersal of termini with interconnection by direct rapid transit, which in time should replace most local flights. New forms of improved air service will then better accommodate the mid- to long-distance traveler.

The crux of the problem is that air and other forms of transportation are struggling to serve cities formed for reasons no longer valid. New growth centers formed around coordinated transit networks will make travel of all types more efficient and more pleasant.

Greenways

How can one wonder why people no longer enjoy walking, when the usual walkway provided is a straight length of concrete pavement at the edge of the street curb, exposed to the roar of the traffic and steeped in its fumes?

We would all like to help with the energy crisis. Yet how can we expect, or wish, our family members to pedal bicycles to school, to shop, or to work when they must move in crowded roadways or along the pedestrian sidewalks? Bicycles and electric carts *are* used in those places where safe, pleasant, separate, and interconnected trails are provided. Where better could they be aligned than through the community open space lands or "greenways"?

Fully as important as the routes of inter- and intracommunity movement by automobile are the networks of pedestrian walks and bicycle trails. At times they may be natural in character, winding along a wooded ridge, through a ravine, or beside a lake or stream. Again, they may be planned as lineal gardens, open to the sky yet embellished with trees, flower beds, and water features. Elsewhere in urban areas they may become architectural, as in roofed or underground corridors with attractive paving materials, lighting, and displays. Always, at best, they will be designed for the use of *people,* and to give them a full measure of comfort and visual satisfaction.

Let the walkways and bikeways touch and reveal the beauty of the natural surroundings. Let them link the points of scenic and historic interest. Let them pass through and connect the recreation places, explore the shopping districts, and disclose the workings of the inner city in all its kaleidoscopic moods. Build into and around them those qualities of interest and charm that people so universally seek. Then will they be willing, at times, to leave their cars behind them and venture abroad, to rediscover the pleasures of moving about at a more leisurely pace by bicycle, or on foot.

Plan pedestrian domains into the cities

They will be the focal points for the structures at their sides and will serve as the passageways and congregating places for the people. Malls,

Within the past several years—for the first time in many decades—the number of bicycles sold in the United States exceeded that of automobiles.

I am an old-time country lane. Now I have been officially vacated and closed. (I never liked automobiles anyway.) I invite you to walk as folks have walked for generations and be friendly with my trees, my flowers, and my wild creatures.
 Sign in Cook County Forest Preserve District
As quoted in *Conservation Quotes*
U.S. Department of the Interior,
National Park Service
January 1953

Would the valleys were your streets, and the green paths your alleys, that you might seek one another through vineyards, and come with the fragrance of the earth in your garments.
 KAHLIL GIBRAN
The Prophet
Alfred A. Knopf, Inc.
New York, 1923

courts, plazas, squares, and public parks—handsomely designed and beautifully furnished—will form the refreshing oases in our otherwise desert cities.

Interconnect community focal points and public gathering places

Such places and the pedestrian routes that connect them are best planned together to provide dramatic approaches and a series of pleasant views. Each time a new space or structure is introduced along the way, the system must be readjusted.

The approach to a building, and the sequence of spaces from which it is viewed, are as important design considerations as the actual structure itself.

Design pedestrian ways and spaces to express and fulfill their purpose

Well-planned walkways will lead people where they want to go, directly when time is important, as in access links between transit stations and office towers, or sometimes indirectly and meandering, as through a park or marketplace.

They will be enclosed where the interest is in shopping windows, market stalls, or other detail; opened partially to enframe a vista, or wide to reveal a view.

Make them convenient by providing reasonable alignment and clear direction. Make them comfortable, with easy changes of grade, nonslip pavements, shelter from winter winds and rain, and relief from the heat of summer. Furnish them with benches, colorful graphics, attractive lighting, water features, sculpture, and planting. Allow them always to pick up and enhance the character of the environs. A well-planned pathway will discover and reveal the best aspects and richest qualities of each district through which it passes.

Separate pedestrians and vehicles

The two are incompatible.

Vehicles require wide, clear channels for uninterrupted movement. Each pedestrian crossing is an inconvenience; each abutting sidewalk a potential hazard.

Pedestrians, like passengers, are also interested in motion, but at an entirely different rate and within spaces of an entirely different quality and scale. They tolerate the disadvantage and danger of on-grade street crossings only until offered something better.

The attraction of customers and businesses from downtown to the outlying regional centers may be largely attributed to the fact that the latter provide drivers with uninterrupted vehicular circulation, while people on foot may move between shops and offices through trafficfree courts and malls.

Connect communities to each other and to urban centers with a system of pedestrian and bicycle trails

Green swaths of varying width may follow the arterial parkways and circulation roads on widened rights-of-way. They may move from park to recreation area along the waterways and through the floodplains. They may join transit routes in places, or merge with forest preserves and conservation areas.

Both walking and travel by bicycle are growing in popularity and soon become favorite forms of recreation where pathways are provided.

Extend urban-suburban greenways to connect with cross-country trails

The same paths that bring nature into the city may lead people out of the city into nature.

Today everyone who values cities is disturbed by automobiles.
Jane Jacobs
The Death and Life of Great American Cities
Random House, Inc.
New York, 1961

The automobile needs accommodation. But so do people's other needs. At present the form of the city reflects only one, and excludes the other.
Serge Chermayeff and Christopher Alexander
Community and Privacy
Doubleday & Company, Inc.
New York, 1963

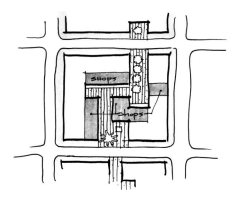

With urban renewal—or starting from scratch—inner block walkways and spaces can create attractive and valuable frontage.

OPEN UP THE BLOCK INTERIORS

Millions of dollars in funds for *"the development, improvement, and use of bicycle transportation, and the improvement of pedestrian walkways on or in conjunction with highway rights of way"* have for years been made available to the states by the Federal Highway Act.

A glaring failure of most regional plans is the lack of access provided the city dwellers to outlying recreation areas or other attractions.

Blueways

How fortunate the region that is blessed with open water!

Such assets as streams, canals, rivers, lakes, and oceanfronts are to be preserved and developed for the enjoyment and use of the public. They are neither to be neglected nor walled off by buildings or other uses that may crowd along the edges. They are rather to be enclosed within open space bands of varying width that extend the valuable frontage deep into the surrounding neighborhoods. People may thus enjoy cycling or walking along the banks or skimming across the water surface.

Often opportunities exist which have been overlooked. Other possibilities which have been lost may be regained only by long-range planning that will lace greenways and blueways together into a grand pattern of interrelated open spaces and waterways.

Develop all possibilities for waterborne travel

Aside from the recreational use by citizens, the economic returns to be enjoyed from the tourist industry more than justify the investment and efforts required. The utilization of waterways for the movement of people and goods may also alleviate highway congestion and form an important aspect of transportation systems. The construction of quays, piers, and marinas, and the installation of navigational aids, can pay rich dividends.

Provide access to the water

New roads, parking areas, and boat launching ramps will usually be required.

Regulate the use of the water surface and edges

Various areas may be zoned for different uses such as wildlife preserve, fishing, swimming, water skiing, and boating. Consideration must also be given to policing the water surface and shoreline activities. Regulations will cover the types of docks, type and size of watercraft, and limitations on noise and speed.

Improve the existing waterways

Most urban areas have ignored their watercourses. There is little access to or enjoyment of the ponds and streams. Views of the rivers are rare, even from the bridges that cross them. There are few water-edge parks, little realization of the inviting potential for water-related living. Lakes and lagoons, long neglected, require major cleanup. Beaches require erosion control, vegetative protection, and recreational improvements. Only when such water bodies are developed and featured will the use of their surface and travel along their edges again become popular pastimes.

Fish and game sanctuary

Marker

Fishing only

Marker

Water ski course. Power boats permitted

Marina and launching

Fishing, swimming and boating (Motor boats prohibited)

Dam

Marker

Fishing only

Lakes and waterways can be zoned to permit and regulate a variety of desirable uses.

ZONE THE WATER SURFACE

Joint-use corridors

As we drive through, or fly over, our countryside—even its most primitive backlands—we are shocked at the great crisscrossing slashes of highways, railroads, and transmission lines that disturb orderly patterns of land development or despoil nature's splendor.

Since most cross-country routes are planned to interconnect and service the urban centers, it is reasonable that they should all be planned together. Yet there are to date few, if any, agencies, at any governmental level, whose job it is to coordinate the various types of alignment. Thus, in the projection of transportation routes, power lines, and utility mains, the new installations seem to be constantly bumping into things and each other. This is disruptive, socially disturbing, politically explosive, and costly in the extreme.

In a few states highway rights-of-way are being acquired with sufficient width to accommodate joint transit routes or bus lanes. This is to be commended and the possibility of full-scale, all-inclusive transportation-transmission corridors fully explored. Within such designated swaths the highway and transit agencies, chronically short of funds, could lease ground and air rights to utility companies.

There is no reason why utility and transmission lines cannot be consolidated with the highway construction, buried in widened berms, or carried on overhead structures. Bridges and tunnels, as well as all other types of crossings, can be so planned as to accommodate the other uses also. The savings in land acquisition, grading, and construction will be enormous; efficiency in operation and maintenance will be increased; public acceptance will be more easily obtained and the regional landscape greatly enhanced.

As far as can be determined, neither the highway, transit, or transmission interests are prohibited from such joint use—nor have they been encouraged by the government to consider it. Mounting public pressures against further intrusion of communities now call for a whole new look.

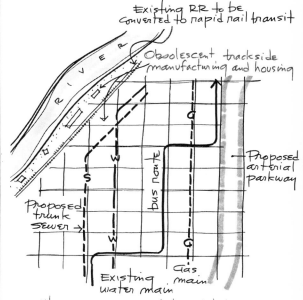

The many necessary but varied lines traversing a region limit other land uses, destroy continuity, and cause frequent disruptions of installation and maintenance.

Record the present condition

This is best accomplished by preparing a series of coordinated "as-built" maps. These will show at the same scale all jurisdictional boundaries, land-use zoning, existing dedicated rights-of-way, and topographical features.

Then, on prints of these base sheets, or on overlays, plot the existing streets and highways, railroads, airways, shipping lanes, and all other routes of transit and transportation movement. Show also the major sewer systems, utility mains, and fuel and power transmission lines.

It is probable that for the first time, in a study of such as-built maps, those charged with the administration, planning, and operation of the study area will understand its physical structure and the way it works, or fails to work.

Coordinate all routes of movement into a revised composite master plan

Using the "as-built" maps as a base, devise through comparative studies a more reasonable long-range diagram for regional transportation.

Such a plan will provide for safe and pleasant travel and maximum accessibility for all forms of transit and transportation. Routes, nodes, and crossings will be fitted to the neighborhood patterns and to the topography. There will be provision for high-speed traffic as well as for more leisurely movement, perhaps by barge, bridle trail, minibus, golf cart, bicycle, or pedestrian path. Intercommunity linkage will be planned through parklike greenways and blueways.

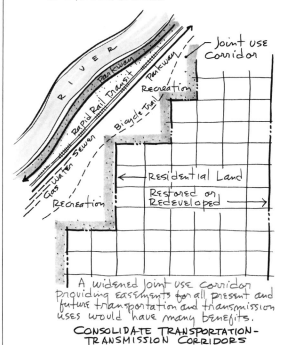

A widened joint use corridor providing easements for all present and future transportation and transmission uses would have many benefits.

CONSOLIDATE TRANSPORTATION-TRANSMISSION CORRIDORS

Further Reading:

Adams, John
Transportation Planning: Vision and Practice
Routledge & Kegan Paul, Ltd.
Boston, 1981

American Society of Civil Engineers and
Charles H. Klohn, eds.
*Joint Usage of Utility and Transportation
Corridors*
New York, 1981

Appleyard, Donald
Livable Streets
University of California Press
Berkeley, Calif., 1981

Carstens, Diane Y.
Site Planning and Design for the Elderly
Van Nostrand Reinhold Company Inc.
New York, 1985

CLM/Systems, Inc.
*Airports and Their Environment: A Guide to
Environmental Planning*
(Prepared for U.S. Department of Transportation)
Cambridge, Mass., 1972

Godwin, George
Traffic, Transportation and Urban Planning
Volumes 1 and 2
Van Nostrand Reinhold Company Inc.
New York, 1981

Meyer, Michael D., and Eric J. Miller
Urban Transportation Planning
McGraw-Hill Book Company
New York, 1984

Owen, Wilfred
The Accessible City
The Brookings Institution
Washington, D.C., 1972

Simonds, John O., ed.
The Freeway in the City: Principles of Planning and Design
U.S. Government Printing Office
Washington, D.C., 1968

Untermann, Richard K.
*Accommodating the Pedestrian: Adapting
Towns and Neighborhoods for Walking and
Biking*
Van Nostrand Reinhold Company Inc.
New York, 1984

U.S. Department of Transportation
*National Transportation Planning Manual,
1970–1990*
U.S. Government Printing Office
Washington, D.C., 1971

U.S. Federal Highway Administration
A Manual for Planning Pedestrian Facilities
U.S. Government Printing Office
Washington, D.C., 1974

Consolidate the transmission lines

Shelving the short-term problems, attempt to combine on the study plans all transmission routes with other transmission routes, with the transportation corridors, or with the projected regional open space system. The resulting plan—while no more than a theoretical guideline for long-range planning discussions—will be eloquent in its message of the advantages of such joint-use corridors.

Designate combined transportation-transmission corridors as part of the future land-use plan wherever feasible

Using the foregoing studies as a guide, take the bold step of defining broad generalized bands which, with modifications, could in time become major joint-use corridors.

Such bands need not detract from the urban or suburban scene. They will provide welcome open space relief and many opportunities for public or taxable multiple use.

They will provide space for present and future highway and transit rights-of-way, transmission lines, and utility mains. They will pay for themselves through savings in future condemnation and acquisition costs, through leases, and through the increased tax yield of abutting lands for which they will provide improved services and access. Interim uses may include parking, material storage, recreation, agricultural fields, or nature preserves.

Who is to own them? Either the local municipalities, the state or the federal government, alone or in combination—or an authority created for this purpose. Once a program is inaugurated, the income from leases will provide a revolving fund.

Reserve the rights-of-way

Most new or enlarged highways planned within metropolitan areas must be sliced through living urban tissue. Acquisition and construction costs are correspondingly high; the problems of displacement and relocation are acute; and environmental stresses severe. Many essential improvement programs are stalled as a result, and many public careers are thereby jeopardized. The same conditions pertain to the installation or expansion of utility mains, transit routes, and transmission lines.

It has become clearly evident that interconnecting rights-of-way of ample width to accommodate all forms of transportation, transit, and transmission should be consolidated into a single network. These will be established, whenever possible, well ahead of area development and reserved by lease or purchase. The economic advantage of such advanced planning is irrefutable. The side benefits may be of equal, or greater, importance.

Consolidate all possible cross-country power-line, pipeline, and roadway routes

Highways and railroads are fairly sympathetic to the terrain through which they pass since they avoid topographical obstructions and move with the contours. Pipelines and power lines, oblivious to grades, tend to follow the straightest possible course as they slash inexorably across hill, marsh, and meadow. As a result of the varying alignments—especially where several routes traverse the same vicinity—the land is cut into wasteful patterns and fragmented with leftover parcels. The mandatory consolidation of all new routes will have many desirable results.

Exploit the multiple-use potential of existing transmission routes

A move to open up for public and private uses the heretofore restricted lands of the public utility companies is rapidly gaining momentum in the United States. Thousands upon thousands of acres of prime land are at stake.

The need for such joint use has been intensified by the rapid urbanization of the properties surrounding the utility service areas. At the same time that the cities have been crowding in upon the utility lands, the companies have needed to expand their rights-of-way in order to meet the increased demands for service. Faced with monumental problems of land acquisition and changing public attitudes, the utility interests have begun to reexamine and modify their traditional policy of reserving their property free from other uses.

In a study by Charles L. Crumpton, the alternate uses of power-transmission rights-of-way have been imaginatively explored and documented. Such uses presently include streets, highways, and parkways, off-street parking compounds, commercial and industrial storage areas, public and private recreation areas, parklands, and golf courses. Agricultural lands and horticultural nurseries frequently share the land with the utility installations. Home and apartment owners have in many cases been granted the right to utilize the right-of-way for an extension of their lawns and gardens and as as community open space.

Utility companies questioned about the possibilities have generally agreed that all such uses, including joint occupancy by other utility companies, would be welcomed under reasonable controls and conditions. Few limitations were stipulated except that because of the matter of safety, buildings, swimming pools, and places of public assembly should not be permitted, nor should such uses as might become unsightly or a nuisance.

The right of joint occupancy is normally granted to private interests by means of an easement or lease agreement which spells out the type and conditions of the use, the fee, and such matters as access and the degree of user maintenance. Land-use rights are often granted to public or quasi-public agencies without charge.

There are many advantages to such multiple use. Utility companies, with an eye to public opinion, are constantly seeking means by which they may improve their image. To let large strips of highly desirable land lie dormant and unavailable is not in their best interest. By sharing their landholdings with the communities they serve, they assume the role of a good neighbor. There are considerable revenues to be gained, especially in leases for commercial and industrial purposes. The maintenance of the right-of-way by joint users is also an economic advantage.

To the public in general there is great promise in this new opportunity to restore to good uses the extensive land reserves which until recently have been "locked up" in the sacrosanct realms of the utility companies.

Convert utility rights-of-way into regional open space connectors

Because of their elongated nature, transmission routes lend themselves ideally to joint use as "greenway" linkage between communities. Park drives, for example, can loop through the corridor and adjacent parcels acquired to supplement the utility company holdings.

Lineal parks of variable width can utilize the transmission swath to provide access to and interconnect the dispersed components of the park and recreation system. Utility easements are admirably suited for such compatible uses as walkways, bicycle trails, bridle paths and, in remote areas, interconnecting snowmobile courses.

Utility companies are spending millions of dollars annually for rights-of-way for transmission lines and therefore are the owners of extremely valuable property. As such, they are responsible for keeping the rights-of-way intact for the purposes for which they were acquired. One of the purposes is to assure a location where electric power transmission facilities may be operated and maintained free from impairment and interference. The ideal solution from the utility's point of view would be rights-of-way with no encumbrances whatsoever. However, this ideal is not realistically attainable. Progress cannot be stopped by the refusal on the part of utilities to allow some non-utility uses on their rights-of-way. Such joint uses must, of course, not only benefit the community, but also, at the same time, not interfere with the utility's operations.

CHARLES L. CRUMPTON
Alternate Uses of Electric Power Transmission Rights of Way within Urban Areas
A thesis presented to the Faculty of
Georgia Institute of Technology 1968

7 The planned community

Little boxes on the hillside
Little boxes made of ticky tacky
Little boxes on the hillside
Little boxes all the same.
There's a green one and a pink
    one
And a blue one and a yellow
    one
And they're all made out of
    ticky tacky
And they all look just the same.

174

The days are past, in most localities, in which a developer could purchase raw land, clear the trees, lay out streets, and sell lots or build houses, stores, or bowling alleys at his own discretion. It has been learned from sad experience that in many such cases the entrepreneur provided only those minimum improvements necessary for quick sales or rentals. Often he neglected to install street surfacing, lighting, erosion control, or even sewers. He would take his profit and leave behind him, as a community burden, the responsibility for providing schools, parks, and all other public services.

Public officials now realize that land development for any purpose should be permitted only if it is accomplished in accordance with a well-considered program for orderly development, under proper controls and procedures.

Acceptable development proposals must:

1. Comply with the zoning and building codes and applicable ordinances.

2. Relate to trafficways, transit and transportation routes, and their projected capacities.

3. Meet the requirements of the police, fire, sanitation, post office, and public works departments.

4. Be meshed with the programs of the school board and the park and recreation authorities.

5. Demonstrate that in its planning the negative environmental impacts have been minimized, the benefits maximized, and that in sum the project will be consistent with the community's long-range goals.

This presupposes that there *is* for the larger community a planning board or commission, a workable program, and the mechanism for guiding the developer of housing, shopping, industrial, or any other type of project, into producing a public asset. If these planning tools do not yet exist, the community officials have not been performing.

The legal basis

As with highways, the form of a community is to a large extent the three-dimensional expression of the laws which pertain to its planning and construction. Such legal controls may prescribe the type of use, the width of the streets, the height of the buildings, the distance between them, and sometimes even their color.

While enlightened controls are a safeguard and boon, outmoded or shortsighted restrictions may do more harm than good. They may even impose rigid patterns of newly created blight upon a naturally beautiful countryside. Often the damage is irreparable. In some localities, for example, regulations require that all streets be laid out, to the horizon, on a monotonous north-south, east-west grid, simply to facilitate the delivery of mail. Again, large tracts of property are sometimes restricted to a single use, without provision for supporting amenities or open space relief. Elsewhere, such artificial limitations as "paper streets," or preestablished section-line canals or roads may set an inflexible pattern for all future landscape planning. Even the restrictive regulations of a sanitation department may have more effect upon a subdivision layout than the conformation of the land or an existing stream.

In sum, the quality of a community's development can be no better than the legal controls which govern its design. How can their effectiveness be tested?

The first and essential step is for the local government, be it county, city, or township, to create a planning commission. This body will appoint a trained director, who will in turn engage the necessary staff and initiate planning procedures. As a result of their studies and recommendations, desirable changes in, and improvements to, the legal controls will soon become apparent.

Establish a planning commission

This influential body is appointed by the jurisdictional government, from which it derives its powers. At best it comprises a progressive, realistic, and idealistic cross section of the community leadership. Members selected from the legal, architectural, and engineering and landscape architectural professions have much to contribute, as do the most respected representatives of the business and cultural institutions. Membership should be made a high honor, with terms of service short and overlapping.

The responsibility of the commission is to define goals, establish policy, review proposals, and recommend action pertaining to the area's physical planning. Its work is to guide, rather than to encourage, new development. Let other groups make their case for growth, the promotion of new business and the provision of a broader tax base. The emphasis of the planning commission is best focused upon *environmental quality* and the creation of those conditions and amenities which will assure for the citizens, their children, and their grandchildren a full, rich, and satisfying life in a community of which they may be justifiably proud.

Create a planning department

The working arm of a planning commission is the *planning department* which is normally created by the governing body at the same time that the commission is formed.

While planning departments sometimes function under a municipality and its council directly, there are many benefits in making the planning director and department responsible to an appointed, nonpartisan commission. Among the advantages are those of continuity, community participation, and the generation of public support for the planning proposals when they are brought to vote.

Prepare a "workable program for community improvement"

One of the first tasks of a planning staff is to aid in the preparation of a detailed program for community development. This is necessary not only for the formulation of meaningful plans and regulations; it is also a prerequisite for participation in most programs involving the flow of state and federal funds to the local government.

By usage, a "workable program" comprises those elements which have been generally tested and accepted as being essential to good municipal management.

A community plan is not a layout of streets and houses, or of viaducts and factories. It is the form of the activity going on.
PAUL AND PERCIVAL GOODMAN
Communitas
University of Chicago Press
Chicago, 1947

177

Out of this discussion of the neighbourhood there appears to emerge four criteria by which the quality of design of these smaller social units may be measured. The first is that the social values to the individual and to the community shall, in case of conflict, outweigh any temporary financial advantage. . . . Secondly the plan must foster family life with widely diverse opportunities for wholesome outdoor as well as indoor social activities . . .

The third of the criteria is the effectiveness of the scheme in promoting friendliness among neighbours. This involves an ability to recognize or to create those physical arrangements which bring pre-school age children and their mothers together almost daily in natural and informal play and talk.

The fourth criteria is the recognition of the rightful dominance of the pedestrian within the social unit centering on the smaller elementary school . . .

G. HOLMES PERKINS, article in
The Future of Cities and Urban Development
University of Chicago Press
Chicago, 1953

The meaning of "community" is one of the basic unresolved questions confronting society and planning today. In the absence of a thorough understanding of community and in the absence of a modern dynamic meaning of community, we are building a physical living environment in which the individual is losing his identity.

PERRY L. NORTON, article in
Planning and the Urban Community
University of Pittsburgh Press
Pittsburgh, 1961

To describe the modern community one would have to explore in detail the potentialities of life for modern man.

LEWIS MUMFORD
The Culture of Cities
Harcourt, Brace and Co., Inc.
New York, 1938

. . . there is an art of relationship just as there is an art of architecture. Its purpose is to take all the elements that go to create the environment . . . and to weave them together in such a way that drama is released.

GORDON CULLEN
Townscape
Reinhold Publishing Corporation
New York, 1971

Develop a comprehensive plan

The planning agency sets about to survey and assess the local resources—physical, social, financial, and administrative. Then, in the light of its program and goals, and often with the help of expert consultants, it works to evolve a series of plans for community improvement. Each aspect of the community life and environmental framework is considered, and proposals are made to bring them all together in a more harmonious relationship.

Planning decisions are incorporated in a series of documents which describe existing and proposed land uses, major thoroughfares, and community facilities.

Three ingredients are essential to effective planning. One is that all plans must be kept current. Secondly, all proposals must be geared to take full advantage of the long-range possibilities. Finally, future plans must be kept generalized to the point that they are flexible and responsive to new factors and changing conditions.

Provide legal controls

Once planning decisions have been made, on even a tentative basis, they are put into effect by the enactment of zoning ordinances and subdivision regulations, and by the adoption of a capital improvements program. These, like the plans which they implement, are subject to constant review and revision. It is desirable to keep them positive and permissive in their wording, rather than restrictive.

Program, plan, ordinances, and regulations together make up the legal mechanism required to guide and encourage the orderly evolution of the community and its environs.

Community components

A community may be likened to a living organism. It has substance, form, and vitality. It requires air, water, and nourishment, and gives off wastes. Perhaps the best way to understand its workings is to dissect the body and examine the parts. Then, sensing the function and importance of each, it can be seen how they all work together.

It could be said that the body of the community is composed of its land-use areas, such as the various types of residential, commercial, and cultural properties. Their size and disposition set the general outline or shape. The skeleton to which they relate is the natural topography with its geological structure, which determines the basic three-dimensional form and much of the community's landscape character. Circulation ways, including streets, transit routes, pedestrian walks, and perhaps canals serve as the veins and arteries. Commerce and industry provide the lifeblood. Energy and communications systems function as the nerves. The institutions—schools, libraries, museums, and churches—symbolize the mind and spirit. The total aspect, or countenance, is attractive only if each of the features is well formed to serve its purpose, and the composite body is healthy and thriving.

Consider the type of community you would like yours to be

What is its purpose? Does it serve the purpose well?

Is it a trade center? Does it have industrial and manufacturing districts as well as commercial, residential, and recreation areas? Are they awkwardly jumbled together and full of frictions, or are they well related and interconnected, yet separated by natural buffers? Is yours an "institutional town," built around a cathedral, medical center, or university campus? Or is it essentially a living community with supporting amenities? Does its plan arrangement express and accommodate the role that it plays? If not, what obvious changes should be made? What desirable features have you found in other communities that you would like to have in your own? Suggest them to friends. Discuss them with civic leaders. Propose them to city council. Remember that there is no force on earth as powerful as a good idea.

Analyze each community component

Are all of the parts in good working order? Are they well planned, efficient, and attractive?

Do the shopping and business office areas have safe and pleasant access? Do they have adequate parking areas—well lighted, planted, and screened from view by low walls, mounding, or hedges?

Are the schools designed as neighborhood focal points and gathering places? Are they combined with recreation areas and open space as school-park units?

Are the business-office buildings grouped into a "campus" and interconnected with pedestrian plazas and courts?

Are churches, libraries, and auditoriums so located as to serve as neighborhood centers?

Is the manufacturing district in good tone? Is it clean and up to date? Or is it blighted with obsolescent warehouses, rusty trackage, and pollution?

A community takes its character and flavor from the spaces and places to which it relates, and from the routes along which the people move. It is judged by the assemblage of the elements—all of the elements—of which it is composed.

Think in terms of systems

A problem common to most communities is congenital fragmentation. Over their years of development many facilities have been built as separate and unrelated projects.

Highways have been constructed a section at a time, often without regard for their function as part of an overall system of traffic movement. Such segmented trafficways may ease local congestion, only to overload other connecting routes.

Park, recreation, and open space lands have often been acquired on a spotty basis, rather than as well-considered and integrated units of a comprehensive plan.

Streets, walks, and trails have been laid out by developers of adjacent properties without interconnection.

Local sewers have been approved and installed to serve immediate needs, without study of projected upland requirements, or of down-valley capacities.

Even water, gas, and power distribution lines are often uncoordinated. Two competing utility companies, for example, may install mains on either side of a single street, or both may serve the same area. Lines, plants, and operations are needlessly duplicated. Such practices are clearly wasteful.

It can be said that all community services that are to be jointly administered, operated, or maintained should be coordinated in their planning stages. It can further be stated that all lines of movement or transmission, being continuous by nature, are best planned as integral segments of a comprehensive system. All must be well related to each other and to the landscape through which they move.

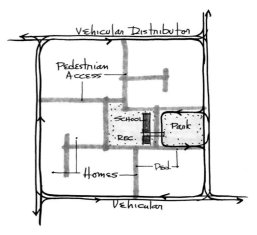

THE SCHOOL AS A NEIGHBORHOOD CENTER

All things considered, the elementary school-park, with its pedestrian walkway approaches, still provides a superior neighborhood focal point and structuring element.

A community that does not plan and build the necessary structures for the common (social) life will remain under a perpetual weight and handicap: its buildings may tower against the skies, but its actual social stature may be smaller measured by effective accomplishment than a decent country town.
  LEWIS MUMFORD
The Culture of Cities
Harcourt, Brace and Co., Inc.
New York, 1938

Land-use patterns

Beauty, by definition, is the perceived harmonious relationship of all the elements in any object, place, or action. If this be so, then the most attractive communities are those in which everything seems to be working well together. This is largely a matter of the allocation and distribution of the land-use areas for housing, schools, shopping, and so on, in relation to each other, the circulation routes, and the topographical features.

Many neighborhoods have been laid out with T-square and compass as rigid, two-dimensional patterns of lots and rights-of-way. Such geometric doodles disregard the living habits of the families and the natural groupings and movements of people, which are so much a part of pleasant community life. Often they also ignore the orientation of streets and buildings to the sweep of the sun, the direction of the prevailing breeze, and the winter winds. Sometimes they even violate natural flood or drainage patterns or destroy irreplaceable landscape features.

Such projects are plagued with troubles from the start. They are cross-grained. They are marked with problems of disruption, conflicts, and excessive costs. They are awkward and usually ugly.

Provide suitable areas for all required land uses

These will be of the best possible size and shape to express and accommodate the community's workable program. The areas defined will be comprised of usable land, with favorable slopes and elevations. Soil types and vegetation will be in keeping with the uses proposed, and the subsurface conditions will be suitable for the excavations and foundations.

All natural and man-made conditions will be considered and carefully weighed. Just as a farmer lays out his fields, orchards, and building sites to best suit all conditions, so will the land planner at every scale of development, be it homesite or townsite, seek the most appropriate land-use arrangements.

Leave greenbelt areas in between

Land-use boundaries are usually best set along ridge or valley lines or separated by streams or waterbodies. Often man-made constructions such as canals, highways, railroads, or transmission corridors serve well as separators between various community districts.

Preplan the transportation routes

At the same time logical *areas* are planned for each type of development, compatible *routes* for all types of traffic movement must be devised to serve them. In many cases these routes may be given a parklike character and may be planned to separate neighborhoods or their various segments. In other cases the trafficways may be elevated or depressed, suggesting the multiple use of the right-of-way to provide such community amenities as parking courts, or recreation areas.

Group the compatible uses

In the layout of land-use patterns it will be found that some elements can be effectively combined while others would be in conflict.

Homes, schools, and convenience centers form a complementary grouping, as do parks, zoos, and botanical gardens. Business offices and

---

The best community . . . is that which provides the best environment for the experience of living.

We should design our neighborhood streets for people, not for fire engines.

EUGENE MARTINI
"Land Planning in Transition," address
Housing Conference
National Design Center
New York, 1963

shopping malls are mutually supportive, as are universities, hospitals, and cultural centers. Manufacturing districts are best related to transportation routes and transmission lines. Farmlands blend well with forest preserves.

Incompatible uses generate frictions and tensions. Complementary relationships create a sense of fitness and well-being.

Fit the size to the use requirements

Each use has its own general order of magnitude that seems most desirable.

In nature, swarms of bees, flocks of birds, and herds of antelope, for example, seem to find this type of balance. In community planning, as well, one may learn from experience and observation the size and set of relationships that seem to work best. As a case in point, a neighborhood courtyard as a social unit will generally be most agreeable when some eight to twelve dwellings are grouped around a common feature or space. One reason is that in larger groupings the adults cannot all gather in one home for a party or special occasion. Another is that their small children at play feel intimidated by the offspring of a larger group, and believe themselves to be surrounded by more enemies than friends. Two or three clustered dwellings do not seem to be enough. The "group" relationship is often lacking among the parents and children alike.

Not only do social groupings seem to have a "right" size, but also each neighborhood facility, such as the elementary school or drugstore, has its own rule-of-thumb range of sizes, shapes, and concentrations. These are, of course, approximate. The genius lies in knowing when and how to adjust the sizes or groupings to meet variable situations and to respond to changing conditions.

Preserve the topographical features

Conserve the floodplains, streams, and rivers and build well back from their edges. Build atop the wooded hillsides and between the mountain slopes. Protect the lakes and lagoons with borders of green parklands and create the neighborhoods and business districts between radiating streets. Ravines, water bodies, forests, rock promontories, beaches—these are the true spectaculars of the region.

If destroyed, they will be lost forever. If conserved and intelligently managed, they will enrich the lives of the people for generations to come and make their communities beautiful and unique.

People, streets, buildings

By age-old tradition urban man has built his structures along the public streets which have afforded access, address, and some degree of protection. But conditions have changed with the coming of the automobile. The public streets and highways have become thoroughfares for massive, and often high-speed, traffic movement. They bring with them pollution and danger, for any path of vehicular movement is a lethal line of force.

In the early 1930s two pioneering American planners, Henry Wright and Clarence Stein, set about to design an automobile-age community in which homes and schools would face inward upon pleasant park spaces, courts, or plazas, while vehicular traffic moved *around* and *between* the compounds to make their necessary con-

It would be wise to confine the size of our neighborhood units in the city and in the country to pedestrian distances in spite of automobiles and planes, for our human stride should determine our space and time conception in our local living space.
WALTER GROPIUS
Rebuilding Our Communities
Paul Theobald
Chicago, 1945

Planners have agreed, at long last, that a unit of manageable size must be the cell from which the city grows. Within such a unit, whether residential neighborhood or commercial center, man's two feet again become a pleasant and efficient means of getting around.
ARTHUR HILLMAN
Community Organization & Planning
The Macmillan Company
New York, 1950

Our client is man—whose body and senses, conditioned through countless centuries of living near nature, yearns to see the sky and the earth and the green and trees . . .
CHARLES BLESSING, address
American Institute of Planners
July, 1959

Foxes have holes and the birds of the air have nests; but the Son of Man hath not where to lay His head.
ST. FRANCIS OF ASSISI
Quoted by Kenneth Clark
Civilisation
Harper and Row, Publishers, Inc.
New York, 1969

The main threads of today's urban patterns are streets, roads and highways. In the fabric of the spreading urban scene, they usually appear in gridiron formation. Their function is a two-fold one. They serve first, as lineations along which all structures designed for human activities are arranged—from maternity hospitals to mortuary, from cathedral to hot dog stand, and from mansions to skid-row saloons. The second function they are expected to fulfill is to serve as tracks for a bewildering number of rubber wheeled vehicles.
VICTOR GRUEN
Centers for Urban Environment
Van Nostrand Reinhold Co.,
New York, 1973

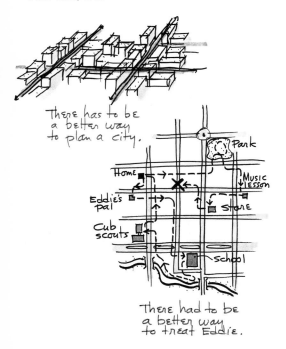

nections. Radburn, New Jersey, and Chatham Village in Pittsburgh remain highly successful examples of their theories put into practice.

It would seem that these models which have such obvious merit would have long ago transformed the science of town and community planning in this country; but the old ways die hard. The planners of the European new towns which have been springing up in the aftermath of World War I have adopted and greatly extended the principles of Radburn. In the United States, however, it is only within the past few years that such new communities as Reston, Columbia, and Saga Bay have again begun to deal firmly and intelligently with the automobile.

There can no longer be the option of clinging to the old ways. The problems of mixing people, buildings, and cars have become so extreme that reasonable decision makers can no longer condone it. The frontage of homes or other buildings upon an arterial street or highway can no longer be considered a right, except as granted as a special exception by the local planning agencies as a reasonable use of property adjacent to a particular trafficway. Cars must be confined to vehicular routes and parking compounds designed for their exclusive use. People and traffic-related functions must be separated, either horizontally, vertically, or both, in order that vehicles may move efficiently, and that within our cities, suburbs, and countryside people may sense again the safety and delight of ways and places planned for the use and enjoyment of ambulating man.

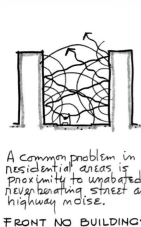

A common problem in residential areas is proximity to unabated, reverberating street and highway noise. X

FRONT NO BUILDINGS ON TRAFFIC ARTERIES

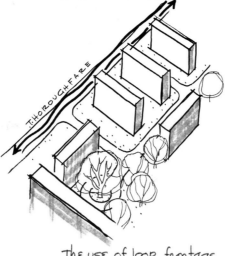

Noise and hazard are both accentuated when buildings face upon busy trafficways.

Buildings set back from, or placed perpendicular to roadways reduce the noise levels and confusion.

PLAN OFF-STREET FRONTAGE TO REDUCE SOUND LEVELS

The use of loop frontage streets or culs-de-sac is an additional improvement.

FACE THE BUILDINGS ON LOCAL APPROACH STREETS

Homes and apartments may turn their backs to the public access streets.

TURN SOUND-ABSORBENT WALLS TO THE TRAFFIC. FACE LIGHTER WINDOW WALLS AWAY.

Face homes and apartments away from the streets

In districts where established land-use patterns or regulations still require building frontage on public street rights-of-way, the design and orientation of the dwelling can help to overcome the problems of sound, light, glare, and the lack of privacy.

Design dwelling clusters around courts or culs-de-sac

The conventional use of high-volume, high-speed traffic corridors as building frontage is senseless. The strange contemporary compulsion to be seen from the highway, to approach one's residence directly from the highway, and to face upon the confusion of the highway, is neither conducive to efficient traffic movement nor to pleasant living.

To function at their best, trafficways should be smooth, uninterrupted channels of flow, without the interference of impinging streets or driveways. To provide a more desirable environment for living, homes should face upon safe and quiet garden-parks.

Enclosure sums up the polarity of legs and wheels. It is the basic unit of the precinctual pattern; outside, the noise and speed of impersonal communication which comes and goes but is not of anyplace. Inside, the quietness and human scale of the square, quad or courtyard. This is the end product of traffic, this is the place to which traffic brings you. Without enclosure traffic becomes nonsense.

GORDON CULLEN
Townscape
Reinhold Publishing Corporation
New York, 1971

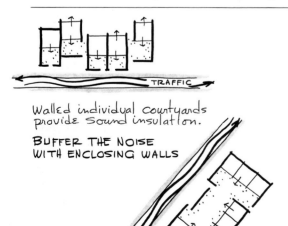

Walled individual courtyards provide sound insulation.

BUFFER THE NOISE WITH ENCLOSING WALLS

On the courtyard may be shared . . .

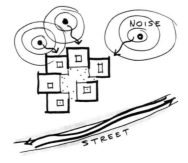

Single or multiple dwellings may face inward upon quiet patios.

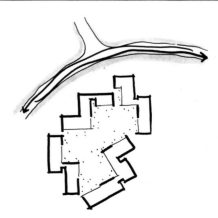

The buildings themselves may be used as sound shields against the passing traffic.

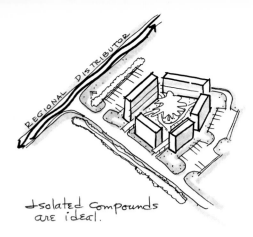

Isolated compounds are ideal.

KEEP HOUSING OFF THE HIGHWAYS...

... one prime way to encourage contacts between neighbors is to put them on a common pathway.

KEVIN LYNCH
Site Planning
MIT Press
Cambridge, Mass., 1971

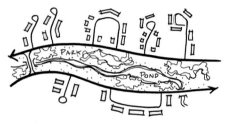

There are many variations to be explored in better relating dwellings and residential clusters to community trafficways.

DIVIDE THE ROADWAYS AND INCREASE THE SETBACK

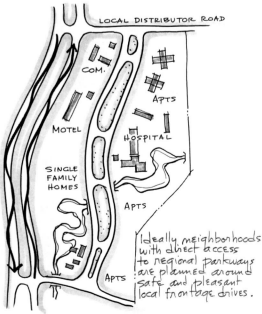

LOCAL DISTRIBUTOR ROAD

COM.

APTS

MOTEL

HOSPITAL

SINGLE FAMILY HOMES

APTS

APTS

Ideally neighborhoods with direct access to regional parkways are planned around safe and pleasant local frontage drives.

CREATE TRAFFIC-FREE NEIGHBORHOODS

Plan isolated living compounds

In new developments where direct building frontage on arterial roads or circulation streets may be prohibited, several noticeable improvements will take place. The roadway, freed of local ingress and egress at each driveway, will be more safe and pleasant. Noise and fumes will be reduced with the reduction of stop-and-go traffic. Homes and apartments will be clustered around motor garden courts or quiet recreation spaces, removed from the trafficways.

Develop trafficfree residential neighborhoods

One reason for the persistent practice of fronting buildings upon streets is the requirement of city ordinances that they be dedicated to a *public right-of-way*. This has been commonly, and erroneously, construed to mean that building sites must be ranged along a public thoroughfare.

Once the idea, and the possibility, of orienting homes and other structures to a dedicated walkway, easement, or commons is accepted, the opportunity is presented for the creation of a vastly superior order of "residential parks." All that is needed is a simple ordinance revision or amendment.

Plan entire communities as residential parks

Such new living environs will recognize and accommodate the essential role of self-propelled vehicles and of mass rapid transit. These will be permitted to circumnavigate, and serve, but not bisect, unified neighborhoods.

Within the inner open space sanctums whole families will be set free—on tricycle, bicycle, or on foot—to move about at leisure within a garden-park setting without regard for the danger of roaring automobiles, trucks, or buses. Such thinking presupposes and makes possible a whole new concept of *community.*

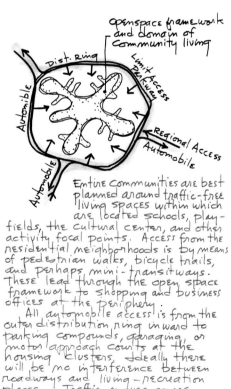

Entire communities are best planned around traffic-free living spaces within which are located schools, playfields, the cultural center, and other activity focal points. Access from the residential neighborhoods is by means of pedestrian walks, bicycle trails, and perhaps mini-transitways. These lead through the open space framework to shopping and business offices at the periphery.

All automobile access is from the outer distribution ring inward to parking compounds, garaging, or motor approach courts at the housing clusters. Ideally there will be no interference between roadways and living-recreation places. Traffic moves more freely; living is far safer and more pleasant.

PROVIDE SEPARATE DOMAINS FOR THE AUTOMOBILE AND FOR COMMUNITY LIVING

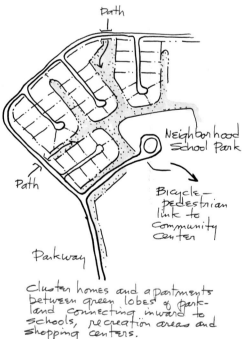

Cluster homes and apartments between green lobes of parkland connecting inward to schools, recreation areas and shopping centers.

LIVING IN A PARK

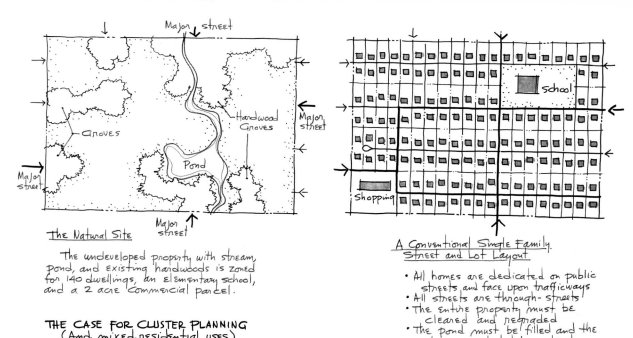

Planned community development (PCD)

Up until a few years ago, if developers owned a piece of land which they wanted to use for housing, they knew what they must do. They must divide the land into streets and lots—each lot as narrow as the law would allow—because of the high cost of installing the heavy traffic-bearing pavement and the large sewers and utility mains which must pass in front of every dwelling. Each house or apartment would face the street—set back a prescribed distance from the front, side, and rear property lines. The driveway entrance to the garage would be cut in from the street or from an alley at the rear.

The developer had no alternative, because this is what all town and city ordinances required. Many still do. The resulting pattern of rigid lots and look-alike homes stretches all around us, often to the horizon. This is middle-income urban and suburban America, and it isn't good enough!

A new breed of land planners, seeking a better way, has proposed a simple solution. Why not, they have suggested, amend the existing ordinances to provide that if a sizable property were involved, say one of 5 acres or more in a single ownership, all zoning restrictions, excepting the number of dwellings for the total acreage, would be waived? The plans for the freer neighborhood layout would be reviewed by the planning department in progressive stages, and would be approved or rejected solely on the basis of performance—the kind of living that the neighborhood would provide.

Homes and apartments could then be grouped with their backs

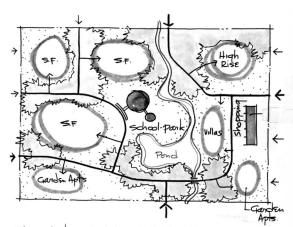

The Clustering of Mixed Single Family and Multifamily Uses (the "PCD," or Planned Community Development approach)

• The same number of housing units are accommodated, but in varying types
• Dwellings face inward to motor courts and outward to neighborhood parkland
• The pond, stream, and trees are preserved, together with the topsoil
• Earthwork is minimized
• The road length, including paving, curbs, utility and sewer mains, is reduced by half
• The school-park, with playfields and meeting rooms, becomes a central neighborhood feature
• Convenience shopping is placed adjacent to a major street intersection
• Safety is increased; monotony is relieved; and property values are raised by the "sense of community."

If we want everything to stay just as it is, everything has to change.

TANCREDI
From *The Leopard*
By Giuseppe Tomasi di Lampedusa

to winding access roads or to motor courts, and could front upon community parks, waterways, or pedestrian plazas. Without the need for rigid lots, the natural site features could be preserved and many new and more livable housing types could be fitted together around them.

Public officials, naturally, have been reluctant at first to try such a novel idea. Some, with more imagination, have agreed on a tentative basis. There have been problems, of course, but the results have proved so successful that more and more municipalities have adopted a Planned Community Development (PCD)* amendment in some form, and the trend is rapidly gaining momentum. The benefits are many.

For homeowners they include trafficfree living, community recreation space just outside their doors, safe pedestrian walkways, and safer vehicular streets. Shops and schools may be reached by a walk or bicycle ride through the park and open space areas where trees, streams, and the natural landforms have been left to enhance the surroundings.

Builders and developers have the advantage of more efficient streets and utility patterns, less site preparation and grading, better drainage, the right to include convenience shopping, better homes in a more attractive living environment—all to be sold or rented at less cost.

Although the PCD concept is still fairly new, and although the ordinances vary widely in their language and effectiveness, they represent a long-overdue and highly promising breakthrough in residential planning. It can be categorically stated that any local government that does not now have on its books a PCD or PUD ordinance, in some form, has not kept up with the times.

Legalize advanced planning techniques in your locality

For the many who would like to maintain or improve the quality of their communities, the most important key lies in the adoption of enlightened planning legislation at the local level that reflects "the current state of the art." A simple amendment to the zoning ordinance is often all that is needed. In other cases the entire system of ordinances, codes, and subdivision regulations is due for a thorough overhaul.

Provide the possibility of planned community development (PCD)

Until recently, as noted, the customary procedure in community planning has been to subdivide a larger property into strips or parcels fronting upon both sides of all public streets. Homes or other buildings have been "shoehorned" onto the lots on the basis of mandatory setbacks from each property line. Further restrictions have usually been imposed in the form of minimum lot sizes; height limitations; general positioning of driveways, parking bays, and garages; and the prohibition of screening hedges or freestanding privacy walls.

These outmoded practices have encouraged developers to clear and level all possible areas of the site and to fit the maximum number of structures within the prescribed building limits. It has resulted in streets which are hazardous and inefficient. Homes and family life are faced upon busy thoroughfares instead of quiet courts or recreation

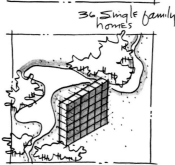

36 Single family homes

36 Dwellings stacked in an apartment tower.

The spread of low density, single family housing is not the answer to land conservation. Where the landscape quality is superior, it is usually better to group the housing units into a multifamily structure.

*Generally synonymous with *planned unit development* (PUD).

spaces. Prodigious amounts of land are wasted in unusable side yards and often front yards which are neither quiet nor conducive to out-of-door living, and many communities have lost all contact with unspoiled nature.

Planned community development, a fresh approach to land planning, has been made possible in many localities through the adoption of a PCD amendment.

Cluster the buildings

"Cluster planning" is a recent and highly desirable outgrowth of planned community development. It means simply that the same total number of dwellings allotted for a given site may be grouped more closely together than under traditional subdivision regulations. A condition is that the land thus saved will be devoted to community open space or other amenities. The more compact arrangement provides savings in grading, paving, utilities, and other costs, and these may be shared with the prospective residents. It is good for all concerned.

An extension of the residential "cluster" concept is being applied to many other uses as well. Shopping centers, industrial parks, business-office and institutional campuses, for example, may be improved by the closer building groupings which yield additional common space.

Of twelve "breakthrough" communities studied by HUD in various parts of the country to explore improved techniques for community planning, not one plan could have been effectuated under traditional zoning procedures. All required the application of the PCD approach.

The more we are together, the merrier we shall be.
  FREDERIC J. OSBORN AND ARNOLD WHITTICK
The New Towns
McGraw-Hill Book Company
New York, 1963

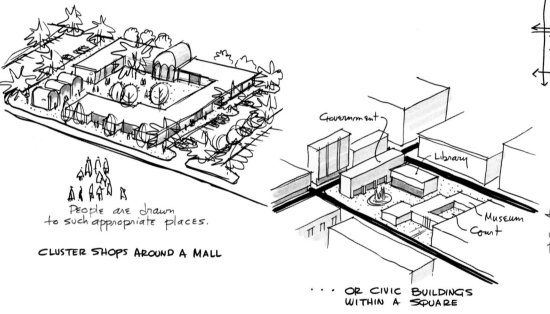

People are drawn to such appropriate places.

CLUSTER SHOPS AROUND A MALL

··· OR CIVIC BUILDINGS WITHIN A SQUARE

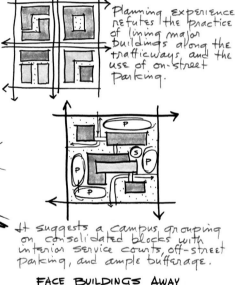

Planning experience refutes the practice of lining major buildings along the trafficways, and the use of on-street parking.

It suggests a campus grouping on consolidated blocks with interior service courts, off-street parking, and ample bufferage.

FACE BUILDINGS AWAY FROM THE PUBLIC STREETS

Include the essential provisions

Planned community development regulations can have far-reaching effects. What they require, permit, and stimulate will set a whole new pattern of landscape development.

To be effective they should refrain from overelaboration and overrestrictiveness. They are best so written as to leave to the developer wide latitude for improvisation, and to the reviewing staff and advisers ample flexibility of choice and authority of decision. Those ordinances which have been most successful have spelled out in clear and simple terms the following provisions:

1. *The types of uses permitted.* It is well to note that convenience centers and services may be provided within residential areas as appropriate.

2. *The gross density allowed.* In the case of residential areas, this should be in substantial accord with the general land-use master

plan. Some "bonus" units may be granted for outstanding developments.

3. *The square feet of floor area.* This applies to commercial, industrial, and institutional uses.

4. *Required parking ratios.* It is helpful to note the percentage of parking stalls to be included beneath, or within, the structures.

5. *Incentives for "cluster" development.* It should be noted that, wherever feasible, preference would be given to proposed plans which have grouped the buildings in such a way as to conserve natural features and open space.

6. *Submission and review procedures.* These should describe the method by which phased plans are to be processed.

Spell out the criteria for plan evaluation

Much of the quality of community plans submitted in accordance with PCD procedures will depend upon the planning-department reviews. It will be helpful, therefore, to prepare as an administrative guideline a set of clear and concise evaluation criteria. This checklist will help to ensure that each plan submitted will be examined in terms of:

1. *Conformity with general plan of community.* The projects must conform with the spirit of the local government's general plan and with its long-range goals.

2. *Soundness of approach.* A sound and realistic planning approach, from the point of view of both the developer and the responsible governmental agency, is essential. The projects, for example, must be economically feasible and the dwellings marketable.

3. *Relationship to the site.* Insofar as reasonable the plan should preserve the best of the natural and man-made features and eliminate any negative aspects.

4. *Effects on adjacent properties.* A good plan should enhance, rather than detract from the surrounding areas and uses.

5. *Demands on facilities and resources.* A check should be made to determine the adequacy of existing or projected traffic networks, sewers, water supply, and energy production. It should also consider the availability of such other needs as schools and fire and police protection.

6. *Environmental impacts.* All positive and negative effects are to be itemized and studied. It is not reasonable to expect that there will be no negative impacts, but rather that they will be eliminated insofar as is reasonable and that, in sum, the benefits to the region will outweigh the negative factors.

7. *Compliance with land development standards.* Those regulations which pertain to environmental protection and enhancement are to be applied. It is of utmost importance, however, that such restrictions as typical right-of-way widths and sections, lot sizes, floor-area ratios, ground coverage, height limitations, and bulk controls are not imposed as requirements. The essence of successful plan review is the maintaining of sufficient control and a high level of "livability," while at the same time permitting and encouraging fresh and creative design. Each new community should be exemplary; each should be unique.

Planning-department reviews, to be effective, must be scheduled as each succeeding phase of the plan is developed. They are to be kept positive and constructive, and geared toward the reaching of agreements in as short a time as possible. It is fundamental that the local government, through its planning commission, retain powers of review and regulatory control through the completion of all construction.

Ensure continuing plan flexibility

In the planning of large-scale developments it is impossible to foresee the changing conditions, new and desirable environmental controls or the design opportunities that may become evident before the project is completed. It is clearly in the public interest therefore, to provide for freedom of change and for refinement of detail as the planning progresses.

This flexible planning framework can be provided by either of two tested approaches. The first entails the official approval of a *generalized development plan* for the proposed community. This will describe graphically and in text the broad concept and plan features. As each subarea of the total plan is carried into detailed planning, and before any construction permits are granted, it is reviewed in stages by the planning department, and approved on the basis of conformity, in all essentials, with the generalized development plan.

The second approach also involves the approval of a generalized development plan and in addition entails the consummation of a legal agreement between the local government and the developer. This agreement, in the form of a covenant running with the land, spells out in detail all the provisions and environmental quality controls that shall govern the detailed planning of each evolving sub-area. This second approach is best suited to the planning of residential developments of "new-town" magnitude.

Community planning checklist

It is helpful to the community planner to compile from experience and observation a list of "dos" and "don'ts." These may stem as well from failures as successes. For the shaping of agreeable living and working places requires constant experimentation, and, admittedly, a good measure of trial and error.

There are no fixed rules—excepting perhaps the established legal statutes. These, if lengthy, are usually more confusing than helpful. If they have been gathering dust for too long in the books, they have no doubt lost their vitality and often deaden any efforts at inventiveness and improvement. And so it is with caution that the following supplementary principles are suggested. They are presented only for consideration and for testing.

Plan, if possible, a complete neighborhood or community

There are many advantages.

To the resident there are benefits of assured schools, churches, recreation, and convenience shopping. Community facilities are "built in." Neighborhood stability is increased and investments are protected. The economies of large-scale operation are passed along to the prospective owners and tenants. Trafficways, pedestrian circulation, and open spaces are planned as unified systems. Many services and

The best plan . . . is one that recognizes its limitation in itself; that planning for everything includes freedom from the plan as one of the greatest things to plan for.
PERCIVAL AND PAUL GOODMAN
Communitas
University of Chicago Press
Chicago, 1947

The great disadvantage of all-at-once design is that people must freeze on the concepts and assumptions of the particular moment. There is no space in time to acquire experience, to test various approaches, no provision for second thoughts, no opportunity to follow through on the happy accidents that always occur.
WILLIAM H. WHYTE
The Last Landscape
Doubleday & Company, Inc.
Garden City, N.Y., 1968

desirable features are possible only when the community is planned as an entity.

To the municipality there is the advantage of optimum land use, and the studied planning of all community components in balanced relationship and in harmony with the topographical features. Order, logic, and reason have more opportunity to prevail.

To the developer accrue the benefits of efficient land acquisition, planning, construction, management, and sales. There are opportunities for creative design and innovative planning not possible in smaller projects. There is the prestige and marketing power of a named community. There is a built-in market for commercial facilities. And there is reason to expect increased long term profits.

Involve the public agencies in the planning process

They have much to offer in data, experience, and knowledge. Consult with them early. Solicit their help. Test their ideas and apply them where sound. It is human nature to favor that plan to which you have contributed; and agency support and approvals are helpful and usually essential.

Relate to the surrounding region

The master planning for a community must extend beyond the project site and immediate environs to include consideration of all extensional elements and factors which have bearing.

Plan at the start for the ultimate growth

While the long-range plans are best kept diagrammatic and open to change, the capacities of all systems should be sized to accommodate all foreseeable demands. Their construction to the point of completion can then be scheduled in reasonable stages.

Establish a feasible density range and land-use allocation

Upon these, to a large extent, will depend the ultimate character, and the economic success of the venture. Optimum densities, like optimum land-use distributions, are determined mainly on the basis of proven performance in comparable situations. While such considerations must be particular to each individual project, it will be of interest to check the projected statistics for comparable communities.

Define the boundaries

Without fencing it in, it is well to mark or suggest the limits of the community. Peripheral greenbelts are effective; they provide protection, identity, openness, recreation, and the space for a bounding access drive. They may also provide the route for subsurface distribution systems.

Natural features such as forest preserves, ridges, ravines, lakes, or watercourses afford excellent definition, as do highways, golf courses, and institutional grounds.

Provide for a balanced community

When development is completed, all land uses and trafficways should work together as a balanced system.

Plan the entrances and approaches with care

Shape the community plan to favor the most convenient and pleasant approach routes, for what one experiences in driving to and from one's home is an important part of daily life. Locate entry points where penetration seems most logical and dramatic and takes fullest advantage of the natural site features. Remember that first impressions are often the most lasting.

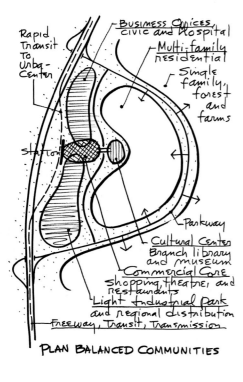

Rapid Transit To Urban Center

Business Offices, civic and Hospital

Multi-family residential

Single family, forest and farms

Station

Parkway

Cultural Center Branch library and museum

Commercial Core Shopping, theatre, and restaurants

Light Industrial Park and regional distribution

Freeway, Transit, Transmission

PLAN BALANCED COMMUNITIES

Provide a descending order of trafficways

A proper roadway system will have a trunk-limb-branch-twig order. Starting with the freeways, it will reduce in magnitude through the regional arterials, major and secondary distributor-collectors, to the local residential streets. Ideally, all will be free-flowing with controlled access, except for the local frontage drives, loops, and culs-de-sac.

Design each roadway, in alignment, section, and detail, to fulfill and express its particular purpose.

Preclude through-traffic movement

Internal trafficways are best devised to provide optimum distribution for the residents and good connections to regional origin-destination points, while yet affording no shortcuts for through traffic.

Align streets and sewers to follow the slopes and contours

Design the roads to serve as the storm-water collectors and conductors. Plan sewers to flow by gravity, and with existing grades. Great savings in grading, trenching, and manhole costs can thus be effected.

Let the topography suggest plan forms

Leave the hills, valleys, streams, ponds, and marshes intact; save the dunes, the pines, and checkerberries; preserve the cypress hammocks, palmetto flats, tidal bays and estuaries, and set homes and apartments around them.

Avoid geometric patterns

A stiff geometric plan layout imposes monotonous regimentation. It fails to respond to the convolutions of the site or to its natural features. Except on a flat or uniformly sloping plane, it is also uneconomical.

Provide community focal points

These may include a pleasant school-park, a handsome church, or a well-designed shopping plaza. They may include too a stream, a lake, a fishing pier, or an attractive community building, a golf course, or tennis club.

All groups of habitations tend to rise, or sink, to the quality level of the places, spaces, and social institutions to which they are oriented.

Give maximum exposure to the best site and community features

This suggests aligning the entrance drives and walkways toward and around them. It suggests also the extending of open space lobes to embrace and better display them and to provide as much frontage as possible that will be focused inward upon them.

Cluster multifamily housing around open space preserves

This provides a pleasant environmental contrast and relieves the pressures of high-density living.

Consider the needs of the people

If our new communities are to be conceived as better places in which to live, they will provide those things which people commonly seek in their living environment. These will include space, comfort, safety, privacy, group encounter opportunities, identity, convenience, interest, variety, and order.

Provide the full range of amenities

It is far from enough to provide only for schools and for shopping. A thriving and progressive community will require a variety of opportunities for intellectual and spiritual stimulation, and for recreation.

In the fertile streets and market place of town and village it is the focal point which crystallizes the situation which confirms "this is the spot." This magnificent clarity illuminates many a community but in many others the chief function of the focal point has been stripped away by the swirl and hazards of traffic . . .
GORDON CULLEN
Townscape
Reinhold Publishing Corporation
New York, 1971

There are two strong, yet diverse trends in housing demand: One is expansive, wanting acreage lots and space and freedom. The other is wanting the town house—no maintenance, no driving. Both trends seek privacy—the one through the insulation of space—the other through turning one's back to the world.
EUGENE R. MARTINI
"Land Planning in Transition," address
Housing Conference
National Design Center
New York, 1963

Text continued on page 207.

The arterial highway corridors will be designed as divided parkways with space at the sides for transit lanes, pedestrian and bicycle paths, and native Florida plantings.

Much of the low-density residential acreage will be devoted to semirural "horse country" living.

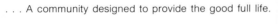

. . . A community designed to provide the good full life.

Equestrian trails will border waterways and weave through open meadows.

Business office and light industrial parks have been planned to provide employment opportunities for residents.

Many of the water storage areas will be set aside as boating and fishing pres

Pedestrian walkways and bicycle trails will link neighborhoods and activity centers.

A planned community

Preliminary proposals for the regional satellite community of Weston, Broward County, Florida (orginally known as Indian Trace).

School-park campuses have been planned throughout the community.

Shopping centers, with professional offices, craft shops, and restaurants, will serve as community gathering places.

Indian Trace (Weston), Broward County, Florida

Most city living rubs people the wrong way. They are disturbed at the increasing distances between home and work, home and school, and home and shopping or recreation areas. They are dismayed at traffic snarls, noise, and fumes. They are alarmed at the dangers of having their children cross busy vehicular trafficways. They see too much of concrete and asphalt, and too little of foliage, fields, or nature. They long for a more rewarding place in which to raise their families.

The alternative to chaotic parcel by parcel development, with dwellings fronting on busy streets, is the commitment of sizable tracts of land to comprehensive and unified planning. An essential feature of such planned communities is that they take their form, stage by stage, from an overall plan which determines from the start the diagrammatic patterns of traffic and land use. Residential, school, church, shopping, work, and recreation areas of proper size and shape are planned in the best possible relationship to each other, to the total site, and to the trafficways which serve them.

Each new community must be designed on a sound ecological basis without undue stress on the natural systems. It should preserve and take its own native character from the landscape features of the site. It should be conceived as a welcome and integrated component of the regional environs, developed in consonance with prevailing social, political, and economic forces.

A master plan must be considered both a commitment and a guideline. It must give the residents assurance that growth will be orderly and in accordance with established limitations of land use and density. It should, however, be kept sufficiently flexible in detail to permit each area as it develops to reflect improved techniques of construction, new standards of environmental quality, and emerging theories of improved land planning.

The approach to the planning of such a new community, Indian Trace, in Broward County, Florida, is outlined in this report.

193

The opportunity

The proper development of land is a matter of far-reaching concern to public officials and citizens alike. It is to the benefit of the entire community that land be planned with foresight and imagination. All too often in the past, considerations raised by groups alarmed at the deteriorating effects of uncoordinated housing and strip commercial development have gone unheeded. More recently, at the ballot box, citizens have consistently expressed their support of more comprehensive planning and environmental controls.

In Broward County the unprecedented population increase experienced in the past two decades will continue in the future,

lated urban expansion. New large-scale communities, which for the most part are built in a natural setting, afford an excellent opportunity for families to live the good full life in neighborhoods freed of through traffic, surrounded by amenities, and with nature close at hand.

Arvida Corporation's 16-square-mile holding of land in a single ownership presents Broward County with a unique and splendid opportunity. Here, ideally situated within the regional transportation network, a new satellite subcenter has been planned for staged development over the next four decades. In character it has been conceived as a spacious rural to semirural Florida community

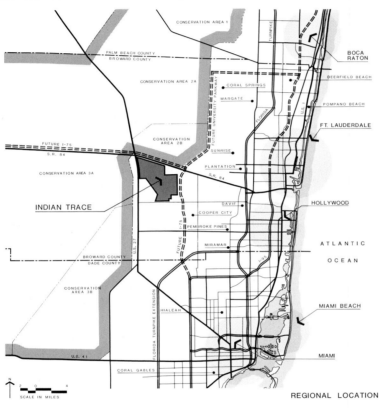

REGIONAL LOCATION

though probably at a slower pace. Homes will be provided in one way or another, either by spot developments, or more hopefully, by unified and complete communities such as the one being proposed by Arvida Corporation.

Totally planned communities are a promising answer to those who protest the continuing sprawl of lot-by-lot and parcel-by-parcel development, for mile after mile, without relief, across the countryside. The new towns of America and Europe have demonstrated clearly the many advantages of clustering homes, schools, and other structures around open water bodies, parks, recreation areas, and nature preserves to accommodate regu-

surrounded by, and interlaced with, lakes and open greenways. Its concept has been derived from the county's stated goals and objectives, and uses and elements to be included are those considered by the county leadership and planning agencies to be most desirable.

The total community plan will be implemented gradually within the procedural guidelines of the county's forward-looking planned-unit-development ordinance. Throughout its entire build-out period, it will be responsive to the best of evolving environmental protection techniques and planning principles.

Planning objectives

From its inception, the planning of Indian Trace has been guided by five governing objectives:

1. Protect and manage the water resources

A dominant feature of the site is its location between Everglades Conservation Areas to the north and west and the C-11 canal to the south. An abundance of water poses both problems and opportunities and makes necessary a highly sophisticated water management system. Its fourfold purpose is to prevent flooding, protect water quality, replenish the underground reserves and develop the water storage areas as prized community assets.

Much of the land to be improved must be raised to levels at or above flood criteria. The extensive excavations required to provide landfill are to be shaped into a network of reservoirs. These will store excess surface runoff and will serve as natural filters to sustain water quality. They will serve also as highly effective recharge basins which will return to the underlying Biscayne Aquifer more water each year than will be withdrawn to meet community needs.

A further beneficial aspect of the water management system will be the creation of a wide expanse of interconnected lakes and waterways. These and the meadows and wetlands around them, will provide habitat for fish, game, and wildfowl, and will supplement the recreational opportunities of the adjacent conservation lands.

2. Create an open space framework

In addition to their primary function, the water storage areas will be designed to provide a magnificent setting of lakes, waterways, and vegetated open space preserves. These will serve to enfold and separate the various development areas to be planned for residential, cultural, business, and other uses.

By their need for both dispersion and continuity, the water management blueways and greenways will penetrate the entire community.

Other spaces will occur in the form of planted parkways, golf courses, recreation areas, and urban or regional parks. By employing the "cluster" concept of building arrangement, structures will be grouped around plazas, courts, or commons, to free additional greenbelt lands for recreation and buffer zones.

Traditionally, neighborhoods have been bound together by highways and streets upon which homes have faced and toward which all life has been oriented. In the community of

Indian Trace, islands of development will be surrounded by usable waterways and green open space.

3. Ensure ease of access and circulation

Diagrammatically, the roadway system is composed of a hierarchy of freeways, arterial parkways, circulation roads, and local frontage streets, loops, and culs-de-sac.

The arterial parkways are planned without building frontage and with widened rights-of-way to provide for separate bus lanes, mini-transit routes, walks, and bicycle trails. As "lineal motor parks," they will feature earth contouring, landscape planting, and attractive signing and lighting. The circulation roads will also be designed with limited frontage and with parkway characteristics. To yield the utmost in safety, T-intersections will be used except at arterial crossings.

While through traffic is not to be encouraged, inward and outward linkages are provided as an integral part of the county's regional transportation and transit network.

4. Define and accentuate the neighborhoods

Utilizing the neighborhood concept, the conceptual plan provides development areas of varying shapes and sizes to accommodate residential arrangements of many types—from relaxed, semirural "villages" to vibrant urban apartment complexes. Each neighborhood will be defined by waterways, greenbelts, or circulation corridors and will be provided with routes of interconnection to activity centers that will develop within the larger community.

Each neighborhood will develop its own individual character with gathering places, focal points, and those amenities best suited to its own particular needs. These may include playlots, parklets, swim and racquet clubs, or other recreation places and spaces. When and where justified, they may include convenience shopping, craft studios, business offices and learning centers.

An essential feature of the neighborhood-plan arrangement, however, will be that while each provides some amenities within easy walking or biking distances, other aspects of the larger community life will be shared by two or more neighborhood or subneighborhood groupings, or by all of them together. School systems, commercial enterprises, and cultural facilities have their own best size and optimum "trade area" and are usually best situated outside and between those residential groupings that they serve. Aside from the residential neighborhoods,

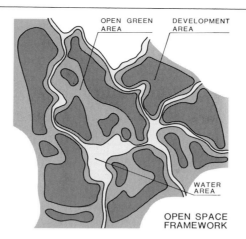

OPEN GREEN AREA
DEVELOPMENT AREA
WATER AREA

OPEN SPACE FRAMEWORK

EXPRESSWAY
NON-VEHICULAR TRAIL
CIRCULATION ROAD
ARTERIAL

ACCESS AND CIRCULATION

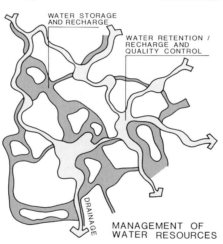

WATER STORAGE AND RECHARGE
WATER RETENTION / RECHARGE AND QUALITY CONTROL
DRAINAGE

MANAGEMENT OF WATER RESOURCES

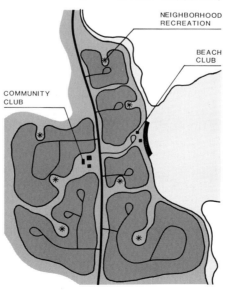

NEIGHBORHOOD RECREATION
BEACH CLUB
COMMUNITY CLUB

NEIGHBORHOODS

there will be other "neighborhoods," or districts, designed as unified shopping malls, light industrial parks, business office complexes, and civic or cultural centers.

5. Provide for the good full life

In the planning of Indian Trace, the overriding consideration has been to create the best possible environment for living. Implicit is the provision of a full range of housing types, amenities and public services, new approaches to the design of safe and efficient trafficways, the need for freedom from pollution in any form, and coordinated systems of schools, parks, and convenience centers. Most of all, the plan expresses the conviction that a progressive community must present a variety of opportunities for intellectual and spiritual stimulation, employment, and economic livelihood, along with excitement, reward, and pleasure in all aspects of daily life.

Survey and reconnaissance

The site

The site is protected on the north and west by established conservation areas. It is bordered by existing and proposed thoroughfares: State Road 84 and proposed Interstate-75 on the north, U.S. 27 on the west, Griffin Road on the south and proposed I-75 on the east.

A neighboring residential community of medium-high density is being developed immediately to the northeast.

The sparse vegetative cover, consisting mainly of sawgrass with scattered Melaleuca, Brazilian pepper, and Australian pine, is of little ecological, economic, or landscape significance. The displacement of the existing flora by imported weed species is an ongoing process. Essentially, the land, in its present state, is unproductive in terms of the regional ecosystem, except for its water storage function.

Site analysis

Sound planning must start with an understanding of all existing conditions and factors which have a bearing on the development process. These conditions pertain not only to the property itself but to the county environs and the larger region of which it is a part.

In exploring the nature of the immediate site, the topographic survey has been supplemented with data secured by detailed field investigations, by soil and water measurements and sampling, and remote-sensing photography. Pertinent and available information, as obtained, is made part of the site-

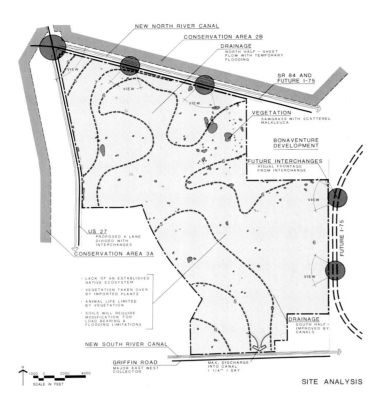

NEW NORTH RIVER CANAL

CONSERVATION AREA 2B

DRAINAGE
NORTH HALF - SHEET
FLOW WITH TEMPORARY
FLOODING

VIEW

SR 84 AND
FUTURE I-75

VIEW

VEGETATION
SAWGRASS WITH SCATTEREL
MALALEUCA

VIEW

BONAVENTURE
DEVELOPMENT

FUTURE INTERCHANGES
VISUAL FRONTAGE
FROM INTERCHANGE

VIEW

FUTURE I-75

US 27
PROPOSED 4 LANE
DIVIDED WITH
INTERCHANGES

6

CONSERVATION AREA 3A

VIEW

· LACK OF AN ESTABLISHED
NATIVE ECOSYSTEM

· VEGETATION TAKEN OVER
BY IMPORTED PLANTS

· ANIMAL LIFE LIMITED
BY VEGETATION

· SOILS WILL REQUIRE
MODIFICATION FOR
LOAD BEARING &
FLOODING LIMITATIONS

5

5

DRAINAGE
SOUTH HALF -
IMPROVED BY
CANALS

NEW SOUTH RIVER CANAL

6

GRIFFIN ROAD
MAJOR EAST WEST
COLLECTOR

MAX. DISCHARGE
INTO CANAL
1 1/4" / DAY

N
1000 0   2000   4000
SCALE IN FEET

SITE ANALYSIS

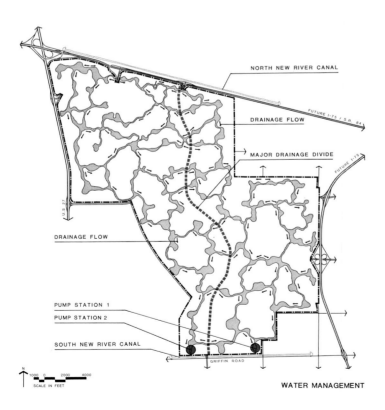

NORTH NEW RIVER CANAL

FUTURE I-75 / S.R. 84

DRAINAGE FLOW

MAJOR DRAINAGE DIVIDE

FUTURE I-75

US 27

DRAINAGE FLOW

PUMP STATION 1

PUMP STATION 2

SOUTH NEW RIVER CANAL

GRIFFIN ROAD

N
1000 0   2000   4000
SCALE IN FEET

WATER MANAGEMENT

analysis documents. These in turn form the basis for continuing research and for all land planning studies.

Regional factors

Within the regional context, much useful information has been made available by the county's planning agencies and departments. The Area Planning Board and the County Planning and Zoning Department particularly have been able to furnish not only excellent background data but also related planning studies and projections as to Broward County's long-range needs and goals.

Eco-determinant mapping

All applicable information obtained from these and other sources has been recorded on a set of eco-determinant maps which, together, define the ecological basis and indicate the long-range constraints and possibilities.

Of some thirty-two maps compiled to date, eight examples are shown.

Community systems

Water management

In this conceptual plan, approximately 3,000 acres of lakes, waterways, and open space will be utilized as water storage areas and as drainageways to conduct excess storm-water runoff to one of two pump stations, at which point discharge will be made into the South New River Canal. Additionally, with the improvement of this canal to increase its capacity, the total water management system will result in a 100-year flood elevation of 7.5 feet mean sea level. The water management map indicates the proposed drainage system and the direction of flow throughout the lakes and waterways.

The water management system will be operated at a normal elevation of 4.0 feet mean sea level, which will provide a positive head of approximately 1 foot above that presently maintained in the area. This head will aid in the recharge of the freshwater aquifer.

During rainy periods, the system will be allowed to reach 5.0 feet mean sea level before discharge is made into the South New River Canal. Discharge into this canal will be at a rate of $1\frac{1}{4}$ inches per day, which is permitted by the Central and Southern Florida Flood Control District. Water that is discharged into the canal will be back-pumped into Conservation Area No. 3A for storage and recharge of the freshwater aquifer.

Prior to entry into the lake system, storm-water runoff will pass through various filters and traps to remove possible pollutants.

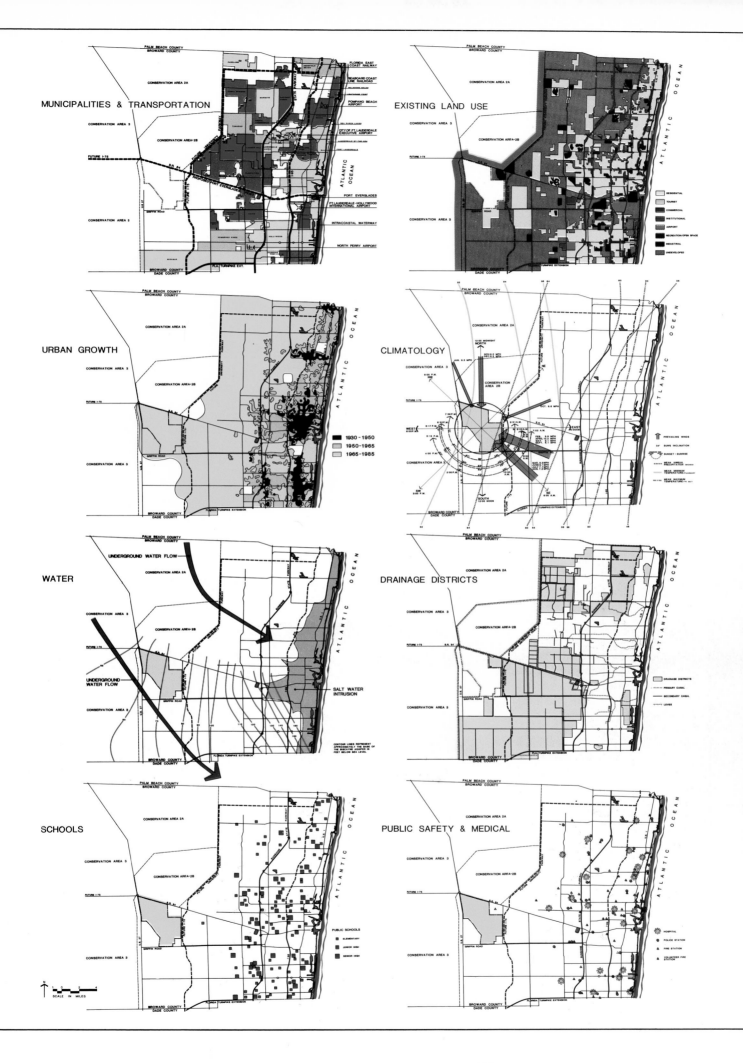

MUNICIPALITIES & TRANSPORTATION

EXISTING LAND USE

URBAN GROWTH

1930 - 1950
1950 - 1965
1965 - 1985

CLIMATOLOGY

WATER

UNDERGROUND WATER FLOW

UNDERGROUND WATER FLOW

SALT WATER INTRUSION

CONTOUR LINES REPRESENT
APPROXIMATELY THE BASE OF
THE BISCAYNE AQUIFER IN
FEET BELOW SEA LEVEL

DRAINAGE DISTRICTS

DRAINAGE DISTRICTS
PRIMARY CANAL
SECONDARY CANAL
LEVEE

SCHOOLS

PUBLIC SCHOOLS
ELEMENTARY
JUNIOR HIGH
SENIOR HIGH

SCALE IN MILES

PUBLIC SAFETY & MEDICAL

HOSPITAL
POLICE STATION
FIRE STATION
VOLUNTEER FIRE
STATION

Grassed swales will be utilized extensively throughout the project as nutrient retainers. A filter barrier system will surround the lakes within the project. As a final screen, and to remove nutrients from the water in the lake and waterway system, aquatic vegetation will be used on the perimeter of the lake sections.

The operation and maintenance of the water-quality aspects of the storm-water drainage system will be the responsibility of an improvement district or homeowners' association.

The maintenance of water quality has been a major determinant in all phases of project planning. The storm-water management system has been designed under the

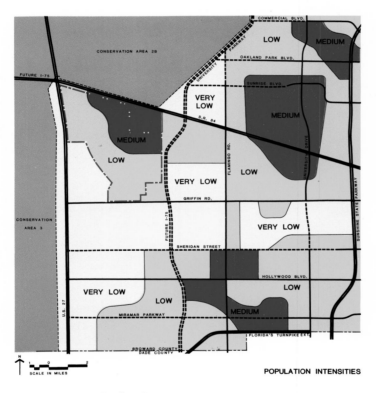

POPULATION INTENSITIES

criterion that water discharged into the South New River Canal is to be equal to, or better than, the quality of the water that presently exists in the canal.

Population allocation

In its recently published Land Use Plan and report, the Broward County Area Planning Board has addressed itself to the distribution of the county's projected population. For the Southwest subregion it has recommended population intensities ranging from very low to medium. With gross residential densities of from eight to twelve dwelling units per acre recently approved within the vicinity, the proposed density for Indian Trace is quite low by

comparison. Here, as has been clearly demonstrated, a large part of the county's anticipated growth can be accommodated without stress upon the planned highway network, public services or natural systems.

Circulation

The free movement of traffic to, from, and within the community has been one of the most important planning considerations. From the start, liaison has been maintained with the State Department of Transportation, the Broward County Area Planning Board, and its Trafficways Committee, the Broward County Transportation Authority, and the Broward County Engineering and Planning and Zoning departments. Among these agencies there is general concurrence with the proposed traffic plan, which has been mutually devised.

Few sites in the county will have comparable access. The property is bounded on three sides by roads presently scheduled as major expressways.

Three types of internal roadways are to be provided—arterial parkways, circulation roads, and local frontage streets. Provision has been made for access to a future regional transit system and for on-site transit. The inclusion of extensive pedestrian trails, bicycle paths, and equestrian trails are a featured aspect of the circulation system.

Arterials These internal traffic arteries, planned as segments of the regional transportation network, are to be controlled-access parkways. Expanded rights-of-way, some planned to exceed 200 feet in width, will accommodate transitways, walks, and bicycle paths.

Circulation roads The secondary level of vehicular distribution will be provided by a system of circulation roads also having parkway characteristics and limited building frontage. The treatment of these curvilinear paths of movement will vary to reflect the landscape character of the neighborhoods through which they pass and to which they provide pleasant access.

Local roads Within the development areas defined by the arterials, local traffic movement will be provided on circulation roads and low-speed frontage streets, loop drives, and motor courts. Residents may accomplish all internal trips to convenience shopping, neighborhood recreation spots, or classrooms without need to use the arterial highways. The circulation and frontage roads in effect form a loosely arranged network which disperses traffic and, by giving multiple choice of movement, reduces the number of vehicles on any one road.

In large outlying areas, the meandering two-lane roads will resemble country lanes in keeping with the rural character of the conceptual plan. In more urban areas they will form winding frontage streets relieved of fast through traffic.

Pedestrian, bicycle, and equestrian trails In a significant effort to reduce the need for automobile use, and to provide popular forms of outdoor recreation, over a hundred miles of pedestrian, bicycle, and equestrian trails have been included as a secondary circulation system.

Transit Space for internal transit routes has been reserved within the major rights-of-way. Additional easements will be delineated in the more detailed planning of the open space areas. It is intended to provide multimodal transit linkage between commercial, recreational, and other activity centers.

Although the county's transit proposals have not yet been finalized, it is anticipated that a future Community Center in Indian Trace will in time be structured around a major regional transit node.

Transport Within the Broward County region there is a critical need for the more

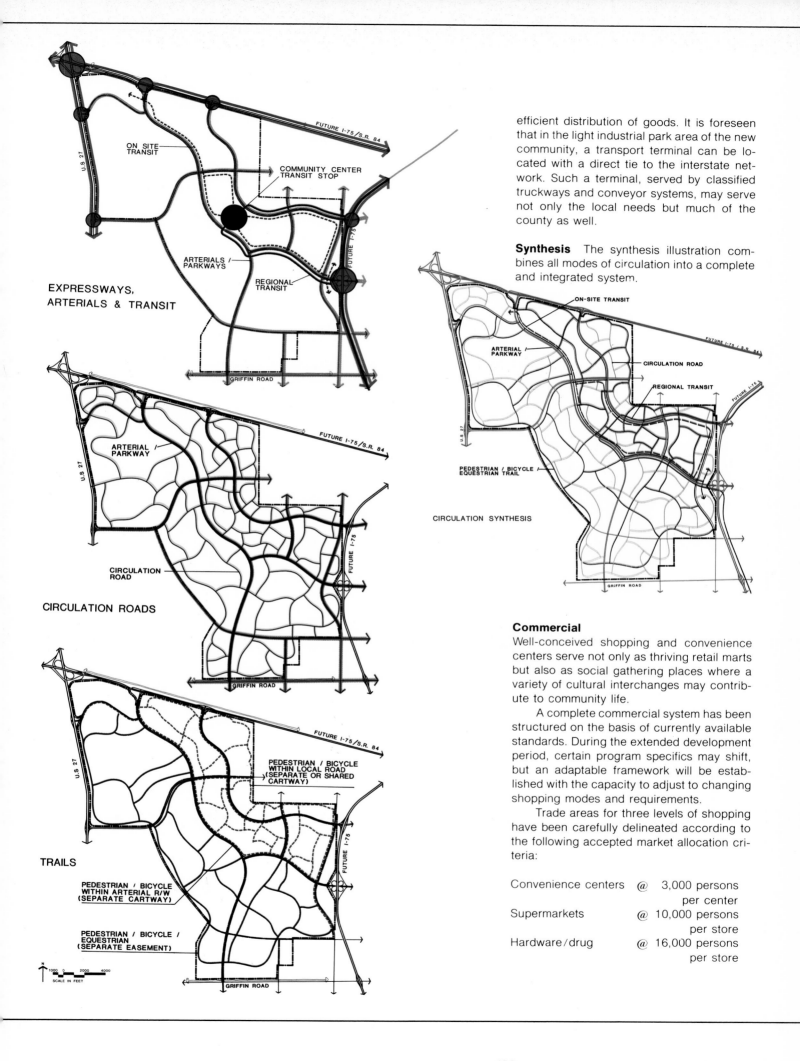

EXPRESSWAYS, ARTERIALS & TRANSIT

ON SITE TRANSIT

COMMUNITY CENTER TRANSIT STOP

ARTERIALS / PARKWAYS

REGIONAL TRANSIT

FUTURE I-75/S.R. 84

U.S. 27

FUTURE I-75

GRIFFIN ROAD

CIRCULATION ROADS

ARTERIAL / PARKWAY

CIRCULATION ROAD

FUTURE I-75/S.R. 84

U.S. 27

FUTURE I-75

GRIFFIN ROAD

TRAILS

PEDESTRIAN / BICYCLE WITHIN LOCAL ROAD (SEPARATE OR SHARED CARTWAY)

PEDESTRIAN / BICYCLE WITHIN ARTERIAL R/W (SEPARATE CARTWAY)

PEDESTRIAN / BICYCLE / EQUESTRIAN (SEPARATE EASEMENT)

FUTURE I-75/S.R. 84

U.S. 27

FUTURE I-75

GRIFFIN ROAD

N
1000 0   2000   4000
SCALE IN FEET

efficient distribution of goods. It is foreseen that in the light industrial park area of the new community, a transport terminal can be located with a direct tie to the interstate network. Such a terminal, served by classified truckways and conveyor systems, may serve not only the local needs but much of the county as well.

Synthesis The synthesis illustration combines all modes of circulation into a complete and integrated system.

ON-SITE TRANSIT

ARTERIAL / PARKWAY

CIRCULATION ROAD

REGIONAL TRANSIT

FUTURE I-75 / S.R. 84

U.S 27

FUTURE I-75

PEDESTRIAN / BICYCLE EQUESTRIAN TRAIL

GRIFFIN ROAD

CIRCULATION SYNTHESIS

Commercial

Well-conceived shopping and convenience centers serve not only as thriving retail marts but also as social gathering places where a variety of cultural interchanges may contribute to community life.

A complete commercial system has been structured on the basis of currently available standards. During the extended development period, certain program specifics may shift, but an adaptable framework will be established with the capacity to adjust to changing shopping modes and requirements.

Trade areas for three levels of shopping have been carefully delineated according to the following accepted market allocation criteria:

Convenience centers	@	3,000 persons per center
Supermarkets	@	10,000 persons per store
Hardware/drug	@	16,000 persons per store

CONVENIENCE
TRADE AREAS

SUPERMARKET
TRADE AREAS

DRUG / HARDWARE
TRADE AREAS

The three levels

1. Specialized retail facilities to serve the entire community have been planned for the Community Center site. Tenants will include department stores, high-quality restaurants, grocery stores, bakeries, boutiques, and shops for custom clothing, shoes, jewelry, and specialized equipment.

2. Neighborhood centers have been located to provide ready access for all residents. These centers have been planned with a supermarket alone or in combination with a drug-hardware store as primary tenants. Other possible tenants may include dry cleaners, branch banks, bakeries, variety stores, and retail clothing shops.

3. In addition, smaller convenience centers containing retail outlets to serve the day-to-day needs of residents have been situated throughout residential groupings to complete the commercial systems.

These components have been allocated to actual sites according to proposed population distribution and highway access patterns. Together, they comprise a balanced and mutually supportive range of well-placed shops and stores which should satisfy most of the needs of the residents at both the neighborhood and community levels. Over the years, this should do much to reduce the need for travel on the surrounding streets and highways.

Employment distribution

The current "Regional Land Use Plan for Broward County," prepared by the Area Planning Board, identifies the site as having potential for two possible industrial areas and

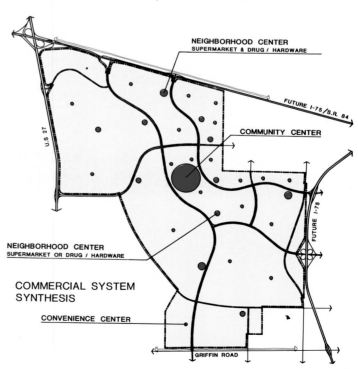

COMMERCIAL SYSTEM
SYNTHESIS

a major commercial complex. These have been incorporated in the Indian Trace community concept plan, for they provide, among other attributes, highly desirable sources of employment. It is foreseen that the "industrial" uses will evolve as a goods-distribution center and as research-oriented business offices and light industrial parks.

The Community Center is to be designed as a campus-type aggregation of civic, cultural, and business structures spaced around a regional transit terminal, central shopping mall, and lake. Additional employment will be provided by the planned tourist center, the school system, golf courses, and by many other types of recreational and public service installations.

As depicted in the accompanying illustration, the employment centers have been so located as to minimize impact on residential areas and circulation routes, while affording convenient employment for residents and nonresidents.

Employment, both during and after construction, will be composed of the following broad occupational types:

Professional, technical, and managerial
Sales
Clerical and kindred
Craftsmen, foremen, and kindred
Laborers

The forty-year community build-out period will help to stabilize the Broward economy. Rather than inducing a surge of transient workers, it will provide instead a steadily increasing employment base for an eventual 23,000 persons. Such employment opportunities, coupled with an adequate supply of moderate-income housing, will be a welcome attribute to a county in which both are presently needed.

Utilities

Water supply and distribution system

Potable water for the development will be obtained from the Biscayne Aquifer, and the recharge available from the development of extensive lakes and large open spaces will make the project more than self-sufficient.

A preliminary water distribution system is illustrated on the water distribution map with approximate locations of ground storage tanks and service pumps. These mains will be sized to provide normal water-use requirements and adequate pressure.

Wastewater collection and disposal system

A preliminary wastewater collection system is illustrated on the wastewater collection map with approximate locations of lift stations and wastewater treatment facilities. The entire system will be phased over the

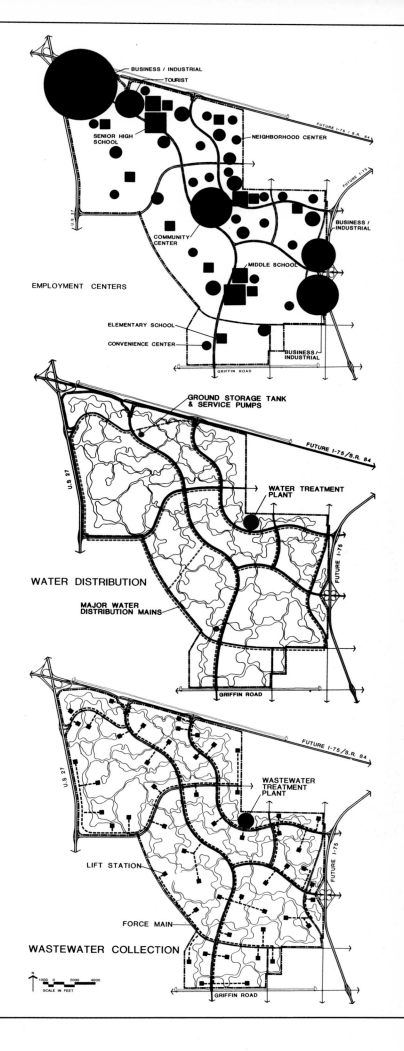

EMPLOYMENT CENTERS

WATER DISTRIBUTION

WASTEWATER COLLECTION

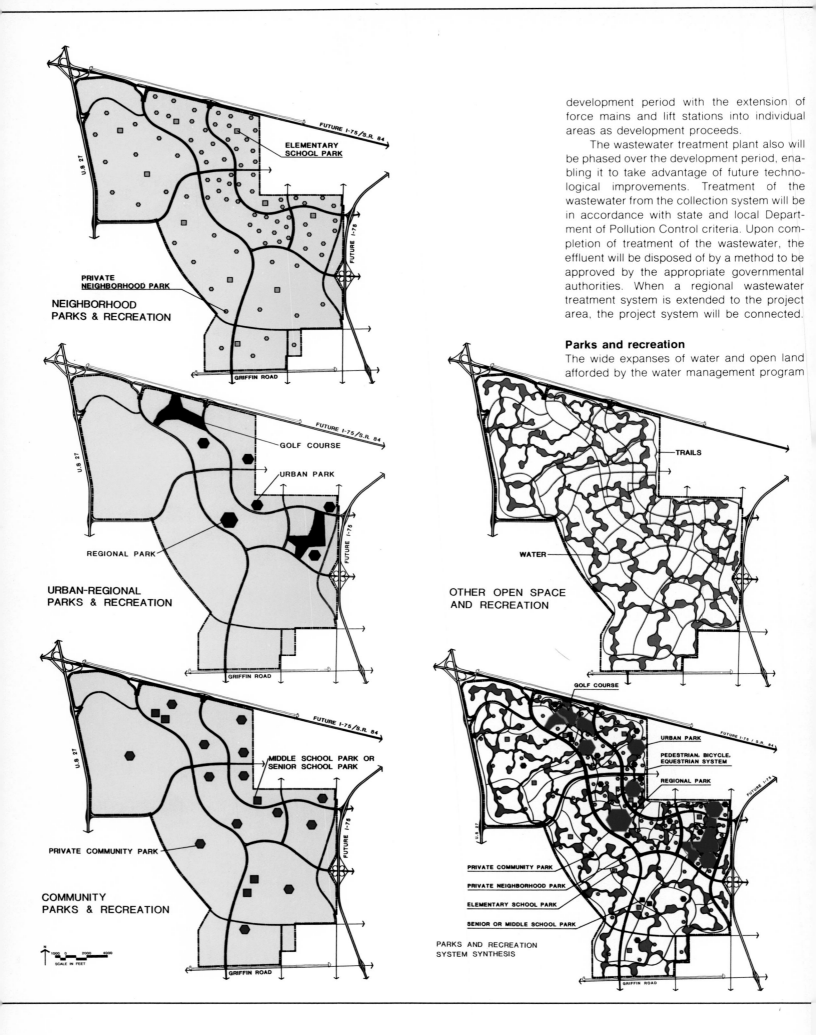

NEIGHBORHOOD
PARKS & RECREATION

ELEMENTARY
SCHOOL PARK

PRIVATE
NEIGHBORHOOD PARK

U.S 27

FUTURE I-75/S.R. 84

FUTURE I-75

GRIFFIN ROAD

URBAN-REGIONAL
PARKS & RECREATION

GOLF COURSE

URBAN PARK

REGIONAL PARK

U.S 27

FUTURE I-75/S.R. 84

FUTURE I-75

GRIFFIN ROAD

COMMUNITY
PARKS & RECREATION

MIDDLE SCHOOL PARK OR
SENIOR SCHOOL PARK

PRIVATE COMMUNITY PARK

U.S 27

FUTURE I-75/S.R. 84

FUTURE I-75

N
1000 0   2000   4000
SCALE IN FEET

GRIFFIN ROAD

development period with the extension of
force mains and lift stations into individual
areas as development proceeds.

The wastewater treatment plant also will
be phased over the development period, enabling it to take advantage of future technological improvements. Treatment of the
wastewater from the collection system will be
in accordance with state and local Department of Pollution Control criteria. Upon completion of treatment of the wastewater, the
effluent will be disposed of by a method to be
approved by the appropriate governmental
authorities. When a regional wastewater
treatment system is extended to the project
area, the project system will be connected.

Parks and recreation

The wide expanses of water and open land
afforded by the water management program

OTHER OPEN SPACE
AND RECREATION

TRAILS

WATER

PARKS AND RECREATION
SYSTEM SYNTHESIS

GOLF COURSE

URBAN PARK

PEDESTRIAN, BICYCLE,
EQUESTRIAN SYSTEM

REGIONAL PARK

PRIVATE COMMUNITY PARK

PRIVATE NEIGHBORHOOD PARK

ELEMENTARY SCHOOL PARK

SENIOR OR MIDDLE SCHOOL PARK

U.S 27

FUTURE I-75 / S.R. 84

FUTURE I-75

GRIFFIN ROAD

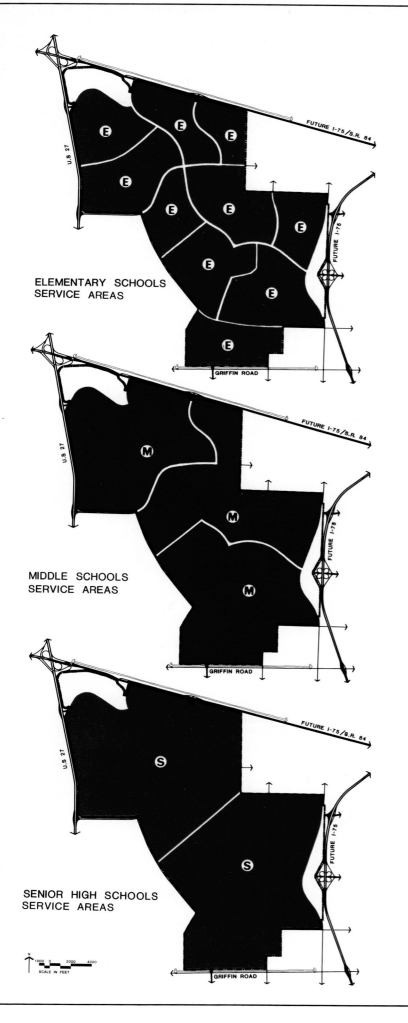

ELEMENTARY SCHOOLS
SERVICE AREAS

MIDDLE SCHOOLS
SERVICE AREAS

SENIOR HIGH SCHOOLS
SERVICE AREAS

give promise of an abundance of recreational
activities.

In devising a complete park and recreation program, full coordination with the
Broward County Parks and Beaches Department has been helpful. The county's present
open space standards require that a total of
10 acres of various types of recreational
land be provided for each thousand people in
the total population. These 10 gross acres of
recreational land may be categorized as follows:

Recreational Type	Acres per 1,000 Population
Neighborhood Park	1.25
Community Park	1.00
Urban Park	2.00
Regional Park	2.00
Other usable open space	3.75

The community of Indian Trace will contain over twice the amount of recreational
land required by the above criteria.

The neighborhood park needs will be
served by the elementary school–parks and
local recreation areas. Middle school–parks
and senior high school–parks will also provide joint educational-recreation facilities.
These, together with scattered tennis courts,
swim clubs, and other private social centers,
will meet and exceed the community park
criteria. The urban and regional park requirements will be met by the allocation of five
urban parks in the locations shown (see illustration), together with a regional park within
the Community Center.

From the beginning, the entire community has been planned as an all-embracing
park, nature preserve, and wildlife sanctuary.
Drives and residential clusters have been
planned around a series of water bodies, golf

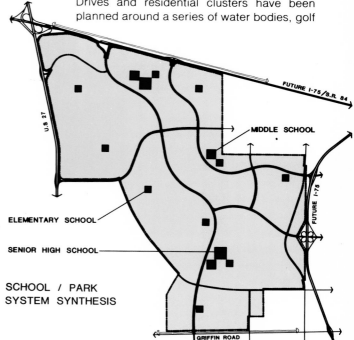

MIDDLE SCHOOL

ELEMENTARY SCHOOL

SENIOR HIGH SCHOOL

SCHOOL / PARK
SYSTEM SYNTHESIS

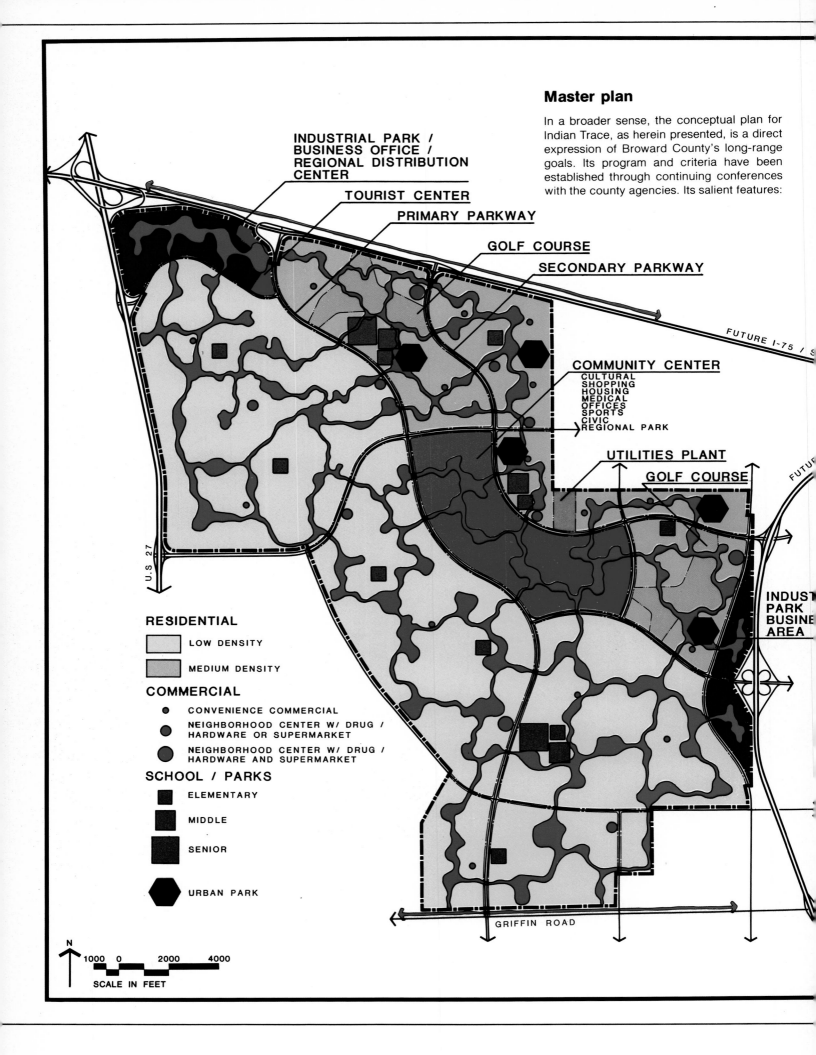

Master plan

In a broader sense, the conceptual plan for Indian Trace, as herein presented, is a direct expression of Broward County's long-range goals. Its program and criteria have been established through continuing conferences with the county agencies. Its salient features:

INDUSTRIAL PARK /
BUSINESS OFFICE /
REGIONAL DISTRIBUTION
CENTER

TOURIST CENTER

PRIMARY PARKWAY

GOLF COURSE

SECONDARY PARKWAY

COMMUNITY CENTER
CULTURAL
SHOPPING
HOUSING
MEDICAL
OFFICES
SPORTS
CIVIC
REGIONAL PARK

UTILITIES PLANT

GOLF COURSE

FUTURE I-75 / S

FUTUR

INDUST
PARK
BUSINE
AREA

U.S 27

RESIDENTIAL

LOW DENSITY

MEDIUM DENSITY

COMMERCIAL

● CONVENIENCE COMMERCIAL

● NEIGHBORHOOD CENTER W/ DRUG /
HARDWARE OR SUPERMARKET

● NEIGHBORHOOD CENTER W/ DRUG /
HARDWARE AND SUPERMARKET

SCHOOL / PARKS

■ ELEMENTARY

■ MIDDLE

■ SENIOR

⬡ URBAN PARK

N

1000 0   2000   4000

SCALE IN FEET

GRIFFIN ROAD

- A low density of 4.08 dwelling units per gross acre.

- The comprehensive planning of a large landholding under a single ownership as a unified satellite community for staged and controlled development.

- Protection of the regional ecosystem by the provision of a scientific water management program and by measures designed to eliminate all significant forms of pollution.

- Retention of large areas of land in its natural state, with development clustered around a series of sizable lakes, interconnecting waterways, and open space preserves.

- Maximization of the recreational use of the water bodies and water storage areas.

- Use of the cluster concept in the planning of all residential, industrial, business office, and commercial areas.

- Establishment of a rural, ranch-country environment of high quality, embracing more urbanized neighborhoods and community, business, and cultural centers.

- Provision of a broad employment base ranging from recreation facilities to business office and industrial park centers.

- Creation of a joint school-park system. This forward-looking approach to the multiple use of school and park facilities, developed in cooperation with the county authorities, should result in substantial savings coupled with a high level of community service.

- Inclusion of civic, cultural, and commercial amenities within each neighborhood as well as within the Community Center.

- Provision of those outdoor recreation opportunities most popular in Broward County. These will include boating, fishing, golfing, swimming, tennis, walking, and riding.

- Accommodation of a wide variety of housing types in the lower-, medium-, and higher-priced brackets.

- Creation of a community that will be made self-sufficient and self-contained, in all ways feasible.

- Application of the planned-unit-development approach as the key to flexible and optimum long-term planning.

With the development of Indian Trace continuing over a period of almost forty years, the planning of such an extensive land area must be a slowly evolving process. If carried forward within the conceptual framework mutually agreed upon and with the continuing guidance, coordination, and direction of the county and its appropriate agencies, it is believed that the new community will be in many ways exemplary, and a notable Broward County asset.

courses, and greenbelts. An extensive network of hiking, biking, and bridle paths will interlace the neighborhoods. Recreation, and the enjoyment of the out-of-doors, will be a featured way of life at Indian Trace.

School-parks

In planning a school system to meet both the initial and ultimate needs of Indian Trace, a major consideration is that the development period will extend an estimated forty years into the future. In the field of education particularly, profound changes can be expected over this period of time. This will be true regarding design and construction of the physical plant, methods of teaching, and even basic philosophy. This suggests that sites of adequate size and optimum location be reserved and that flexibility be retained to permit response to growth and changing conditions

Installations at the initial stage, nevertheless, must relate to present-day criteria. The educational planning data supplied by the Broward County School Board on student generation by housing type, student groupings, number of students per school, and size of school sites have been most helpful and have formed the basis for the development of the Indian Trace community school system.

Student generation As a general rule, it can be stated that as housing units increase in density, the number of children per unit decreases. County data on student generation anticipates the following yield:

Housing type	Students per Dwelling unit
Ranchette	1.00
Single Family	1.00
Townhouse	0.80
Garden Apartment	0.20
Mid-Rise Apartment	0.08

Statistically, these students are anticipated in the following grouping percentages:

Elementary	46%
Middle	24%
Senior	30%

County criteria for school and site sizes are as follows:

School type	Optimum No. of students	Size (acres)		
		School	Park	Total
Elementary	765	6	4	10
Middle	1,580	13	4	17
Senior	2,300	26	4	30

As illustrated on the maps each school type and site has been located with studied relationship to the residential groupings to be served.

School-park combination In programming the new schools, it is proposed to combine them with neighborhood and community parks. In this way a complete educational and recreation program can be operated jointly on a full-time, year-round basis. Multiple use of the parking and recreation areas and specially designed school-building wings will provide expanded opportunities at a substantial cost savings. Lighted parking lots, ballfields, and game courts, for example, will be available not only for school use, but for communitywide nonschool recreation as well.

School and park officials have welcomed the chance to apply their experience and knowledge to the planning of such advanced systems on this extensive county subregion.

Community systems synthesis

To complement the recreational facilities and opportunities in the nearby Everglades, and to protect the natural quality of the existing landscape, an extensive open space system has been designed. This system establishes the basic nature and rural character of the community. All residential neighborhoods will have excellent access to dispersed recreation areas and community activity centers.

Major parkways and collector roads within the community will have limited building frontage and will be heavily planted. Local streets, due to their spacing and design, will be two-lane country roads with low speeds and limited volumes. This dispersal of traffic flow will allow the parkway system to enhance the community's rural atmosphere.

The extensive waterway network, a result of a comprehensive water management analysis, will be utilized for communitywide water-oriented recreation activities.

Two kinds of open space will be provided. Broad bands of land used for water management purposes will be laced throughout the community and have the additional purpose of providing a wide variety of active and passive recreational opportunities. This system, incorporating extensive bicycle, equestrian, and hiking trails, will structure and connect all residential, educational, commercial, and other community uses.

In addition, local private recreation areas

will be located in each residential cluster to provide swimming, tennis, and other similar facilities.

The synthesis of these components will provide a community unique in its character and living environment.

Environmental quality

In evaluating the environmental factors affected by the improvement of this property, it is important to note that a construction program of approximately forty years is anticipated. The following conclusions have been made within the context of this extended development period.

Air quality
Air quality in Indian Trace, as in all developments, will be affected by vehicular traffic, construction equipment, and industrial activities. Each of these contributors will comply with prevailing state and local standards for quality control.

Since the exhaust fumes from automobiles are a principal source of air pollution, the arterial roads have been planned as controlled-access roadways. The fact that they will be substantially free of stop-and-go traffic will materially reduce the volume of emissions over the conditions that prevail on conventional grid street patterns. In addition, the provision of an extensive open space framework will provide natural ventilation for the building groupings. Even the prevailing winds will help to protect the air quality since the predominant direction of air flow will be away from populated areas and toward the conservation areas and the Everglades which lie to the north and west.

Water management
Approximately 3,000 acres of the project area will be devoted to lakes, lagoons, canals, dry swales, and open space in residential areas. This storage system will permit the water from the primary recharge areas to reenter the Biscayne Aquifer. It will discharge into the South New River Canal at a rate permitted by the Central and South Florida Flood Control District. Surface runoff water will be retained in a system of ponds and connecting canals.

Noise
While there will be a temporary increase in localized noise levels during the construction phases, no continuing noise problems of major consequence are anticipated. After development is completed, noise levels will be greater than the ambient noise levels that

presently exist, but this increase will be comparable to the increase in other developed communities and should not adversely affect the region.

Noise levels below those experienced in other urbanizing areas of the county are to be expected. Factors contributing to noise abatement will be free-flowing and planted trafficways, the relatively low density of the community, and the concept of off-highway building groupings with frontage precluded on all major streets.

Animals
Preliminary reconnaissance of the property revealed the presence of little significant animal life and no endangered species.

It is foreseen that the extensive network of water bodies, waterways, and wetlands together with their naturalized edges and cover will provide habitats for many types of fish, indigenous wildlife, and migratory birds. These possibilities are being fully explored with the Florida Game and Fresh Water Fish Commission as planning proceeds.

Wastewater disposal
Wastewater will be collected on-site and processed in a treatment plant which is to be located within the project boundaries. Disposal of treatment plant effluent will be by a method to be approved by the Broward County and State Departments of Pollution Control and other local and state health agencies.

Water supply
The source of potable water for the project will be the Biscayne Aquifer, and the recharge available from the development will make the project more than self-sufficient for water supply purposes.

Solid waste
Initially, trash and garbage collection will be by privately owned companies franchised by Broward County. This waste will be disposed of through Broward County facilities. The Broward County Commissioners have expressed a determination to supervise solid-waste disposal throughout the entire County, including the municipalities. The problem of solid-waste disposal can be solved only on a countywide or regional basis, and only when it is considered as a valuable resource from which processed metals, glass, and chemicals can be recovered and recycled and from which organic material may be converted into energy. As Broward County moves toward new disposal techniques, Arvida Corporation

will cooperate in all ways feasible and assume its pro-rata responsibility regarding the overall solution.

Moreover, on the condition that the air and water quality of the community would not be adversely affected, Arvida Corporation stands ready to accept as a by-product of advanced waste treatment, substantial quantities of inert and sterile residual "soil" and composts for use in creating a new landscape of hills and ravines within the community boundaries.

Power
The Florida Power & Light Company will furnish all power required at Indian Trace. On-site generators will be available for emergency conditions.

Historical
Five archaeological sites have been recorded by the Broward County Historical Society. Future studies will be conducted and a plan devised to protect sites of significance.

Public safety
There will be a Volunteer Fire Protection System approved by the Broward County Fire Control Commission and County Commissioners. Police protection will be provided through the Broward County Sheriff's Department.

Traffic
With its frontage on U.S. State Route 84 and the proposed I-75, the community of Indian Trace will enjoy a high level of accessibility to and from the supporting region. Few other areas of the county will be as directly served.

Arvida Corporation, working in close cooperation with those agencies of the county and state most concerned with transportation planning, has designed a roadway network which provides continuity to the countywide system and accommodates all projected internal and external movements.

No overloading of the trafficways is expected within the Department of Transportation's period of programmed construction. The ultimate traffic generated by this project, when routed through the planned external road system, is not expected to exceed acceptable levels on any major highways or their ramps.

Transit
Planning includes the provision of an internal diversified system of "people movers." Interconnected pedestrian paths, bridle trails, bikeways, transit routes, and reserved bus lanes are envisioned.

Text continued from page 191.

Incorporate the best of the proven features

A sampling of some of the newer and more successful communities reveals that a number of innovative concepts have been applied in their planning. These include:

1. The planned community development (PCD) approach.

2. The filing of an environmental impact assessment.

3. A water resource management plan.

4. The use of parkways and nonfrontage circulation drives.

5. A combined school-park system.

6. A unified community open space framework.

7. Pedestrian paths and bicycle trails.

8. Planned cultural and convenience centers.

9. Provision of employment opportunities.

10. Land leasing.

11. Cluster planning.

12. Residential, business-office, and commercial condominiums.

13. Underground electrical distribution.

14. A homeowners' association.

15. A tax improvement district.

16. The transfer of development rights from ecologically sensitive land to land better suited for construction.

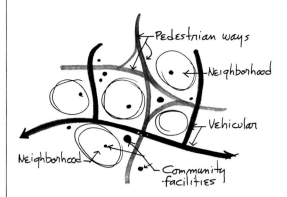

Depending upon their type and area of service, community facilities, such as schools, play areas, shopping, churches and social centers may be located either within, or between the various neighborhoods.

LOCATE COMMUNITY CENTERS TO BEST SERVE THEIR PURPOSE

Although any plan is essentially the scheduling of specific means to definite ends, it is possible to become so preoccupied with the planning operation itself as to overlook the general purposes which are being achieved or subverted.
CATHERINE BAUER

Understand the importance of phasing

Development will best proceed in such a way as to *extend* trafficways and utility lines with a minimum of unused installation and front-end investment. Avoid the waste of hop-skip construction and scattered maintenance. Each area is best "developed out" before the next is started. Bring materials and equipment in from the rear, and retreat as construction progresses.

Put your best foot forward if you can, for the first areas opened up tend to set the tone of the whole community. Build in the base and demand for shopping and other facilities as they are provided. Create successes; they generate other successes.

Build in the maintenance program

Plans for community operation and maintenance must be considered concurrently with the plans for development. The successful maintenance program will come on strong at the start and keep ahead all the way.

Develop protective covenants to govern all construction

Enforce them uniformly. Include provisions for architectural design review, sensitive site development, and environmental protection.

Round out the professional planning team

Expert consultants from related disciplines should be called upon as needed.
One column of figures by an experienced economist,
one report by a trained sociologist,
one diagram by a traffic engineer,

may spell the difference between a community's ultimate failure or success.

Know the political climate

No plan is worth the conceiving if it cannot be effectuated. More often than not, local political powers if unfamiliar with a plan will tend to delay or block it. If included in the planning, kept advised, and educated as to the merits of proposals, they will be more willing to support them. It is essential to politicians, and their constituents, that they be kept informed.

Know the economic limitations

The purpose of planning is not only to prevent the costly mistakes of haphazard growth. Its chief aim is to produce, through a comparative study of plan alternatives, the best possible community—at a cost the residents can afford.

Community planning must be considered the production of a marketable commodity—dwellings and developed parcels of land—in a highly competitive market.

Keep checking the estimates

Devise an accurate system of development cost analysis. Check it against the projected cash flow and anticipated returns. Improvements and amenities must be kept within feasible limits.

Group the higher-density clusters near the community entrances

This provides the convenience of ready access for most people and reduces the volume of traffic through the more dispersed residential sectors.

Separate people and vehicles

Each on-grade crossing of a pedestrian and vehicular trafficway means danger to the pedestrian and interruption of traffic flow.

Plan roadways as free-flowing lines of vehicular movement. Reserve the use of pedestrian areas and walkways for pedestrians alone. Even bicycles should move through the community on their own separate trails.

Provide greenways and open spaces within the neighborhoods

Give relief and form to the housing groupings by arranging them around open parklets and interconnecting meadows.

Leave room for individual expression

Within the framework of the master plan, and certain unifying controls, give ample latitude for that variety which can come only from individual efforts. All residents should have some area that they may treat as they wish.

Apply the test of human experience

Lift yourself up in your imagination and trace through the proposed community the children on their way to school, mothers with strollers on their way to shop, the business people and laborers as they leave for work in the morning and return in the evening to their homes, guests who are visiting for the first time, and those who deliver the milk and the mail and the paper each day. If for any of these the experience is one of inconvenience, hazard, frustration, or displeasure—the plan requires further study. If for each resident, worker, and visitor the community plan affords a sense of well-being and pleasure—the plan is well conceived.

The neighborhood is essentially a spontaneous social grouping, and it cannot be created by the planner. All he can do is to make provisions for the necessary physical needs, by designing an area which gives the inhabitants a sense of living in one place distinct from all other places, and in which social equipment, like schools and playing fields, are conveniently located.

FREDERICK GIBBERD
Town Design
Architectural Press
London, 1967

Reduce densities at the periphery

Land-use intensities, and building-height profiles, will usually taper downward as they approach the property edges. This both strengthens the community center and pleases adjacent landowners.

Provide protection from external detractions

The best protection from the intrusion of undesirable neighboring influences is the instigation of favorable zoning. Where peripheral nuisances exist, their blighting effects may be lessened by so aligning community entrances, drives, and clusters as to orient away from them or to be screened from them by natural ground forms, construction, or planting.

Develop for each community its own unique "custom" site hardware

The character of a community can be greatly enhanced by the provision of a few well-designed components, such as screen walls, street furniture, lighting, a family of directional and identification signs, and a coordinated system of symbols, colors, and graphics.

Name the streets

The difference between living on "86th Street" and "White Oak Drive" is a considerable difference. Street names can downgrade a community or lift it to a level of distinction. Names should grow out of the character of the site or the tradition of the area, and should be "picture" names which call to mind pleasurable images, such as: Granite Ridge Road, Hemlock Hollow Drive, Sassafras Knob, Strawberry Lane, Stonycreek Way, or Spyglass Hill.

Develop a master planting plan

Preserve and feature the natural growth. Work mainly with native plant materials in simple swaths and masses. Trees will best predominate. Select a theme tree, several supporting trees, and a small palette of supplementary plants for 95 percent of the planting. Each plant will be used to a purpose—as for shade, screening, windbreak, backdrop, sculptural accent, or floral display. Use plantings to reinforce landscape forms, to strengthen lines of movement, to provide spatial and visual enframement, and to articulate the plan.

Sound landscape planting can only evolve as a continuing and integral aspect of the total site-planning process.

Respond to the local climate

Obviously, the pattern and structure of a community in the desert, with its drying winds, blazing sun, and oppressive heat, should be different from that planned in low, humid country. In the desert the community would dig in, take to the hollows, group the structures tightly with their backs to the searing winds to front on a man-made oasis. In the hot humid situations the patterns would be more open. Structures would take advantage of the slightest rise and face into the welcome breeze. A fine community, whatever the locality, must be conceived in full response to all climatic factors.

Attend to the microclimate as well

Within an urban area of a 1-mile radius, the temperature at ground level on a hot summer afternoon may vary as much as 30 degrees from place to place, depending upon such local conditions as elevation, vegetation, moisture, breeze, materials of construction, colors, texture, and the presence of sunlight or shade. In the wintertime, variations of temperature from space to space within the area may be almost as

For most Americans, the residential neighborhood provides the major environmental experience. Most adults recall vividly and often nostalgically the neighborhoods where the most impressionable years of childhood were spent, the places associated with early experiences of birth and death, sickness and health, friendship, marriage and all the intimate ceremonies and activities that lend deep emotional significance to family life.

These formative experiences are inevitably enhanced and enriched in attractive, well-ordered neighborhoods . . .

From Sea to Shining Sea
A Report on the American Environment—
Our Natural Heritage
By the President's Council on Recreation and Natural Beauty
U.S. Government Printing Office
Washington, D.C., 1968

extreme. Since comfort and health are goals of community design, it would seem only sensible to consider all such factors. For some reason that is hard to explain, they are often completely ignored.

At the scale of community planning this implies such concerns as the preservation of the natural vegetation and ground covers. It means protecting the level of the subsurface water tables which maintain soil moisture content and surface temperatures. It means utilizing the tempering effects of the lakes and bays, of the marshes and watercourses. It means, too, making use of the thermal air currents that exchange each day as the sun's energy is exerted upon the surface of open water.

It dictates the grouping of hot-climate housing around cool water bodies, with careful adjustment to the sweep of the sun and the play of the welcome breezes. It suggests placing heat-prone paved surfaces in the lee of structures and the provision of a shade tree or palm frond canopy.

In the cooler or colder latitudes it implies the alignment of streets and open space axes across the storm winds, while yet shaping them to catch the full play of the lighter summer airs. It means the provision of good air drainage and the avoidance of ridge exposure or damp frost pockets.

Not only the site plans but the structures as well, in their plan arrangement, materials, and conformation, must be designed in full awareness of, and sensitivity to, the climate and microclimate.

Environmental quality controls

It is no longer sufficient for development of any kind to be governed by local codes alone. The full range of construction projects—from housing to industrial park, from playlot to pumping station—must be made subject to review and approval by a fully qualified environmental protection unit.

If a subdivision plan is submitted, for example, a preliminary examination will be made to determine whether or not the use is reasonable in terms of need, location, and general ecological impact. It will be reviewed in the light of the desirable nature and magnitude of growth in the affected locality, for expansion is not necessarily good. It will be appraised in the context of existing and projected land-use and circulation patterns, and it will be checked against the inventory of significant natural and historic resources that make an area agreeable and unique. If it passes preliminary muster in respect to these overall criteria, it will then receive further scrutiny in all particulars.

Care will be taken to assure that water bodies, streams, and drainageways are preserved; that such vegetative cover as woods, native shrubs, sods, and dune grass are conserved and protected in all ways feasible; and that grading and erosion are kept to a minimum. Complete water-supply, storm-drainage, and sewage-disposal studies will be required. Pollution of all types will be considered and minimized. The effects of internal traffic generation will be assessed against the regional highway and transit system and capacities.

Community planning is an art, but one in need of a large scientific advisory board, chaired by an expert in biology.
RICHARD NEUTRA
Survival Through Design
Oxford University Press
New York, 1954

Power demands, gas needs, and requirements for telephone and all other public services must be resolved. School, park, and open space areas will be allocated.

In large-scale development, or where the nature of the project is otherwise critical, it may be required that developers, in exchange for necessary zoning revisions or approvals, enter into an agreement with the governing body to guarantee a high level of environmental quality throughout the life of the installation by recording protective covenants which will run with the land.

It must be recognized that no project can be constructed without disturbing the land and affecting to some degree the fragile balance of nature. It is deemed imperative, however, that the negative effects be minimized, the positive contributions maximized, and that the benefits be such that, all factors considered, the development when completed will be in the best public interest.

Provide the official mechanism

Effective environmental protection and control requires a legally constituted council, agency, or officer with adequate authority, budget, and staff. This unit has seemed to work best under one of the following situations:

1. *As a division of the planning department.* If the department is well-established and strong, or if the director has special competency in environmental matters, this is usually the most desirable arrangement. Proposals and recommendations are presented to the local government either directly or through the planning commission.

2. *As staff to an ex-officio council comprised of the appropriate department heads.* Regularly scheduled meetings are required, at which time development proposals and planning-staff analyses are submitted for review and recommendation. Again, final decisions are normally made by the local governing body.

3. *As staff to a nonpartisan advisory commission* appointed by, and responsible to, the chief administrative officer.

Each jurisdiction must review its particular situation and form a unit to best fulfill its needs.

Establish review procedures

Broad policy directives, information, and various forms of aid will no doubt continue to flow from the federal and state governments. Regional criteria will normally emanate from the county agencies. But it will be left to the local governments to implement policy and to determine their own standards and procedures for processing development applications.

Issue landscape development standards

Many progressive municipalities have discovered the need for uniform requirements governing site construction. They have prepared a looseleaf manual of landscape development standards which give detailed instructions in such matters as grading, erosion control, drainage, walk and driveway construction, curb cuts, lighting, signing, screening, and even planting installations. This manual, made authoritative by a supporting ordinance, is of great help to the public and officials alike, and does much to raise the quality of the area's landscape improvements.

Further Reading:

Ahlbrandt, Roger S., Jr.
Neighborhoods, People and Community
Plenum Publishing
New York, 1984

Cary, Lee J., ed.
Community Development as a Process
University of Missouri Press
Columbia, Mo., 1983

Deasy, C. M., and Thomas E. Lasswell
Designing Places for People, A Handbook on Human Behavior
Whitney Library of Design
New York, 1985

Dowden, C. James
Community Associations: A Guide for Public Officials
Published jointly by ULI and Community Associations Institute
Washington, D.C., 1980

Francis, Mark, Lisa Cashdan, and Lynn Paxon
Community Open Spaces
Island Press
Washington, D.C., 1984

Griffin, Nathaniel M.
Irvine—The Genesis of a New Community
Urban Land Institute
Washington, D.C., 1974

Hester, Randolph T., Jr.
Planning Neighborhood Space with People
Van Nostrand Reinhold Company Inc.
New York, 1984

Moore, Colleen Grogan
PUD's In Practice
Urban Land Institute
Washington, D.C., 1985

Real Estate Research Corporation
The Costs of Community Sprawl: Environmental and Economic Costs of Alternative Residential Development Patterns at the Urban Fringe
Prepared for the Council on Environmental Quality, Department of Housing and Urban Development, and the Environmental Protection Agency
Washington, D.C., 1974

Sommer, Robert
Social Design
Prentice-Hall
Englewood Cliffs, N.J., 1983

Whyte, William H.
Cluster Development
American Conservation Association
New York, 1964

8 Urbanization

For more than seven out of ten Americans, home is an urban setting—not only the place of residence, but the site of most experience. By the year 2000 . . . nearly nine out of ten Americans will dwell in urban areas.

From *Sea to Shining Sea*
A Report on the American Environment—
Our Natural Heritage
By the President's Council on Recreation and Natural Beauty
U.S. Government Printing Office
Washington, D.C., 1968

A city is a concentrated and more or less permanent grouping of people and activities. In its evolution each city repeats to a greater or lesser degree the development of all cities. We find in most contemporary metropolises the vestiges of the crossroads trading post, the fortification, the public square, the marketplace, the cathedral, the court, and the capital.

From the dawn of civilization until recent times people have banded together for protection—as in the walled and fortress cities of Europe and the Orient. In America, too, many of our urban centers had their genesis in an armed encampment. St. Augustine, Pittsburgh, Detroit, and Fort Worth, for example, had their beginnings as forts.

Other cities like New York, Chicago, and San Francisco have formed from the start as centers of trade and commerce. Towns and cities have seemed to spring up almost spontaneously at those nodes where highways cross other highways, railroads, or rivers, or where they converge at a port. Other municipalities have grown up around educational institutions or in locations rich in natural resources or scenic splendor.

As long as the advantages offered by a city—safety, convenience, and opportunity—have outweighed such disadvantages as peril, pollution, and high taxes, the city has continued to thrive. When, however, the sum of the disadvantages has come to exceed the benefits of urban living, those citizens who could afford to move out have done so. We have witnessed in this century an unprecedented exodus of the wealthy, the employers, and the workers from the city centers—to create suburban dormitory towns and satellite commercial hubs. This centrifugal movement, accelerated by the advent of the automobile, has sapped many core cities of their vitality, and created a vacuum no-man's-land to be invaded by émigrés of lesser means and often lesser productivity. The costs of services have exceeded tax revenues until socially, economically, and physically, most of our larger cities are in dire straits, moving from crisis to crisis.

To add to their woes, they have expanded to the point where access and movement are no longer efficient. They have been fractured by a craze of trafficways and burst apart by huge parking compounds in attempting to accommodate and store the hoard of space-demanding automobiles that have borne in upon them. They are no longer compact. They are no longer concentrated. Unless, or until, such cities can be reshaped and redeveloped, they will have forfeited their ability to fulfill their essential purpose, which is to provide their supporting regions with efficient centers of intensive activity.

Fortunately, at the very time when the urban needs are the greatest, there have come into being those new concepts and techniques of urban redevelopment, transit and transportation planning, and environmental protection which can provide the means of salvation and give our American cities a new lease on life.

Let us consider the possibilities.

What should a city be?

To consider a town or a city as if it were essentially a *habita-*

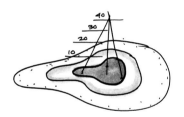

The closer the center of efficient concentration . . . the higher the rents and land values

URBAN LAND VALUES

tion is to harbor a misconception. To understand its nature as a prerequisite to its planning, replanning, or improvement, it must be studied with a much broader view which encompasses the full range of human endeavors. All nodes or ganglia in the urbanizing network, with its strands and globs of varying conformation, are centers of *production, operation,* or *regulation.* Ideally, they perform, in sum, all the functions necessary to physical, spiritual, and intellectual life. Considered in this context, it can be readily seen that *all* contributory activities not only *belong* but are *essential to* a well-balanced city. The problem of urban planning therefore, reduces itself simply to the task of providing space for each necessary component and fitting it in wherever it works the best.

Various activities suggest certain conditions most conducive to their success. Where the requirements are similar and the activities are compatible, they may be grouped in such a way that they form a mutually beneficial cluster. These clusters, or constellations, may in turn be interrelated to form larger galaxies spaced about the more dominant urban nuclei.

Recognizing that all human affairs are in a constant state of evolution and flux—it would seem that the best organizational system for a city is one which:

1. Provides for each type of activity the most favorable situation possible in terms of location, circulation, and amenities.

2. Groups or accommodates the spontaneous grouping of complementary activities.

3. Arranges all elements freely into the best possible relationship to each other and the surrounding environs.

Form and content

Many men have said in many different ways that the ultimate criterion for the form of an object or a place is that it be a direct and lucid expression of its function. An airplane, for example, is designed to fly. A knife is shaped to cut. A house is planned as a dwelling. The more fully and more precisely each fulfills the particular needs of the particular user, the better its design. So it is with a city, or any part thereof.

The best city, clearly, is that which best fulfills the needs, and aspirations, of the people who will live and work within its sphere of influence.

Form follows function.
LOUIS SULLIVAN
The Architecture of Fantasy
Ulrich Conrads and Hans G. Sperlich
Praeger Publishers, Inc.
New York, 1962

Until quite recently most city planning has dealt mainly with two-dimensional diagramming of street patterns and its subdivision into blocks and lots.

Specifications for urban development have comprised, traditionally, generalized limitations by zoning and negative regulation by code or ordinance.

The form of most American cities is not the result of a stimulating philosophic concept or creative design as much as it is the resultant of a multiplicity of deadening restrictions.

Accommodate each necessary function

When people look to the city as a place in which to live, work, trade—or for any other purpose—they seek out that location and those conditions best suited to their needs. The more and the better the options, the better the city from their point of view.

Since all activities require location and space, it is evident that the full range of pursuits must be considered and the best possible locations and conditions provided and fitted together into the urban plan. Experienced planners are alert to emerging and changing needs and

Our human nature was created, not as some imagine in treetops and caves, but in that invisible city. It was there that we learned the art of living together . . .
JOSEPH HUDNUT

Men came together in cities in order to live; they remain together in order to live the good life.
LEWIS MUMFORD

This great good that we enjoy . . . that august thing the Romans adored above all their gods, the town, "Urbs."
ANATOLE FRANCE

Civilization is inseparable from urban living.
CAROL ARONOVICI

Trade and exchange are what have formed cities.
HENRY S. CHURCHILL

A city plan is the expression of the collective purpose of the people who live in it or it is nothing.
HENRY S. CHURCHILL

What is the city but the people.
WILLIAM SHAKESPEARE

Show me your city, and I will tell you what are the cultural aims of its population.
ELIEL SAARINEN

The city is in fact the physical form of the highest and most complex types of associative life.
LEWIS MUMFORD

A city is the expression of the diversity of social relationships which have become fused into a single organism.
SIGFRIED GIEDION

The city, as one finds it in history, is the point of a maximum concentration for the power and culture of a community.
LEWIS MUMFORD

An urban form that would properly reflect all the pressures of our time would be capable of sustaining balanced life within it, without need for escape. It would be a fully functioning framework for ecological equilibrium.
SERGE CHERMAYEFF AND CHRISTOPHER ALEXANDER

A town, like a flower, or a tree, or an animal, should at each stage of its growth, possess unity, symmetry, completeness, and the effect of growth should never be to destroy that unity but to give it greater purpose . . .
EBENEZER HOWARD

After apportioning the alleys and settling the main streets, the choice of sites for the convenience and common use of citizens has to be explained; for sacred buildings, the forum, and the other public places. And if the ramparts are by the sea, a site where the forum is to be put is to be chosen next to the harbour; but if inland, in the middle of town. But for sacred buildings of the gods under whose protection the city most seems to be, both for Jupiter and Juno and Minerva, the sites are to be distributed on the highest ground from which the most of the rampart is to be seen.
VITRUVIUS

For town planning is first and foremost a human issue: its problems are by no means exclusively technical and economic. It can never be carried on satisfactorily without a clear understanding of the contemporary conception of life.
SIGFRIED GIEDION

The battle of the second half of this 20th century is that against blight in our urban centers where two-thirds of our population lives.
CHARLES P. TAFT

The paradox of cities, as we all unhappily realize, is that they are necessary for most of us. They are, as of now, perfectly adequate to work in, but they are not livable in. Constructive solution: they must be made livable.
PHILIP SNOW

The Future . . . In the contemporary city the green openness will go far beyond the parks, flowing through and connecting the superblocks. Not only will every building open on views of fine old trees and distant hills, but broad belts of green which will be close by for agriculture or forests for great sport fields or hiking, boating, fishing, swimming, skating or just for solitude in the peaceful valley or the wilds.
CLARENCE S. STEIN

Love of town is a human passion which may not be suppressed by advocates of the Simple Life and the Return to Nature. . . . For human life gravitates townwards; even when it emigrates and settles in lands of prairie and forest, cities spring up about it; nothing, indeed, is more certain than the fact that, at the touch of humanity, the wilderness blossoms with the town.
HOLBROOK JACKSON

There are advantages to be gained from the gathering together of people to form a town. A single family living in the country can scarcely hope to drop into a theatre, have a meal out or browse in a library, whereas the same family living in a town or city can enjoy these amenities. The little money that one family can afford is multiplied by thousands and so a collective amenity is made possible. A city is more than the sum of its inhabitants. It has the power to generate a surplus of amenity, which is one reason why people like to live in communities rather than in isolation.
GORDON CULLEN

Only the city can afford the arts in their broadest and most developed sense, because it takes population to keep art centers alive and flourishing. The same reasoning applies to great medical centers which require the most nearly complete clinical facilities, to management headquarters of banking and big business, and to many mercantile establishments which have to be close together.
ROBERT MOSES

The city is man's greatest invention: an intellectual powerhouse, a store of learning and of the most diverse energies.
THEO CROSBY

Intricate minglings of different uses in cities . . . represent a complex and highly ordered form of order.
JANE JACOBS

At every step the city itself was my teacher in everything. The tradesmen in the market, the waiters, the porters, the peasants, the workmen—all were surrounded by that astonishing atmosphere of light and freedom I have not found anywhere else.
MARC CHAGALL

Great old cities are like tolerant grandmothers. They represent to their children a world vaster than one can explore or exhaust, and one is happy merely to grow up under their all embracing protection.
LIN YUTANG

Utopia, then, lies in this city around us; and it must be planned and realized, here or nowhere, by us as its citizens—each a citizen of both the actual and the ideal city seen increasingly as one.
PATRICK GEDDES

Long live Utopia! . . . It is, in fact, the only thing that survives.
HERMAN OBRIST

Since we are becoming to an ever increasing degree an urbanized nation, the future of our cities will decide our future as a free democratic society
ROBERT FUTTERMAN

To plan we must know what has gone on in the past and feel what is coming in the future.
To plan cities one must believe in life.
SIGFRIED GIEDION

It must namely be borne in mind that whatever is considered to be best for man, from the point of view of inner cultural growth, must be established as the governing principal in the shaping of a healthy urban environment.
ELIEL SAARINEN

If we would lay a new foundation for urban life, we must understand the historic nature of the city, and distinguish between its original functions, those that have emerged from it, and those that may still be called forth.
LEWIS MUMFORD

The question is can we find the enlightened leadership to direct and to utilize our technological prowess to humanize, to beautify, and to make economically viable our great urban centers?
JULIUS STRATTON

Efficient organization of activities in space becomes an even more critical metropolitan problem when one adds in the satisfaction which the citizens of the city derive from the web of interaction.

LOWDEN WINGO, JR., editor
Cities and Space
Johns Hopkins University Press
Baltimore, Md., 1963

To understand and describe this complex interaction which is city life—both activities and physical environment serving each other, adjusting to each other, conditioning each other—it is possible to begin with activities or with their physical setting, but neither can be understood without the other.

JOHN RANNELLS
The Core of the City
Columbia University Press
New York, 1956

keep adjusting their charts and checklists to keep supply and demand in balance. This process is akin to "dead reckoning" in navigation, in which a course is set from experience, observation, and by intuition, and then adjusted as each new "input" is received.

List and apportion the proposed land uses

The zoning map of each town, city, and metropolitan area comprises a patchwork of land-use areas depicted in various colors. Ideally these

Contemporary land uses in representative American cities

City	Population	Land area (sq. mi.)	Population per sq. mi.	Residential	Commercial	Industrial	Institutional	Streets and highways	Transit	Public parks and recreation	Other open space
1,000,000 and over											
Chicago, IL	2,992,000	228.1	13,117	31.3	7.5	5.1	4.2	24.6	12.0	7.6	7.7
Philadelphia, PA	1,647,000	136.0	12,110	30.0	6.8	7.3	5.8	14.5	8.0	9.6	18.0
Detroit, MI	1,089,000	135.6	8,031	42.0	5.0	8.0	5.0	29.0	—	6.0	5.0
Houston, TX	1,706,000	565.2	3,018	30.0	7.6	8.7	1.6	*2.0	—	2.9	47.2
*Freeways only											
500,000 and over											
Cleveland, OH	547,000	79.0	6,924	33.4	3.8	11.2	4.9	15.6	4.6	7.3	19.2
Indianapolis, IN	710,000	352.0	2,017	17.1	0.8	0.9	2.4	9.8	1.2	2.8	65.0
Milwaukee, WI	621,000	95.8	6,482	30.6	2.5	5.0	4.0	21.2	9.0	8.0	19.7
San Diego, CA	960,000	322.1	2,980	16.6	1.7	3.2	14.6	11.9	—	4.6	47.4
250,000 and over											
Albuquerque, NM	351,000	108.6	3,232	9.1	2.2	1.2	0.7	15.1	—	0.6	71.1
Atlanta, GA	426,000	82.3	5,176	43.3	5.2	5.2	5.1	17.2	—	6.0	18.0
Buffalo, NY	339,000	41.8	8,110	32.1	8.9	7.1	6.5	22.2	8.3	4.7	10.2
Cincinnati, OH	370,000	78.0	4,743	35.1	8.3	2.5	5.3	12.4	7.0	9.5	19.9
Nashville-Davidson Co., TN	462,000	479.5	964	23.4	2.8	0.6	0.1	6.2	1.8	2.7	62.4
Toledo, OH	344,000	84.3	4,081	19.9	4.3	9.2	3.6	13.0	—	5.8	44.2
Portland, OR	366,000	109.0	3,358	27.1	2.6	5.0	3.4	20.5	—	10.0	31.4
Newark, NJ	314,000	24.1	13,029	20.0	5.0	12.2	14.3	16.9	4.6	9.0	18.0
100,000 and over											
Dayton, OH	181,000	54.4	3,327	38.0	3.7	8.0	2.8	20.0	—	17.9	9.6
St. Petersburg, FL	241,000	55.9	4,311	40.9	4.1	1.4	5.5	22.7	1.2	4.7	19.5
Yonkers, NY	191,000	18.3	10,437	31.8	4.4	1.9	17.8	18.1	4.9	6.0	15.1
Des Moines, IA	191,000	66.1	2,890	35.0	5.0	7.0	8.0	14.0	—	7.0	24.0
Syracuse, NY	164,000	23.8	6,891	36.0	3.8	5.3	6.2	26.5	—	7.8	14.4
Flint, MI	149,000	32.7	4,557	34.0	4.0	7.0	4.0	23.0	2.0	7.0	19.0
Davenport, IA	102,000	60.1	1,697	13.9	0.9	2.0	1.8	15.2	—	3.6	62.6
Durham, NC	102,000	29.5	3,458	41.9	3.5	1.3	3.8	12.9	3.0	2.9	30.7

1. All listings indicate, by best approximation, the percentage of land actually devoted to the use described, as opposed to "paper zoning." (From a recent survey conducted by The Environmental Planning and Design Partnership.)
2. Areas of consolidated city/county governments, and western cities in general, reflect high percentages of "Other open space."
3. The majority of land in "Other open space" category is composed of vacant properties.
4. Where no separate breakdown is shown for "Transit," it may be assumed to be included in "Streets and highways."
5. Population and area figures are taken from The Statistical Abstract of the U.S., 1986. U.S. Department of Commerce, Bureau of the Census.

have been established in size, shape, and location to best accommodate the foreseeable functions of urban life. Ideally, also, these land-use zones have been conceived in best relationship to each other, to the topographical features, and to the various routes of transport and interconnection.

Since the city as a living organism is in a constant state of evolution, the conformation and nature of the designated use areas must be amended periodically to reflect new social needs and political decisions. The areas are planned for their optimum long-range and "ultimate" use. Once described, they become locked in by an increasing number of constraints and tend to be self-perpetuating. They are not easily expanded or changed.

These things being so, the tendency in urban planning has been to grossly oversize the land-use zones. This leads to wasteful and inefficient *dispersion* rather than to the desirable *concentration* of activities. Moreover, a phenomenon of American cities is that, even at build-out, the actual utilization of most broadly defined use zones seldom exceeds 80 to 90 percent of the land coverage or density permitted. This is because the balance of the property is either vacant, devoted to uses of lesser intensity, undergoing renewal, or tied up in litigation.

As one promising solution, it is proposed that the ultimate land use of all property be zoned, as best it can be determined, but that within each zone, an outer variform band be designated for *potential* use and landbanked until at least 75 percent of the land assigned to *current development* has been committed to construction. Landbanked reserve lands could be devoted to a wide range of interim open space uses, taxed accordingly, and reconsidered for permitted construction only on the basis of demonstrated need.

Each urban area will have its own unique possibilities and particular zoning requirements. No standard criteria can be uniformly applied. As a means of comparison however—and as a point of departure—a checklist has been prepared to show the latest tabulation of land uses by area in representative American cities.

Ensure ease of movement

Not only do people seek that atmosphere or situation most conducive to their activities; they seek in their living environment the opportunity to move at will from one scene to another. The city dweller seeks as relief from urban frenzy the tranquillity of nature. The nature lover seeks at times the urbanity of the city. The suburbanite may be drawn now to the field or forest and again to the teeming city square. The more diversified the available choices and the more vivid the contrasts, the more stimulating the milieu.

Accessibility to the possible choices is dependent both upon relationships of position and upon means of locomotion. If one lives within easy reach of a wide variety of experiences, it is enough to be able to walk from one place to another. Where distances are greater, mechanical means of locomotion—such as bicycle, car, or rapid transit—are required. There are thus two magnitudes of scale. One is *pedestrian*, the other *vehicular*. In all metropolitan areas there are paths of movement, and places designed for the sole use of pedestrians. Others are planned for the use of the automobile or transit-transport vehicles. The two realms must be interrelated but kept separate and distinct. Most failures in the physical planning of our cities result from a failure to recognize and differentiate between the two incompatible types of use and the two incompatible scales.

At the pedestrian scale a distance of approximately one-half mile, or a travel time of from five to ten minutes maximum, has been used

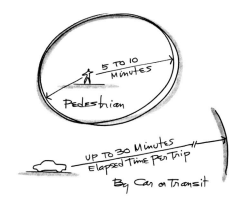

ACCEPTABLE DAILY TRAFFIC RANGES

Depending upon the means of locomotion to be employed, the desirable distance between changes of ambience is normally within the range of spontaneous and natural travel.
GERHARD SIXTA
Urban Structure
A Report of the Burnaby Planning Department
Burnaby, B.C., Canada, 1971

In the eighteenth century it took man ten minutes to get from the outskirts to the center of his city. In the nineteenth century it took twenty minutes. Today, despite the fact that we own vehicles capable of transporting us at a hundred miles per hour, it takes, on the average, forty minutes.
WOLF VON ECKARDT
A Place To Live
Dell Publishing Co., Inc.
New York, 1967

as a workable measure. By vehicle, a range of half an hour or less is considered to be acceptable, except in the case of more significant changes, as from seaside to mountain, or from rural to urban center.

Provide unity with diversity

Walter Gropius, founder of the Bauhaus and one of the great architectural educators of the twentieth century, has held this to be the chief characteristic of all inspired design. That building, park, or city is best, which most precisely fulfills its many variable functions, which provides the richest flow of sequential impressions or desirable experiences, and which combines all the elements into an expressive whole.

Allow for change

As society and human needs keep changing and as technology continues to advance, it is essential that cities and their surrounding regions respond to and accommodate the evolution. They must be able to replace obsolescent tissue and to reestablish constricted channels of movement. Like the roots, trunk, and limbs of a tree, they must provide the basis for regenerative growth. A static city, like a static tree, is dead.

Planning goals

A city can be no better than it aspires to be.

It has been recorded that in 1266 Kublai Khan, who was to consolidate an empire greater in extent than that of Alexander or the Romans, set about to build, on the northern plains of China, a fitting capital, the city of Ta-tu. This city, the present-day Peking, is considered by many to be among the most magnificent of all time. As was the custom, Kublai Khan first gathered his scholars about him to discuss its nature and purpose. They would plan, they decided, a governmental center and earthly paradise in which man might find himself *in harmony with God, nature, and his fellow man.* With such a lofty concept the genius of the city was assured.

The planners went on to spell out their goals in more detail.*

The walls which surround the city shall be impregnable. They shall be fronted with deep, water-filled moats, and shall be double-gated to form at each entrance a compound where all who enter may be subjected to surveillance by the guards. Each gate shall be commanded by a drum tower which shall sound the times of the day and control all passage through the city portals.

The avenues, from gates to central parade ground, shall be broad and straight and of a width to accommodate two passing regiments. At the intersection of the avenues, from north to south and east to west, an inner walled city shall be set aside as the court of the royal family. Here at the center of Ta-tu the Khan shall govern his people from his throne of Jade.

The city reservoirs shall be dug wide and deep to form lakes and lagoons of pure water which shall be undefiled. The earth

---

* The following excerpts from the planning objectives for Ta-tu, "the Great Capital," have been set down by the author, as well as his memory serves him, from oral translation, in 1939, of an original manuscript in the library of a former architect to the Imperial Court.

removed in their excavation shall be formed into hills overlooking the lakes. Upon the slopes and tops shall be constructed the temples and governmental buildings so that all people may look up to see their golden roofs emblazoned against the sky. The water edges and the hills shall be planted with flowering trees and plants, gathered for this purpose from all the provinces, and the streets shall be lined with cool and fragrant groves.

The residences of the officials shall be placed along streets which shall wind beside the waterways and amongst the hills. Each residence shall be walled to ensure privacy—the most highly regarded of all blessings—in which the master may instruct his children, write poetry, and discuss important matters with his friends.

The market places shall be kept apart from the military roads. They shall be suited especially to their purpose—and kept confined and in compression.

Finally [the Khan's advisors concluded], we shall plan no parks within Ta-tu. Rather, the whole of the capital city shall be conceived as one great all-encompassing garden park within which hills, lakes, roadways, and structures shall be planned and built together.

Few contemporary cities are influenced in their long-range development by such compelling goals. Yet clearly, they should be. For without the broad vision and well-defined objectives, a metropolis can only be uninspired, uninspiring, and mundane.

The city is an open book in which to read aims and ambitions. When it is built in a disorderly manner and the inhabitants are indifferent to its appearance, they automatically reveal this attitude. They are like the unwashed, unshaven, and untidy person who enters a social gathering and makes a poor exhibition.

ELIEL SAARINEN
The City—Its Growth, Its Decay, Its Future
MIT Press
Cambridge, Mass., 1965

The first task of the planner is to clarify and define objectives.

Define the goals and objectives

These will describe for the city and each aspect of its development the conditions to be achieved.

Record the existing conditions

Such a comprehensive analysis will normally provide all useful information on the following elements:

Land uses

Residential
Commercial
Industrial
Institutional, public, and semipublic
Park, conservation, and open space lands
Others, as appropriate

Physiographic characteristics

Topographic
Drainage
Geological
Meteorological
Ecological
Hydrological
Other significant features

Community facilities

Civic and municipal buildings
Public safety installations
Medical and welfare centers
Educational
Cultural
Entertainment
Recreation

Utility systems

Energy generation and distribution
Water
Communication
Gas and liquid fuels
Storm and sanitary sewers
Solid-waste recycling

Circulation systems

Streets and highways
Multimodal transit
Transportation routes and termini
Air, rail, and water facilities
Bicycle trails
Pedestrian walkways

Population analysis

Trends
Characteristics
Settlement patterns
Projections

Housing

Types, densities, and condition
Supporting amenities
Community focal points
Community boundaries
Needs

Economic base

Trends
Profiles
Thresholds
Potential

Fiscal analysis

Tax structure, base, and rates
Assessment levels
Debt levels
Debt service status
Capital improvements program and budget

In the planning context:

A *goal* is an idealized end toward which an individual or society may strive.

An *objective* is attainable. It describes a direction or course of action by which a goal may be realized.

A *policy* is an officially adopted objective or set of objectives.

A *criterion* is a measure by which the attainment of an objective may be evaluated.

The chief value of planning lies not in dealing with exigencies as unrelated problems, but in shaping overall policy, and guiding future events.

IRA BACH
As quoted in *The Freeway in the City*
The Report of the Urban Advisors to the
Federal Highway Administration
U.S. Government Printing Office
Washington, D.C., 1968

Prepare a comprehensive program

This will set the frame of reference for and give impetus to the long-range planning. It will include detailed statements as to:

1. *Planning rationale*
   Concept
   Policy and objectives
   Standards and criteria

2. *Land-use goals*
   Development structure and growth patterns
   Land-use types and descriptions
   Environmental quality controls
   Economic improvement
   Sociopolitical considerations

3. *Traffic and transportation plan*
   Transportation systems

Transit
Major transmission routes

4. *Community facilities*
   Public buildings
   Safety systems
   Medical and welfare
   Educational
   Cultural
   Entertainment
   Recreation plan

5. *Housing and renewal plan*
   Private and public improvements
   Innovative programs
   Priorities

Initiate studies and planning

For each area of consideration—such as trafficways, neighborhoods, parks, schools, and so forth—first convert the program into detailed standards and criteria and then into study solutions. To be meaningful, each study proposal should include notes as to costs and a brief environmental impact assessment. All such studies are best evolved through the process of comparative analysis, moving always toward improved performance within the limits of feasibility.

As the studies progress, conclusions or directions are recorded on a set of *long-range development plans*. These may be published from time to time and "approved in principle" by the governing bodies. But it is essential that they be considered no more than recommended guidelines. They must always be kept flexible and responsive to new factors and changing conditions.

Put the plan to work

No plan is worth preparing unless it can be translated into reality. A crucial aspect of the planning process is therefore the formulation of a feasible implementation program to be reviewed and updated each year. It will comprise:

1. *A capital improvement plan*
   Long-range proposals
   Costs
   Methods of financing
   Priorities

2. *A capital budget*
   Income-level projections
   Proposed expenditures
   Debt limits
   Funding

3. *A legislative program*
   Federal, state, and county
   Local
      Zoning ordinance
      Subdivision ordinance
      Housing code
      Building code
      Landscape development standards
      Environmental protection ordinance

A proper implementation program describes priorities, establishes costs and means of funding, defines legislative needs, and assigns agency responsibilities.

Social scientists, anthropologists, and others who have studied the situation appear to agree on nine points which presumably comprise the minimum requirements of man in what could be a successful urban system. All other facets of city planning should be means to this end.
1. *Livable shelter.*
2. *Effective urban services.*
3. *Reasonable security.*
4. *Hope for personal and community improvement.*
5. *A source of income, a sense of belonging.*
6. *Reduction of the waste that increases living costs and frustrates citizens.*
7. *A fresh look at cultural and recreation facilities.*
8. *A solution to the transportation problem.*
9. *A minimum of pollution and ecological disruption.*

FRED SMITH
Abstract of proposals presented in
Man and His Urban Environment
A Report of the Man and His Urban
Environment Project
Room 5600, Rockefeller Plaza
New York, 1973

The social basis of the urban order and, therefore, the most important instrument for today's urban planning, is the limitation of population in both directions, maximum and minimum, in relation to a functionally determined part of the urban area.

ERNEST FOOKS
X-Ray the City
Ruskin Press
Melbourne, Australia, 1946

I do not think that it is the task of the planner to accomplish social, economic reform: that way dogmatism lies, and authoritarianism of whatever complexion, right, left or religious. The planner should try to understand the effect technology has on living, and to adapt the physical form of the city accordingly.

HERBERT L. MARX, JR.
Community Planning
H. W. Wilson Company
New York, 1956

Cities throughout all ages are not merely means of accommodation, they are expressions of a concept of life, of the feelings, thoughts, and strivings of human beings. In the space-organization and form-order of cities, social and community life find their true physical expression.

ERNEST FOOKS
X-Ray the City
Ruskin Press
Melbourne, Australia, 1946

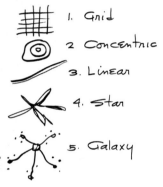

1. Grid
2. Concentric
3. Linear
4. Star
5. Galaxy

Each diagrammatic city form has its faults and advantages

THE FIVE BASIC PATTERNS OF URBAN DEVELOPMENT

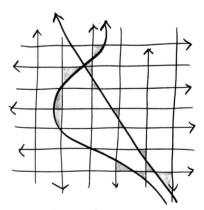

A diagonal or curvilinear roadway which crosses a grid street pattern develops fragmented parcels which are difficult to use.

THE GRID TRANSECTED

Patterns for growth

What's the best shape for a city?

A discussion as to the ideal pattern for the layout of a contemporary metropolis may seem an esoteric exercise. But there are lessons to be learned; the first of which is that the diagrammatic plan of a settlement of any magnitude has far-reaching consequences for everything which follows.

There are five basic forms of urban structure—the grid city, the concentric city, the linear city, the star-shaped city, and the galaxy city with its core and clustered satellites. Each has its inherent advantages and disadvantages. Each is better suited to a particular combination of functional requirements and landforms.

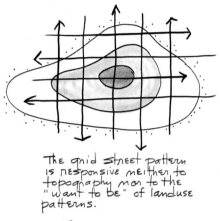

The grid street pattern is responsive neither to topography nor to the "want to be" of landuse patterns.

THE GRID

The grid

The difficulties presented by the conventional grid system of block layout and traffic movement become apparent as soon as the trafficways are superimposed on a plan showing either existing or proposed land uses. The streets divide the community into a rigid and wholly artificial framework.

Grade separations of street crossings are cumbersome and costly. Without them each intersection becomes a point of conflict and hazard. The movement of both vehicles and people must become intermittent, and therefore inefficient. Streets and arterials, being fixed in their direction if not actual position, are at the mercy of topography and often do violence to the natural landscape. There is little opportunity to respond to grades, or to the winds, sun direction, or drainage patterns.

The grid pattern of street and highway layout does have the advantage of providing a simple method of street addressing and postal distribution. It also lends itself to easy lot and parcel layout and is suited to the four-square methods of traditional building construction. In theory, it must be conceded, it does also allow a certain degree of flexibility in that land uses may expand across the grids. But the grid, the mark of our American town planning, has left its uncompromising and indelible stamp upon far too many sections of the landscape.

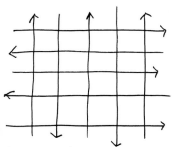

The Conventional Grid

Provides ease of orientation.
Is adapted to right-angle building construction.
Creates four-way intersections which maximize traffic hazard.

The larger the squares or rectangles the more efficient the layout.

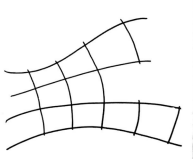

The distended grid

Affords partial response to topography.

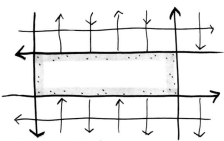

The Superblock

Larger, elongated land-use areas have many advantages over the smaller grid street blocks.
Through-traffic is eliminated.
Regional traffic movement is improved on widened distributor parkways.
There is greater site planning flexibility within the larger parcels, permitting campus-type, or cluster, building layout.
Interior vehicular traffic is eliminated and safety thereby increased.
The interiors of the expanded blocks can be returned to pedestrian uses and community space.

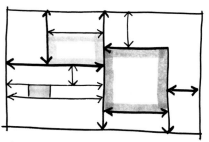

The Modified Superblock

Discontinuity of roadways precludes through-traffic movement.
Multiple-choice traffic patterns are provided.
The T-intersections are safer than normal two-way crossings.
This arrangement yields maximum flexibility in parcel size and shape.

VARIATIONS ON THE GRID STREET PATTERN

The Hexagonal

Has the advantage of discouraging through-traffic.
Three-way traffic intersections are an improvement.
Where the area of each unit can be made large enough, there are good applications for limited use.

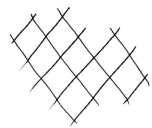

The Diamond

Has few, if any, advantages over the grid or hexagonal.
Has all the disadvantages of both.

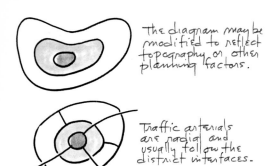

The diagram may be modified to reflect topography or other planning factors.

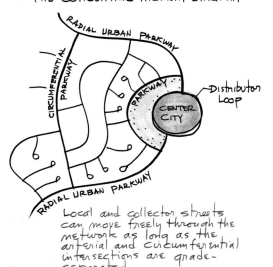

Traffic arterials are radial and usually follow the district interfaces.

THE CONCENTRIC HIGHWAY DIAGRAM

RADIAL URBAN PARKWAY

CIRCUMFERENTIAL PARKWAY

PARKWAY

CENTER CITY

Distributor Loop

RADIAL URBAN PARKWAY

Local and collector streets can move freely through the network as long as the arterial and circumferential intersections are grade-separated.

MAINTAIN THROUGH-TRAFFIC MOVEMENT ON ALL RADIAL AND CIRCUMFERENTIAL URBAN PARKWAYS

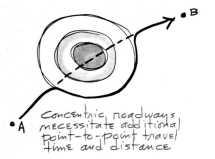

• B

• A

Concentric roadways necessitate additional point-to-point travel time and distance

THE CIRCUITOUS BYPASS

Keep the urba-centers in compression, to squeeze out obsolescence; keep available space in demand, and intensify interaction.

CONFINE THE CBD AND OTHER ACTIVITY CENTERS

Concentric traffic movements are well-suited to the urban metropolis or to regional subcenters.

The concentric

The concentric diagram for urban development is one in which activities are concentrated at the core and supported by rings of varying width and land use. As one moves outward from the core, the use of the land normally diminishes in intensity. Traffic and transit arterials are circumferential or radial. The circumferential routes will follow and separate the interfaces of the various land-use bands. The radial connectors penetrate to the central business district, the bull's-eye of the target, giving the traveler the option of circumnavigating all or part of the city, or of moving directly inward to the zone desired. It can be seen that with the grade separation of all major intersections, it would be hard to devise a more efficient diagram of traffic movement and distribution.

There are certain disadvantages. Orientation is more difficult. Also, in the concentric-circle diagram the trafficways must circumvent large areas of the city with increased distance involved.

The circular distributor loop defines, and therefore constricts, the limits of the central business district (CBD). While this might seem undesirable, it is instead considered an attribute, since most experienced urbanists hold that an optimum and ultimate area distribution should be assigned and *held* to keep all systems in balance over the long-range development period. Such planners would propose that constriction is essential to keep the activity centers vital, and that as new urbanization is required, supplementary centers should be located elsewhere.

The advantages of the concentric scheme are manifold. On a relatively level or mild terrain it combines ease of concentration and separation of uses, with logical organization. Circulation routes of all types can be planned into the environs with a minimum number of crossings. Transportation, transit, and transmission corridors may be readily incorporated in the long-range plan, to provide for future expansion.

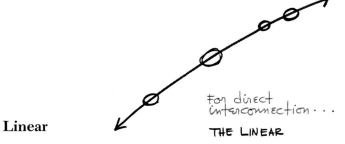

For direct interconnection...

THE LINEAR

Linear

The linear form of urbanization is expressive of movement, and particularly of rapid transit or new modes of guided transportation. As such it has many applications in new-town development.

In the Stockholm metropolitan area, as an example, a dozen or more new outlying communities have been linked to the center city with radial transit lines that weave through the open countryside. These linear paths of high-speed movement connect directly to transit portals at the central plaza of each community in turn. Around these stations and plazas are clustered the apartment towers and shopping malls which serve the transit users. The communities are thereby provided with optimum interconnection, and the proud city of Stockholm, structured around the transit hubs, has been sustained and revitalized.

The concept of interconnecting rapid transit routes and spaced-out nodes of concentrated institutional, commercial, or recreation centers can be envisioned as a highly efficient and desirable means of metropolitan organization. Travel by automobile is not diminished, but is instead improved. Freed of local traffic, the highways can be designed as controlled-access parkways moving through agricultural lands and natural preserves, with interchanges outside of, and serving, each development node.

The linear pattern of settlement is admirably suited to attenuated ridge, valley, and river-basin development, although it applies fully as well to flat and undifferentiated topography. In newly developing areas it has few significant disadvantages and many points in its favor.

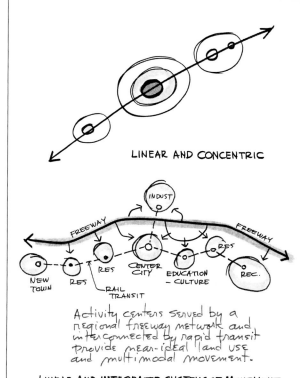

LINEAR AND CONCENTRIC

Activity centers served by a regional freeway network and interconnected by rapid transit provide near-ideal land use and multimodal movement.

LINEAR AND INTEGRATED SYSTEMS OF MOVEMENT

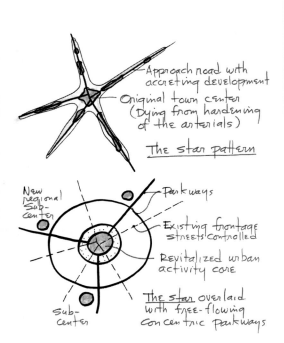

Approach road with accreting development

Original town center (Dying from hardening of the arterials)

The star pattern

New regional Sub-center

Parkways

Existing frontage streets controlled

Revitalized urban activity core

Sub-center

The star overlaid with free-flowing Concentric Parkways

REMEDIAL ROADWAYS

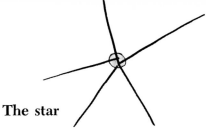

The star

The star conformation is not recommended for new cities or even smaller communities. It is described only because it is so common. It is the often unconscious result of spontaneous urban growth. As farm roads or trade routes converged on the early town center, homes, shops, and other development formed along the roadways—more intensively toward "down town."

Once established, the pattern tends to perpetuate itself in spite of the problems, which become serious. For as expansion continues and traffic volumes swell, there is increasing conflict between the pressures of development and the pressures for road widening. How many towns and cities have struggled with, and still struggle with, this vexing problem!

One planning solution is to overlay the star with a new concentric highway pattern, with limited-access (parkway) radials approaching through the intervening web to a central distributor loop as illustrated. Within the loop the city center will have room to expand and will be blessed with near-perfect regional access. At the intersection of the new circumferential parkways and star rays, new subcenters of various types can be planned and, in time, accommodated.

Each satellite subcenter can develop its own galaxy.

Galaxy

The galaxy city pattern is usually formed of a central core surrounded by a freely arranged constellation of satellite clusters. Such groupings are less ponderous than either the concentric or linear systems and far less rigid and demanding than the grid. They are expressive of either a flat or, more usually, an undulating or irregular landscape and are readily adjusted to the natural features and topographical forms.

Satellite groupings may be planned with care into the region around the central body, and interconnected with either direct or meandering transit-transportation spurs. Each component, as well as the total galaxy, may be surrounded and insulated by open space to preserve the best landscape features. Trafficways may be located with greater selectivity, and often with less demand for capacity.

This pattern has both the disadvantages and advantages of dispersion. On the negative side, lines of linkage are less direct and there is a lack of close interaction between the various components. More extensive land areas are also required. The overall benefits of satellite or cluster groupings are so obvious, however, that their application in some form or combination is fundamental to all systems of large-scale land planning.

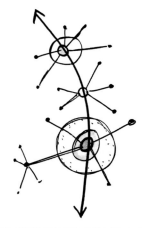

LINEAR, CONCENTRIC, AND SATELLITE
IN WORKING COMBINATION

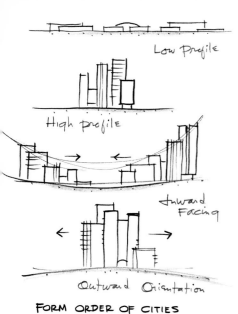

Low Profile

High profile

Inward Facing

Outward Orientation

FORM ORDER OF CITIES

If nature in her actions were not governed by the principle of correlation, cosmos would dissolve into chaos.

Particularly in building of cities, we must learn to understand that, it would prove just as disastrous to the city, if the principle of correlation did not exist, as it would prove to the landscape—to the "city of nature"—if the same principle should cease to function.

ELIEL SAARINEN
The City, Its Growth, Its Decay, Its Future
MIT Press
Cambridge, Mass., 1965

⊙ University
△ Stadium · Sports
◎ Civic Arena (Conventions)
▣ Cultural (Museum · Library · Symphony)
▢ Theatre District
△ Marina
Ⓣ Airport
⟵⟶ Retail Shopping (Mall)
▣ Govt. Center
▲ Trade
◉ Industrial Park
▢ Business Office Campus
⊕ Zoological Garden
▢ Park · Recreation · Open Space
▪▪ High Rise Apartments
▪▫ Midrise Apartments
▫ ▫ Low Density Residential

DIAGRAM FOR A CITY

Consider the purpose

The form of urbanization of any type must be expressive of, and conducive to, its function. Settlements established for defense, for trade, for industry, or as residential or recreation centers, will each have their own distinctive characteristics. Each must be precisely designed to operate fully and effectively. And so it must be for development of every scale and category, if it is to be successful.

List and describe the components

Urban planning is somewhat like fitting together all the pieces of a puzzle. Before the assembly is attempted, it is well to make sure that all the parts have been accounted for.

Arrange the major elements into a logical diagram

As in the construction of a building, it is important that the structural framework be well suited to the building type and site. It is at this stage of planning, when the basic urban structure is to be established, that the choice must be made between variations of the grid, concentric, linear, or galaxy patterns of land use and traffic arrangements. It must also be determined whether the community is to be condensed or dispersed, high or low in profile, and oriented inward to open centers or outward to the surrounding landscape.

Adjust the diagram to fit the topography

Where development "fights the topo," the problems are manifold. The additional accumulative time, effort, and cost involved in blasting, excavation, filling, drainage, and erosion control may be enormous. Besides, the natural quality of the landscape is destroyed, and a new and artificial landscape must be created.

Conversely, where, by sensitive planning, development is fitted to, and integrated with, the natural landscape, the results are consistently better. A community which has been designed in harmony with nature borrows of its strength and returns to the landscape a fitness of its own.

Provide a desirable balance of development, trafficways, and open space enframement

When, and only when, these three ingredients of urbanization are brought into proper balance can the communities function as they should, and can life for all people of the region be fulfilling.

The character of towns springs in the main from their natural setting, the mood and abilities of their inhabitants and the materials which lie at hand, with climate and latitude determining the degree to which the town can open itself out to the sun and air.
GORDON LOGIE

Why not also cities that identify themselves in terms of their region, their cultural heritage, their activities?
GEORGE MCCUE

229

The agglomeration syndrome

The megalopolitan mess that has accreted like a cancerous growth along the main highways from Boston to Washington, from Palm Beach to Miami, from South Bend to Chicago, and from Burbank to Los Angeles—to cite but a few examples—results from a series of fallacies. Most of the horrible mishmash has derived from three lingering misconceptions:

In transportation considerations the benefits should accrue to the public that bears the cost.
DAVID BOND
Unpublished memo

1. *People have the right to front homes and business enterprises along all roads, including arterial highways.* While this was, indeed, the historical pattern of development in the times of the horse and buggy, it is no longer valid in the era of high-speed automotive travel.

   Highways, and major circulation roads, are built with public funds for the express purpose of moving vehicles rapidly and efficiently. The use of these roadways as building frontage is in no way consistent with this primary objective. Each point of egress or ingress at the right-of-way edge imposes dangerous interruptions and reduces the capacity for through-traffic movement. One traffic light, for example, or a single exit ramp from a roadside apartment or shopping mall, may reduce the capacity of a highway lane by half. As few as ten access drives per mile may completely vitiate the purpose for which the road was constructed. Why should private enterprise be granted this privilege at the expense of the taxpayer and highway user?

   The strip commercial slums that line so many dreary miles of our clogged roadways must be outlawed, for they are murderous. They kill the sense of community; they kill the landscape; and they kill the trafficway as an effective route of vehicular movement. A highway will become stagnant and "die" from peripheral misuse as quickly as a lake will die, or eutrophy, from the misuse or pollution of its shoreline.

2. *Public lands should not be acquired until needed.* A second fallacy is the premise that when the demand for a facility is great enough, it will somehow be forthcoming.

   In many otherwise progressive communities it is specifically provided by law that neither school nor park sites, nor land for other public purposes, may be acquired prior to the time of actual construction. The intention, of course, is to preserve agricultural lands in their present use and to discourage speculation. Both of these commendable objectives can be achieved as well by the official adoption of a comprehensive land-use plan, by zoning, and by tax laws designed to make continued farming, recreation, conservation, and other such uses of open space land economically feasible.

The advantage of acquiring sites well ahead of their need is that they may be purchased at the locations best suited to the future use, and at uninflated prices. If the acquisition of public properties must be delayed until the time when construction is imminent, it means that the municipality must then bid for the land in competition with the developers whose projects the facilities are to serve. By then the most desirable sites will probably have been taken, development patterns will have been established, utility systems and trafficways designed without consideration of the new public use, and often condemnation proceedings will be necessary.

To assure communities the ability to predesignate and pre-purchase sites and rights-of-way, new legislation may be needed. Enabling bills or ordinances should provide for such desirable features as rights of continued occupancy by the present user, temporary leasing, and the joint purchase of lands by several agencies for multiple-use opportunities.

3. *Growth is always desirable.* A third and common myth is that growth equates with progress. On the contrary, in spite of unremitting promotional efforts by the local chambers of commerce, there is a strong case to be made in most established communities *against* further expansion. While in some instances well-planned development may be in the public interest, in other cases it may destroy the community or bankrupt the very enterprises that so glibly invited it in.

A pleasant New Hampshire town, for example, may be completely discombobulated by a new residential neighborhood that overwhelms its schools, depletes its water resources, and requires more public improvements than can be underwritten by its tax yield. An established and thriving commercial district may wither and die because of a new suburban shopping mall. New industrial plants so eagerly sought, and perhaps even subsidized, may downgrade the character of an entire region. They may impose heavy traffic loads upon existing streets; they may shift the centers of gravity and cause new and less desirable groupings; they may usurp favorite hiking, hunting, or fishing grounds; or they may bring with them new types and critical levels of pollution.

Where suitable land is available, and where public services are adequate or can be easily augmented, an infusion of new development *may* be beneficial—but only provided it satisfies three essential conditions. It must be compatible with the situation which exists; it must be consistent with long-range community objectives; and the benefits from its presence must exceed its negative impacts. The proof of satisfying all three criteria lies with the promoter. If his facts are correct and his case is sound, it can be demonstrated to the agencies and in open public hearings. Otherwise, his proposal should be defeated, and his petitions denied.

Towns are biological phenomena. They have hearts and organs indispensable to the accomplishment of their special functions. They may, in the wake of anarchy, lose their vital nature and degenerate into vast parasitic conurbations. But the very factor which permits their growth—mechanized speed—ends by reducing them to an absurdity.
LE CORBUSIER

To look at the plan of a great city is to look at something like the cross-section of a fibrous tumor. Seen in the light of space needs today there are not any unnatural concentrations of tissue but more and more painfully forced circulation, comparable to high blood pressure in the human body.
FRANK LLOYD WRIGHT
When Democracy Builds
University of Chicago Press
Chicago, Ill., 1945

Traffic is not important. What is important is how people live. There is no gain in cutting a few minutes' traveling time if the result is an unsatisfactory environment at the end of it. There is no gain in adequate parking for everybody if it involves a half mile walk across asphalt to do your shopping.
THEO CROSBY
Architecture: City Sense
Reinhold Publishing Company
New York, 1965

No cheap or reasonable solution can be expected to urban traffic congestion as long as cities think they must be open-air parking lots and throughways for commuters.
EDWARD HIGBEE
The Squeeze—Cities Without Space
Apollo Editions
New York, 1962

And the first lesson we have to learn is that a city exists, not for the constant passage of motor cars, but for the care and culture of men.
LEWIS MUMFORD

The motor car has completely upset the form of the city. I feel that the time has come to make a distinction between the viaduct architecture of the car and the architecture of man's activities.
LOUIS I. KAHN
The Notebook and Drawings of Louis Kahn
Edited by Richard S. Wurman and Eugene Feldman
MIT Press
Cambridge, Mass. 1974

Massive agglomeration—urbanization out of control—has been marked by a tragic handover of irreplaceable land resources to misguided and unchecked economic exploitation. It is time to ring the bell.

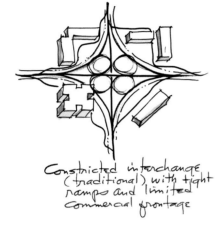

Design all arterial highways and distributor roads as controlled-access greenways

Perhaps no other single improvement will make such an immediate and significant contribution to sound metropolitan planning. New strip commercial development will be precluded at one blow.

People will drive from their homes to work and to activity centers along pleasant tree-lined drives. Communities will be planned as quiet enclaves within the highway network. Neighborhood convenience and regional shopping centers will no longer face directly upon roadways but will be designed as self-contained courts and malls. Trafficways will be reserved for the free and safe movement of traffic. Community life will be focused inward upon trafficfree places and spaces linked by pedestrian paths.

Plan the interchanges as open space nodes

The preferred location for many enterprises has long been the intersection of two important roads. From the point of view of the entrepreneur, the more important the highways, the better is the site. There can be no doubt that such a location affords the business venture a high degree of exposure and a prominent regional "fix." Such development is generally encouraged by the local officials who welcome the high commercial tax yield.

But this common practice of crowding motels, restaurants, filling stations, and fried-chicken emporiums tightly in upon the roadway intersections has a number of negative aspects. The business entranceways and exits often interfere with through-traffic movement. Signing and lighting systems are thereby complicated and highway safety jeopardized. Moreover, each interchange attains a commercial and often shoddy mien, and the entrance to the adjacent districts is through a business core.

It is proposed that, as a more desirable alternative, each interchange of the regional arterial system be planned as an attractive motor park and that crossing points be so located that this is made possible. At the perimeter of the park will then run a service-loop road upon which the enterprises will front. Set back from the intersection, they will impose less interference, command even better exposure across the park foreground and enjoy much-improved ingress and egress. They will also be farther removed from the nuisance of traffic sounds and lights.

The arterials, now freed of strip development along their routes, and with each node designed as a green portal to the communities served, will assume the quality of a handsome parkway system.

Preplan the entire district

In the absence of an enforceable plan for orderly growth, urbanization spreads across the landscape like a dread and consuming disease. It first

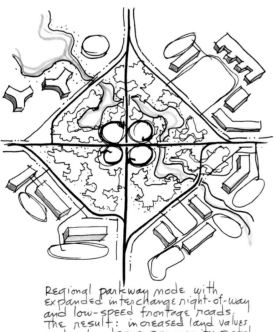

Constricted interchange (traditional) with tight ramps and limited commercial frontage

Regional parkway mode with expanded interchange right-of-way and low-speed frontage roads. The result: increased land values and a handsome community portal.

DESIGN THE INTERCHANGES AS ATTRACTIVE GATEWAYS

forms in nodules along the major circulation routes, then follows back along feeder roads and paths of least resistance to infect the surrounding countryside. In the early stages the blight is only an irritant; soon, however, it gains momentum as a rampaging epidemic. It leaps from hilltop to valley, destroying the natural cover and forming lesions of erosion and scars of corruption wherever it touches down. It breaks out at last within established farming communities—raising spot land values and increasing tax assessments. From that time, the farmsteads, dairy herds, vineyards, and orchards are doomed. Neither woodland, meadow, nor marsh are spared as the entire region soon succumbs to a malignant fester of incompatible uses and disruption.

Harassed officials, long since unable to check the building fever once started, must turn to the hopeless task of connecting the scattered settlements with roads and sewers, and providing, with inadequate funds, the services which they demand.

With advanced planning, a locality can protect the well-being of thriving farmlands and the integrity of other desirable areas against the threat of such scatteration. Or compatible forms of development may be invited in, under control, as a welcome regional attribute.

Designate, and reserve or purchase, all public lands required

The time to purchase public lands is when they are available. For cities with a perennial lack of funds, one possibility to be explored is that of land purchase by bonds, to be retired in full or in part with income received from the lease of development rights or easements for compatible uses on a long-term or interim basis.

With advance area planning the patterns of future land uses and highway-transmission corridors can be defined for a community, a county, or an urbanizing region. The limits of future development clusters, together with their projected densities, can also, and should be, established. With this data at hand, it is a simple matter to prepare a diagrammatic layout of all lands needed for future schools, parks, roadways, and other public uses.

While such a long-range plan may be modified in detail by unforeseen circumstances, *it will never be achieved at all unless, having been conceived, it is implemented.* This can be accomplished by its incorporation into the comprehensive area plan and its reservation by zoning. A more certain way is to purchase outright—as far in advance as possible—all public lands which will be required by anticipated growth.

How fortunate the citizens whose officials have had such foresight!

Limit development to the acceptance capacity of the ecosystem

Land areas and water bodies have a limited tolerance for use. Food chains, natural vegetation, soils, currents, aquifers, and water edges and land conformation can stand only so much alteration. When levels of use or abuse are exceeded, the unfortunate ramifications may extend far beyond the project site and wreak havoc throughout wide and distant reaches of the surrounding environs.

Seldom is the balance of nature changed for the good. Imbalance is usually attended by drastic deterioration of the landscape character, by slippage, erosion, and sedimentation, and by irreparable damage to the existing fauna and flora.

Yet nature is tough and durable. She will accept and adjust to a remarkable degree of tugging and hauling, provided ascertainable limits are not exceeded. It can thus be seen that a first step in the planning for any land area, from garden site to metropolitan region, is the conduct of an ecological survey as a guide to all development, and against which its environmental impacts can be tested.

The fragile strands that make up the web of checks and balances were woven by forces of nature. When the weight of man's activities are thrust upon one strand repercussions are often felt in portions of the web quite remote from the area acted upon and may remain unseen until other strands break under the stress. The end result can be the complete collapse of entire systems.

Coastal Zone Management in Florida
Report of the Florida Coastal Zone
Coordinating Council, 1971

The modern city is losing its external and formal structure. Internally it is in a state of decay while the new community represented by the nation everywhere grows at its expense.

DON MARTINDALE, translator and editor
The Theory of the City
The Free Press
New York, 1958

Metropolitan America is in a squeeze. The space it uses for living and to make a living has become cluttered to the point of frustration. Efforts to relieve congestion are feeble by comparison with the forces that make it worse. Urban decay, suburban sprawl, rising taxes, clogged highways, distressed railroads, poor public schools, higher prices to food consumers, lower prices to food producers, disappearing recreational space—these and other penalties of living in our time are not isolated ills. They are symptoms of the same deadly disease. This illness lowers the standard of living while wages rise, and it threatens to make a corpse of a once vibrant social organism. What is this malady? How did we contract it? Why does it provoke so many forms of weakness which seem unrelated at first glance? Finally, is there a cure?

EDWARD HIGBEE
The Squeeze—Cities without Space
Apollo Editions
New York, 1962

Dull, inert cities, it is true, do contain the seeds of their own destruction and little else. But lively, diverse, intense cities contain the seeds of their own regeneration, with energy enough to carry over for problems and needs outside themselves.

JANE JACOBS
The Death and Life of Great American Cities
Random House, Inc.
New York, 1961

Weep not that the world changes. Did it keep a stable, changeless state, it were cause indeed to weep.

WILLIAM CULLEN BRYANT
As quoted in *Conservation Quotes*
U.S. Department of the Interior,
National Park Service
January 1953

Instead of striving to make permanent the passing forms and shapes of meaning it would be more creative if [men] entrusted themselves to the natural processes of change and so refused to become ensnared in surface patterns.

LAURENS VAN DER POST
The Seed and the Sower
William Morrow & Company, Inc.
New York, 1963

Blight

Decay, filth, and aching slums have long been the curse of cities. Why?

A study of this phenomenon shows that the causes are as many and varied as the foibles and sins of man himself. The contributing factors change from era to era and from place to place, and include the whole range of social, economic, and political ills. But while conditions in our contemporary cities are far from ideal, there are few knowledgeable cynics who will not begrudgingly concede that the extremes between the fair and foul have been lessened over the years. Today there are promising signs of public concern, and massive urban aid and self-help programs at work, which are gradually bringing improvement.

Yet blight and the slums remain. The patterns of their incidence are generally consistent. In a business district, for example, the signs of decline are familiar. Along a thriving street will appear the "closing out" or "bankruptcy" announcements, then the "store to let" signs, the vacancies, and soon the vandalism. As leases run out there will be the emigration of the better stores to the newer shopping districts. The old-time merchants will rally in a futile attempt to shore up the sagging district, and then, eventually, will come the total collapse.

In residential areas the decline may start with an untidy neighbor. With loss of pride, the abutting property owners may neglect their maintenance. Dwellings will begin to change hands, at first by sales and then by rentals. The "solid citizens" will leave while the leaving is good. Rezoning appeals will be granted, sometimes as political favors, to give tax relief for those who remain. "Zither lessons" and "colonic irrigation" signs will begin to blossom in the windows. Minority-group tenants, often displaced elsewhere by urban reconstruction, will crowd into the area, paying exorbitant rents for shoddy rooms. Absentee owners, squeezing out the maximum profit, will neglect repairs to the point of total dilapidation.

If there be a law of blight, it is this: *Once deterioration in any form has been allowed to start in any area, it must be checked immediately by repair or replacement; otherwise the decay will run its full course.* It is the old story of the rotten apple. The longer the delay and the more extensive the spread, the more drastic the cure required.

Act fast when the first signs of blight appear

Urban health, like human health, is largely a matter of good habits. If a district, whatever the type, is kept clean, attractive, and in good tone, decay is less apt to establish a foothold. Bad housekeeping or disrepair should never be ignored. Spalled paving, burned-out light bulbs left dead in the lamps, peeling paint on a home or storefront, or the first appearance of overflowing trash cans left out beside the curb should be the signal for alert and positive action. If neighborly banter and serious persuasion are not effective, public health laws and police power should be invoked.

Form an owners' association

Ten individuals, acting alone, have the force of ten separate hammer blows. Ten, as a group, can deliver the force of a sledge.

The best time for the creation of an association, or civic action group, is when area pride is running high. Its purpose then can be the positive functions of promotion and improvement. A desirable side effect will be the generation of group spirit and the guarding against all threats to the local scene.

If such an association, or committee, must be formed on an emergency basis, it acts with less effectiveness; but act it must, if the well-being of the area is at stake. Only group action can save it.

Contain, and excise, the spots of dilapidation

Considered as a disease, which it is, blight can be clinically treated. If quickly diagnosed by those concerned, mild treatment may suffice. If the disease is allowed to progress, more drastic cures, including major surgery, will soon be required.

Reverse the trend

The best defense is an attack. At the first signs of deterioration, or preferably before, the launching of a neighborhood improvement program can stimulate positive action. Architectural renovation, and the installation of attractive new walk pavings, lighting, or street plantings can upgrade the appearance of a whole street—improving morale, increasing sales, and raising property values.

Expand the improvement area

"No man is an island"; and no residential block or business district stands alone. Homes, shops, institutions, and communities are interdependent and interacting.

It is to little avail, for instance, if a local shopping street is upgraded while the supporting residential neighborhood is permitted to run down. While each individual or local effort at property improvement sets a commendable example, improvement is doubly effective as part of a total areawide campaign. Some cities, such as Philadelphia, Pittsburgh, Chicago, Dallas, and Los Angeles, have, with dynamic civic leadership, achieved a remarkable renaissance of a whole metropolitan region.

Blight is not a matter of crowding, age, mixed uses, or the low income of occupants. Some of the world's most vibrant urban areas and delightful neighborhoods are marked by just these characteristics.

Blight is disrepair, decay, unsafe or unhealthful conditions; it is unbearable noise, stench, filth in the streets, rats in the basement, and cockroaches in the kitchen.

Progress occurs when people cooperate.
HAL BURTON
The City Fights Back
The Citadel Press
New York, 1954

[*It might be assumed that*] *an "island of good" would favorably affect "the swamp of bad" immediately surrounding it. Unfortunately, . . . the reverse has proven true.*
ROBERT A. FUTTERMAN
The Future of Our Cities
Doubleday & Company, Inc.
Garden City, N.Y., 1961

Urban renewal

The deterioration of cities usually starts with the central business district, or the smaller outlying commercial cores. It moves outward gradually in an ever-widening ring, advancing first along the radial trafficways. This is caused by the fact that when buildings become obsolescent, it is often more convenient and less costly to replace them outside of the central city. It is mostly a matter of economics. When renovation or expansion becomes necessary, each owner must weigh the advantages of the existing location against the disadvantages of high real estate values and property taxes, difficulties of access, and other facts of urban life. When the balance is tipped in favor of relocation, the outward migration begins.

If zoning provisions so allow, the new stores or office buildings are often constructed at the edge of the urban core and within the retreating residential fringe. Or they may relocate farther outward in a newly forming regional center.

In either case, the city government is left in a double bind. Faced with shrinking revenues and increasing demands for services and improvements, its only recourse, historically, has been to pile on additional property taxes. This, in turn, accelerates the centrifugal wave. In its wake, each vacancy tends to invite an influx of less desirable uses. Where buildings are demolished, they are often replaced with parking lots or garages, leaving gaping deserts of parked automobiles between the stores and office towers. With each new vacancy, and with each drop in the level of concentrated business activity, the CBD becomes less attractive to new primary business ventures. Inevitably, in the past, large areas of the urban centers have sunk into a state of bleak disrepair and hopeless poverty. Such, in the United States, was the condition of every large metropolitan core at the start of the century. In this light it may be painful to remind ourselves that one of the surest tests of the cultural level (civilization) of a people is the nature of the cities that they build—or fail to rebuild by encouraging regeneration.

It is only within the past several decades that a promising cure for advanced urban blight has come into being. The program, known as *urban renewal*, is currently administered by the Department of Housing and Urban Development (HUD). Although it got off to an awkward start, and although the techniques are still in the stage of testing and evolution, the process has been successfully applied in a number of states and is now gaining wide acceptance. To date, the emphasis has been mainly on renewal by *replacement*. In some cases this is indeed the required specific. But it is proposed that the hope of our cities lies even more in the stimulation of *self-help* and *rehabilitation* programs such as the incentive plans sponsored by HUD.

The seeds were sown in the Federal Housing Act of 1937. This for the first time provided a legal basis by which a city could take the initiative in combating deterioration. Essentially, it empowered local governments to establish a redevelopment authority, chartered by the state. To the authority was granted the right to acquire, through condemnation proceedings if necessary, private and dilapidated properties which it could then improve and resell or lease for private development. It thus made possible the assemblage of composite holdings of sufficient size to permit the creation of a whole new revitalized subdistrict. The land could be planned by the authority for its "highest and best use" in relation to the overall city pattern. Pockets of blight could be removed and healthy areas supported. Aside from the environmental upgrading, the city government would gain from a stronger tax base and from the decreased need for fire and police protection and other public services.

With funds flowing to the authority from the state and federal grants in aid, with borrowing power, with the city contributing its share in the form of street and other improvements, and with the returns from the sales or lease of redeveloped parcels, such a renewal or redevelopment agency can stage a massive and revolving program of urban improvement.

Create an authority

The first step in redevelopment is the obtaining of a charter by act of the state legislature. With respected—and representative—civic leaders named to the redevelopment authority board, with a competent director appointed, and with well-trained staff assembled, the program is off and running.

Priority areas must then be established and proposals for funding submitted to the state and to HUD, unless private financing is elected.

Start with the central business district (CBD)

Within a metropolitan area the central business district is the nerve center and dominant focal point. As such, its condition has great effect upon the city's vigor and well-being. It is also the ganglion most susceptible to deterioration and most responsive to treatment.

While each situation will have its own unique problems and opportunities, recent experience has shown that there are considerations common to the revitalization of all urban cores. These are outlined in the following paragraphs.

Reexamine its purpose

The urban center is at best an intensified nucleus of governmental, business, and cultural activities. Only those uses and services which are specifically required to support and sustain such activities, or to enrich the daily experiences of those who will be drawn, to work or live, downtown should be permitted space within the central confines.

Just as each city has its own distinctive nature and characteristics, so should its polarized center. The core should build upon regional strengths and capacities and answer to regional needs. It should epitomize the best that the region can produce and express its full flowering.

Constrict the size of the center city

A study of the existing plan of any downtown area will suggest the natural center of gravity. Around this point may be described a circle that can be distended to include those thriving CBD functions which are to be maintained. As a guide it is proposed that an area of approximately 300 acres, having a radius of some 2,000 feet, be used as a trial precinct within which all primary business and governmental functions be confined. Only those cultural facilities, such as libraries, museums, symphony halls, and cathedrals, which are to serve both the entire region and its urban center should be invited within the circle. While hotels and a limited number of apartment towers will be accommodated by zoning, land for most of the urban apartments will be reserved adjacent to, but outside of, the ring.

Adjustments to both the size and conformation of the redescribed CBD area must, of course, be made in the case of each actual center under study. The main concern is that the sprawling core be reduced in area to a point of high concentration, and the marginal and noncontributory uses be supplanted.

By thus reducing the size of the core, all buildings will be within easy walking distance and a pedestrian scale restored. As a function of supply and demand the vacant and obsolescent properties will again become desirable for rehabilitation or new building sites. Further, the intensity so essential to a vibrant inner city will have been assured.

Preclude the outward extension of the CBD

As the pressure of concentration raises internal real estate values, there will be appeals to permit the construction of major business uses "just outside" the redefined center. These must be firmly resisted, since

Planning involves the coordination of human activities in time and space, on the basis of known facts about place, work, and people: it involves the modification and relocation of various elements in the total environment for the purpose of increasing their service to the community.

LEWIS MUMFORD
The Culture of Cities
Harcourt, Brace and World
New York, 1938

. . . the first ingredients of any future plan is the provision of simple and effective machinery to encourage constant renewal of the fabric of the city . . .

G. HOLMES PERKINS, in
The Future of Cities and Urban Development
By Robert A. Futterman
Doubleday & Company
Garden City, N.Y., 1961

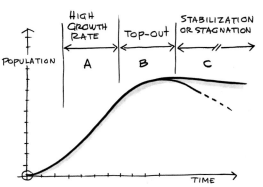

A. Growth varies with immigration attractions, alternative locations, resources, and available services.

B. Maximum population and build-out of usable land. Because of zoning imbalances, title difficulties, transition, demolition, and rebuilding lag, at least 15% of developable property is vacant at any one time.

C. Urban health depends upon a reasonable balance of housing, jobs, environmental quality, and taxes.

Declining population is usually caused by centrifugal development and a lack of regenerative incentives or mechanisms. With administrative vision, civic support, and the application of new renewal techniques, many older cities are being revitalized and enriched. Montreal, Toronto, Boston, Atlanta, Chicago, and San Francisco are examples.

THE GROWTH OF AN URBAN METROPOLIS

The growth of the American city in the past century has meant the extension of paved streets and sewers and gas mains, and progressive heightening of office buildings and tenements. There is a curious confusion in America between growth and improvement.

LEWIS MUMFORD
City Development
Greenwood Press, Inc.
Westport, Ct., 1973

they would at once relieve the planned intensity and reinitiate the cycle of deterioration.

To preclude the breaching of the tightened boundary, it is well that it be set along a dominant natural barrier such as a river, palisade, deep ravine, or shoreline. An open space barrier may be provided in the form of a circumferential park reserved to serve also as a corridor for future surface and subsurface transportation or transmission uses. In many instances the most logical barricade will be provided by the construction of an inner distribution beltway feeding parking structures on either side.

Stop the automobile at the edge

Except for passenger buses moving along well-defined transitways, and except for transportation vehicles confined to subsurface tunnels—no automobile (of the conventional types now in use) will be allowed to penetrate the magic circle. The center city can thus be reformed compactly around a trafficfree system of pedestrian ways and spaces, resembling in scale the narrow streets and delightful plazas of Venice. Mini-trams, electronically motorized cabs, cycles, moving beltways, and escalators will supplement internal modes of pedestrian circulation.

Automobiles will approach the replanned city centers along radial parkways and the inner circumferential ring to garaging in towers or subsurface parking decks at the edge of the business district. From garage to district center will be no more than a pleasant five-minute walk along open-air greenways or through bustling underground passageways as in Montreal's Place Ville Marie or Washington's L'Enfant Plaza.

Bring transit into the ring

Rapid transit runs from the farthest regional hinterlands to the urban nuclei will be frequent and direct. In the outlying districts transit-related towns and communities will develop in clusters around attractive new stations.

Within the city, the central transit interchange at the heart of the business district will recall, but far exceed in convenience, activity, and delight, New York's old "Grand Central." Other modes of transit, by busways, skyways, and waterways, will be planned to or through the city as appropriate.

With the automobile removed from the streets and centers, rapid transit will become again a way of life for an increasingly large proportion of the metro population.

Provide tunnels and underground terminals for the distribution of goods

No doubt the chief contributors to urban traffic constipation are the delivery trucks and service vehicles. Blocking lanes and sidewalks, they bring traffic to a standstill and impose enormous costs to the city in person-waiting-hours. By all reason, goods should be delivered from points outside the CBD ring by subsurface routes to internal distribution points, from which they can then be transported locally, and still underground, by motorized carts, forklifts, or pneumatic tubes.

Build a multilevel garden city

The city of the future will rise in terraced decks above its service and utility levels. Its modular, interlocking base, extending horizontally and vertically in response to need and topography, will support the office towers, domes, and other urban structures. All will be served by the transit system and all will be interconnected by escalators, flying walkways, and high-speed lifts. Concentrations will be much greater than in our present downtown areas because of the removal of vehicular streets and space-consuming garaging. Offices will be surrounded by, and will look down upon, a parklike and interconnecting network of garden courts and pedestrian walkways enriched with fountains, sculpture, foliage, and handsome pavings—perhaps under lofty geodesic domes for protection and climate control.

Preserve the historic landmarks

In any renewal plan great care must be taken to preserve not only the "historic monuments" but also the "lesser" structures that trace the course of the city's development from its earliest beginnings. Montreal, Boston, Philadelphia, and San Francisco give us inspiring examples of how this can be done. Here new towers rise in dramatic contrast and complete compatibility with the fine old buildings marked for historic preservation. Many of these have been sensitively adapted for use as charming restaurants, shops, and in-town residences.

Urban renewal moves slowly. But block by block, our fractured inner cities can be unified and given new form and vitality if their reconstruction is conceived as part of an overall plan which is sound and compelling.

---

10 Axioms for urban revitalization

1. *Keep the urba-centers* compact*

   Concentrate the business, governmental, and cultural functions.

   Stop spread and proliferation which normally leave rings of dilapidation in their wake.

   Limit the ultimate size by physical barriers—such as a park band, waterway, or ring road.

   Squeeze out the vacancies and noncontributing uses. In such condensed centers, with area and space at a premium, real estate values are high.

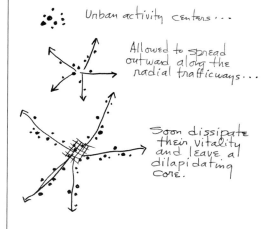

Cities work best in compression.

Urban activity centers...

Allowed to spread outward along the radial trafficways...

Soon dissipate their vitality and leave a dilapidating core.

2. *Provide a regional transit hub*

   Create a multilevel terminal near the center of concentration.

   Construct grade-separated rapid transit approaches.

   Route the surface transit vehicles—such as buses, minibuses, and taxis—along reserved rights-of-way.

   Incorporate all modes of external and internal movement into an integrated system.

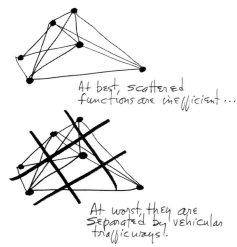

At best, scattered functions are inefficient...

At worst, they are separated by vehicular trafficways.

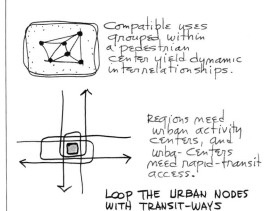

Compatible uses grouped within a pedestrian center yield dynamic interrelationships.

Regions need urban activity centers, and urba-centers need rapid-transit access.

LOOP THE URBAN NODES WITH TRANSIT-WAYS

---

* Dominant *urban activity centers* may be of varying types—such as governmental, financial, trade, business office, cultural, medical, residential, entertainment—or several in combination.

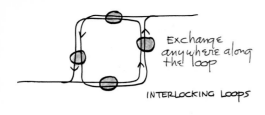

Exchange anywhere along the loop

INTERLOCKING LOOPS

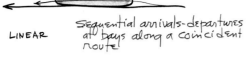

LINEAR

Sequential arrivals-departures at bays along a coincident route

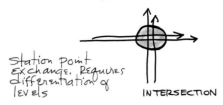

Station point exchange, requires differentiation of levels

INTERSECTION

THREE METHODS OF TRANSIT-TO-TRANSIT INTERCHANGE

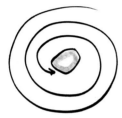

The efficient and pleasant "homing in" to the new urban centers is a plan requirement.

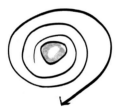

Free and orderly dispersion is a necessity too.

ACCESS AND EGRESS BY CAR MUST BE PLANNED

3. Plan for peripheral automobile access and storage

Design circumferential bypass routes in the form of controlled-access parkways.

Bulk-store those automobiles with the urba-center as their destination. Parking towers, terraces, and compounds adjacent to the inner distributor ring will have direct and convenient access to various forms of people movers.

Accommodate a limited amount of premium and short-term parking within the office structures or roofed parking decks. Access by grade-separated approach ramps will be a mandatory requirement.

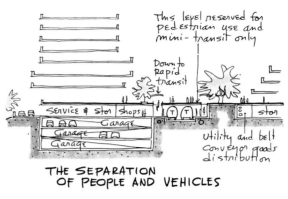

This level reserved for pedestrian use and mini-transit only

Down to Rapid transit

Service & Stor shops

Garage
Garage
Garage

Utility and belt conveyor goods distribution

THE SEPARATION OF PEOPLE AND VEHICLES

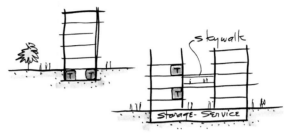

skywalk

Storage-Service

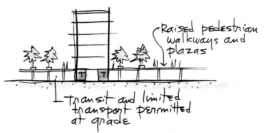

Raised pedestrian walkways and plazas

transit and limited transport permitted at grade

SEGREGATE PEOPLE, VEHICLES, AND SERVICE-STORAGE FUNCTIONS

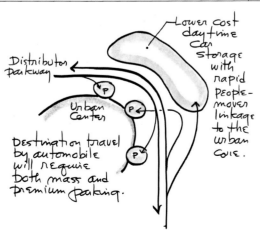

Lower cost daytime car storage with rapid people-mover linkage to the urban core.

Distributor Parkway

Urban Center

Destination travel by automobile will require both mass and premium parking.

KEEP THE CARS TO THE EDGES

Bulk Parking

Premium

Short Term

PROVIDE PERIPHERAL CAR STORAGE

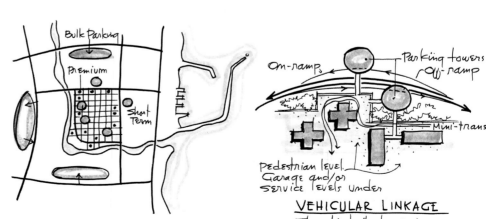

On-ramp

Parking towers Off-ramp

Mini-transit

Pedestrian level. Garage and/or service levels under

VEHICULAR LINKAGE
The distributor ring, car storage, and pedestrian office plaza

4. Convert the urban center from automobile to pedestrian scale

Eliminate the conventional streets and parking areas.

Exclude the personally operated vehicle from all pedestrian levels.

Transform the public rights-of-way into an interconnecting network of walkways, malls, courts, and plazas. Consider all-weather comfort.

Reserve routes for evolving forms of local transit such as monorail, moving chairs, and cubicles that can move swiftly along a horizontal or looping pathway.

5. Group the like activities

Maximize convenience and intensify interactions.

Typical groupings will include those functions related to:

> Government
> Finance
> Business offices
> Retailing
> Trade
> Dining and entertainment
> Culture

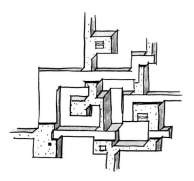

PROVIDE CONGREGATING PLACES AND ALL-WEATHER PEDESTRIAN MALLS, ARCADES, AND WALKWAYS

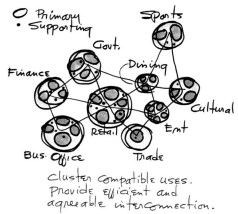

Cluster compatible uses. Provide efficient and agreeable interconnection.

GROUP LIKE ACTIVITIES.

6. Incorporate the supporting uses

In addition to the primary central-area functions, plans and zoning will accommodate and encourage the inclusion of such ancillary uses as professional offices, specialty shops, restaurants, cafés, bars, clubs, and studios that give variety and interest.

7. Include centralized services

These will range from such basics as energy production and solid-waste processing to advanced systems of computerized accounting and subsurface storage and goods distribution.

8. Bring art and nature into the city

Refresh the urban environs with tree-shaded courts, terraced gardens, and roof-deck recreation parks.

Face outward to waterbodies and wooded preserves.

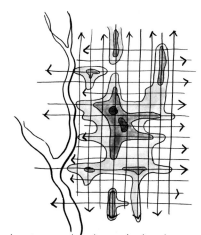

The typical urban district is a machination of frictions. It spreads out along its divisive trafficways, and dissipates its strength.

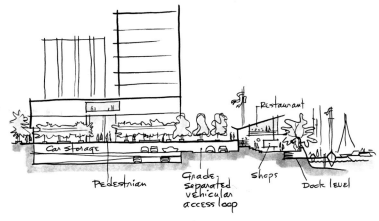

LET CITY DWELLERS ENJOY THE WATER EDGES

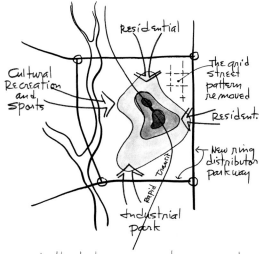

In the techniques of urban renewal lie the key to creating a system of free traffic movement, intensified business activity, and organic urban form.

THE RESHAPING OF AN URBAN CENTER

241

Build into the new traffic-free urban centers the delight and charm of the old European cities.

ENCOURAGE FREE PLAN ARRANGEMENT

Face inward to planted ways and spaces around which the shops, bookstalls, cafés, and other features of pedestrian interest may be located.

Furnish the center with sculpture, murals, pools, splashing fountains, and handsome lighting and graphics.

Consider gardened shopping arcades with retractable roofs, domed conservatories, and variform exhibit halls, libraries, and museums.

Provide the spatial (and legislative) structure within which the city may be enhanced by private enterprise.

9. *Rehabilitate the surrounding areas*

   Redevelop adjacent areas of blight into new residential neighborhoods.

   Provide them with their own convenience and recreation facilities.

   Link them by freeway to the open countryside and by rapid transit to the regional activity nodes and to the center city.

10. *Keep the plans free and flexible*

    Develop a creative conceptual framework in terms of land use, systems of movement, and services.

    Modify and improve the plan whenever new techniques emerge or new opportunities are presented.

    Encourage freedom of choice and innovative design.

    Prepare a staged program for implementation. Include provision for the necessary administrative unit, staff, legislation, and capital funding.

    Launch an all-out drive to accomplish the first-phase objectives.

The new-town movement

It is generally conceded that Sir Ebenezer Howard was the father of the new-town movement. A self-taught sociologist, he became concerned with the crowded and distressing conditions in the British industrial cities and proposed that town and country must be married. Out of the union, he prophesied, "would spring a new life, a new hope, a new civilization." He conceived of a better mode of living in spaced-out "garden cities." Here, he reasoned, homes and factories could be planned together in such a way that people could live close to their work, children would walk in safety to their schools, and each family could have its own plot for a garden.

By the early 1930s a team of American planners had adapted Howard's theories, to provide a new type of community which was designed particularly for the automobile era. These men, led by Henry Wright and Clarence Stein, produced the plans for Radburn, New Jersey, a highly successful community which was to establish precedents for most new towns built since. A distinguishing feature of Radburn is that cars and service vehicles circulate on the outside and in zones separated from the living and pedestrian areas. Homes and apartments are grouped with entrances, garages, and service areas oriented to approach drives and to parking courts, while living and sleeping areas are faced inward toward lawns, play areas, and gardens. Vehicular traffic thus moves much more freely and safely than in the conventional grid patterns, while homes and community life are focused on pleasant open spaces, not on busy city streets.

The American new-town plans were in turn to serve as models for those to be built in England, Scandinavia, and later all of Europe after World War II. As a result of the massive wartime destruction, Europeans were faced with the need to provide both housing and employment centers for a large percentage of the population. Since 1945, thirty or more new towns have been planned and brought into construction in Great Britain and Scandinavia alone. Each has brought fresh new thinking and improvements. Most of these new communities are located well outside of urban areas. All received heavy governmental subsidies and were subject to strong centralized design and management controls.

The more recent new towns of the United States have been built in response to burgeoning population expansion and to relieve the crushing strain on the overburdened urban centers. They have been devised as a logical and hopeful answer to the common malaise of urban sprawl caused by the spread of single-family homes dotted for mile upon mile without relief across the landscape. They have been built, in the main, as unified components of urbanized metropolitan areas. They have been developed to a large extent with private capital and thus with much greater freedom and flexibility in their planning than their counterparts in Europe.

Plan a unified community

Something in the American tradition has engendered a need for the sense of "belonging." Our early villages and towns had their own special locale and neighborhood life—usually focused upon the town hall, church, and general store. Even the urban neighborhoods, with strong ethnic ties, had their focal points and favorite gathering places. Such close-knit residential groupings have given way for the most part to vast and seemingly boundless deserts of look-alike city blocks and homogenized suburbs. Often, not only the neighborhood boundaries are missing, but schools and shops as well.

In response, there is evident an increasing demand for more humane communities and "new towns" where dwellings, schools, shopping places, and recreation and employment centers are all planned together within a parklike environment.

Respond to regional needs

Within the next thirty years, despite hopeful programs of birth control, the population of the United States will probably increase from its current 200 million level to 300 million persons. The problems of housing this multitude are, and will be, immense. Construction on a lot-by-lot, or parcel-by-parcel, basis is unthinkable, since it could only extend the vast expanse of homes and apartments crowded haunch to haunch along the local streets. A far better approach to housing is the grouping of medium-density housing clusters around courts, parks, recreation spaces, or water bodies. New, self-contained, and fully planned communities are the promise of the future, especially in those regions where population growth is to be concentrated.

In most growth areas there is also need for new plant sites and other employment centers. It is well that these be incorporated in the plans for each new town.

Further Reading:

Bacon, Edmund N.
Design of Cities, revised editio.
The Viking Press, Inc.
New York, 1974

Basile, Ralph, et al.
Downtown Development Handbook
Urban Land Institute
Washington, D.C., 1980

Bell, Gwen, and Jacqueline Tyrwhitt
Human Identity in the Urban Environment
Penguin Books, Inc.
Baltimore, Md., 1972

Boyer, M. Christine
Dreaming the Rational City: The Myth of American City Planning
MIT Press
Cambridge, Mass., 1983

Cassidy, Robert
Livable Cities: A Grass-Roots Guide to Rebuilding Urban America
Holt, Rinehart and Winston
New York, 1980

Chandler, Tertius, and Gerald Fox
3000 Years of Urban Growth
Academic Press, Inc.
New York, 1974

Coppa, Frank J., and Philip C. Dolce
Cities in Transition: From the Ancient World to Urban America
Nelson Hall
Chicago, 1974

DeChiara, Joseph, and Lee Koppelman
Urban Planning and Design Criteria (Third Edition)
Van Nostrand Reinhold Company Inc.
New York, 1982

Fein, Albert
Landscape into Cityscape
Van Nostrand Reinhold Company Inc.
New York, 1981

Haar, Charles M.
Land-use Planning: A Casebook on the USE, MISUSE, and RE-USE of Urban Land (3d ed.)
Little, Brown and Company
Boston, Mass., 1976

Further Reading (cont.):

Hough, Michael
City Form and Natural Process: Towards a New Urban Vernacular
Van Nostrand Reinhold Company Inc.
New York, 1984

Jacobs, Jane
The Death and Life of Great American Cities
Random House, Inc.
New York, 1961

Magnago Lampugnani, Vittorio
Architecture and City Planning in the Twentieth Century
Van Nostrand Reinhold Company Inc.
New York, 1985

Mumford, Lewis
The City in History, Its Origins, Its Transformations, and Its Prospects
Harcourt, Brace & World, Inc.
New York, 1961

Robinette, Gary O., ed.
How to Make Cities Liveable
Van Nostrand Reinhold Company Inc.
New York, 1984

Rossi, Aldo
The Architecture of the City
MIT Press
Cambridge, Mass., 1985

Spirn, Anne Whiston
The Granite Garden
Basic Books, Inc.
New York, 1984

Spreiregen, Paul D.
Urban Design: The Architecture of Towns and Cities
For the American Institute of Architects
McGraw-Hill Book Company
New York, 1965

Teaford, Jon C.
The Twentieth-Century American City
Johns Hopkins University Press
Baltimore, Md., 1986

Whittick, Arnold, Editor-in-chief
Encyclopedia of Urban Planning
McGraw-Hill Book Company
New York, 1974

Wrenn, Douglas M., et al.
Urban Waterfront Development
Urban Land Institute
Washington, D.C., 1983

Develop a comprehensive plan

All new towns take their form, stage by stage, from an overall plan which determines from the start the diagrammatic patterns of land use and traffic movement. This will relate to the metropolitan master plan, which should be modified to include it. Through many and continuing sessions, the new-town plan will be checked and coordinated with all the various departments concerned—on federal, state, county, and regional levels.

Traffic studies will determine the location of the community entranceways or portals, the distribution roads and culs-de-sac, loops, motor courts, and local frontage streets. Residential, school, church, shopping, work, and recreation areas of proper size and shape will be planned in the best possible relationship to each other, to the total site, and to the trafficways which serve them.

A master plan must be considered both a commitment and a guideline. It must give the residents assurance that growth will be in accordance with established limitations of land use and density. It should be kept sufficiently flexible in detail, however, to permit each area as it develops to reflect improved techniques of environmental protection, and emerging theories of land planning.

Provide a variety of housing types

The mark of the more successful new-town communities is the diversity of housing types, locations, and price ranges available. A broad base of lower-density one- and two-story homes is usually provided in the outlying areas adjacent to a peripheral water edge or open space preserve. They may vary from single-family homes on spacious lots, to more compact living units, attached or detached, arranged in bars or clusters. Most new towns or villages feature, however, a predominance of apartments grouped about lakes, meadows, golf courses, parks, and neighborhood focal points. The high-rise towers are most often sited within 2,000 feet of the transit plaza and town center, for maximum convenience and to provide a resident clientele for its restaurants, theaters, and shops. Some dwellings will thus be stacked in towers as part of a dynamic urban scene, while others will be spaced out in a more relaxed and natural setting.

Accept and accommodate the automobile

Contemporary families have a predilection for and are dependent upon their cars and want to park them as closely as possible to the doorways of their homes. The automobile and delivery and service trucks are simply facts of life. To ignore them as important planning factors would be as pointless as to let them overrun the entire community.

In the better communities the traditional grid layout of streets has disappeared completely. The master plan provides instead a hierarchy of vehicular roadways from freeway, to controlled-access parkway, to private-frontage streets. Traffic moves freely around the outside of each neighborhood with access loops and culs-de-sac penetrating inward to the parking bays and courts. Cross-community travel is discouraged by the circuitous roadway alignment. T-intersections replace the more hazardous X street crossings. Safety, and the separation of people and moving vehicles, is a constant consideration in all aspects of the land planning.

Travel by automobile is a form of daily recreation, and care should be taken to design pleasantly curving drives and shaded streets with enframed views of community features. Even the parking bays and courts will be developed as motor gardens where cars are parked beneath a canopy of foliage and between attractive planting beds.

Apply the "planned community development" or "PCD" approach

In essence, this means that rather than first subdividing the land into single lots or building parcels, it is instead allocated to study units of five or more acres. Within these larger units, buildings, streets, and amenities are arranged freely on a "performance basis" to achieve the most pleasant and workable relationships. Only after thorough study by comparative analysis is the favored scheme selected and the parcel lines finally fixed.

Another feature of PCD is that most of the normal subdivision restrictions—such as right-of-way widths, building setbacks, and public street frontage—are waived by the jurisdictional government and the plans are submitted in prearranged stages for agency review. When the various county or metro departments are kept closely involved in the land and traffic planning, they will often suggest new and helpful procedures and adapt their larger plans to implement those of the new community.

Perhaps the greatest single lesson to be learned in the PCD planning process is the benefit of full and continuing consultation and cooperation with planning, traffic, school, and recreation officials.

Create new forms of building "clusters"

As has been previously noted, a promising innovation in land planning is the "clustering" of homes and other buildings in compact arrangements about approach courts, malls, or other open places. Usually, and desirably, the buildings are dedicated with frontage upon the central open space right-of-way or easements leading to it, rather than upon the community circulation streets.

With overall densities prescribed, the building groupings are compressed, with a saving in such land improvement costs as paving, curbs, and utility runs, while the normal side yards and front and rear setbacks are squeezed out and allocated to the blue and green of waterways and community open spaces. With imaginative design, dwellings attached on one or more sides may be faced inward or outward upon private courts, giving a whole new dimension of indoor-outdoor living.

New-town centers, and even their business office and industrial parks, are also planned on this advanced basis.

Plan the new towns for people

In new-town planning the needs of the citizens who will live there are to be given top priority. It is not enough that amenities be designed into the scheme of things; they must also be placed in the best possible relationship to the people who will use them.

Two levels of facilities are provided. Those which will serve the entire community—such as town center, junior and senior high schools, an inn, country club, convention center, or industrial park—are each placed on their own "campus," easily accessible by car along interconnecting parkways.

Those which will be used by the residents on a neighborhood basis are placed in close proximity to the homes and within easy reach by safe and pleasant pedestrian walkways, bicycle paths, or by automobile along local streets. Each neighborhood will have its own or shared elementary school or schools and its convenience center where one can find a well-stocked grocery, hardware, or drugstore; keep a dental appointment; have a ballet lesson; or linger over a sundae. Churches, theaters, meeting rooms, and firehalls, too, are considered important elements of each neighborhood plan. In those cases in which a neighborhood is too small to support its own elementary school or local convenience centers, these are placed between the

The farmer, in his daily life, spends the day about his farm buildings, ploughlands, and meadows. He does not rush from place to place to get his work done, but quietly organizes his usual day within the comparatively limited area of his farm. Consider also the natural relationship between living and working in the hamlet, village, and small town. In this quiet and livable atmosphere, much can be found which the large cities would do well to emulate. Because this relationship between living and working is based on natural selection, and because it contributes so greatly to fuller and happier living, it must be accepted as the primary premise in the creating of functional order in urban life, no matter whether the community be small or large.

ELIEL SAARINEN
The City—Its Growth, Its Decay, Its Future
MIT Press
Cambridge, Mass., 1965

Human contacts, now limited by social barriers, would easily expand in a city where everyday life was harmoniously conceived within a planned frame.

JOSE LUIS SERT
Can Our Cities Survive?
Harvard University Press
Cambridge, Mass., 1942

The city is the supreme expression of a people's cultural level.

EDWARD HIGBEE
The Squeeze—Cities without Space
Apollo Editions
New York, 1962

neighborhoods to be served and interconnected with walks and bicycle trails as well as access drives.

Planned into the new towns will be provision for such community activities as playhouse performances, adult education classes, craft programs, art festivals, public assemblies, concerts, conferences, and all those big and little features that make for the good, full life.

Make recreation a daily experience

From the beginning, a new town is ideally planned as an all-embracing park, arboretum, and bird sanctuary. Drives and building clusters are designed around a series of open lands and waterways, which double as recreation spaces.

Recreation starts at home. Privacy for gathering with family and friends is considered so essential that interior courts, secluded balconies, and enclosed patios are generally provided, as are small individual garden spots for each home or villa. Where possible, streams, ponds, lakeways, or beach are made part of every neighborhood to freshen the breeze, provide the sound of lapping water, and to give people the chance to get splashing wet. Within each residential grouping are small play spaces or miniparks which often include swimming pools, shelters, game courts, and seating at the water's edge or in the shade of an overhanging tree.

Cooperative planning with park and recreation officials will help to describe a network of community parks and parklets, scenic drives, bicycle trails, and interconnecting walkways. The school authorities should also be invited to join the team in the planning of a joint school-park system. Here, on specially designed campuses, a complete educational and recreation program can be operated on a full time, year-round basis. Multiple use of the parking and recreation areas and the school buildings makes possible a varied and expanded program at substantial tax savings. Lighted ballfields, for example, are available not only for school use, but also for communitywide nonschool recreation as well. Such additional public and private features as golf courses, stables and riding trails, tennis compounds, swimming clubs, and marinas are included where conditions permit.

Even the new-town nuclei are planned as regional living-working-recreation activity centers. Architectural terraces constructed over concealed parking decks will face inward to central courts and fountains, around which will rise apartments, offices, shops, theaters, museum, playhouse, restaurants, and cafés.

Only in a parklike environment with recreation as a common experience and with nature always close at hand can all members of the family find a full measure of satisfaction in their daily lives. This, after all, is the purpose, and the promise, of the new-town movement.

Why not?

A combination of planned communities and new towns supporting and linked by rapid transit to new or revitalized urba-centers . . .

all conceived in dynamic equilibrium within a salubrious regional landscape setting . . .

where the best of the agricultural lands and natural features have been preserved . . .

and environmental protection assured.

This is the possibility, and the goal of the planning visionary. This is the broad outline of urbanization at its evolving best.

[In London] Birds and doves sing in the backyards, in commons, in squares, in three-treed squarelets, and in parks. The most valuable and central real estate is wasted on parks. One practical royal lady once asked how much it would cost to convert the public parks to royal use and was told by her Prime Minister, "Two crowns, Madame," and he may not have been exaggerating greatly. Londoners have held and fought for their greens tenaciously and, when necessary, violently. A Londoner will bear much, accede to much, tolerate a good deal more, but do not touch a blade of his grass.

KATE SIMONS
London, Places and Pleasures
Capricorn Books
New York, 1971

You see things as they are; and you ask "Why?" But I dream things that never were; and I ask "Why not?"
GEORGE BERNARD SHAW

Urbanization

OUR URBAN TRAFFIC-TRANSPORTATION ROUTES HAVE SLASHED OUR CITIES ASUNDER AND ALL BUT DESTROYED THEIR PRIMARY FUNCTION AS CENTERS OF INTENSIVE BUSINESS AND CULTURAL ACTIVITY.

Variations on the theme of a guest article appearing in the "Urban America" issue of *Consulting Engineer* magazine.*

* March–April 1974.

The metropolis of the future

• There will be no vehicular streets within the city centers.

• All buildings will face inward upon pedestrian greenways, malls, and plazas.

• Intensive activity nodes will be formed around the regional transit termini.

• Optimum urban land-use and roadway capacities will be predetermined and controlled.

• Multimodal transit and transportation facilities will be planned and operated as integrated systems.

• Activity centers of varying types will be dispersed throughout the metropolitan region as satellites of the urban nucleus.

• A network of transit-transportation-trans-mission corridors will be acquired as public land, and reserved for future uses. Leasing revenues will offset acquisition costs.

• All major roadways and transit lines will move through the regional open space framework.

• All highways will be "classified."

• An innovative array of trafficways and vehicles will provide unprecedented levels of mobility and service.

Despite the recent decline in the national birthrate, the best projections of our demographers now show an anticipated increase of approximately 100 million people in our country by the year 2000. By then more than eight out of ten Americans will have gravitated to urbanizing regions. Why? Because, in the vernacular, that's where the action is.

Highway canyons and parking deserts have destroyed the vital interconnections and sapped the city centers of their strength.

All this means that within the next twenty to twenty-five years for every two persons presently residing or working within our crowded cities there will probably be three. It can well be imagined that to accommodate this massive influx, and to provide the essential mobility both between and within urban centers, entirely new concepts of city and transportation must by then have been evolved.

The mobile society
Ours is a society on wheels. Cars, trucks, and buses stream, day and night, along the highway networks, forcing their way through constricted suburban channels and flooding into the cities. Twice each workday at the peak hours there is a rolling tide of vehicles, surging inward upon the urban centers in the morning and outward after office hours.

The effects on the countryside, suburbs,

and cities alike have reached critical proportions as new highway corridors voraciously swallow the hills and valleys, as expressways disrupt residential districts, and as huge parking compounds wedge the cities apart and preclude their essential interactions.

The law of real estate economics
People seeking a location for any enterprise or purpose will pay as much as they can afford to gain that situation which provides the most desirable relationships, with a minimum of frictions.

The desirable relationships are those of access; suitable and pleasant surroundings; a concentration of friends, clients, or customers; and the presence of public services and other amenities. The frictions most often involve the movement of people and goods. They may be measured in terms of inconvenience, costly delays, frustration, or actual

danger. They occur when pedestrians must cross vehicular streets or transitways. They occur each time a passenger car or bus must slow down or stop at an intersection, rather than zoom freely along a nonfrontage arterial street or parkway. They occur each time a delivery is delayed. There are frictions of inefficiency, annoyance, and added cost whenever vehicles are interposed, at grade, within any pedestrian activity area—business-office center, school, campus, residential neighborhood, or park.

It can be seen that workable land areas and systems of circulation can only be planned together. This is usually a four-part process. First, areas of proper size, shape, and character are allocated to accommodate each of the various uses proposed.

These "land-use" parcels then are fitted to each other and to the topography. As a third step, interconnection is provided be-

Urban activity centers, when split apart by trafficways, have lost their chief reason for being.

tween the parcels and the regional points of origin-destination. Finally, the areas, topography, and linkage are adjusted to achieve the highest possible level of performance for the good of most of the users at any given time.

In the accompanying diagrams dispersed centers of regional activity (urba-centers) are linked to the center city by both highways and rapid transit. The urba-centers may be commercial, industrial, cultural, residential, or recreational in character. In all instances they will be clustered densely around pedestrian courts and interconnecting malls.

Transitways will provide direct connection between central terminals. In the open countryside trains or trams will move at flashing speeds through scenic corridors. Within the activity centers they will connect by illuminated tubes or terraces to portals at the very heart of each urbanized core. The regional

highways will move around and between, but never through, the activity nodes, as controlled-access parkways.

An urban transportation planning checklist

The field of highway engineering has made remarkable progress within the past two decades. These have seen the extension of federally aided highways to a transcontinental network of well over a million miles. They have brought to near completion the Interstate Highway System, begun in 1956, which will link 90 percent of all cities having populations of 50,000 or more.

Advanced techniques of planning, design, and construction have provided the United States with the highest level of mobility—and some of the most efficient and beautiful highways—in the world. Yet it is clearly evident, within our urban areas particularly,

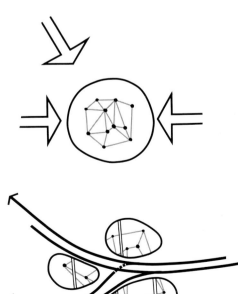

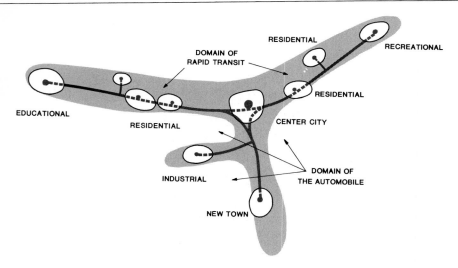

Transitways. Direct internal linkage of urban activity centers will be provided by rapid transit (rail, busway, and/or by aerial tram).

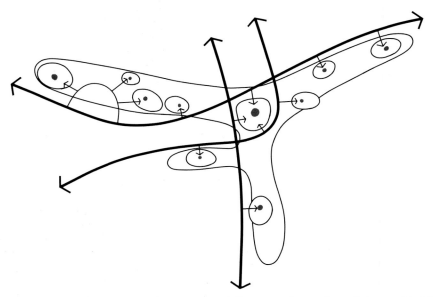

Highways. External access to the urba-centers and the supporting region will be provided by urban parkways. (Scenic freeways without trucks.) Transportation vehicles will move on their own independent routes.

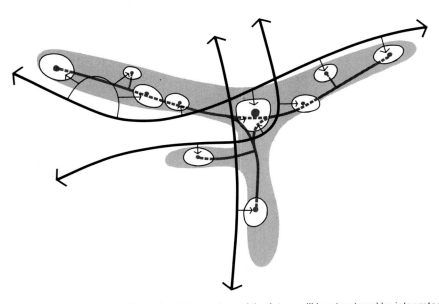

Movement and interconnection. The urbanizing regions of the future will be structured by integrated transit and transportation systems.

that new approaches to transportation planning are urgently needed.

In devising more workable systems of movement within and between the cities of the future, it is proposed that the following principles be considered, and applied.

1 *Coordinate highway considerations with the comprehensive planning of every city and region.* It is not enough to espouse this principle in theory. The location and design characteristics of each street and highway segment should, in fact, be established by a competent planning body concerned with the shaping of each community and its traffic-ways into a balanced and integrated system. Proper weight must be given to providing convenience, safety, beauty, and economic strength to every area served.

Without an overall concept of how the various components of the city and its supporting region will work together, it is unlikely that the transportation system, no matter how well engineered, will serve its many functions.

2 *Define the activity centers.* The urban metropolis is composed of ways and places. The ways are paths of circulation for people, vehicles, and goods. The places are land-use areas of varying sizes and types, each planned primarily to accommodate business activities, governmental functions, housing, and educational, medical, cultural, or recreational facilities.

It can be said that for each type of activity the more cohesive the area and the more convenient the interactions between the participants the more successful the center will be. To this end, the major activity cores should be constricted in area to intensify the ease and scope of desirable interactions. In such concentrated nodes all opportunities for interchange will be accessible by a few minutes of travel on foot or by escalator, elevator, or mini-transit. As a general rule, travel time between any two points within an urban activity center should not exceed fifteen minutes, or a maximum distance of from 3,000 to 4,000 feet.

In such metropolitan focal points as Rockefeller Center, Place Ville Marie, L'Enfant Plaza, the Ginza of Tokyo, Hotorget of Stockholm, or the Kurfurstendamm of West Berlin rentals are high, vacancies rare, and the urban experience is one of exhilaration and pleasure. In their planning and design, concentration without congestion is the key.

At best, all urban activities might be combined in one dynamic core—the central business district or CBD. This is possible in the small to medium-size city. In the larger cities, however, reasonable travel-time distances would be exceeded. In such instances compatible and mutually supportive activities are best grouped into satellite urba-centers spaced out around the center-city nucleus. Each activity core should be afforded its own residential base, convenience shopping, services, and recreational facilities.

3 *Connect the centers with rapid transit.* The primary reason for the existence of these centers is to provide the optimum concentration of related activities and choices. The more compact the grouping (whatever its nature) and the closer the components (within the limits of adequate space and efficient interaction), the more dynamic the center and the more desirable the address.

A second prerequisite is that they are readily accessible to as many people as possible within the urban sphere of influence.

Each urban center should therefore be planned in tiers and towers above the garage and transportation levels and around its pedestrian courts and transit mall, with direct linkage to all parts of the regional system.

4 *Keep the interstate highways out of the inner city.* In the future all interstate freeways should terminate at the outer beltway, circumscribed at a distance ranging from 2 to 10 miles from the city core, and containing all urban activity nodes. Small cities may have but one. Within the beltway, all arterials will best be designed with parkway characteristics, and will be one of three distinctive types: the *urban parkway,* including the radials and circumferentials; the *distributor ring* surrounding either the center city or one or more of its satellite activity cores; and the *urban busway,* reserved for the movement of buses, cabs, or other motorized transit vehicles. Each will be designed to fulfill its own and particular function.

5 *Plan "urban parkways" to provide interdistrict access.* Access to and between metropolitan activity nodes or urba-centers, be they residential complexes, business office or commercial cores, institutional centers, or recreational parks, will best be provided by urban parkways. These controlled-access radial and circumferential arterials will weave between the areas of concentration. They will move along ridges or watercourses as lineal vehicular parks which, together with adjacent open-space lands, will form the district boundaries. Neither trucks, direct driveway access, nor building frontage are to be permitted, and intersections will be spaced out to a minimum of 660 feet (one-eighth mile) to ensure the free movement of traffic.

6 *Develop a new type of urban arterial, the "distributor ring" as the primary inner distributor loop for metropolitan centers.* Unlike the conventional downtown freeway it will not interpose a wide cleavage canyon, or wall, through built-up areas. It will not disrupt activity centers, and it will not introduce through-traffic that has no desire to be within the center city. Rather, its corridor will circumvent and bound the business district and other activity centers. It will be fed by radial connectors from the outer interstate beltway and the inner circumferential parkway rings. The roadways will be multilevel, often sepa-

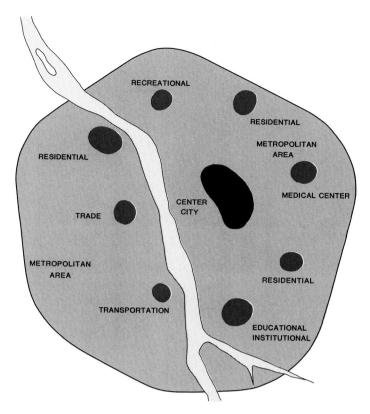

Where demands for space within the center city exceed the limits of convenient interconnection, new satellite urba-centers must be spaced out around the central core.

rated, and moving in tunnels, flyovers, or terraced decks. Multiple use of the roadway will be a common characteristic.

It will provide high-speed ramps and parking decks and towers planned integrally above, below, and adjacent to the roadway. Trucks and transit buses will move on separate levels. It will compose the major means of vehicular traffic access and distribution for the center city and its urban center satellites. Each of the latter may also have its own distributor ring.

As a secondary but important function it will serve each activity center as a circumscribing boundary which will limit its natural tendency to expand and thus decay. It will ensure the compression and convenience that are so essential to a vital urban core.

7 *Create separate urban "busways."* Since each transit bus in operation can replace as many as twenty to thirty private automobiles on the highways and eliminate the need for their parking space within the city confines, the use of buses is obviously to be encouraged. Yet the success of transit by bus, as well as by rail, is dependent upon speed and well-maintained schedules. Neither is possible in peak-hour highway traffic jams, often caused by the buses themselves. They, like transportation vehicles, cannot be geared to move at the same pace, or to travel in the same lanes, with the smaller and faster private automobiles.

A successful innovation by the Virginia

Department of Highways has been the designation of separate lanes for the exclusive use of transit vehicles. A single lane with a widened sweep at stops will suffice. Preferably, a pair of such busways will provide movement both into and out of the cities concurrently. In congested corridors, however, a single lane may be designated for one-way movement in rush hours only. Ideally, bus-transit lanes will be separated, by alignment, grade, or visual screening, from adjacent paths of vehicular movement. They may be routed independently or integrated with the urban parkway system.

8 *Encourage the multiple use of the corridor.* With up to 30 percent of urban real estate now devoted to traffic right-of-way, it can be seen that the possibility of recouping some of this tax-ratable land for building sites, parking, or recreation purposes would be welcome. This is being accomplished, with increasing success, through newly developing techniques of multiple use. Essentially, this involves the purchase or lease of the space above, below, or alongside the roadway. This may be arranged by public agencies or private developers with concurrence of transportation authorities and planners.

The first such uses were mild, as in the extension of parking lots or play courts beneath portions of elevated streets. In time, however, structures were planned to flank and bridge the highways or transit routes, until now in some instances segments of the trafficways are being planned from the start as integral parts of extensive architectural complexes.

The Department of Transportation has declared itself "ready to work with the nation's cities, to seek new and bold uses of the joint development concept to achieve maximum use of that part of our scarce urban land which must be devoted to highway transportation."

9 *Provide access to buildings from local streets and approach courts.* In addition to the major thoroughfares above described there will be located between the city centers, and at their peripheries, several types of local frontage streets. These will include residential motor courts, loop streets, culs-de-sac, and vehicular malls.

Within our new cities no buildings will front upon through-traffic arterial roadways.

10 *Integrate urban streets with the districts served.* A further innovation will be the classified approach street or urban way. This will not so much resemble a roadway as a lineal motor plaza designed to receive and accommodate passenger automobiles and transit vehicles. Its sole purpose will be to provide vehicular access and egress to the adjacent structures. It will loop inward and outward from the urban arterials to become an interrelated element, and to assume the function and character of the area through which it moves. It will be freed of on-grade intersections, and its through lanes, often divergent, will be separated from pedestrian ways.

A residential urban way, for example, will loop into the district on one-way multilevel terraces to give visual exposure and a direct approach to the apartment compounds and towers. It will be widened, or lanes will diverge, at entrance courts. Speed ramps will connect to parking tiers and to other garaging facilities.

An urban way through an industrial complex will become industrial in use and appearance, with passenger cars and transit vehicles providing access to office approaches at upper levels while freight and service vehicles move to warehouse areas below. Differentiated channels of such transportation roads may branch off from the peripheral truckways to penetrate deep within the urbanized cores to terminals and service platforms.

An urban way through a theater-amusement-restaurant district will be theatrical in its nature. It will move freely from marquee to glittering marquee, and from twinkling and glowing pedestrian way to brightly illuminated plaza. It will give the theatergoers and restaurant clientele a welcome degree of access by cab, car, or transit vehicle. Parking will be in adjacent towers or on decks within the structures. During business hours the same facilities will serve contiguous office clusters.

Institutional urban ways will become a diversified component of the campus plan. Civic urban ways will be so closely coordinated with architectural and landscape architectural design that they will resemble motor-approach courts and vehicular-access malls. Commercial urban ways will be so thoroughly integrated with the shopping spaces and offices that it will be impossible to distinguish roadway from structures. Such streets will not only become more architectural in form; they will be architecture.

11 *Design new traffic-free centers.* In the communities and cities of the future the transit and transportation ways and terminals will be planned integrally from the start. They will be key factors in setting the community diagram and patterns of development. These routes of vehicular movement will differ greatly from those that exist today in type, layout, section, and relationship to uses and structures around them. They will be designed exclusively for free movement of people and goods.

Gone will be the rigid grid pattern of small blocks and all-purpose streets.

The traditional grid city will be replaced by spaced-out, multilevel residential, business office and cultural centers, and commercial malls. Traffic will move freely through the open space parklands between. Since each center will have its own restaurants, shops, and service areas the needs for vehicular movement will be minimized.

Cars, at grade, will be permitted only as far as the periphery of each center, except as they penetrate on levels reserved for vehicles and goods. They will be located under or over the pedestrian courts and terraces. Pedestrian levels and spaces will be traffic-free. With such a plan organization the city will be efficiently served, not usurped, by the transportation system.

12 *Exclude automobiles from the urban-center cores.* Personal desires and tradition notwithstanding, experience has proven that private vehicles cannot be permitted to function as a means of conveyance of people or goods within the urban activity centers. They usurp too much essential space in trafficways and parking compounds. They conflict with pedestrian movement. They disrupt the concentration of activity which gives the city its vitality and its main reason for being.

13 *Stable the automobile at the edge of the centers of urban concentration.* Since a large proportion of those who approach the urban-centers will continue to arrive by private vehicles (even in the face of heavily taxed parking privileges) parking must be provided. Space requirements alone will dictate multilevel garages, which may be constructed by parking authorities adjacent to or over the distributor rings, with direct connection to the urban cores by pedestrian walkways, moving chairways, or mini-transit conveyances.

14 *Ban delivery trucks from the city streets.* The movement of goods to and through the urban activity centers has traditionally been handled by freight trucks jamming their way through the city streets or parked along their edges. Each delivery has thus disrupted movement not only within the vehicular roadways but also along the abutting pedestrian sidewalks. It would be hard to conceive a less efficient method of transporting materials or goods.

New transport systems within the urban-centers will include grade-separated truckways, conveyor belts, and pneumatic transport-tubes. These will link local distribution centers to nearby terminals reached in turn by rail, boat, or interstate trucks.

15 *Provide transport trucks with a system of classified freightways.* The daily recitation of woes by the overhead traffic-copter usually dwells on the theme that access to employment centers is blocked by low-speed commercial vehicles. A single tractor-trailer grinding uphill may reduce, by half, the capacity of a 10-mile freeway lane. Each morning and evening on the city approaches, passenger cars must creep along behind trucks while thousands of valuable work hours are lost. Conversely, trucks and motorized trailers, needing access to the urban centers, must force their way through streams of the faster and more maneuverable passenger vehicles. Clearly, the two types of traffic are incompatible.

The concept of creating within each metropolitan region an independent system of truck routes, terminals, and urban distribution lines has long been discussed by transportation engineers and planners. It is time to build them. They may be routed through industrial districts, transportation corridors, and utility rights-of-way to major terminals. From these, local deliveries can then be handled with increased efficiency.

Trucking firms pay huge sums for the right to move on highways. By all logic they should have their own specially designed routes, with wider cartways, heavier slabs, swing-out lanes on uphill grades, and other useful features. The total time cost per passenger mile traveled and ton cost of goods delivered by such a dual system will be substantially reduced.

With the distribution of goods accommodated at levels reserved for this purpose and with automobiles stored at the periphery of urban centers, the public streets may be replaced with attractive pedestrian courts, ways, and plazas around which the buildings will be grouped. The lively charm of the old European and Oriental towns and cities can thus be regained, and improved upon, within the contemporary context.

16 *Route freeways through the open countryside.* The expressways of the future will continue to form the free-flowing interstate networks. They also will serve as the primary means of high-speed vehicular movement between cities, past metropolitan centers, and around concentrations of activity. While providing direct connection with the arterial parkway systems, they will avoid traversing unified communities or highly developed urban districts.

They will be constructed as one-way roadways, converging only at major interchanges and will be characterized by their rural and scenic qualities. The rights-of-way will be spacious, the landscape features will be carefully preserved, and the natural or agricultural character of the abutting lands assured through regional land-use controls and scenic-conservation easements.

Where opportune, access will be provided to low-speed scenic-historic byways that loop and wind through the countryside between interchanges.

17 *Plan highways as the framework for development.* Just as the railroads in the late 1800s and early 1900s opened up and set the pattern for the economic growth of our country, so will many of the planned highways of the future be designed to serve this purpose.

Freeways, parkways, and urban arterials will set the basic framework for new cities and metropolitan satellites. Transportation corridors and terminals will be structured as the spine of new industrial districts. Recreation roads with wide naturalized rights-of-way will provide city dwellers with access to state and national forest lands, newly created reservoirs, and back-country vacation regions.

18 *Consider the full range of environmental impacts in highway location.* Much may be contributed to the environment of urbanizing regions when highways are located and designed by a process of comparative analysis that weighs all positive and negative effects of the alternatives. These include not only economic considerations but social, historical, recreational, and ecological values as well. The positioning of a highway corridor and the design of its roadway, intersections, and interchanges usually will determine more than any other factors the use and character of the landscape through which it moves.

Most state highway systems have been planned primarily to meet transportation needs and to provide essential access and service to communities and to property. These highways are also the major outlets for the recreation of our people. Driving for pleasure is the nation's most popular outdoor recreational activity and deserves full attention in the financing, design, and construction of the highway system.

Transportation departments will be encouraged to give appropriate consideration to design for maximum retention of landscape character and increasing emphasis on the environmental aspects of highway construction. In addition, they will be mandated to protect the highway from the traffic conges-

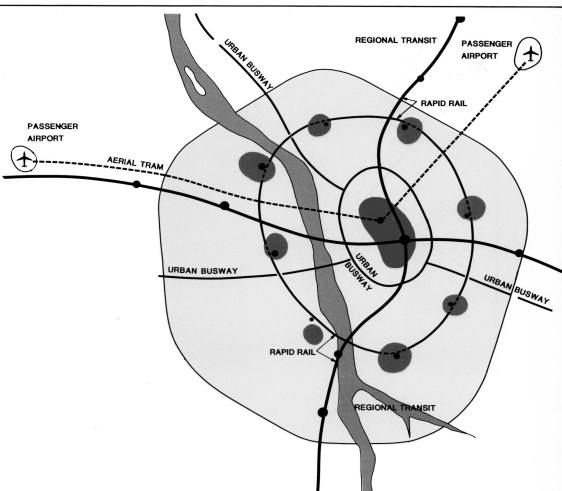

Transitways will loop freely through the metropolitan region, providing direct internal connection to terminals at the heart of activity nodes.

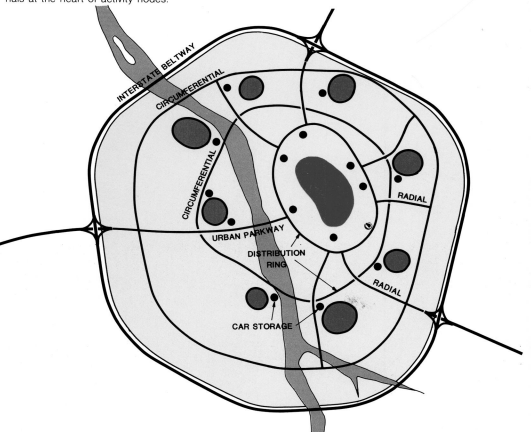

The urban highways of the future will provide maximum access and interconnection with minimum disruption. They will move freely between, but not through, urban centers. None will have building frontage.

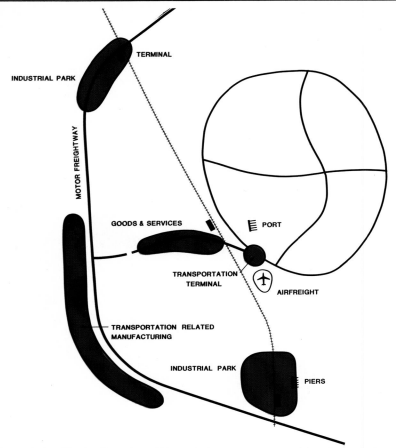

Transportation. Trucks, like trains, will have their own separate corridors. Integrated transportation systems will serve regional distribution terminals and transport-related districts.

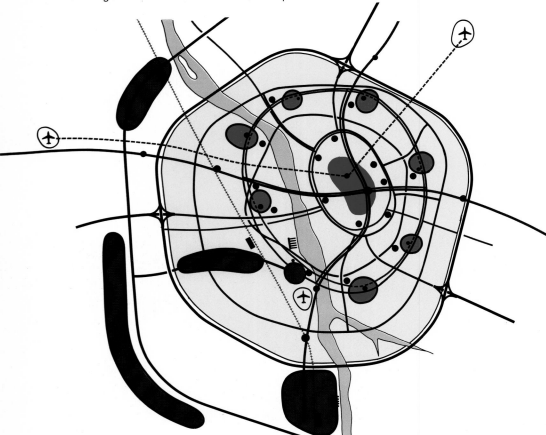

The future urban metropolis. The center city, as the regional nucleus, will be a towered and terraced pedestrian domain surrounding the transit portals. It will provide, within its computerized matrix, the optimum mix and density of business, civic, and cultural activities. Other activity nodes will supplement and complement the center-city functions. All will be linked externally by free-flowing parkways and will be served internally by varied means of transportation.

tion, hazard, and loss of roadside beauty generated by unrestricted roadside commercial and residential development.

What one knows of a city or region depends, to a large extent, upon what one sees from its highways.

19 *Provide the congested cities with interim relief.* Until the city centers can be converted through long-range planning into unified pedestrian domains, temporary measures will be enforced to reduce the debilitating effects of urban traffic and car storage. This is necessary not only to restore the functional efficiency of the city, but also to reduce the present critical levels of air pollution caused by the chief offender—the automobile exhaust.

Within the next decade most American cities will act to control the amount of vehicular traffic in one or more of the following ways:

● Develop mass transit systems.

● Collect tolls on bridges and key access points.

● Establish exclusive bus and car pool lanes on the approach highways.

● Create peripheral parking compounds with new forms of rapid transit linkage.

● Ban the construction of additional in-town parking space and reduce present inventories.

● Enact an urban-parking surcharge tax.

● Prohibit all on-street parking.

● Eliminate daytime deliveries.

● Restrict taxi cruising.

● Disperse certain functions (such as medical, university, and sports centers) to satellite locations.

20 *Reduce the need for traffic movement.* The solution of the nation's monumental transportation problem does not rest alone with the provision of more and more highways. A recent and significant approach lies in the design and redevelopment of communities and cities in such a manner that the need for people to move about by automobile is drastically reduced. Until recently this has been considered a desirable goal in terms of convenience and economics. Now, in the light of the emerging energy crisis, it has become mandatory. It can be accomplished by the planning of new, almost self-sufficient satellite communities where housing, shopping, recreation and employment centers are planned together for ease of accessibility. It can be achieved also in the reshaping and regrouping of the components of existing communities and cities by the gradual process of redevelopment. It can be effected by designing new highways and transit routes in such a way that urban activity centers will be at the same time concentrated, spaced out and provided with rapid interconnection.

In this architectural model for San Francisco's Golden Gateway Center one may sense the promise of intensive, humanized cities yet to come.

Evolution of the city

In the democratic scheme of things one would expect our cities to tend toward the accepted ideal, to become more and more what the people, government, and urbanologists believe that they should become. To observers of the American scene this slow transformation toward the "ideal" has been clearly evident. Also evident is the well-documented fact that from time to time attitudes toward the city have changed considerably.

From the start of this century, for example, the generally held concept of the best possible city has undergone a series of rather remarkable transitions. The notion of the *city beautiful,* seeded in the Columbian Exposition, introduced the era of civic art, with its boulevards, spacious parks, and statue-studded public gardens. This was to give way, in Depression times, to the *socialized city* of

public housing, welfare programs, and massive federal aid. Next came the *planned city* with the advent of zoning, planning agencies, redevelopment authorities, and broadened powers of eminent domain. New computer techniques and "systems analysis" presaged the *efficient city* of comprehensive highway, utility, and communications networks. Burgeoning population and mass migrations to the urban centers triggered an urgent public demand for the *ecological city* in which man might put an end to all forms of pollution and devise a more salubrious living environment. Almost concurrently, the sheer density of urban concentrations and attendant traffic congestion have brought a loud clamor for new means of achieving mobility within our metropolitan regions. The emphasis now is concentrated on the *accessible city*.

While one new goal does not necessarily replace the others, for they are often combined or coalesced, it does revise priorities of funding and planning effort. We may thus expect, in the years immediately ahead, intensified experimentation in the development of new modes of urban transportation. The future urba-centers will be formed between looping highway-transmission-transit corridors. They will be sheathed with open space parklands and interlaced with refreshing greenways and blueways. Hived megastructures of interlocking cubes and garden spaces, open and enclosed, will be terraced densely above and around the regional transit nodes. All forms of movement and distribution will be infinitely more efficient. Cities will be more dynamic; and the urban experience will be richer and more rewarding.

9

Regional planning

Regional planning is the conscious direction and collective integration of all those activities which rest upon the use of the earth as site, as resource, as structure.

LEWIS MUMFORD
The Culture of Cities
Harcourt, Brace and World, Inc.
New York, 1938

The concept of the balanced city must now be widened to the balanced region.

LEWIS MUMFORD
The City in History
Harcourt, Brace and World, Inc.
New York, 1961

To consider a city or town as an entity separate and apart from the extensional landscape—its suburban, rural, and wilderness matrix—is like trying to understand the phenomenon of planet Earth outside the context of the planetary system. The Earth and its celestial framework constitute one great interrelated, interacting whole, and can only be comprehended on this basis. So it is with the city and its supporting region.

Most environmental considerations extend beyond the borders of political subdivisions. Individual cities or urbanizing counties in the metropolitan areas cannot plan as if they were islands unto themselves. Rural counties also can plan more effectively on a regional basis. Rapid population growth and shifting concentrations of people, with their urgent needs for land, water, and *systems* of transit, transportation, and utilities have made regional action in most areas an absolute necessity. Most local governments now have the power to join in regional development councils or regional park authorities or regional planning commissions. A number have done so. But far too few have taken advantage of these opportunities.

One has only to look at disorderly urban and suburban growth to see that there is little coordination between the land-use, traffic, or conservation planning of the separate jurisdictions. A central city, for example, feels it cannot afford to acquire open space in the adjoining county, and the suburban county considers that it has plenty of open space and doesn't intend to provide park space for the central city. The result is a complete stalemate which will inflict uncontrolled development on the overall area and a rash of rehabilitation and reclamation projects on succeeding generations.

All local governments would do well to join in regional planning efforts—to learn what the others are doing, to keep advised of the state and federal programs, and to work together toward that plan which is best for all concerned.

Life-style objectives

When considering planning in the *regional* context, the problems and opportunities transcend those of cities, suburbs, and rural counties, and embrace the whole spectrum of human needs.

In the *regional* perspective there exists for the planner the opportunity to "bring it all together" into the best conceivable and attainable living environment.

Here, in this larger framework, man's structures and activity areas can be conceived together in harmony with nature.

Here, particularly, the emphasis can be on quality.

Here, at last, is the opportunity to provide a rational setting for a balanced society.

What, then, are the human needs to which a regional plan should respond? What are the goals that they suggest? Perhaps it is possible to reduce them to specifics . . .

The city is one thing, a place of dynamic activity . . . the countryside is another, with its own rhythm and its own beauty. The two environments need and complement each other.
THEO CROSBY
Architecture: City Sense
Reinhold Publishing Corporation
New York, 1965 (paperback)

Eliminate monotonous uniformity

Provide a variety of choices in life-style and location. Plan each activity center "in broad brush" as a unique and special place, expressive of its use and natural setting.

Encourage creativity

This can be accomplished *by providing only the development framework* (the transit-transportation routes and generalized land-use patterns) *within which individual freedom of choice* will be encouraged and stimulated. Codes and ordinances will be *permissive* rather than *restrictive. Incentives* for innovative planning will replace the traditional *penalties.*

Within the broad constraints essential to systematic organization, design decisions that affect a homeowner should be left to the homeowner. Decisions regarding a street should be made by the people on the street. Decisions relating to a town square should be made by those who will use the square. Decisions that have bearing upon a suburban or agricultural community are best made by those whose lives will be directly affected.

Ensure a sense of community

People need to belong. Many are lost and disoriented in the sprawling, formless backwash that makes up most of our urbanizing regions.

Historically, those settlements have been most agreeable, and those citizens most fulfilled, where the city or community, and each subneighborhood thereof, "reads" as a cohesive and identifiable unit. The conceptualizing and distribution of such unique and variable units—each surrounded by open space preserve—is perhaps the chief work of the regional planner.

Promote social interaction

Within each residential or business neighborhood, a rich mix of building types and uses is to be not only permitted but encouraged. This is one of the more important keys to perpetuating the charm and vitality so much esteemed in the older European and Oriental countryside and cities. It is the polarization of classes, the clinical isolation of uses and groups, that have robbed so many of our newer communities of their life and vibrancy.

Provide a multitude and variety of public *places*—the tot lots, the playfields, the plazas and malls—where people may meet or congregate. Plan networks of circulation *ways* to make the places easily and pleasantly accessible.

Provide a full range of cultural opportunities

The deployment and siting of such attractions as colleges, libraries, museums, stadiums, and zoos will have much to do with the quality of the regional living environment. Just as nature should be brought into the city, so should many of the cultural and recreational facilities traditionally reserved for the city be moved out into the adjacent suburban and rural districts.

Far outside of Copenhagen in the Danish countryside is to be discovered the Louisiana museum, surely one of the most delightful in the world. Ronchamp, chapel extraordinary, is well removed from the nearest of the larger French cities. In America many cultural centers of various types have also moved into the hinterland—among them Chautauqua, the Red Rocks Amphitheater, the Chicago Botanic Garden, Aspen's Summer Institute, the International Music Camp at Interlochen, and Florida's Disney World.

If the man who builds is perceptive to the processes of nature, to materials and to forms, his creations will be appropriate to the place; they will satisfy the needs of social process and shelter, be expressive and endure.
IAN MCHARG
Unpublished memo

In a sense it can be said that seeking to discover unities in the world is the whole business of our mental activity . . .
HENRY V. HUBBARD
Introduction to the Study of Landscape Design
MIT Press
Cambridge, Mass., 1974
(Reprint of 1917 ed.)

. . . The separation of man and nature, of townsmen and countrymen, can no longer be maintained; . . . the entire planet is becoming a village; and as a result, the smallest neighborhood or precinct must be planned as a working model of the larger world.

For esthetic and intellectual stimulus, the suburb remains dependent upon the big city: the theater, the opera, the clubs, the orchestra, the art gallery, the university, the museum are no longer a part of the daily environment. The problem of reestablishing connections, on a regional rather than a metropolitan basis, is one of the main problems of city planning in our time.
LEWIS MUMFORD
The City in History
Harcourt, Brace and World, Inc.
New York, 1961

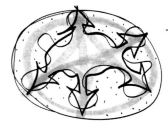

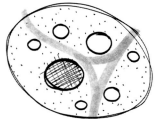

REGIONAL GROWTH ALTERNATIVES
THE Choice: Unlimited Proliferation
Or A Union Of Coherent Communities

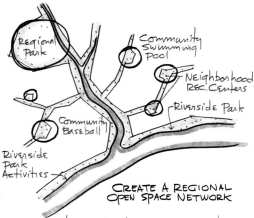

CREATE A REGIONAL
OPEN SPACE NETWORK

The regional openspace system should sheath and protect, or reclaim, the waterways and edges. It can accommodate active, neighborhood community and metro recreation centers. It can also provide pleasant pedestrian and bicycle or mini-transit linkage and facilitate park and recreation maintenance.

Keep nature always close at hand

Fundamental to regional planning and orderly growth is the concept of intensely developed urban cores with supporting communities and activity subcenters spaced out in the surrounding landscape.

To heighten the experience of nature appreciation, all possible routes of movement within a developing region will be conducted along the blueways, or through the fields and woodlands which separate and embrace the development clusters. Within each activity center, in turn, and penetrating the densest city nucleus will be areas reserved for earth, water, and foliage—so that all people may experience, and take delight in, their instinctive ties with nature.

Make beauty a feature of everyday life

Beauty is an attribute sensed when "all things are working well together." It presupposes the elimination of all negative or incongruous elements—including all forms of pollution.

It can be seen that *beauty* and *happiness* are often synonymous. Both are most keenly experienced when the relationships between people are right—and where people find themselves living and working in harmony with nature.

An ecological survey

Each rational approach to the use of land—be it for a garden, a farmstead, or a new community—begins with a study of the earth and its natural processes.

Gardeners will seek a plot of rich, loamy ground protected from the winds, well-drained, yet close enough to the water table to draw upon its moisture. They will adjust their rows to the sweep of the sun so that all plants will receive the light required for photosynthesis.

Farmers will fit their orchards and fields to the land conformation and to the soil types and depths. Their furrows will be plowed along the contours so that water and rain will be retained to seep into the ground. Their buildings will be protected from the storms, yet lifted above the frost pockets, and out of the dews and damps. Their homes will receive the summer breezes, but not after these breezes have played across the barnyard coops and pens. Barn and hayloft will be kept "crosswind" and out of the path of flying sparks from the chimneys.

The community planner's diagrams will begin with a layout of land uses fitted to the topography. The trafficways of various types will be traced along gently rising and falling grades not only to provide desirable access and views, but also to ensure gravity flow of the storm-water mains and sewers within the rights-of-way. The best of the natural cover will be preserved, the best of the landscape features conserved, as the planner seeks in all ways to develop systems of harmony.

But in addition to natural phenomena it can be seen that other influences will have a telling effect as well upon the use of the landscape. These have to do with man-made "improvements" to the land, and the legal, economic, and other constraints which have been placed upon it. Roadways, utility easements, tax assessments, or zoning, for example, may be more critical than the character of the property itself. All such factors have direct bearing upon land use, life patterns, and thus upon *human ecology*, which in biologic terms deals with the relationships between humans and their environment. It is significant that within the broader sociological context, the term *ecology* connotes the spacing of people and institutions, and their interdependency.

Ecological determinants

An ecological survey is essentially an exercise in awareness. It is a systematic investigation of those factors, or "eco-determinants," which deal with the relationship of humans, and all attendant forms of life, to the natural and man-made environment. As such it provides the base and basis for all sound land-use planning.

How is such a survey conducted? Simply by obtaining, and recording in any orderly and useful form, the information required. The findings are usually assembled under three main category headings—*physiographic, topographic,* and *cultural* data. A checklist follows:

All good planning must begin with a survey of actual resources: the landscape, the people, the work-a-day activities in a community. Good planning does not begin with an abstract and arbitrary scheme that it seeks to impose on the community: it begins with a knowledge of existing conditions and opportunities.

LEWIS MUMFORD
The City in History
Harcourt, Brace and World, Inc.
New York, 1961

Eco-determinants

(*A list of ecological factors to be considered in the planning and design of all land and water areas*)

I Physiographic (*Nature's forms, forces, and processes*)

1. *Geology* (The physical history of the earth and the rocks and soils of which it is composed)
   a. Bedrock strata: sections and outcrops
   b. Surface geology: soil types by classification
   c. Bearing capacities
   d. Soil stability: susceptibility to faults, slides, erosion, and subsidence
   e. Soil productivity: Composition and condition

2. *Hydrology* (The science that deals with the occurrence, circulation, and distribution of the water of the earth and the earth's atmosphere)
   a. Streams and water bodies
   b. Inundation: tides and flooding
   c. Groundwater: tables, aquifers, and recharging basins
   d. Surface drainage
   e. Erosion
   f. Siltation

3. *Climate* (Generally prevailing weather conditions)
   a. Temperatures
   b. Humidity
   c. Precipitation
   d. Sunshine and cloud cover
   e. Prevailing winds and breezes
   f. Storms and their incidence

4. *Biology* (The study of life and living matter)
   a. The biologic community
   b. Plants
   c. Birds
   d. Animals
   e. Fish and aquatic life
   f. Insects
   g. The ecosystem: values, changes, and controls

II Topographic (*Land-surface configuration and features*)

1. *Land conformation*
   a. Land-water outlines
   b. Relief
   c. Slope analysis

2. *Natural features*
   a. Land
   b. Water
   c. Vegetative cover
   d. Landscape values
   e. Scenic values

3. *Man-made features*
   a. Metes and bounds
   b. Trafficways
   c. Buildings and structures
   d. Site improvements
   e. Utilities

III Cultural (*Social, political, and economic factors*)

1. *Social influences*
   a. Community resources
   b. Community attitudes and needs
   c. Neighboring uses
   d. Historic values

2. *Political and legal constraints*
   a. Political jurisdiction
   b. Zoning
   c. Rights-of-way and easements
   d. Subdivision regulations
   e. Environmental quality standards
   f. Other governmental controls

3. *Economic factors*
   a. Land values
   b. Taxing structure and assessments
   c. Regional growth potential
   d. Off-site improvement requirements
   e. On-site development costs
   f. Cost-benefit ratio

Eco-determinants: Social, physiographic or other factors which have a bearing upon the working or planning of a land-water area as an ecological unit.

Plot, on transparent sheets, and shade in three or more values of gray, each type of eco-determinant. The darker the tone the more severe the constraint. A composite overlay of the pertinent sheets will define by gradation of lighter values the areas or routes best suited for development. The lighter, the better.
While this technique* is not intended to be precise, it serves as a useful guide in preliminary planning and for defining those locations to be subjected to further study.

* Adapted from McHarg

ECO-DETERMINANT OVERLAYS

Initiate an ecological survey of the region

An important requisite of regional planning is that all physical, social, economic, and political resources and constraints be inventoried and plotted, on a continuing basis.

List the eco-determinants to be investigated

For each new aspect of regional study it will be helpful to prepare a comprehensive checklist of all data, or eco-determinants, which will have bearing on the specific project under consideration. These will vary in scope and degree of detail from study to study and from area to area. The location of an airport, transit system, or industrial park in Arizona, for example, would require no information on flood tides, or the relative productivity of estuarine lands, while along the Gulf Coast this might be critical.

Within a given region there will also be variations in the type and amount of eco-data needed. The location of a highway segment, for instance, will require entirely different information than that to be used in the designation of a park and open space system, or the determination of the limits of a floodplain zone.

Get all, but only, the data required

The mark of a competent survey is that it be complete, accurate, and well organized. It should, however, provide only that information needed for the study at hand. Extraneous data clutters the maps, clogs the files, and soon becomes outdated.

The technique of data gathering is a science in itself. Essentially, one gathers material from the most authoritative sources, cross-checks wherever possible, and uses the collection process as an opportunity to meet and interview the agency heads and others who will contribute to, or be affected by, the conduct of the studies.

Systematize the findings

Most information is best recorded on a set of coordinated base maps. These are of a uniform and appropriate scale, to facilitate interpretation and to provide the possibility of transparent overlays. Supplementary and background reports are keyed to the maps by reference numbers and are filed for easy retrieval. Those survey maps are most useful which give clear, concise, and direct exposition of essential facts.

The annotated maps and reports together record the findings of the ecological survey and comprise for the study project the *eco-determinants.*

Prepare a site-analysis diagram

From the information provided by the eco-determinant maps and reports, those responsible for the survey will usually prepare a *site-analysis diagram* and a set of planning criteria or *land-use guidelines.* For who is better qualified to interpret the findings of an ecological survey than those who have prepared it?

The more important landscape values and planning constraints are noted on a *site-analysis diagram,* which summarizes the eco-survey findings. Those features or conditions which most directly affect the planning are graphically abstracted. Even such obvious factors as heavy rock outcrops or deep muck deposits are often overlooked unless their presence is underscored. More subtle considerations such as the direction of the prevailing breeze, or the existence of a utility easement, may be of equal design importance. The complete and well-substantiated site-analysis map is as indispensable to the land planner as the navigation chart to the coastal pilot.

The eco-survey maps and site-analysis diagram as they are prepared will contain a store of unprocessed data. These must be translated into useful design conclusions and land-use guidelines. If the conclusions are sound and the guidelines explicit, the character—and often the entire plan diagram—will have been established.

By way of an analogy, experienced architects find it helpful to begin the design of a structure by making a simple statement describing the character desired. All aspects of the design as it proceeds are then checked and tested against this preliminary specification. The architect, for example, might say of a residence to be built at the head of a rocky Pennsylvania gorge that it would be natural in character and constructed of rough-sawn beams and uncut native stone. The roof of heavy-butted cedar shakes would be shaped like a folded wing, set low above the entrance court, and rising steeply toward the throat of the ravine to command the full view of tumbling stream, hemlocks, and mountain sky. Windows of varying heights and widths would be let directly into the deep stone walls at random to reveal additional facets of the woodland scene. Broad, cantilevered decks of white oak planking would be terraced down the slopes and overhung with balconies. Bold triangular shapes would dominate both the plan forms and framing, to recall and accentuate the dynamic quality of the site.

Or again, in another locale, the design guidelines might call for a simple one-story structure of interlocking white brick cubes set down on a birch-enframed meadow. Each disciplined cube would be topped with a low-profile concrete dome. Sliding glass panels of uniform width and full wall height would be framed in bronze channels. Floors of black slate would extend in a plane to a low-walled exterior patio to overhang a small circular swimming pool lined with white vinyl plastic. The native wild grasses and flowers of the field would be left unmowed to the building walls.

In each case the brief descriptive statement has in effect set the architectural theme and character, from broad concept to smallest detail.

So it is also with the land-use guidelines derived from visits to the site, from study of the eco-survey maps and from review of the site-analysis diagram. In a few well-considered statements the theme and approach to the planning of any project, within the regional context, may be essentially determined.

In every design problem we must work from the general to the particular, and from the particular to the general, simultaneously.
JERZY SOLTAN
In conversation

Land-use allocation

In all areas of human endeavor the planning process is one of research (perception), analysis (deduction), and synthesis (application).

Research. In the conduct of an ecological survey, the facts are first gathered and organized for ease of reference and interpretation. The survey documentation may vary in depth from a single map upon which preliminary findings are recorded to a comprehensive coverage by map sets and detailed reports exploring the full range of ecological factors. The nature of the study, the fragility or difficulty of the site, and the complexity of the project will together determine the extent of the investigation required.

Analysis. When assembled, the maps and reports are studied in the light of the particular problem or project at hand, and deductions are reached. These are normally recorded in the form of a *site-analysis diagram*, and *land-use guidelines*.

Synthesis. The third and final step in the planning process is the application of the findings to the design solution.

Having accomplished the necessary investigations and recorded the findings in the form of eco-determinant maps and correlated reports, and having from this data prepared a site analysis and set of land-use guidelines, one is now ready to proceed with the actual process of land-use planning. This will involve the designation of areas for *preservation*, *conservation*, and *development*, and the subsequent allocation of land for the various uses and paths of movement. As the planning and project design continues, these land-use areas and ways are adjusted and brought into the best possible relationship to each other, to the program requirements, and to the project site.

Define the areas to be preserved

Within most landscape areas there are outstanding features which should be left untouched. A strand of beach, extensive beds of submerged turtle grass, a mangrove forest, a rise of sea oats, a historical ruin—such are the elements that give a region its essential quality. Destroy them and they are lost forever. Preserve them, and the land, the environs, and life for the observers will long be the richer for it.

A study of the project eco-surveys will reveal those site areas and elements which are of highest ecological value. These should be outlined on the plans and protected in the field against the threat of damage or destruction. Often the presence of an unsuspected feature will be of great benefit to the proposed development, provided the feature may be preserved. In other cases existing landscape "superlatives" have been deemed so visually important, or so critical to the region and its ecosystem, that to preserve them the project plans have had to be drastically modified or abandoned altogether.

Denote land for conservation

Often, in addition to key areas to be *preserved* intact, there will be those of secondary, yet important, landscape value. These may well be set aside for *conservation*, and such limited development as may be compatible. Here the land conformation and the outstanding natural features and vegetative covers will be left undisturbed. The borders of streams and water bodies will be left in their natural state. Beaches, dunes, and wetlands will be carefully protected.

Recreation areas, parkways, pedestrian paths, and bicycle trails will be "fitted into" the conservation areas in such a way as to minimize any negative impacts. In some cases recreational, residential, or other structures may be grouped on *development* enclaves within the larger conservation area boundaries.

Outline the development areas

In most areas, sections can be found where there are few limitations to reshaping or construction. Perhaps because of prior use, or lack of natural distinction, the land lends itself to alteration. Such areas will be designated on the survey maps as the primary potential *development* sites.

Explore the plan alternatives

Once the *preservation*, *conservation*, and *development* areas have been allocated and the land-use guidelines formulated, it is time at last

---

The less of our landscape there is to save, the better our chances of saving it. It is a shame we have to lose so much land to learn the lesson, but desecration does seem a prerequisite for action. People have to be outraged. Most of the new land-use legislation and the pioneering programs did not come about as the result of foresighted, thoughtful analysis. They came about because people got mad over something they could see. Some of the most significant legislation can be traced to a small local outrage—a line of trees being chopped down for a highway, a meadow being asphalted for a parking area.
WILLIAM H. WHYTE
The Last Landscape
Doubleday & Company, Inc.
Garden City, New York, 1968

Planning a priori is dreaming . . . that indispensible scheming towards the future.
ELIEL SAARINEN
The City—Its Growth, Its Decay, Its Future
MIT Press
Cambridge, Mass., 1965

for the planner to begin his conceptual studies. With firsthand knowledge of the site and its environs, and with a well-organized body of background maps and data at hand, the alternative plan concepts can now be fully explored.

Schematic solutions are best kept diagrammatic. They need not be carefully drawn or detailed in the initial trial process. It is enough at first to record only the essentials of a scheme. If it bears up in comparison with other studies, it can then be further developed.

Experience has shown no workable substitute for the mind-bending process of checking out all possibilities. While some land planners may be content with their first plan proposal, and defend it to the bitter end, more seasoned professionals have learned that first concepts are seldom the best. Occasionally the inspired scheme may burst forth at once like the dawning of the morning sun, but usually the superior plan solution must be arrived at through the arduous process of "cut and try," with constant refinement and adjustment.

Select the preferred land-use pattern

This is achieved through the process of *comparative analysis* in which a number of alternative concepts are carefully weighed and evaluated. The best solution will be that which:

1. Best satisfies the program requirements.

2. Is capable of implementation.

3. Provides the maximum benefits at the least total cost.

In the comparative analysis of the various land-use proposals, it is recommended that the *systems* approach be applied. Essentially, this requires that a competent team be selected to conduct the review and make its recommendations. With the team leader named, the next order of business is to define the objective of the group effort and explain the review procedures. The "decision unit" is appointed at the start. It may comprise the entire review team, a subcommittee, or a jury. It is only important that the decision makers be present at all review sessions to hear each scheme presented and its pros and cons fully discussed.

The main difference between a "systems" review and the bureaucratic decision process is that, in the former, each member of the team, and each expert who may be called upon for testimony, may speak his mind freely on an equal basis. Too often bureaucratic decisions are made by officials who are pressed for time and who speak only with those next above or below them in the rigid chain of command; thus they seldom hear the key issues discussed by those who know most about them.

All values that can be quantified on a numerical basis should be. Where relative values cannot be accurately quantified—as, for example, in the appraisal of a historic or scenic resource—the review team must rely upon expert opinion.

In analyzing the alternative schemes presented, the study team should be satisfied that all reasonable plan approaches have been explored. Those schemes which seem less feasible will be rejected. Those which contain the seeds of a good solution may be improved as a result of discussion. The better alternative concepts will be selected and evaluated in greater detail. As the review proceeds and as understanding of both the regional needs and the ecological possibilities and constraints is expanded, it is important that the team be empowered to suggest changes in the governing planning program.

When finally the review-team decision makers are satisfied that they are familiar with the alternative land-use proposals and their

Planning is the rational process of orderly evolution.

A plan is no better than the means devised by which it can be effectuated.

Ecology has a counterpart in the field of technology with the development of systems analysis. A space missile, for example, is a combination of systems—each composed of sub-systems—for propulsion, guidance, enclosure of passengers, and communications. The effects of all activities within each system and sub-system must be measured not only by the efficiency of the single system but also by their effects on other systems.

Similarly, a human environment is composed of various systems and sub-systems, including a residential system, a park system, an educational system, a commercial system, an industrial system, an agricultural system, a communications system, and a transportation system. The goal of all these systems should be a total environment capable of satisfying the broadest range of human needs.

From Sea to Shining Sea
A Report on the American Environment—
Our Natural Heritage
By the President's Council on Recreation and
Natural Beauty
U.S. Government Printing Office
Washington, D.C., 1968

The planning process is a systematic means of determining where you are, where you want to be, and how best to get there.

Planning is the guidance of the quantity and quality and rate and nature of change.

implications, and when they have heard all pertinent views and sufficient argument, they will make their recommendations. Even such well-founded recommendations must be, of course, subject to periodic review and to change if compelling new factors may be from time to time introduced.

The plan elements

The regional plan is a graphic representation of the way the region works. Its makeup is disarmingly simple. Transit and transportation routes of various types are shown in solid, dashed, and dotted lines in tones of gray to black, depending upon their importance. Lands devoted to residential use are indicated in yellow for low-density housing, orange for medium density, and tan to brown for multifamily apartments in the high-density range. Commercial uses are shown in red; industrial in plum; institutional lands in dark blue-gray; water in light blue or turquoise; and parks and open space in tones of light to forest green. This color code, like scientific nomenclature, is universally understood. (Those of us who, tiring of the conventional palette, have tried to change and improvise, have only managed to get our map readers, and ourselves, thoroughly confused.) In addition to land uses, major public facilities are often shown and labeled. These may include such installations as airports, locks, lighthouses, piers, and terminals.

In actuality, the regional plan comprises two or more overall land-use maps—one showing the conditions which exist, and the other, or others, the proposed land-use patterns and routes at any projected time in the future. Maps are kept constantly updated. They are supported by explanatory text, by charts, graphs, tables, and by supplementary reports. These show in greater detail the nature and interrelationships of the various plan components.

Planning is for people. It is an easy matter to become so bogged down in the mass of maps and statistics that the human basis for planning is forgotten. The only justification for regional planning, however, is to find ways to improve the living and working environment. An agreeable living environment is largely a matter of *quantity, quality,* and *interrelationships.*

The kinds of questions that need to be asked are:

What kinds of jobs and positions will exist? Will there be enough? Will the employment centers be easily accessible from the residential areas? Or must one drive for miles to work, and grind in low gear along overcrowded highways?

What improved types of transit and roadways are being planned? What of schedules and capacities? How direct and parklike are the routes?

What advanced kinds of educational, medical, and cultural facilities will the region provide? Will there be training centers for all age groups and for all types of skills? Will there be opportunities for continuing education?

Will complete medical care and treatment be available—from local doctor, to diagnostic clinic, to general hospital?

Will there be concert halls, libraries, theaters, zoos, botanical gardens . . . ?

What kinds of outdoor recreation are to be provided? Can one swim, hike, sail, and fish and find a secluded spot for a picnic?

Will all members of each family be able to enjoy those amenities that give them a sense of well-being? Will needs and capacities be in balance? Will movement from place to place be pleasant and efficient? Will interarea vehicular travel be reduced by making each subregion more self-sufficient?

Again let the planner be clear on this point; his chief purpose is to help provide for the present and future people of the region all those elements and relationships which will make their lives more pleasant and rewarding.

Give homes and housing preferential treatment

Within *development* areas, except where special circumstances may otherwise dictate, residential uses are usually given first consideration. They are best sited in areas of topographical interest, where the residents may "be at home with nature."

Dwellings will be grouped off to the side of, but not facing upon, the circulation roads. Low- to medium-density housing will be located in planned neighborhoods and communities near convenience centers. Concentrations of higher-density housing are best located near rapid transit terminals, freeway intersections, or contiguous to major employment, recreation, or commercial centers. All dwellings will be protected from through traffic, from noncompatible uses, and from noise and glare.

Reassess the residential land-use inventory

Unbuilt-upon areas designated for residential development will be reviewed periodically. Unneeded acreage will be rezoned for agricultural or other open space purposes. New residential land will not be released until that presently so designated and having adequate roads, sewers, and other improvements has first been "built out" and utilized.

Isolate, or insulate, housing developments

Ideally, residential areas will be planned as enclaves within or abutting conservation or other open space lands, with low-profile dwellings placed at the periphery. Residential uses will be encouraged adjacent to, and screened from, highway and transit corridors, but only when adequate shielding is provided by embankments, walls, or greenbelts. Buffer strips will also be established between housing and commercial or industrial areas, to eliminate visual or other frictions and to maintain property values.

Preclude the improper location of residential uses

The use of land for residential purposes will be prohibited within preservation areas, floodplains, tidal estuaries, or where it might contribute to the pollution or silting of streams or water bodies. It will not be permitted adjacent to surface water-supply resources or in areas unsuitable for septic tanks and lacking in adequate sewage disposal systems. It will also be precluded on lands rich in mineral or other extractive deposits and from industrial districts, or areas of potential hazard, such as sites adjacent to airports or unstable slopes, or lands subject to mine subsidence.

Differentiate between, and accommodate, the various types of commercial use

Regional commercial centers are those of suburban character which are developed primarily to serve a regionwide trade area. They are to be distinguished from the urban central business district (CBD) of metropolitan regions, and from neighborhood and community business and shopping centers which are more local in nature.

Each type has its own tried and proven requirements of location, acreage, floor area, parking ratios, and related components. These, of course, are always subject to change and improvement.

Encourage planned commercial clusters

Strip development, the construction of commercial enterprises with frontage directly upon the public arterial or circulation roads, will be prohibited. Except for isolated neighborhood or apartment convenience shops, and such uses as artist studios and professional offices, all commercial and business-office space should usually be located in centers planned especially for this purpose. This pattern can be reinforced by the gradual elimination of the scattered and unrelated business uses in between.

In commercial cluster planning it is important to provide sufficient supporting area in addition to the restricted building sites. For besides safe and pleasant access, all commercial centers will need land for parking and service compounds, attractive landscape development, and buffering.

Group the highway services

Highway-related commercial enterprises—such as service stations, garages, automotive supply stores, and car or trailer sales lots—will be located near arterial intersections or freeway interchanges. These, also, are best clustered around a motor-access mall, or circulation loop, and kept off the major roadways.

Consider new forms of commercial land use

There are a number of promising developments in the planning of commercial "parks." The best of these highly successful off-highway and out-of-city business centers occur in those regions that enjoy progressive planning and zoning laws and strong regulative controls. Such shopping, design, entertainment, or business-office centers form their own urbanized satellite of intensive use and convenience and provide all supporting amenities within a spacious campus setting. Where such facilities complement and supplement the regional urba-centers, rather than diffuse them, they are to be in all ways encouraged.

Locate industrial and other employment sites near areas of dense population

Commuter time and the peak-load strain upon highways and transit systems will thus be reduced. While there are benefits in living close to one's work, it is important that housing and employment districts be isolated visually and that access roads and uses be kept separate.

Combine industrial uses also into self-contained "parks"

Regional industrial activities include manufacturing, research and development, wholesale trade and distribution, warehousing and storage, and extractive processes. Various combinations of these can be advantageously grouped. All are best closely related to transportation and transmission corridors and to airports, harbors, freeway interchanges, and to rapid transit stations.

Such industrial districts and their routes of access and connection will be subject to strict pollution controls and to landscape quality standards. Some nuisance-type industries, such as foundries, power-generation plants, mining and heavy manufacturing, will be isolated or perhaps prohibited in many metropolitan or scenic regions.

Locate institutions to best serve the needs of the people

Most schools, churches, and hospitals are planned as part of, or between, the neighborhoods and communities that they serve. Other institutions, such as the great cathedrals, libraries, museums, and medical complexes, are more urban in character and relate to the metro centers. Among these, however, there is a growing trend to establish subcenters throughout the surrounding region. Mini-zoos, branch libraries, mobile health units, church workshops, summer theaters, and music camps may be dispersed to "reach out" to the people.

With improved highways and rapid transit, other institutions, traditionally bound to the cities, have moved to the open countryside. Convalescent hospitals, colleges, botanical gardens, and arboretums, for example, find that suburban and rural locations often provide more benefits to the users, at less cost, than the urban sites.

Use regional transit and transportation routes as multimodal linkage

Traditionally, regional transportation planning has been viewed as the provision of an adequate network of highways and streets. Sometimes the concept of reserved bus lanes or a rapid transit route has been introduced, or hiking and biking trails proposed. Such planning falls far short of the possibilities. There is need for a fresh, creative, and total approach to the safe, pleasant, and efficient movement of people and goods. This will envision a complete and integrated system embracing all modes of inter- and intraregional travel.

Included will be such features as:

Urban and suburban cores reserved for the use of public transit vehicles only.

The banning of freight and diesel trucks from all urban arterials.

The provision of transportation-transmission routes through industrial-commercial areas of concentration.

Innovative methods of freight transportation, providing rail and truckway ingress to major terminals. Subdistribution systems to use-centers employing subsurface tunnels, tubes, and beltways and specially designed electric-powered surface vehicles and conveyors.

Classified ports, airports, and heliports, each reserved for the exclusive and particular handling of passengers, goods, or mail.

Airports, of various types, surrounded by protective open space lands, and so located as to ensure direct and easy access to activity centers.

Linkage, at flashing speeds, of ports and urban nodes by monorail or other grade-separated shuttles.

Independently routed busways and the use of reversible freeway bus lanes.

New types and sections of passenger-vehicle roadways planned and acquired on the basis of future, rather than present, needs.

Full utilization of all multiple-use and air-rights possibilities.

Corridors of sufficient width to accommodate all anticipated highway,

Every year over 1 million acres of farmland are converted to urban or suburban uses.

All cities are vassals of farm technology. Unless the farmers can produce many times what they need to feed themselves, the population of the hungry cities will melt back to the countryside. What has made possible the rapid growth of American cities is the growing scientific efficiency of farming, which gave the cities not only food but—increasingly with the years—a surplus population no longer needed in the fields.

ROBERT FUTTERMAN
The Future of Our Cities
Doubleday & Company, Inc.
Garden City, N.Y., 1961

The maintenance of the regional setting, the green matrix, is essential for the culture of cities . . .

LEWIS MUMFORD
The City in History
Harcourt, Brace and World, Inc.
New York, 1961

Agriculture includes the wooded land, . . . the rocky ridgetops, the lakes and rivers, the swamps, marshes and shellfish grounds, as well as our working farms.

And so agriculture gives a sense of beauty and pleasure. It may be the pleasure of a beautiful view. It may be the satisfaction, a very special pleasure, of work accomplished on a farm or in a garden. It may be the satisfying taste of . . . fresh milk, of homegrown fruit, of sweet corn fresh from the summer field, of tomato's lush ripeness fresh from the vine. This we have known and cherished. Unless we decide wisely now, these pleasures and these satisfactions, these treasured values of our land, could and no doubt will vanish.

JOHN N. DEMPSEY
An Environmental Policy for Connecticut
Report of the Governor's Committee on
Environmental Policy
New Haven, Conn., 1970

The rural landscape is primarily the workshop of agriculture, yet in the form in which it was bequeathed to us in the last century it was one of the finest works of functional art in the world. If it is to remain so there must be an understanding of its present composition and a realization that it was born of conscious design as well as of economic expediency.

SYLVIA CROWE
Tomorrow's Landscape
Architectural Press
London, 1956

Millions of city dwellers have moved out to the country. They arrive and settle down and in so doing they cause the destruction of the country. The result is a vast sprawling built-up area encircling the city . . .

PETER BLAKE
The Master Builders
Alfred A. Knopf
New York, 1960

transit, and pedestrian uses combined in a natural setting.

The inclusion of recreation roads, waterways, walks, and bicycle trails into the green- and blueway systems.

Second only to the sensitive allocation of regional land-use patterns is the provision of the best possible means of access and interconnection.

Preserve the agricultural lands as a base

These "breadbasket" lands, which also supply our timber and natural fibers, are to be protected assiduously. They are an essential part of our economy. They provide much-needed breathing space, and they are a cherished extension of our American rural tradition. Once fragmented by unplanned development or taxed into oblivion, they can never be restored to the region.

Inventory and protect other open space lands

The green and blue matrix of a region—that forms the grand setting for human constructions and habitations—will be composed of unbuilt-upon lands and water areas of widely varying types. Agricultural fields and woodlands will most often predominate. In some regions, however, state and federal forests, parks, wildlife management preserves, fish and game lands, military installations, and sites within the jurisdictions of the Army Corps of Engineers or the Coast Guard will comprise the bulk.

All public parks and parkways are part of the inventory, including those built to serve local communities. Where highways or circulation roads are planned as controlled-access parkways, with trucking excluded, their entire right-of-way will be considered as open space. Semipublic holdings such as conservation lands and historic sites are included, as are institutional grounds, golf courses, and private clubs. Airports, cemeteries, joint school-park sites, university campuses, and campus-type employment centers all make their contribution. Industrial holdings such as reservoirs and transmission rights-of-way add extensive swaths. The aggregation will be rounded out by floodplain, stream-land, and steep-slope zoning, and by a host of smaller plazas, parklets, trails, and overlooks, each adding its welcome space.

One of the most valuable functions of a regional planning commission is that of ensuring the existence, regulation, and multiple use of a unified, and interrelated, open space system.

How to describe a total, regional, open space framework

In general terms "open space land" may be considered to be any significant area which is not covered by buildings, vehicular traffic-ways (pavement or tracks), parking storage, or other manufacturing or service facility. In certain instances, built-upon land may be restored to the "open space" category by such commendable techniques as "air-right" and "multiple-use" design.

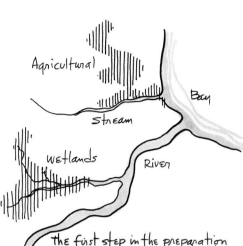

The first step in the preparation of an open space plan is to plot on a suitable base map the topographical features. These will include all significant areas of wetland, water, farm land, forest and other unbuilt-upon property.

DEFINE THE LAND AND WATER BASE

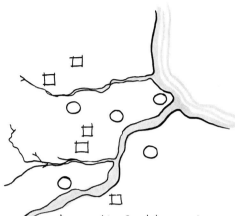

Existing public facilities such as military installations, parks, zoos, botanic gardens, conservation areas and school and university campuses will be located. Also shown will be such private holdings as industrial parks, institutional grounds, cemeteries, campsites, golf courses and other recreational uses.

LOCATE THE MAJOR PUBLIC AND PRIVATE FACILITIES

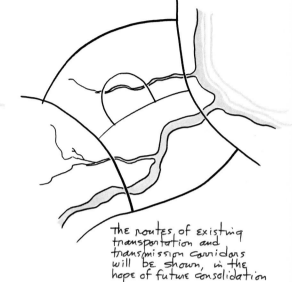

The routes of existing transportation and transmission corridors will be shown, in the hope of future consolidation

INCLUDE THE TRANSPORTATION – TRANSMISSION CORRIDORS

Existing neighborhood and community facilities of less than twenty-five acres will together make a significant contribution. These will include public schools, athletic fields, playgrounds, parks, nature preserves, historic areas and comparable sites. Smaller private open space lands and waters will yield their welcome share also. These will include recreation areas, estates, preserves, and open portions of larger developments. Such linear or interconnecting routes as equestrian and bicycle trails will be indicated in the larger scale mapping.

DD THE MINOR STRUCTURING ELEMENTS

New development and rehabilitation opportunities will suggest themselves – to relate to, and expand, the regional open space framework. Such regional assets as a new university or community college campus, an industrial park, a new community, a government center or a recreational park and marina can become important open space nodes.

DESCRIBE NEW OPEN SPACE OPPORTUNITIES

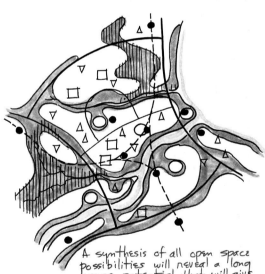

A synthesis of all open space possibilities will reveal a long range potential that will give new meaning and thrust to the regional planning effort.

IMPLEMENTATION

1. Establish an open space policy
2. Survey the existing conditions
3. Project the future possibilities
4. Plan a coordinated system
5. Act to accomplish the plan

PUT IT ALL TOGETHER

Structuring

A well-devised plan layout establishing the diagrammatic structure of each region is nothing short of essential to its orderly growth. If, however, the designated land uses and relationships are not expressive of the regional character, all sorts of frictions will be generated. If the free movement of people and goods is not assured, there will be costly inefficiencies and troublesome delays. If *all* the needs of the people who will live and work within the region have not been considered and accommodated, there will be persistent rumblings of discontent. If the planning framework does not provide the opportunity for adjustment and constant renewal, deterioration is bound to occur.

In allocating the plan elements, the planner will discover a number of built-in "givens" which will largely influence the evolution of the regional structure. Key topographical features—such as

BLUEWAY-GREENWAY SYSTEM

Natural corridors will be defined along the regional drainageways. They will include, wherever possible, the marshes, waterbodies, rivers and their tributary streams, together with their side slopes and floodplains. This scenic network will protect the watershed, accommodate many forms of recreation, and provide for the region an interconnecting network of parkways, bicycle paths, and pedestrian trails.

ACTIVITY CENTERS

Locations and appropriate land areas will be established for all projected centers of regional activity. These will include the urban core, communities, industrial parks, institutional and business office campuses and recreation places. All other land excepting that required for the transportation-transmission corridors will be reserved for agricultural, forest, nature preserve, and other compatible uses.

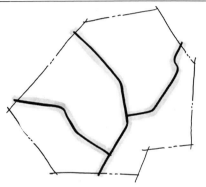

TRANSPORTATION-TRANSMISSION CORRIDORS

These will provide access and interconnection to the activity centers. They will be wide enough to accept routes for highways, transit, and transmission lines simultaneously, and to ensure adequate screening and visual quality.

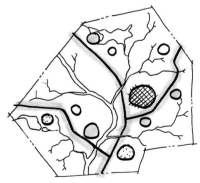

A COMPOSITE PLAN FOR THE REGION

Here the best of the natural features are preserved; activity centers are so located and sized as to permit their optimum function; routes of movement and transmission are direct and consolidated; and all land uses are planned together in harmony with each other and the regional landscape.

hills, ravines, and water bodies, for example, will suggest some land-use patterns and dictate others. Extant roads and railways, together with major utility installations, are usually so firmly established that, with slight modification, they must be accepted and incorporated into the plans. The disposition of existing agricultural lands and natural areas is also significant, for it is much easier to weave them into the open space system than to eke out new openings within the built-up sectors.

Prevailing concentrations of sound development are of course to be respected, as are all traditional land uses, and even the attitudes of the property owners. The possibility of attracting new and desirable development is also a factor to be considered in the planning process, as is the "jurisdictional climate," which may encourage progressive entrepreneurs or drive them to other locations.

If the projected plans for the region are contrary to the will of the populace, or if they drastically disrupt the natural and man-made order of things, they are doomed to forceful opposition and eventual failure. If, on the other hand, they respond to the nature of the land and promote systems of harmony, the region will achieve, stage by stage, through the process of logical evolution, the fulfillment of its highest potential. The goal of the planner in this regard is therefore the preparation and effectuation of a regional diagram that brings needs, land-use patterns, and all environmental factors into balance. If this goal is achieved, each region will realize not only its highest and best use, but also its own distinctive character.

Move with the terrain

No matter what the landscape base—be it prairie, hill country, mountain range, or coastal plain—the topography is an eloquent and persuasive determinant of the region's land-use structure. Where plans are conceived in harmony with nature's features, forms, and forces, the results are sound and pleasing. Where nature is violated, conflicts are generated, disruptions occur, costs rise, and blight is a usual consequence.

Utilize existing transportation routes

The most dominant lines on a regional map are those denoting the railroads and the highways. This is rightly so, for access and the movement of people and goods are prerequisites to the use of most properties. It can be generally stated that the better the access, the more valuable the land.

Since the acquisition of rights-of-way and the building of highways, canals, and transit lines is costly in the extreme and a heavy tax burden, it is logical that existing routes be fully improved and utilized to accommodate the traffic generated by the best use of adjacent lands. These contiguous and supporting areas will in turn be so planned, and development so guided, that it is in balance with the capacities of the routes.

Where the alignment of existing roads or railroads—or where the location of ports, airports, or terminals—are inconsistent with the evolving long-range goals of a region, they will be phased out or relocated. Where new routes are required, they will be planned as multi-use corridors to serve the transport, transit, and transmission needs of the related lands.

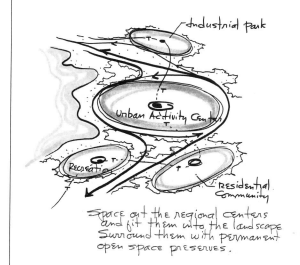

Space out the regional centers and fit them into the landscape. Surround them with permanent open space preserves.

DISPERSE AND INTERCONNECT THE REGIONAL COMPONENTS

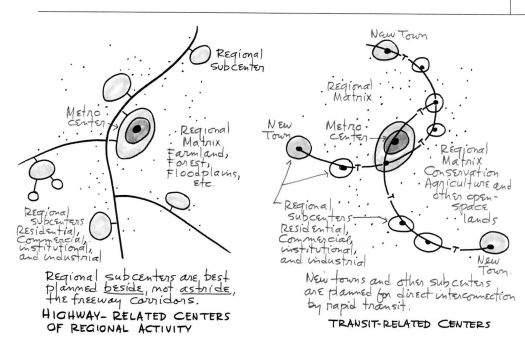

Regional subcenters are best planned beside, not astride, the freeway corridors.

HIGHWAY-RELATED CENTERS OF REGIONAL ACTIVITY

New towns and other subcenters are planned for direct interconnection by rapid transit.

TRANSIT-RELATED CENTERS

The two systems of land use and movement are then coordinated.

THE REGIONAL STRUCTURE

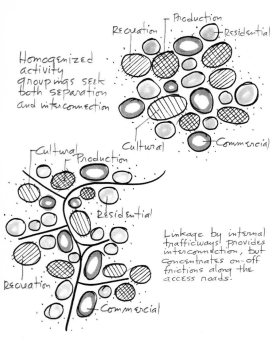

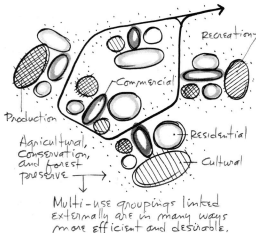

THE DYNAMICS OF LAND USE STRUCTURING

The chaos of non-relation is probably worse in America than anywhere else in the world.

IAN NAIRN
The American Landscape
Random House, Inc.
New York, 1965

Where future transportation facilities are planned, and particularly in newly urbanizing areas, their routes are to be determined with great care. These routes and the placement of the activity centers which they will serve can at once ensure (or forever preclude) a sound development structure for the region.

Build around utility installations

These, like roads and railways, represent substantial investment and are bound to be influential in determining regional patterns of growth. Their beneficial aspects—the provision of water, power, waste disposal, and other services—will be utilized to the fullest. Their negative features—various types of pollution and visual detraction—will be ameliorated or eliminated insofar as may be technically and economically feasible. Recently, new levels of public concern, and sometimes indignation, have resulted in significant improvements in the design and operation of utility installations.

Designate locations for regional subcenters

Within the study region locate and describe a logical arrangement of existing and proposed subcenters. These might be residential, institutional, commercial, or industrial, alone or in combination.

Each will be so placed and sized as to best accommodate and serve its designated purpose, with all brought into balanced relationship. All will have well-defined man-made or natural topographical boundaries and will be served by projected transit-transportation routes.

Provide for new towns and planned communities

As regional subcenters, or closely related to them, they will be connected as well by transit to the metropolitan core. Especial consideration will be given to employment and recreation opportunities.

Designate activity subcenters, not zoning districts

Many of the problems of county and regional planning have stemmed from the traditional approach, borrowed from city planning, by which the entire land area is subdivided into land-use zones. It is proposed that such zoning by district encourages erosion of the regional open space matrix, makes transportation planning extremely difficult, and forces the sale of agricultural property because of the artificial inflation of taxes based on the potential land use.

Instead, the entire region might better be considered a green-blue matrix reserved for the most part for agricultural, forest, floodplain, conservation, recreation, or other open space uses. Within this matrix, at logical resource centers and interconnected by projected trafficways, activity subcenters of various types could then be designated. These allocated subcenters could be studied in greater detail as their need developed—to expand outward from each nucleus as additional area might be required and as services would then be extended. With this approach, the hop-skip development patterns of regional fragmentation could be precluded to the benefit of all.

Match development to resources

Ecological sensitivity and land-carrying capacities must determine the limits of future growth—rather than the artificial configurations of zoning.

A serious error in the premise of conventional zoning is that land-use patterns tend to follow property and political boundaries rather than the more significant lines of environmental limitations and potential.

The overuse of land or the improper balance between population (development) and environmental constraints may be expected to produce one or more of the following consequences:

1. Draw-down of the water table and aquifer.

2. Decreased water quality resulting from contamination and perhaps saltwater intrusion.

3. Disruption of natural drainage patterns.

4. Erosion and siltation.

5. Increased surface runoff and downstream flooding.

6. Local climatic changes.

7. Air, noise, and visual pollution.

8. Extension of traffic and transit networks.

9. Increased demand for energy, power generation, and transmission lines.

10. Need for additional solid-waste disposal.

11. Alteration of plant and animal communities.

12. Destruction of natural and scenic features.

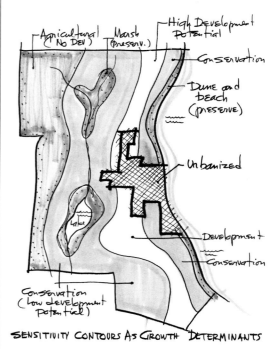

SENSITIVITY CONTOURS AS GROWTH DETERMINANTS

Zoning as a useful planning tool has consistently failed when variances or increased densities are easily granted. The resulting lack of effective regulation in land development has produced an array of difficult and costly environmental problems.

As an alternative, it is proposed that after a reasonable cut-off date all undeveloped private land be returned to an agricultural or a preservation land-use category and so taxed. Such lands would then be classified by degree of ecological sensitivity as a future guideline. Development permits would be granted only upon demonstration that a proposed use was compatible with regional goals, was suited to the proposed site and that acceptable levels of service would be provided by logical extension.

Consolidate land uses

Uncontrolled growth by "scatteration" is wasteful. Great swaths of the natural landscape are usurped and fragmented to provide for the use of the few. Roads and utility lines—and eventually water and sewer mains—must be extended to uneconomic lengths to serve isolated dwellings or projects. When the proliferation of incompatible uses is also allowed as part of the mix, the opportunities for sound development are seriously impaired.

Only when land-use patterns are predetermined and established by localized zoning can the best use be made of the region's land resources.

Preserve steep slopes and narrow ravines as permanent open space through a program of conservation easements and tax incentives

Using a concept developed by Charles Eliot for the preservation of open space lands related to private development, the owners of unbuildable slopes and narrow ravines or other areas of scenic quality could be induced to sell such areas to a public conservancy or regional park authority for a nominal sum and thence be relieved of taxes on the lands conveyed. Preestablished use controls or restrictions on the land sold would permit good conservation and forestry practice and allow public access for passive recreation such as hiking, picnicking, and nature study. The construction of active playfields or recreation structures could be precluded in those areas where they might be a nuisance. Such a program could well result in a cohesive system of open space lands around which future developments would be formed.

Fit the regional plan to the topography

Reserve the plateaus and buildable slopes for construction, the ridges and valley floors for traffic movement, and the natural drainageways for the gravity flow of storm drainage and waste water.

By tradition and logic the level plateaus have been used for building sites. High land values and new techniques of construction will tend to preempt the use of the lesser slopes for new forms of building.

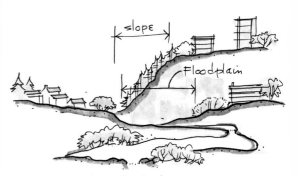

Build on the higher ground and plateaus. Preserve the steeper slopes and flood-prone valleys as community open space.

PRESERVE THE SLOPES AND FLOODPLAINS

275

Describe and enforce a program of floodplain zoning

> Most regions are interlaced with an extensive pattern of stream and river floodplains. The existing and projected limits of the 100-year flooding should be scientifically described and the construction of homes or other structures prohibited within the areas of potential hazard. This would preclude the need for public relief or restitution for flood damage sustained. Floodplain lands may be zoned and used for agricultural, conservation, or recreation purposes including private or public campgrounds, parks, parkways, and golf courses.

Parks, recreation, and open space

An agreeable region provides for its people all types of outdoor recreation. The list is long. It might well begin with the urban parks, plazas, and squares which are the public gathering places. These are best interconnected with shaded pedestrian walkways and furnished with fountains, benches, and attractive lighting to make them safe and pleasant. In addition there will be the horticultural gardens, museums, aquarium, aviary, and zoo, and for the sports enthusiasts the athletic fields, stadium, and arena. There will be the concert shells and amphitheaters. There will be parkways, picnic areas, golf courses, and swimming pools. Where water frontage permits, one may find public beaches, fishing piers, and marinas. For the nature lover there will be hiking, biking, and bridle trails, forest preserves, fishing lakes, hunting lands, and plant and wildlife sanctuaries. Each region will provide, within the limits of its resources, all possible forms of recreation to give its citizens pleasure and instruction.

To ensure a complete park and recreation system, it is essential that each locality provide for its own particular local needs. Each neighborhood and community has, for example, the responsibility to install an adequate system of play lots, athletic fields, and local recreation places.

At the municipal level, towns and cities operate for their citizens such larger recreation installations as zoos, marinas, and public beaches which the individual communities could not themselves provide. Often, and ideally, two or more towns, cities, or counties may participate in a joint program to provide such additional features as scenic drives, waysides, hiking trails, golf courses, beaches, and boat launching ramps.

Regional parks or forest preserves will supplement other community or municipal recreation facilities by providing large conservation areas for nature appreciation, field and natural-water sports, and picnicking. Development is best limited to the provision of access roads and parking areas, toilets, shelters, water supply, and rough-mowed meadows around which picnic tables are grouped. Game courts, swimming pools, or golf links are not recommended. The emphasis is on nature.

Between 25 and 35 acres per 1,000 population should normally be designated for the creation of regional parks or forest preserves of from 1,000 to 3,000 acres each. Up to two-thirds of this area can be "borrowed" from adjacent public lands or waters.

In acquiring the sites, consideration should be given to depleted and eroded farmlands, refuse dumps, spoil banks, gravel pits, and strip mines. With regrading and reforestation, these blemishes on the landscape may be transformed into attractive properties.

Beyond the local and regional facilities, the state has an obligation to develop a system of state parks and recreation areas. These usually include forest and nature preserves, hunting lands, fishing lakes, recreation access roads, and historic sites and buildings.

The federal government, in turn, is concerned with the preservation and development of natural and historic superlatives of national significance. Such monuments as those of Gettysburg, Mount Vernon, and Muir Woods are examples, as are the Blue Ridge and Great Smoky parkways, Yosemite, the Redwood National Park, and that within Florida's Everglades.

The essential feature of a superior recreation system is that it be *complete*. It must be an interrelated and well-balanced hierarchy of parks and open spaces of all types, ranging from a neighborhood hiking trail to a great national seashore—each contributing its own unique and important part to the whole.

Plan ahead

Many cities and counties have by tradition acquired land for parks and recreation as well as for other public purposes mainly on a parcel-by-parcel basis, as properties become tax delinquent. This has resulted in a patchwork agglomeration of poorly suited, poorly placed lands which are expensive to develop and difficult to maintain. Farsighted administrators have, by contrast, developed and kept current a detailed, well-balanced, and *complete* program of needs and possibilities and have vigorously sought out for acquisition those properties best suited for the varying purposes. The benefits of the latter approach—as demonstrated, for example, in Milwaukee, Cook County (Illinois), and San Francisco—can be readily observed.

Consider changing needs

Most park and recreation systems are archaic. They were built to reflect customs which are outmoded and to serve neighborhoods which no longer function as neighborhoods. They have not responded to emerging social patterns and demands. With burgeoning populations, more leisure time, and rapid urbanization, the need for recreational facilities *of the right kind and in the right locations* has been greatly intensified. In localities where these are inadequate or outdated or where a sound and creative policy and program do not exist, professional consultation may be needed.

Determine reasonable standards

In all stages of park and recreation planning it is essential to know *how much land is required* and *how it should best be distributed*. For municipal systems, considering acreage requirements first, there have been two generally accepted guidelines for determination—the *area-population* and the *area-percentage* ratio methods.

It will be informative for each municipality to check itself against these two scales, provided the *average* is not considered the optimum. The chief value of such a comparison is to define those examples which fall outside the norm and to learn *why* they vary. Perhaps the

To live pigeonholed within a "rectangle standing on end" from which there is nowhere to go except into a car and onto a highway, or for a walk along a continuous stretch of grass, is not urban living at all. In an urban environment one should be able to lead, on both sides of the wall, a life that has a complete gamut of experiences—a life that is pleasant as well as interesting, reposeful as well as exciting.

Progressive Architecture *magazine*
October, 1961

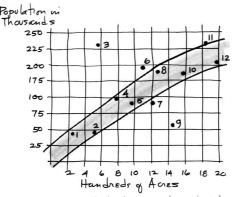

Population in Thousands

Hundreds of Acres

Assume that the numbered dots represent the land holdings in twelve typical American cities, in acres per 1000 population. The dark band indicates a generalized median. It would be instructive to park and recreation officials and planners to visit comparable cities to check the reasons for variation in the amount of land acquired, and for an appraisal of actual needs and performance.

Why do cities #3 and #9, for example, lie so far outside the band? Perhaps one may demonstrate greater need because of topography. Or one may suggest means by which the population may be adequately served with less land, as by the application of new multiple-use techniques, or the innovative planning of smaller and more intensively used facilities.

COMPARATIVE ANALYSIS · P&R LAND HOLDINGS

A serious error persists in much of our recreation planning . . . to judge the demand for recreation facilities solely by observing present recreational habits and multiplying the current participation rates by anticipated future populations . . . there is too facile a tendency to beguile oneself with computing ratios and performing arithmetic operations, as a substitute for meaningful recreational planning activity.

JOHN V. KRUTILLA AND JACK L. KNETSCH
From Annual Report of the Citizens' Advisory Committee on Environmental Quality
Washington, D.C., 1972

variants may demonstrate that *more* land is required on a percentage, or acres per population, basis to meet contemporary needs. Or perhaps they may demonstrate that by innovative planning, *less* acreage may actually be required.

Check area-population ratios

For over a century urban planners have been applying, as a rule of thumb, the ratio of ten acres of well-lying land per thousand population. It has been felt that this should accommodate all municipally owned and operated parks and recreation areas within the metropolitan area. Included would be such special areas as parkways, arboretums, forest preserves, beaches, marinas, city-owned golf courses, cultural and sports centers, plazas and squares. Excluded would be extensive water area, unusable land, school playgrounds and athletic fields, and such private or semiprivate facilities as scout camps, sportsmen's clubs, commercial pools and marinas, residential swimming pools and game courts, and country clubs. Out-of-city or regional parklands would also be excluded.

The acquisition programs in many urbanizing areas are presently based on this time-tested ratio which most authorities believe to be generally sound, although many consider it minimum. On the other hand, few large established cities have been able to achieve such desirable ratios, especially in densely populated districts with soaring land values. It has been proposed that a more realistic standard for cities of 500,000 population would be 8 acres per thousand, while for cities of over a million the figure might drop to 6.

It is not reasonable, of course, to apply one standard across the country uniformly, for each locality has its own special needs and resources. In every case where a standard is used as a guide, the following modifying factors should be considered:

1. Accessibility to other park and recreation areas such as national, state or regional parks, U.S. forests, or state forests.

2. Accessibility to open countryside, woodland, streams, rivers, lakes, seashore, mountains, and other natural attractions.

3. Nature of the locality—rural, urban, suburban, static or growing.

4. Population characteristics such as density, employment, income level, age, habits, and patterns of distribution.

5. Topography and climate.

6. City and regional land-use and traffic plans.

7. Cost and availability of land.

8. Effects of rehabilitation and urban renewal.

9. Private and commercial facilities.

On the following page is a table comparing, for some of the larger cities, the acreage of recreation land provided per thousand citizens.

Check area-percentage ratios

A second approach is that of providing for park and recreation uses a "reasonable percentage" of the total city land area. Roughly 10 percent has been considered adequate for traditional park and recreation land allocation. This assumes that conditions of the land's usability and distribution are ideal, and excludes the land needed as a reserve against population expansion. Again, a consideration of adequacy must include the same factors of modification that have previously been noted.

Even so, such a standard, used alone, ignores the fact of the wide disparity in urban population densities and other characteristics. Ten percent of the total city area allocated to recreation lands would approximate the "recommended" 10 acres per thousand population only where the average density is 10 persons per gross acre. In large cities where the population ratio is much higher, the application of this guideline would clearly fail to provide for even existing needs.

Apply the "planned-system" approach

A third, and more definitive, method of land-requirement calculation is suggested. Stated simply, it is proposed that in planning for the needs of a metropolitan region, or any part thereof, the first step should be the preparation of a comprehensive program for a complete and interrelated park, recreation, and open space *system*. Each component and facility to be provided should be described and listed, together with the type and amount of land or water area required. Such a program should be based upon both current and projected planning data and a fresh analysis of emerging social patterns. Then, on the basis of an ecological survey, the program would be applied to the regional diagram and fitted with sensitivity to the landscape. The proposed plan could then be viewed as a whole and tested on the basis of performance. Everything would work well together, because it was planned that way.

A tabulation of the land needed to accommodate this system and to provide sufficient land reserves to assure bufferage and flexibility will give the most, and only, realistic projection of area requirements. Such a plan will indicate also the location and the priority of desirable

Recreation land–population ratio comparisons

City	1970 Population [1]	Area for park and recreation lands [2]	Ratio: acres per thousand population
Boston	641,071	6,900	10.76
Denver	514,678	16,686	32.42
Detroit	1,511,482	5,954	3.94
Houston	1,232,802	4,762	3.86
Kansas City	507,087	7,355	14.50
Los Angeles	2,816,061	15,947	5.66
Memphis	623,530	4,981	7.99
Milwaukee	717,099	14,264	19.89
New Orleans	593,468	442	0.74
Philadelphia	1,948,609	9,822	5.04
Phoenix	581,562	18,696	32.15
San Antonio	654,153	4,455	6.81

Area-percentage ratio comparisons

City	Total area (acres)	Area for park and recreation lands [2]	Percentage ratio of park and recreation to total
Boston	29,440	6,900	23.44%
Denver	60,928	16,686	27.39
Detroit	88,320	5,954	6.74
Houston	277,696	4,762	1.72
Kansas City	202,752	7,355	3.63
Los Angeles	296,768	15,947	5.37
Memphis	138,496	4,981	3.60
Milwaukee	60,800	14,264	23.46
New Orleans	126,144	442	0.35
Philadelphia	82,240	9,822	11.94
Phoenix	158,656	18,696	11.78
San Antonio	117,760	4,455	3.78

Source: U.S. Department of Commerce for year 1970.

1. Comparable data for 1980 or later not available.

2. Exclusive of other open space lands.

land acquisition, a situation much preferable to the norm, in which the recreation program is determined by arbitrary patterns of land-taking.

Ensure optimum distribution

Fully as important as the *amount* of land is its proper *distribution*. Some cities, of necessity, have had to acquire land where and as it became available. Others have developed tracts of land which are no longer well located in relation to their purpose. Those cities which have landholdings comprised of many unsuitable or inaccessible parcels—or which continue to maintain outmoded parks—impose upon their citizens a high development and operational cost while providing a low quality and quantity of recreation opportunities. How then are recreation ways and places best located?

One determinant is that they will be *people oriented*. They will serve best when each component of the system is placed as close as possible to the people who will use it.

The better recreation places will also be *resource oriented*. They will be so situated as to take fullest possible advantage of the outstanding natural and man-made features of the locality—its hills, valleys, streams, and perhaps a lake or harbor, as well as its circulation nodes, landmarks, and activity centers.

In the light of these two criteria it is proposed that in neighborhoods and communities particularly, the conventional central-park concept be reconsidered. The neighborhood playfields will be placed adjacent to the elementary school and the community athletic fields adjacent to the junior-senior high schools—all in combined *school-parks* operated by the school and park authorities jointly. Such school-parks will then become true neighborhood and community centers, open year round, daytimes, evenings, and weekends. The park playfields and courts will be available for use in the school athletic courses without duplication. The school meeting rooms, auditorium, rest rooms, locker rooms, and gym will be used in the after-school and summer recreation programs, again without duplication, and make use of the school's trained teaching staff and fully equipped physical plant.

The many smaller park and recreation elements will be located throughout the neighborhoods. In the densely built-up apartment districts of the city these will have to be distributed where space can be found. They will become the neighborhood mini-parks, the block gathering places, the hose and hydrant "splash" courts, a basketball backstop on a 20- x 30-foot strip of paving, a bench or two set in the shade of a sycamore tree, or a space in which to set up chairs around a mobile television, projector, or sound unit.

In the more open residential areas, portions of the neighborhood parks will be linked to such natural features as streams, rock outcrops, or a commanding hilltop and may be left completely natural, or improved with a parking space or shelter. Dispersed units of the community park and recreation system may even take the form of mowed floodplain meadows, miles-long bicycle paths, or shaded sitting enclaves around the city reservoirs. The possibilities for new types of parks and new approaches to recreation planning are limitless.

Certain it is that recreation needs are changing and that these needs must be satisfied. Perhaps the most significant feature of the parks and recreation facilities of the next decade will be innovative patterns of distribution.

Join in comprehensive planning efforts

The pattern of recreation uses, as well as that of all other land uses and trafficways, can be meaningful only if integrated with a comprehensive plan for the entire metropolitan region. Each political subdivision, with its own planning staff or professional consultants, must plan for its own local needs. These efforts must be coordinated with those of city and county planning agencies, which in turn will form a working relationship through a regional planning commission, association, or council with other agencies on a regional or statewide basis. The activities within each state in turn, are best coordinated through a strong central agency or council such as Wisconsin's Department of Natural Resources, Vermont's Agency of Environmental Conservation, or Pennsylvania's Department of Environmental Resources. Only through orderly planning processes can the needs of the people at each governmental level be defined and accommodated. And only through enlightened state leadership can the multiplicity of demands be balanced and brought into consonance with federal programs and the flow of state and federal funds.

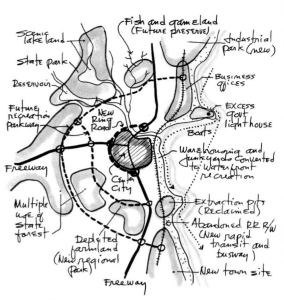

A SYSTEM OF INTERCONNECTED PARK AND RECREATION LANDS

Acquire the sites

Although funds for development may not be available, or the specific needs fully established, suitable lands should be acquired, or reserved through zoning, while they are still available and before their cost becomes prohibitive. During the past few years both state and federal governments have done much to stimulate wise acquisition through the provision of legislation, guidance, and financial aid.

Devise a network of recreation-land connectors

Parkways, aerial tramways, rail transit, busways, boats, bicycle paths, and pedestrian routes may be aligned, where compatible, through:

1. Abandoned railroad, trolley, or canal rights-of-way.

2. Redevelopment areas.

3. Utility easements.

4. Reclaimed dumps, junkyards, landfills, strip mines, borrow sites, and gravel pits.

5. Depleted farm or forest land.

6. Agricultural lands, on scenic or conservation easements.

7. Private holdings such as golf courses and planned subdivisions.

8. Public open space lands as a multiple use.

9. Continuous topographical systems such as ridges, watercourses, ravine and valley drainageways, floodplains and wetlands.

Plan a regional open space system

Recreation places and open space lands are best considered together as integral parts of a regional open space plan. This will greatly increase recreation opportunities, while at the same time yielding many other side benefits. It will conserve woodlands and forest, ensure the continued agricultural use of farmlands and watersheds threatened by spot development. It will protect water reserves by retaining runoff, reduce the siltation of streams and water bodies, and afford relief from flooding. It will insulate residential areas from airports, commercial, and industrial areas. It will create natural breaks and breathing spaces. It will provide for routes of interconnection between centers of urbanization. It will at the same time preserve as part of the regional environment its scenic, historic, and ecologic treasures.

Once designated, the permanance of the open space domain must be ensured by public dedication, easements, purchase or gift, and by appropriate zoning.

I assert the environmental policy of the state . . . (region) . . . to be that all practicable means and measures shall be used, in a manner calculated to foster and promote the general welfare, to create and maintain conditions under which man and nature can exist in productive harmony, to protect the cleanliness of the air and the purity of the . . . waters and to protect the natural, scenic, historic and aesthetic qualities of the . . . environment for the benefit of this and future generations.

JOHN N. DEMPSEY
An Environmental Policy for Connecticut
Report of the Governor's Committee on
Environmental Policy
New Haven, Conn., 1970

The environmental impact statement

In recent years, as a condition of obtaining governmental grants in aid, zoning, or in some cases a construction or excavation permit, it is frequently required that an applicant submit a statement describing the anticipated impacts of the proposed use. In other cases information must be supplied from which the reviewing agency will itself assess the impacts. Bureaucracy being what it is, it can be imagined that from locality to locality and from agency to agency the requirements for such a statement are far from uniform. It can also be foreseen that the amount and detail of information considered necessary will be constantly expanded and elaborated upon until whole shelves full of plans and studies may be demanded for a single application. The insistence by the reviewing agency of such exhaustive submissions often results in unreasonable delays or severe financial hardship. This is far from the intent of the congressional sponsors who originally recognized the need and value of an environmental impact assessment, and envisioned it as a concise exhibit appended to the project proposal at the time of its review. Its essential features were to be—and continue to be:

1. A description of the location and nature of the project and a tentative construction schedule.

2. A listing of all foreseeable *negative* impacts, their degree of severity, and the means by which they have been ameliorated insofar as feasible in the project planning.

3. A listing of all the *positive* environmental features and implications, and a notation as to how these benefits have been increased through scientific analysis and competent design.

4. An accurate appraisal of the overall community gain or loss.

These are the basic elements of a sound impact statement. They, and the data to support them, are all that is actually needed.

Impact assessments must be reasonable as to the kinds and amount of information required. They must be objective and fair if the process, and the environmental cause, is to gain and hold public support. Rights in property are to be respected and the possible alternative uses of the land considered. It would be patently wrong and irresponsible, for example, to deny the use of a property for long-term development as a planned community "because it would have adverse effects"—when the use was in accordance with the regional plan, when the carrying capacities of the land were not exceeded, and when there was no reason to expect any other use of the property except uncontrolled parcel-by-parcel construction. Judgments in each case should rather be based on the central question "In the light of feasible possibilities, would or would not the project proposed be in the best long-range public good?" The foreseeable alternatives must be weighed one against the other. It must also be recognized that all land uses—even farms, parks, and playgrounds—have their negative impacts too.

The best and most logical means of assessing the environmental impacts of an extensive or long-term project is by staged and supplementary submissions. This is in all ways consistent with accepted planned community development (PCD) procedures. The first-phase submission would be based on the overall use and design concept. It would deal mainly with the questions of whether the project was compatible with community goals and appropriate to the site and whether it would be, *in sum*, of social and economic benefit. If the conceptual plan were approved, succeeding submissions would build upon the assumption that the overall project was justified, and would deal only with that level of detail necessary to assure that the component parts, as further studied and brought under review, were consonant with—or an improvement upon—the original proposal. Each component as reviewed would be expected to prove its own case as a sound and workable unit.

A proper environmental assessment, or a more complete and official EIS (environmental impact statement), is not to be considered as a *final test* to be applied after the plans are completed. It best serves its purpose if started concurrently with the initiation of the planning process and is used throughout as a checklist and guide in the comparative analysis of the various studies. The final report then becomes in effect a summary statement of planning accomplishment. Together with that data *which is essential*, it will describe the proposed plan as it has evolved, and discuss its suitability and impacts.

Already, in the relatively short time during which they have been a requirement, impact statements have been remarkably effective in reducing misuses and abuses. They hold great promise provided they gain and maintain continuing public endorsement. To this end it is important that review procedures be constantly improved. Improvement will come in the form of centralized governmental responsibility, simplification, and the processing of the more extensive projects in supplementary increments. Each level of government will request only that information necessary for a determination of impacts at its level of jurisdiction. Clearly, whenever a local government is capable of making its own determination of local effects and values, it should have the right to decide.

Start the "EIS" early

Begin with a comprehensive listing of all the environmental concerns and an indication as to how each is to be addressed. Initiate those investigations which will be necessary. Determine and apply to the planning acceptable quality standards and criteria. Use the checklist in comparing and "weighting" the alternative plans. Let the studies respond to the findings—since a sound plan and a meaningful impact analysis should interact. Let the statement develop with the plan.

Work with the agencies

Start at the top. Contact and discuss with each department down the line the problems and possibilities. Borrow from the experience and

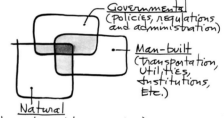

Governmental
(Policies, regulations and administration)

Man-built
(Transportation, Utilities, Institutions, Etc.)

Natural
(The ecological basis of life)

No Environmental planning considerations can be meaningful unless they respond to, and meet the requirements of, all three interacting systems.

THE THREE CONTROLLING SYSTEMS

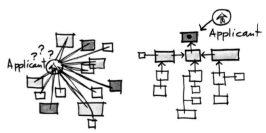

Applicant

Applicant

In all matters relating to environmental protection, resource management, and the review of development proposals by governmental agencies— it is essential that a clear chain of command be established, and authority centralized.

STREAMLINE THE AGENCY REVIEWS

283

insight of those who are closest to the scene. Obtain the latest directives and materials. Return periodically to discuss the proposals as they develop. Project review is best accomplished through cooperative planning sessions and workshops. The ideal impact statement would be a simple confirmation of concensus.

Reduce the negative effects

At best these would be eliminated entirely. Seldom is this possible. In the construction stage, at least, such adverse consequences as noise, erosion, glare, and temporary stress are almost inevitable. It should be demonstrated, however, that all such problems have been considered and that effective measures have been taken to reduce to acceptable levels all forms of pollution or disruption.

Increase the safeguards and benefits

At the same time that the adverse effects of a proposed development are being reduced through conscientious study, the positive values should be maximized. It should be remembered that the worth of a project to a community is the ratio of its *total* benefits over its *total* economic and social cost.

Conduct the environmental impact analysis in a constructive vein

If treated as "another governmental imposition" and approached on the defensive, it will be largely negative! If, conversely, it is recognized as a highly effective means by which the "fit" of a project may be assured, its stress minimized, and its lasting benefits increased, the analysis may prove helpful in many ways.

It can be a bridge to the responsible agencies.

It can be a method of systematic testing.

It can be a means of demonstrating, and publicizing, the attributes of a proposal.

It can give solid evidence that the petitioning agency or group is in fact doing its best to protect the environmental integrity of the region and serve the best interests of its people.

Regional government

There can be no doubt that in an urbanizing region there is need for planning which looks beyond the boundaries of the governmental jurisdictions of which it is composed. Planning cannot stop at the city or township line. Transportation, utilities, and park and recreation systems, for example, can only be designed effectively on a regionwide basis. This is especially true of the whole range of environmental considerations such as energy production, waste disposal, air pollution, water quality, and resource planning, each of which requires the broader point of view. A persuasive case can also be made for areawide traffic regulations, courts, schools, zoning, and even government itself.

Where each jurisdiction has its own, and often conflicting, codes and regulations, or where tax millages, or the quality of schools and education vary widely, there are bound to be tensions born of the inequities; there is confusion; and there is wasteful duplication of funds and effort. The more crucial result of such

A negative policy of not disturbing the old cannot . . . for long succeed.

We must *disturb [the landscape] to survive . . .*

The answer ". . . is the conscious adaptation of our habitat to new conditions by controlled land use planning."
 NAN FAIRBROTHER
New Lives, New Landscapes
Architectural Press
London, 1970

myopic planning, however, is the sporadic, piecemeal mishmashing of the landscape.

This lack of coordination—a condition which prevails in our country—points to the need for a mechanism by which those concerns which are regional in nature may be approached on an areawide basis. There are several possibilities, each of which has been tried with varying degrees of success. The most direct is the consolidation of smaller governmental units into a countywide, or regionwide, *metro* government with the authority to perform certain well-defined functions. Another approach is that of a council of local governments, with proportionate representation and a permanent working staff to tackle mutual problems. Or a regional *authority* may be formed, by state charter, to handle some particular aspect of the regional planning and operation. Again, the various political units may make per capita contributions toward a cooperative study by a permanent staff or a team of consultants selected for this purpose. In a more general sense, it is incumbent upon the state to provide regional planning guidelines, financial incentives, and model legislation.

Whatever the means, it is only through multijurisdictional cooperation that the benefits of regional *systems* may be realized.

Consider the metro form of government

There are many arguments in its favor. By the consolidation of departments and staff, endless duplications of planning and operation are eliminated and performance improved. Combined systems of streets, utilities, and recreation areas, for example, are more efficiently constructed and maintained. Costs are lowered; levels of service raised; and built-in continuity assured.

The chief deterrent to such cooperative effort is, of course, the reluctance of each local government to relinquish its sovereign powers. Since this is understandable, a precondition of consolidation must be a guarantee that each locality can preserve its own identity, retain its administrative leadership, and continue to perform those functions particular to its needs.

The more successful metro governments are those in which broad underlying powers have been vested by charter, but to which have been delegated by the constituents only those specific assignments which are clearly best handled on an overall regional basis.

Form an interim coalition

Until such a time as a full-scale regional agency can be organized, or perhaps in its place, there are many means by which cooperative planning may be achieved. Joint study committees, coordinating councils, or authorities may be formed to carry out a wide variety of assignments. It is desirable, but not necessary, that all political units within the study area be represented. It is only necessary that each political subdivision have the opportunity to review and approve, or reject, the proposals that affect it.

Look to the state to help in regional planning

The help is there, or should be. Most states have enabling legislation by which they may delegate the needed powers to regional governments. Others are prepared to furnish planning assistance through one or more of their agencies. Many are able to provide financial incentives on a participating basis.

If any plan or research program is to be successfully applied, it must have strong public backing, financial especially. To this end, planners and engineers should present to the public an accurate picture of the conditions actually existing in their community or metropolitan area, and the reasons why a given plan is necessary for their own individual protection and benefit.

H. LOREN THOMPSON
Environmental Engineering and Metropolitan Planning
Northwestern University Press
Evanston, Ill., 1962

Reason must prevail.
JOEL KUPERBERG
In conversation

Further Reading:

Blunden, John, ed., et al.
Regional Analysis and Development
Harper & Row, Publishers, Inc.
New York, 1973

Bosselman, Fred, and David Callies
The Quiet Revolution in Land Use Controls
Prepared for the Council on Environmental Quality
U.S. Government Printing Office
Washington, D.C., 1971

Brower, David, ed.
Wildlands in Our Civilization
Sierra Club
San Francisco, 1964

Ehrlich, Paul R., et al.
Human Ecology: Problems and Solutions
W. H. Freeman
San Francisco, 1973

Eltringham, S. K.
Wildlife Resources and Economic Development
John Wiley & Sons, Inc.
New York, 1984

Fairbrother, Nan
New Lives: New Landscape: Planning for the Twenty-first Century
Alfred A. Knopf, Inc.
New York, 1970

Glikson, Arthur
The Ecological Basis of Planning
Edited by Lewis Mumford
Nijhoff
The Hague, Netherlands, 1971

Hall, Peter
The Theory and Practice of Regional Planning
Pemberton Books
London, 1970

Isard, Walter, et al.
Ecologic-economic Analysis for Regional Development
The Free Press
New York, 1972

Jackson, John Brickerhoff
Discovering the Vernacular Landscape
Yale University Press
New Haven, Conn., 1984

The new land ethic

Looking back, we find we owe much to the pioneers. Those hardy men and women were imbued with the New World spirit of getting ahead, of seeking new opportunities, of competition, free enterprise, of using their hands and their minds and their ingenuity to open up the land and "conquer the wilderness." But in their zeal they viewed the land as a limitless resource. It was there to be claimed, farmed, mined, or cut over for timber until the resource was expended. Then they "pulled up stakes" and moved on. Always there seemed to be more and better land ahead . . . to be used, and again exploited.

There were notable exceptions to the general despoliation. There were homesteads and farms well cared for; there were villages and towns well planned; there were holdings of land well managed. But though the open land has long since been claimed, the bent for exploitation has persisted, sometimes with devastating effects. Until recently the public has lacked the power to check the flagrant misuse of land or its disastrous consequences. The traditional attitude has been "It's my land and I'll do with it what I damn please, and nobody's going to stop me." This attitude on the part of individuals, corporations, and governmental agencies is now at last being challenged.

There is an emerging view that each parcel of land is related to all others, and that land use should be so limited as to preclude adverse effects on the neighbors or the environs. It is at the regional level that this new approach is becoming most evident. It is now being stated, and accepted as governmental policy, that a projected use for any property may be allowed provided—and only provided—that it is consistent with the long-range community goals, compatible with contiguous land uses, and buildable without significant damage to the environment, and provided that adequate public services are, or will be, available.

These criteria are so new that in most localities they have not as yet been formalized by code or ordinance, or by workable review and permitting procedures. But the concept has been widely accepted, and in many areas it is presently being tacitly enforced.

This changing concept of land rights and use is of great significance. It has now become fundamental to the planning of every developing region.

The essence of good planning

It is possible that the evaluation of sound regional planning can be reduced to four simple tests:

1. *Is the proposed use suitable?*

It must first be ascertained that the land or water area is to be devoted to its "highest and best use" consistent with federal, state, and regional land-use plans (if these have been formulated) and with community goals.

2. *Can it be built without exceeding the carrying capacity of the land?*

The use should not be permitted if it would impose significant stress upon the natural systems. In case of question the filing of a simplified environmental assessment statement could well be required. This would describe the nature of the project, its negative impacts (there are always some), and its benefits (which should outweigh the negative effects). The statement should address itself to at least the following checklist of environmental considerations:

1. Natural ecological systems

2. Water supply and quality

3. Air quality

4. Noise pollution

5. Erosion

6. Flooding

7. Historic sites

8. Landscape features

9. Flora and fauna (rare or endangered species)

10. Open space integrity

3. *Will it be a good neighbor?*

Is the proposed use complementary and complimentary to the existing and proposed uses in the neighborhood? Or will it have harmful physical or visual effects? Will it reduce property values or force tax increases? Will it destroy, or preserve, cherished landmarks? A well-conceived, well-designed project—be it a bridge, service station, home, or play lot—should enhance, not harm, its environs.

4. *Can adequate levels of public service be provided?*

At all stages of its construction and use the proposed improvement should have available all public services required, without overloading of trafficways, power or water supply systems, storm sewers, waste treatment plants, fire and police facilities, and (in the case of residential development) the schools and recreation areas. Not only should all such facilities be "on-line" when needed, but the local government should be assured that the developers and users will bear their fair share of the cost.

If these four questions can be answered "yes," there should be no reason for opposition. The proposed development should make a welcome contribution to the diversity, and vitality, of the region.

Further Reading (cont.):

Lovejoy, Derek, ed.
Land Use and Landscape Planning Techniques
Barnes & Noble, Inc.
New York, 1973

MacDougall, E. Bruce
Micro-computers in Landscape Architecture
Elsevier Science Publishing Company
New York, 1983

Mackaye, Benton
The New Exploration: a Philosophy of Regional Planning
University of Illinois Press
Urbana, Ill., 1962

Passmore, John
Man's Responsibilities for Nature; Ecological Problems and Western Traditions
Scribner
New York, 1974

Real Estate Research Corporation
Infill Development Strategies
Urban Land Institute and American Planning Association
Washington, D.C., 1982

Reilly, William K., ed.
The Use of Land: A Citizen's Policy Guide to Urban Growth
(Sponsored by Rockefeller Brothers Fund)
Thomas Y. Crowell Co.
New York, 1973

Smart, Eric
Making Infill Projects Work
Urban Land Institute and Lincoln Institute of Land Policy
Washington, D.C., 1985

Smart, Eric et al., in conjunction with the Recreational Council of ULI
Recreational Development Handbook
Urban Land Institute
Washington, D.C., 1981

Strahler, Arthur N. and Alan H.
Environmental Geoscience: Interaction Between Natural Systems and Man
Hamilton Publishing Co.
Santa Barbara, Calif., 1973

U.S. Outdoor Recreation Resources Review Commission
Outdoor Recreation for America
Study report: 27 volumes on specific topics
U.S. Government Printing Office
Washington, D.C., 1962

10 Dynamic conservation

. . . to promote greater knowledge
about the earth's resources—its
waters, soils, minerals, plant and
animal life; to initiate research
and education concerning these
resources and their relation to
each other; to ascertain the most
effective methods of making them
available and useful to people; to
assess population trends and
their effect upon environment;
finally, to encourage human
conduct to sustain and enrich
life on earth.

The Conservation Foundation
A statement of purpose
The Conservation Foundation Annual Report of 1964
New York, 1964

Conservation, in its generally accepted meaning, is defined as the wise use of our resources.

Conservation is intelligent cooperation with nature.

Conservation is humanity caring for the future.
NANCY NEWHALL as quoted in
Encounters with the Archdruid
By John McPhee
Farrar, Straus and Giroux, Inc.
New York, 1971

The conservation idea covers a wider range than the field of natural resources alone. Conservation means the greatest good to the greatest number for the longest time. One of its great contributions is just this, that it has added to the worn and well-known phrase, "the greatest good to the greatest number," the additional words, "for the longest time," thus recognizing that this nation of ours must be made to endure as the best possible home for all its people.
GIFFORD PINCHOT, quoted in
Annual Report of the Citizens' Advisory Committee
on Environmental Quality
Washington, D.C., 1972

The practice of conservation is an act of patriotism and the understanding of it, the preaching of it, and the contribution to it, are parts of the fundamental duties of a citizen in a free society.
SHERMAN ADAMS
As quoted in *Conservation Quotes*
U.S. Department of the Interior,
National Park Service
January 1953

Conservation need not be static—the unreasoning and jealous safeguarding of the status quo. It is not inimical to either development or progress. Indeed, true progress can be attained only when development and conservation are carried forward hand in hand, when they are planned together, and are complementary.

As a systematic approach to the care and wise use of our earthscape, the conservation movement has four chief goals. The first is the protection of the world ecosystem in such a manner and to such a degree that life and health on our planet may be sustained. This entails the *preservation* of those critical lands and waters which are vital to the life-giving food chain, to the relative stability of our water edges and landforms, and which are necessary to the replenishment of our aquifers. A second goal is the *conservation* of an adequate supply of open space lands. These may be used for many purposes such as farming, forestry, or recreation, provided the use be such that the essential quality of the landscape remains unimpaired. A third concern is the allocation of ample and suitable land for all types of *development*, and the regulation of construction and operations to preclude all forms of pollution. A fourth and equally important aspect of conservation is to ensure the use of our lands and waters in such a way that their educational, and scenic values may be maximized.

A new and creative approach to conservation envisions a grand strategy for resource management and environmental protection. It calls upon the federal government, every state, and each local jurisdiction to formulate and implement its own plan of action.

A comprehensive plan*

In addressing the central issues of resource management and environmental protection, each state and local government is in need of a workable plan of action. While varying from locality to locality in scope and particulars, the essential features of each plan will be much the same.

Its purpose will be the application of planning, legal, and management techniques to promote the optimum use of natural and man-made assets and to assure the best possible life for all citizens at least social and economic cost.

The comprehensive plan will deal with such natural attributes as rivers, beaches, and forests and their best utilization. It will seek to conserve the farmlands, fisheries, mineral deposits, and freshwater reserves. It will concern itself with matters relating to growth and population distribution. It will act to set guidelines for future planning and responsible development. It will take steps to preclude pollution and environmental degradation in any significant form. And it will look to the future to provide those measures necessary to bring the landscape, people, and their habitations and constructions into sound relationships.

* With thanks to the Florida Department of Administration, Division of State Planning, for permission to include excerpts from the publication *State Comprehensive Plan.*

The comprehensive plan will describe for each area of concern a statement of purpose or *goal* toward which effort will be directed. Each *goal* will be supported and amplified by a list of specific *policies*, or recommendations for action. These in sum, will constitute the plan.

While each locality will have its own special problems, possibilities, and priorities—the following listing of goals and policies is suggested as a good working start.

1. Planning and research

Goal: To devise and apply a systematic approach to the process of data gathering, analysis, programming, planning, and resource management.

Policies: (*Note:* Policy statements are to be prepared describing recommended action in the various areas of concern. This sample listing may be expanded or modified as appropriate.)

1. Organization
2. Authority and governmental relationships
3. Advisory board
4. Centralization of plan coordination
5. Mandatory submission by other agencies of all land-water use proposals
6. Interagency and interdepartmental liaison
7. Survey, research, and other grants
8. Map and study assembly
9. Planning approach
10. Review procedures
11. Public participation
12. The plan and report
13. Implementation
14. Exercise of controls

2. Inventory of resources

Goal: To survey and record on a scientific and continuing basis the location, nature, and condition of all physical resources.

Policies:
1. Survey coordination
2. Methods of data gathering, storage, and retrieval
3. Standardization of base maps, terms, and format
4. Natural systems
5. Man-made systems
6. Freshwater supply
7. Topographic, geologic, hydrologic, ecologic, and other investigations
8. Agricultural and forest lands
9. Submerged lands, wetlands, and estuaries
10. Unique natural and scenic features

3. Growth and population

Goal: To formulate a procedure for establishing the optimum population and distribution patterns based on land-carrying capacities.

Policies:
1. Current demographic profiles
2. Population and growth projections
3. Independent study of land-water tolerances by indexed land unit
4. Definition of a generalized land-use plan
5. Delineation of growth areas
6. Public service extension alternatives
7. Study of social, economic, and growth dependencies
8. Comparative analysis of options
9. Optimum land use, growth, and public service matrix
10. Guidelines for implementation

4. Land development

Goal: To provide the conceptual and administrative framework for sound and creative development.

Policies:
1. Long-range objectives
2. The conceptual model (plan)
3. Zoning
4. Growth management
5. Transfer of development rights
6. High-benefit, low-impact development
7. Planning guidelines
8. Controls and incentives
9. Private rights in property
10. Public landholdings
11. Interagency coordination
12. Reviews of development proposals
13. Adjustments to the model
14. The public interest

5. Housing

Goal: To assure sound and agreeable housing and neighborhood environs for all citizens.

Policies:
1. Acceptable standards
2. The existing condition
3. Measure of need
4. The private sector
5. The public role
6. Rehabilitation
7. Planning aid and incentives
8. Cluster development
9. Planned communities
10. New towns

6. Urbanization

Goal: To facilitate the shaping of urban centers that will express and accommodate contemporary life at its most intensive level of interchange.

Policies:
1. Urban sprawl
2. Urban renewal
3. Need for intensive activity centers
4. The alternatives
5. Types and locations
6. Conceptual guidelines
7. The car and the city
8. Rapid transit linkage
9. Cargo movement and servicing
10. Urban open spaces

7. Parks, recreation, and open space

Goal: To create a permanent land-water open space system, together with interrelated recreation areas and parks.

Policies:
1. New approaches
2. A balanced system
3. Ridges, water edges, and floodplains
4. Paths of movement
5. Land acquisition
6. Holding patterns and interim uses
7. Community recreation
8. The school-park
9. Other multiple-use opportunities
10. Environmental attributes

8. Environmental protection

Goal: To prevent the degradation of the earth, air, water, natural systems, or man-made environment.

Policies:
1. Ecologic survey
2. Evaluation of capacities and tolerances
3. A total program
4. Standards and criteria
5. Monitoring
6. Recommended procedures
7. Review of land-use proposals
8. Assessment of impacts
9. Regulation and control
10. Reclamation and restoration
11. Research
12. Public education

9. Goods and services

Goal: To relate levels of production to the best long-range utilization of reusable, renewable, and finite resources.

Policies:
1. Inventory
2. Projection of needs
3. Alternative sources of supply
4. Reduction of use
5. Increased production efficiency
6. Matching production to supply
7. Conversion
8. Recycling by regulation

10. Transportation

Goal: To promote a unified system of transportation, transit, and transmission facilities of the highest order.

Policies:
1. The present network
2. New modes and techniques
3. Transportation as a structuring element
4. Urban activity centers
5. Regional satellite nodes
6. Streets and highways
7. Transit
8. The movement of cargo
9. Transmission
10. Joint-use corridors

11. Energy production and distribution

Goal: To so regulate energy demands and production as to bring them into better balance with resources.

Policies:
1. Present needs and facilities
2. Projected demands
3. Regulation of consumption
4. The planning of more self-sufficient communities
5. Improved building and automotive design
6. Increased production efficiency
7. Solid-waste conversion
8. New installations
9. Alternative sources of power
10. Energy as a regulator of growth
11. Impacts and control

12. Agricultural use of the land

Goal: To preserve the integrity of agricultural landholdings.

Policies:
1. Definition of prime agricultural lands
2. Classification by types and use
3. Agriculture as the basic zoning classification
4. The halt of "scatteration"
5. Tax and other incentives
6. Reduction of zoned development land inventories
7. Reassembly
8. Soil and water conservation
9. Restoration and reforestation

Brower [describing the creation of the world] invites his listeners to consider the six days of Genesis as a figure of speech for what has in fact been four billion years. On this scale, a day equals something like six hundred and sixty-six million years, and thus "all day Monday and until Tuesday noon, creation was busy getting the earth going." Life began Tuesday noon, and "the beautiful, organic wholeness of it" developed over the next four days. "At 4 P.M. Saturday, the big reptiles came on. Five hours later, when the redwoods appeared, there were no more big reptiles. At three minutes before midnight, man appeared. At one fourth of a second before midnight, Christ arrived. At one-fortieth of a second before midnight, the Industrial Revolution began. We are surrounded with people who think that what we have been doing for that one-fortieth of a second can go on indefinitely. They are considered normal, but they are stark, raving mad.

DAVID BROWER *as quoted in*
Encounters with the Archdruid
Copyright © 1971 by John McPhee
Farrar, Straus and Giroux, Inc.
New York, 1971

Natural and scenic resources

The land and water expanses of planet Earth have fed and supported man from the time of his beginnings. Wherever his first forays or later migrations have led him, he has stood in awe of the wonder and beauty of the landscape unfolding before him. He first learned to gather its bounty and then to cultivate its plains and hillsides for the production of food and fiber. For thousands of centuries he learned to make his peace with nature, devising intricate religious rites in efforts to assure an abundance of water, game, and crops. Nature was to be revered and propitiated. The relationship between man and environment has been, in the main, direct and rewarding.

It is only within the past few centuries that the people of the Western world, in their arrogance, have set out to conquer nature, to wrest from her meadows, forests, and waters far more than required to meet human needs—to deplete, lay waste, and to squander. It is this new contemptuous attitude toward nature to which we, haplessly, have fallen heir. It is this recently acquired habit of wanton destruction, this acceptance of mass slaughter of wildlife to the point of extinction, this compulsion to reshape and reorder the landforms and waterways, that has led us in the United States to ravish and befoul to a shameful degree this "Land that we love."

We have joined the Western cultures, and lately even those of the East, in a frenzy of ruthless exploitation. As our attitude toward nature has changed, as our technical capacity for devastation has increased, and as our population has doubled, redoubled, and redoubled again, we have taxed the ecosystem to the breaking point. We have threatened, on a massive scale, the biosphere itself. Those scientists whose work it is to study our relationship to nature have amply documented their warnings that unless we drastically change our ways, the realm of nature, as we have known and enjoyed it, is doomed to rapid and certain destruction. Within our lifetime and that of our children one-fourth of our land will have been drained, leveled, built upon, or paved. Our lakes and seas may have succumed to eutrophication, and the air we breathe may have become charged with fumes to the point of near suffocation.

Yet there is room for encouragement. Within the present decade our country has been stirred by a sense of revulsion at the prevailing condition. There is an urgent demand for reform. There is a new yearning for a way of life again attuned to nature's way. There is emerging a whole new ethic of environmental protection. And there is still time, for nature possesses a boundless capacity for self-healing and regeneration.

To end exploitation and pollution; to relearn, expand, and teach an understanding of the natural processes; to preserve and conserve the best of our resources; and to bring our development, and our lives, into harmony with the world of nature about us: these are the goals, and this the new role, of a reoriented, intensified, and compelling conservation movement.

Protect the superlatives

Thanks to the efforts of such dedicated conservationists as John Muir, Theodore Roosevelt, Gifford Pinchot, Laurance Rockefeller, David Brower, Russell Train, and untold legions of their peers, our national heritage of lands and waters preserved in the public domain is rich beyond measure. Thousands of square miles of scenic lands, forest preserve, fish and game sanctuary, and watershed have been acquired by the federal and state governments to be held and administered for the long-range good of our citizens.

Yet there is still much "labor in the vineyards," if the remaining areas of critical concern are to be spared from destruction. Such areas are those unique to the nation, its states, and to all localities—in terms of ecological contribution, recreational use, and scenic, historic, or cultural values. Each governmental unit, acting in the best interest of the people it represents, has the clear obligation to acquire by purchase or easement those threatened resources of most importance. All other lands and waters of regional, state, or national concern are to be protected by new or existing legislation, by those agencies which are responsible, and with all the powers that they can command.

In this regard a national land-use policy providing incentives and guidelines to the states for comprehensive land-use planning is an instrument of great promise.

One of the most important legacies that we can bequeath to future generations is an expanse of protected land and waters that will enrich the opportunities for recreation and make the wonders of the earth and sea available to all who wish to learn from and enjoy them.

Only two kinds of landscape are fully satisfying. One is primeval nature undisturbed by man; we shall have less and less of it as the world population increases. The other is one in which man has toiled and created through trial and error a kind of harmony between himself and the physical environment. What we long for is rarely nature in the raw; more often it is an atmosphere suited to human limitations, and determined by emotional aspirations engendered during centuries of civilized life. The charm of the New England or Pennsylvania Dutch countryside should not be taken for granted, as a product of chance. It did not result from man's conquest of nature. Rather it is the expression of a subtle process through which the natural environment was humanized, yet retained its own individual genius.
RENÉ DUBOS
Environmental Improvement (Air, Water, & Soil)
The Graduate School,
U.S. Department of Agriculture
Washington, D.C., 1966

Environment moulds our minds more than a textbook.
RICHARD NEUTRA
An interview
Architectural Record
January 1966

Despite our long preoccupation with urban problems and resource planning, we have not yet been able to formulate a workable plan for national growth.

The conservation of our natural resources and their proper use constitute the fundamental problem which underlies almost every other problem of our national life.

THEODORE ROOSEVELT

For conservation of the human spirit, we need such places as Everglades National Park where we may be more keenly aware of our Creator's infinitely varied, infinitely beautiful, and infinitely bountiful handiwork. Here we may draw strength and peace of mind from our surroundings. . . . Here we can truly understand what the Psalmist meant where he sang: "He maketh me to lie down in green pastures, He leadeth me beside the still waters; He restoreth my soul."

HARRY S. TRUMAN

The National Park System of the United States already represents a dream come true—a dream so splendid that it is difficult to appreciate its reality.

RAY LYMAN WILBUR

The national parks of America represent as wise an investment as the American people have ever made. It is an investment in health, recreation, education and in something as simple and as profound as love of country—love of the unique and wonderful natural fabric that is the foundation of America.

Editorial, *The New York Times*

There is nothing so American as our national parks. The scenery and wildlife are native. The fundamental idea behind the parks is native. It is, in brief, that the country belongs to the people.

FRANKLIN D. ROOSEVELT

It is interesting to note that the principle of keeping untouched the choicest parts of the American landscape has not only met the unquestioning approval of all its people, but the system has fairly been adopted into the life of the folk.

NATHANIEL SHALER

Cities call—I have heard them. But there is no voice in all the world so insistent to me as the wordless call of these mountains. I shall go back. Those who go once always hope to go back. The lure of the great free spaces is in their blood.

MARY ROBERTS RINEHART

Climb the mountains
  and get their good tidings;
Nature's peace will flow into you
  as sunshine into flowers;
The winds will blow their freshness
  into you and the storms
  their energy, and cares
  will drop off like autumn leaves.

JOHN MUIR
Quotations selected from *Conservation Quotes*
U.S. Department of the Interior,
National Park Service
January 1953

Indians had no sense of private property, private land. The idea of individual human beings owning pieces of the earth was to them at first incomprehensible and when comprehended, a form of sacrilege.

JOHN MCPHEE
Encounters with the Archdruid
Copyright © 1971 by John McPhee
Farrar, Straus and Giroux, Inc.
New York, 1971

We need the tonic of wildness.
JOHN MUIR

Thousands of tired, nerve-shaken, over-civilized people are beginning to find out that going to the mountains is going home; that wilderness is necessity; and that mountain parks and reservations are useful not only as fountains of timber and irrigating rivers, but as fountains of life.

HENRY DAVID THOREAU (1845)
Walden

Preserve the wilderness

When the first settlers beached their landing boats on our eastern shores, the American wilderness stretched in one vast unbroken sweep from the Atlantic to the Pacific. Except for a few more or less permanent Indian villages, the primeval landscape knew man only as an unobtrusive visitor—tracing his way along unmarked paths, or pausing to harvest its game or gather from its bounty.

To the pioneer, however, the untamed wilderness must have seemed threatening, and sometimes overwhelming. It was to be pushed back. The forests were there to be cleared; the marshes and wetlands to be drained. Plains and prairies existed to be crossed. Stream and river edges and the shores of water bodies were to be opened up as sites for farmsteads and settlements. Today, several centuries later, the wilderness has receded into the remote back reaches of the continent. Most men and women now spend their lives without ever experiencing the majestic solitude and grandeur of an untrammeled landscape—where birds, animals, and vegetation survive in their wild and natural state.

As primitive areas disappear, they become more esteemed. And so it was that in 1964 the Wilderness Act set aside 9 million acres within the national park, national forest, and National Wildlife Refuge holdings as the beginning of a wilderness system. Its purpose was to ensure permanent protection to a vestige of the American wilderness. Procedures were established by which the system could be expanded, and from that time additional millions of acres of undisturbed lands, waterways, shores, and islands have been added to the store of natural treasure.

Within each state there remain those surviving traces of yet wild country which cry out for preservation, as part of either the national or regional preserves. Where they exist and *before* they are threatened with roads, dams, or any other of man's constructions, it is incumbent upon sport and conservation groups to marshal their forces in an effort to save as much as they can.

I went to the woods because I wished to live deliberately, to front only the essential facts of life, and see if I could not learn what it had to teach, and not, when I came to die, discover that I had not lived.

HENRY DAVID THOREAU
Walden

Wilderness areas are first of all a series of sanctuaries for the primitive arts of wilderness travel, especially canoeing and packing.

I suppose some will wish to debate whether it is important to keep these primitive arts alive. I shall not debate it. Either you know it in your bones, or you are very, very old.

ALDO LEOPOLD
A Sand County Almanac
Oxford University Press
Fair Lawn, N.J., 1969

A week in the high country is a purge of certain civilized notions, and a month would be better. The idea that all food must come in cans and bottles, that we must live in a sort of cocoon where the air is always 70 degrees, that heat and transportation must be generated by an ancient legacy of fuels left over from a time that will never be repeated, that everything wild must be killed or tamed, that all the land must be owned and every foreigner is suspect, these and a hundred other old-habit ideas crumble at timberline, because in the alpine economy there is neither room nor time for such extravagance.

ERNEST BRAUN AND DAVID CAVAGNARO
Living Water
Copyright © 1971 by The American West Publishing Company, Inc.
Used by permission of Crown Publishers, Inc.

The chief biologic and economic reason for preserving wilderness areas is that they do preserve the balance of nature; that they are the refuge of the predators, who are constant in their value to us; that they are great reservoirs of the serene order of nature, where things work the way they ought to. They are the right answers in the back of the book, from which we can get help in solving our problems outside them, when we make a mess of things, as we usually do.

DONALD CULROSS PEATTIE
As quoted in *Conservation Quotes*
U.S. Department of the Interior,
National Park Service
January 1953

Without enough wilderness America will change. Democracy, with its myriad personalities and increasing sophistication, must be fibred and vitalized by regular contact with outdoor growths—animals, trees, sun warmth and free skies—or it will dwindle and pale.

WALT WHITMAN
As quoted in *Conservation Quotes*
U.S. Department of the Interior,
National Park Service
January 1953

But there is another part of being human, a part that man has strived to express since he first painted pictures of animals on the walls of ancient caves—beautiful, sensitive pictures that tell us more about ourselves than a thousand spaceships, dams, or factories will ever tell. It is this part of us that loves the mountains and the sea; that listens for the cricket chirp, the quiet rustling of aspens, or the crash of the storm-surf; that marvels at the tiny egg of a hummingbird hatching or a thunderstorm being born. It is this part of us that flows with the river and water of life, that tempers our extravagance and urges us to live by nature's carefully arranged economy.

ERNEST BRAUN AND DAVID CAVAGNARO
Living Water
Copyright © 1971 by The American West Publishing Company, Inc.
Used by permission of Crown Publishers, Inc.

Wilderness has answers to questions that man has not learned to ask.

1) *Why is the wolverine the only mammal free of arthritis?*
2) *How many discoveries like quinine, or the antibiotic properties of abalone blood lie undiscovered in the wilderness?*
3) *Wilderness is a bench mark, a touchstone. In wilderness we can see where we have come from, where we are going, how far we've gone. In wilderness is the only un-sullied earth sample of the forces generally at work in the universe.*

KENNETH BROWER
The Environmental Handbook
Edited by Garrett DeBell
Ballantine Books, Inc.
New York, 1970

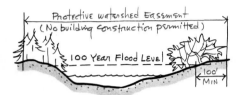

HOW TO PRESERVE A WATERWAY

Leave the natural alignment, section, and covers intact. Define a protective watershed easement extending landward for 100' minimum from the limits of the 100 year flood.

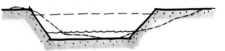

WATERWAY DESECRATION

The traditional "flood control" measure of straightening, widening, and rip-rapping or walling of the stream or river channels must be fought to a stop. Such treatment accelerates the runoff, reduces recharge of the water table, eliminates the natural vegetation and wildlife and destroys the character of the land.

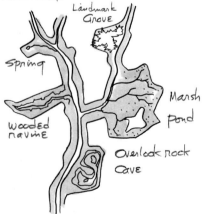

PROTECT THE WATERCOURSES

The proposed "protective watershed easements" will be extended wherever feasible to include the best of the natural features along the rivers and tributary streams. The easements may be converted in time to public ownership by purchase, gift, transfer of development rights, or in payment of overdue taxes. Most future uses of the abutting and downstream lands will benefit from such stream and landscape conservation.

Save the wild rivers

Pouring down through the forests and rocky gorges of most of our upper watershed basins there remain—almost miraculously—long stretches of pristine river. The water is clear and cold, the riverbed in its natural state, and the edges still clothed in moss, ferns, undergrowth, and virgin timber. Sometimes, the unspoiled reaches of the stream extend deeply into the inhabited country of the lower valleys and plains. They have remained wild up to now either because they lie within the holdings of some state or federal agency, or because they have been inaccessible. Some still exist in spite of strong political pressures to dam them for power or water supply or to log off the forests along their edges. With new-found champions among the citizenry, and with new public awareness of their ecological contribution and recreational value, they are being protected at last by acquisition and by the agencies and jurisdictions entrusted with their care.

Few experiences could be more rewarding to friends of the natural landscape than a successful campaign to protect and preserve a stretch of such a waterway.

Preserve our domestic waterways

By good fortune all navigable waterways of our nation have been placed by law within the jurisdiction of the U.S. Army Corps of Engineers. Sometimes in the past their treatment of this vast water empire has left much to be desired. Their extensive channel dredging, flood-control operations, and other "improvement" projects have been carried out with a singleness of purpose that often ignored the serious environmental and ecological implications. Thousands of miles of beautiful river have been dredged to a uniform section and walled with concrete. Thousands of acres of wetland have been needlessly drained, and thousands of acres of prime woodland needlessly inundated. In fairness it must be said that most of these transgressions were instigated at the request of local political leaders and were responsive to the public temperament of the times.

Recently, most undertakings of the Corps have been carried forward in cooperation with the planning and other agencies of each region, and with commendable attention to environmental protection. As the agency responsible for the largest construction program in the history of mankind, the Corps has recently formulated a systematic approach to installation planning designed to ensure a high level of site improvement. The Corps has initiated also a program by which as part of its operation it is providing unsurpassed opportunities for water-based recreation. One of the most promising aspects of our awakened federal conservation conscience is the new orientation of the Corps, and the exercise of its power to expand the water-edge holdings as part of the public domain. In this way the environmental integrity of much of its great waterway network can in time be assured.

Conserve and expand our forests

In writing of his boyhood in Michigan, Bruce Catton, the noted Civil War historian, has lamented that the majestic beauty of unbroken white pine and hardwood forest has succumbed to the donkey engine and the steam locomotive. The bigger part of many states had been treated, not as a region where people might live happily ever after, but as an expendable resource. The trees were gone and those who had "opened up" the country were left with thousands of acres of stumps and broken, eroded land.

Thousands of square miles of the depleted forest lands Catton described have since been restored to full productivity. Over the years

they have been gradually acquired as part of the vast national forest and state forest holdings, and have been replanted for timber production and watershed protection. They exemplify the work of government at its best.

Our public, and private, forest lands are being managed with advanced techniques and programs that match and often excel those developed in the famed Black Forest of Germany. New directions include the multiple use of the forest lands for recreation, for fish and wildlife preserves, and for scientific study. These state and federal programs deserve our full support.

In addition to public holdings, the local woodland and forest area can be dramatically expanded by school, scout, and sportsmen's reforestation projects and by farm tree plantings on depleted land.

Guard the coastal wetlands

How welcome and timely is the recent flurry of state and federal legislation designed to halt, at last, the desecration of our coastal estuarine and saltwater marshes. It is remarkable in what a short space of time the "inexorable" pressures of development have finally been overcome and the right to indiscriminate "bulkheading and filling" denied.

There is an important lesson here. When the true value of a resource is finally understood, and the consequences of its possible loss made clear to those people affected—and when their will is made firmly known—long-standing attitudes and political positions can be quickly reversed.

Our Michigan forests vanished in little more than half a century, partly because the country needed lumber but even more because it had developed new ways to fell trees, move them to the mills, transform them into boards and get the boards to market. Because it could do these things faster it had to do them faster. The maddening thing about a technological improvement is that it must be used to the limit. Natural resources have to be treated as expendable. New devices have to be used at full capacity; new processes have to be tuned up, perfected, developed until they can be replaced by something better. Our founding fathers had seen constant improvement as the basic law of life and the blind force that dominated the new society agreed with them. The difference was that the fathers thought the improvement must take place in the people, while the new power believed that it should take place in machines. Where the machines would take the people who worked so untiringly to improve them is still an open question.

BRUCE CATTON
Waiting for the Morning Train
Doubleday & Company, Inc.
New York, 1972

Acquire the remaining lakeshores and beaches

In the 1950s the National Park Service conducted a survey of the nation's coastlines and of the Great Lakes shorelines. These influential studies defined and described the last of the undeveloped beaches, shores, and islands and made a persuasive case that the most significant of the undeveloped strands should be purchased and protected with government funds. Much of this rare waterfront property has since been brought into the public domain.

Various states have recently made their own studies and plans by which the yet available beaches and shores might be made part of their forest, fish and game, state park, or other conservation holdings. In many cases the efforts were too late—and public access to the lakes and ocean has been denied to the thousands who might otherwise have enjoyed the pleasures of fishing, boating, and swimming.

Where the opportunity for the public acquisition of wateredge lands still exists, the drums should now be sounding.

Save our receding rural landscape

Just as the wilderness was initially pushed back and eroded under the pressures of expansion and development, so too in a following wave has our rural landscape been fast disappearing. Uncontrolled growth has followed the highways and utility installations to disrupt the farming communities and their fields, woodlots, and grazing lands alike. Coupled with such incursions, agricultural land is frequently assessed according to its "fair market value." The resulting taxes may be so high that they preclude the existing use. Many a farmer has thus been forced to sell his land for other, and often marginal, uses. Today few agricultural counties are immune to the blighting effects of hop-skip housing, trailer parks, junk-car yards, gas stations, and commercial strip development. Why? Because the protection of our agricultural regions and the quality of the rural landscape has not yet been considered an issue of critical concern.

When "save our farmlands" contingents have become as vocal as those committed to "save the redwoods" and "save the wild rivers," we will soon have the comprehensive land-use planning, zoning, and tax incentives to do the job. The first crucial step is the formation by each county of an active planning commission.

Inventory the most valuable assets

Whatever the area under study, be it the whole of the nation and its resources, a region, or any part thereof, it is well for those concerned with its planning to define, by mapping, those areas and features which are unique, or which can make the greatest contribution to the living environment. No matter what the present ownership or the existing condition, they are to be included and described.

An untouched coastline or lakeshore is, of course, of immense intrinsic worth and is to be assiduously protected. Yet equally so is a fertile farm valley with its irreplaceable mantle of topsoil and its farmsteads, vineyards, and orchards. The forested hillsides and ridges all make their own contribution, as do the rivers and their floodplains and the fresh- or saltwater marshes.

The smallest stream, even if now polluted or buried beneath the public dump, can be restored, with care, and rehabilitated to add its share to the landscape, and to the well-being of the people.

Formulate a plan for their best utilization

Having "inventoried" and plotted the topographical features of most value, there remains the task of planning for their best long-range use and protection.

As a helpful approach it is proposed that the study area be divided into three categories. The first will include all areas which, it may be determined, should be *preserved* in, or restored to, their natural state. The second category will include those natural or improved lands which should be *conserved* in their present condition or use, or planned in such a way that the existing landscape character will remain essentially unchanged. The third category will comprise those lands set aside for the *development* of various types of housing, school, commercial, manufacturing, and institutional uses. The hypothetical treatment of a small tract is shown as an example.

It would be hoped that the preservation and conservation areas will be formed into a unified assemblage of open space lands, around which, and perhaps within which, planned development will occur.

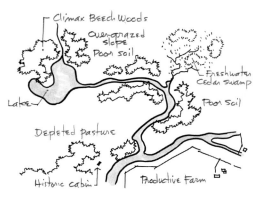

AN EXISTING TRACT UNDER PLANNING CONSIDERATION

In assessing the possibilities begin by allocating — from your own intuitive experience if necessary — those areas that seem best suited for preservation, conservation, and development.

Implement the plan

The map upon which the three categories of preservation, conservation, and development have been allocated will serve, together with the ecological survey and site analysis, as a key resource document in all subsequent regional planning.

Only when all projected uses have been brought into consonance with the character of the land will a sound master plan be produced. This is, of course, a continuing process, requiring constant reappraisal, adjustment, and readjustment.

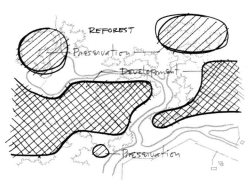

A PRELIMINARY ASSESSMENT OF THE LAND USE POTENTIAL

The beech forest, cedar swamp, and historic landmark are to be preserved. The depleted upland with sparse vegetative cover and no significant attributes is noted as being suited for possible future development should the need be demonstrated. All other land and water areas are marked for conservation. Included are the productive farmlands, the lake and waterways and their banks, and the best of the secondary woodland. Reforestation is prescribed to protect the lake and stream from siltation.

Historic landmarks

Just as the preservation and proper utilization of our natural landscape heritage is a moral obligation, so also is the guardianship of our historic heritage. Historic sites and buildings have educational, esthetic, and patriotic value that cannot be measured in dollars and cents, despite the fact that a travel industry of the first magnitude is based upon their attraction to visitors.

Wherever they exist, historic sites and structures are threatened, at one time or another, by misuse, deterioration, urban expansion, highway construction, or other development. Their preservation requires a crusade carried forward with the power of legislative authority, by the efforts of many individuals and groups, and on many different fronts. An essential requisite is that each state have the governmental apparatus for coordinating historic preservation activities and for fitting the surviving sites into the pattern of its planning for the future.

Create a historic landmarks commission

Such a commission, formed within the state government by legislative act, will be empowered to designate, preserve, and manage historic landmarks and districts. It will recommend on assessments for their taxation. It will also have the authority to receive gifts and bequests of property and funds and, under certain conditions, to acquire property by purchase or condemnation.

Conduct a survey of historic sites and buildings

Listed in an official register will be those buildings and properties which, because of historic, associative, architectural, esthetic, or archeological values, qualify as landmarks possessing statewide or national significance.

Certify and register the landmarks

The commission may certify registered landmarks by entering into agreements with the owners, whereby conditions governing the preservation and use of the properties can be imposed in return for the eligibility to receive certain benefits. In hardship cases, these may include grants of funds for the purposes of preservation and restoration. In cases of need, tax abatements may also be offered or relief may be given for a specified number of years as a condition of privately financed restoration. Guarantees can also be given against seizure of such properties by other agencies under the power of eminent domain.

Acquire and administer those which are threatened

The commission can acquire registered landmarks by gift, purchase, or bequest, or in the event that they are in danger of being sold or damaged by misuse, can exercise its power of acquisition by condemnation.

Coordinate statewide activities

All historic preservation programs being conducted within the state will be coordinated by the commission. Counties and municipalities will be encouraged to establish local commissions for the preservation, promotion, and development of their historic assets, especially the buildings and sites which do not meet the specifications of statewide or national interest, but which nevertheless reflect the cultural development of the communities in which they are situated.

A state program for outdoor recreation

In embarking upon a conservation program, the first and most basic step is a legislative statement of policy to guide the state and its political subdivisions, and to broaden and clarify the necessary legal authority.

This statement should declare, among other things, that the preservation of permanent open space is a public necessity, and that the use of public funds and the exercise of various legal powers to acquire and preserve appropriate lands and waters, including the acquisition of easements or other limited rights, would be for a public purpose.

The present lack of such a legislative assertion within many states often limits the acquisition of open areas by cities, towns, and counties to public parks, playgrounds, and other areas for intensive use. Much of the land required under farsighted open space plans will not be actively used and therefore could not now be legally acquired with public funds. Some may be needed to preserve scenic or other values without being open to the public at all, being left in agriculture, pasture, estates, or marshes. Other lands, such as forest preserves or golf courses, can be open to light public use. Outright ownership of the land is not always necessary if scenic easements or development rights can be acquired. But the cities, towns, and counties of many states do not presently have this power.

Legislation necessary for accomplishing these objectives will

Text continued on page 310.

Dynamic conservation

Virginia's Common Wealth

A state program for outdoor recreation. From a report prepared for the Virginia General Assembly

This study, conducted by a state recreation commission, under the chairmanship of Hon. FitzGerald Bemiss, was broadened in scope to address itself to the conservation, protection, and best use of the full range of Virginia's natural, scenic, and historic resources. The Virginia General Assembly, recognizing the need to protect and make available to the people the rich and varied splendors of the Virginia outdoors, directed the commission to:

• Inventory the federal, state, and local outdoor recreation resources and facilities in Virginia and estimate what will be needed in the future.
• Determine what the state could do to meet these needs.
• Determine what local governments could do and how the state should help them through new legislation, financial aid, and planning assistance.

• Consider ways of encouraging individuals and private enterprise to join with local and state efforts for the preservation of the state's natural superlatives and the creation of a permanent open space framework.

This program, together with a recommended budget and enabling legislation, was adopted by the Assembly in 1966. Under the guidance of the Virginia Commission of Outdoor Rec-

reation, created at the time, progress has been made in the implementation of all proposals, and the good work continues. The study has become a model for environmental action, and in many ways its proposals are even more timely and pertinent today.

Virginia's land and waters have abundantly nourished its citizens, in body and in spirit, for nearly four centuries. To neglect these natural attributes—to abandon their conservation, to let heedless exploitation consume them or remove them from reach of the great majority of our citizens—is to sell their birthright for a mess of pottage. Once sold, it cannot be recovered. Virginia's resources, abundant as they are, are neither inexhaustible nor indestructible.

Today a sharp change is taking place. The face of Virginia is taking on a new character as it becomes urbanized and industrialized in its commitment to progress. The progress is manifested by population growth and concentration, by increased income, by more cars, better roads, and more leisure time.

But these forces, which increase the demand for outdoor recreation, are also threatening the very landscape features which are basic—our brooks and woods, our farms and shorelines.

The problem is that the average person—and especially the city dweller—is having a harder and harder time finding the outdoors.

- It is being marred or demolished.
- It is being walled off with "no trespassing" signs.
- It is being consumed by unplanned urban sprawl.

But such devastation is not an inevitable result of growth and progress. It is inefficiency. There is plenty of room in Virginia for both

development and for open space. The key is effective land use.

Thus we do not have to choose between material progress and an agreeable environment. We must have both. But we can have them only if we decide now the kind of environment we want—and shape our programs to bring it about.

The major findings of the commission

There is a strong and growing demand for more outdoor recreation opportunities. The population is increasing dramatically. Not only are there more and more Virginians; increasingly, they are living closer and closer together. Yet they have more leisure time than ever before, they have higher incomes, and they have more automobiles. These are the dynamic factors behind Virginians' demand for access to the Virginia outdoors and for places to walk, to swim, to launch a boat, to camp—to loaf and refresh themselves.

Existing facilities are inadequate for present demands. This is true in all resource categories—from high-density neighborhood parks to remote natural areas. There is a serious deficiency in number, location, and variety of state parks.

The need for action is most urgent in metropolitan areas. Three-fourths of Virginia's population will soon live in these areas. Meanwhile open space for outdoor recreation is being consumed, spoiled, or made unavailable at an alarming rate.

The term outdoor recreation *must include the entire Virginia outdoor environment.* The most popular forms of outdoor recreation are the simplest ones—driving, walking, swimming, and picnicking. So outdoor recreation must involve state parks and the roads which take people to them; municipal parks and playgrounds and habitable communities; access to ample, unpolluted water; historical sites and harmonious countryside. All of these are outdoor recreation resources and they must be dealt with as interrelated parts of the total environment in which Virginians work, play, and live.

Each individual, with the government at all levels—local, regional, state, and federal—has a job to do. Individuals, nongovernmental organizations, and private enterprise are providing many outstanding recreation opportunities. Virginia has benefited greatly from broad individual concern for the Virginia landscape. Garden clubs, conservation organizations, nonprofit historical-preservation corporations, service clubs, and others like them should be aided and encouraged by the state in every possible way. The state should also encourage private enterprise and the travel industry to develop outdoor recreation facilities and to provide the services needed in support of public facilities.

The demand intensifies and the supply diminishes

Population growth—and increasing income, mobility, and leisure time—are creating soaring demands for recreation places and facilities. These are needed throughout the state, in relation to its mountains, rivers, forests beaches, countryside, neighborhood woodlots and fields.

Needed also are more city parks and playgrounds; more state parks, picnicking and camping sites; more access to rivers and lakes for swimming, boating, and fishing; pleasant paths to walk on and roads to drive on; and a properly treated historic and cultural heritage.

The supply of places is shrinking. Each year more fields and streams are bulldozed, more historic buildings razed, more shorelines and woodlands made unusable or inaccessible. The diminishing supply of facilities is less and less adequate as demand soars.

The ever-increasing pressure of need includes all categories of outdoor recreation.

Each of the charts on the opposite page says, "More, More, More." More people, more net income per person, more leisure hours, more need for spiritual and physical recreation.

Not shown is the destructive burden the increased need will place upon our existing recreation places if we permit the demand to outrun the supply.

More and more and more . . . more time for living creates more demand for outdoor recreation.

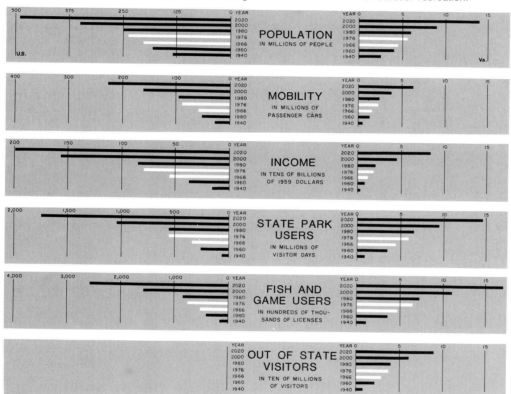

Population growth in Virginia almost duplicates the national pattern of more and more and more.

American families are mobile. With improved roads and cars they drive extravagant distances in search of the limited recreation areas.

We have more money for leisure. The higher the family income the greater the demand for recreation facilities and the greater the willingness to be satisfied only with the best.

The numbers of state and out-of-state visitors to parks and other recreation areas increases, but so does the average number of days each spends in a recreation area. The demand is thus compounded.

More hunting and fishing licenses, more sportsmen fishing our coastal waters, create a demand for more access roads, more camping facilities, more public shoreline, and more breeding and hatching facilities.

More out-of-state users of Virginia recreation areas reflect an increasing economic resource as well as a challenge to meet a growing demand.

These are America's favorite outdoor pleasures

They are the simple pleasures—walking, for example, and playing games, and driving through the American countryside. But they require space, under the sky, amongst the trees, beside the waters.

They refresh and strengthen a nation because they are fundamental to human development—to balanced living.

It all adds up to more demands upon the limited supply of recreation resources.

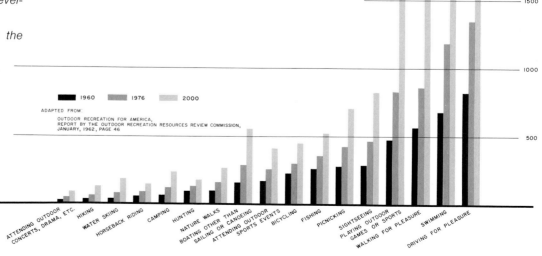

SOURCE: BASED UPON U.S. CENSUS OF POPULATION, 1960, WITH INTERPRETATIONS BY VIRGINIA DIVISION OF INDUSTRIAL DEVELOPMENT AND PLANNING.

1960 POPULATION
2020 POPULATION

1
682,731
4,270,000

6
312,159
840,000

219,007
450,000

8
112,241
190,000

10
47,601
80,000

7N

2
542,729
2,240,000

4
300,532
980,000

9
61,981
110,000

5
485,526
450,000

7S
319,922
670,000

3
882,520
3,720,000

The Virginia Outdoors Plan

The Virginia Outdoors Plan is an investment in our inheritance. Properly tended it will pay good dividends and appreciate in value. To be effective the effort must be comprehensive, and it must be a continuing one.

For this reason the Virginia Outdoors Plan looks to the year 2020 in its concept of what can and must be done to protect and develop the Virginia outdoors. If the plan is launched soundly and put on the right course, it will be continued with increasing effectiveness in the years which follow.

The recommendations of the study commission fall into five general categories:

1. A state policy and a continuing comprehensive program to protect the quality of the Virginia outdoors and to make its resources available to its people.

2. A permanent Commission of Outdoor Recreation to analyze supply and demand, and to lead and coordinate state, local, and federal activities.

3. State action to plan, acquire, and develop outdoor recreation places and facilities and to encourage, assist, and guide local and regional governments.

4. Local and regional action to meet local and regional needs for planning, acquisition, and development.

5. Encouragement for individuals and private enterprise to make their essential contribution to the total program.

The ten study regions

Recreation opportunities must be provided where the people now are and where they will be in the foreseeable future. The left bars represent 1960 populations, the middle bars represent 1980, and the right bars project the populations in 2020.

Two basic criteria determine the adequacy of recreation places. They are, (1) the nature of the resource and (2) its relation to population centers. To facilitate the use of these criteria, the state has been divided into regions, on the basis of physiographic and population characteristics. Although these regions have internal demands which may be met internally, the regions should not be considered as independent entities. They are highly interdependent in terms of people and of resources.

Regions 1–4 are major urbanizing areas, containing over 60 percent of the population.

Regions 5–10 are predominantly rural.

Compare the projected population growth rates of each group and consider them in terms of recreation demands.

The following pages show for each study region* the major existing outdoor recreation facilities administered by governmental agencies—federal, state, and regional. They do not include such local recreation areas as athletic fields, school playgrounds, or other in-city parks.

Also shown are the commission's proposals for adding outdoor recreation opportunities. It is not suggested that these will meet all demands until 2020, but only that on the basis of resource characteristics and demands of people, these proposals, if undertaken promptly and seriously, will be the backbone of a worthy program. Many other locations were suggested by interested citizens. The fact that they are not included in the commission's proposals does not indicate disapproval but simply a lower priority in terms of character of, and need for, the resource.

The commission has purposely avoided indicating precise locations, preferring to show only general areas for detailed analysis and action by the proposed permanent Commission of Outdoor Recreation and by appropriate local and regional agencies.

*Note: Three of the ten study regions included in the full report are shown on the following pages as examples.

Region 1 Washington-Fredericksburg

This is Virginia's fastest growing region. Its population increased from 404,000 in 1950 to 683,000 in 1960, and is predicted to be 1,800,000 in 1990— almost a threefold increase in thirty years. The headlong flood of residential and commercial development (in Fairfax County alone 4 square miles of open space go to single-family dwellings each year) has created a serious shortage of outdoor recreation. By the year 2020 the population is estimated to be 4,270,000. This alone makes the case for prompt action.

There is no state park in this, the state's most populous region. The efforts of the Northern Virginia Regional Park Authority and the Fairfax County Park Authority have brought forth good but limited facilities—certainly not enough for present and growing demand. The sound plans of the Northern Virginia Regional Planning Commission should be the basis for regional development.

The federal government is taking the lead in the planning of the Potomac River and in the development of the George Washington Country National Parkway. It also is concerned with other major features of the area, including Prince William Forest Park, Manassas Battlefield, and Balls Bluff Battlefield. The proposed Commission of Outdoor Recreation should coordinate the state's program with these federal projects for the greatest benefit to the people of Virginia. This cooperation will be particularly important since the George Washington Country National Parkway along the Potomac River will be a highly desirable link between the metropolitan population and proposed outdoor recreation areas.

Proposals

State parks

1 Bull Run Mountain rates high priority. This attractive mountain terrain is closer than any similar resource to the metropolitan center.

2 The Widewater area on the Potomac below Washington rates high priority in offering a full range of water-based recreation opportunities.

3 The Blue Ridge foothills offer a logical general recreation site.

4 The Conway-Robinson Memorial State Forest environment offers space for high-density development adjoining state forest land which by deed must be preserved in its natural state.

5 The Kelly's Ford area on the Rappahannock offers desirable recreation in its present state—unpolluted, and with white-water rapids. If and when a dam is constructed at Salem Church at a later date, the design of the park could be altered to fit the impoundment.

State or regional parks

6 The Short Hill area of Loudoun County.

7 The Goose Creek area west of Dulles Airport.

Regional parks

8 Potomac Overlook, a site selected by the Northern Virginia Regional Park Authority.

9 Bull Run–Occoquan Park, now in existence, is to be greatly enlarged and improved by the Northern Virginia Regional Park Authority.

10 River Bend–Great Falls Park, an existing area, to be enlarged and improved by the Fairfax County Park Authority in coordination with the federal government.

11 Mason's Neck, an enlargement of the existing Pohick Bay Park, now owned by the Northern Virginia Regional Park Authority, in coordination with the state and federal government.

12 A new park to be developed adjacent to Prince William Forest Park, with a lake created in cooperation with the Commission of Game and Fisheries on the Lake Burke Plan.

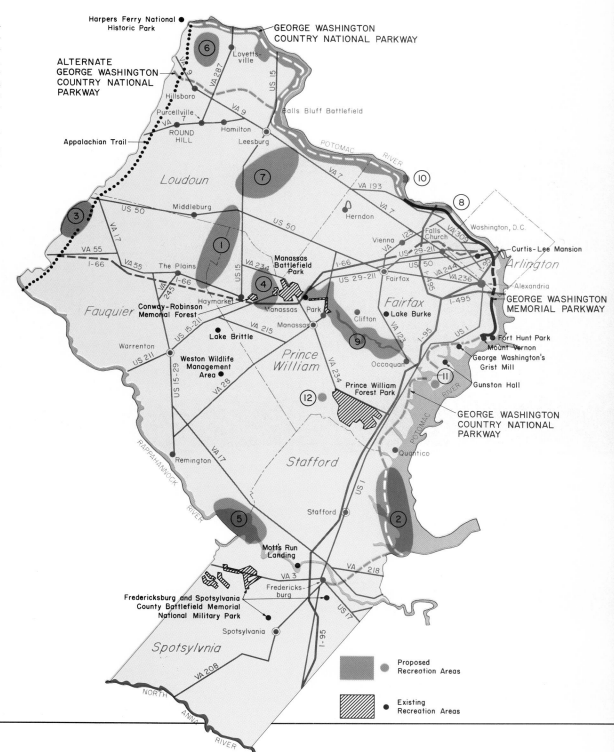

Region 3 Hampton Roads

Surging population growth and shrinking outdoor recreation space characterize this region. Its 1960 population of 883,000 is expected to increase to 1,800,000 in 1990, and to 3,720,000 in the year 2020. As in other metropolitan areas, the acquisition and development of public outdoor recreation facilities has been severely inadequate. This is particularly serious in this region because of the great appeal of the beaches and the other waterfront areas, which draw not only from the immediate metropolitan area, but from across the state, and indeed from the entire eastern seaboard.

There is urgent need for additional state parks. Some of the individual localities have done well on local projects, but both the scale of the resources and of the demand require strong regional planning and regional action.

The individual cities of this region have good recreation programs. All would benefit from more active participation in regional planning and development of interrelated resources.

Proposals
State Wildlife Management Area

1 Approximately 50,000 acres of Dismal Swamp, including Lake Drummond, should be acquired as a wildlife management area. This deserves high priority. A small part of the area, bordering on Lake Drummond and the feeder ditch, should be preserved as a natural area with foot and boat access to the lake.

State Parks

2 A substantial ocean beachfront should be made available for public use on the Atlantic Ocean south of Virginia Beach. Public access to ocean beachfronts is diminishing rapidly and this project deserves high priority.

3 Seashore Park is the state's most popular and unique park. It should be diligently protected, and the state should make certain that if Fort Story ever becomes surplus property, this area is added to Seashore Park.

4 The lower Chickahominy near its confluence with the James would serve plantation-country visitors and complement other area attractions.

5 A state park in Isle of Wight County on the James River would provide water-based recreation for the metropolitan population south of the river.

6 A site on the Blackwater River should be acquired for future development.

7 A camping and service area near Dismal Swamp should be considered as a base from which people might visit the Dismal Swamp wildlife management area and natural area.

Regional Parks

8 Goodwin's Island, a low sandy island at the mouth of the York River.

9 Lower York and Chesapeake Bay, including sites at Big Bethel, Hampton and Lee Hall Watershed Reservation.

10 Grand View Beach, facing on Chesapeake Bay.

11 Nansemond River and Nansemond County lakes provide attractive areas available for public recreation development.

Region 8 Northern Tidewater

One of the plainest facts of outdoor recreation is that the people want access to clean water. They like to camp beside it, swim in it, ski on it, and just loaf near it. No other region in the state has such a wealth of water-based resources. In the area are three major rivers—the Potomac, the Rappahannock, and the York, which flow into the Chesapeake Bay to the east. Acquisition of points of access and of park sites for camping, boating, and swimming on these rivers, as near as possible to the Bay, needs immediate consideration.

In addition to these assets, there is on both peninsulas a wealth of historic sites which will be made more readily available by the proposed George Washington Country National Parkway from the Washington metropolitan area to Yorktown. The proposed state parks near the mouth of each of the great rivers are perhaps the highest-priority proposals. Linked and coordinated in their development with the proposed George Washington Country National Parkway, they will constitute an incomparable asset to the area and to the entire state.

Immediately to the west and south is the urban crescent. With its swelling population and rapid improvement of roads, there is a critical need to be met. Properly developed, the area's great resources will provide incomparable recreation opportunities to millions of people, with great economic benefit to the region.

Proposals
State Parks

1   The Smith Point area at the mouth of the Potomac. The Coan River area is an alternative for consideration as a regional park.
2   Mathias Point on the south bank of the Potomac in King George County.
3   Near the mouth of the Rappahannock in Lancaster County. This is one of the state's most popular boating and fishing areas.
4   Either the Smoot Farm area on the Potomac River East of Fredericksburg or a site on the Rappahannock River between Fredericksburg and Port Royal.
5   Mathews County on the Chesapeake Bay above New Point.
6   Dragon Run, a clean stream of great beauty which should be acquired as a state forest for later development as a state park and natural area.
7   York River near Gloucester Point. This is another of the state's most popular boating and fishing areas.
8   The Lower Chickahominy near its confluence with the James. This would serve the plantation-country visitors and complement other area attractions.

State Natural Area

9   Windmill Point is typical of a number of small, distinctive, low-lying waterfront areas which are valuable in their natural state as wildlife habitat and as nature preserves. The Commission of Outdoor Recreation should consider the inclusion of this type of resource in the natural areas system.

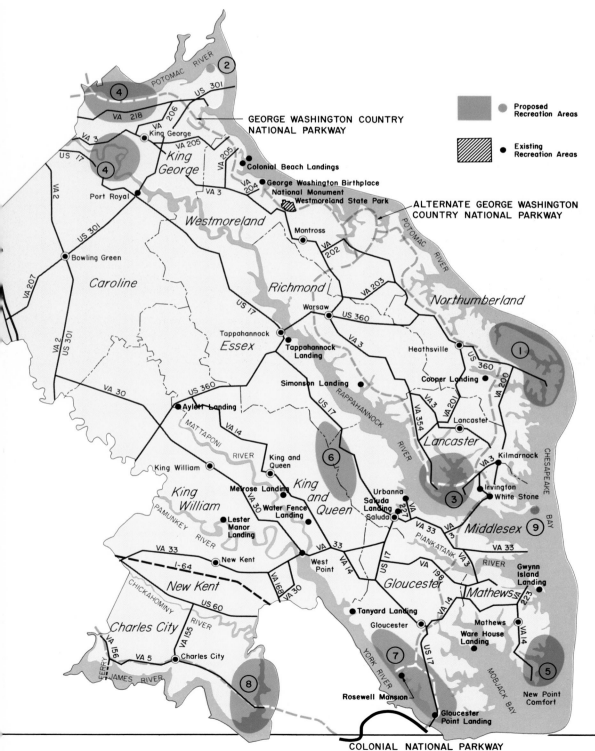

Summary of recommendations

1 Adopt a state open space policy. In embarking on a program of conservation and development of its natural resources for the public benefit, the first and most basic step is a legislative statement of policy to guide the state and its political subdivisions, and to broaden and clarify the legal authority necessary to implement the program.

2 Create a Commission of Outdoor Recreation. An independent state agency is needed to guide and coordinate continuing statewide implementation of the Virginia Outdoors Plan. It should advise the governor on resources and needs, coordinate the outdoor recreation activities of local, state, and federal agencies, provide technical assistance to localities, and receive and allocate federal land and water conservation funds.

3 Enlarge and improve the state park system. The present number, location, and condition of state parks and recreation areas is inadequate. Within the next ten years land should be acquired for 36 new parks, 20 of which should be developed within this period. Facilities in existing parks should be improved and increased. The Division of Parks should be given an expanded staff to administer the program.

4 Aid localities in resource conservation and development. Local governments have a vital role in the Virginia Outdoors Plan. They must take the initiative in the use of local resources for local benefit. Unfortunately, available local powers are not sufficiently used. Their use should be encouraged. The state should aid localities in three ways: (1) research, guidance, and technical assistance, (2) matching funds, and (3) provision of legal powers.

5 Encourage greater use of regional planning commissions and regional park authorities. Natural resources conservation and development problems and opportunities, more often than not, extend beyond the borders of political subdivisions. Where two or more localities share a common problem, regional action is an absolute necessity.

6 Establish a system of scenic byways and provide for recreation access roads. All across Virginia are roads of incomparable charm and historic significance. These roads should be identified and their character protected for the general enjoyment of Virginians and as a prime attraction to visitors. Many major recreation attractions do not have adequate access roads.

7 Make our highways more pleasant. A substantial part of all leisure time is spent on the highways. Driving itself is regarded as a prime recreational activity. The design of roads and their amenities should recognize this fact.

8 Accelerate the program of the Commission of Game and Inland Fisheries. More fishing lakes, more boat launching ramps, and more public hunting lands are needed (especially in eastern Virginia), than are being provided through revenues from commission licenses and fees.

9 Encourage the multiple use of public lands to allow maximum recreation opportunity consistent with the land's primary purpose. This offers many practical and economical opportunities to achieve a broad range of outdoor recreation on land originally acquired for a single purpose. The state forests should be incorporated into a system of forest preserves to conserve lands and waters for future public recreation or other compatible uses.

10 Encourage advance planning and land acquisition in areas of major water impoundments. These large man-made reservoirs offer great recreation and development potential which can only be realized fully when the state and the localities involved consider in advance the problems of public access, recreation areas, pollution control, and zoning.

11 Develop the recreation opportunities created by soil and water conservation districts. Substantial lakes, created for soil and water conservation, offer important local or regional recreation sites. Localities should acquire sufficient land around these lakes to allow recreation for the general public benefit.

12 Recognize the vital role of the individual and private enterprise. Virginia benefits greatly from the facilities and services provided by private enterprise, from the activities of nonprofit conservation groups, from associations devoted to historic preservation, and from the travel industry. These should be encouraged and relied upon to the greatest extent practical.

13 Undertake a study of the relation of land taxation to the preservation of open space. Preferential assessment and tax deferral have been tried with various difficulties and questionable results in a number of states. Present land-taxation practice is nevertheless a factor which requires further study in the interest of the preservation of open space.

14 Provide for the acquisition of scenic and conservation easements. The easement can be an economical and effective device for retaining the scenic character, and ownership, of land. Through it only the development rights are acquired and the private owner retains the right of land use for farming and other purposes not destructive of scenic or ecologic values.

If a desired scenic or conservation easement cannot be acquired at a price substantially less than the cost of full ownership, then the government should consider outright purchase.

15 Initiate water-resource and river-basin studies. It is increasingly clear that present demands on Virginia's rivers—their waters and their shorelines—require comprehensive river-basin research and planning to conserve our most vital resource and a prime recreation asset. There is no provision for this type of research and planning in Virginia and only an uncoordinated scattering of agencies concerned with various aspects of water—such as groundwater, surface water, and pollution.

Important aspects of such river-basin studies will be floodplain zoning, pollution control, and water management considerations.

16 Accelerate marine-resources and beach-erosion study. There is far too little understanding of the natural forces which control our marine resources, our saltwater marshes, and the shape of our beaches and islands. There is inadequate understanding of the extent to which man can intrude on these without destroying them. These values require intensified study.

17 Provide guidelines for planned communities and cluster development. State and local agencies should facilitate private entrepreneurial development of new communities and new types of housing subdivisions which meet acceptable standards and preserve the quality of the general outdoor environment.

18 Create a Historic Landmarks Commission. Virginia has no policy or program for the protection of its vast historical treasure. An agency is needed to catalog and evaluate historic and cultural buildings and sites, and to develop plans and programs for their protection. This is an economic resource which is being grossly exploited or destroyed.

19 Establish the Virginia Outdoors Foundation. The foundation can be of substantial help in the encouragement of private gifts and bequests of lands and waters of recreation value. Virginia has benefited in the past from private generosity. The foundation is intended to facilitate private philanthropy.

20 Establish the Virginia Outdoors Fund to implement the Virginia Outdoors Plan. State funds must be provided to meet the state's part of the total plan and to aid the localities in meeting theirs. The state general fund appropriations will be matched by federal land and water conservation funds, constituting the Virginia Outdoors Fund.

21 Create greater awareness of the value of natural resources and environmental geography. The basic cause of inattention to the rapid consumption and destruction of our outdoor recreation resources is ignorance of their nature and value. The state must develop programs for the awakening of a conservation conscience in the public interest.

Legacy

A comprehensive study of outdoor recreation resources is a new thing for Virginia. The problem to which the study is devoted is new. The commission has had to learn as it proceeded.

The study commission feels that it has performed its assignment. It has inventoried the resources and facilities; it has analyzed the present and future demand; it has indicated areas of responsibility; and it has offered a plan of action. Throughout this process the commission has sought and received information and advice from hundreds of Virginia citizens and from authoritative sources across the nation. Large numbers of people attended the commission's five public hearings, furnishing invaluable suggestions.

But not for a moment does the commission maintain that it has covered all aspects of this very broad subject—a subject which indeed touches all the people and all the natural resources in Virginia. The commission's effort has been to show the values that are threatened, to introduce the concept that they are worth conserving and developing for lasting public benefit, and to suggest the first steps on a basic course.

If Virginia continues to grow and develop over the years to come at even the present rate, we can see plainly that individual citizens will have to give to the *quality of development* the same emphasis which over the past generation they have been giving to *quantity of development*. After all, the purpose of all our endeavors is not just to amass more money, more goods, and more impressive statistics—but to attain the requisites of a good life, the opportunity to enjoy the things we have acquired; a place of pleasure, dignity, and permanence which we can pass on to future generations with satisfaction and pride.

Text continued from page 300.

authorize appropriate state and local public bodies to acquire, by purchase or otherwise, such rights or title in property as will provide a means of preserving open space. It will authorize such acquisitions by eminent domain procedure, in which the public necessity is determined by the governing body. It will require such acquisitions to be in conformity with the official comprehensive land-use plan for the area, and limit the diversion of property once acquired unless replaced by property of equivalent public benefit and value. It will permit open spaces to be leased or conveyed with limitations on use and development that will preserve their open character. It will provide for tax reductions in the case of easements or other limited acquisitions. The term *open space land* should be broadly defined to include all properties required for the preservation or conservation of the state's natural, scenic, agricultural, recreational, and historic resources.

It is important to note that supportable conservation practice embraces the enjoyment and *use* of open space land consistent with the protection of its ecological values.

Expand and renovate the state park system

The number of state parks provided generally falls far short of meeting present and growing demands. New state parklands should be selected and acquired on the basis of two criteria:

1. *The character of the resource:* Does it offer the type of outdoor recreation opportunity which people want?

2. *Its location in relation to numbers of people:* Is it within convenient distance for day or weekend use?

Land and waters which meet these requirements become more scarce and more expensive each year. The importance of prompt site evaluation and acquisition cannot be overemphasized.

A second basic action calls for enlargement and improvement of the facilities in the present parks and recreation areas. A worthy state park system should not only meet the desire of the people for opportunities to enjoy the outdoors; it should pay the state dividends in the form of citizens made happier and wiser by contact with the state's rivers, fields, hills, and beaches, an experience re-creating strength and perspective in an age when they are greatly needed.

A superior state park system will serve as an attraction to visitors and to the most desirable types of development in the surrounding region. It will bring economic activity where it will be highly beneficial, and will prove in all ways to be a sound investment.

Include recreation areas and natural areas within the state park system

State parks, usually ranging in size from 2,000 to 10,000 acres are planned to give the public a chance to visit and enjoy the state's more scenic areas. Emphasis is on camping, boating, swimming, and hiking in natural surroundings.

State recreation areas, usually administered by the same division, supplement the state parks by offering high-density uses, such as marinas, skiing, trailer camping, and picnicking wherever suitable sites become available, and often within state forest or fish and game lands.

Natural areas are small outdoor museums for the safekeeping of those few rare spots where the ecology is as yet undisturbed by man and where there exists a natural condition of great distinction. These are available for observation and study under regulations designed to conserve the natural values.

Nature is not to be regarded as a refuge from life, but as an invigorator of it and a stimulus to body and mind.

CHRISTOPHER TUNNARD
"Gardens in the Modern Landscape"
The Architectural Press, London
Charles Scribner's Sons
New York, 1948

Consolidate the state forest holdings

The better state forest programs have two important functions. The first is the protection and scientific management of existing forests. The second is the reclamation and reforestation of depleted, eroded, or otherwise devastated lands. Both objectives can best be achieved when the holdings are acquired in large cohesive tracts, often embracing entire mountain ranges or interconnected stream and river basins. It is important that they be acquired "out ahead" of development while the properties are inexpensive and when many may be tax delinquent.

In practice, the timber of state forests is harvested by private operators and the revenues shared by the state with the local counties. Hunting within the forests may be permitted and managed through cooperative agreements with the Fish and Game Commission. State parks and parkways may also be included within the boundaries.

Traditionally, state forests have been located in the "outback" regions, but suburban and even in-city forests offer promising opportunities for watershed protection, recreation, and the provision of an open space buffer and preserve.

Create additional fish and game preserves

In every state without exception more fishing lakes, more boat launching ramps, and more public hunting lands are needed.

New fishing waters should be purchased or leased with local funds supplemented by state and federal contributions. As a condition of acquisition there should be assurance of suitable access roads and sufficient supporting land around the streams or lakes to provide for parking, camping, picnicking, and the enjoyment of nature.

Where feasible, fishing lakes ought to be constructed in state parks or forests. This would broaden the recreation opportunities of the park and forest, while saving acquisition and operating costs.

While private lands will no doubt continue to meet a large part of the hunting requirements, priority should be given to the provision of public hunting grounds in those regions of the state where rapid development is consuming or overcrowding areas presently available for hunting.

Enact floodplain zoning

Large swaths of land adjacent to streams, wetlands, or water bodies, being subject to periodic flooding, are not suited for uses which would be damaged by inundation. Yet, being low, moist, and fertile, floodplains are ideally suited for agriculture and recreation.

Progressive localities, regional planning commissions, or the state itself, if necessary, will undertake studies leading to the legal description and mapping of floodplains and the enactment of legislation to govern their use. Typically, all lands lying within the 100-year flood-stage contours, as modified from time to time by flood-control installations, will be zoned for agricultural, recreational, or transportation-transmission uses. An additional bordering strip of 100 feet minimum width should be protected by easement or purchase wherever feasible. All housing, commercial, or other similar construction will be precluded within these areas. By this single device, and in the interest of public health and safety, huge periodic losses and governmental flood-relief programs may be eliminated and marginal land development forestalled.

Floodplains make a welcome contribution to the regional open space network. The forest preserves of Cook County and Chicago, for example, have utilized thousands of acres of such low-lying lands to lace the region with broad green meadows, waterways, and reforested parklands around which most of the better new housing, institutional, and business-office development of the region has been attracted.

Small ponds can be formed by damming a stream.

On large lakes can be dug on level floodplain land with the earth shaped into low hills and reforested mounds.

Existing Vegetation

Lake

Newly formed hills with native trees

Existing Vegetation

CREATE NEW FISHING PONDS AND LAKES WITHIN PARK AND FOREST HOLDINGS

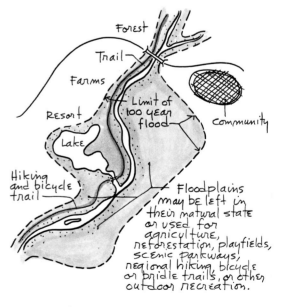

Forest

Trail

Farms

Resort

Lake

Hiking and bicycle trail

Limit of 100 year flood

Community

Floodplains may be left in their natural state or used for agriculture, reforestation, playfields, scenic parkways, regional hiking, bicycle or bridle trails, or other outdoor recreation.

ZONE AND CONSERVE THE FLOODPLAINS

Encourage soil and water conservation

The objectives of soil and water conservation efforts are to prevent the erosion of soils and the silting of waters and to conserve water resources. This is accomplished mainly by encouraging and aiding good soil treatment practices and by the construction of farm ponds and larger water-supply and flood-prevention reservoirs.

Under the Federal Soil Conservation Service program, the study of a prospective watershed site must show economic justification sufficient to warrant construction of a dam. If a dam is indicated, the federal government pays for that portion of the dam which serves as flood control, with the local government paying for additional water supply and storage.

Although recreation is not the primary concern of the Federal Soil Conservation districts, their larger lakes offer excellent opportunities.

Gear land taxation to regional planning objectives

As urban growth spreads across suburban and rural farmland, land values and taxes increase to the point of either driving or enticing the farmer to sell his acreage. The result is frequently a leapfrogging of spot developments which either destroy or consume all open spaces and which yield as a consequence a disorderly and unattractive community.

It is proposed that the best means of retarding this process is the regionwide designation of logical satellite activity (development) nodes and the land-banking of all remaining nonurban lands for agricultural or other open space use. Corresponding adjustment of land appraisals will help to gain public support.

Two other devices have been widely discussed. They are preferential *assessment*, and deferred *taxation*. *Preferential assessment* means that land is assessed for taxes according to its use, rather than its "fair market value." *Deferred taxation* means that a part of the taxes are not collected until the land is sold or its use is changed. The purpose of such plans is to give an incentive to continue farming in the outskirts of urban areas, but neither of them guarantees even the temporary preservation of open space. They only serve the landowner who wants to stay in the farming business rather than take a big immediate profit on the sale of his property.

The subject is important. It would benefit many urbanizing areas if farmers chose to, and could afford to, keep their lands in cultivation. Continued rapid urbanization is raising serious questions about the adequacy and equity of present land assessment and taxation procedures.

Create a conservation foundation

Most states can now accept private gifts of land, money, or other property and have been the beneficiary of the generosity of citizens who have donated property for the protection of natural beauty or historic values. There are, however, occasions in which a separate foundation might better encourage and facilitate private philanthropy.

The foundation should be governed by a board of trustees, to be appointed by the governor. It should be empowered to accept, hold, and administer gifts and bequests of money, securities, or other property in support of the state's conservation program.

Acquire conservation easements

It is often economical and practical for a jurisdiction to acquire less than fee title in property to protect its scenic and conservation attributes. This means, in effect, obtaining the development rights but

West Germany has protected its countryside from sprawling suburbs, even while economic priorities favored all-out growth. This Oregon-sized nation of 60 million people maintains 29 percent of its land area in forests, 55 percent in farmland. Though German cities long ago broke out of their medieval walls, seen from the air today they seem confined by invisible walls rigidly defining the edges of development.

One essential ingredient of this story of successful land planning is the concept of development land *and* non-development land. *Only property owners within the zone designated for development may subdivide and urbanize their land.*

The extraordinary result . . . is an engaging mix of vital cities and tranquil, productive countryside—a harmonious contrast inviting to Americans who are eager to contain sprawl and to guard diminishing open spaces.

WILLIAM K. REILLY
Conservation Foundation President
Thoughts on the Second German Miracle
Conservation Foundation Letter
August, 1976

leaving the land for the owner's use and enjoyment.

The arrangement can be of great value in instances where new construction, billboards, or unsightly roadside clutter threaten a scenic vista, a historic environment, or an approach to a place of recreational or cultural significance.

If a desired scenic easement cannot be secured at a price substantially less than the cost of full ownership, then the governing body should consider outright purchase and leaseback for private use under suitable restrictions.

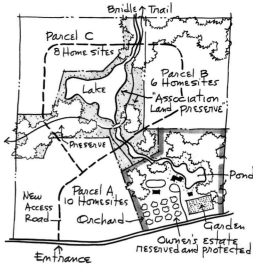

THE PRECONDITIONED SALE OF LAND

Owners wishing to sell or lease a portion of their property for development may do so according to a preliminary layout plan, and with whatever covenants or controls they may wish to place upon it. These may include point of access, schematic layout of the circulation drive, number of dwellings permitted, type of structures, rights of plan and architectural approval, limits and treatment of "Association Land" to be preserved, etc. Often such preplanning increases, rather than limits, potential land values.

Effectuate all multiple-use possibilities

Most public lands are acquired for a single purpose—as for fishing or hunting, forest management, conservation, or school playgrounds. Often these lands can serve multiple purposes without impairment of the primary use, thereby serving more people more economically. There are numerous examples.

The extensive holdings acquired by the U.S. Army Corps of Engineers for flood control and navigational improvements are being opened up for such water-based recreation as fishing, boating, and camping. Camping areas on state fish and game lands are quite practical also, since they are available to hunters and anglers during the season and are heavily used at other times by the general public. Hunting is permitted on some large federal military sites. The U.S. Forest Service, concerned mainly with the protection of timber and watershed preserves, offers a growing number and variety of recreational experiences.

Rural highway rights-of-way are being widened and improved with scenic pulloffs and picnic areas. Urban freeways are now designed to accommodate parking, playgrounds, and even buildings within, under, and over the roadways. Many urban communities have benefited from developing neighborhood parks adjacent to school playgrounds, thus providing a combined facility which is utilized during the summer months for recreation programs and which is available year round for community use.

These examples indicate the soundness of the multiple-use concept and suggest its broader application.

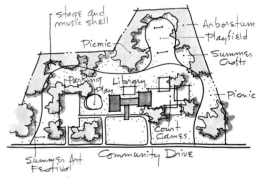

THE SCHOOL-PARK CAMPUS

When schools, playfields, and park are planned together, everybody gains. The school playlots and athletic fields can be used full-time and year-round. Meeting rooms, library, auditorium, and parking courts serve a double purpose. The salaries of staff members can be augmented by summer craft and recreation counseling, and the school becomes a true community center, in a park.

Land preservation by private owners

Assuming the accomplishment of a regional plan by which development and the natural landscape are to be brought into balance, a critical problem remains. *How is the open space land to be acquired?* As in the past, a large share must be purchased with public funds. But the public treasury is limited, and although the rate of acquisition is being accelerated, the new lands added cannot keep pace with the needs—especially in urbanizing areas where real estate values are soaring and where development spreads relentlessly across the fields and woodlands. It is not until the open land is used up that its loss becomes so keenly apparent and its need so urgently felt.

Since most of the remaining open space is in private ownership, conservationists are now looking to the private owners for help. In a persuasive booklet, the Open Space Institute has outlined a number

"Stewardship" may seem an abstract concept, but there are many means for its concrete expression. An owner who is philanthropically inclined might donate land for open space use to a park authority or a conservation organization. A person who wishes to sell his land might participate in the design of a subdivision to assure that some valuable open space remains. The estate owner who would like to continue to live on his property just as it is or bequeath it intact to his heirs, might convey an "open space easement" to preserve the open character of his land, remove the pressure for development, and stabilize his taxes at a level he can afford.

CHARLES E. LITTLE AND ROBERT L. BURNAP
Stewardship
The Open Space Institute
145 E. 52 Street
New York, N.Y. 10022

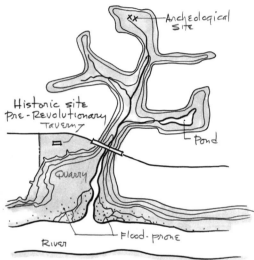

COMMUNITY OPEN SPACE CREATED BY GIFTS OF PRIVATE LAND

Donations of unbuildable land, or grants of conservation easements, with suitable use restrictions, have tax and other benefits to the owners. The community also gains by preserving its scenic-historic assets.

Every farm woodland, in addition to yielding lumber, fuel and posts, should provide . . . a liberal education. This crop of wisdom never fails, but it is not always harvested.

ALDO LEOPOLD
A Sand County Almanac
Oxford University Press
Fair Lawn, N.J., 1969

of means by which private landowners may manage, develop, or dispose of their holdings in such a way as to protect the natural quality of the landscape, while contributing to the appearance and livability of the surrounding community. The essential ingredients are a love for the land, and a sense of stewardship.

Offer excess lands for sale to guardian agencies

Excess property, or that not suited for other purposes, may make welcome additions to highway corridors, park lands, greenbelts, or other open space systems. Even exhausted farmlands or extraction pits are often eagerly sought by conservation groups or by public agencies, for rehabilitation. The thoughtful disposition, and thus protection, of such surplus land is a community service. It may also bring income, while enhancing the value and use of the property remaining.

Contribute scenic-historic features to a conservancy

Historic structures or scenic areas of a farm or estate—such as marshes, streams or ponds, ravines, outcropping ridges, or wooded slopes—may be given away while yet preserved for the enjoyment of the property owners and their heirs. Simple covenants going with the gift and land may limit the public use to hiking, nature study, or to its off-site viewing only.

The lands conveyed become tax free. The donation of larger tracts in stages may become a significant factor in wise inheritance planning.

Grant scenic and conservation easements

Often lands adjacent to a highway, park, or private development may add much of scenic quality or contain wetlands, woodlands, or other areas of ecological value. In some cases, the owner who wishes to retain the property and continue its present use may be willing to convey to a public agency, or to another property owner, certain rights to the land. These rights may be granted in the form of a scenic or conservation easement. The easement will legally describe and limit the uses to which the land in question may be put, as well as the terms of its preservation and care.

The gift or sale of such rights has many benefits. Both parties are assured of environmental protection; the grantor is normally given tax abatement; and new construction is forestalled.

A variant of the "preservation by easement" approach is the purchase of the land in fee, with an agreeable leaseback arrangement. Much of the farmland along the Blue Ridge Parkway has been sustained in use by this means.

Consider the shared use of private lands

Owners, as a public service or as a source of income, may elect to share the use of their property with others. This can be done in a number of ways, as by posting their land as a game preserve or by admitting schoolchildren and others for nature appreciation and study. It may be opened to campers, or to hunters and fishermen, on a lease or fee arrangement. A pathway easement may be leased or granted as a link in a hiking or bicycle trail. Often the affording of views to or across their acreage may in itself add much to the pleasure of those who live in or move through the region.

Precondition the sale of land to be used for development

Land need not be handed over "carte blanche" to developers or speculators for whatever use they may have in mind. If their motives are good, they should have no objection to a certain amount of preplanning. This could well include the designation of key areas or features to be preserved, and the provision of greenbelt screening and protection. Even points of access may be defined by covenant, as may types of use, building heights, densities, and the general disposition of drives, structures, and parking areas. The right of review and acceptance of the development plan may also be agreed upon.

Such preconditioning of the property sale need not reduce its value. It may, however, be a crucial factor in protecting the quality of the surrounding community.

Apply the "cluster-planning" approach to land development

As long as the pressures of increasing population persist, it is inevitable that a good part of our present open space inventory must in time be devoted to new housing, institutions, and business centers. Even when the land is to be intensively used, however, much can be done to preserve its natural character.

This can be accomplished by the application of the principle of cluster planning, as elsewhere described in this book. This fairly recent innovation in land development provides for the planning of more compact building arrangements to allow increased space between the groupings. By this device natural features may be preserved and green enframement and focal use areas provided. Often, a community or homeowners' association is formed to care for the common land and facilities.

Assure the land needed for public use

If open space land is to be saved and made available for the use and enjoyment of those who are to live in our communities, it must be set aside at the time of the community planning. Adequate land for schools, parks, and buffers, as well as for the conservation of the best of the landscape features must be built into the neighborhood plan. That land which is needed for the use of the neighborhood solely will be provided by the developer, and its cost included in the sales price or rental of the dwelling or other buildings. This will be made a condition for the granting of rezoning or building permits. If the parcels are so limited in size that this is not feasible, then an equitable sum should be contributed by the developer on a pro rata basis to be applied to the purchase of property suitable for this purpose.

Such additional land as may be desirable for open space needs of the larger community should be predesignated and purchased with public funds.

Organizing for action

Ultimately, all ideas and actions flow from individuals. It is a person, not a group or a government, that is first concerned with a condition and decides to do something about it. In the field of conservation and environmental planning, it is the individual who sniffs the first acrid traces of polluted air, who becomes alarmed at the degradation of a scenic valley, or who determines to save a favorite hill or pond. Once motivated, the individual will seek alliance with others having interest in the same cause—to gain more leverage and clout.

In seeking help and guidance, a citizen will normally do well to look first to the government.

Nationally, in broadest terms, the whole federal government

Further Reading:

Austin, Richard L., ed.
The Yearbook of Landscape Architecture: Historic Preservation
Van Nostrand Reinhold Company Inc.
New York, 1983

Chanlett, Emil T.
Environmental Protection
McGraw-Hill Book Company
New York, 1973

Clark, John
Coastal Ecosystems—Ecological Considerations for Management of the Coastal Zone
The Conservation Foundation
Washington, D.C., 1975

Conservation Foundation
National Parks for the Future: An Appraisal of the National Parks As They Begin Their Second Century in a Changing America
Washington, D.C., 1974

Costonis, John J.
Space Adrift: Saving Urban Landmarks Through the Chicago Plan
The National Trust for Historic Preservation
University of Illinois Press
Urbana, Ill., 1974

Little, Charles E.
Challenge of the Land: Open Space Preservation at the Local Level
Pergamon Press
New York, 1969

Little, Charles E., and Robert L. Burnap
Stewardship
The Open Space Institute
New York, 1965

McPhee, John
Encounters with the Archdruid
Farrar, Straus & Giroux, Inc.
New York, 1971

may be considered a conservation unit. After all, it is fundamentally responsible for the health and well-being, and the orderly development, of the nation. Such a view conveys a whole new attitude toward conservation, and toward government itself. Each federal department has in fact been given, at the cabinet level, a mandate to conduct its affairs and to coordinate its activities in such a way as to ensure environmental protection. A separate "inspector general" agency, the EPA, has been created to cut across departmental lines and report directly to the President on environmental matters. Congress enacts the basic conservation legislation, and congressional representatives provide an open line between their constituents and the particular federal agency most concerned with the problem in question.

Each state, in turn, is responsible for the conservation and best use of its own resources. The implication would seem to be that each state government has established a clear and orderly legal and administrative framework for carrying out its work. This is not the case. Most states have far to go in formulating effective conservation programs such as those of Florida, California, Virginia, Connecticut, Michigan, and Vermont.

Each region, county, and local jurisdiction has its own areas of responsibility and its own work to do.

An increasingly important role in environmental protection and planning has been assumed by nonprofit organizations such as the Conservation Foundation, the National Land Trust, the Trust for Public Land, the Nature Conservancy, and the National Trust for Historic Preservation. Appealing to the public and to industry for support and contributions, they have channeled funds into a broad range of critical projects that would otherwise have gone wanting.

Many other private associations and clubs are also wielding telling influence. Included in the growing list of such effective groups are the Sierra Club, the National Audubon Society, and the National Wildlife Federation, for example. They have awakened widespread interest in nature through their superb publications and led highly successful crusades against formidable threats to cherished natural landmarks. Other exemplary programs are those of the American Forestry Association, the Izaak Walton League, the Wilderness Society, and that of the National Council of State Garden Clubs, which has undertaken an advanced training course in landscape appreciation and planning for many thousands of its members.

Professional societies have become vocal and articulate. Student groups have marched in protest, canvassed from door to door enlisting support, and have worked elbow to elbow up littered ravines and stream beds in ardent demonstration cleanup projects.

Within the pages of our books and magazines and Sunday supplements we are reading of the new crusade. Our theaters are dramatizing the issues. Our radios and televisions are preaching the word.

These are heartening signs.

Further Reading (cont.):

Roosevelt, Nicolas
Conservation: Now or Never
Dodd, Mead & Company, Inc.
New York, 1970

Sale, Kirkpatrick
Dwellers In the Land: The Bio-regional Vision
The Sierra Club
San Francisco, Calif., 1985

Scott, Randall W., ed.
Management and Control of Growth: Issues, Techniques, Problems, Trends (3 vols.)
The Urban Land Institute
Washington, D.C., 1975

Sheaff, Richard D.
The Formation of Land Trusts and Watershed Associations
Society for the Protection of New Hampshire Forests
Concord, N.H., 1970

Smith, Guy-Harold, ed.
Conservation of Natural Resources,
4th ed.
John Wiley & Sons, Inc.
New York, 1971

Smithsonian Institution, Center for Natural Areas
Planning Considerations for Statewide Inventories of Critical Environmental Areas: A Reference Guide
Washington, D.C., 1974

Watt, Kenneth E. F.
Principles of Environmental Science
McGraw-Hill Book Company
New York, 1973

Wolf, Peter
Land In America: Its Value, Use and Control
Pantheon Books
New York, 1981

Keep your congressional representatives conservation-minded

Remember that they are under constant pressure from special-interest groups and lobbies to lower quality standards, controls, and penalties. Let them hear from your side. Make it clear that a majority of their constituents have an active concern in environmental protection and are watching their performance and voting record.

Know your state program

Keep the names and addresses of your state legislators at hand. Let them know of your interest in conservation. Ask to be kept informed. Work particularly for:

1. A progressive legislative package which will provide the required authority, machinery, and funds essential to a strong conservation program.

2. A state commission on the environment.

3. A state conservation foundation.

4. State guidance and aid to local governments in environmental protection.

Thump for regional planning

Only on a regional basis can most environmental problems—such as air and water pollution, noise, flooding, and lack of open space protection—be studied and resolved.

Just as individuals gain strength and direction in group action, so do towns, cities, and counties gain by joining in regional planning and conservation programs. Local officials, however, are reluctant to share their authority or budgets, and sometimes drag their feet. Political persuasion may be necessary.

Join a conservation group

In most localities an active club, society, or conservancy has already been formed and is eargerly seeking new members. Choose the one which you believe to be most effective. If none exists, form your own group to help on any particular project that seems to be needing attention. Or go it alone, if you prefer. The growing conservation movement is the sum of such group, and individual, efforts.

Become a local "watchdog"

The place to solve problems is where they occur.

Most instances of local pollution, or other environmental degradation, can be stopped, and often quickly, if they are brought to the attention of the proper authorities, by enough people, and with enough persuasive force. But first they must be documented, by description or photograph, and reported. A good place to start is with your local conservation groups, public officials, and press. The person to start it is you.

A better world in which to live can only be made possible if concerns, and hopes, are translated into action.

A healthy environment, a balanced ecology—is for the benefit of everyone. Why is it that a cause which is approved by the majority is so blindly neglected in government policy decisions?

Mainly because the passive support of a majority will have no real power until conservation becomes a major election issue. And the majority can only express itself on a few such issues at a time. People don't get a chance to vote directly on the issues. They can only vote for a candidate and all his platform at once. Thus it is not enough for people to want clean air and water. They must demand it with such intensity that they refuse to vote for a man who would deny them, no matter what else he has to offer. Until this happens, pollution will continue to get worse.

MARION EDEY
The Environmental Handbook
(edited by Garrett DeBell)
Ballantine Books, Inc.
New York, 1970

The ideal government is one in which those elected truly represent the will of the people—for the good of all.

Nothing great was ever achieved without enthusiasm.

RALPH WALDO EMERSON
As quoted in *Conservation Quotes*
U.S. Department of the Interior,
National Park Service
January 1953

Environmental improvement is not something to be achieved at once by any sweeping governmental mandate.

Environmental improvement is perhaps most importantly the sum of myriad group and individual actions.

Any act—small or large—which makes a place (*any* place) more attractive or more livable is a gain in a worthy cause.

In the past few years the public has been aroused from long-term apathy to an eagerness for environmental quality. We have come to realize that our land and our water and our air are essential to the well being of our nation. We have come to know that environmental quality is not the aberration of a few eccentrics but that it must be a first priority of the public business. We are at the crucial point, however, where the easy part, the public realization and acceptance of the need is over. Now we must stop the speechmaking and begin the hard action.

HENRY L. DIAMOND, quoted in
Annual Report of the Citizens' Advisory Committee
on Environmental Quality
Washington, D.C., 1972

LOOKING AHEAD

A search for quality

Improving the environment
should not mean only correcting
pollution or the other evils of
technological and urban growth.
It should be a creative process
through which man and nature
continue to evolve in harmony.
At its highest level, civilized life
is a form of exploration which
helps man rediscover his unity
with nature. In the words of
T. S. Eliot,

We shall not cease from
    exploring,
And the end of all our
    exploring
Will be to arrive where we
    started
And know the place for the
    first time.

RENÉ DUBOS
Environmental Improvement (Air, Water, & Soil)
The Graduate School
U.S. Department of Agriculture
Washington, D.C., 1966

We are the product of our culture. As we have believed, as we have aspired, so we have become. Our attitudes and actions change, but only as our values change. It is as simple, and altogether as complex, as that. If this be so, then let us first look back and appraise the course which has led us into our present condition. Then, it is hoped, we may take a corrected heading.

We are a new country. Ours is a young culture in a new land. Think now; it is not yet five short centuries since Columbus guided his tiny *Santa Maria* along our southern shores. We are, relatively speaking, a newcomer in the established family of nations. We are of pioneering stock, in a burgeoning, boom-town, push-forward, bust-wide-open country. If we are to understand ourselves, we must recognize first and foremost the fact of our rambunctious youth.

We are a free country. This spirit of freedom is in the blood and must be reckoned with. Much of what we have been, are, and will be, is bound up in this freedom of enterprise. We are proud and jealous of our individual rights and do not like to be told what to do.

Group actions to help others—the barn raisings, threshings, quilting bees, and flood relief for the people of the neighboring or distant town—lie at the heart of our tradition.

We are a democratic country. Since the long ago time of Athens' golden age, our land is the first to be governed by the common vote for the common good.

These things are of great significance to an understanding of our American people, our history, and our future.

A time of transition

By the late 1800s there had been established in the United States a social system ruled by big business and by men of great private wealth. These were the clients of our early engineers, architects, and landscape architects. These were the days of the building of transcontinental railways, the sumptuous railroad resorts, the great estates, and public gardens replete with magnificent sculptural groupings and monumental fountains. This was the age of elegance. There were many things to commend this period of our history, but there were social undercurrents that presaged a change, and change was soon to come.

The times through which we have been passing since the turn of the century have been transition times. They have been marked with wars, depressions, camping "hippies," marching blacks, race riots, and student revolt against the draft. They have seen the rise of labor unions, social security, and Medicare. They have ushered in the era of the motorcar, national highway networks, unprecedented mobility, and migrations to the West and South. They have brought the population explosion, the energy shortage, critical levels of pollution, the accelerating devastation of our natural landscape, and at last a determined crusade, sparked by our youth, to protect our living earthscape.

The years of our lives have been years of experiment, of metamorphosing values, of rapid growth, of confusion and often chaos.

This is not surprising to those who have sensed these things to be the mark of a generally peaceful but deep-seated social revolution. We have experienced a shift from the era of the great private fortunes and minor governmental control to an era of waning individual power, strong central government, increasing group pressures, and astronomical government budgets. This shift has left its imprints.

Social gains

Hunger, abject poverty, illiteracy, human degradation and misery—the products of every major civilization from earliest recorded times—have been remarkably reduced in our nation. Further advances are being constantly pressed. There is evidence on every hand of a newly intensified social concern.

Our class structure is less stratified than ever before. There is much less of a gap between our underprivileged and our elite. This has many obvious advantages and gives promise of a new social stability.

We have as a society become so proficient and so demanding that the niceties of our parents' time are considered to be the necessities of our own. Ours is a time of unprecedented abundance.

We have developed our productive capacity and technical know-how to the point where our horizons are almost unlimited.

We have gained a new leisure which, if well applied, should lead us into new levels of cultural gain.

We are coming to understand the negative effects of overpopulation and are beginning to take effective measures to stabilize our growth.

There is new respect for others. Until recently, individuals could use their property as they liked, without regard for their neighbors. This is no longer so. New planning concepts, zoning powers, restrictions, and controls have provided cities and suburbs with the means by which senseless exploitation and disruption may be curbed and more orderly development assured. We are learning to accept regulation within reason, and to gear our planning decisions and our actions to the long-range good of the group. Yet the changes have not all been for the better.

Social losses

Where, now, are our rugged individualists? The epoch of the unique bold spirits is passing. We accept and teach conformity as a positive social value. The very qualities of free thought and individual enterprise that founded and developed our nation are being discouraged by our educational systems and by our government. This is a loss that no nation can afford.

Where are our "taste-makers"? As late as the start of our present century there was a wealthy social class that had developed a high artistic consciousness and a love for the finer things of life. Its members were the patrons who collected art and who commissioned the artists. They were the public benefactors. These men and women of position have been forced by taxation to abdicate their

We must think anew, we must act anew, we must disenthrall ourselves.
Abraham Lincoln (1862)
Quoted in *Saturday Review*
December 18, 1975

321

In the present century, we have come to live increasingly on capital resources—of oil, coal, and other minerals—using up in a few generations what it took tens of millions of years of Earth time to accumulate.

The future landscape of America is in the hands of businessman.
Nation's Business

role of artistic arbiters. There have been, as yet, few successors . . . except perhaps the advertising agencies and the publishers of our glossy magazines.

Where are our craftsmen? The rise of the labor unions, despite their need and benefits, has spelled the demise of excellence. This has been a tactical error of policy, for the unions could have contrived to ensure fine craftsmanship rather than preclude it, and thus worked in the public interest as well as for union gain. But labor is misusing its power and is employing its muscle to limit productivity, reduce quality, and discourage innovation. In a competitive world market this poses a serious threat to our national prosperity.

Where are our artists? One sure measure of a culture is the position it gives the painter, the sculptor—those gifted with creativity. Our present culture is one in which the highest esteem is reserved for the scientist. The artist in our times works on a low level of economic reward and social recognition. The painter is in the attic. The sculptor labors in the converted garage.

Where is our sense of quality? We have come to accept somehow, without question, the fact that we find along our highways the brash conglomeration of the dairy cream, the used-car lot, the pottery stalls with pink concrete flamingos, and whitewashed concrete deer. Our furniture is produced by machines. Our carpets, cars, and dinnerware are mass-produced. Our children's toys are punched out of the flimsiest of plastics. We live in a chewing-gum, push-button, soda-pop atmosphere of poor taste on a mass basis. Our lives are steeped in mediocrity. We need desperately those individuals who understand quality and therefore demand it.

What of our living environment? Are we conserving our natural heritage? Hardly. Almost everywhere that man has laid his hand, he has brought disruption and ruin. We have chopped, plowed, burned, bulldozed, stripped, mined, and dredged without control or reason. Our highways have been gouged through the hills and lined with trash and clutter. We have befouled our rivers and oceans and charged our atmosphere with deleterious matter and poisonous fumes. Our cities are machinations of friction. They are oriented to their traffic and service ways rather than to open parklands, plazas, and refreshing courts and malls.

These things have not happened through malice or through willful, destructive intent. They have happened because in the rush and exuberance of "opening up" our land, we have placed the emphasis on the right of the individual—on the freedom of exploitation—rather than upon a concept of the highest good for succeeding generations.

Economic influences

It is an unfortunate commentary on our times that our society is governed to perhaps an unprecedented degree by the dictates of economics. The sole measure of sound project planning has too often become the index of its revenue-producing potential over its gross development cost.

It is obvious to all professional planners that to function in our time they must "face the realities" and be prepared to substantiate their proposals on an economic basis. It is reasonable that they employ the techniques of the feasibility study, capital improvement programming, and operational financing. They must consider cash-flow situations, governmental aid programs, and tax benefits. They must be alert to, and react to, economic opportunities.

They will fail in their responsibility, however, if they do not make clear, on every possible occasion, their conviction that the feasibility of a project must also be determined on the basis of its long-range social implications.

Although a planned community would provide much needed and desirable housing, if it would drastically lower a subsurface water table or preclude the public enjoyment of a beach or seashore, it is not feasible.

No matter how favorable the balance sheets, if a proposed industrial complex would spew a cloud of dust or stench into the atmosphere, or contaminate a river, it can no longer be tolerated.

A projected freeway, fully warranted on an economic cost-benefit ratio basis alone can no longer be considered acceptable. Feasibility studies, to have meaning, must also include a full evaluation of the effects of alternate modes and routes, or no further routes, upon the social, historic, and ecological values of the region to be served.

Economic justification, so absolute in the past, can no longer be considered reason enough to give license to either the private entrepreneur *or a public agency* to act against the long-range public good.

Politically speaking

We have moved into a period of "big government," of increased federal powers, of increased federal influence, and of increased federal emphasis. All other spheres of government—city, county, and state—have experienced the same mushrooming trend. Social welfare is now a national concern rather than the concern of the family or neighborhood. The government has in recent years launched major programs for the benefit of the needy, the underprivileged, and the aged.

Planning, also, is now approached on a governmental basis, with increasing federal participation in all community, county, and state development programs. These include those of land use, transportation and community planning, conservation and urban affairs.

We have come to keep our eyes on Washington for the solution of local, as well as national, problems. We look instinctively to the government for assistance and regulation, and thus come to accept "guidelines" and "standards" and conformity to program. There are possible gains in such regulation and government aid—but there are also hazards.

The guides and "minimum standards" of the Federal Housing Administration (FHA) and Public Housing Administration (PHA) programs, for example, have produced in our country a flood of the most sterile and unimaginative housing in the contemporary world. Their minimum standards have produced minimum quality. Their fixed regulations and "review by the manual" have produced dreary standardization. Nor has the promise and great potential of the federal Department of Housing and Urban Development (HUD) so far been realized. Its projects have been swamped in a bureaucratic sea of forms, reports, standards, criteria, and endless paperwork. There is hope, however, that new streamlined programs may be conceived to stimulate, rather than hamper, creative environmental planning and design. If so, HUD may yet exert its resources to help revitalize our cities, give an orderly structure to our developing regions, and create new and largely self-sufficient communities where life may be more vibrant and satisfying.

Environmental protection also has recently come under the federal purview. The National Environmental Policy Act, for example, has exerted a powerful influence for good in this increasingly popular cause. The federal government is presently looking beyond our national boundaries toward participation in a global strategy for resource conservation and pollution control.

In recent years, we have made those gains which are fundamental to a socialized democracy, and we have experienced those losses which are inherent in a socialized democracy. Our system guarantees to the individual certain rights and thus gives importance to the individual as a sociopolitical unit. It has given increased status to labor. The lower economic classes have been "social-legislated" up the scale. The upper economic classes have been taxed down the scale. We have produced a broad central band in the social spectrum and are becoming a middle-class country. This middle class and the government acting in its interest have now assumed the dominant role.

The new technology

Our way of life has changed more in the past 200 years than in the previous 10,000, more in the past 20 years than in the preceding 200.

Our culture is perhaps best described as a technological culture. The life we know is to an unprecedented extent the life provided by our new technology. Within the last half-century, the old general store has been transformed into the regional shopping center; the rutted wagon road to the controlled-access expressway; the one-seater plane to the planet-orbiting spacecraft . . . and all the signals are "Go!"

New systems of communications have linked us directly with all mankind and made us citizens of the world, whether or not we like it, and whether or not we understand or can yet cope with the many implications.

New methods of transportation and transit have reduced travel time and distances to fractions of their former magnitude. We are a society moving in vehicles—the most mobile ever known. The automobile is the symbol of our time. The biggest single problem of our urban, suburban, and regional planning is traffic. Our greatest development potential lies in the devising of new systems and patterns for the movement of people and goods.

New dietary, medical, and surgical advances have relieved us of immeasurable pain and suffering and almost doubled our life expectancy.

New methods of goods production—automation, computer programming, and the like—have increased our manufacturing capacity to the point where we can produce more of almost every commodity than we can possibly use.

New techniques of energy production give hope that in the not-too-distant future we may have clean and abundant power.

New military weapons and the potential of total destruction have presented us with a threat to the very survival of the human race. We are a society motivated more by fear than by high purpose.

We have put so much emphasis on the technological process that we have become the servants of our machines. We have created an artificial age. We have abrogated nature and strained our patient Earth to the limits of tolerance. But even as nature seems ready to capitulate, new counterbalancing forces are at work within our society.

We have begun to rebel against the end products of our technology—against the stark air-conditioned cells we call our offices; against the mechanized cubes we call our homes; against the barren windblown canyons of our cities. We are sickened as we survey the extent of our pollution. We are beginning to sense that life in such surroundings does not satisfy. We, as a nation, are beginning to recognize the need for a more salubrious living environment in which we may find again the simple satisfactions of life.

In every part of the world, the interplay between man and nature has commonly taken the form of a true symbiosis—namely a biological relationship which alters somewhat the two components of the symbiotic system in a way that is beneficial to both. Such transformations, achieved through symbiosis, account in large part for the immense diversity of places on earth and for the fitness between man and environment so commonly observed in areas that have been settled and have remained stable for long periods of time.

. . . by using scientific knowledge and ecological wisdom we can manage the earth so as to create environments which are ecologically stable, economically profitable, esthetically rewarding, and favorable to the continued growth of civilization.

RENÉ DUBOS
B. Y. Morrison Memorial Lecture
Annual Meeting, American Association for the
Advancement of Science
Washington, D.C., 1972
(Lectureship established by the Agricultural Research
Service of the U.S. Department of Agriculture)

Cooperation with nature can lead to new forms of creative expression. Man has tradi-tionally found expression in music, poetry, painting, the performing and plastic arts, in the sciences, in industrial technology. Only recently has he begun to give this impulse expression on a large scale in the art and science of designing his environment.

From Sea to Shining Sea
A Report on the American Environment—
Our Natural Heritage
By the President's Council on Recreation and
Natural Beauty
U.S. Government Printing Office
Washington, D.C., 1968

That made me think . . . of the events or causes that might bind this great, sprawling heterogeneous and frequently anarchic country together. No such cause will bind every fragment in the society. I doubt if doomsday would do that. But partial and temporary binding is better than none, and for the next few years would be therapeutic. Here I believe environmentalism, antipollution, conservation, Save the Earth, call it what you like, is one of the answers. Among the people I have talked to . . . this is by long odds the nearest approach to a common concern.

C. P. SNOW
"Hope for America"
Look magazine
December 1, 1970

Looking ahead

As we seek a way of life yielding less distress and greater fulfillment;

in which our humanitarian horizons may be broadened, scientific inquiry extended, and technology advanced;

in which a determination to improve our physical environment will be a strong guiding compulsion;

and in which we may find inspiration and enjoy the rich cultural attributes of urbanity,

while yet sensing ourselves to be always at home with nature, and our lives attuned to nature's processes;

we might well commit ourselves, and our resources, to the achievement of these ten compelling goals:

1. *Stabilize the population.* René Dubos, the eminent biologist, has observed that most of the environmental problems in the modern world have their origin in the rapid increase of world population. There are those who believe that with the advent of ''the pill'' the population upsurge has at last been brought under control. Far from it. Although the *rate* of increase has diminished within the past decade, it is anticipated that without the introduction of yet unforeseen factors, the present United States population of slightly over 200 million will be increased to a total of approximately 300 million by the end of this century. This coupled with the increasing migration to our cities would mean that for every two persons now living or working within our crowded urbanizing regions, there will by then be three. The resulting stress upon our water and food supply, energy production, waste removal, and transportation systems could well defy solution.

2. *Reverse the trends of environmental pollution.* To put it succinctly, worsening conditions of pollution in America have reached such alarming proportions that an aroused public has at last been moved to action. The indignation of the people has finally become so vocal and so purposeful that the ponderous wheels of government have been set into motion. With the passage of the National Environmental Policy Act a special federal agency, the Environmental Protection Agency, has been formed and given broad powers to oversee all programs relating to the protection of our environment.

    Significant progress has been made in the development of some standards and some control procedures and in arresting some of the more flagrant abuses, especially where public health has been threatened. The start has been promising, but lest we become lulled into complacency, it should be noted that within the foreseeable future the annual tonnage of pollutants discharged into our atmosphere and water bodies is expected to *increase*, rather than *decrease*. Although the amount of pollution per person will be reduced, the reduction will be more than offset by the increase in national and world population. Further causes are the fact of the global energy crisis and the reluctance of the nations of the world, to date, to pay the price of a full-scale antipollution campaign.

Since government is the ultimate, though sometimes recalcitrant, instrument of the people, and since pollution in all forms can be reduced by existing technology to acceptable levels, the people, through their governments, will achieve in time that degree of environmental quality that they demand and are willing to pay for.

It is a generally accepted thesis that we are the products of our heredity and environment. If we then wish for ourselves and children a better world in which to live, our options are simple and clear.

3. *Revise our tax laws.* To understand development trends and patterns, it is necessary first to understand the tax laws, loopholes, and inequities by which they were to a large extent created. Entrepreneurs routinely locate business ventures, and corporations move their plants, to escape or to mitigate one tax situation or to take advantage of another. New communities are planned in direct response to tax gains and losses. Thriving farm communities are often forced out of production because their fields and orchards are taxed on the basis of appraised or salable market value rather than upon the agricultural use. In every developing region desirable open space lands are being sold off to escape the rising assessments.

The waste of resources resulting from inequitable and unbalanced property taxes is a national disgrace. Perhaps the fundamental approach is wrong. Taxes on land or real estate encourage the maximum profit taking rather than the optimum use. They discourage, rather than stimulate, first-rate development. They tend toward dispersion rather than consolidation. High local taxes drive off the enterprises on which they were levied. Mills are abandoned, homeowners move, and farms are put up for sale, only to increase the burden upon those who elect to remain. Fluctuations in tax levies from place to place and from year to year result in a transient society, business losses, and an unstable economy.

Could it be that the whole concept of the property tax is outmoded, and that *all* revenues should be raised instead by taxes on the sale of goods, and on net earnings? The advantages would be many. In any event, a thoroughgoing federal tax reform bill (and perhaps a constitutional amendment) is needed to provide a fair and uniform system of assessment and collection on a national basis. Aside from the psychological benefits, the savings in resources and energy consumption could be immense.

4. *Reduce our energy consumption.* Haul down the pennants, fold the tents, the carnival is over, and no doubt it is all for the best. The gaudy days of our super-horsepower, automated chariots

In the last few years the American people as a whole have made it clear that they do care what kind of country our affluence is creating. They do care about the quality of the air they breathe, about the quality of the water they use, and the beauty of the land that surrounds them.

They have been willing to dip into their pocketbooks and invest in a better environment.

LAURANCE S. ROCKEFELLER
From *The Quality of Our Environment—The Challenge to Landscape Architects*
An address before the American Society of Landscape Architects
Niagara Falls, Ontario, 1968

The further away the goal, the more certain the way.

KURT THEODOR SCHIRRMACHER
The Architecture of Fantasy: Utopian Building & Planning in Modern Times
Ulrich Conrads and Hans G. Sperlich
Praeger Publishers, Inc.
New York, 1962

are numbered, as are the roaring forays of the souped-up cycles, snowmobiles, and palatial summer power craft that have guzzled great drafts of oil and gas and shattered the peace of our lakes and countryside. They are passing symbols of the heyday of our insatiable appetite for automotive power.

Americans have squandered more horsepower and kilowatts per person, by double and triple, than are used by people anywhere else. Our extravagant vehicles, gadgets, lighting, heating, and our loosely extended patterns of transportation and power distribution have consumed more energy, by a hundred times, than has been needed to keep us mobile, safe, and warm. Our projected demands, as differentiated from needs, have risen on a curve far exceeding population rise, in spite of the warnings by our experts that fuel reserves are in critically short supply.

Power is pollution, at least in all its present forms. It is mine acid leaching into the streams, oil spills and leakage, the thermal pollution of rivers and lakes, nuclear fallout and radioactive residues. It is smoke and fumes. Clean power, as by solar or tidal energy, or by nuclear fusion, is still some years in the offing in terms of economically feasible production. Until it is available, and while our demands must be met in the main by fossil fuels, we will be forced to curtail, drastically, our energy consumption. And our lives will be better for it.

5. *Encourage the creation of planned communities.* On the face of it, it would seem that local governments would do all in their power to implement the planning and construction of well-planned communities and new towns. The alternative is the endless scatteration of traditional parcel-by-parcel development in which a builder acquires a lot or parcel of land along a dedicated street, and builds in compliance with local, and often outmoded, ordinances and building codes. He assumes no responsibility or cost for the provision of schools, parks, recreation, open space, water supply, sewage or solid-waste disposal, employment centers, cultural facilities, or most of the other amenities which make for wholesome community life.

Parcel-by-parcel developers have relatively few problems. The public agencies are geared to record their standard plat plans and issue building permits without delays.

When, however, a development group acquires interest in a large tract of land and sets about the comprehensive planning of a unified and total community, it seems that the jurisdictional government and all its agencies are joined in a league against them. Plan reviews are exhaustive and difficult to schedule. In many cases the requirements for background and supporting information would seem to be devised to provide data that should properly have been assembled and furnished by the agencies themselves. Extensive dedications of land for street rights-of-way, parks, school sites, and conservation areas are assumed to be an obligation. Commitments for escrow payments to be applied for off-site improvements may be demanded, together with environmental protection controls far exceeding existing levels.

Such unusual costs, coupled with those of extraordinary planning and engineering fees, presentations, hearings, delays, and the preparation of exhaustive impact reports are often so formidable that the developers are forced to abandon their plans in full or in part, and resort to the sale of undeveloped parcels.

Yet in most urbanizing regions such balanced and more self-sufficient communities are the best, and perhaps *only*, hope for orderly development. It would be to the advantage of the municipalities, as well as the state and federal governments, to encourage and support such endeavors in all ways possible, rather than to block or delay them. They would do well to initiate *planned community development (PCD)* procedures, streamlined reviews, tax incentives, and even loans to help offset the extremely heavy front-end costs involved in large-scale, comprehensive planning.

It can be seen that the same problems and principles apply to the comprehensive planning for any large land development, such as for unified industrial parks, business-office complexes, commercial centers, institutional campuses, and recreation areas. Where a development group is willing and able to "plan it all together" in close cooperation with the responsible governmental agencies and in consonance with the long-range regional plans and objectives, their efforts should be in all ways supported. This is community planning at its very best.

6. *Provide for the free and separate movement of people, vehicles, and goods.* Wherever there is life and activity, there is need for circulation. Thriving residential communities cut off from downtown or the surrounding countryside soon deteriorate. Bustling shopping centers wither whenever a major sector of their trade area is denied ready access. Industrial districts blocked off from the free flow of materials or personnel become inefficient and noncompetitive. Churches, hospitals, concert halls, or sports arenas are forced to relocate when their parishioners, patients, or patrons are no longer able to reach them conveniently. When cities, neighborhoods, or ventures fail, it is usually because of a breakdown in circulation ways and distribution systems.

Our failures to provide for the safe and efficient movement of people within our cities and lesser communities occur mainly when persons on foot must cross busy streets and highways. This intermittent movement is wasteful in the extreme. Yet our traditional business and residential communities repeat the senseless grid pattern for square mile after square mile. Far more efficient and pleasant is a plan arrangement by which traffic moves *between* groupings of buildings which face inward upon pedestrian ways and spaces. People thus move from building to building, or from place to place, within a pleasant parklike environment. Vehicles, free of the intersections and cross traffic, may also move without interruption.

In the more recent and more successful shopping, business-office, and apartment malls, as in the industrial parks and institutional campuses, people, automobiles, and delivery trucks are all separated by varying route alignments or differences in grade.

Both within and outside of the cities, the failures in the circulation of private automobiles, transit buses, and transport vehicles usually come when the same roadway is shared by all three. Such sharing is illogical, not only because of the differing rates of speed, but also because the three types of vehicles have varying points of origin and destination, and require differing roadway characteristics. A more workable, and far more acceptable, system will provide separate routes and specialized roadways for each type of vehicular movement.

7. *Restore our sick and sundered cities.* Our cities are in need of help. Not palliatives, not tonic infusions, but major surgery.

Historically, cities have been the regional centers of intensive commercial and cultural activity. They have been concentrated, often compressed by ancient moats or walls. Their chief reason for being has been to provide a rich multiplicity of opportunities, choices of vibrant interactions. These are best afforded, as in the medieval town centers or oriental bazaars, where at a pedestrian scale, the distances to be traveled are short and the variety great. For centuries these vital cities have withstood, or recovered from, the attacks of armies and the scourge of plagues. But the contemporary cities of the world have been invaded by an insidious enemy, the automobile, that has all but destroyed them as unified entities.

The pedestrian ways and plazas have been usurped by the car. The essential connections between shops, offices, residences, and restaurants have been severed by streets and avenues streaming with vehicular traffic. Huge parking compounds have moved in to take over, as apartments and businesses retreat, and as evermore trafficways are constructed to maintain the interconnections. Department stores, offices, and banks have joined the exodus to escape the delays and frictions of traffic. Hospitals, cathedrals, and even the governmental complexes have left the city, to form their own more cohesive subcenters, only to be followed and hounded by the ubiquitous automobile.

The facts are irrefutable. Our cities will regain their strength, and their very reason for being, only when the scourge of the automobile is brought under firm control. They will regain their vitality when intensive activity "urba-centers" are restructured over rapid transit portals and around pedestrian ways, plazas, and interconnecting malls. They will attain new efficiency and appeal when the transportation of goods and services is provided on separate levels by new forms of

Further Reading:

Adams, Robert, et al.
The Fitness of Man's Environment
Smithsonian Annual II
Smithsonian Press
Washington, D.C., 1968

Bronowski, J.
The Ascent of Man
Little, Brown and Company
Boston, 1973

Brubaker, Sterling
In Command of Tomorrow: Resource and Environmental Strategies for Americans
Johns Hopkins University Press
Baltimore, Md., 1975

Church, Thomas D., Grace Hall, and Michael Laurie
Gardens Are for People
(Second Edition)
McGraw-Hill Book Company
New York, 1983

Clark, Kenneth
Civilisation
Harper & Row, Publishers, Inc.
New York, 1969

Clawson, Marion
America's Land and Its Uses
Johns Hopkins Press
Baltimore, Md., 1972

Fein, Albert
Frederick Law Olmsted and the American Environmental Tradition
G. Braziller
New York, 1972

Jellicoe, Geoffrey and Susan
The Landscape of Man
The Viking Press, Inc.
New York, 1975

Maddex, Diane, ed.
Master Builders: A Guide to Famous American Architects
National Trust for Historic Preservation
The Preservation Press
Washington, D.C., 1985

McHarg, Ian L.
Design With Nature
The Natural History Press
New York, 1969

transpo-conveyors served by regional terminals on classified freightway routes.

In the new cities, the automobile will be stored in peripheral towers, or on terraced decks beneath the activity tiers. They will sweep around and between (but not through) the urban cores on controlled-access parkways aligned through the regional hinterland. In the future urban metropolis the activity centers will be restored to the people and will regain their essential compression. The personally operated vehicle, in whatever forms it may evolve, will provide an important means of inter-urban access.

8. *Support statewide land-use planning.* The welcome environmental legislation of the past decade has dealt mainly with pollution and with ameliorating the negative effects of government-backed installations. It has done little to protect our most valuable resource, the land itself. The biggest single threat to that 70 percent or more of the American landscape now held in private ownership is its uncontrolled subdivision and use, and its helter-skelter development.

Landowners have traditionally believed themselves to have the sole right of decision as to the use of their property. Within recent years, it is true, the concepts of comprehensive planning, zoning, and land-use controls have been tried and tested with encouraging results; but outside of our more urbanized areas they have not been generally applied. They should be.

Many established land holding and development companies are dedicated to long-range programs of first quality land improvement. Their well-conceived communities, subdivisions, office parks, shopping malls, golf courses, and marinas have made a welcome contribution to the American scene. They continue to demonstrate the excellent and creative works that can be achieved by advanced techniques of land planning under the free enterprise system. Such well-considered use of the land is the best hope of most regions and is to be fostered in all ways possible.

Unfortunately, other land sales promoters and operators are not as scrupulous. They deal only in speculative sales, with minimum investment, maximum quick profit, and no concern for the long-term effects on the land or locality. In every state such opportunists race to secure extensive tracts of open land for recording and sale in lots and parcels as investment opportunities. The "opening up" of such land too often comprises clearing, grading, and the scratching-in of unpaved streets without storm runoff systems or erosion control. Other thousands of acres are being mined, often without adequate controls, for gravel, coal, or chemicals. Forests are being destroyed, marshes drained, and fields and pastures converted to dumps and stockpiles. From a transcontinental plane there would appear to be few expanses of our countryside not presently being marred, or ruined, by such unregulated activities.

Further Reading (cont.)

Naito, Akira, and Takeshi Nishikawa
Katsura, A Princely Retreat
Kodansha International Ltd.
Tokyo and New York, 1977

Neuschatz, Alan
Managing the Environment
Washington Environmental Research Center and U.S. Environmental Protection Agency
U.S. Government Printing Office
Washington, D.C., 1973

Oldham, John, and Ray Oldham
Gardens in Time
Lansdowne Press
Sydney, N.Y., 1980

Simonds, John O.
Landscape Architecture: A Manual of Site Planning and Design
(Second Edition)
McGraw-Hill Book Company
New York, 1983

Spirn, Anne Whiston
The Granite Garden
Basic Books, Inc.
New York, 1984

Stegner, Wallace, and Page Stegner with Eliot Porter
American Places
E. P. Dutton
New York, 1981

Teilhard de Chardin, Pierre
Building the Earth
Dimension Books
Wilkes-Barre, Pa., 1965

Whyte, William H.
The Last Landscape
Doubleday & Company, Inc.
Garden City, N.Y., 1968

In the face of this desecration, however, and perhaps because of it, a new land ethic is emerging. It would treat all land, including that in private ownership, as a *public resource*. As such, its use would be made subject to the public good and to compliance with a land-use plan developed by each state. This simple idea, which is gaining wide acceptance and support, could do more to ensure the good husbandry of our landscape than any other measure yet devised.

The best land-use planning would reserve to the public all sizable water areas and all water rights. It would limit the types of construction permitted within floodplains. It would designate the lands best suited for agriculture and for forest management. It would indicate those lands, waters, and landscape features to be preserved in their natural condition, and it would define those areas best suited to various types of development. The categories would be broad, with detailed land-use planning, zoning, and control reserved to the local governments. The sum of such statewide land-use plans would, and it is hoped *will*, constitute a national plan for the use of all our lands and waters.

9. *Protect the world ecosystem.* Only within recent years have we come to realize the extent to which we are accountable for the destiny of planet Earth and all life upon it. Unfortunately this realization has come, not through advancement in the science and politics of planetary management, but through the accumulating evidence that the by-products of our new technology are poisoning the biosphere to the point where all living creatures will soon be adversely affected.

The problems are worldwide in their dimension and demand worldwide solutions. While there are today in existence many groups dealing with environmental matters on an international scale, most efforts are directed toward research, or deal with a limited aspect of the total problem.

As is true in all matters requiring concerted action, no program can be more effective than the mechanism or organization established to define the objectives and carry it forward to fruition. There is urgent need for a powerful world council created with environmental protection as its one, all-encompassing goal. It must be conceived and formulated at the highest diplomatic and scientific levels, and provided with the authority and awesome budget required for full and coordinated action on all fronts. Only by such a well-directed, forceful, and systematic approach can the trends of deterioration be reversed and the very survival of mankind be assured. There are a number of possibilities.

George F. Kennan, the distinguished American diplomat, has suggested* as the functions of such a body:

a. The provision of adequate facilities for the collection, storage, retrieval, and dissemination of information on all aspects of the problem.

---

* In an essay, "To Prevent a World Wasteland" from *The Crisis for Survival*, William Morrow and Company, New York, 1970, p. 226.

b. The coordination of research and operational activities which now deal with environmental matters at the international level.

c. The establishment of international standards in environmental matters, and the provision of advice and help to governments and organizations in their efforts to meet these standards.

d. The framing of proposals for international action in matters relating to the high seas, the Arctic and Antarctic, the stratosphere, and outer space.

To stem the tide of deterioration in the human living environment will be an all-pervading concern of our next generation. This can only succeed if the people of all nations come to consider the planet Earth as their mutual dwelling place and join forces to care for it, together.

To see the earth as it truly is, small and blue and beautiful in that eternal silence where it floats, is to see ourselves as riders on the earth together, brothers on that bright loveliness in the eternal cold—brothers who know now they are truly brothers.
ARCHIBALD MacLEISH

The age of Nations is past. The task before us now, if we would not perish, is to build the earth.
PIERRE TEILHARD DE CHARDIN
Building the Earth
Published by Dimension Books
Denville, N.J., 1965
Copyright 1965 by Dimension Books

The management of the planet, whether we are talking about the need to prevent war or the need to prevent ultimate damage to the conditions of life, requires a world government. This will be the test of man's vision and greatness.
NORMAN COUSINS
Saturday Review
March 7, 1970

10. *Work assiduously for peace.* War is the absolute despoiler, the utter destroyer, and the ultimate polluter.

The words *war* and *pollution* share the unsavory connotation of disruption, ugliness, and waste. Conversely, the words *peace, health, beauty*—and *happiness*—all bring to mind the concept of things working well together, and in balance.

If we with our aggressive tendencies must wage war, then let it be a constructive war against *all* forms of degradation. Let it be a compelling crusade for a better world—of harmony between nation and nation and between the people of all nations and the bountiful Earth, their home.

Appraisal

How is it that of all earth's creatures, humans are the only species to poison themselves, the waters of the earth, and the whole of the biosphere, with the by-products of their workings?

Is it through ignorance of the condition? Hardly, for even the obvious facts are thoroughly convincing.

Is it from lack of ability to effect a remedy? Not likely, for with determination we could within a few years reduce our indices of air and water pollution to one-tenth the present levels.

Is it that we put individual gain above the health and well-being of the group? If so, wise and patient nature must be watching with curious interest as the aberrant homo sapiens "experiment" self-destructs.

Or is it just human frailty that we become so engrossed in new ideas and contrivances that "lesser" concerns are pushed aside until they reach crisis proportions?

Could it be that in time we can have it both ways, a high standard of living, with all the creature comforts, and at the same time a clean and wholesome environment? The facts would indicate that we can, and no doubt will, when we are willing to pay the price, and when we make the search for quality in our landscape and in our lives a national, and worldwide, commitment.

In the words of philosopher Teilhard de Chardin:

> *There is now incontrovertible evidence that mankind*
> *has just entered upon the greatest*
> *period of change the world has ever known.*
>
> *The ills*
> *from which we are now suffering have had their seat*
> *in the very foundations of human thought.*
>
> *But today something*
> *is happening*
> *to the whole structure of human consciousness*
>
> *A fresh kind*
> *of life is starting.*

It is not too late. Neither in America nor in any broad region of the world has the damage to the earthscape passed the critical point of no return. Nor are we running out of land—yet. Here, we are still blessed with great reaches of unbroken wilderness. Our coastal beaches still stretch for thousands of miles along the Atlantic, the Pacific, and the Gulf. Our lake shores and river edges still largely retain their natural form and condition. Our hills and mountain slopes are for the most part still clothed in forest, and our broad valleys are well-watered and rich with fertile soil.

This is not to aver that up to this point we have managed well, for there is damning evidence to the contrary. Clearly, things have been getting out of hand. There has been, in truth, precious little concern for our natural heritage. And there has been, until recently, almost no attempt at scientific land and resource planning. We are despoiling our landscape and polluting our water and atmosphere to a shameful, and increasingly harmful, degree. Such waste and corruption must be stopped. There is need to conserve, reclaim, restore, replace, and consolidate. There is need to formulate a strategy for long term growth and development—an evolving plan to bring people, production, and nature into better balance.

We have been hearing the strident cries of alarm and the warnings of doom and impending disaster. These have been well-meant and often all too accurate. In sum they have been a highly effective force, for they have created a timely apprehension and an urgent demand for environmental controls.

But it is time now to cease the hand-wringing and the litany of lament. It is time for the bold and positive view. It is time to concentrate on those things, big and little, that need to be done—and to get on with the job.

Pierre Teilhard de Chardin
Building the Earth
Published by Dimension Books
Denville, N.J., 1965
Copyright 1965 by Dimension Books

All of our towns and cities and suburbs together occupy only 2 percent of our land.

Environmental planning is the development of strategic means for ensuring the best possible living conditions for all forms of life.

We went out to Bell's Bay for a picnic last night, and what we
saw was some kind of miracle. Several years ago when we were
there the beach was so strewn with beer cans, garbage, and
broken glass that we couldn't find a place to swim—or even a
spot for a bonfire. This time the whole bay was clean. The long-
haired guitar-and-bikini kids had gathered their trash in boxes
and bags and carried it out to the road for pickup. They told us
that most folks who use the beach have been doing this now
for some time.

Wavering Skeptic

Index of quotation sources